Probation

Key readings

Probation presents a comprehensive selection of 'key readings' in community penalties. It is divided into six parts, each with a detailed introduction from the editors. Part A showcases central policy perspectives on the role, tasks and significance of the probation service since its inception in 1907, demonstrating the key shifts in political opinion that have taken place. Part B considers the history and development of probation and other community penalties, including accounts of the emergence and origins of such penalties. Part C looks more theoretically at these developments, illustrating the extent of professional and academic debate about the purpose of probation in a changing criminal justice climate through the models of practice that have been proposed and elaborated on at different times in the history of the service. Part D examines practice, including some of the key programmes that have been developed, such as day centres, drug programmes, intensive supervision projects, together with innovative experiments in community engagement. It covers various techniques and approaches to working with offenders, such as casework, groupwork and partnership working. Part E includes various articles on the theme of diversity, a longstanding concern of probation staff. Finally, Part F looks at the arguments around effectiveness, including how it is measured and the Nothing Works/What Works debate.

Probation: key readings will be essential reading for practitioners, trainees and students of probation.

George Mair is Professor of Criminal Justice, Liverpool Hope University. He has researched and published widely on community penalties. His most recent book is *Redemption, Rehabilitation and Risk Management: a history of probation* (Routledge 2012). He was a member of the Merseyside Probation Board between 2001 and 2007.

Judith Rumgay recently retired from the London School of Economics where she was Reader in Social Policy.

'At a time when probation in England and Wales faces its deconstruction as a public service, this indispensable collection of readings will serve as a treasure trove of policy, research and practice-based writings on a much-neglected and hugely important part of the criminal justice system. Anyone who wants to understand, to improve or to transform probation should be required to read this book first.'
Fergus McNeill, Professor of Criminology & Social Work, University of Glasgow, Scotland

'This book offers a timely and fascinating overview of policy developments, theoretical debates and practitioners' views and experiences throughout the rich history of probation in England and Wales. A must-read for all who are interested in the successes and challenges raised by community penalties.'
Sonja Snacken, Professor of Criminology, Penology and Sociology of Law at the Department of Criminology, Vrije Universiteit, Brussels

'George Mair and Judith Rumgay are both eminent researchers and writers on criminal justice, and in this volume they have put together a definitive collection of key texts and sources for the study of probation. Everyone interested in this field will benefit from their fascinating selection, and from their helpful commentaries, which put the selected readings in context. This deserves a place on every criminologist's bookshelf.'
Professor Peter Raynor AcSS, Swansea University, UK

Probation

Key readings

Edited by George Mair and Judith Rumgay

Routledge
Taylor & Francis Group

LONDON AND NEW YORK

First published 2014
by Routledge
2 Park Square, Milton Park, Abingdon, Oxon, OX14 4RN

and by Routledge
711 Third Avenue, New York, NY 10017

Routledge is an imprint of the Taylor & Francis Group, an informa business

British Library Cataloguing in Publication Data
A catalogue record for this book is available from the British Library

Library of Congress Cataloging-in-Publication Data
A catalog record has been requested for this book
Rumgay, Judith, 1952-
Probation : key readings / George Mair and Judith Rumgay.
pages cm
ISBN 978-0-415-67148-4 (hardback) – ISBN 978-0-415-67149-1 (pbk.)
1. Probation–Great Britain–History. 2. Alternatives to imprisonment–Great
Britain–History. I. Mair, George. II. Title.
HV9345.A5R86 2013
364.6'30941–dc23
2013008579

ISBN13: 978-0-415-67148-4 (hbk)
ISBN13: 978-0-415-67149-1 (pbk)

Typeset in Baskerville
by Saxon Graphics Ltd, Derby

Printed and bound by CPI Group (UK) Ltd, Croydon, CR0 4YY

Contents

Sources and acknowledgements

The editor and publisher would like to thank the following for their kind permission to reproduce copyright material.

Part B Probation history: alternative perspectives

The extract from Peter Young, 'A sociological analysis of the early history of probation', *British Journal of Law and Society*, 3(1), 1976, pp. 44–58 has been reproduced with permission of Blackwell Publishing Ltd.

The extract from William McWilliams, 'The English Probation System and the Diagnostic Ideal', *Howard Journal* 25(4), 1986, pp. 241–260 is reproduced with permission from Blackwell Publishing Ltd.

The extract from Elizabeth R. Glover, *Probation and Re-education*, 2nd ed. (London: Routledge and Kegan Paul), 1956, pp. 15-25 is reproduced with permission from Taylor and Francis Books.

The extract from Maurice Vanstone, 'A history of the use of groups in probation work: Part 1 – from "clubbing the unclubbables" to therapeutic intervention', *Howard Journal* 42(1), 2003, pp. 69–86 is reproduced with permission from Blackwell Publishing Ltd.

The extract from Ken Pease, 'A brief history of community service', in K. Pease and W. McWilliams (eds.) *Community Service By Order* (Edinburgh: Scottish Academic Press), 1980, pp. 5–13 is reproduced with kind permission from the author.

Part C Theoretical models

The extract from Stanley Cohen, 'It's all right for you to talk: political and sociological manifestos for social work action', in R. Bailey and M. Brake (eds.), *Radical Social Work* (London: Edward Arnold), 1975, pp. 76–95 is reproduced with permission from Hodder Education.

The extract from Robert J. Harris, 'The probation officer as social worker', *British Journal of Social Work* 7(4), 1977, pp. 433–443 is reproduced with permission from Oxford University Press.

The extract from Malcolm Bryant, John Coker, Barry Estlea, Sheila Himmel and Ted Knapp, 'Sentenced to social work?', *Probation Journal* 25(4), 1978, pp. 110–114 is reproduced with permission from Sage.

The extract from Anthony E. Bottoms and William McWilliams, 'A non-treatment paradigm for probation practice', *British Journal of Social Work* 9(2), 1979, pp. 159–202 is reproduced with permission from Oxford University Press.

The extract from Hilary Walker and Bill Beaumont, *Probation work: critical theory and socialist practice* (Oxford: Basil Blackwell), 1981, pp. 159–173 is reproduced with permission from Blackwell Publishing Ltd.

The extract from William McWilliams, 'Probation, pragmatism and policy', *Howard Journal*, 26(2), 1987, pp. 97–121 is reproduced with permission from Blackwell Publishing Ltd.

The extract from Rob Canton, 'Working at the margin, campaigning at the centre', *Probation Journal*, 34(3), 1987, pp. 97–100 is reproduced with permission from Sage.

The extract from Judith Rumgay, 'Talking tough: empty threats in probation practice', *Howard Journal*, 28(3), 1989, pp. 177–186 is reproduced with permission from Sage.

The extract from Mike Nellis, 'Probation values for the 1990s', *Howard Journal*, 34(1), 1995, pp. 19–44 is reproduced with permission from Sage.

The extract from Ken Pease (1999) 'The probation career of Al Truism', *Howard Journal* 38(1), 1999, pp. 2–16 is reproduced with permission from Sage.

The extract from Judith Rumgay, 'The barking dog? Partnership and effective practice', in G. Mair (ed.), *What Matters in Probation* (Cullompton: Willan), 2004, pp. 122–145 is reproduced with permission from Taylor and Francis Books.

Part D Supervision: practice and programmes

The extract from A. W. Hunt 'Enforcement in probation casework', *British Journal of Criminology* 4, 1963–64, pp. 239–252 is reproduced with permission from Oxford University Press.

The extract from Christine Weaver and Charles Fox, 'The Berkeley sex offenders group: a seven year evaluation', *Probation Journal*, 31(4), 1984, pp. 143–146 is reproduced with permission from Sage.

The extract from Tim Chapman, 'Political motivation and probation practice', *Probation Journal*, 33(1), 1986, pp. 8–12 is reproduced with permission from Sage.

The extract from John Smith, 'Antabuse of probation: an example in practice', *Probation Journal*, 33(1), 1986, pp. 13–16 is reproduced with permission from Sage.

The extract from Members of the Demonstration Unit, 1981–84, Inner London Probation Service, 'Increasing the use of Probation', *Probation Journal*, 33(3), 1986, pp. 87–90 is reproduced with permission from Sage.

The extract from David Bale, 'Using a "Risk of custody" scale', *Probation Journal*, 34(4), 1987, pp. 127–131 is reproduced with permission from Sage.

The extract from David Millard, 'Looking backwards to the future?', *Probation Journal*, 36(1), 1989, pp. 18–21 is reproduced with permission from Sage.

The extract from Nigel Spencer and Pat Edwards, 'The rise and fall of the Kent Control Unit: a local perspective', *Probation Journal*, 33(3), 1986, pp. 91–94 is reproduced with permission from Sage.

The extract from Jeff Bowe, Linda Crawley and John Morris, 'Inner city disturbances: lessons from Liverpool 1985', *Probation Journal*, 34(1) 1987, pp. 10–12 is reproduced with permission from Sage.

The extract from Michael Sheath, '"Confrontative" work with sex offenders: legitimised nonce bashing?', *Probation Journal*, 37(4), 1990, pp. 159–162 is reproduced with permission from Sage.

The extract from George Mair, 'Specialist activities in probation: "confusion worse confounded"?', in L. Noakes, M. Levi and M. Maguire (eds.) *Contemporary Issues in Criminology* (Cardiff: University of Wales Press), 1995, pp. 251–258 is reproduced with permission from University of Wales Press.

Part E Diversity

The extract from Bruce Carrington and David Denney, 'Young Rastafarians and the probation service', *Probation Journal*, 28(4), 1981, pp. 111–117 is reproduced with permission from Sage.

The extract from Richard Pinder, 'On what grounds? Negotiating justice with black clients', *Probation Journal*, 29(1), 1982, pp. 19–23 is reproduced with permission from Sage.

The extract from Jim Lawson, 'Probation in St. Pauls: teamwork in a multi-racial, inner-city area', *Probation Journal*, 31(3), 1984, pp. 93–95 is reproduced with permission from Sage.

The extract from Mary Davies and Gillian Stewart, 'Prostitution and the Absolute Discharge strategy', *Probation Journal*, 34(2), 1987, pp. 51–53 is reproduced with permission from Sage.

The extract from Pat Carlen, 'Feminist jurisprudence – or women-wise penology?', *Probation Journal*, 36(31), 1989, pp. 110–114 is reproduced with permission from Sage.

The extract from Patrick Williams, 'Designing and delivering programmes for minority ethnic offenders', in S. Lewis, P. Raynor, D. Smith and A. Wardak (eds.) *Race and Probation* (Cullompton: Willan), 2006, pp. 145–163 is reproduced with permission from Taylor and Francis Books.

Part F Effectiveness

The extract from K. Pease, S. Billingham and I. Earnshaw, 'Community Service Assessed in 1976', *Home Office Research Study 39* (London: HMSO), 1977, pp. 3–10 is reproduced with kind permission from the authors.

The extract from Steven Folkard, 'Second thoughts on IMPACT', in E.M.Goldberg and N.Connelly (eds.) *Evaluative Research in Social Care* (London: Heinemann), 1981, pp. 81–97 is reproduced with permission from Heinemann.

The extract from George Mair, 'What works – nothing or everything ? Measuring the effectiveness of sentences', *Home Office Research Bulletin 30*, 1991, pp. 3–8 is reproduced with kind permission from the author.

The extract from Peter Raynor, 'Community penalties and Home Office research: on the way back to "nothing works" ?', *Criminology and Criminal Justice* 8(1), 2008, pp. 73–87 is reproduced with permission from Sage.

The extract from Steve Stanley, 'What Works in 2009: progress or stagnation?' *Probation Journal* 56(2), 2009, pp. 153–174 is reproduced with permission from Sage.

The extract from Mike Hough, 'Gold standard or fool's gold ? The pursuit of certainty in experimental criminology', *Criminology and Criminal Justice* 10(1), 2010, pp. 11–22 is reproduced with permission from Sage.

Acronyms

ACE	Assessment, Case management and Evaluation system
ACOP	Association of Chief Officers of Probation
ACPO	Assistant Chief Probation Officer
ACPS	Advisory Council on the Penal System
AGM	Annual General Meeting
APSW	Association of Psychiatric Social Workers
BME	Black and Minority Ethnic
BQS	Better Quality Services
CAB	Citizens' Advice Bureau
CB	Cognitive Behavioural
CCETSW	Central Council for Education and Training in Social Work
CCPC	Central Council of Probation Committees
CJA	Criminal Justice Act
CND	Campaign for Nuclear Disarmament
COS	Charity Organisation Society
CPO	Community Punishment Order
CPO	Chief Probation Officer
CPS	Crown Prosecution Service
CQSW	Certificate of Qualification in Social Work
CRAMS	Case Recording and Management Software
CRE	Commission for Racial Equality
CRO	Community Rehabilitation Order
CRO	Criminal Records Office
CRP	Crime Reduction Programme
CSAP	Correctional Services Accreditation Panel
CSO	Community Service Order
DCA	Department for Constitutional Affairs
DCPO	Deputy Chief Probation Officer
DHSS	Department of Health and Social Security
DOM	Director of Offender Management
DTC	Day Training Centre
DTTO	Drug Treatment and Testing Order
DTU	Differential Treatment Unit
EEM	European Excellence Model
FDR	Fast Delivery Report
FMIS	Financial Management Information System

FPN	Fixed Penalty Notice
GOR	Government Office of the Region
HMIP	Her Majesty's Inspectorate of Probation
HMT	Her Majesty's Treasury
IAPS	Interim Accredited Programme Software
ILPS	Inner London Probation Service
IMPACT	Intensive Matched Probation and After Care Treatment
ISM	Intensive Supervision and Monitoring
IT	Intermediate Treatment
LSI-R	Level of Service Inventory - Revised
MAPPP	Multi-Agency Public Protection Panel
MSC	Manpower Services Commission
NACRO	National Association for the Care and Resettlement of Offenders
NAG	NAPO Action Group
NALGO	National And Local Government Officers association
NAO	National Audit Office
NAPO	National Association of Probation Officers
NDPB	Non-Departmental Public Body
NEC	National Executive Committee
NICE	National Institute for Health and Clinical Excellence
NOMM	National Offender Management Model
NOMS	National Offender Management Service
NPD	National Probation Directorate
NPS	National Probation Service
OASys	Offender Assessment System
OGRS	Offender Group Reconviction Scale
OSD	Operational Support Division
PSD	Petty Sessional Division
PSR	Pre-Sentence Report
R&R	Reasoning and Rehabilitation
RCT	Randomised Controlled Trials
RDS	Research Development and Statistics
RoC	Risk of Custody
RPU	Research and Planning Unit
SER	Social Enquiry Report
SGC	Sentencing Guidelines Council
SIPU	Special Intensive Parole Unit
SIR	Social Inquiry Report
SNOP	Statement of National Objectives and Priorities
SPO	Senior Probation Officer
STEP	Skills Training and Employment Programme
STOP	Straight Thinking On Probation
TDA	Take and Drive Away
TEC	Training and Enterprise Council
USI	Unlawful Sexual Intercourse
WORP	Women's Offending Reduction Programme
YJB	Youth Justice Board
YOP	Youth Opportunity Programme

Introduction

The probation service in England and Wales is the smallest and least known of the traditional criminal justice agencies. Compared to the police with around 139,000 full-time equivalent (FTE) police officers at 31 March 2011 (Home Office 2011), or the prison service with almost 50,000 staff (Ministry of Justice 2012a), probation has far fewer staff (18,000 FTE on 31 March 2012; Ministry of Justice 2012b) and its annual budget is much lower than both. Police dramas (both fictional and documentary) flood our televisions; prisons are also regularly shown on our screens. Probation, however, is – to all intents and purposes – absent. The service's activities simply do not arouse the dramatic excitement that is inspired by the hot pursuit of serial killers or prison escape. Yet the significance of the probation service is out of all proportion to its size, budget and public image. Probation is involved with the police (especially in Multi-Agency Public Protection Arrangements), with the courts (by providing pre-sentence reports for sentencers), and with prisons (via pre- and post-release supervision). It works with the victims of crime, has worked with defendants threatened with remand in custody (bail information schemes), and with the Crown Prosecution Service in trying to avoid prosecution where possible (Public Interest Case Assessment schemes). In addition, the service is the lead organisation (working alongside a wide variety of voluntary and private sector agencies) in dealing with offenders sentenced to a community order or suspended sentence order by the courts. Moreover, what might be called the English model of probation has been significantly influential in the development of probation work in Eastern Europe since the fall of communism two decades ago. The reach of the probation service is considerable; it lies at the very heart of the criminal justice system and it is difficult to imagine how that 'system' would function effectively without it. The probation service, alone of all the criminal justice agencies, works at all stages of, and with all participants in, the system.

However, despite its significance – and partly as a result of its low public profile, which is rooted in the way it has tended to work with offenders – probation has never been a 'sexy' topic for criminologists. The police and prisons have always attracted far more academic attention than probation. Conference presentations tend to include many papers on the police or prisons and relatively few on probation. Even in simple matters such as the way in which the annual *Probation Statistics* were published in the 1980s and 1990s in a loosely bound, somewhat makeshift format, compared to the *Criminal Statistics* or the *Prison Statistics* where a much more professional binding was used, the message was clear that probation was not really that important. This seems to us a strange conclusion, given the impressive scale of the probation service's enterprise; for example, on 31 December 2011 a total of 234,528 individuals were being supervised by the probation service (all those on court orders plus all pre- and post-release supervision; Ministry of Justice 2012c), compared to a prison population on 30 December 2011 of 86,778 (Ministry of Justice 2011). This was being accomplished by a probation staff complement that was less than half that of the prison service, yet we are regularly treated to cries of crisis in the custodial sector.

Notwithstanding the lack of comparative quantity in probation studies, there is quality to be found. Furthermore, many of the debates that have been anchored in probation work have resonance for wider criminological discussions. Indeed, it is within the sphere of probation that many of the most passionate debates about criminal justice have taken place. Moreover, in the current age of concern about failures in the system and the ineffectiveness of criminal justice policy, the probation service's relative scarcity of scandal has – ironically – fed the lack of interest in its endeavours rather than encouraged eagerness in learning its lessons.

In addition – and this is a problem for other areas of criminological study too – there is a tendency to forget the past. In the rush to drive forward with new research and analyses, the past and what it might have to tell us about probation (or the police or prisons for that matter) becomes marginalised, its relevance forgotten or ignored. This was particularly noticeable when, with the creation of the National Probation Service, 2001 became a Year Zero with probation's rich history being airbrushed out of the picture. We suspect that this was not simple forgetfulness; it encouraged staff to adhere to new methods of working and new organisational arrangements, and it discouraged them from laying claim to historical and local 'traditions' and thereby jeopardising the impact of the new, national service.

Ironically, another reason for the marginalisation of probation's past is that more academics do now seem to be working in the field of community penalties. Long-standing scholars of probation such as Loraine Gelsthorpe and Peter Raynor continue to carry out important work and younger ones such as Shadd Maruna, Fergus McNeill and Gwen Robinson are bringing fresh and stimulating insights to bear. With the number of publications in the field growing, helped along by a rejuvenated *Probation Journal*, and more international contacts (e.g. the European Working Group on Community Sanctions and Measures, CREDOS – the Collaboration of Researchers for the Effective Development of Offender Supervision), it is not difficult to relegate to the background earlier studies in the excitement of new research concerned with a rising tide of political, administrative and programmatic innovations.

However, it is one thing to try to change by putting the past behind you, but entirely another matter almost deliberately to forget more than 100 years of development and productive work with offenders. Without a contextual and historically grounded understanding of the probation service's rich history of professional debate and grass-roots innovation, as well as changing policy perspectives on its role and significance, it is impossible to make sense of its current position in the criminal justice system. For the past 25 years, government attempts to remould the probation service and its activities have themselves been moderated – for better and for worse – by the strength of the service's powerful traditions. And as we write (in the middle of 2012), the threats to probation seem to be more dangerous than ever: a rehabilitation revolution that has stalled before it started, contestability underway, the introduction of payment by results, and professional deskilling in areas of complex work (e.g. the disturbing increase in Fast Delivery Reports to the courts which now comprise more than half of court reports, and the number of Probation Service Officers which is now greater than the number of qualified Probation Officers), and plans for a major review of probation and community sentences (Ministry of Justice 2012d; Ministry of Justice 2012e). Even while the government makes encouraging moves to return some much-needed discretion to probation staff by relaxing National Standards and piloting an Offender Engagement Programme, such developments are threatened by serious budget cuts.

This volume is intended to ground and contextualise the various developments taking place in probation rather than to add to the growing number of commentaries on them. It aims to pick out key articles, reports, studies and debates in probation that have had critical resonance for the development of the service since its official beginnings with the Probation of Offenders Act 1907. These will either continue to have something to say to current issues or represent missed opportunities, moments when probation might have followed a different path. They are not intended to represent a fixed canon of probation studies, although we obviously think that our choices are important pieces of work. Rather, we hope that the readings presented here will stimulate discussion, remind readers that probation has a lengthy and challenging history, and help to establish probation's rightful place as a key criminal justice agency.

As is the way with any such attempt to record key events, transitions and debates in a century-old agency (particularly one that has enjoyed impassioned argument as much as probation has), we expect that readers will disagree with some of our choices, and we would be delighted to hear about such disagreements and why your preferences should have been included. But given the self-imposed constraints we have worked under, we believe our choices to be fully justifiable.

We agreed at an early stage that to make the project manageable we would have to make hard decisions about topics to include and exclude. We decided to focus on community penalties – most particularly the probation order – with regard to adults aged 17/18 and older; thus, we will not be concerned with community penalties for juvenile offenders (although we are fully aware that prior to the 1960s probation orders were very much a disposal for young offenders). Nor have we attempted to cover the work carried out by probation officers with prisoners, either pre- or post-release – although over the last 30 years this has been an increasingly significant aspect of probation work (indeed, it currently constitutes almost 50 per cent of those supervised by the service). And finally, we have focused on readings from England and Wales, although we have also included what we believe to be an important contribution from Northern Ireland, and two from Robert Martinson. This is certainly not to imply that influential work has not been carried out elsewhere, but it is the case that probation in England and Wales has been more influential in other countries than it has been influenced by them (although a strong argument could be made for the original service to have been modelled on that in Massachusetts). To embrace the wider United Kingdom would have introduced substantial differences of agency history, structure and ethos that, if overlooked in their detail (for which there is inadequate space), might have appeared more neglectful than flattering to those whose professional lives are bound up in them.

We begin with a substantial section on government and other 'official' reports, as the slowly enveloping embrace of governmental control has been a key theme in the development of the probation service; and it is one that continues today. This 'official' history is balanced by a following section that examines other historical accounts of probation. It attempts to illuminate the realities of probation officers' (and others) thoughts about their work and practices against this backdrop of prescription from the centre. The next two parts examine, first, theoretical models of practice and, second, specific programmes and methods for dealing with offenders. Part E focuses on diversity – an issue that has always been of considerable significance for probation, despite changes in the ways in which that significance has been understood, and one that the service continues to grapple with today. Finally, Part F looks at effectiveness, a topic that probation managed to avoid for almost 70 years but that has since become a hugely controversial matter and which could have major implications for the future of the service.

We have chosen to focus for the most part on the first century of the probation service's existence. Most of the readings are more than 20 years old and this has been a deliberate choice. More up-to-date contributions are easily available, particularly in this electronic age, and this explains what might seem to be a surprising lack of Home Office/Ministry of Justice research publications. Older material, however, which reveals the breadth of probation's imagination and experience, is more difficult to discover and access. This problem, in our view, exacerbates the contemporary enthusiasm noted above for living entirely in probation's present, albeit that this 'present' is in constant flux, subject to ever more rapid and radical change. We hope that those with long experience of the probation service will appreciate renewed contact with its remarkably varied experience. We hope, too, that newcomers to the service will be proud to learn that they are part of such a rich tradition of innovation, imagination and passionate vision.

The task of pulling together this book has taken us far longer than we had planned; a tribute in part to the range of material that we had to consider for inclusion. We are very grateful to Nicola Hartley and Tom Sutton of Routledge for their unfailing support and encouragement and their willingness to put up with our requests for extensions to the deadline for delivery of the manuscript. David Ashton was cheerfully helpful in the scanning of numerous articles.

George would like to acknowledge the debt he owes to Carmel for her patience, good humour and love; thanks too, to Ruth and Ethan – just for being themselves – and not forgetting Sophie this time! He is also very grateful to Judith for making working together a pleasure and wishes to apologise to her for disrupting her retirement.

Judith would like to thank Mary and Stuart at the Radzinowicz Library, Institute of Criminology, Cambridge for their patience and generosity, not least in helping to trace some writings on the flimsiest of clues; George for being unfailingly tolerant and constructive; and on a personal level, much is owed as always to Alan for his patience and encouragement.

References

Home Office (2011) *Police Service Strength England and Wales, 31 March 2011*. London: Home Office.

Ministry of Justice (2011) *Prison population bulletin – weekly 30 December 2011*. Available at www. justice.gov.uk/statistics/prisons-and-probation/prison-population-figures.

——(2012a) Data taken from a Freedom of Information request. Available at www.justice.gov. uk/downloads/information-access-rights/foi-disclosure-log/prison-probation/foi-75741-hmps-staffing-data.doc.

——(2012b) *National Offender Management Service: Human Resources Workforce Information Summary Report – Quarter 4 2011/12*. Available at www.justice.gov.uk/statistics/prisons-and-probation/probation-workforce-quarterly-2011–2012.

——(2012c) *Offender management statistics (quarterly) – October to December 2011*. Available at www.justice.gov.uk/statistics/prisons-and-probation/oms-quarterly.

——(2012d) *Punishment and Reform: effective probation services*. London: The Stationery Office.

——(2012e) *Punishment and Reform: effective community sentences*. London: The Stationery Office.

Part A

Probation: an official history

Introduction

Like skinning a cat, there are a number of ways to examine the history of probation and in this opening section of the book we provide what is essentially an official account of the development of the service, relying for the most part on Acts of Parliament, reports of departmental committees and government or government-sponsored proposals. We begin with the 1907 Probation of Offenders Act (Reading 1) which set in motion the whole process after the false start of the 1887 Probation of First Offenders Act. The 1907 Act is – unlike Acts of Parliament today – remarkably brief and somewhat vague, especially in its confusion over what we know as probation with binding over (release on recognizance without supervision) or dismissal. Unfortunately, probation's reputation for being a soft option (still firmly in place today) is encapsulated in the Act's opening section where probation is seen as being equivalent to no punishment at all. The Act also contains the classic phrase that provided the foundation of probation work for almost 100 years when it lists as one of the probation officer's duties to 'advise, assist, and befriend' the offender. At this stage, there is little indication of any desire by the Home Office to have anything to do with the direction or control of probation work, apart from section 7 which permits rules to be made.

It is impressive that the 1909 Departmental Committee report (Reading 2) is so positive about probation's value – despite the fact that no research or analysis had been carried out to demonstrate this. And this faith in the efficacy of probation is a thread that can be followed for much of the next 50 years or more; the lack of firm evidence to demonstrate effectiveness becoming more glaring as the decades pass. The report encourages some Home Office intervention in the organisation of probation, but is quite clear that there should be no such thing as a Central Probation Commission – thereby emphasising the significance of probation as a local initiative – and no Chief Probation Officers as local justices of the peace were the managers of probation officers. The recommendation to form a Probation Officers' Society was quickly acted upon in 1912 when the National Association of Probation Officers (NAPO) was formed. Another Departmental Committee reported in 1922 (Reading 3), again opening with a clear statement of belief in probation's effectiveness. While voluntary societies were the main source for probation officers, the need for better education and more training for recruits is emphasised, marking the beginning of the end for the police court missionaries. Consistency is a theme of the report – in the use of probation in different areas, in pay, in caseload, in the kind of officers employed – and this is a topic that continues to haunt the probation service. Although slow and indirect, government control is inexorably growing, as can be seen particularly in recommendations 18 and 22.

By the time of the Departmental Committee on the Social Services in Courts of Summary Jurisdiction 14 years later (Reading 4), the Home Office is being urged to 'accept greater responsibility for the general administration, supervision and direction' of the service (recommendation 45). By this time, probation is becoming established on a rather more professional footing and the missionary societies are on their way out (recommendation 36). The need for appropriate training is emphasised, the appointment of Principal Probation Officers is encouraged as is specialisation, and a full list of probation tasks is given – including reports to the courts and after-care of young offenders, both of which significantly increased the range of responsibilities for probation officers. In 1961 the Streatfeild Committee reported (Reading 5), emphasising the significance of probation reports to the courts – but not just as background and contextual information to help sentencers in deciding on a sentence; reports are expected to contain an informed opinion (*not* a recommendation) about the effect of a sentence on an offender. This was a major development for probation work, widely understood as recognition of a professional, specialised service within the courts.

The most substantial examination of the probation service in the second half of the twentieth century was that of the Morison Committee which reported in 1962 (Reading 6). The Committee's report is of similar length to that of the 1936 Departmental Committee on the Social Services in Courts of Summary Jurisdiction (Reading 4) but while the 1936 report contains only 56 recommendations, the Morison Committee report makes 157. Many of these advocate no change in what probation was doing and in that sense the report can be seen as a lost opportunity to explore critically what probation work was, what it might become, and how it should be organised. The need for more probation officers is noted, although the report is surprisingly diffident about the need for high educational standards in recruits. Probation officers are acknowledged as professional caseworkers and the service as a social service located in the courts. After 50 years of generally good relations with the Home Office, tensions are beginning to emerge between the department and the service – tensions which would be exacerbated as the years pass. Interestingly, given the current use of Fast Delivery Reports (FDRs) by the courts (in the July–September 2011 quarter almost seven out of ten reports to magistrates' courts were FDRs), the Morison Committee's view of such reports is that they are 'a poor substitute for a full social enquiry' (recommendation 5).

Perhaps the best known of all official reports into probation is that carried out by the Advisory Council on the Penal System (ACPS) in 1970 – better known as the Wootton report after its chair, Baroness Wootton of Abinger (Reading 7). The Wootton report is remembered almost solely for recommending the introduction of community service as a sentence of the court, yet it also proposed the deferment of sentence, intermittent custody and combining probation supervision with a fine or a suspended sentence of imprisonment. The chapter of the report presented here focuses on the case for introducing community service which is seen as a constructive activity to be carried out with volunteer non-offenders on evenings and weekends. Community service was introduced in the 1972 Criminal Justice Act with three notable changes from the Wootton proposals: first, it would only be available for offences liable to imprisonment; second, the proposed maximum of 120 hours was doubled to 240; and third, community service was to be a new court sentence without the option of making it a condition of a probation order. Community service proved to be a hugely popular sentence and radically changed the probation service: it was intended as an alternative to a custodial sentence; it involved no social work with offenders; it heralded the arrival of a new group of staff who were not trained probation officers; and it encouraged much greater liaison between probation and voluntary agencies than hitherto had been the case.

Four years after the Wootton report, the ACPS produced another report that – if its recommendations had been accepted – would have had an even greater impact upon the probation service. The main probation-related proposal of *Young Adult Offenders* (Reading 8) is for the introduction of a supervision and control order that would not require the offender's consent (then necessary for a probation or community service order) and where a probation officer could apply to a magistrates' court to grant up to 72 hours detention for an offender who had not actually committed another offence or breached the requirements of the order but was believed to be about to do so. Predictably, probation staff were outraged by such a proposal and it is perhaps fortunate that a combination of economic problems and a change of government in 1974 meant that the report's proposals were never accepted. But the Younger report's idea for a supervision and control order – from the viewpoint of the early twenty-first century – looks remarkably prescient (and a separate recommendation for a custody and control order encapsulates, essentially, the suspended sentence order) and it is fascinating to speculate what the future for probation would have been if these proposals had been acted upon by government in the mid-1970s.

When the *Statement of National Objectives and Priorities* (SNOP) was published in 1984, the probation service response verged on an apocalyptic feeling that the world was coming to an end. Yet SNOP was – certainly with the benefit of hindsight – a rather innocuous document (Reading 9). As earlier readings have shown, the Home Office had been slowly taking control of aspects of probation since its introduction, so what was the problem with issuing a short paper suggesting that, because resources were limited, decisions were needed about setting priorities for the various objectives of the service? Local probation areas were not used to being given such direction by government – even though SNOP was little more than a very gentle nudge. Perhaps more significant, though hardly noticed at the time, is the word 'National' in the title of the document. There were 56 local probation services in England and Wales in 1984 and they remained remarkably independent with their chief probation officers having a great deal of autonomy; not a situation that would have been welcomed by the Conservative government of the time. Following SNOP, government intervention in probation began to increase and moves towards a more centralised service became more noticeable; for example, five years later the first National Standards were introduced for community service.

If SNOP was – in reality – a fairly gentle reminder that ultimately government had control, then the Green Paper *Punishment, Custody and the Community* (Reading 10) represented a loud wake-up call for probation. In the first place, the term 'punishment' is used repeatedly in the Green Paper; this was not a word that was normally associated with probation work. Second, suggestions such as changing the hours of community service, increasing the length of a day centre requirement, extending the use of tracking and introducing home curfews to be enforced by electronic monitoring, were all intended to make community penalties more punitive. In addition, a new and more demanding community sentence was proposed and here one can see the first hints of what became, 25 years later, the community order. Most troubling of all was the discussion (which comes at the end of the excerpt) about who might be responsible for the organisation of the new punishment in the community. Greater private sector involvement is mooted as one possibility, but the threat of setting up a new organisation entirely (presumably if the probation service did not cooperate) is also discussed (para. 4.4). The Green Paper offered considerable opportunities for the probation service; the invitation to move to centre stage in the criminal justice system was blatant but very clear dilemmas about its future direction lay between the lines.

The 1996 White Paper *Protecting the Public* (Reading 11) shows a very different probation service. The priorities set out for it (paragraph 7.4) are a far cry from 'advise, assist and befriend', a revised and more demanding set of National Standards is in place, and trials of the electronic monitoring of curfew orders are underway. The probation service is not, of course, responsible for electronic monitoring (largely due to officers' refusal to welcome tagging with open arms when it was introduced), but it is significant that this lies at the heart of a new community penalty (the curfew order) which is organised and operated by private sector companies. The idea of a single, integrated community sentence – a proposal contained in the Green Paper *Strengthening Punishment in the Community* (1995) which preceded the White Paper – is not to be pursued, although within a decade a new government would take it forward. And the cherished, longstanding principle of asking an offender to consent to a probation or community service order is under threat. *Protecting the Public* was the final statement of intent regarding criminal justice by the Conservative government which had been in power since 1979, when it had been elected on a promise to crack down on crime (among other things). The various Conservative administrations had indeed changed the probation service in many ways, the fundamental nature of which was perhaps most expressively encapsulated in the removal of its training base in social work in the face of considerable opposition from within and without the organisation. However, even greater changes were to come when the Labour Party won the 1997 election.

Just over a year after winning the election, the new Labour government published its plans for the probation service and these carried further the developments that had been initiated by their Conservative predecessors. *Joining Forces to Protect the Public* (Reading 12) is a consultation document that is obsessed with modernisation – a key theme of New Labour. Despite fears that it would propose a merger between the prison and probation services, this was considered to be 'a bridge too far' (para. 2.38). It did, however, propose a radical restructuring of the probation service so that it would become a unified national service (which, given the changes of the previous years had begun to seem inevitable) with a national leadership and 100 per cent government funding replacing the previous split between central and local funding. The much vaunted independence of the individual probation services was, therefore, under threat. Somewhat foolishly, new names were suggested for the proposed new national service – none of which made much sense and most of which were ridiculed – and it was suggested that the community orders themselves might be renamed. The three main bodies representing probation – the Association of Chief Officers of Probation (ACOP), the Central Council of Probation Committees (CCPC) and NAPO – were not opposed to a national service in principle, but, not surprisingly, were keen to retain some local autonomy. The Criminal Justice and Court Services Act, 2000 created the National Probation Service (NPS) which officially came into being in April 2001; at the same time the probation order was renamed the community rehabilitation order, the community service order became the community punishment order and the combination order, with a great leap of imagination, became the community punishment and rehabilitation order. History was being carelessly jettisoned in the name of progress.

The document that introduced the new National Probation Service to the public was entitled *A New Choreography* (Reading 13), although it remained unclear about what dance had to do with the cultural change that was envisaged. The language of *A New Choreography* is radical with 'stretch objectives', and 'strategic imperatives'; the NPS is unequivocally and immediately claimed as 'a law enforcement agency' and the service's image is 'to be that of a "hawk-like professional", sharp and keen-eyed' (rather aggressive imagery that would not have been associated with probation officers up to this time). The Executive Summary of the document is ambitious and business-oriented and the nine 'stretch objectives' are linked to challenging targets which in turn are related to financial incentives intended 'to improve performance and to meet the targets agreed'. At the same time as the NPS was building this new organisational structure, it was heavily engaged in taking forward the What Works practice agenda under the guise of Pathfinder programmes, developing the new drug treatment and testing orders introduced in the Crime and Disorder Act, 1998 and learning to work in partnership with the police as part of the Multi-Agency Public Protection Panels which were part of the Criminal Justice and Court Services Act that had introduced the NPS. This constituted a big agenda for a service that had been consistently undermined by government for more than a decade.

Patrick Carter's review of the correctional services reported in December 2003 and the government's response came the following month (Reading 14). This would represent remarkable speed if the Carter report had indeed been given serious in-depth consideration by the Home Office after its publication, but perhaps would be less surprising if Carter's work and conclusions had been discussed with government in advance. The Home Office was in complete agreement with Carter's conclusions and announced its intentions to implement them surprisingly quickly. Fines needed to be revitalised to take some of the pressure off the probation service as far too many low risk offenders were clogging up NPS caseloads. Electronic monitoring should be expanded and more demanding community sentences should be developed (it would be an interesting exercise to trace how often the need for more demanding community sentences had been expressed during the previous 20 years). Carter's most significant proposals were accepted without qualification: a National Offender Management Service (NOMS) was to be introduced within six months (by 1 June 2004), merging the prison and probation services; and contestability (market testing by another name) was to be introduced so that private and voluntary sector organisations could compete to manage offenders in the community. The NPS had been operating for just three years, had scarcely been given time to settle down and had been subject to no evaluation of its effectiveness; yet it was to be consigned to history. The introduction of market testing, despite the invocation of the rhetoric of partnership, threatened to destroy the coherence of the probation service.

To contrast the language of the Ministry of Justice document *Capacity and Competition Policy for Prisons and Probation* (Reading 15) with that of any government report on probation from 20 years previously shows how far matters had developed. *Capacity and Competition* reads as if dealing with offenders in the community is a marginal issue for probation – indeed, in the extract reproduced here, offenders scarcely exist. The language is clearly borrowed from the commercial sector:

We are building new capacity and implementing competition to deliver a step-change in the efficiency and cost-effectiveness of the delivery of services. We are looking to deliver high quality, flexible, modern public services which can meet our needs into the medium term.

Even the promise that services to courts would be excluded from competition did not necessarily mean that probation would remain the provider; other public sector agencies could provide these if required.

As we write, unpaid work is undergoing contestability (community service always seemed to be one of the most likely candidates for market testing) and the landscape for probation will be changed utterly when the exercise is completed. South Yorkshire probation staff have been ordered out of three prisons due to conflicts of interest as the Probation Trust is involved with G4S in planning to submit a bid to run the three prisons (as reported in the *Guardian* on 1 March 2012). National Standards have been relaxed by the coalition government, but this is not necessarily a matter for rejoicing on the part of probation workers as this development will simply make it easier for private and voluntary sector organisations to bid to take over tasks previously regulated by strict standards.

Tracing the official development of probation – especially in the last 30 years – can only lead to a fairly pessimistic view of its future. While there can be no doubt that probation, like any organisation, needed to change with the times, the service's reluctance to accept this or at least to agree on the nature of that change, coupled with a heavy handed and unconsidered approach on the part of successive governments has led to a situation where it is almost impossible to envisage a healthy and vibrant probation service existing in ten years time. Yet, notwithstanding the acknowledged resistance on the part of the probation service, the organisation has undergone more radical change than any other criminal justice agency. It is hard to discern, within an increasingly rapid flow of official documents, the true causes of government's complaints.

1   The Probation of Offenders Act, 1907

1. Power of courts to permit conditional release of offenders

(1)   Where any person is charged before a court of summary jurisdiction with an offence punishable by such court, and the court thinks that the charge is proved, but is of opinion that, having regard to the character, antecedents, age, health, or mental condition of the person charged, or to the trivial nature of the offence, or to the extenuating circumstances under which the offence was committed, it is inexpedient to inflict any punishment or any other than a nominal punishment, or that it is expedient to release the offender on probation, the court may, without proceeding to conviction, make an order either:

(i)   dismissing the information or charge; or

(ii) discharging the offender conditionally on his entering into a recognizance, with or without sureties, to be of good behaviour and to appear for conviction and sentence when called on at any time during such period, not exceeding three years, as may be specified in the order.

(2)   Where any person has been convicted on indictment of any offence punishable with imprisonment, and the court is of opinion that, having regard to the character, antecedents, age, health, or mental condition of the person charged, or to the trivial nature of the offence, or to the extenuating circumstances under which the offence was committed, it is inexpedient to inflict any punishment or any other than a nominal punishment, or that it is expedient to release the offender on probation, the court may, in lieu of imposing a sentence of imprisonment, make an order discharging the offender conditionally on his entering into a recognizance, with or without sureties, to be of good behaviour and to appear for sentence when called on at any time during such period, not exceeding three years, as may be specified in the order.

(3)   The court may, in addition to any such order, order the offender to pay such damages for injury or compensation for loss (not exceeding in the case of a court of summary jurisdiction ten pounds, or, if a higher limit is fixed by any enactment relating to the offence, that higher limit) and to pay such costs of the proceedings as the court thinks reasonable, and, if the offender is under the age of sixteen years, and it appears to the court that the parent or guardian of the offender has conduced to the commission of the offence, the court may under and in accordance with the Youthful Offenders Act, 1901, order payment of such damages and costs by such parent or guardian.

(4)   Where an order under this section is made by a court of summary jurisdiction, the order shall, for the purpose of revesting or restoring stolen property, and of enabling the court to make orders as to the restitution or delivery of property to the owner and as to the payment of money upon or in connexion with such restitution or delivery, have the like effect as a conviction.

2. Probation orders and conditions of recognizances

(1)   A recognizance ordered to be entered into under this Act shall, if the court so order, contain a condition that the offender be under the supervision of such person as may be named in the order during the period specified in the order and such other conditions for securing such supervision as may be specified in the order, and an order requiring the insertion of such conditions as aforesaid in the recognizance is in this Act referred to as a probation order.

(2)   A recognizance under this Act may contain such additional conditions as the court may, having regard to the particular circumstances of the case, order to be inserted therein with respect to all or any of the following matters:-

(*a*) for prohibiting the offender from associating with thieves and other undesirable persons, or from frequenting undesirable places;

(*b*) as to abstention from intoxicating liquor, where the offence was drunkenness or an offence committed under the influence of drink;

(*c*) generally for securing that the offender should lead an honest and industrious life.

(3)   The court by which a probation order is made shall furnish to the offender a notice in writing stating in simple terms the conditions he is required to observe.

3. Probation officers

(1)   There may be appointed as probation officer or officers for a petty sessional division such person or persons of either sex as the authority having power to appoint a clerk to the justices of that division may determine, and a probation officer when acting under a probation order shall be subject to the control of petty sessional courts for the division for which he is so appointed.

(2)   There shall be appointed, where circumstances permit, special probation officers, to be called children's probation officers, who shall, in the absence of any reasons to the contrary, be named in a probation order made in the case of an offender under the age of sixteen.

(3)   The person named in any probation order shall,-

(*a*) where the court making the order is a court of summary jurisdiction, be selected from amongst the probation officers for the petty sessional division in or for which the court acts; or

(*b*) where the court making the order is a court of assize or a court of quarter sessions, be selected from amongst the probation officers for the petty sessional division from which the person charged was committed for trial:

Provided that the person so named may, if the court considers it expedient on account of the place of residence of the offender, or for any other special reason, be a probation officer for some other petty sessional division, and may, if the court considers that the special circumstances of the case render it desirable, be a person who has not been appointed to be probation officer for any petty sessional division.

(4)   A probation officer appointed for a petty sessional division may be paid such salary as the authority having the control of the fund out of which the salary of the clerk to the justices of that petty sessional division is paid may determine, and if not so paid by salary may receive such remuneration for acting under a probation order as the court making the order thinks fit, not exceeding such remuneration as may be allowed by the regulations of such authority as aforesaid, and may in either case be paid such out-of-pocket expenses as may be allowed under such regulations as aforesaid, and the salary or remuneration and expenses shall be paid by that authority out of the said funds.

(5)   A person named in a probation order not being a probation officer for a petty sessional division may be paid such remuneration and out-of-pocket expenses out of such fund as the court making the probation order may direct, not exceeding such as may be allowed under the regulations of the authority having control of the fund out of which the remuneration is directed to be paid.

(6)   The person named in a probation order may at any time be relieved of his duties, and, in any such case or in case of the death of the person so named, another person may be substituted by the court before which the offender is bound by his recognizance to appear for conviction or sentence, or, if he be a probation officer for a petty sessional division, by a court to whose control that officer is subject.

(7)   In the application of this Act to the City of London and the metropolitan police court district, the city and each division of that district shall be deemed to be a petty sessional division.

4. Duties of probation officers

It shall be the duty of a probation officer, subject to the directions of the court-

(*a*)   to visit or receive reports from the person under supervision at such reasonable intervals as may be specified in the probation order or, subject thereto, as the probation officer may think fit;

(*b*)   to see that he observes the conditions of his recognizance;

(*c*)   to report to the court as to his behaviour;

(*d*)   to advise, assist, and befriend him, and, when necessary, to endeavour to find him suitable employment.

5. Power to vary conditions of release

The court before which any person is bound by his recognizance under this Act to appear for conviction or sentence may, upon the application of the probation officer, and after notice to the offender, vary the conditions of the recognizance and may, on being satisfied that the conduct of that person has been such as to make it unnecessary that he should remain longer under supervision, discharge the recognizance.

6. Provision in case of offender failing to observe conditions of release

(1)   If the court before which an offender is bound by his recognizance under this Act to appear for conviction or sentence, or any court of summary jurisdiction, is satisfied by information on oath that the offender has failed to observe any of the conditions of his recognizance, it may issue a warrant for his apprehension, or may, if it thinks fit, instead of issuing a warrant in the first instance, issue a summons to the offender and his sureties (if any) requiring him or them to attend at such court and at such time as may be specified in the summons.

(2)   The offender, when apprehended, shall, if not brought forthwith before the court before which he is bound by his recognizance to appear for conviction or sentence, be brought before a court of summary jurisdiction.

(3)   The court before which an offender on apprehension is brought, or before which he appears in pursuance of such summons as aforesaid, may, if it is not the court before which he is bound by his recognizance to appear for conviction or sentence, remand him to custody or on bail until he can be brought before the last-mentioned court.

(4)   An offender so remanded to custody may be committed during remand to any prison to which the court having power to convict or sentence him has power to commit prisoners. In the case of a child or young person under the age of sixteen, he shall, if remanded, be dealt with wherever practicable in accordance with the provisions of section four, subsection one, of the Youthful Offenders Act, 1901.

(5)   A court before which a person is bound by his recognizance to appear for conviction and sentence, on being satisfied that he has failed to observe any condition of his recognizance, may forthwith, without further proof of his guilt, convict and sentence him for the original offence or, if the case was one in which the court in the first instance might, under section fifteen of the Industrial Schools Act, 1866, have ordered the offender to be sent to a certified industrial school, and the offender is still apparently under the age of twelve years, make such an order.

7. Power to make rules

The Secretary of State may make rules for carrying this Act into effect, and in particular for prescribing such matters incidental to the appointment, resignation, and removal of probation officers, and the performance of their duties, and the reports to be made by them, as may appear necessary.

2 Report of the Departmental Committee on the Probation of Offenders Act, 1907 (1910)

Home Office

Summary of conclusions and recommendations

(1) That the Act has already proved to be of great value in a large number of cases, and that actively used, when the conditions allow, it may become in the future a most useful factor in our penal law.

(2) That, partly owing to misapprehension of its scope, partly to its novelty, and partly to objections that have no solid foundation, the courts in many places have not made use of the powers of the Act in a considerable proportion of the cases in which they might properly be applied.

(3) That, supplementing the memorandum issued when the Act came into force, the Home Office should send a communication to every justice of the peace drawing attention to the provisions of the Act, and suggesting its more frequent use in proper cases.

(4) That a directory of probation officers should be prepared and annually revised by the Home Office.

(5) That the Home Office should draft model forms for the use of the courts, embodying the best features of the forms now in use, and couched in as simple terms as possible.

(6) That one official at the Home Office should be specially charged with the duty of keeping in touch with probation work, and of furnishing information with regard to it.

(7) That, except possibly in the case of some rural districts where offences are rare, at least one paid probation officer should be appointed at each court. The appointment of honorary probation officers may also be most valuable, but such appointments should be regarded as a supplement to, and not a substitute for, the employment of regular probation officers.

(8) That, where practicable, probation officers, specially qualified, should be appointed to deal with children and young persons; but that no attempt should be made to enforce section 3(2) of the Act, relating to the appointment of special children's probation officers, with a greater rigidity than Parliament intended.

(9) That a probation officer should be required by the terns of his appointment to undertake the supervision of offenders charged elsewhere, who live, or come to live, within his area.

(10)   That, as a general rule, police officers should not be appointed probation officers; and that, where they are so appointed, they should not also be employed on ordinary police duties.

(11)   That where an officer is regularly employed by the court, payment should be made by salary rather than by fee.

(12)   That, when payment is by fee, the amount of the fee should take into account any time spent by the officer in making preliminary inquiries.

(13)   That the scale of fees provisionally fixed by the Home Office for the metropolitan police courts is too low.

(14)   That the system of a fixed allowance for travelling or out-of-pocket expenses should be abolished, and that the sums actually expended by the officer on these accounts should be refunded to the officer, subject to a maximum and to the approval of the court.

(15)   That it is not desirable that a Central Probation Commission should be appointed.

(16)   That it would be useful if a Probation Officers' Society were formed to assist in the dissemination of information and in the development of probation work.

(17)   That generally it is neither desirable nor necessary that a chief probation officer should be appointed in each area to enlist assistants and to control the work of subordinate officers.

(18)   That, where possible, the justices should endeavour, for dealing with cases of lads and youths, to enlist the services of young men experienced in social work among working lads.

(19)   That care should be taken to secure that the district assigned to a probation officer should not be unmanageable through its extent, and that the number of cases he should be required to supervise should be limited as suggested in paragraph 46.

(20)   That in the case of a probationer who lives in a district other than that of the court before which he is charged, the officer in the former district should undertake the supervision.

(21)   That registers should be kept by the courts showing the results of the probation in each case.

(22)   That the probation officer should, if possible, be present in court at the hearing of the case, but that the result of any preliminary inquiries which he has made should not be communicated to the court till it has reached a conclusion on the truth of the charge.

(23)   That the probation officer should explain to the probationer the meaning of the probation order in the presence, where practicable, of the person in whose custody the probationer is, or of a responsible officer of the court; that he should keep a book containing a record of his cases, with entries of the visits paid and other particulars; that he should report to the court from time to time, as directed by the court, on the conduct of the probationer.

(24)   That the justices should require their officer to report without delay cases in which the probationer disregards the conditions of his recognisance; and that the probation officer should carefully guard against undue laxity in reporting any misconduct of the probationer to the court.

(25)   That, except in unusual and urgent cases, probation should be kept distinct from charitable relief.

(26) That the probation officer should not be employed to collect fines by instalments, where time has been given for payment.

(27) That when an offender has failed to observe the conditions of his recognisance, the duty of applying for a summons or a warrant against him should lie upon the police, and not upon the probation officer.

(28) That it is desirable that in every petty sessional division, by an informal arrangement among the justices, one or more justices should give special oversight to the probation work of the district.

(29) That the success of probation work would be promoted if justices would assist the probation officer in enlisting the help of local social agencies, and possibly in forming local committees to co-operate in the work.

(30) That a probation period of less than six months is, in most cases, of little use; that in a large number of cases a period of twelve months is desirable, and, in some, a longer period.

(31) That the Act should be amended to remove doubts as to whether under section 5 of the Act there is power to 'vary the conditions of the recognisance' by extending the term of supervision.

(32) That ... legislation should be introduced to enable the court to include a condition as to residence in an institution in the case of offenders over the age of 16; but that in such cases a probation officer should be appointed to visit the institution.

(33) That section 2(2) (b) of the Act should be amended so as to empower the court to impose the condition of abstention from intoxicating liquor in any case where the court is satisfied that the offence was committed in consequence of the habit of taking intoxicating liquor in excess.

(34) That the court should be given a somewhat wider latitude in fixing the conditions of a recognisance than section 2(2) of the Act now allows.

(35) That it should be made clear that an offender should be given an opportunity, by means of a summons, of showing cause against a proposed variation of the conditions of his recognisance.

(36) That the procedure for the recovery of damages, compensation, and costs should be simplified.

From Home Office, Report of the Departmental Committee on the Probation of Offenders Act, 1907: Report *(London: HMSO), 1910, pp. 13–15.*

3 Report of the Departmental Committee on the Training, Appointment and Payment of Probation Officers (1922)

Home Office

Summary of conclusions and recommendations

(1) Probation is of great value as a means of reformation and is economical. Magistrates should always consider the possibility of using it, and the organisation of Probation Officers should be sufficient for this purpose.

(2) Probation should be used at an early stage in the offender's career, but where it has definitely failed its use should not as a rule be repeated.

(3) The existing law is generally speaking adequate.

(4) The extent to which probation is used varies considerably in different places, both as regards young offenders and adults. Probation would with advantage be used much more freely in many Courts. Every Court should have a Probation Officer at its disposal.

(5) Probation Officers should continue to be appointed by the Courts and paid by local authorities as at present. It is not desirable that they should be appointed by the State.

(6) It is not necessary that the appointment of Probation Officers should be reviewed annually by the Courts except for the first two years after appointment.

(7) It is not desirable to separate probation work from other missionary work in the Courts

(8) Many persons are now employed as Probation Officers who are not properly qualified for the work.

(9) Wherever possible Probation Officers should be employed only on probation work and similar missionary duties. Where the work at one Court does not justify the appointment of a full-time officer it is desirable to arrange that two or more Courts should share the services of the same officer.

(10) The Societies who have hitherto provided Probation Officers have done most valuable work, and, though some Courts may prefer to appoint their own officers, others can rely on the services of these Societies.

(11) Women officers should be appointed as a rule to supervise women probationers, and specially qualified officers should be appointed to look after children.

(12) Volunteer officers can often give valuable assistance and their employment under proper supervision should be encouraged. The paid Probation Officers should make greater use of voluntary agencies in carrying on their work.

(13) Probation Officers should not be given too many cases or too large districts. No absolute standard can be fixed, but the amount of work and nature of their duties should be supervised by the magistrates.

(14)   As the value of probation depends on the character and personal qualities of the Probation Officer, great care must be exercised in their selection. There is need in the Probation Service for men and women of higher education and better training, and Societies who provide Probation Officers should be advised to improve the education and training of their candidates.

(15)   The remuneration of Probation Officers is unsatisfactory in many places, both as to method and amount. It is suggested that full-time officers (men) should receive not less than £200 at the age of 30 and rise to £350 at the age of 45. Women should receive £150 and rise to £250. Travelling and other incidental expenses should be paid. Where the officers are provided by a Society the local authorities should pay an adequate proportion of the salary. The remuneration of part-time officers should be by salary or fixed annual sums, and should be fixed according to the average amount of work. The system of paying by fees should be abandoned except for isolated cases.

(16)   No general superannuation scheme for Probation Officers is practicable. Societies should be encouraged to establish adequate schemes for their own officers to which both the local authorities and the officers might contribute.

(17)   The creation of a paid Government Commission to control and develop probation work is not desirable.

(18)   The Home Office should continue to act as the Central Authority and should be assisted by an Advisory Committee having a paid secretary.

(19)   The supply of Probation Officers will depend largely on the services of voluntary Societies, especially the Police Court Mission, which should be reorganised on broader lines.

(20)   In London there should be one Police Court Mission. Better organisation and supervision is required, in which the members of the Advisory Committee who are selected from London should assist.

(21)   In provincial towns the magistrates should appoint a small committee of their own members to select Probation Officers and generally supervise their work. In counties endeavour should be made in suitable cases to organise the work on County lines.

(22)   A Government grant should be given eventually towards the cost of probation.

(23)   It is suggested that juvenile adults sentenced to prison for three months or more might be placed under supervision on their release for a period of six months.

> *From Home Office,* Report of the Departmental Committee on the Training, Appointment and Payment of Probation Officers *(London: HMSO), 1922,*
> *pp. 22–24.*

4 Report of the Departmental Committee on the Social Services in Courts of Summary Jurisdiction (1936)

Home Office

Summary of recommendations

(17) No person should be placed on probation without full enquiry into his previous history and present surroundings. ...

(18) The present procedure should be simplified. There is no need for the recognizance, and a simple supervision order based on the consent of the offender should be substituted. The power to require sureties should be retained. The name of the probation officer should not appear on the order. The prescribed conditions should be simplified.

(19) Greater use should be made of the power to order the payment of damages, compensation and costs, and to vary or discharge probation orders.

(20) If a probationer disobeys the conditions of the order, it is important that it should be enforced. The wording of the 'good behaviour' condition should be varied to make it clear that liability to punishment for the original offence does not depend merely on the commission of a new offence. The summons or notice to a probationer brought up for disobedience should state in what way his conduct is regarded as unsatisfactory.

(21) The responsibility for the supervision of the probationer and for the enforcement of the order should rest with the probation authority for the area in which he resides. Transfer should follow change of residence.

(22) Suggestions are made as to the way in which the duties of the probation officer should be performed [with regard to home visits, reporting, finding work for the probationer, attendance at court, etc.].

(23) The present Home Office scheme for the payment of grant in respect of residence in approved hostels should be made more elastic, and should be extended to cover residence in other hostels and in suitable lodgings.

(24) The power to insert in a probation order a condition of residence in a home should be limited to six months, and should be confined to institutions approved by the Home Office.

(25) It should not be necessary to obtain the consent of the local authority to expenditure on maintenance in hostels, lodgings or homes, when required by a probation order.

(26) The services of a probation officer should be available at Assizes and Quarter Sessions whenever the question of making a probation order is likely to arise. Arrangements should be made for the principal probation officer or other experienced officer to attend as liaison officer.

(27)   The liaison officer should be allowed to present to the Court the reports of other probation officers. ...

(29)   The various social services which are carried out by probation officers should be recognised as part of their official duties as well as the supervision of probationers.

(30)   Apart from conciliation, these services include:

(i)   Social investigation in cases other than those in which a probation order is likely to be made.

(ii)   Investigation as to means under the Money Payments (Justices Procedure) Act and otherwise.

(iii) Supervision of persons ordered to pay fines.

(iv)   Collection of monies. Probation officers should not act as collecting officers but they may be able to assist the persons responsible for payment to avoid default by receiving instalments of fines and other payments.

(v)   Applications in bastardy. Where an applicant for a bastardy order requires advice this should if possible be provided by reference to a solicitor or legal aid society. Where this cannot be arranged the probation officer may be able to help with advice as to procedure, but care must be taken to avoid abuse.

(vi)   Adoption enquiries. Ordinarily the local authority is the most suitable guardian *ad litem* but in exceptional circumstances the probation officer may be employed.

(vii) Escorting to institutions.

(viii) Supervision of juveniles in need of care or protection

(ix)   Assistance in the administration of the Poor Box or other Court Fund.

(x)   After-care. Where other arrangements cannot be made probation officers may assist with after-care connected with approved schools and Borstal institutions but they should not engage in the after-care of discharged prisoners or convicts. Any payments for this work should be paid to the probation authority, and it should be supervised in the same way as the probation officer's other duties.

(xi)   Miscellaneous. The advising of the many miscellaneous applicants who come to the Courts is valuable work, but care should be taken that there is no interference with the probation officer's other duties.

(31)   The appointment of probation officers should rest with the Probation Committee.

(32)   The principle of combination should be applied to every petty sessional division, except the larger county boroughs. The county will ordinarily be the most effective unit for combination, but local circumstances may need different arrangements. In some cases it may be necessary to combine more than one county.

(33)   In a Combined Area there should be a central Probation Committee, responsible for matters of organisation, and local Case Committees with the duty of case supervision.

(34)   The Case Committee should take into consultation persons of social experience, who are not Justices. The probation officer, or one of the probation officers, should be the secretary of the Case Committee and the Clerk to the Justices

should be an *ex officio* member. In a Single Area the work of case supervision should be carried out by one or more Case Sub-Committees.

(35)   It should be the duty of the Probation Committee to make arrangements for the efficient performance of probation work at Assizes and Quarter Sessions. The machinery for bringing probationers before Courts of Assize and Quarter Sessions for breach of conditions requires consideration.

(36)   It is essential for the efficient development of the probation service that in future it should be organised on a wholly public basis. There is, however, ample scope for the co-operation of the missionary societies in the social services of the Courts.

(37)   The general rule should be to provide for full-time appointments. Even in the smallest Combined Area there should be at least one full-time probation officer and in most cases one of each sex. Existing part-time officers doing virtually full-time work should be eligible for appointment as full-time officers.

(38)   In some scattered areas it may be necessary to give the full-time officer the assistance of 'probation officers' assistants'. Such appointments should be subject to Home Office approval, and the probation officers' assistants should work under the direction of the full-time officers, and should not spend more than a limited part of their time in the work. Their remuneration should not exceed £50 per annum without Home Office approval.

(39)   Principal probation officers should be appointed wherever this is justified by the size of the staff or other considerations. In some of the larger areas it may be necessary to appoint deputy principal probation officers. Where the appointment of a principal probation officer is not justified the duties ordinarily performed by a principal probation officer should be carried out by an experienced probation officer. Where the amount of work and responsibility is substantial there should be power to make an allowance of £25 or £50 per annum for these duties.

(40)   Voluntary help may be of great assistance to the probation officer in individual cases, but it should be carefully supervised. Voluntary officers cannot take the place of paid ones.

(41)   The power to appoint persons other than probation officers to exercise supervision should be repealed.

(42)   Greater specialisation is desirable, but it should not be carried so far as to prevent officers from obtaining experience of all branches of the work.

(43)   Adequate provision should be made for office accommodation and equipment, transport and clerical assistance.

(44)   The present Rules as to the expenses of probation officers should be revised.

(45)   The Home Office should accept greater responsibility for the general administration, supervision and direction of the probation service. The responsible officials should keep in close touch with the probation authorities, and the Secretary of State should be given a general power of inspection to satisfy himself that a reasonable standard of efficiency is being maintained.

(46)   The Home Office should be assisted by an Advisory Committee representative of all the interests connected with the probation service on the lines of the present Advisory Committee.

(47)   The National Association of Probation Officers has rendered valuable assistance in the development of the probation service. Consideration should be given to

the question of summoning from time to time regional conferences of probation officers, Justices and other interested persons.

(48)   The Home Office as probation authority for London should work through a Committee as at present. One or two members with experience of social work might be added. In London it will probably be necessary to appoint not only a principal probation officer, but also deputy principal probation officers, at least one of whom should be a woman. Case supervision should be provided for on lines similar to those of Case Committees elsewhere.

(49)   The organisation in London should include not only the Metropolitan Police Courts, the Juvenile Courts, the London Sessions and Central Criminal Court, but also the Petty Sessional Courts.

(50)   The qualifications for appointment as probation officers require revision as indicated in the Report.

(51)   The improved scales of salary given in the Report are required to attract a sufficient supply of suitable candidates.

(52)   It should be the duty of the Probation Committee to make sure that the probation officer receives sufficient opportunity for relaxation and recreation and so to regulate the hours of work where there is more than one officer to provide for a proper alternation of duties, and to allow annual holidays of at least four weeks.

(53)   Retirement should be optional at the age of 60 at the wish of the officer or the appointing authority and should be compulsory at 65.

(54)   A probation officer needs two kinds of training:
   (i)   a broad study of the principles of modern social work such as can be gained by a University social science course.
   (ii)   a short specialised training in the work of a probation officer (or 'Probation Course').

(55)   The best means of ensuring that candidates for appointment as probation officers receive this training is through an extension of the experimental Home Office training scheme. The Home Office should appoint a Central Board on which the appointing authorities and the Universities with social science departments should be represented. This Board should make periodical selections of candidates for training, and should determine the appropriate training for each of the selected candidates. All should take the probation course. It would depend on the qualifications of the candidate whether a social science course was necessary. There should be close co-operation between the Board and the appointing authorities, who, on the occurrence of a vacancy, would choose between available trained candidates. Candidates selected for training would be paid a subsistence allowance. The cost of the scheme should be shared between the Home Office and the local authorities.

(56)   Facilities should also be provided for the training of existing officers.

From Home Office, Report of the Departmental Committee on the Social Services in Courts of Summary Jurisdiction *(London: HMSO), 1936, pp. 140–145.*

5 Report of the Interdepartmental Committee on the Business of the Criminal Courts (1961)

Home Office

Summary of recommendations

(9) ... the cardinal principle is that every sentence should be based on comprehensive and reliable information which is relevant to the objectives which the court has in view. ...

(13) The probation service and the police should, on request, give the court all the information they can about the effect of a sentence which was specially intended to deter potential offenders. ...

(17) Reports by probation officers:

(a) All concerned should recognise that a probation report may properly supply the court with information about the offender and his background which is relevant to his culpability or to stopping him from offending again and with an opinion as to the likely effect on the offender of probation or some other form of sentence.

(b) (i) An opinion given to the court about the likely effect of a form of sentence should be based on relevant knowledge of the effect of the form of sentence to which it relates and on general research into the results of sentences.

(ii) Those concerned with the training and supervision of probation officers should consider how, in this respect, the experience of the probation service as a whole, together with the results of researches, can best be made available to individual probation officers.

(iii) The opinion should be freely expressed but should in terms be confined to possible ways of diverting the offender from his criminal career (which is only one of the considerations in the court's mind).

(c) Pre-trial enquiries.

(i) It should be permissible for a probation officer to make enquiries about a person accused of an offence but unconvicted, provided that the accused person is given the opportunity to object and does not object.

(ii) At all courts a probation report should be available upon conviction, and any necessary pre-trial enquiries should be made, in all cases where the accused does not object and

(a) is 30 or under, or

(b) has not been previously convicted, or

(c) has recently been in touch with the probation service.

Individual courts may add to these minimum categories, and the probation liaison officer should be able to authorise the preparation of a report in a case not falling within them.

(iii) The probation officer should be supplied with an advance copy of the police statement of antecedents, and should avoid, so far as is possible, duplicating the police enquiries or repeating in his report facts contained in the police statement.

(iv) A report prepared before the trial should, where possible, be sent to the court at least 24 hours before the hearing and should invariably be taken into account by the court before passing sentence.

(v) The clerk to the committing justices should see that the probation liaison officer at the superior court is promptly notified whenever a person is committed for trial or sentence.

(vi) Where the defendant is on bail, the probation officer should arrange for any medical examination which appears to be necessary, subject to the prior approval of the clerk of the court of trial. Where the defendant is in custody, the probation officer should mention the matter to the prison medical officer.

From Home Office, Report of the Interdepartmental Committee on the Business of the Criminal Courts *(London: HMSO), 1961, pp. 122–124.*

6   Report of the Departmental Committee on the Probation Service (1962)

Home Office

Summary of conclusions and recommendations

(1)   The functions of the probation service have, in general, developed to meet needs which probation officers are best equipped to meet. The range of functions which probation officers undertake should not be narrowed. ...

(3)   Probation officers are well fitted to meet the courts' needs for enquiries about offenders whether or not a probation order is in prospect. The probation officer's report should be known as a 'social enquiry report'.

(4)   It is most desirable that a social enquiry report should be considered before a court makes a probation order and full social enquiries should be made wherever possible. The courts should not be under a statutory obligation to make them.

(5)   An enquiry made when a case is 'put back' for a few hours after a finding of guilt is a poor substitute for a full social enquiry; but there may occasionally be cases in which delay for enquiries before making a probation order would not be justified.

(6)   Probation officers should make social enquiries before trial only if the accused person, having had the opportunity to object, has not done so.

(7)   If a probation officer is able to form an opinion about an offender's likely response to probation he should express it in reporting on his social enquiries.

(8)   There is not scope at present for more than the most gradual development towards reporting by probation officers on offenders' suitability for methods of treatment other than probation. ...

(14)   Probation work has become more complex and demanding since the report in 1936 of the Departmental Committee on the Social Services in Courts of Summary Jurisdiction. The probation service is now a profession, requiring professional training and skill. The probation officer is a professional caseworker employing, in a specialised field, skill which he holds in common with other social workers. He is also, however, the agent of a system concerned with the protection of society. ...

(28)   Duties under supervision orders are appropriately placed upon probation officers: but it should remain for the courts to decide whether a probation officer will be the most appropriate supervisor in a particular case.

(29)   A money payment supervision order is in no sense a substitute for a probation order. A probation officer should be used for money payment supervision only

where the limited supervision he can exercise may avoid a default otherwise likely to occur.

(30) Every effort should be made to avoid probation officers having to collect instalments of fines.

(31) The after-care duties of probation officers have appropriately been placed upon them. A very considerable expansion of the probation service would be needed before probation officers could undertake the after-care of all those for whom the Criminal Justice Act, 1961, enables it to be provided. ...

(34) Probation officers should continue to be available for *guardian ad litem* duties in England and Wales. ...

(35) Probation officers who undertake enquiry work for the divorce courts into questions concerning the welfare of children may appropriately, at the request of the judges, attempt reconciliation of the parties. This work should be recognised in planning staffing. ...

(38) Probation officers should continue to undertake matrimonial conciliation at the request of the courts. It should be made clear beyond doubt that this is a statutory function of the service. ...

(42) The probation service is well placed to help people in matrimonial trouble who approach probation officers direct or are referred to them by other agencies. Without this help many such people would be without recourse. ...

(49) The probation service is essentially a social service of the courts. ...

(52) Further combinations of probation areas can profitably be made. Unless there are exceptional circumstances, any probation area which cannot sustain a staff of six or more probation officers (excluding a principal probation officer) should be merged in a larger administrative unit. ...

(54) There are no substantial grounds for criticising the way in which the Home Office has carried out its role as central authority but strained relationships have developed, for a variety of reasons, between the Home Office and probation committees and between the Home Office and the service. ...

(58) Full inspections of probation areas are desirable at about three-yearly intervals. ...

(63) The Home Office should exercise a degree of control and guidance which reflects the legitimate national interest in the service, but the present apparatus of control is not wholly apt for this purpose. ...

(73) The scope for specialisation in the probation service is severely limited but, where practicable, the division of work among the members of a group, according to their aptitudes, interests and experience, should be encouraged. There should not be any general movement towards specialisation in particular types of work, such as after-care or matrimonial. ...

(100) The rapid expansion of the service in England and Wales has not kept pace with the increase in work and it has been necessary to admit a high proportion of untrained persons. It would be unrealistic at present to set a date after which such appointments are forbidden. The training the direct entrants receive after appointment is not an acceptable alternative to full training before appointment. Every effort should be made to release them for full length training as this becomes possible. ...

(103) Recruitment to the probation service cannot be confined to specified 'types' of personality or to people with narrowly defined experience or qualities.

Selectors can best be guided by a broad description of the work of probation officers such as was prepared by the Institute of Industrial Psychology in 1946. ...

(104) There is room in the service for a range of educational and intellectual attainment. The normal standard for acceptance for training should be no lower than that of the school certificate or the general certificate of education at ordinary level, and a substantial proportion of more highly qualified men and women are needed. But a minimum educational qualification should not be rigidly applied. ...

(108) Research is needed into ways of assessing probation officers' work. Case-loads should be treated as guides to the appraisal of total 'work-loads'. In so far as reference to case-loads may still be helpful the standard for a man should be fifty. It is questionable whether the theoretical grounds for distinguishing the standard case-loads of men and women are justified.

(109) In England and Wales, expansion will be necessary in the near future to a strength of rather more than 2,000 whole-time officers. A further increase to 2,750 may be necessary in the next few years. ...

(121) From the earliest possible date every probation officer should receive not less than two years' training before appointment. In the immediate future one year Home Office courses for students aged over 30 should continue; but candidates of this age should be considered for university training if they are willing and are accepted by universities. Admission of students over 30 to two year 'general' courses should also be arranged. ...

(144) The maximum of the salary scale for the basic grade of probation officer should be £1,350 a year. The minimum should be £750. Starting pay should depend on age for officers who have not attained the age of 28.

From *Home Office,* Report of the Departmental Committee on the Probation Service *(London: HMSO), 1962, pp. 147–155, 158–161.*

7 Non-Custodial and Semi-Custodial Penalties (1970)

Advisory Council on the Penal System

Chapter 3 Service to the Community

The idea in principle

32.   Voluntary service has deep roots in the social life of this country. It has for long been a feature of many multi-purpose organisations such as the Scout movement, the Women's Royal Voluntary Service, youth clubs, the Churches, Toc H and a host of others, often in conjunction with local Councils of Social Service. Recently, the idea has come into fresh prominence with the emergence of organisations created for the specific purpose of providing such service, and with the involvement of young volunteers still at school. For illustrations of the wide variety of projects included in such voluntary community service, ranging from constructional enterprises for the benefit of the community as a whole to acts of personal service to individuals, we are greatly indebted to representatives of the organisations concerned whom we have consulted. The examples quoted included: constructing adventure playgrounds; clearing beaches and country paths; helping with reclamation projects and restoring canals; cleaning up churchyards; redecorating and restoring churches and church halls; landscaping hospital grounds; clearing bomb-sites; planting trees; repairing railings; making and repairing children's toys in hospitals and children's homes; helping in hospital wards and kitchens, and in clubs for the physically handicapped; maintaining the meals on wheels service at week-ends; and helping the elderly or needy in various ways, e.g., visiting, decorating their homes, gardening and distributing clothing. In all cases, care is taken to ensure that the use of volunteers does not prejudice the position of paid employees: local Councils of Social Service each have a trade union representative amongst their members. In general, the work is such that if it were not done by unpaid labour it would not be done at all.

33.   Some of these tasks would seem suitable for offenders, although a few would not; there would, for example, be obvious difficulties in some tasks involving close personal contact with individuals, many of which would in any case require greater continuity than a court order would afford. But in general the proposition that some offenders should be required to undertake community service should appeal to adherents of different varieties of penal philosophy. To some, it would be simply a more constructive and cheaper alternative to

short sentences of imprisonment; by others it would be seen as introducing into the penal system a new dimension with an emphasis on reparation to the community; others again would regard it as a means of giving effect to the old adage that the punishment should fit the crime; while still others would stress the value of bringing offenders into close touch with those members of the community who are in most need of help and support.

34.   These different approaches are by no means incompatible. A court order which deprived an offender of his leisure and required him to undertake tasks for the community would necessarily be felt to have a punitive element. What attracts us, however, is the opportunity it would give for constructive activity in the form of personal service to the community, and the possibility of a changed outlook on the part of the offender. We would hope that offenders required to perform community service would come to see it in this light, and not as wholly negative and punitive.

35.   The importance which we attach to the reformative value of a community service scheme for offenders has led us to the conclusion that offenders performing community service at the behest of the courts should, so far as is practicable, do so in association with volunteer non-offenders. While we do not rule out entirely the performance of community service by groups consisting solely of offenders (we explore this question further in paragraph 45), we would regard it as a mistake if this became the normal style of the new proposal; for this would, in our view, be likely to give the whole scheme too strong a punitive flavour, and would cut off offenders, both from the more constructive and imaginative activities, and from the wholesome influence of those who choose voluntarily to engage in these tasks.

36.   We have, therefore, in mind a scheme which would rely substantially on voluntary community service agencies, and we discuss in paragraph 46 the kind of relationship with these agencies that we envisage. It is true that there are many areas in which voluntary agencies do not operate; and it has been suggested to us that in such areas the best course would be to stimulate the setting-up of an all-purpose voluntary agency. But this is a bridge which need not be crossed yet. Community service for offenders would have to be built up gradually, and its development is unlikely to outstrip the development of local voluntary community service. In any case, in view of the need for legislation it would be some time (see paragraph 61) before our recommendations could become effective.

37.   We have not attempted to categorise precisely the types of offender for whom community service might be appropriate, nor do we think it possible to predict what use might be made by the courts of this new form of sentence. While inappropriate for trivial offences, it might well be suitable for some cases of theft, for unauthorised taking of vehicles, for some of the more serious traffic offences, some cases of malicious damage and minor assaults. We have considered whether it should legally be confined to imprisonable offences, and while in general we would hope that an obligation to perform community service would be felt by the courts to constitute an adequate alternative to a short custodial sentence, we would not wish to preclude its use in, for example, certain types of traffic offence which do not involve liability to imprisonment. Community service should, moreover, be a welcome alternative in cases in

which at present a court imposes a fine for want of any better sanction, or again in situations where it is desired to stiffen probation by the imposition on the offender of an additional obligation other than a fine. It might also be appropriate as an alternative to imprisonment in certain cases of fine default. We do not, however, think that it should be possible to combine a requirement to perform community service with a fine in respect of the same offence; community service and fines should be alternatives.

38. We recognise that community service might be particularly valuable in the treatment of the young offender, especially in view of the association which we envisage with volunteers, many of whom are teenagers; indeed, such service is one of the forms of treatment which are envisaged for offenders under 17 by the Children and Young Persons Act 1969. But we do not think that it should be confined to any particular age group. There is in our view considerable scope for application of this new sentence to adults. Not all volunteers are young, and some middle-aged or even elderly offenders of either sex might well profit from working for the benefit of those in need; and, for offenders thought to be suffering from domestic isolation, community service might well prove to be a less sterile treatment than deprivation of liberty.

39. We have therefore attempted to devise a scheme under which a court could order an offender to carry out in his leisure time, over stated period, a specified number of hours of community work. We envisage that, generally speaking, this should involve attendance only during evening or week-ends, though we do not exclude participation in residential projects. But we do not include in this context any proposal for full-time, compulsory service, which we regard as fundamentally different in principle from the scheme we have in mind. Our views on this alternative are elaborated, in connection with the general possibilities of compulsory paid work as a penalty, in Chapter 5.

40. Before making an order for community service, the court would need to satisfy itself that the offender was capable of undertaking such service and was reasonably likely to be co-operative; and it would need to have sanctions available in the event of non-compliance with the order. The court would not itself specify the work to be done; that would have to be arranged by or through an agency acting on its behalf. Our conclusions as to the choice and function of such an agency, which we recognise to be crucial to the whole success of our proposal, will be found in paragraphs 47–52.

41. In some State and municipal courts in the USA, for example, it is a common practice to require traffic offenders to carry out work in hospitals; and in West German juvenile courts the power to issue directives to young offenders has been used for similar purposes in an imaginative and sometimes striking fashion, e.g., by sending young drunks to help in homes for inebriates in order to bring home to them the consequences of alcoholism, or by sending those who rob old people to help at weekends in old people's homes. We are alive to the attractions of such proposals but it is not our primary intention to make the punishment fit the crime; should this occur we would expect it to be as much a matter of accident as of design. We are particularly anxious to avoid decisions which might smack of gimmickry and so undermine public confidence. The scheme we have in mind, therefore, is intended not to compel the offender to undergo some form of penance directly related to his offence, which would

have only a limited application, but to require him to perform service of value to the community or to those in need.

Existing experience of community service by offenders

42.   Experience of the present practice of employing prisoners and borstal inmates on extra-mural work has some relevance to our inquiry. In these cases some work is undertaken for government and voluntary bodies without charge for labour, one of the best-known examples being the clearing of the Stratford-on-Avon canal. Some paid work is also done for local authorities and hospital group management committees, who pay the full labour cost. Additionally, in some cases prisoners have been encouraged to perform voluntary unpaid community service outside working hours. It is a feature of all these schemes that offenders volunteer for the work, and that they often perform it alongside non-offender volunteers. The value of this experience for our purpose is however, limited, inasmuch as volunteering affords offenders in custody a welcome opportunity of getting outside the institution for a time, and does not raise the administrative problems inherent in a non-custodial scheme. At the same time, success in the employment of prisoners alongside volunteers supports the view that we have expressed in paragraph 35. We understand also that local arrangements are sometimes made under which probation officers and hostel staff have been successful in encouraging young offenders to participate in voluntary community service schemes.

Finding and organising the work

43.   We see three conditions as crucial to the attainment of our objective, namely, (i) a steady, sufficient and varied supply of tasks to be carried out by offenders, (ii) machinery for linking the offenders with the organisation responsible for the provision of these tasks, and (iii) machinery to give effect to the order of the court. Since we envisage a scheme which makes use of voluntary organisations, we have turned to them for advice about a supply of tasks, and we have been assured that there is an abundance of opportunity for community service, both in work with or for individuals and in constructional projects. But the administrative problems involved in promoting a sufficient range of suitable tasks and in matching these tasks to offenders – who would not come in a steady flow and who would represent a wide range of ability, and possibly of willingness to co-operate – would be considerable. It would be necessary to ensure that offenders participating in joint schemes did not slack, and to provide not only for supervision on the actual performance of the job, but also for the court to be satisfied that its sentence was being effectively carried out. So far as the former type of supervision is concerned, however, we would hope that, if sufficient care is taken in the selection of the offenders who are to work alongside volunteers, the normal operational supervision undertaken by the persons or organisations for whom the service was provided would usually be enough.

44.   Difficult problems are raised by the question how much information about offenders working alongside volunteers should be disclosed, and to whom.

Here something may perhaps be learned from experience of cases where prisoners work alongside volunteers: but this analogy is limited, and our proposal necessarily raises even more complex and delicate issues, on which we think that it would be premature to lay down hard and fast rules in advance of practical experience. These questions should, in our view, be the subject of thorough discussion on the spot between the parties concerned, and the decisions reached would not necessarily be in all cases identical. At the present stage we would only say that we are not disturbed by the possibility that the presence of offenders might deter voluntary workers. Few volunteers are likely to regard offenders as a class apart, and in general, the voluntary organisations which we have consulted think that offenders could safely be absorbed into groups of volunteers. From the offender's point of view, we recognise that there might be attractions in secrecy, but there is always a danger of leakage. In any case, it would appear to be necessary, for many practical reasons, that the voluntary association responsible for the organisation of community service should know which of its workers were offenders and which volunteers. This does not, however, mean that detailed particulars of the offences committed by the former should be disclosed by the court; nor should information identifying offenders automatically be passed on to the authorities in charge of any institution, such as a hospital or old people's home, on whose behalf the community service is undertaken and by whom it is supervised. On all these questions experience may in due course suggest general principles to be followed, but here we must again emphasise that, in the initial stages of the scheme, decisions can only be reached after careful consideration of all the circumstances of each individual case.

45. The proportions of offenders and volunteers engaged in any particular task would, no doubt, vary from one project to another. In exceptional cases we would not rule out the possibility that some tasks might be undertaken by groups composed entirely of offenders. If court-ordered community service is to make a real impact as an alternative to custodial treatment, it will need to embrace a range of offenders some of whom may require closer and firmer supervision than a voluntary agency could reasonably be expected to exercise. Even if the reformative value of community service would be diminished where offenders are not working side by side with volunteers, we think that, if the projects are imaginatively chosen, there may well be scope for some groups of offenders to work on their own in situations in which they are not publicly identifiable.

The relationship with the voluntary agencies in the community service field

46. We come now to the critical question of the link between the courts and the voluntary agencies. These agencies could not be expected themselves to provide the courts with all the services that would be required, and it would, therefore, be necessary to establish some intermediate organisation whose functions would include reporting to the courts, before sentence is passed, on offenders' suitability for community service; assessing their capabilities; arranging with the voluntary agencies what work the offenders should do; ascertaining whether the work had been satisfactorily performed; providing

any necessary equipment and transport where these were not available from any other source; maintaining records and referring back to the court those offenders who failed to report or to work to an acceptable standard.

The organisation to administer community service

47.   After examining the various possibilities we have come to the conclusion that these functions would most appropriately be assigned to the probation and after-care service. To set up a new national organisation with local offices would be extremely expensive and would compete for staff with both the prison and the probation and after-care services. Nor do we think it practicable, at least in these present circumstances, to look to the local authority department to undertake these tasks. Our choice therefore lay between the prison and the probation and after-care services.

48.   Although in some areas, the prison service might be relatively well placed to allocate offenders to particular projects, to receive them from the courts and, where necessary, to supervise them and to transport them to and fro, we do not think that prisons would in principle be suitable as reporting centres. Moreover, they are not well distributed geographically, and their use for this purpose might involve serious issues of security.

49.   The probation and after-care service, on the other hand, is a locally-based service with an extensive network of local offices. It exists to serve the courts, and it carries out a widening range of duties connected with the treatment of offenders in the community. It has a tradition of working through the use of general community resources. Some aspects of the new functions which we envisage, such as the assessment of individual offenders and their allocation to appropriate tasks, would not be very remote from existing probation duties. We have discussed the matter in general terms with representatives of the Conference of Principal Probation Officers, the National Association of Probation Officers and the Central Council of Probation and After-Care Committees; and with the agreement of the Chairman of our parent Advisory Council we have also had discussion with the Advisory Council for Probation and After-Care. We have been greatly encouraged by the reaction of these bodies to our proposals. They have all readily accepted the proposition that the probation and after-care service would be the appropriate organisation to administer a scheme of community service for offenders. A power to order community service would in their view represent a significant addition to the range of disposals available to the courts; and they would think it entirely appropriate for local probation and after-care committees to assume responsibility, in collaboration with local voluntary bodies, for giving effect to such orders.

50.   We accept that it would be necessary to strengthen the resources of the service for these new functions, particularly on the administrative side, and that there might well be a need for a new type of appointment (at a relatively high level) in large urban areas. Such an appointment would, moreover, be in keeping with the present tendency towards diversification within the service resulting from the new demands recently imposed upon it. In addition, special training

might be necessary for probation officers responsible for offenders required to undertake community service.

51. We recognise that we have not precisely defined the detailed relationship between the probation and after-care service and the voluntary agencies. This is deliberate: to work out this relationship would require much discussion between representatives of the service and the agencies (and no doubt of the Home Office also); and whatever arrangements resulted would need to be regarded as provisional and subject to adjustment in the light of experience. The broad pattern of arrangement, as we now see it, is that the local probation and after-care service would maintain regular contact with any local community service agency which would thus be in a position to make suggestions about suitable placing of offenders required to undertake community service. Each offender would report to the local probation officer or some alternative centre; and his initial placement, as also subsequent contact concerning his performance of the task allotted to him, would be a matter for arrangement between the voluntary agency, the organisation or person for whom he was working, and the local probation and after-care service. This would be the usual procedure; but occasionally it might be expedient for arrangements to be made directly between the probation and after-care service and those wishing to make use of the offender's services without the intervention of a voluntary agency.

52. A harmonious relationship between the probation service and the voluntary agencies would clearly be essential to the operation of the scheme. Each of the voluntary agencies has its own individual philosophy and objectives, but all share an over-riding concern with the needs of the community. We find nothing in this which is in any way incompatible with our proposal, but we recognise that the agencies would need to be on their guard lest the interests of the community should be subordinated to the urgency of finding occupation for a flow of offenders sent by the courts.

The order of the court

53. As regards the form of the court order, a choice lies between, on the one hand, a new statutory provision (which might, for example, be modelled on the attendance centre order) and, on the other hand, an extension of the conditions which may be inserted in a probation order to include a direction to undertake community service. Both the Advisory Council for Probation and After-Care and ourselves found the choice between these alternatives difficult, and there was some divergence of opinion among the representatives of the probation and after-care service with whom we discussed the matter. Some took the view that it should be possible for the court to order community service directly in cases where the supervision normally exercised by a probation officer appeared to be unnecessary, even though the probation and after-care service would, as we have proposed, still be responsible for giving effect to the order. Others argued that, if the probation and after-care service were to run a scheme on behalf of the court, the logical course would be for community service to be a condition of a probation order, and that the concept of probation ought to be widened accordingly, so that even those offenders who did not

appear to need support at the time of their court appearance could receive it, should the need arise during the currency of the order. An offender's assumption of the responsibility of community service might, it was suggested, of itself precipitate some personal crisis in which the guidance of a probation officer would be helpful. In any case, probation should be developed as a method of treatment of a wider spectrum of offenders than heretofore.

54.   In our view there are three main arguments in favour of making community service a condition of a probation order. In the first place, it is undesirable to multiply new forms of court order without good reason. It would certainly minimise confusion if the courts were able to avail themselves of a well-established and familiar form of order which is already used to ensure compliance with directions as to residence in a hostel or submission to mental treatment, rather than to be required to accommodate themselves to an entirely new type of order. Secondly, a probation order would afford a ready-made means of continuing support and supervision during and after the period of community service and of ensuring that an offender was not ordered to undertake community service unless he was willing (or at any rate not resolutely unwilling) to do so. Thirdly, a probation order would provide an established procedure in cases where the offender failed satisfactorily to perform the required service.

55.   On the other hand, we see several objections to this proposal to make performance of community service a condition of a probation order. Such a requirement, even though linked with supervision by a probation officer, needs to be seen, both by the courts and offenders, as a new form of treatment standing in its own right. The creation of a new form of order would be a guarantee that the courts would see it in that light and would use it accordingly, and that they would not regard it merely as an 'extra' in a probation order. A separate order would also make it easier for the offender to understand what was being required of him, and would obviate the risk that the use of a probation order merely as a vehicle for a novel type of sanction would blur the traditional concept of probation. A further objection is that an offender suitable to perform community service may not necessarily need the supervision and guidance which a probation order provides, and that it would be a misuse of such an order for it to be employed merely as a means of giving effect to a community service requirement. Nor is a probation order essential as a means of establishing an offender's willingness to undertake community service. Whatever the form of the order the courts would be required to attach to it a notification on the part of the person to whom it applied of his consent to its terms.

56.   The arguments in favour of either of the two methods of imposing an obligation to undertake community service do not seem to us so compelling as to justify exclusion of the other alternative. We, therefore, recommend that the court, having satisfied itself by a social enquiry report as to an offender's suitability to undertake community service, and having ascertained that he consents to this course, should be empowered *either* to make a probation order with a condition requiring such service, *or* to issue a direction to undertake community service unaccompanied by any probation order: and that in every case the choice between these methods be left to the court's discretion.[1] In the exercise of this

discretion the court will no doubt distinguish between, on the one hand, offenders who do not appear to require help or supervision in their personal lives, or to whom the obligation to attend regularly at a probation office might seem an unnecessarily irksome addition to the obligation of community service, and on the other hand, those who seem likely to benefit significantly from the friendship, advice and support which a probation officer can give. There would need to be provision for dealing with breaches of a direction to undertake community service, such as failure to report or to work satisfactorily. The court should have power to deal with minor breaches by imposing a fine, and with more serious transgressions by revoking the original direction and dealing with the offender in any way in which he could have been dealt with for his original offence.

57.   The order of the court would need to specify the total period of service to be performed, within a maximum to be prescribed by legislation. We suggest that this overall maximum might be of the order of 120 hours. We think it preferable not to specify in legislation any maximum number of hours of work to be performed on any one occasion, so that there would be complete freedom to fit in with arrangements for volunteers. It would clearly be undesirable for a very long period to elapse before the service was completed: one suggestion made to us was that the order might provide for a maximum period of six months during which the community service should be completed, within a probation order of two years' duration. We think, however, that, since there might be changes both in the offender's circumstances and in the programme of work which would hamper the implementation of the order, it might be preferable to leave the supervising probation officer to decide within what overall period the order should be carried out. It would be for this officer to instruct the offender when first to report for work, and it would be open both to him and to the offender to apply to the court for variation or cancellation of the community service requirement, as with any other condition of a probation order.

58.   If, as we propose in paragraph 37, community service is used in some cases of fine default it would seem necessary to provide a special maximum number of hours which the courts may order where the defaulter is under 21, since it would seem inconsistent to enable the courts to order up to 120 hours in default in such cases, in view of the fact that there is a maximum of 12 (or 24) hours for defaulters ordered to attend an attendance centre. ...

The need for experiment

61.   We are conscious that there are many imponderables and many practical difficulties involved in a community service scheme for offenders. We do not think that it would be profitable to work out further details on paper; in the last analysis the only way of discovering whether schemes will work is to try them out. We should have welcomed experiments within the framework of existing law, but we are advised that as the law stands a probation order cannot properly include a requirement of community service; probation is at present an alternative to the imposition of a sentence and what we are proposing would clearly constitute a sentence. Our proposal must, therefore, await new

legislation. But even when the necessary statutory provision has been made, it seems to us essential that a few pilot schemes should first be established in different parts of the country in order to test the practicability of the whole idea of community service. In this connection we are glad to report that a number of local voluntary agencies have expressed themselves as very ready to set up pilot schemes of community service for offenders in their areas: there is certainly no lack of goodwill.

62.   We would recommend further that the statutory provision empowering the courts to order community service or to include it as a condition of a probation order should (on the lines of the attendance centre or detention centre provisions in the Criminal Justice Acts) be exercisable only as and when individual courts have been notified that appropriate facilities are available. This procedure would ensure that the general framework within which each local probation and after-care committee proposed to give effect to the order of the court would be subject to central approval, so as to safeguard consistency of standards and to preserve the status of the system; and it would, additionally, provide an opportunity for indicating to the court the broad age range or ranges for which local work would be suitable.

The need for evaluation

63.   Finally, we would strongly urge that, as with any new penal experiment, provision for systematic study of the working of the community service project should be incorporated in the scheme from the outset. While we attach importance to the need for the experiment to be evaluated from the beginning, we should emphasise the dangers of drawing premature conclusions from early experience. We hope, therefore, that the most careful consideration will be given to the design of an appropriate research project.

From Advisory Council on the Penal System, Non-Custodial and Semi-Custodial Penalties *(London: HMSO), 1970, pp. 12–21.*

Note

1   The technical question arises as to whether an offender directed to perform community service should, like an offender placed on probation, be deemed not to have been convicted for purposes of record. We are content to leave this to the legislators.

8 Young Adult Offenders (1974)

Advisory Council on the Penal System

Chapter 10 Treatment in the Community

260. In this chapter we set out our proposals for developing and expanding the arrangements for the non-custodial treatment of young adult offenders, building upon the existing probation system. *In particular, we propose the introduction of a new non-custodial order which we have called a supervision and control order.* The purpose of this order is to give to the courts a means of imposing on a young adult offender to whom they might at present feel obliged to give a custodial sentence a degree of supervision and control which would enable him to be dealt with in the community. The new order would be administered by the probation and after-care service but would be distinct from a probation order – which would remain available to the courts – and is intended to deal with a class of offender who would not normally be considered suitable for probation. The order would include a wide range of standard requirements – discussed in greater detail later on – which could be invoked at the supervisor's discretion. *The making of the order, unlike a probation order, would not require the consent of the offender,* and the order would not be 'instead of sentencing him'. ...

267. Our proposal for a new type of non-custodial sentence is based on two important considerations. First, the supervision and control order gives the supervising probation officer a greater measure of control and freedom of action in exercising supervision. Because the order would be made without the consent of the offender, the probation officer would have a different kind of responsibility for intervening in the conduct of the case by bringing into effect any requirements contained in the order without having to rely on the agreement of the offender. Though the techniques used in the treatment involved in implementing a particular condition would be comparable to techniques used in probation, the authority given to the probation officer implies powers of enforcement in bringing the condition into operation. The sanctions available to the supervising authority in case of the offender's failure to co-operate or in the event of breach of conditions of the order are discussed below. In particular, an entirely new proposal is made that, in certain circumstances, the supervising officer should have power to detain the offender temporarily on application to a magistrate.

268. Our second important consideration in proposing the new power is that it should encourage the courts to use, and the public to accept the use of, non-custodial measures on relatively serious offenders for whom an order of the

court which depended on their consent does not seem appropriate. This wider judicial and public acceptance would, we hope, in turn stimulate further provision of resources and facilities in the community which would be available for use both in support of the new measure and for supervision of those released to the community under a custody and control order.

269.   Underlying both the considerations outlined above is the contrast between the probation order and the supervision and control order in regard to the need for the offender's consent. We recognise that there are some who will not easily accept a new form of supervision by probation officers which does not require consent. But supervision imposed without the offender's consent and administered by the probation service is not a novelty. It is a feature of statutory after-care supervision and of the new suspended sentence supervision order. A statutory requirement of consent to a supervision and control order would not be appropriate, since it is intended that the order should permit the imposition of types of control to which it would be unrealistic to expect the offender to give genuine consent at the outset of the order. It is of course true that, if the order is to be effective, there must be a measure of acquiescence on the offender's part, but the relationship between supervisor and offender will, at least initially, be based more on obligation than on consent. *Before imposing the order, the court should consider a social enquiry report and satisfy itself that there is at least a reasonable probability of the obligations being accepted by the offender.* If, in the event, they were not, the order would no doubt break down and the offender would have to be brought back to court. But to pretend that the order was based on freely given consent would be unreal.

The order and its requirements

270.   Thus, the supervision and control order would supply a means of placing a young adult offender under a quite strict form of control by a probation officer. *The order would be available in respect of any offence punishable by imprisonment in the case of an adult* (i.e. in a narrower class of case than a probation order). *We would recommend that the maximum duration of a supervision and control order should be two years* rather than the three year maximum for probation, in recognition of the greater element of control and intensity of contact: *provision should be made for early termination on the application of the supervising officer, given a good response on the part of the offender.*

271.   It would be an important feature of the order that it would make available to the individual supervisor a standard range of requirements which could be invoked at his discretion unless the court in making the order had specifically excluded any of them. *The requirements of the order would be substantially the same as those which we recommend that the Secretary of State should be enabled to apply at the time of releasing an offender from custody under a custody and control order ... Thus the requirements would be*
    (a) to keep in touch with the supervisor as required by him;
    (b) to be of good behaviour;
    (c) to work in employment approved by the supervisor;
    (d) to reside in a place approved by the supervisor (including an approved probation hostel);

    (e) to avoid any places of resort specified by the supervisor; and

    (f) if required by the supervisor, to undertake a specified course of education or work training, whether residential or non-residential.

We envisage that *the Secretary of State would have power to add or modify the available requirements by statutory instrument.*

272.   *It is essential that the court, when making a supervision and control order, should explain to the offender what the potential liabilities under the order are,* including his liability to temporary detention (see paragraphs 283 to 288 below) *and that the offender should be given a notice in writing setting them out.* The court should ensure that he clearly understands that any requirements imposed upon him during the course of the order are authorised by the court at the time of sentence and are not to be regarded as being arbitrarily imposed by the supervisor. The latitude allowed to the supervisor in deciding the timing or precise incidence of the conditions allowed by the court order has as its object to permit treatment to be varied flexibly in accordance with the offender's changing needs, without the necessity for reference back on each occasion to the court.

273.   We shall not attempt to spell out in detail how the supervising officer would use his discretion, within the terms of the supervision and control order, to carry out his obligation to supervise and control. This would be determined by the needs of the individual offender. We limit our comments to a few points which seem to us to involve new administrative provisions or a novel approach.

274.   Clearly a requirement with regard to residence will be important. Under our proposals hostel residence will continue to be available both as a requirement of a probation order and also as an option available to the supervisor under a supervision and control order. There is a particular need for an increase in non-custodial residential provision for offenders in the form of hostels, lodgings and flatlets which will enable young adult offenders to be kept in the community while at the same time giving them a stable background which may have been lacking in their normal environment. This will be the more important if a greater proportion of offenders in this age-group is to be treated non-custodially. ...

275.   As regards education, work training and similar activities, we see scope for a range of different approaches. One approach which may well prove valuable and relevant to the needs of young adults is the day training centre, particularly if (as the initial experience of the experimental centres set up under the 1972 Act seems to suggest) the centres can develop not as premises where educational and training activities take place exclusively but as somewhere for people to meet and develop a common identity and purpose and from which they could go out to make use of existing community facilities. The impression of those members of the Council who visited the United States and saw day centres for young adult offenders, particularly in California, was that this kind of facility should be developed for young adult offenders here also. *Consideration should be given, in the light of further experience of the experimental centres, to adding attendance at a day training centre to the list of standard requirements available in a supervision and control order,* just as it is a requirement that can be inserted in a probation order.

276.   But non-residential training of the kind we envisage does not necessarily require the formality of a centre from which it is organised. As indicated above

probation officers are accustomed to encouraging those under their supervision to make use of many kinds of community facility which bring them into contact with non-delinquents – for example specifically educational activities, social and recreational clubs, and adventurous outdoor activities of the Outward Bound type. There is every reason to suppose that this process would extend to young offenders made subject to a supervision and control order. Indeed, the greater emphasis on control which the order will impart into the supervisor/offender relationship, and the greater concentration of supervising effort which will be necessary under the order, should mean that more can be done under a supervision and control order than under a probation order to influence an offender in those ways. Whether it is done under the aegis of a formal requirement (paragraph 271 (f)), or informally, will vary with the circumstances and indeed, once a proper relationship has been established under the supervision and control order, will probably not greatly matter. These are after all activities towards which the offender can be led but not driven.

277.   Some of these considerations apply to *community service*. As introduced in the 1972 Act this is a separate court order and not a condition in a probation order. It will be apparent from what has been said about our concept of the supervision and control order that community service is the kind of activity which it would be useful to be able to require an offender to carry out under a supervision and control order as well as under the existing community service order under the 1972 Act. The Home Office Guide to the Act, prepared for the use of magistrates and others, describes the community service provisions as aimed at providing 'a power which the courts and the public will see as a viable alternative to the shorter custodial sentence', and 'envisaged as a means of imposing the sanction of deprivation of leisure for a constructive and outward-looking purpose, which will enable the offender to give something back to the community against which he has offended and will in some cases bring him into direct contact with members of the community who most need help and support'. These features of community service would make it particularly valuable as an instrument of control available to the supervising officer under a supervision and control order.

278.   There is a complication in adding the performance of community service to the list of standard requirements available in a supervision and control order. It arises from the question of consent. Section 15(2) of the 1972 Act provides that a court shall not make a community service order unless the offender consents. We understand that a condition requiring an offender to perform community service would, if imposed without the offender's consent, be held to contravene Article 4(2) of the European Convention for the Protection of Human Rights and Fundamental Freedoms, and the International Labour Convention of 1930 for the Suppression of Forced or Compulsory Labour. Therefore, if the performance of community service were made a standard supervision and control order requirement, it would have to be subject to the qualification that the formal consent of the offender had first been obtained. We do not regard this as a serious obstacle, particularly since the performance of community service, like participation in the educational and other activities discussed above, must involve the *de facto* consent of the offender whether or

not there is a formal requirement; we should therefore like to see community service made, with the qualification about consent, one of the possible requirements under a supervision and control order. If, however, it were decided to leave the performance of community service outside the formal scope of a supervision and control order, it could still be treated as an example of the involvement in community activity towards which a supervising officer should guide an offender under his charge. This would then be no more than has been the position under the probation system. But in any event, what matters is that young adult offenders subject to a supervision and control order should where appropriate take part in this sort of activity; the precise means by which it is arranged is of secondary importance.

Provisions for dealing with breach of requirements of a Supervision and Control Order

279. Since it is our intention that the supervision and control order should be used to deal with offenders of a more difficult kind than those who are at present put on probation, and since the order is to be imposed without the offender's consent, the demands made upon supervisors will be heavy and it is important to consider carefully what powers they may need to secure compliance and deal with breaches of requirements.

280. A main purpose of the order being to avoid committing the offender to custody, the supervising officer must in the first instance attempt to deal by persuasion, rather than sanctions, with a failure on the part of the offender to co-operate. He will have considerable latitude in the application of requirements, for instance with regard to residence or avoidance of certain places of resort, but such variations are to be seen as treatment measures rather than as sanctions for failure to carry out other aspects of the order.

281. *We propose that, if the offender shows whether by failing to keep in touch with the supervising officer or by committing specific breaches, that he does not intend to carry out the requirements of the order, the supervisor should have power to take him before a magistrates' court. The court should then have power to deal with the breach by fine or any other non-custodial disposal available to it.* This would include the power to make a community service order; if an order was to be used in this way, we recommend that the minimum of 40 hours to be worked, as laid down in the present Act, should not apply.

282. The imposition of a non-custodial penalty by the court would not terminate the supervision and control order. *There should however be the power in extreme cases,* such as blatant refusal by the offender to comply with the requirements of the order, *to revoke the order and substitute an alternative sentence, which should take account of the extent to which the offender had complied with the original order.*

Temporary detention

283. In the discussion which we have had both in this country and abroad about the difficulties of handling young adult offenders in the community, our attention has been called to the view of experienced supervising officers that a breakdown of a supervision order might sometimes be prevented if they were able to take quick and decisive but essentially short-term action to detain an offender,

either on the commission of a breach or in anticipation of some behaviour on the part of the offender which would threaten the continuance of the order. We have therefore given careful thought to the possibility of providing supervising officers with a power which might meet this requirement and so permit the treatment of offenders to continue despite some temporary crisis in the supervisory relationship.

284.   In our investigation of methods employed in California we found that a practice has developed whereby a supervising officer occasionally has an offender removed to temporary detention. The detention of a probationer has to be followed within 48 hours by a court appearance unless, as is frequently the case, he is released by that time. The practice is used in order to provide a short-term penalty for misbehaviour under supervision or a cooling-off period when a breakdown is feared. The most significant feature of this arrangement is that detention is essentially an interlude in the course of supervision in the community and is used with the specific purpose of making it possible for the supervision to continue and of avoiding resort to a custodial sentence. Those who have experience of this practice emphasise the importance of being able to take immediate action, so that the offender sees his detention as a direct consequence of what he has done.

285.   Adapting this system to conditions in this country, *we recommend that a supervisor administering a supervision and control order should be empowered to apply to a magistrate for a warrant authorising the arrest of the offender giving reasons why he thinks such action is justified. The magistrate would then have power to issue a warrant, which would be executed by the police, permitting the offender's detention for a maximum period of 72 hours.*

286.   We propose that the ground on which a magistrate might make an order of this kind would be that he was satisfied either that a breach of the requirements of the order had been committed, or that the supervising officer had reasonable ground for believing that the commission of an offence or other breach of the order was in contemplation; and that in either case the temporary detention of the offender might avoid the necessity of taking the offender before the court for revocation of the order.

287.   It follows from what has been said that the period of temporary detention should be used by the supervising officer to bring home to the offender the likely consequences of his behaviour, so that supervision in the community could be resumed. It would therefore be necessary to hold the offender in detention reasonably near to where he lived and for the supervisor to have easy access to him. We do not think that police cells would be an appropriate place of detention. In cases where the offender offered some measure of co-operation, it might be sufficient to order him to reside in a hostel, but *in most cases he would have to be detained in the nearest establishment designated for the reception of young adults.*

288.   We appreciate that this proposal for the temporary detention of a young adult offender, to whom the court has given a non-custodial sentence, would be an innovation in the present British system and raises questions both of principle and of practical administration, which will require full discussion among the various authorities involved in its implementation. We feel sure that the practical problems can be solved if the principle is accepted. The principle

which has underlain our thinking on this issue has been that, if difficult and unstable offenders are to be effectively supervised in the community instead of being placed in custody, the supervising officer must be given adequate means of dealing with temporary periods of crisis, which are bound to arise. These means must provide a way of surmounting a passing crisis in such a way that supervision can be resumed when it is over. Breaches of the requirements of a supervision and control order are to be expected, and the purpose of this new provision will be frustrated if a breach is normally followed by return to the court and termination of the supervision. Arrangements are however needed to ensure that the offender's rights are protected and that the courts retain ultimate control over the decision whether a person should be deprived of his liberty. We consider that the arrangements we have proposed provide sufficient protection.

Implications of these proposals for the probation service

289. Our proposals for making wider use of supervision and control of young offenders in the community ... have important implications for the probation service. This is particularly true of the proposal for a supervision and control order, which will call for the exercise of more extensive and intensive supervision and control of categories of offender who are likely to prove more difficult than those who are customarily put on probation. We have had some discussion of our proposals with representatives of the probation service, but we have thought it best that formal consultations with the service should take place at a later stage, when these proposals can be considered in the wider context of our published report.

290. We see the role of the probation and after-care service in regard to the new supervision and control order as consistent with recent developments in the functions of the service. We have stressed the differences between the new order and a probation order, and these will inevitably be reflected in the daily duties of probation officers. But the functions of the service have long since been extended beyond the administration of probation orders into after-care and more recently parole. Under the Criminal Justice Act 1972 they are being further extended into responsibilities for community service, day training and suspended sentence supervision. In all these the traditional duty of the probation officer to 'advise, assist and befriend' has been preserved, but the concept of the consent of the person supervised has been eroded and the element of control has been increasingly emphasised. Similarly, while the final decision on the disposal of a probationer following a breach of a probation order remains with the judicial authority, in parole and after-care the decision to recall or to revoke a licence is taken by the executive authority, after receiving a report from the officer in charge of the case, whose opinion on the need for recall or revocation of licence plays an important part. It is true that in these cases the responsibility of the individual probation officer is modified to the extent that the final recommendation rests with his superiors. Similar protection could be provided under our proposals to probation officers administering a supervision and control order, subject only to the need to avoid administrative delay in the operation of temporary detention.

291.   For these reasons we do not think that our proposals involve any violation of the basic principles of the probation and after-care service. On the contrary, since their fundamental purpose is to keep as many young offenders as possible out of custody, we believe rather that they represent a realistic modification of traditional practice, which is essential if the underlying objectives of the service are to be attained in the conditions which exist today.

From Advisory Council on the Penal System, Young Adult Offenders
(London: HMSO), 1974, pp. 89–97.

9 Probation Service in England and Wales

Statement of National Objectives and Priorities (1984)

Home Office

1. This statement of national objectives and priorities for the Probation Service in England and Wales has been prepared as part of the Home Secretary's developing strategy for dealing comprehensively with all aspects of crime and of the treatment of offenders. The strategy recognises not only that the criminal justice agencies – the police, the courts and the probation and prison services – must work closely together, but also that effective action requires the collaboration of other statutory and voluntary bodies and the support of all members of the community in their ordinary lives. As an agency drawing on social work skills and working within the criminal justice system and also within local communities, the Probation Service can make a unique contribution in providing a link between the offence and the offender, and in the wider social context in which offending takes place and in which preventive action has to be taken if results are to be achieved. It is therefore particularly important that the work of the Probation Service should not be dissipated and that its resources should be used to full effect.

2. The efficient and effective use of resources is primarily the responsibility of area probation committees and their chief officers, who must assess their local needs and circumstances and design local programmes to meet them. These programmes must, however, reflect consistent principles which cannot just be determined locally. This statement of national objectives and priorities has therefore been prepared in the Home Office, following consultation with the Service's representative organisations – the Central Council of Probation Committees, the Association of Chief Officers of Probation and the National Association of Probation Officers – as a basis on which area services can construct their own plans and deploy their own resources to best effect. The statement, like the local programmes based on it, will be reviewed and modified at appropriate intervals to take account of changing demands and opportunities and of the effects of the change on other services.

3. The duties, powers and functions of the Probation Service in England and Wales are established by statute – principally the Powers of the Criminal Courts Act 1973, as amended by the Criminal Law Act 1977 and the Criminal Justice Act 1982. This statutory framework is complemented by the Probation Rules of which a new consolidated set is due to come into operation in 1984. The main duties of the Service are the provision of advice to the courts; the supervision of offenders in the community subject to probation, supervision and community service orders; the provision of welfare services to offenders in custody; and the

after-care of offenders released from custody including the supervision of those released on licence. The Service also has duties arising from the civil jurisdiction of the courts. The locally based organisation of the service and its special position in the criminal justice system have attracted to it other less well-defined but important tasks. In the past these were mainly directed towards working with the offender in the community and to limiting the distress involved in the break-up of families; more recently the service has also become increasingly involved in the community's wider response to offending, for example through participation in schemes providing housing, education and employment or in the support of victims.

4.   The Service remains as always concerned with reducing the incidence of crime and related social breakdown, and with enabling offenders to achieve more satisfactory ways of life. However, the character of the Service and the volume, scope and variety of its work have changed dramatically since its origin in the voluntary police court mission at the end of the last century. The pace of change has accelerated considerably in the last twenty years.

5.   As well as providing advice to courts and undertaking the supervision of offenders subject to probation and supervision orders, the Service is now operating in penal institutions, providing day centres, running schemes of community service and intermediate treatment, and engaging with a wide range of statutory and voluntary agencies in a variety of activities. In 1963, 94 area probation services employed some 2,000 probation officers and some other staff and the annual cost was about £4.5 million. In 1983, 56 area probation services employed nearly 6,000 probation officers and about 5,000 ancillary and other staff; the current cost in 1983–84 is expected to be about £150 million. The task of running the Service has therefore become more demanding, both managerially in terms of the size, variety and complexity of the resources involved, and professionally in terms of the demands which are made on the objectivity, judgement and commitment of individual probation officers and those responsible for their professional development and supervision.

6.   At a time when recorded crime and public concern about crime have been increasing, the Probation Service has constantly to ensure that its work is effective, that it is relevant to the needs of the community which it serves and that it has the confidence both of the courts and of the public at large. There must be a continual process of interaction with other agencies and other interests – locally between probation committees, the management and staff of area services, the courts, the police, the prison service, local authorities, local government services, educational institutions and a variety of voluntary organisations; and centrally between the representative organisations and central Government, especially the Home Office. New opportunities and demands are opening up in the fields of preventive work, mediation and reparation, where the service is already involved to some extent and where its experience, knowledge and skill should enable it to make a significant contribution.

7.   New activities and new interests of this kind inevitably raise questions of resources. The provision made by the Government is intended to allow the Probation Service to grow by rather more than three per cent in 1984–85 as

compared with 1983–84. But the response to changing needs and circumstances cannot always be the provision of extra resources. The first task must be to check that existing resources are being deployed in a cost-effective way. It can then be seen how far any new requirements can be met by adjusting priorities or adopting new methods of working with the resources that are already available. The following paragraphs are intended to provide the context in which such an examination should take place.

Purpose, objectives and priorities of the Probation Service

I.   The Probation Service, together with others involved in the criminal justice system, is concerned with preparing and giving effect to a planned and co-ordinated response to crime. It must maintain the community's confidence in its work, and contribute to the community's wider confidence that it is receiving proper protection and that the law is enforced.

II.   The main purpose of the Service within the criminal justice system is to provide means for the supervision in the community of those offenders for whom the courts decide that it is necessary and appropriate.

III.   In pursuance of this purpose, the service has the following principal tasks:
(i) the provision of reports to the courts which may include reasoned advice on sentencing;
(ii) supervising offenders subject to probation, supervision and community service orders;
(iii) providing through-care for offenders sentenced to custody, and exercising supervision after release in cases where required by law.

IV.   The Service has other statutory tasks arising from the civil work of the courts in relation to matrimonial disputes and the welfare of children.

V.   In fulfilment of these purposes, and in the discharge of its statutory responsibilities, the Service should seek to attain the following specific objectives:

A   *Working with the courts*
(i)   concentrating the provision of social inquiry reports on cases where a report is statutorily required, where a probation order is likely to be considered, and where the court may be prepared to divert an offender from what would otherwise be a custodial sentence;
(ii)   maintaining the confidence of the courts in the ability of non-custodial measures to cope with a wide range of offenders.

B   *Supervision in the community*
(iii)   ensuring that each area probation service is able to accept and put into effect as many orders as the courts decide to make, especially in cases where custodial sentences would otherwise be imposed;
(iv)   maintaining a range of facilities which, used in conjunction with probation and supervision orders in suitable cases, will increase their effectiveness and thereby the Service's capacity to cope with the widest possible range of offenders;
(v)   ensuring by clear planning and follow-up action that the supervision, support, advice and guidance available to offenders under probation or supervision orders, through the exercise of social work skills and

use of available facilities, are applied as efficiently and effectively as possible in each case so that the risk of offending is reduced, to the benefit of the offender and of the community.

C   *Through-care*

(vi)   assisting prisoners while in custody, and in preparation for and following release;

(vii)   ensuring that offenders under statutory supervision comply with the requirements of their licences, and assisting them so far as possible to make a successful and law-abiding adjustment to ordinary life.

D   *Other work in the community*

(viii)   encouraging the local community in the widest practicable approach to offending and offenders, taking account of the influences of family, schools and other social factors and of the potential contributions of other agencies;

(ix)   developing the service to the wider public by contributing to initiatives concerned with the prevention of crime and the support of victims, and playing a part in the activities of local statutory and voluntary organisations;

(x)   civil work: providing services to courts in accordance with statutory requirements.

VI.   In the allocation of resources towards these objectives, the following broad order of priorities should be followed:

(a) The first priority should be to ensure that, wherever possible, offenders can be dealt with by non-custodial measures and that standards of supervision are set and maintained at the level required for this purpose.

(b) Resources should be allocated to the preparation of social inquiry reports on the basis that standards will be similarly set and maintained, but that reports will be prepared selectively in accordance with the objective set out above.

(c) Sufficient resources should be allocated to through-care to enable the Service's statutory obligations to be discharged (including the reduction in the minimum qualifying period for parole). Beyond that, social work for offenders released from custody, though important in itself, can only command the priority which is consistent with the main objective of implementing non-custodial measures for offenders who might otherwise receive custodial sentences.

(d) The Service should allocate sufficient management effort and other resources if necessary to ensure that each area probation service is making an appropriate and effective contribution to wider work in the community (objective D). The scale and pace of development will depend on local needs and the opportunities available.

(e) The proportion of resources allocated to civil work should be contained at a level consistent with local circumstances and the foregoing priorities.

VII.   The extent to which this order of priorities will involve a redistribution of resources or a change in the existing priorities of area probation services will vary according to the circumstances of the service concerned. In general it may be expected that priority (a) will continue to engage an increasing proportion of the Service's total resources; that (d) will engage an increasing amount of energy or management effort but not necessarily of total manpower; and that (b), (c) and (e) will involve some reappraisal of methods to establish the scope for using the existing or a slightly reduced level of resources to better effect.

From Home Office, Probation Service in England and Wales: Statement of National Objectives and Priorities *(London: Home Office), 1984.*

10 Punishment, Custody and the Community (1988)

Home Office

Part III Proposals for Punishment in the Community

Components of punishment in the community

3.8 The Government believes there is scope for reducing the use of imprisonment by introducing a form of punishment which leaves the offender in the community, but has components which embody the three elements identified in Part I, punishment by some deprivation of liberty, action to reduce the risk of offending and recompense to the victim and the public.

3.9 Punishment in the community would place a range of requirements on the offender, which include making some recompense for the crime. The arrangements could include many features of the present disposals, community service, compensation, going to a day centre or an attendance centre. The restrictive elements might include close supervision of the offender's whereabouts, residence at a particular place, or confining the offender to his home during specified hours. Other restrictions might be forbidding particular activities, or staying away from particular places. Legislation might be introduced which would enable any or all of these elements to be combined in a single supervisory order.

Compensation

3.10 The Criminal Justice Bill makes changes in the arrangements for compensation orders. The Government hopes that these changes will increase the use of these orders. It has been suggested that the courts should be able to pay the total sum awarded to the victim immediately and then recover the money from the offender. The victim would benefit by having the compensation more quickly but the direct link between the offender's payments and the victim would be lost. Meanwhile the court and the Exchequer would, in effect, be lending the outstanding money.

Should the courts be empowered to pay the whole sum to the victim immediately from fine income and then to recover the money from the offender?

Reparation

3.11 Consideration has also been given to the possibility of making direct reparation by the offender to the victim an element in the new arrangements. Between

1985 and 1987, the Home Office funded four experimental reparation schemes, enabling a victim and offender to meet, on an entirely voluntary basis, to discuss the offences and, if possible, to arrange reparation. One of the schemes linked reparation to police cautioning as an alternative to prosecution. Two others assessed it as a possible adjunct to other court disposals for offenders in magistrates' courts. The fourth examined the potential for diverting offenders in the Crown Court from custody. A report on the assessment of these schemes will be published later in the year. In some schemes, there seemed to be confusion about whether reparation was for the benefit of the victim or a means of rehabilitating the offender.

3.12   Victims should not be placed under pressure to co-operate in arrangements for reparation and no victim should feel under any obligation to take part in such arrangements. Nor should a victim's decision on reparation affect the court's decision in sentencing the offender. It would be unjust if the severity of a sentence depended on the victim's willingness to take part in reparation and it would place undue pressure on some victims. On the other hand, mediation between the offender and the victim could be useful when they are known to each other and are likely to remain in contact, for example, as neighbours or colleagues at work.

Would it be desirable for the probation service to arrange such mediation informally, when it would be helpful? Should direct reparation by the offender to the victim be restricted to monetary payments by compensation orders paid through the courts?

Community service

3.13   General reparation to the public can be made through community service. Legislation might enable community service to be imposed either as a separate disposal or as part of a wider supervisory order. The present maximum is 240 hours (120 for 16 year olds) and the minimum is 40 hours. The Court of Appeal has equated 190 hours of community service with 9 to 12 months of imprisonment.

3.14   A lower minimum could result in the order being used for less serious offenders. A longer community service order is useful in requiring the offender to accept the sustained discipline of regular attendance. But experience has shown that community service orders of more than 200 hours are more likely to be breached. An order of more than 200 hours requires the offender to attend at least 30 work sessions over a period of several months. The location may well be inconvenient but he will be expected to report punctually. The demands which a long period of community service make are therefore considerable, especially for offenders whose way of life is disorganised.

Should the minimum of 40 hours for community service (the equivalent of a working week) be altered? Could it be higher or lower? Should the present maxima be changed?

Day centres

3.15   Under existing law, the period of attendance at day centres cannot exceed 60 days. The 60 day period may extend over six months with the offender usually attending two or three days a week. Because the period is defined in days rather than hours, the offender's time can be occupied more fully by requiring him to attend for 12 hours each day. However, stress on long hours for their own sake may not be the best way of using day centres. In practice, the impact which day centre attendance can make on an offender may reach its peak after less than 60 days. However, for some offenders a longer period of attendance may be beneficial.

3.16   The programmes in day centres should be geared to the types of offending prevalent in the areas. Programmes designed to bring home the consequences of what an offender has done and to change his or her outlook are essential in every centre.

Should the maximum period for attending a day centre be increased from 60 to 90 days? Are there new elements which should be essential in the provision made by day centres?

Restrictions on liberty

3.17   There are a number of ways in which offenders' liberty could be restricted and the public protected by deterring reoffending. 'Tracking' is a term used broadly to cover various schemes which use ancillary probation staff to maintain regular and frequent contact with offenders under supervision in the community. Experimental schemes set up in West Yorkshire, including some schemes working with adults and young adults, involve the tracker contacting the offender, either face to face or by telephone. At first, this is done daily. The tracker discusses with the offender how he or she will spend his or her time and maintains contact with schools, clubs and other places where the offender intends to go. These contacts usually become less frequent over time. Tracking is at present limited to 60 days for adults. There has been no central evaluation of the success of these schemes in diverting offenders from custody or in preventing offending during or after the period of supervision.

Should tracking be used more to reinforce supervision and some control over offenders? Should it be available for longer, possibly up to three months?

3.18   More restrictions could be introduced by legislation which could allow the courts to make an order confining an offender to his home during specified hours. This is done in some jurisdictions in the United States. Such requirements punish by severely restricting an offender's liberty. They may also reduce the opportunities for reoffending, but they cannot prevent it if the offender is determined to reoffend. An offender confined to his home could still receive stolen goods, and engage in drug trafficking or drug abuse. Before imposing an order, the court would need to take account of the offender's circumstances. Those living in poor or isolated accommodation might have to be provided with a hostel place if the condition is to be enforceable. The court would also have to consider the effects of the requirement on the offender's family, other people sharing the same accommodation, and neighbours. There are also the interests of landlords.

Should the courts be given powers to require offenders to stay at home at specified times? If so, should there be guidelines on the length of the curfew and a maximum period for which it could be imposed, possibly three months?

3.19   The main constraint on such an order is the likely difficulty of enforcing it. Curfews for juveniles are meant to be enforced with the co-operation of parents, though in practice this is not always forthcoming. Young adults are much less likely to be living at home with their parents although it is an objective of the Government's social security policies to encourage them to do so until they are in a position to support themselves financially. Many adults will be living fully independent lives. Personal visits to the offender's home by a supervisor, especially in unsocial hours, would be expensive. Observance of a curfew might be checked by telephone calls, but only if the offender had a telephone. As a consequence, the offender would be tempted to violate the order because of the low risk of detection.

3.20   Electronic monitoring might help to enforce an order which required offenders to stay at home. It is used for this purpose in North America. Less restrictively, it could help in tracking an offender's whereabouts. By itself, electronic monitoring could not prevent reoffending, though it might limit opportunities to commit offences to a degree which a court would consider justified diversion from custody. There are two main types of monitoring equipment in use in North America. In some systems, the offender wears a miniature transmitter which emits a continuous signal. This retransmitted from his home, e.g. by telephone, to a central monitoring point and the offender cannot move very far away from the telephone without alerting the central monitoring system. In other systems, the supervisor uses the signal from the monitoring tag to verify that the offender is in a specified place, either in response to random telephone calls from the central monitor or in calls at a prearranged place. North American experience may not be directly relevant to England and Wales; for example, monitoring is used in the United States to divert from custody some offenders who would not be at risk of a custodial sentence in England and Wales.

3.21   It would not seem necessary, or desirable, to use electronic monitoring as an additional restraint on offenders who are dealt with in the community at present. The main justification for its use in England and Wales would be to enforce tracking or an order requiring the offender to stay at home for a limited period, thereby making it possible to keep out of custody offenders who would otherwise be in prison. The Home Office is evaluating various forms of equipment.

It would be helpful to have views on the usefulness of electronic monitoring in keeping more offenders out of custody.

3.22   Consideration has been given during the last 10 years to the possibility of introducing some form of intermittent or weekend imprisonment. In a consultation document on 'Intermittent Custody' (Cmnd 9281) the Government asked for views on the possibility of a semi-custodial sentence, which would involve detention for only part of the day or part of the week. This would be an alternative to full custody; a partial deprivation of liberty might be preferable to full imprisonment for many of the less serious offenders who were receiving custodial sentences. However, for intermittent custody to work effectively, the offenders would have to be sufficiently reliable to report each week to serve their sentence. It would therefore be unsuitable for rootless and unstable offenders. Employed offenders would not be suitable for day prison, but could be considered for prison at weekends.

3.23   Many of those who responded to the consultation document considered that intermittent or weekend custody was more likely to replace non-custodial measures than full custody. There was no agreement on the kind of offenders for whom it would be suitable or the form it might take. Given the considerable likely cost of providing the necessary facilities and of tracing offenders who did not turn up and bringing them back to court, the Government concluded that the possible advantages were outweighed by the probable disadvantages. The Government has considered the arguments again and reached the same conclusion.

3.24   However, there are other ways of restricting an offender's liberty at weekends. For example, the courts could require offenders to refrain from taking part in particular activities, such as attendance at football matches or other sporting events or to stay away from specified places connected with the offence, for example, specified streets, pubs or clubs, shops.

Would such restrictions be useful and enforceable?

Drug and alcohol abuse

3.25   The programme for the offender could also include regular attendance at work, education or training and treatment for misuse of alcohol or drugs. There is often a link between drug misuse and offences against other people, such as robbery, burglary or theft. But, although more co-ordinated and intensified effort is being put into the care of drug misusers who go to prison, the chances of dealing effectively with a drug problem are much greater if the offender can remain in the community and undertakes to co-operate in a sensibly planned programme to help him or her to come off drugs. Such a programme would aim, in the first instance, to secure a transition from illegal consumption to a medically supervised regime designed to reduce the harm caused to the individual by drug taking and would be based on a realistic plan for tackling the addiction in the context of his or her other problems. The process might well take time, but the programme could be varied as progress was made. Monitoring by urine tests by the agency providing the treatment could be part of the regime.

Is this the right approach?

Parole

3.26 A Committee under the chairmanship of Lord Carlisle QC is reviewing the arrangements for parole. The Committee is expected to report later in the year. Some of the proposals for supervising offenders as part of their punishment in the community might be helpful in supervising offenders on parole or given earlier release from custody to serve part of their sentence in the community.

A new sentence

3.27 These proposals might be brought together in a new supervision and restriction order, enabling the courts to make requirements which might include:
- compensation to the victim;
- community service;
- residence at a hostel or other approved place;
- prescribed activities at a day centre or elsewhere;
- curfew or house arrest;
- tracking an offender's whereabouts;
- other conditions, such as staying away from particular places.

In the formal requirements of the order there would inevitably be an emphasis on restrictions and on compulsory activity, but there would be room for positive and voluntary elements as well. The programme for the individual offender might include encouraging regular attendance at work, education or training and treatment for substance abuse.

3.28 The aim of the order would be to make a sharp initial impact on offenders but perhaps to allow them to progress to less rigorous forms of supervision, subject to good behaviour, and under judicial supervision. ...

3.29 There should be simple and straightforward procedures for varying requirements which were no longer necessary or practical or if an offender's circumstances changed. Otherwise, they would be oppressive. Moreover, the possibility that the requirements could be relaxed should give the offender an incentive to co-operate. The courts' confidence in the orders will be greater if variations in the order are not made entirely at the discretion of the offender's immediate supervisor. There should be some judicial oversight. One possibility is a supervising magistrate, who would have oversight of the order until it is completed. The magistrate would be able to vary the order, either relaxing the requirements if good progress is made or, if necessary, reimposing requirements if the offender's response deteriorates, without actually breaching the order. The arrangement would have the advantage of keeping the magistrates in touch with an offender's subsequent behaviour.

Would judicial supervision be helpful in making the new sentence effective, and how might it be exercised?

3.30 Because a supervision and restriction order would be intensive in its initial stages, the minimum length might be 3 months, compared with 6 months for probation. The maximum might be 18 months or 2 years, since it is doubtful whether intensive supervision could be sustained for longer periods. This suggests that where an order is imposed for longer than 12 months, the requirements should be reviewed no later than 12 months after the beginning of the order. It would be possible to set different maximum limits for the Crown Court and the magistrates' courts. There would need to be a procedure for ending an order early if the offender received a custodial sentence for a further offence. It might also be sensible to allow the order to be ended by the court on the initiative of the supervisor, if the offender was responding well and no longer required intensive supervision.

3.31   Sanctions for failing to meet the requirements of an order might, depending on the seriousness of the offence, be a fine, imposing more demanding requirements, e.g. a curfew, or revoking the order and resentencing the offender for the original offence to a term of imprisonment. If the requirements are made too demanding, it is more likely that the offender will fail to complete it satisfactorily and this could result in his imprisonment. This would defeat the purpose of the order. It is therefore essential that offenders should be assessed very carefully at the sentencing stage and there should be realism in the use of requirements.

3.32   A new supervision and restriction order could be introduced in addition to the existing disposals or it could replace some of them. There seem to be three main possibilities:

- an enhanced probation order, in addition to existing penalties;
- a new order, replacing probation orders, community service orders and possibly attendance centre orders; and
- a new order, in addition to the existing penalties.

3.33   Extending the requirements for probation orders would give the courts flexibility to tailor the disposal to individual offenders, but it would confuse the new controlling requirements with the welfare objective inherent in the present concept of the probation order, which is that it is imposed 'instead of sentencing' (section 2 of the Powers of Criminal Courts Act 1973). A new order, which replaced existing orders, would also be flexible and the courts would still be able to give some offenders a disposal which amounted to a probation order without any punitive elements. On the other hand it might encourage the courts to impose too severe a penalty and make them more reluctant to use supervision a second time for an offender who had failed to complete an earlier order satisfactorily. Adding a new order to the existing disposals would have the advantage that it would not disturb existing penalties, which are working well. Leaving the other disposals in place would make it clear that the new order was reserved for those for whom other disposals were not sufficient. This might encourage discriminating use of the order.

3.34   Both the sentencing structure of maximum penalties set out in legislation and the sentencing guidelines within these maxima given in the decision of the Court of Appeal are based on the principle of keeping proportionality between the offence and the sentence. The punishment should fit the seriousness of the crime; it should not be excessive or lenient. Since the new order, with its component elements, would be more severe than any of the present disposals, except custody, it follows that it should be used for more serious offenders, who at present would be given a custodial sentence.

3.35   The objectives of these proposals would be frustrated if the order was used for those already given community service orders or placed on probation. Both the courts and probation service will need to be clear about the purpose of the new order, and the probation service will have a particular responsibility to put clear proposals for each offender before the court. The courts will need to know why the probation service considers that the new order would be suitable for an offender and the programme which the offender will be expected to pursue. The kind of activities to be made available could usefully be discussed locally and judges and magistrates will need to see for themselves the work which is being done, if they understand its objectives and to have confidence in it. Even so, there is a risk that the order will be used for offenders who would receive community disposals now and it may be desirable for the legislation to define the circumstances in which the new order should be used.

3.36   Because the new order would be flexible, it could be used repeatedly for persistent offenders. Indeed, community service could already be used repeatedly for recidivists, since it involves both restrictions on liberty and reparation to the community. There is no reason for the courts to give a custodial sentence, unless the offence itself is serious enough to justify it.

3.37   It costs about £1,000 to keep an offender in prison for four weeks. The cost of punishment in the community should not exceed the cost of imprisonment, which is a more severe sentence. If the courts are to have a wide discretion with powers to place a range of requirements on offenders, they should take account of the costs to taxpayers of carrying out requirements. The courts will therefore need regular and up-to-date information about the cost of imprisonment and of the individual components of the new order, e.g. the cost of a day's attendance at a day centre (now about £30), the cost of 10 hours of community service (about £35), the cost of tracking an offender (about £15 a day). While the suitability of a penalty cannot be measured solely in terms of cost, the total cost of the requirements for an individual offender could be a useful check on whether the penalty is proportionate to the offence.

It would be helpful to have comments on the proposals for a new order set out in paragraphs 3.27 to 3.37. ...

Part IV Organising Punishment in the Community

4.1   At present, the supervision of offenders in the community is the responsibility of the probation service. Probation officers supervise offenders on probation and they make arrangements for community service, though the work is normally supervised by ancillary or other staff. The probation service has extensive links with other local services, voluntary organisations and the community generally, which would be helpful in developing the arrangements for a new order. Moreover, if a new order were to be used effectively, the courts would need information about both individual offenders and the programmes which an offender would follow. This would build on the kind of information already provided by the probation service to the courts in social inquiry reports. On the other hand, the new order would contain additional elements of control which some members of the probation service might perceive as inimical to their approach to working with offenders.

4.2   There are great opportunities for the probation service. In the short term, no other existing service or organisation is better placed to take responsibility for supervising punishment in the community. The police have no role in the punishment or supervision of offenders; the limited exception is running attendance centres, which is done by some police officers in their spare time and this is much appreciated by the Government. The prison service is used to exercising control over offenders, but it is not organised or well placed to supervise offenders in their homes. Prison officers generally lack the right training and experience for supervising offenders in the community. Private sector security organisations may be able to play a part in some aspects of the new arrangements, e.g. by monitoring curfews, but it would be difficult for them yet to take on the wide-ranging responsibilities involved in supervising offenders throughout the country, for example, by ensuring that offenders act in accordance with the requirements of their order and in initiating breach proceedings if they do not. Nor could many voluntary organisations working with offenders be expected to take this on.

4.3   One possibility would be for the probation service to contract with other services, and private and voluntary organisations, to obtain some of the components of punishment in the community. The probation service would supervise the order, but would not itself be responsible for providing all the elements.

4.4   Another possibility would be to set up a new organisation to organise punishment in the community. It would not itself supervise offenders or provide facilities directly, but would contract with other services and organisations to do so. The organisation could be part of the Home Office. Alternatively, it might be a separate non-departmental public body with a Director, a small permanent staff and possibly a governing Board drawn from those with relevant experience. The new organisation could contract for services from the probation service, the private or voluntary sector and perhaps for some purposes from the police or the prison service. The Prison Department already contracts in this way for services of probation officers in prisons, and the Central After-Care Association operated similarly until the probation service assumed direct responsibility for prison after-care in the 1960s. A new organisation would be able to set national standards and to enforce them, because they would be written into contracts.

The Government would welcome views on the possibility of setting up a new organisation to take responsibility for the arrangements for punishment in the community, and providing services through contracts with other organisations.

From Home Office, Punishment, Custody and the Community *(London: HMSO),*
1988, pp. 9–15, 17–18.

11 Protecting the Public

The government's strategy on crime in England and Wales (1996)

Home Office

Chapter 7 Community Sentencing

7.1   The Government's aim is to ensure that community sentences are effective forms of punishment and to reduce the risk of further crime. They are available for offences which are so serious that a financial penalty will not suffice, but not so serious that only a prison sentence is justified. Offenders have to undergo physically, mentally or emotionally challenging programmes, and are required to conform to a structured regime. The courts may specify any additional requirement in the interest of securing the rehabilitation of the offender or protecting the public from harm or further crime – for example, a requirement for drug or alcohol treatment, or to reside in a specified place, or not to approach or contact the victim.

7.2   The punishment also includes the prospect of a prompt return to court if the offender fails to comply with the requirements of supervision, so that the court can decide the appropriate course of action. This may mean a prison sentence if the original offence or offences attracted the possibility of custody.

The role of the probation service

7.3   It is the probation service's responsibility to supervise adult offenders in the community, so that they lead law abiding lives, in a way which minimises risk to the public. The 54 local probation services in England and Wales provide a wide range of community service placements providing unpaid work for the benefit of the community and a wide range of demanding and constructive activities and other forms of supervision. Supervision will include work to confront offending behaviour, so that offenders are aware of the impact of their crimes on their victims and the community; and work to instil a greater sense of personal responsibility and discipline, aiding re-integration as a law abiding member of society.

7.4   The Government sets priorities for the probation service on the basis of a rolling three year plan. The Home Secretary's priorities for the probation service are:

- to ensure that community sentences provide a tough and demanding punishment which is effective in reducing crime;
- making community supervision safer for the public by enhanced risk assessment, enforcement and management; and

- improving both the quality of service delivery and the use of resources.

7.5   Her Majesty's Inspectorate of Probation undertakes a rolling programme of local area Quality and Effectiveness inspections, as well as regular thematic inspections into specific areas of service delivery.

National Standards for the supervision of offenders in the community

7.6   The Government published the first National Standards for the work of probation services and social services departments in 1992. After a comprehensive review, revised National Standards were published jointly by the Home Office, the Department of Health and the Welsh Office in March 1995. The new standards improve and strengthen the supervision of offenders.

7.7   The 1995 National Standards for the supervision of offenders in the community are the required standards of practice for probation services and social services departments in England and Wales, in relation to the supervision of offenders in the community and in providing services to the courts. The revised National Standards ensure that community sentences are demanding as punishments, that supervision is rigorous and that offenders are returned to court promptly if they fail to comply with the requirements of supervision, for the courts to consider appropriate action. The standards:

- protect the public from further offending by requiring effective supervision of offenders;
- make clear to the private and voluntary sector partners with whom probation and social services work how they are expected to meet these standards;
- provide a framework for good practice and a basis for demonstrating accountability for probation staff and local authority social workers;
- provide clear guidance on the preparation of reports, supervision of offenders and how to proceed when offenders behave unacceptably; and
- make it clear to offenders what is expected of them and what action will be taken if they fail to comply with the requirements of the standards.

The role of parents

7.8   The courts have power to bind over the parents of young offenders, to require their attendance at court and to order them to pay any fines or compensation arising from the child's offending behaviour. The Government has taken steps to strengthen these powers and included new provisions in the Criminal Justice and Public Order Act 1994 which allow the courts, in passing a community sentence, to bind over the child's parents to ensure compliance with the sentence. The provisions are aimed at those parents who might not otherwise give their children the support that is needed. Failure to comply with the binding over order can lead to a fine of up to £1,000.

Electronic monitoring of curfew orders

7.9   The Criminal Justice and Public Order Act 1994 allows trials of electronic monitoring of curfew orders to take place in selected areas. This new community sentence was established on a national basis in section 12 of the Criminal Justice Act 1991. Pilot trials of electronic monitoring commenced in July 1995 at three locations: Manchester, Reading and the County of Norfolk. The area of the trials was subsequently extended in November 1995 to include the whole of Greater Manchester and Berkshire.

7.10   The objectives of the trials were:
- to establish the technical and practical arrangements necessary to support the electronic monitoring of curfew orders;
- to ascertain the likely cost and effectiveness of curfew orders in relation to court sentences; and
- to evaluate the scope for introducing electronic monitoring of curfew orders on a selective or national basis.

7.11   It is too early to make a final evaluation of the trials so far, but they have already proved the potential value of electronic monitoring as a highly flexible, restrictive community sentence with a part to play in punishing offenders and reducing crime. The curfew order is a significant restriction of liberty with the courts empowered to sentence for up to 2,000 hours over a period of six months. The technology has so far proved successful in monitoring offenders whom the courts want off the streets, and has ensured that the courts' sentences cannot be evaded without serious consequences. The slightest breach of a curfew order or attempt to tamper with the equipment is detected, and investigated by the contractors immediately. No violations are ignored, with warnings given for the most minor infringement. Offenders who continue not to comply are returned to court.

7.12   The courts are keen to test the new curfew order fully, but the Magistrates' Association has pointed to the need for more time for magistrates to get used to the sentence and has suggested that more courts might be involved. In the light of these views, the trials have been extended for more courts in the trial areas to use the sentence. The Government is also carefully considering the scope for wider application of electronic monitoring.

Why change is needed

7.13   The Government published a Green Paper 'Strengthening Punishment in the Community' in March 1995 seeking views on proposals designed to improve understanding and confidence in community sentences.

7.14   The current range of community orders (the probation order, the community service orders, the combination order, the curfew order, the attendance centre order and the supervision order) provide the courts with a variety of sentencing disposals, taking into account the seriousness of the offence, suitability, the degree of restriction of liberty imposed and the age of the offender. The present array of community orders have been established over several years and do not provide sentencers with the widest possible choice of sentencing options.

7.15   Despite recent initiatives to reinforce rigorous standards for the supervision of offenders, community sentences are often portrayed as a 'soft option' and perceived as such by the public. The Green Paper 'Strengthening Punishment in the Community' recognised the need to address this perception by strengthening the hand of sentencers in passing a community sentence. It proposed that there should be more choice and flexibility in sentencing options, and that the purpose and content of community sentences should be made clear at the point of sentence, thus increasing public understanding of supervision in the community.

7.16   The Green Paper proposed:

- the introduction of a single integrated sentence replacing and incorporating the present range of community orders in the adult courts;
- the matching of sentence elements to the three principal purposes of punishment in the community: restriction of liberty; reparation; and the prevention of re-offending;
- the court's role should be to address these purposes of punishment; to decide whether one or more should be met in the sentence passed; and to determine the balance between a wider range of sentence elements to match the punishment;
- the courts should have increased discretion to determine the content of community sentences in individual cases, either singly or in combination, and increased choice and flexibility in the range of supervisory or reparative activities provided by the probation service;
- the courts should also have more consistent access to information on the progress and outcome of community sentences; and
- the present requirement that offenders consent to community orders should be removed.

Responses to consultation

7.17   Comments on the proposals in the Green Paper were asked for by 16 June 1995. 181 written responses were received from organisations and individuals. Meetings were held with key organisations including two consultative seminars for sentencers at which participants took part in a sentencing exercise to try out the proposed integrated community sentence.

7.18   The responses revealed general support for the further development of community sentences, greater clarity about the content of community sentences at the time they are passed by the courts, a wider range of sentencing options and more information for the courts. However, some respondents considered that a single integrated community sentence was unnecessary because the current community orders already provided a sufficient range of options.

7.19   The results of the sentencing exercise suggested that sentencers would welcome greater choice and flexibility in combining elements of community service, supervision, treatment or other constructive activities when passing a community sentence in suitable cases. It was also clear that some sentencers may not fully utilise the opportunities already available to them, particularly in the use of additional requirements to a probation order.

Good practice and better liaison

7.20   The consultation process revealed considerable support for more and better liaison between sentencers and probation services in discussing and developing the range of supervision opportunities locally. The Government welcomes the initiative suggested by the Magistrates' Association, the Justices' Clerks' Society and the probation service organisations to launch local development work to enhance community sentences. The Home Secretary and the Lord Chancellor have decided to support the principle of demonstration projects with the aim of increasing public and sentencer confidence in community sentences. Discussions with interested bodies are taking place on the way in which these projects should be run and evaluated. They are likely to include increases in the range of requirements as part of supervision; better information for the courts; clear indications by the courts as to the purpose of a community sentence; and action to improve the enforcement of community sentences including speeding up the process by which offenders are brought back to court if they fail to comply with the terms of their sentence.

7.21   In addition to the measures proposed in the Green Paper, the Government is also considering whether the range of community sentences available to the courts could be widened, to ensure that imprisonment should not be used unnecessarily. One interesting possibility, which will be evaluated, would be the use of electronic monitoring to restrict liberty in the community.

Issues which require legislation

7.22   Legislation would be required to bring in some of the changes proposed by the Green Paper, including the abolition of the requirement for the offender's consent to a community sentence. Legislation would also be required to introduce other possible changes to the community sentencing framework which the Government has identified as potentially desirable, including:

•   the provision of a new power to suspend the operation of a community sentence pending the outcome of an appeal against conviction or sentence. This is particularly relevant where an offender is sentenced to a number of community service hours. Under the current law, the offender is required to undertake community service hours immediately even if an appeal against sentence is outstanding. The Government consulted on this proposal in 1994 and there was some support for the availability for such a power in appropriate cases; and

•   the introduction of community sentences for fine default. Legislation would be needed to provide sentencers with a power to impose a period of community service in the case of persistent fine defaulters. The Government will consult sentencers, the probation service organisations and other key organisations on the need for a new community service disposal in order to improve the effectiveness of the fine enforcement system. Such a disposal could be introduced on a pilot basis in the first instance.

The way forward

7.23   In the light of the response to the public consultation on the proposals in the Green Paper, the Government has decided to support the principle of local demonstration projects designed to show how far changes in approach by the courts and the probation service, in accordance with the principles set out in the Green Paper, but within the current law, may increase public and sentence confidence in community sentences.

7.24   The Government recognises that there is support for legislation to tackle a number of community sentence issues. Consultation with sentencers, the probation service and others with an interest will take place on issues not covered in the Green Paper. In the light of these consultations, and the progress of the demonstration projects, the Government will keep the case for legislation under review.

From Home Office, Protecting the Public: the government's strategy on crime in England and Wales *(London: HMSO), 1996, pp. 36–39.*

12 Joining Forces to Protect the Public

Prisons–Probation – a Consultation
Document (1998)

Home Office

Chapter 2 A Modern Probation Service

I. *Modernising the organisational framework*

2.1   Successive Governments have neglected the organisational framework which
supports the work of probation officers. A series of Acts of Parliament have
merely served to consolidate an outdated reflection of a service that has been
engaged in change and modernisation for many years. Legislation still directs
probation officers to 'advise, assist and befriend' offenders. This is completely
out of line not just with the expectations of the courts but also with the reality
of the work which probation staff undertake day in and day out.

2.2   The service now rightly recognises that its core function is public protection,
even though a great deal of its important work in this area for the time being
goes unsung. The legislative framework needs to be brought up to date in this
respect. Moreover, in reflecting the modern probation officer's role, the
statutory duties will need to be to confront, challenge and change offending
behaviour and to recognise punishment as a central part of that process. This
should help the public to understand and value more highly the work which
probation staff do on their behalf.

II. *A more accountable service*

2.3   Legislation needs, however, to go beyond 'duties' to the organisational
structure of the probation service. It is a fragmented organisation, with 54
autonomous units free to deploy the resources allocated by central Government
as their committees see fit. There is only limited accountability to central
Government. By modern standards, the lack of democratic accountability even
at local level is a concern. The Committees have done and continue to do
excellent work on a voluntary basis, but the new probation services they have
helped to create now have outgrown their organisational origins.

III. *Organisational networks*

2.4   To deliver its goals the service needs to be more accountable and better
organised to develop its work in close co-operation and partnership with
central Government, the Prison Service, the police, mental health services,
health authorities, local authorities, the CPS, victim support groups, TECs, and

a range of voluntary sector groups and others. It must be organised to reflect the modern focus of its core business and the purpose of these partnerships: the protection of the public from predictably dangerous offenders under supervision in the community; and from those who pose a more general risk of reoffending.

IV. Co-terminosity

2.5   There are also too many probation services. The boundaries lack co-terminosity with many key partners, particularly the police. The present organisation also too readily leads to:

- **inconsistent performance between one area and another;**
- **some unacceptable standards in certain areas of service delivery;**
- **too much left locally to *ad hoc* arrangements rather than strategy; and**
- **differing interpretations of best practice.**

There is little relationship between the performance of different area services and the resources which they use – or indeed with anything else.

2.6   These are features of the present system rather than criticism of individual committees and chief officers. A great deal of effort has been made, especially in the last year, to develop relationships with the Prison Service and other partner bodies.

V. Increased cost-effectiveness

2.7   Fragmentation also inhibits efficiency and value for money. There is no doubt that a unified approach to support services, generating economies of scale, would increase significantly the scope for improved cost-effectiveness. The pressure to reduce public spending is a reality for all public services and the Probation Services is no exception. We need to ensure that organisational arrangements provide managers with the greatest possible flexibility to deliver economies while maintaining the high standards of service delivery.

VI. Responsiveness to new technologies

2.8   We need a service better able to take forward new national strategic developments. New technologies offer opportunities for service to be delivered in new ways and more cost-effectively. For example, electronic monitoring can provide a cheap and effective means of imposing tighter supervision on offenders; of imposing discipline on chaotic lives; of reintegrating offenders more effectively into society; and an inescapable means of detecting breaches of court orders. A new service needs to embrace such technologies and to incorporate the opportunities they offer into their strategies for confronting and impacting on offending behaviour, thus making better and more focused use of probation core competences and skills.

VII. *National leadership*

2.9 As well as a clearer national direction, the service also requires stronger national leadership forging an alliance with central Government to create the best environment for delivering the Service's aims. The problem is not simply the lack of a single probation service voice: it is that there is nobody who can be seen to be responsible for delivering on service-wide commitments.

2.10 We do not consider that it is in the interests of efficiency and effectiveness for probation service managers to attempt to serve several masters. Lines of accountability and command must not be blurred. The Home Secretary is ultimately responsible for delivering improved public protection and he must be in a position to move swiftly and effectively to ensure high and consistent levels of performance. He will be answerable to Parliament for the success or failure of policies directed at reducing re-offending. The constitutional arrangements must therefore enable him to take proper political responsibility for the Service.

2.11 **We therefore consider that the Service should be directly and unequivocally accountable to Ministers and through them to Parliament.**

VIII. *New names and language*

2.12 It is important that the names, language and terminology used by the services should give accurate and accessible messages about the nature and aims of their work. Some of the terms used have been criticised, for example because:
- they are associated with tolerance of crime (e.g. 'probation' which can be seen as a conditional reprieve), or
- they can be misunderstood (e.g. 'community service' which sounds like voluntary activity), or
- they are too esoteric to be understood outside the two services (e.g. 'throughcare' which sounds more associated with the 'caring' services).

2.13 The term 'probation service' does not appear in primary legislation, but the terms 'probation committee', 'probation order', and 'probation officer' do. Changes to these names would therefore require primary legislation. Probation is a long established concept, well understood internationally, and probation practice in this country has enjoyed a high reputation in other countries. These are not sufficient reasons, however, for avoiding change that would bring other benefits. The probation services' strong position internationally rather makes it easier to give a new lead.

2.14 We have no strong preference on the potential name for a new unified National Probation Service so long as it is capable of inspiring public confidence in the work of that Service. The Review has considered names such as:
- **'the Public Protection Service'**
- **'the Community Justice Enforcement Agency'**

We recognise the strong and varied views on naming the Service that will exist within the services and more widely. Other possible names are:
- The Offender Risk Management Service
- The Community Sentence Enforcement Service
- The Justice Enforcement and Public Protection Service

- The Public Safety and Offender Management Service
- The Community Protection and Justice Service

We do not intend to list all the possibilities here, but we want to hear your views on naming the new service and any alternative ideas.

2.15   'Throughcare' is the term which lies at the heart of much of the two services' joint work. It is unlikely to be properly understood outside of the prison and probation worlds, and conveys little to the public about the important and difficult work that is being done in this area. Even sentencers may be uncertain about what it comprises. We think that public and sentencer confidence would be enhanced if the focus was on the ultimate goals of 'throughcare' – high quality sentence planning in the community. Our preference is for this work to be called simply '**Resettlement**', but again we are ready to consider any views you may have.

2.16   We shall want to look again at structure and names of the present community orders themselves in the light of community sentence demonstration projects which have been running in Shropshire and Teesside. The evaluation of those projects is now being completed and will be published separately.

IX. A new unified National Probation Service

2.17   Our preferred option for structural and organisational change is for a unified National Probation Service which we believe will:

- maximise the scope for the change agenda described in Chapter 4 to make positive impacts on the Aims described in Chapter 1 and for overcoming the obstacles to improved integration with the prison service described in paragraph 1.10;
- provide the greatest scope for modernising the probation service and for bringing its outdated statutory framework into line with the work it is now doing with offenders;
- increase its democratic accountability;
- maximise public and sentencer confidence in community punishments;
- significantly increase the scope for improved joint working and planning with the Prison Service by creating a better match nationally through parallel hierarchies and points of contact;
- allow us to take responsibility for the enforcement of community punishments and public protection so that there can be a smoother transition of policy and our public commitments into operational effectiveness;
- offer the greatest scope for meeting the requirements and for producing savings and greater cost-effectiveness through the provision of shared support services; and
- provide for a new and modern Service with clear national leadership able to influence and participate at the highest levels of central Government.

2.18   With both the Prison and Probation services having parallel hierarchies, significantly increased scope would be generated for improved integration and better strategic planning across the field of corrections. As a national Next Steps Agency, the employees of the new Service would be directly employed by the Home Office, with a line of command leading to the Home Secretary: a clear and unequivocal line of accountability, opening up new and better opportunities for joint decision-making.

2.19 Against the background of our vision for the future of the criminal justice system, the main building blocks of the new service would be 42 individually managed operational units matching the 42 police and CPS areas allowing local partnerships to flourish both within and without the criminal justice system. The new Next Steps Agency would be managed centrally by a Chief Executive to whom local chief officers would be accountable.

2.20 A key issue is whether a regional dimension is necessary within the national organisation, whether to secure the savings generated through shared support services, or to achieve necessary co-ordination with the Prison Service, to secure accountability to Headquarters, or for any other reasons. The regional element could form part of the National HQ, be capable of working at regional level, and be accommodated there only when needed. The flexibility to organise support and administrative services appropriately needs to be driven by the demands of improved cost-effectiveness not geography. Best practice might mean some of those services being organised nationally or regionally. But if such a regional element is essential, we believe that it should be administered with a light touch leaving local chief officers sufficient flexibility, authority and scope for local innovation in operational matters. We shall be commissioning further work on the options for delivering support services.

2.21 In this context, however, we must remember that the impetus for modernising the Probation Service came first from our desire to secure the objective of improved joint effectiveness (see Chapter 4) with the Prison Service which will itself be administered on the basis of ten regions matching the geographical areas of responsibility of the Government Offices of the Regions (GORs) and Wales. A regional dimension within the National Probation Service's organisational arrangements therefore appears to be necessary to promote efficient joint working at regional area management level, within the respective national headquarters, to take forward important joint work, such as that associated with the long term aim of having prisoners housed within their home regions in order to improve resettlement. Similarly, co-operation at regional level with a range of other bodies may produce valuable gains, for example, in Wales with the forthcoming Assembly and the Welsh Health Service.

2.22 The transition to a national Service should also be made in a way which ensures a proper balance between individual offender casework and community-based approaches to crime reduction as envisaged in the Crime and Disorder Bill. This will need to be managed carefully to avoid any shift in emphasis which detracts from the community-based initiatives. We believe that the required balance can be achieved within the structural model we have described.

2.23 Our goals in developing this radical organisational restructuring would therefore be:
- **a better balance between the national and local priorities;**
- **maximum local operational discretion and authority;**
- **an appropriate emphasis on community-based crime reduction initiatives;**
- **organisational arrangements contributing to improved outcomes on joint effectiveness with the Prison Service;**

- **a streamlined national Headquarters;**
- **a light touch regional component;**
- **co-terminous boundaries with the police and CPS;**
- **improved cost-effectiveness.**

2.24 Start-up and transitional costs associated with the creation of a unified national service would depend on the detail of the organisational arrangements put in place. For example, the inclusion or exclusion of a regional dimension. Establishing these costs requires further work to inform our decisions. Preliminary estimates prepared in the course of the Review suggest that savings in the longer term would be over £20 million annually. This supports our view that a unified national service would be more cost-effective than the existing arrangements. Again we need to look at this work in more detail.

2.25 We are therefore particularly interested to hear views about:
- **our view that a unified National Probation Service is the right way forward; and**
- **how the management relationships between the local area, regional dimension and central Headquarters should be organised.** ...

XII. *Funding*

2.32 The creation of a unified National Probation Service as a Next Steps Agency forming part of the Home Office would end the arrangements whereby 80 per cent of the Service's funding is provided by the Home Office and 20 per cent by local authorities. A national service would be centrally funded. This would break the existing financial tie between probation services and local authorities. But this ought not in any way to affect the development of partnership arrangements relating to local crime reduction strategies under the Crime and Disorder Bill.

XIII. *Partnership at local level*

2.33 We want local decision-making to be less constrained by central Government, and favour increased local accountability. A National Probation Service therefore also needs to provide mechanisms which are responsive to local needs and circumstances, secures effective and meaningful input from the community, and ensures that the agency works constructively in partnership with local authorities and other organisations at local level. A variety of mechanisms might be appropriate. Formal and informal joint working in partnership with local authorities and those other local bodies which help to deliver public protection services, will be vital to promote a whole range of desirable outcomes locally. Approaches to joint working could range from some form of forum for the exchange of ideas to joint delivery of services through pooled budgets. One idea would be the establishment of 42 local reference groups or advisory boards within the overall national probation framework. These might provide a forum through which local stakeholders, including victim support groups, local authority representatives, ethnic minority groups and other members of the community can influence the way in which local plans are prepared and delivered. Moreover, these groups could have a developing role to play in influencing the direction of community-based approaches to crime reduction.

2.34   Such boards should also include representatives of the local judiciary and magistracy, who will remain amongst the most important users of the probation service. But such representation will not do away with the need for good and close liaison at individual court level to ensure that the probation service meets high service standards. This improved sentencer liaison could also include jointly arranging what offender programmes or activities are available locally and their effectiveness. Amongst other things this would help provide systematic feedback to sentencers about the results of their decisions.

2.35   **We want to hear from interested parties about how we can most effectively preserve the elements of local influence within an overall national framework. We would welcome views on how to secure joint working with local authorities and others, on methods of joint working that are most likely to be fruitful and on what would be necessary to allow this to happen.**

2.36   **We want to hear your views on whether local reference groups or advisory boards represent the right approach and what the composition of such a group should be. Equally important is the question of how the members of such a group/board should be appointed and who should appoint them? Finally, we would welcome views on the extent to which joint working with local authorities and others should be encouraged, on methods of joint working that are most likely to be fruitful and on what would be necessary to allow this to happen. We would also welcome views on the extent to which such advisory boards might have a role in relation to the handling of complaints directed at probation service staff.**

2.37   These issues will need to be examined in conjunction with our consideration of the possible case for changing the role of HM Inspectorate of Probation to meet the requirements for an independent element in dealing with complaints against staff. ...

XIV. *Rejecting merger with the Prison Service*

2.38   In coming to our views on the need for a unified National Probation Service, we have carefully considered the case for merging the existing probation services with the Prison Service. We have rejected it for several compelling reasons. First, while there are areas of joint enterprise there are also separate responsibilities specific to each service, for example maintenance of prison security on the one hand and the enforcement of effective supervision of offenders in the community on the other. Second, even potential savings in support services would have to be balanced against the management cost of merger, disruption to staff and the difficulties of renegotiating major IT initiatives, for example the Prison Service Quantum project. Our view is that a merger is a bridge too far. The Prison Service and the Probation Service should therefore remain separate services within the criminal justice system and we have no current plans to merge them.

From Home Office, Joining Forces to Protect the Public: Prisons–Probation – a Consultation Document *(London: The Home Office), 1998, pp. 7–12.*

13 A New Choreography – an integrated strategy for the National Probation Service for England and Wales (2001)

Home Office

Executive Summary

The New Choreography

The new National Probation Service (NPS) has brought fresh aims and duties for probation, it has accelerated the development of effective ways of working with offenders and it has created new central and local structures.

The new Service has a clear, unambiguous remit to be a public service that protects the public, operates and enforces court orders and prison licences, and rehabilitates offenders to law abiding lives.

The collective aim is that the National Probation Service should:

- by 2004 establish itself as a world leader in designing and implementing offender assessment and supervision programmes that effectively reduce re-offending and improve public safety; and
- by 2006 be recognised as a top performing public service as benchmarked by the European Excellence Model (EEM).

As a high level strategic framework, the *New Choreography* uses the concept of 'stretch objectives' and it indicates the nine areas where the greatest challenges or changes lie, and these are as follows.

Accurate and effective assessment and management of risk and dangerousness

To be effective, probation staff must be able to differentiate individual offenders, their crime and their victims in order to take the steps necessary for greater public protection and to match offenders with the programmes most likely to reduce reoffending.

The basic tool will be OASys (the Offender Assessment System), jointly developed by the NPS and the Prison Service. By 2003, assessment of risk and dangerousness and of offenders' needs will be taking place in all cases supervised and in all reports prepared.

Where offenders have the potential to be of high risk there is greater urgency still. Under a national framework, and following the requirements of Sarah's Law, the service will build on the establishment of Multi-Agency Public Protection Panels (MAPPPs), reviewing existing arrangements and collaborative protocols and extending the use of hostels or measures such as electronic monitoring.

More involvement of victims of serious sexual and other violent crime

The NPS objective is to develop co-ordinated policy and practice frameworks by 2002/3 and to rapidly expand this using a combination of leadership and direction, resources additional to those identified in SR2000 and targets to improve victim satisfaction, including work from our own baseline survey.

As well as all new accredited programmes containing modules on victim awareness and changing offenders' behaviour, the Service will achieve a more 'victim centred approach', encouraging, where appropriate, restorative justice and reparation.

Offender programmes that have a track record in reducing reoffending

The NPS is committed to evidence-based (What Works) practice and Government targets dictate that we should reduce the reconviction rate of those under the supervision of the Service by 5%. For those who misuse drugs the target is 25%.

This will be achieved by the roll-out of independently accredited evidence-based programmes that will be consistently available across the country. NPS priorities will lead to more programmes aimed at community reintegration and resettlement and a greater emphasis on the reduction of reoffending in community punishment orders (formerly community service orders).

Local delivery will match local crime profiles and priorities. Attention will be directed to persistent offending by drug-misusers and those other persistent offenders who account for a disproportionate volume of crime.

Intervening early to take young people away from crime

The NPS will aim to provide – directly or in partnership – a range of bail support, community interventions and resettlement services that have been designed and assessed for their suitability for this age group. Programmes developing thinking and problem solving skills should feature strongly.

The NPS will strengthen the relationship with the Youth Justice Board (YJB) and apply the lessons from evidence-based practice to young adult offenders.

Enforcement

Confidence in probation relies on the extent to which staff correctly enforce the terms of orders and licences. The objective is for the Service to fulfil National Standards in 90% of cases requiring breach action by staff. Probation areas will be expected to reflect this priority in their annual plans and, as an incentive, enforcement has been given major weighting in the NPS performance management framework.

Providing courts with good information and pre-trial services

Gaining the confidence of judges and magistrates is a key strategic imperative.

The NPS has targets to improve the timeliness of reports and to increase the proportion of specific sentence reports.

Valuing and achieving diversity in the National Probation Service and the service it provides

Inclusiveness, equality and fairness are required to ensure simple justice. They also make an organisation effective and responsive and enable it to command the confidence of a diverse public.

The NPS will weave these values and expectations into its development and planning. No one should be excluded from the NPS or our services because of their gender, race, ethnicity, religious beliefs, disability or sexual orientation.

Encouraging progress is being made in many areas and the proportion of minority ethnic staff in the Service is already above the target set by the last Home Secretary (9.9%, against a target of 8.3%). However, there are problems. For instance, the numbers of Asian staff is disproportionately small and retention for all minority ethnic staff is poorer than for white.

Although the good proportion of chairs and members of new local probation boards from minority ethnic groups is an achievement, the low numbers of minority ethnic managers needs urgent attention. Additionally, the number of female managers and chief officers does not reflect the number of women working with offenders at the front line.

Service delivery, and especially ethnic monitoring, will continue to receive attention so the NPS can be sure it is doing all it can to make services available and meaningful to the full range of offenders and victims who come into contact with the Service. Our response to disability will become a priority area for development.

Building an excellent organisation

The European Excellence Model (EEM) will be an empirical, self-assessment tool, sign-posting the way to the achievements required. The NPS will, *inter alia*, be concentrating on up-grading skills, staff retention, workforce planning, reviewing systems of pay and rewards and recruitment policies.

Financial systems are being changed to meet the needs of the new structures, to allow new audit arrangements and to establish common business processes. Information is recognised as being critical to all NPS activities and new strategies for information management and IT will be developed as the basis for future systems.

National, regional and local probation structures, mirroring boundaries shared by other criminal justice agencies and others, will be used to ensure strategic collaboration and provide mechanisms for communications, consultation and policy development.

Building an effective performance management framework

A bespoke performance management framework using several components incorporating the European Excellence Model (EEM) and that meets the requirements of the Better Quality Services (BQS) strategy is being constructed. This will assist continuous improvement and contribute to the creation of the 'mixed economy' that will be needed to improve effectiveness and efficiency.

The framework will introduce a financial incentive to improve performance and to meet the targets agreed as part of SR2000.

From Home Office, A New Choreography – an integrated strategy for the National Probation Service for England and Wales *(London: National Probation Service)*, *2001, pp. 1–3.*

14 Reducing Crime – Changing Lives

The government's plans for transforming the management of offenders (2004)

Home Office

Annex – the Government's Response to the Carter Report

Report Findings – a new approach is needed to ensure offenders are punished for their crimes, the public is protected and the appropriate help is available to reduce re-offending. This will ensure the system is focused on the ultimate goals of reducing crime and maintaining public confidence.

31.   We agree with this **vision** which is entirely consistent with the reform programmes we have been pursuing and the new sentencing framework created by the Criminal Justice Act.

Targeted and rigorous sentences

Report Findings – Building on the measures set out in the Criminal Justice Act, there needs to be:
- *a renewed focus on paying back to the community*
- *fines rebuilt as a credible punishment*
- *more demanding community sentences*
- *more extensive use of electronic monitoring*
- *greater sanctions and help for persistent offenders*
- *more effective use of custody*

32.   We agree the need for an increasing emphasis on **paying back to the community** building on our Restorative Justice Strategy described previously. The use of reprimands and final warnings within the youth justice system is proving very successful. We intend to develop a similar approach for low risk, low harm adults building on the new conditional cautions in the Criminal Justice Act. This will not be a soft option and our aim will be to link conditional cautions to financial reparation to the victim, community work, etc.

33.   As discussed earlier, the Government has already launched a strategy that has significantly improved the level of **fine** enforcement. The creation of the Unified Courts Agency (in shadow form from April 2004, and formally in April 2005) together with a new focus on enforcement performance and legislative measures to support it directly supports the revitalising of the fine as a sentence. We do not therefore accept the recommendation that responsibility for fine enforcement should be moved from the Court Service.

34.   Revitalised fines should replace a very substantial number of the community sentences which are currently given to low risk offenders. In practice such offenders get little if any supervision from the National Probation Service and a fine which is paid would be a more effective and appropriate sentence. We have also extended the use of fixed penalty notices (FPNs), which provide a means of dealing quickly and effectively with low level criminal behaviour. We aim to extend their use for other offences and expect to see increasing use being made of them by the police.

35.   The report recommends the introduction of a day fine system where the fine is set as a number of days which can then be multiplied to take account of an offender's ability to pay. This would require primary legislation and is something we will explore further. The day fine would only be available for offences that would go to court (i.e. excluding fixed penalty and minor offences). Prison would be available for non-payment linked to the number of unpaid days.

36.   The Criminal Justice Act introduces a generic community sentence around which much more **demanding community sentences** for more serious offenders can be built. We fully support the report's findings that there should be a gradation in community sentences based on a risk assessment of offenders. We agree that there should be intensive supervision and monitoring (ISM) for the highest risk offenders. We have already been testing such an approach through the Intensive Change and Control Programme. Once fully developed ISM should replace prison sentences for the increasing number of relatively low risk and first time offenders who have been given prison sentences in recent years.

37.   **Electronic monitoring** has proved very successful and its use has been expanding rapidly as described above. The use of such new technology to provide a means of monitoring the location of offenders under supervision in the community will be an increasing feature of correctional services in the future. We are already developing a pilot of satellite tracking technology which could enable offenders to be continuously and accurately tracked.

38.   The Criminal Justice Act introduces a new principle for **persistent offenders**. The new sentencing framework will provide sentencers with a range of new disposals, short of a full time prison sentence, to enable them to impose tough and flexible sentences on persistent offenders. However, the new principle will mean that a progression up the sentencing scale towards custody of increasing length is inevitable if offenders continue to re-offend.

39.   The Act also makes clear that a court must only pass a custodial sentence if it is of the opinion that the offence or offences are so serious that neither a fine alone nor a community sentence can be justified.

A new role for the judiciary

Report Findings – There needs to be greater emphasis on judicial self-governance ensuring compliance to guidelines. In the short term, when capacity is fixed, the Sentencing Guidelines Council needs to provide guidance that takes account of the capacity of prison and probation. Over the medium term the Sentencing Advisory

Panel needs to provide evidence on what works to reduce crime and increase public confidence. This will form the basis for changing the capacity of prisons and probation.

40. We established the **Sentencing Guidelines Council** (SGC) through the Criminal Justice Act. Members of the Council are currently being recruited with a view to its first meeting in early March [2004]. The Council will over time formulate a comprehensive set of guidelines, and cost and effectiveness are factors it is statutorily required to take into account in devising them. One of the first matters we will ask the Council to consider is the generic community sentence (also introduced by the 2003 Act) which has the potential to divert offenders, who would otherwise have received custody, to more demanding community sentences. We are already providing comparative sentencing information to magistrates' courts and criminal justice system areas and will consider with DCA and the Lord Chief Justice how best to develop this. A key issue we want to pursue as soon as possible is how to eliminate general sentencing drift and unjustified variations in sentencing severity between areas.

41. We have information on the cost effectiveness of different disposals and interventions, and models to predict future correctional service workloads. We will share these with the Council, the Sentencing Advisory Panel and others.

A new approach to managing offenders

Report Findings – A National Offender Management Service should be established, led by a single Chief Executive, with a clear objective to punish offenders and help reduce re-offending. Within the service there should be a single person responsible for offenders. This would be separate from day-to-day responsibility for prisons and probation. This new structure would break down the silos of the services. It would ensure the end-to-end management of offenders, regardless of whether they were given a custodial or community sentence.

42. We will from 1st June this year [2004] introduce a new **National Offender Management Service (NOMS)** with responsibility for both punishing offenders and reducing offending. The new service will provide end-to-end management of offenders, regardless of whether they are serving their sentences in prison, the community or both.

43. We will also appoint immediately a Chief Executive of NOMS who will begin setting up the organisation and will lead the new service. The key roles of the Chief Executive will include:
    - being accountable to Ministers for reducing re-offending and delivering other agreed outcomes from the new service and for the efficient operation of public sector providers;
    - overall responsibility for strategic developments including policy and standards, strategic finance and human resources etc;
    - ensuring increased contestability in the provision of correctional services;
    - sitting on the National Criminal Justice Board and acting as an observer on the Sentencing Guidelines Council to provide advice on the capacity of NOMS to deliver.

Contestability

The Government are not interested in using the private sector for its own sake, whether in prisons or in the community. We want the most cost effective custodial and community sentences no matter who delivers them. The experience with the Prison Service's use of the private sector has been extremely positive. Four private companies successfully run nine prisons (shortly to grow to eleven). Many prisoners and visitors to these prisons speak positively about the way they are treated by staff. More significantly, the threat of contestability in running prisons has led to dramatic improvements in regimes and reductions in cost at some of the most difficult public sector prisons. So effective has contestability been that the public sector have won two prison contracts back from private sector operators and in the last few weeks, responding to the threat of the private sector, Dartmoor and Liverpool Prisons have transformed their performance. We intend therefore to encourage the private and 'not for profit' sectors to compete to manage more prisons and private and voluntary sector organisations to compete to manage offenders in the community. We want to encourage partnership between public and private sector providers and the voluntary and community sectors which harness their respective strengths. As a market develops, offender managers will be able to buy custodial places or community interventions from providers, from whatever sector, based only on their cost effectiveness in reducing re-offending.

44.   A new National Offender Manager will be appointed as soon as possible. The National Offender Manager will report directly to the Chief Executive and will be responsible for reducing re-offending and managing the budget for offender services. But we believe that the task of integrating the management of offenders whilst in custody or under supervision in the community is best managed at regional level where effective links can be forged and joint strategies developed with complementary services, including health, education, and employment. Therefore reporting to the National Offender Manager will be 10 Regional Offender Managers responsible for end-to-end management of offenders in the nine English regions and Wales. The Regional Offender Managers will be responsible for ensuring effective case management of individual offenders. They will source the prison places, community punishments, supervision and other interventions required for their offenders through contracts with providers from the public, private, 'not for profit' and voluntary sectors within their region and elsewhere.

45.   The public providers of prison places, community punishments and interventions will report directly to the new Chief Executive to whom they will be accountable for the efficient operation of the services. The public sector prison service will be a delivery arm of the offender management service but with custodial places financed by offender managers who will prescribe the interventions made with offenders in prison. The Prison Service has, in practice, been a Next Steps Agency in name only for some years. Its formal status as an Agency, in theory semi-independent of the Home Secretary, will end and it will become an integral arm of NOMS but with continued substantial day to day operational freedom.

46.   The Youth Justice Board will remain an NDPB with responsibility to the Home Secretary. Funding and oversight of the YJB will rest with the Chief Executive of NOMS.

Implications

Report Findings – The proposals will target resources more effectively and should keep numbers under supervision lower than currently forecast. However, this relies critically on the Sentencing Guidelines Council. At the same time there is the issue of old and unsuitable prisons. Depending on the business case, they could be replaced by new, larger and more suitable institutions, providing better value for money.

47.   The report estimates that the proposal it makes could check the projected increase in the numbers in custody (80,000 by 2009 rather than 93,000 as currently projected) and under supervision in the community (240,000 rather than 300,000). We believe this is possible with substantial revitalisation in the use of fines, a range of community sentences, some of which are significantly more demanding than at present, and a step change in sentencing practice. The proposal outlined in this paper will provide the effective infrastructure to enable these changes. But as the report notes, the change in sentencing practice depends critically on the role of the SGC and judiciary. They have a pivotal role in helping ensure we can align the capacity of correctional services to deliver with the demand placed upon them by sentencers. They are also crucially important in ensuring we use the available capacity of correctional services as cost effectively as possible and consistent with the needs of justice.

48.   The report highlights the issue of replacing old and unsuitable prisons stock. We believe there is an excellent value for money case for a replacement programme to create a new generation of larger prisons with the facilities needed to deliver effective programmes designed to reduce re-offending. New large prisons could also provide economies of scale which would allow us to close some smaller prisons and redirect resources to community punishments. We are preparing a detailed investment case to explore further with Treasury colleagues.

Implementation team

Report Findings – The first step should be to set up the implementation team, who will need to set out a timetable for the next four years.

49.   We will set up as soon as possible a project team reporting to the Correctional Services Board which is chaired by the Minister for Correctional Services. The Board consists of senior representatives from the Home Office, DCA [Department of Constitutional Affairs], HMT [Her Majesty's Treasury] and No. 10, as well as a number of non-executive directors who provide external, independent challenge.

From Home Office, Reducing Crime – Changing Lives: the government's plans for transforming the management of offenders *(London: Home Office), 2004, pp. 12–15.*

15 Capacity and Competition Policy for Prisons and Probation (2009)

Ministry of Justice

Competition: probation

Competition to provide probation services has been limited to date. Previously, the Government has set probation boards a non-mandatory subcontracting target (5% in 2006/07 and 10% in 2007/08). This target was successful in some areas, increasing participation by private and third sector organisations in the delivery of probation services. We want to build on this by developing a range of providers from the public, private and third sectors, to drive competition, efficiency and innovation.

Probation trusts

The Offender Management Act received Royal Assent in July 2007, enabling private and third sectors to participate more fully in the market for probation services. By creating new organisations, Probation Trusts, to deliver services on behalf of the Justice Secretary, the intention is to increase the challenge to deliver high quality probation services from a range of providers, which will, in turn, drive efficiency and innovation.

The standards a Probation Board must demonstrate, to become a Trust, are high. Areas assessed include: leadership; performance management; local engagement; and effective resource use. If Probation Boards fail to become Trusts, other arrangements will need to be made to replace them. Boards can propose to be amalgamated with successful neighbouring Trusts, or alternatively, its services will be competed in the open market.

Services provided to courts by the probation service, will be excluded from competition, as they are reserved to the public sector by statute. Alternative arrangements for public sector delivery will be made for court services, in areas where other probation services are contracted out.

Best value in probation

Where the Probation Trust programme is aimed at improving organisational capabilities of probation, the Best Value framework is a method for driving up quality and value for money of the services provided by probation areas.

Launched in November 2008, the Best Value framework will enable probation areas to demonstrate, in a transparent way, the value for money of their services, and to drive improvements in the economy, efficiency and effectiveness of their service delivery.

Best Value reviews will initially be triggered centrally, with NOMS Agency identifying priority services for review. Standard specifications will be developed for the price and quality of probation services. Probation areas, in partnership with the local DOM [Director of Offender Management], will then review their own service delivery against these standards.

Where services are found to be underperforming, probation areas, in consultation with DOMs, will either propose performance improvements or be required to go to the market to seek an alternative provider.

Community Payback and Victim Contact are priorities for Best Value review in 2009. At least 25% of these services will be competed in the open market. Standard specifications are currently being drawn up.

- Specification for Community Payback will be available in April, Victim Contact will be completed shortly after;
- Probation areas will compare their services, on cost and performance, for six months, from September this year [2009];
- Competitions resulting from the comparison will begin in April 2010.

Once the Best Value framework is embedded into the way probation areas review the performance of services, reviews can take place on a regional or local level. These reviews will be informed by the picture of nationally benchmarked, standard specifications, built up during the initial programme. ...

Measuring success

We are building new capacity and implementing competition to deliver a step-change in the efficiency and cost-effectiveness of the delivery of services. We are looking to develop high quality, flexible, modern public services which can meet our needs into the medium term.

We are *not* setting market share targets because we are neutral in relation to who delivers services, as long as they are delivered in an efficient and cost-effective fashion. We are however willing to set targets for the quantity of provision which has been subject to competition.

We will look to measure success through delivering improvements in the following measures:

- The delivery of a net capacity of 96,000 prison places by December 2014.
- The successful delivery of competitions for new prisons, delivering an agreed quality at an efficient price.
- Prison contracts awarded to deliver efficiency savings on current spend, where current spend exists.
- Replace all probation boards with Trusts or alternative providers by 2011.
- The successful delivery of competition for at least 25 per cent of probation services which have been subject to the Best Value process.
- The successful embedding of the Best Value process in probation, allowing the launch of regional and local assessments.

We expect competitive pressure to apply beyond those prisons and probation services which are subject to competition. We expect to see a trend in improvement across the sector as a result. Where service providers fail to deliver to acceptable standards, we will use competition when necessary.

From Ministry of Justice, Capacity and Competition Policy for Prisons and Probation *(London: Ministry of Justice), 2009, pp. 12–13, 15.*

Part B

Probation history: alternative perspectives

Introduction

While the first section of this volume focuses upon official accounts to provide a history of probation, this section uses a variety of contributions to offer a different perspective on the development of probation. The first of these, by Peter Young (Reading 16), offered a new and challenging way of examining the origins of the probation service. Young's claim that 'probation emerged as a policy measure generated out of the relationship between classes in the later 19th century' makes a radical break from the conventional histories of probation such as Fred Jarvis' (1972) *Advise, Assist and Befriend,* Joan King's *The Probation Service* (in its third edition by 1969) and Dorothy Bochel's *Probation and After-Care* which was published in the same year as Young's article. His emphasis on competition and contestation rather than following the old-fashioned Whig approach to history suggests a very different view of the beginnings of the probation service, although still stressing the significance of the Evangelical movement and the rationalisation of charitable endeavour.

Cecil Leeson (Reading 17) was one of the key early supporters of the new probation service following its creation (if indeed it can be claimed that a probation *service* was created) by the 1907 Act. Leeson worked as a probation officer before the war and was to become secretary of the Howard Association in 1916 and later secretary of the Magistrates' Association. The book from which our extract comes – *The Probation System* – was the first full-length study of probation in the UK. Leeson argues that perfunctory work with offenders must be avoided, that probation officers should deal with suitable cases (reminding us that the nostrums of the Effective Practice or What Works initiative around 90 years later were not exactly novel), and that there is a need for national organisation of probation work – although its purpose would not be, as he emphasises, 'to standardise the work of individual probation officers'. The kind of arguments put forward by Leeson played an important role in generating criticism of the work of the police court missionaries and in encouraging the professionalisation of the probation service.

Another, equally important early figure was William Clarke Hall, a stipendiary magistrate who advocated state control of probation and terminating the system of dual control whereby the Church of England Temperance Society managed its police court missionaries alongside probation officers who were managed by local justices. His book, *The State and the Child,* was published in 1917, just three years after Leeson's; but the extract here (Reading 18) comes from a collection of essays covering probation in a number of countries (with a focus on the USA) edited by Sheldon Glueck and published in 1933. Clarke Hall's essay sums up the development of probation in England (*sic*) over the 25 years since the 1907 Act. He is strongly in favour of the use of volunteers to assist qualified, professional probation officers who would be managed by chief probation officers. Like Leeson, he wants 'a uniform state service', and he discusses a number of factors that would be conducive to success, among them firm enforcement of orders and greater psychological input to the examination of offenders.

While the work of the police court missionaries might have been associated with a certain amateurism, even they understood the importance of keeping offenders to rules. Jo Harris' book, *Probation: a sheaf of memories*, was published in 1937, but his account of working with young offenders is deeply rooted in the early days of probation work (Reading 19). Harris' book reads like an overly sentimental Victorian novel but he is emphatic about the significance of having rules that had to be adhered to and that were relevant to the individual's case. He takes his work with offenders seriously. Perhaps his most fascinating practice is the ritual burning of the recognisance form upon successful completion – a nice touch which might do with reconsideration today under the contemporary psychological principle of positive reinforcement.

Sewell Stokes' book, *Court Circular*, although published after the Second World War is based on his time as a probation officer during the war. In the extract here (Reading 20), he identifies two very different kinds of probation officer: the old-fashioned Mrs Gage ('a comfortable old body, self-educated and unable quite to pronounce the word "psychiatric"') who is representative of the dying breed of police court missionaries, and the young, educated, trained Miss Baneystock who has come to probation 'straight from a course of lectures on the psychiatric treatment of delinquents'. Stokes was an untrained recruit to the service (or The Work as he terms it), so not surprisingly is not very sympathetic to Miss Baneystock and her theories. In his – perhaps somewhat biased view – it is Mrs Gage who is seen as the more effective probation officer, although the end of the war signalled the end of police court missionaries and the triumph of professionalism in probation.

Bill McWilliams was one of the key commentators on probation in the second half of the twentieth century, and his quartet of articles exploring changes in the conception of probation work represents a significant achievement. McWilliams – like so many of those who have written thoughtfully about probation – worked as a probation officer before becoming an academic. The extract presented here (Reading 21) is from the third of his four essays. In it he discusses one of the key evolutionary shifts in probation – 'from a service devoted to the saving of souls through divine grace to an agency concerned with the scientific assessment and treatment of offenders'. In other words, and harking back to the previous extract, how Miss Baneystock triumphed over Mrs Gage. McWilliams shows how diagnosis became the key issue in probation work, lying at the heart of the casework approach. By the time of his writing, this 'diagnostic ideal' was already breaking down (for a number of reasons) and he notes the limitations of the diagnostic methodology that contributed to this.

The next extract (Reading 22), from a book by Elizabeth Glover which was first published shortly after the end of the Second World War, shows the continuing influence of religion on probation work – even as late as 1956. Glover emphasises the importance of psychiatry and psychology for probation and – indirectly – shows the practical influence of the medical model (also noted by Bill McWilliams). She argues that probation must not only seek to respond to the immediate problems that led to the offence, but also needs to work on helping the offender to build up resistance 'so that he does not easily fall prey to infection again'. For the latter aim, Glover considers moral health to be the key and she argues that four factors comprise the foundation of this. One of these – 'faith in a living God' – might strike us today as an attribute that sits rather uneasily with the significance of psychiatry/psychology. For Glover, there was no contradiction; indeed, at the conclusion of the book she states unequivocally that '[it] is the merit of the probation system that it is consonant at once with modern psychiatric science and with Christian faith and teaching' (Glover 1956: 271).

In 1958, the *British Journal of Delinquency* published a special number celebrating the fiftieth anniversary of the probation service. One of the articles was by Frank Dawtry (Reading 23), general secretary of NAPO between 1948 and 1967, who was far more concerned with looking forward than with a nostalgic review of the past. He notes that there were three departmental committees that examined the work of probation in its first 28 years and these had considerable influence on the development of the service. Given the number of changes in probation work enumerated by Dawtry since the last of these committees in 1936, it is no surprise that he argues for the need 'for a public assessment to be made of both the work and the organization of the Probation Service'. The list of issues he sets out for a new committee to examine suggests a pressing need to bring the probation service up to date. Early in 1959, the government announced that a major review of probation was to take place and the Morison report was published three years later.

Academic work on the relationships between probation officers and their superiors is notable for its absence. Indeed, we might well ask just who are 'the bosses'? Marjory Todd who became a probation officer in middle age and worked during the 1950s and 1960s lists a number of possibilities and outlines the inconsistencies that can emerge as a result of different opinions (Reading 24). Originally, of course, magistrates were 'the bosses' of probation officers and – although as Todd points out, by the time she is writing they no longer play such a role – their influence on probation work could still be profound. They could be authoritative and sympathetic; they could be cold and distant; they could be crassly insensitive; they could be brusque and rude. Probation officers have to deal with such magistrates directly in their role as 'servant of the court', but they also have to deal with the impact of such magistrates on offenders, especially juveniles. Would these kinds of behaviour towards offenders be found in today's magistrates' courts? And, if so – given the unpredictability of individuals – how would contemporary probation officers see the professional role?

By the 1980s there was a feeling that traditional one-to-one work with offenders was becoming somewhat marginalised in favour of groupwork; day centres and specified activities were the flavour of the day. Typically, groupwork was seen at the time as a novel approach to working with offenders, but as with so many so-called novel approaches, this one had roots deep in the history of probation, as Maurice Vanstone (another probation officer turned academic) perceptively points out (Reading 25). The developments in groupwork charted by Vanstone mirror those that occurred in supervision, particularly with the move from practical help to more scientific casework. The advantages and disadvantages of working with groups of offenders were noted by those involved in setting them up and running them well before their heyday in the 1980s, as Vanstone shows. Perhaps most significantly, groupwork changes the nature of the relationship between the probation officer and the offender, and training is seen to be vital (if not always forthcoming) for those who wish to work in this way.

Community service orders (CSOs) were introduced by the 1972 Criminal Justice Act following the recommendations of the Wootton Committee (see Part A), and might be acknowledged as perhaps the greatest success story of the probation service in the second half of the twentieth century (although this would depend upon one's definition of success). Today, as the unpaid work requirement for community orders and suspended sentence orders, they are the most commonly used requirement. Ken Pease, whose research into community service as a member of the Home Office Research Unit was highly influential, writing only a few years after CSOs had become nationally available, provides an overview of their origins and development (Reading 26). He shows how a number of changes were made in the process leading up to the passing of the Act, most of these resulting in the 'toughening up' of the order. Throughout its history, community service has been regularly criticised for inconsistent practices which might result in injustice, and Pease notes that from the very beginnings of the six experimental schemes there were a number of differences in practice and administration. These differences were never resolved as CSOs were rolled out nationally, and it is such discrepancies in practice that were partially responsible for the first National Standards to be introduced being those for community service in 1989.

The final extract in this section (Reading 27) is a speech given by David Faulkner, at the time a deputy secretary in the Home Office, at a conference held at the Institute of Criminology in 1989 to discuss the role of the probation service. It was at this period that government was promoting the idea of probation moving 'centre stage' in the criminal justice system; and the service was being encouraged to cooperate by a combination of carrots and sticks because of its central importance to the plans set out in the Green Paper *Punishment, Custody and the Community* (1988), the White Paper *Crime, Justice and Protecting the Public* (1989), and carried to fruition in the 1991 Criminal Justice Act. Faulkner stresses the importance of probation but emphasises that it is now a criminal justice service and no longer a social work agency. Probation is in the punishment game. The speech also points to a number of other issues that were to take on greater significance in the coming years: leadership and management; research and statistics; the organisation of local services; whether probation should be the sole provider of the services it used with offenders; whether there is a need for probation officers to hold a social work qualification. Faulkner's final words now echo with a profound irony: 'we have an interesting and exciting time ahead of us'. Indeed, we did, although – as always among probation officers and commentators – opinions vary as to whether the nature of that interest and excitement has been positive or negative.

References

Home Office (1988) *Punishment, Custody and the Community.* London: HMSO.
——(1989) *Crime, Justice and Protecting the Public.* London: HMSO.

16 A sociological analysis of the early history of probation (1976)

Peter Young

The objective of this article is an attempt to provide an explanation of the history of probation in nineteenth-century English society. The thesis argued is that probation emerged as a policy measure generated out of the relationships between the social classes of that period. More specifically the origins of probation are located in the ideological perception by middle-class reformers of the nature, cause and content of social problems and the directed social action that was contingent upon this perception. In order to ground this argument, two closely inter-related themes will be developed. First, a description and analysis of the organisation of ideology in this historical period will be given. Second, this article purports to be an excursion into that familiar historical realm which is concerned with explaining how social work grew from diffuse charitable beginnings to a relatively organised, governmental and bureaucratic present.

Given these wider and more generalised concerns this article could hardly claim to give a detailed, exhaustive historical account of the origin of probation – rather it attempts to isolate criteria that are necessary for any sufficient explanation of this phenomenon. The intention of the article is thus to develop an analytical framework within which a more detailed and empirically secure description could be situated.

To achieve this objective I will first consider those explanations that have been offered by historians to account for the origins and growth of social work and probation, observing not only the content of their arguments, but also the form and structure they take. The aim here is to explicate the ideological overtones and basic organisational themes of these accounts and expose them to critical scrutiny and comment.

The most commonly propounded thesis for the existence and motivation of social workers in cities of the nineteenth century is that their reforming zeal stemmed from the interaction of an Evangelical spirit with the ethos of a peculiar middle-class entrepreneurial philosophy. Whilst noting the existence of these two ideologies, historians emphasise however the predominance of this Evangelical spirit as the prime causal agent, describing it as having a generalised and pervasive influence not only on Victorian society in general, but on the middle-class in particular. For example, Young and Ashton (1956: 28) state: 'To most of the middle-class the economic theories … came at second hand, but their religious experiences and convictions were personal and real, the product very largely of the Evangelical movement.'

Whilst Evangelicism is portrayed as providing an overarching ideology, it is to its subsidiary effects that these authors point in accounting for the immediate forces that pushed 'missionaries' into positive action. Consequently, a Puritan combination of a 'consciousness of sin', as Webb put it, with a generalised compassion towards the 'disadvantaged' in Victorian society are isolated as the twin motivational criteria that finally account for the spread of charitable giving. Thus Lynd (1945: 418) argues: 'Then when a beggar or a scandal thrust a specific case squarely into attention, the pent-up guilt over general conditions flooded to release in doing something about the specific case.'

Further, as the middle-class progressed to more than a junior partner's share in parliament and government, this charitable spirit was supposedly translated into legislation to correct specific cases. Consequently, a convergent movement between the legally and religiously-based charitable spheres is portrayed, promoted by this essential similarity of ideological outlook. For example, in explaining the present-day nature of probation, J. King (1958: 3) contends that: 'Thus the legal and religious approaches converged towards the conception of probation as we know it today.'

Moreover, this growing convergence is seen as being strengthened and extended by the re-organisation of charity giving by such bodies as the Charity Organisation Society (C.O.S.). Originating in 1869, the progress of this organisation is explained by historians as the outcome of a reactive movement whose purpose was to rectify the practices of the indiscriminate alms-giver, by re-instating a rationalised system of charitable giving without, as it was so often put, 'demoralising character'. This new form of charitable giving was not only supposedly more efficient but apparently also brought coherence to middle-class living by 'balancing' or 'binding' potentially conflictual elements implicit in this life-style. As Young and Ashton (1956: 29) describe it:

> Business morality and religious morality overlapped. Many of the commercial and manufacturing classes, laissez faire in their economics were evangelical christians. Philanthropy was the bridge in many cases between their business dealings and their christian conscience.

As well as accounting for the presence of charitably-based social work, this explanation is also normally used to argue a parallel case concerning the relationship between the broader significance and consequence of social work and more basic social structural changes. Not only is social work seen as a balm to middle-class conscience, but more importantly, is characterised as heralding the growth of a new form of political and economic freedom for society. Social work agencies – like the probation service – are conceptualised as mediating between the conflicting ideologies of State interventionism and laissez-faire individualism. Embracing an argument influenced by Dicey, social historians like Lynd contend that intervention was a logical outcome of social changes which, though surfacing in the 1870's and 1880's, were implicit in Benthamite individualism. Intervention, we are told, emerged from the conflicts endemic in an ideology that encapsulated the opposing strands of untrammelled economic competition and Evangelically based humanism. As a result, freedom was no longer defined in negative terms – as freedom from constraint – but positively, as freedom through a limited collectivity. As Lynd (1945: 426) puts it:

> But if certain kinds of authority in society might be a potential for human good, then it becomes possible to consider what kind of structuring of power might achieve this end. Such consideration revived recognition of the relation between economic and political power.

Thus intervention by official or quasi-official bodies became legitimated by this ideology. The period of laissez-faire was eclipsed, apparently, and the ground-work laid for the growth of a new political democracy. For example, Lynd (1945: 424) continues her case in the following manner: 'Collectivism and social security as the eighties developed them are not freedom, but they help to prepare the soil in which freedom may grow.'

Progress in English society was thus guaranteed. Of importance is that these new philosophies are seen by historians not as discontinuities in culture but as organic developments from the preceding social milieu. Middle-class ideology and activity thus become the core feature of a self-adjusting mechanism that united social structure together in holistic fashion. Potential conflicts or exceptions to the organism were apparently neutralised or absorbed by the changing nature of middle-class activity. Interventionism, marked by the spread of social work, was merely the first stage of a movement, so these authors imply, whose apotheosis is a development in political consciousness, 'from preventing bad government to planning good government' (Lynd 1945: 426).

To complete the tale, these social historians also point to the increased pressure and organisational power of a newly mobilised and increasingly more sophisticated labour force to influence political institutions and processes to pass favourable enactments. English society, we are asked to believe, was thus liberalised and opened – these changes finding ultimate codification in legislative activity which 'broke out' in isolated decades, this 'trend' culminating in the 1945–49 rash of welfare laws (for the most detailed general history that endorses this explanation see Bruce 1961).

More specifically, social work is not only viewed as sharing in this progress, but also as beckoning it by operating as a sort of index of the more fundamental underlying social and philosophic changes. In the histories of probation this type of account is best rendered in the book edited by Joan King (1969). For example, we are told that in the late nineteenth century, 'the state had accepted responsibility for providing the means of reformation' (King 1958: 198), or again that:

> Change in the probation and after-care service, as in the social services as a whole, is a product of broader social change. ... It is part of the attempt to adapt social institutions to meet both old and new needs more effectively and more fully. The possibility of progress depends upon the ability not merely to withstand change, but to seize and harness its opportunities.
>
> (King 1969: 40)

Taken in total these various works, as well as others not mentioned (such as Marshall 1971; Pinker 1971; Woodroofe 1962), constitute a generalised type of explanation organised around key thematic ideas and events. Dominating all is the emphasis on the contribution of middle-class reformers to the revitalisation of English national culture. The England of today is portrayed as being intimately linked to the springs of the new middle-class collectivism that flourished in the last decades of the nineteenth century. Social work, nurtured by this environment, is characterised as a symbol of the essence of this movement. A unilinear developmental process is thereby described which connects present-day political freedom with this middle-class ideology. Indeed, the impression is given that the concepts of 'welfare' and 'representative government' become almost substitutable and interchangeable. The past is seen as inexorably leading along a pre-determined pathway that terminates in the natural state of welfare society. Similarly the history of probation – its reform, expansion and 'institutionalisation' – mark the signposts that make clear the way to any who happen to wander.

With the basic questions posed in such a way the job of the historian is reduced to merely filling in the missing details; to 'flesh out' the year to year advancement of welfare, noting temporary set-backs and possible diversions, but assuming always that the goal is clear, universally agreed upon and universally agreeable. The thesis thus suffers from a premature closure of its parameters. The object to be researched (the history of welfare, social work or probation) takes second place to the purpose of engaging in research which amounts to an expression of faith in the essential rightness of English society. Consequently serious historiography is replaced by biased, misplaced hagiology.

The general critical point made in the above analysis was that the purported explanation of the history of social work and probation is infused with an ideological optimism that pre-determines what themes are to be isolated and what significance is to be attached to them. Moreover, it is also contended that this ideology is not arbitrary in nature but of a particular type that makes these histories of social work, as Briggs (1964) has noted, the modern counterpart of the Whig historiography of the nineteenth century. To deepen the analysis it must now be established not only how this ideology affects the nature and type of information brought to support this Whig interpretation, but also how this evidence is utilised.

It is suggested that the key to unlocking these problems is to be found not in observing what this explanation includes and comments upon, but more in observing and analysing what it ignores, to note the silences as well as the utterances. Thus this article is not necessarily concerned to deny the 'facts of the case', but instead to explicate and contest the process whereby these facts were selected, held up to examination and finally given ontological status as events 'in history'.

This argument may be grounded by considering areas of silence that surround two central concepts in this 'Whig' social history. First, the explanation and utilisation of the idea of reformers as specifically middle-class reformers will be examined. The intention here is to bring to light the extreme selectivity of evidence that severely restricts the empirical adequacy and coverage of this thesis. Second, the explanation of the significance of charity in nineteenth-century social structure will be examined, illustrating in this example the theoretical restrictions implicit in the way its basic question is posed.

To take the first example, it may be observed that in establishing the importance of the middle-class as the prime historical agent involved in charitable giving, Whig social historians treat these groups as a clear, homogeneous unit. We are told that charity, and with it probation, spread because groups of like-minded people became repelled by conditions in English society. Thus, to follow this explanation, the history of nineteenth- and twentieth-century democracy becomes a history of the progress of all those who can, by dint of occupational background, be called middle-class, shopkeepers, industrialists, commercial gentlemen, doctors and many others. However, the core problem here is whether the categorisation of these different occupations as a unitary middle-class is adequate. Certainly in terms of the evidence culled by the historians discussed here it is. All those with incomes within the brackets and limits of such occupations are implicitly assumed to be middle-class people who will necessarily exemplify an identical commitment to the Evangelical–entrepreneurial ideology. Thus the utilisation of utterances emanating from any of these groups is taken as an example of an apparently *middle-class* utterance in which all like bodies would share. What is striking here is the way this explanation handles its evidence as though its meaning is quite clear and unproblematic. 'History' is treated as a resource that, in a relatively simple manner, provides examples and illustrations of how present-day structures clearly emerged from yesterday's context. Consequently, this Whig history proceeds by a number of assumed and over-simplified stages that prematurely purport to establish their thesis before sufficient evidence is amassed.

This tendency to one-sided over-generalisation becomes quite clear upon a more stringent examination of the nature of charitable giving in the mid to late nineteenth century. We do not find a situation in which charitable endeavour was dominated by one homogeneous middle-class throughout the period, but instead it becomes clear that a variety of different groups within the middle-class in fact monopolised and organised this activity at different periods. The ramifications of this heterogeneity of groups were considerable, for each had a differing conception of the nature, shape and purpose of charitable giving.

For example, in the 1870's – the decade in which the first police-court missionary was appointed – charity was dominated by the professional sections of society working through the highly centralised C.O.S. Unlike other charitable bodies, the *raison d'être* of the C.O.S. was to practise what they called 'scientific charity'. This was charity that was supposedly rationally organised and specifically intended to avoid 'demoralisation of character' and pauperism.

Underlying the peculiar nature of C.O.S. practice was an analysis of social problems that focused upon what they referred to as 'the indiscriminate alms-giver'. Indeed, considerable C.O.S. energy was spent in combating this activity as it was seen as the sole cause of England's social problems and vices. Dr Guy, a member of the C.O.S. argued:

> If you will bring about the due punishment of this vice … if you will … handcuff the indiscriminate alms giver, I will promise you … these inevitable consequences; no destitution, less poor-rates, prisons emptier, fewer gin shops, less crowded mad houses, sure signs of under-population and an England worth living in.
>
> (Bosanquet 1895: 3–4)

Whilst the C.O.S. may thus have dominated charity in the 1870's, a quite different pattern is evident in the preceding decades. For example, in the 1860's charitable endeavour was monopolised by these indiscriminate alms-givers, which had the effect of focusing attention on pauperism as a specific type of social problem. Hence this decade was distinct from the 1870's in two ways. Not only had the nature and purpose of charity changed, but there was also a concomitant shift in the perception of what constituted *the* social problem to be rectified by missionary action (see, for example, Stedman-Jones 1971: chapters 12–15). The salient point here, however, is that, like the members of the C.O.S., the indiscriminate alms-giver was also a member of what Whig historians refer to as the middle-class. To be more exact, the indiscriminate alms-giver belonged to what Victorians called the 'new middle-class' – the second generation of small industrialists, shop-keepers, the petit-bourgeoisie.

A picture therefore emerges of various groups within the middle-class competing and contesting against one another in the charitable realm. These intra-class relationships had considerable influence on the development of distinct ideological positions and emphases. For example, the established middle-class moralised those middle-class groups below them as much as they did the working class. As B.G. Orchard put it:

> Christians of cultural minds and refined manners … were thus separated by a wide gulf from the seething crowd of those who had no grandfathers, and who, whatever their energetic ambition might aspire to in the future, had no past which they could talk about.
>
> (cited in Simey 1951: 82)

Equally, in their own way, the professional middle-class, speaking through the C.O.S., moralised and condemned these new arrivals. Commenting on the flood of the new middle-class to the suburbs, the C.O.S. stated: 'They have retreated before the advance of the poorer classes abandoning in their flight … any social rule over their neighbours … their isolation in suburban comfort is a sign of defeat' (Stedman-Jones 1971: 244).

Far from there being a homogeneity in outlook and activity between all these different groups, it is apparent that there were considerable and significant variations in emphasis upon the giving of charity and degree of commitment to the Evangelical–entrepreneurial ideology – indeed to the whole notion of being middle-class. Thus these explanations that simply categorise all marginally similar groups as middle-class and then assume a similarity of ideology and activity amongst them, seriously underestimate the considerable dynamics of the social processes involved.

The consequence of this argument is not to deny historians the ability to talk of and use the concept of 'middle-class' when applied to nineteenth-century history. At one level of abstraction this is permissible. The point is rather that given this example Whig historians of social work are not warranted in claiming that their thesis is established in terms of the evidence they use to support it. As this example has illustrated, the nature of charitable giving in the nineteenth century was as much an outcome of a struggle over scarce moral resources by middle-class people as it was a struggle over scarce material resources by working-class people. The theoretical lacuna in the approach of these historians is to collapse, and identify as the same, the concepts of occupational group and social class. Simply locating the job and income level of an individual or group is not sufficient evidence for the further categorisation of them as class members. Further, this example illustrates how the ideology implicit in Whig histories of social work circumscribes the nature of evidence used to substantiate its thesis. The scope and coverage of material is highly limited, containing silences and absences at points where other available evidence might confute the interpretation offered. Thus a highly systematic evasive process is initiated that entrenches the conceptual and empirical restrictions that inhere in these works.

We find a similar position with regard to the second example; that of how these Whig historians explain the social significance of charity. The general thesis they embrace is that charitable giving operated as a mechanism whereby the progressive, developmental forces in English society could be extended to a population – the working class – that did not so readily share in them. Charity was both a way of indicating the politically open nature of English society and a method of raising the material and moral standards of this population to a point where they could reap the potential benefits and fruits of this society. Again these historians approvingly quote evidence to support this thesis. The nature of this evidence is usually a selection of statements that invoke the principles of self-dependence and independence – the general thesis of self-help (see Young and Ashton 1956: chapters 3–7; Lynd 1945: chapters 3, 8 and 11). Charity is consequently viewed as a means of inculcating this philosophy.

For example, Whig histories normally locate the institutionalisation of the self-help philosophy in the enactment of the 1834 Poor Law based on the economics of Nassau Senior and others. Moreover, we are asked to believe that subsequently other administrative agencies, including prisons, converged upon these principles by adopting the ideology of 'less eligibility'. Thus again the continuous expansion of English society is affirmed. However, even accepting that this story is largely correct, the question still remains whether this acceptance equally commits historians to interpreting charity as a beneficent political gift?

Again upon a more stringent examination of the historical situation one finds an extreme selectivity in the utilisation of evidence that not only over-simplifies the dynamics of the social processes involved, but also clearly underestimates the existence of alternative nineteenth-century ideological perceptions concerning charity. These alternative ideological perceptions do not portray a picture of charity in terms of its beneficence but instead stress the role of charitable giving as a directed attempt to coerce a miscreant, working-class population to a better life, defined in terms of these entrepreneurial middle-class values.

The middle-class attempt to moralise society via charitable giving held an implicit political theme based upon a certain perception of the nature of an ideal society. Part and parcel of the middle-class entrepreneurial ideology was the notion of society as an 'open system', of a society founded in and guaranteed by the principles of individualism. English society could only continue in its progress if all within it shared this competitive ethic. As Malthus put it:

> If no man could hope to rise or fear to fall in society, if industry did not bring its own reward, and indolence its punishment, we could not hope to see that animated activity in bettering our own condition which now forms the master-spring of public prosperity.
>
> (cited in Perkins 1969: 254)

Given a generalised political philosophy of this nature, assuming the unity of individual and societal utility, then those who did not seem to share in the 'goods' of a society manifesting these principles could only be defined as either politically dissenting or morally aberrant. The definition of social problems by middle-class reformers thus followed and extended this reasoning. However, these pundits were potentially in conflict. As much as the entrepreneurial ideology stressed the significance and importance of *all* in society sharing a similar outlook, it also stressed the right of the individual to pursue his own ends. Thus to define those who were not manifestly gaining from an individualist philosophy as politically dissenting was problematic, as such a definition implied a rationality and legitimacy to beliefs. If these beliefs were rational and legitimate to hold, then the very principles of the rightness of a society structured on individualism were challenged.

The solution for these Victorian pundits was therefore to define these miscreant individuals as being a social problem on account of their own moral laxity or failing.

Hence the nineteenth century marks the growth of an analysis of social problems as being due not to economic or political reasons, but to individual moral ones. Thus, H. Dendy (1895: 82), writing on the 'Industrial Residuum', stated that: 'The qualities which are characteristic of members of the Residuum are not distributed with any reference to money income.' Indeed, Dendy continues her argument by completely inverting the 'materialist' analysis of social problems and stressing the importance of character as the prime-mover. 'Taking this type of character as one of our data, we may now ask about its effect upon the economic position of its possessor' (Dendy 1895: 87).

Charity given to relieve this situation was thus that which attended to 'character'. However, it is suggested that it is not adequate to interpret this activity purely in terms of it being a beneficent political gift. By concentrating on self-help charitable endeavour contained a point of vital political significance. It functioned as the effort of the middle-class to legitimate the essential correctness of their individualist vision of a particular type of social order. Its intention was to instil and inculcate the miscreant working-class population with a similar notion of social order and so to receive its endorsement of the continued progress to social and political dominance of the middle-class. Thus Cobden could write:

> Mine is the masculine species of charity which would lead me to inculcate in the minds of the labouring-classes the love of independence, the privilege of self-respect, the disdain of being patronised or petted, the desire to accumulate and the ambition to rise.
>
> (cited in Perkins 1969: 137)

This increases the significance of the practices of the indiscriminate alms-giver in the 1860's. His activity, which was a corruption of this conception of charity, amounted to an indirect political assault not only on the social dominance of the established middle-class but also upon the whole edifice of middle-class ideology. Thus the directed efforts of the C.O.S. in the 1870's to counter indiscriminate giving also gain in importance as a political activity. The machinations of the C.O.S. were an attempt to reinstate the principles of the entrepreneurial ideal in a new and more subtle form. Whereas before charitable giving had been an open political act, the professionals of the C.O.S. transposed this ideology into a social and moral philosophy whose political edge was blunted. As G. Young (1960: 23) puts it, the liberal professions attempted to:

> disengage the disinterested intelligence, to release it from the entanglements of party and sect ... and to set it operating over the whole range of human life and circumstances.

The consequence of the C.O.S. was to add a humanistic perspective to charitable giving and thus attempt to legitimate both the structure of an hierarchical English society and the vitality and potency of the entrepreneurial ideal. Historically the contribution of the professional middle-class to the development of nineteenth-century English society can be regarded, to quote Marx (1970: 52), as 'these active conceptualising ideologists, who make it their chief livelihood to develop and perfect the illusion of this class about itself'.

The historians so far discussed completely underestimate this element in charitable giving and the significance given it by middle-class reformers. With this example, however, the selectivity of empirical evidence can only be accounted for by explicating the manner in which the basic questions are posed and not simply by commenting upon restricted empirical coverage. Rather than conceptualising the motivation that lay behind charitable endeavour in societal terms – as a property of the social order – these Whig historians conceive of the motivation that lay behind charitable endeavour in highly reductionist terms, as a property of atomised, individualistic activity. The account given of motivation works on a type of commonsense psychology in which beliefs for action and ideology are treated as conceptual equivalents. Ideology is conceived of as a psychological process whereby beliefs are causally linked to action. The concept of ideology thus undergoes a severe methodological reductionism. These Whig histories, with few exceptions, consequently lack a conception of ideology as a social process binding structures together. Further, these histories also assume a direct, one-to-one relationship between social structural position and ideological commitment. The ideology of middle-class missionaries can thus be assumed to be unproblematic as soon as occupational position is located (see for example, Althusser 1971).

Given this context Whig social histories thus tend to ignore, or simply not conceptualise, the social function of nineteenth-century charitable giving. As this second example illustrates, charity had not only intended social functions they do not record, but also highly significant unintended ones, which makes their general interpretation of it as a beneficent political gift somewhat inadequate.

The Whig interpretation of the origins of social work can thus hardly be said to be adequate in terms of empirical coverage or conceptual power. By noting the silences in this thesis it has been possible to demonstrate the somewhat distorted version of history it conveys. We seem faced with a situation where researches have been co-opted by the very ideology of liberalism that ought to have been the topic for investigation. Consequently, this thesis is actually pre-determined in content and argument even before investigation begins. Once its basic utterance is proclaimed much else is silenced.

Two issues remain. First, I will consider the ramifications of these assertions for the history of social work and probation. Second, I will attempt to integrate and tie together themes that are already implicit in the preceding analysis, but which need coherent explication. By so doing, I will attempt to ground my major thesis that probation emerged as a policy measure generated out of the relationship between classes in the later nineteenth century, although it is conceded that this argument will be both somewhat brief and speculative.

The general thrust of Whig histories of social work is to suggest that it functioned as an element in the middle-class attempt to stabilise society by extending a beneficent gift to a deprived working-class population. In what is perhaps the most sophisticated of these histories, that of Lynd, the explanation of this situation is further tied to an organic, functionalist analogy of society. Middle-class activity is portrayed as the essential mechanism whereby a healthy social structure was maintained, 'health' being defined in terms of a liberal philosophy stressing the unity of individual and social utilities. Thus the growth of social work is described as a natural and essential feature of English social structure.

The thesis argued in this article finds considerable superficial agreement with this Whig interpretation. For example, it too considers that middle-class activity in the form of social reform and charitable giving functioned as a stabiliser of English social structure. However, it differs from the Whig thesis both at the level of how this state of affairs should be explained and what implications can be drawn from this explanation.

It is contended that charitable activity, including probation, operated as a mechanism which politically incorporated a possibly oppositional working-class culture into an institutional and cultural structure based on middle-class values and ideologies. Thus social work should not be seen as a gradual liberalisation and democratisation of society, but as a directed attempt to circumscribe the scope of legitimate action and life styles available to working-class people. As McGregor (1957: 155) has argued 'From the thirties onwards middle-class people were continuously digging channels by which working-class demands could be drained away from the foundations of property.'

It is suggested that social work and social reform are but one example of how such a channel was dug. To quote McGregor once more, social policy can thus accurately be conceived of as deriving 'essentially from professional middle-class anxieties to maintain the stability of social institutions' (1957: 156), rather than as deriving from right-minded people who, on the basis of compassion alone, journeyed into working-class areas. Hence it is to this milieu – the relationships between social classes – that the historian must look for a context in which such anxieties and ideologies operated. The history of social work, including that of probation, must consequently, in part, be a history of how this incorporative process took place and operated in the nineteenth and twentieth centuries.

As this argument stands, its major deficiency is to suggest a crude conspiracy model of society; that evil-minded men so manipulated social forces as to maintain the stability and privileges of their socially powerful and advantageous positions. A clear, two-class model of society is thus suggested, by which all social processes are apparently to be explained. However, this is far from the case this thesis wishes to embrace. For example, it was illustrated above that the specific nature and content of ideologies is to be accounted for as much in terms of *intra*-class relationships as in terms of *inter*-class relationships. The conflictual elements in the relationship between the C.O.S. and the indiscriminate alms-giver are of prime importance for a full understanding of the humanistic, social and moral philosophy of the 'scientific' social workers of the C.O.S. Thus the individualistic moral analysis of social problems by social workers in the 1870's is indicative of the basic structural arrangements that characterise this decade. The consequent desiccation of this mode of analysis in the 1880's following the publication of Booth's work and such events as the London housing crisis and dock strike, are similarly indicative of changed structural arrangements in this period.

To appreciate the particular religious emphasis implicit in the ideology of police court missionaries, it is important to note they originated as social workers who functioned outside the existing governmental framework. Appointed by the Church of England Temperance Society, they were originally concerned with correcting drunkenness rather than general criminal behaviour. Although this religiously influenced group did not manifest an ideology at variance with that of other social workers in this period, the considerations detailed here further confute analysis in crude, two-class, conspiracy terms.

Further, it would be quite incorrect to suppose that working-class culture did not embrace a philosophy of self-help identical to that of the middle-class pundits described here. The late nineteenth century marks a rise in self-help and providence societies originating purely in the working class. Moreover, there is again an interesting parallel with middle-class living, as these providence societies were not initiated by *any* member of the working class, but specifically by those who belonged to the 'labour aristocracy' of Victorian cities. Further, the leadership of these groups very often espoused an ideology embracing an individualistic moral perspective. Thus one leader of the labour aristocracy in Edinburgh expressed the hope that: 'if the Co-operative element were to pervade society more generally than it did at the present time, a vast amount of the misery and crime, consequent upon intemperance and improvidence, would be altogether unknown' (Gray 1974: 29).

A pattern of heterogeneous groups within an overall class-structure therefore emerges in a way that exactly parallels the situation of the middle-classes in the nineteenth century. Indeed, it was this very factor that provided the foundations of one of the core mechanisms by which middle-class charitable giving incorporated working-class culture. The distinctions made between the 'deserving' and 'undeserving' poor, between the 'respectable' and 'unrespectable' poor were key elements in the actual coercive processes employed by middle-class gurus. Thus an analysis which suggested – as did that of the C.O.S. and other social workers – that the subordinate groups, the 'undeserving' and the 'unrespectable' working-class, were subordinated precisely because of their moral laxity had the implication of embracing those who belonged to the other half of these important distinctions. Consequently this effected a major stage in negotiating not only the legitimation of the philosophy of moral individualism but also that of the middle-class life-style that generated and reflected this philosophy.

The practice of social work in this period may thus be envisioned as operating, in part, by a process of 'cultural desiccation'. In shifting the emphasis in the practice of a self-help philosophy from the older, economic principles of 'less-eligibility' to a new humanism, the police court missionaries successfully transposed politics into morality and thereby opened up a new inroad into working-class culture. By tapping the Evangelicism that was by then traditionally a part of working-class culture, social workers helped to ratify the distinctions between different groups already made by this class. In consequence, the ideology of moral individualism became reified and thus able to deny its very status as ideology. Once this position was achieved, the ideology could develop a pervasive sense of naturalism that obviated the need to look beyond its boundaries for a legitimation of its own existence.

A pre-condition for the success of late nineteenth-century charity – that both giver and receiver shared a similar analysis of the problem that caused them to be in such a situation in the first place – was thus made possible by the 'quasi-institutionalisation' of some middle-class cultural patterns. Viewed analytically the process of 'cultural desiccation', and the resultant incorporation, was an emergent property of the concrete practice of these ideological formations and not an end-product of the exercise of naked, absolute power. In this context it becomes all the more important to analyse the concrete situations that underlie the particular ideological formations one is describing. To follow Althusser (1971), it is thus only possible to talk of the history of *specific ideologies* rather than of ideology in general.

Neither Whig histories nor conspiracy theory seems capable of embracing such a mode of analysis. Both amount to an affirmation of faith in the moralisms implicit in their foundations and do not provide a paradigm from which an adequate analytic framework can be crystallised. The suggestions of this article, that this framework can only be found in an analysis of the relationship within and between classes in the nineteenth century, are but the starting point from which a more informed history of the penal system could proceed.

From Peter Young, 'A sociological analysis of the early history of probation',
British Journal of Law and Society, *3(1), 1976, pp. 44–58.*

References

Althusser, L. (1971) *For Marx.* London: Allen Lane.

Bosanquet, H. ed. (1895) *Aspects of the Social Problems.* London: John Murray.

Briggs, A. (1964) 'The welfare state in historical perspective', in C. Schottland, ed. *The Welfare State.* London: Harper and Row.

Bruce, M. (1961) *The Coming of the Welfare State.* London: Batsford.

Dendy, H. (1895) 'The industrial residuum', in H. Bosanquet, ed. *Aspects of the Social Problems.* London: John Murray.

Gray, R.Q. (1974) 'The labour aristocracy in the Victorian class structure', in F. Parkin, ed. *The Social Analysis of Class Structure.* London: Tavistock.

King, J. (1958) *The Probation Service.* 2nd ed. London: Butterworths.

——(1969) *The Probation Service.* 3rd ed. London: Butterworths.

Lynd, H.M. (1945) *England in the Eighteen-Eighties.* London: Oxford University Press.

Marshall, T.H. (1971) *Social Policy.* London: Hutchinson.

Marx, K. (1970) *The German Ideology.* New York: International Publishers Edition.

McGregor, O.R. (1957) 'Social research and social policy in the nineteenth century', *British Journal of Sociology* 8 (2): 146–157.

Perkins, H. (1969) *The Origins of British Society.* London: Routledge and Kegan Paul.

Pinker, R. (1971) *Social Theory and Social Policy.* London: Heinemann.

Simey, M.B. (1951) *Charitable Effort in Liverpool.* Liverpool: Liverpool University Press.

Stedman-Jones, G. (1971) *Outcast London.* London: Oxford University Press.

Woodroofe, K. (1962) *From Charity to Social Work in England and the United States.* London: Routledge and Kegan Paul.

Young, A.F. and Ashton, E.T. (1956) *British Social Work in the Nineteenth Century.* London: Routledge and Kegan Paul.

Young, G. (1960) *Victorian England: portrait of an age.* London: Oxford University Press.

17 Defects of the probation system (1914)

Cecil Leeson

The defects of the probation system are defects of administration, rather than of principle, and are traceable largely to misapprehensions of the nature of the system arising from its extraordinarily rapid growth. The defects consist chiefly in (a) unsuitable probation officers, (b) unsuitable cases, (c) too short probationary periods, and (d) inadequacy of organisation and control.

The question of unsuitable probation officers has been already partly considered [not too old but not too young, adequate education and training, experience of the social conditions of those they have to deal with, and the right kind of personality]. It should be added, however, that even where the system is administered by fully competent officers, there is, in certain circumstances, still a danger that it may become perfunctory. For example, no matter how efficient and conscientious the probation officer may be, if he is permitted by the court to be overladen with cases, the result will be as bad as though he were neither conscientious nor efficient. The officer must have time enough for frequent home visitation, and for interviewing his charges at places other than their homes; he must be able to keep up-to-date in regard to their behaviour; and, above all, if he is to keep his head above his cases, he must have a margin of time not ear-marked at all, but in reserve, partly to draw upon when the needs of any case demand it, but chiefly to enable him to keep a normal outlook. The importance of personality in the probation officer has always been recognised: what is not always recognised is that when the officer is swamped with cases the result is the elimination from probation of everything except its routine, and the possible wrecking of the instrument through which the system operates. Where an officer is expected to 'look after' anything up to a hundred cases, to visit them – not to call, merely, but really to know all these people, assimilate their varying points of view, throw himself into their lives, understand their temptations, and make their interests his own – and where, in addition, there are letters to be written, registers to be posted, employers to be interviewed, and court to be attended, then it is small wonder that probation sometimes becomes perfunctory and meaningless. What happens in such circumstances is that the probation officer degenerates into a mere inspector. The intensive, constructive work of probation becomes impossible; the 'personality' of the officer is negative, he has to lower his ideal – and with it that of the probation system.

The second defect of probation is in its application to unsuitable cases. No offender, reclaimable or otherwise, should be released on probation, unless his individual interests are reconcilable with the interests of the community. This elementary condition is emphasised because extensive use of the probation system does not always appear to have been differentiated from indiscriminate use. Probation is not a panacea for every ill-doer, even though he be a juvenile or a first offender. As is pointed out by Mr A.W. Towne, of the New York State Probation Commission,

> ... to fail to place the offender under a vigorous corrective discipline when such a course is clearly indicated by the circumstances of the offence, and the previous character and present disposition of the offender, is an evil only less serious than to imprison the offender when the circumstances would justify his release on probation.

One method by which the number of unsuitable cases may be reduced is to refrain from applying probation to epileptic or defective children. The ordinary methods of probation fail to reach children of this kind; and, since it is from these that the criminal problem of the future will chiefly come, it is necessary that they be provided for by the institution of court clinics, where mental and physical abnormalities may be discovered and dealt with.

The release of unsuitable offenders on probation has led some critics to say that, so far at any rate as adult offenders are concerned, probation is simply a method of 'turning criminals loose on society'. Waiving the obvious retort that every method short of hanging is open to the same criticism, it is possible to show that probation is not only not a danger, but is, as is claimed for it, of positive constructive value to society. In 1910, after probation had been operative for thirty-three years, the State of Massachusetts appointed a commission to consider, among other things, the question whether there was in the State any increase of criminals. The commission reported in 1911. Its investigations revealed a diminished ratio of crime to the population; and, after commenting on 'the enormous value' of probation 'in reshaping the lives of children' (State of Massachusetts 1911: 45), and on 'its proven worth as a substitute for imprisonment, and as a means of reformation' (p. 46) in the case of adult offenders, the commission made a definite recommendation for the 'extension of the system of probation ... as a substitute for imprisonment' (p. 50). In view of the fact that in the two years immediately preceding this report, 29,500 offenders were released into society on probation by the courts of Massachusetts, the commission's findings and recommendation are particularly reassuring. The real position under this head is well summed up by a committee of the American Institute of Criminal Law and Criminology (1910: 11), which after an investigation of adult probation in 1910 reported that

> ... the fancied dangers to society arise, not from the application of the probation system, but from the misapplication of it, through judicial ignorance and error, to cases to which it is not suited.

The third defect to which the probation system is liable is too short probationary periods. In fixing the period of probation, it should be remembered that the chief object is to accomplish, or create conditions whereby to accomplish, permanent changes in the habit of mind of the offender, in his outlook on life, and in his surroundings – and this not merely to the extent of enabling him to conform to the minimum standards of honesty and general conduct required by law, but in order that the whole standard of his life may be raised so as to put him in a fair way of achieving real worthiness. Such an ideal cannot be attained quickly. To create the conditions for it, to get the offender in the necessary frame of mind, is not merely a question of months, but of years. So far from this having been generally realised, however, it is a common thing to find periods of two or three months specified as the probationary term. For really constructive work, such brief terms are useless; nor are they of much use in training offenders merely to keep within the law. The first few weeks of probation are usually full of unpleasant memories – of arrest, of being escorted to the police station by the constable under the gaze of friends and relatives, of the night time in the cell, of the public trial – and these are usually quite enough to keep the tyro 'straight' for a while. It is not during the period when these memories are fresh that the offender needs help. It is when they grow dim, when the old public-house or the old street corner begins to call him again, and he is emboldened to seek out his old associates – it is at this time that the probation officer should be at hand, with an alternative to the street corner or public-house, with an introduction to more wholesome companions and healthier interests than are to be found there. The offender seldom needs help in the making of resolutions – they pour out of him in the cells of a police station; but – and here is the point as it affects the fixing of the term of probation – it is in a period of reaction that his resolutions have to be kept; his former weaknesses, reasserting themselves, threaten to dislodge the better inclination, and, in the absence of the confidence which the probation officer can inspire, they will succeed. Thus the period of probation should be of sufficient length to cover this period of reaction. This is the reason that probation results covering periods of less than twelve months are scarcely worth the paper they are printed on.

The fourth defect of the probation system is lack of organisation, not so much amongst its administrators in individual courts, as in the country as a whole. Local courts are, presumably, responsible to the Home Office; but, at the time of writing, there exists no body whose business it is to supervise, develop and co-ordinate probation work on a national basis. True, it is impossible, undesirable even, to standardise the work of individual probation officers. The case in hand will be treated as the officer in his discretion thinks fit, and any suggestion from above will probably be a mistaken one. But there is no reason at all why the general conditions under which probation work is done should not be properly organised. Locally, the several units of probation administration (the voluntary and salaried probation officers, that is) should be immediately responsible to a chief probation officer; the chief probation officer, in turn, to be responsible to a committee of local justices. Nationally, there should be created a special permanent branch of the Home Office to exercise general oversight and supervision of probation work. Amongst other things, this special department would seek to develop the probation system throughout the country, to stimulate backward courts to action, to effect some arrangement whereby cases could be transferred from one locality to another, when that course was advisable; to publish annually a list giving the name and address of every probation officer appointed under the Probation of Offenders Act, 1907, and to supply a copy to each probation officer, magistrates' clerk, and clerk of quarter sessions and assize; to supply a guide to magistrates and probation officers giving the text of statutes immediately affecting probation, with the necessary memoranda and explanations, and a copy of the home Office Probation Rules; to issue an annual report; to have supreme oversight over the work of probation officers; to appoint one or more travelling supervisors of probation work, and to publish their reports.[1]

From Cecil Leeson, Defects of the Probation System *(London: P.S. King and Son),*
1914, pp. 175–184.

Note

1   Since the above was written, the Home Office has created a special department to deal with
    questions relating to children, including juvenile probation and children's courts; what we
    now require is a similar department for adult probation – and the scope of both widening
    on the lines set out above.

References

American Institute of Criminal Law and Criminology (1910) *Report on Adult Probation.*
State of Massachusetts (1911) *Committee to Investigate the Question of the Increase of Criminal, Mental
    Defectives, Epileptics and Degenerates.*

18 The extent and practice of probation in England (1933)

Sir William Clarke Hall

I. Historical sketch

Probation in England owes its beginning rather to individual experiment than to any philosophical conception of principle. Cases came from the courts where it was obvious that the particular act of delinquency was due to a temporary lapse on the part of the offender which would in all probability never recur. In such cases humane and enlightened judges and magistrates were reluctant to pass a sentence of imprisonment which would involve complete ruin, not only to the delinquent himself, but also to his family.

The difficulty was sought to be avoided by the passing of a merely nominal sentence or the adjournment of the case generally. The Summary Jurisdiction Act of 1879 gave power to the justices, although finding a defendant guilty, to discharge him, under certain conditions, without the infliction of a penalty. In 1887 the legislature recognized the elementary principle of probation by the passing of the First Offenders Act. This Act gave no power to the courts to place the offender under supervision. The danger, however, of discharging persons who had been found guilty of a criminal offence without any supervision and without any guarantee that the offence might not be repeated, soon became obvious and the practice arose in some courts of requesting the Police Court Missionary appointed by the Church of England Temperance Society and attached to the courts, to interest himself in the delinquent and assist him in making a fresh start in life. In 1907 this practice received direct legal sanction by the passing of the Probation of Offenders Act, which empowered the court to place the offender under the direct care of a probation officer who was at first, in the majority of cases, the Police Court Missionary who had previously carried out similar duties voluntarily and unofficially. This Act, however, provided for the appointment and payment of probation officers and regulated their duties and powers. Its provisions are applicable not only to 'first offenders', but to those who by reason of age or mitigating circumstances may be dealt with efficiently on probation.

The discretion of the court under the Act is very wide and the extent to which its provisions are used varies greatly in different courts and districts. In some, old offenders are never placed on probation; in others the benefit of the Act is frequently extended even to these. In one court, where the Probation Act is very largely used, the statistics were taken for the year 1929 with regard to old offenders. Five previous convictions were deemed to constitute 'an old offender'. On this basis 14 'old offenders' were placed upon probation, the mitigating circumstances in their cases being that they had never had a real chance of reformation and seemed capable and desirous of taking such a chance if it were afforded to them. The numbers of previous convictions in the 14 cases were 60, 21, 19, 18, 14, 9, 7 and several fives. Eight of the fourteen did well on probation, six failed and some have since been sent to prison. It is submitted that this result fully justifies the treatment. A man with five previous convictions will almost inevitably commit a fresh offence after a further sentence of imprisonment. That 60 per cent of these men did not do so when placed upon probation surely makes it worthwhile to have given them this chance. To those who failed to take it, the knowledge was at least brought home that the administration of the law was designed to help them towards reformation. Only too often habitual criminals justify their mode of life to their own consciences by such plea as: 'I never had a chance; there was nothing else for me to do'. It must be borne in mind that in very many of these cases, even of old offenders, the charge before the court was only that of being 'a suspected person', for which the maximum sentence allowed by English law is only three months' imprisonment; a sentence which can have no possible reformative effect.

II. Children and probation

However hopeful the probation system may be, even in certain cases of 'old offenders', it is obviously far more promising in the cases of those who are only just beginning to enter upon a criminal career. It is for this reason that, from a sociological point of view, the juvenile courts are of paramount importance. It cannot be doubted that the majority of habitual criminals, either actually begin their career of crime, or are prone, by reason of their circumstances, surroundings or temperament to criminality, at a very early age. This first beginning, or these tendencies, are in a very large number of cases capable of cure where the right treatment is administered at a sufficiently early age. It is indeed open to question whether criminality in its early stages is not *always* curable save in a very few abnormal cases. Until recently no country in the world has really set itself to the discovery of the cure or to its application at the earliest possible time. The right treatment of the child falling, or about to fall, into delinquency will do more to diminish crime than all the repressive punishments that have ever been inflicted, or than all the most skilled efforts of the most efficient police force.

Juvenile courts in England were established by the Children Act of 1908, which at the same time prohibited the sending of children under 16 to prison save under very special circumstances. Section 111 provides that the trial of children under 16 shall take place either in a room or building separate from the adult court, or at a time when the adult court is not being held, and that the public shall not be admitted. There are not in England, as in most other countries, any 'children's judges' appointed for the special purpose. In London four Metropolitan Magistrates are nominated to preside at the eight London Juvenile courts, assisted by two lay justices, one of whom must be a woman; but this duty is in addition to the ordinary work of the Metropolitan Magistrate in his adult court. Throughout the rest of England children's cases are tried by the unpaid justices of the peace sitting at a time, or in a room or place, away from the adult court for that purpose. Liverpool and Birmingham alone possess courts erected specially for the hearing of children's cases, the latter court having been the splendidly generous gift of Mrs Barrow Cadbury.

The problem of the delinquent child and the right treatment of his case is a very serious and a very difficult one. Its proper solution depends upon very special knowledge and experience in the presiding magistrate and postulates the devotion of much time and thought. No child can safely be placed upon probation without a very full and complete investigation into the underlying causes which brought about his delinquency; but this investigation necessitates one remand at least, or often a series of remands, and these remands cannot be arranged for if the bench before which the case comes again is entirely differently constituted. A few of the larger cities have sought to avoid the difficulty by electing a permanent chairman always to preside in the juvenile court. It is submitted that the problem can be adequately solved only if and when there is some one experienced and responsible person to devote himself particularly to this work. To further this end there should be specially selected justices sitting for at least three consecutive months with a permanent chairman always presiding.

To provide special probation officers dealing only with children would of course be impossible throughout the country, but it should be done in all the larger centres of population where the number of cases justify such an appointment.

In London there are (1931) 14 such probation officers appointed, and these appointments, unlike those in the provinces, are made direct by the Home Office. The officers are all women and the competition to obtain such a post is very keen. There is in consequence no difficulty in securing the best possible candidates. They are now mostly graduates of a university and have all taken courses in sociology and economics.

In the provinces generally the boys over 14 are placed under the care of the adult male probation officer and the boys under that age, together with the girls, under the care of the adult woman officer. Where probation fails, or where the home conditions or other circumstances make the success of probation impossible, there are in England Home Office schools to which the young offender may be sent. These schools have reached a very high degree of efficiency and it is doubtful whether they can be surpassed by those in any other country.

III. Adults and probation

No one can now doubt that the Probation Act of 1907 has more than justified its existence. The criminal statistics for 1928 show that there were during that year a total of 16,566 men, women and children placed on probation under it. The continual increase in the use of the Act is shown by a comparison with the figures for the year 1908 when 8,021 men, women and children were dealt with thereunder. In the year 1920 a Departmental Committee was established to inquire and report on the training, appointment and payment of probation officers. That committee issued its report in 1922. It contained valuable testimony to the system and advocated its wider use.

The Act of 1907, whilst conferring full powers upon the local authority to appoint and pay probation officers, left it entirely to the discretion of these authorities to make, or refrain from making, such appointments. The consequence was that in many districts no such appointments were made. The evil was remedied by the Criminal Justice Act 1925, which made the appointment of probation officers obligatory for every probation area throughout England. As, however, it was obvious that there were many such districts where the entire services of a probation officer were not needed, the Act provided for the creation of 'combined areas', sanctioned by the Secretary of State, each such 'combined area' acting as a unit for the purposes of appointment.

At present, therefore, every court in England must place itself in the position of having a probation officer on whose services it can rely when called upon.

IV. Probation officers

Probation officers may be 'full-time', 'part-time', or voluntary. It is obvious that probation work can be best and most efficiently carried out by full-time probation officers and these should be appointed wherever possible. There are, however, many districts where even a 'combined area' does not need the whole-time services of an officer, and in such cases reliance must be placed on an officer one part of whose time is devoted to other work. This is at best but an unsatisfactory arrangement. The part-time officer is often very poorly paid and his double duties are difficult to reconcile. The tendency should always be to transform him into, or supersede him by, a full-time officer. Only too often the fact that a part-time officer is so much cheaper to maintain induces the authorities to retain him as such when the amount of work would justify a whole-time officer. Voluntary probation officers may be of the highest value in probation work, but the best method of utilizing their services does not yet seem to have been fully realized. A probationer is, after all, a person who has offended against the law and in many cases offended seriously. For his future conduct the court is itself to a large extent responsible and that responsibility should rest upon the shoulders of an official probation officer and not of a mere volunteer. On the other hand, no official can in a wide area exercise direct supervision over all those placed under his care. It is submitted, therefore, that while every order of the court should be made in the name of its own responsible officer, the services of volunteers should in many instances be called in for the actual supervision. If in every town, and even village, some suitable person should be found to undertake this duty, the efficiency of probation work would be greatly increased and the work of the probation officer enormously lightened. The reports of the volunteer workers should be sent in the first instance to him and he should remain responsible for their actions. The system suggested would go far to solve the religious difficulty and enable the Churches through an appointed representative to secure spiritual help and advice to the probationer. There are also many cases where a volunteer could visit the home without any suspicion of carrying with him the 'criminal atmosphere' which is sometimes thought to accompany a court official. In very many cases, also, the official probation officer can obtain most valuable assistance from employers of labour, from club superintendents, Boy Scout leaders, etc. The assistance indicated would in no way interfere with, or diminish the authority of, the official probation officer, but rather strengthen it.

V. Appointment and selection

The appointment of probation officers in England is regulated by the Criminal Justice Act, 1925, and the Statutory Rules made under it. Outside the metropolis the appointing authority is the probation committee. This committee is in its turn appointed by the justices of the particular Petty Sessional Division or of the 'combined area'. The choice is largely unfettered, but the applicants must be over 25 years of age and generally under 35. In exceptional cases they may be over 35 but under 40 years of age. Every appointment must be notified to the Secretary of State and is in the first instance for one year only. At the end of the first year it may be made permanent with his approval.

A feature of the probation system peculiar to England is the position of certain religious societies in regard to it. As has already been noted the initiation of the probation system was due to a large extent to the work of police court missionaries appointed mainly by the Church of England Temperance Society.

In recognition of the services thus rendered, Section 4 of the Act of 1925 dealt specially with the appointment of missionaries of voluntary societies and provided for the payment *to the Society* of the salary of such officer. This arrangement has given rise to considerable controversy. On the one hand it is contended that it creates a dual authority over the probation officer and tends to raise sectarian difficulties; on the other hand it is urged that a definite religious vocation is essential in probation work and the courts secure the services of a man whose position enables him to perform wider missionary functions than would be undertaken by a merely official probation officer.

Since there are in England no prescribed tests and no necessary examinations, the responsibility of the selection of a particular officer is great, for upon the wisdom of the choice the whole success of the work in the district to which he is appointed will rest.

The system has certain disadvantages. The majority on the committee of one area may, for instance, chose to elect persons possessed of no intellectual gifts and with very few educational advantages. In other areas these qualities may be deemed essential. To one committee religious fervour may make the strongest appeal; to another a wide understanding of human nature. To one a course of study in social and economic questions; to another mere general experience. As a partial remedy for these anomalies the Home Office has now initiated a scheme of training for candidates for this service and a special committee has been appointed for their selection. When chosen the candidates undergo a course of training for such time as may be necessary, not exceeding in any case three years. Each candidate will be required to undergo a course of study in sociology and economics at a recognized university, if he has not already done so, and will gain practical experience by assisting the regular probation officer in various courts.

The drawback to the scheme is that the local committee are under no obligation to select one of these trainees and may choose, for purely local or personal reasons, candidates who have neither training nor experience. So far, however, the scheme has worked fairly well; all those who have as yet completed their training have obtained appointments; but the number actually trained under the scheme corresponds to only about half the number actually appointed. The scheme itself therefore must be regarded as merely experimental.

During the period of training each candidate receives a grant of £150 a year, the same amount being paid alike to men and women. The salary on appointment varies somewhat in different districts, the minimum for a full-time officer being £150 a year.

In London and Middlesex, where the probation officers are appointed by and under the control of the Home Office, the initial salary (1931) is £220 for men and £170 a year for women. This salary is increased every year for seven years by £10, thus rising to a maximum of £370 for men and £250 for women. It is hoped that this may be adopted as a minimum throughout the country.

In England, with three exceptions, there are no 'chief' or 'special' probation officers and it is manifest that, on the figures given, the salary is not one to attract *of itself* highly educated men, though it does so in the case of women. A simple and comparatively inexpensive way of remedying this drawback would be the appointment of more chief probation officers at a considerably higher salary. That there should be, as at present, no higher prize to which to look forward, either in salary or position, does not tend to encourage the best candidates to apply, or when appointed to strive to the utmost to make themselves thoroughly efficient. That many do so in spite of this want of encouragement, is no fair answer. Most curates, for example, however great their vocational call may be, do look forward to a wider and more responsible sphere of influence and better means for the support of their wives and the education of their children. It is greatly to the honour of existing probation officers that in spite of poverty and with no better worldly prospects before them, they do such splendid work and display so loyal a devotion to their calling.

Although to strangers the English system, here briefly indicated, may appear somewhat haphazard and unscientific, it does possess the supreme advantage of being both vital and vocational. The English probation officer is no mere official bound by regulation and routine, but a man or woman who is devoting his, or her, life to the doing of a great work for humanity and who is almost wholly untrammelled in the doing of it. To combine technical efficiency and regularity of practice with individual effort and effective personality is by no means easy. Some other countries lay greater stress upon the former; this country has undoubtedly tended to concentrate upon the latter.

VI. The National Association of Probation Officers

Not only has the position of a probation officer in England been in the past a very onerous and underpaid one, but he has had too often to fight a lonely battle without sympathy, help or support and he has been the member of no organization (unless he happened to be the servant of a society) which could champion his cause or voice his difficulties. Impressed by these facts Mr S.G. Edridge, OBE, the Clerk to the Croydon Justices and one of the pioneers of probation work in England, conceived the idea of forming a National Association of Probation Officers. The carrying out of this idea was greatly fostered and encouraged by the Departmental Committee appointed in 1909 to inquire into the working of the Probation of Offenders Act which recommended:

> The stimulus which is needed to maintain the efficiency of probation work, and the initiative necessary to promote the adoption of whatever methods are found most effective, cannot be provided by a Government Department alone. We are of opinion that nothing would be so likely to provide that stimulus and initiative as the formation of a Society comprising and managed by the probation officers themselves. It would provide the means of disseminating information and a theatre for the discussion of questions of common interest.

The Association began its career in 1911 under great difficulties. In the beginning, money for the initiation and support of the movement was difficult to obtain, for its members could only afford very small subscriptions. None the less the zeal and energy of Mr. Edridge carried on the work until the year 1928 when the Association had the good fortune to secure the sympathy and support of the Earl of Faversham. Leaving Eton at the age of 18, he had determined to gain for himself a wider knowledge of social conditions and of the world generally. Choosing South Africa, he became himself a probation officer in Johannesburg and worked there for two years with Mr. H.E. Norman as his official colleague. Returning to England in 1926, he became deeply impressed with the great need for improving the position of English probation officers and strengthening their organization. During a tour in the United States he lectured on this subject and gained the sympathy of Mrs. Margaret Carrington. Her generous munificence placed the National Association on a more sound financial basis and enabled it to secure the services of Mr. H.E. Norman as secretary and to obtain permanent offices in London. Since then the work of the Association has progressed rapidly. It has enrolled 782 probation officers, justices' clerks and magistrates, and publishes a quarterly journal under the title of *Probation*. Lord Faversham is now its President and he devotes much time, energy and money to the cause, but the difficulties of the Association are by no means over, for the fund supplied by Mrs. Carrington will soon be exhausted.

VII. The Home Office and probation

Although, as has been seen, the control of the Home Office over probation work is strictly limited, the central government has throughout shown a very keen interest in the subject and a sincere desire to see the system more fully developed. A special department is devoted to the joint subjects of probation and delinquent children.

The head of this department is Mr. S.W. Harris, CB, CVO, who has thrown himself heart and soul into the work and proved to be one of the best and most loyal friends of the probation officer. Many departmental committees have considered and reported on the subject and there are three permanent committees who advise upon it. One deals with the problem outside London, one with that in the Metropolis and Middlesex, and the third exists to carry out and supervise the new training scheme.

Before the passing of the Criminal Justice Act of 1925 there was no one who had any legal duty to share the responsibility of the probation officer, or to take any interest in his work. It is true that many justices in different parts of the country did themselves individually take such an interest, but this was purely voluntary kindness on their part. The Act and the statutory rules made under it have now created this legal duty and placed upon the Probation Committees a statutory obligation to exercise a direct supervision of their own officer, to interview him from time to time and to go through his reports on the cases placed under his charge. This duty may be well and carefully done, as it is in some districts, or neglected, as it is in others. The function of the Home Office is to produce, as far as possible, a uniformity of practice amongst the local authorities and to awaken and encourage their interest in the question; but it is upon these authorities that the burden of appointment and supervision in reality rests. In London the supervision of the probation officer, the advice and help he needs and the consideration of his cases, fall upon the Metropolitan Magistrates of each court and this duty is one of the most interesting and useful parts of their work.

VIII. Difficulties

The probation system in England has as yet by no means reached the maximum of efficiency and has still many obstacles to overcome.

In this country nearly all social reforms are tentative and experimental. While this method of progress has the great advantage of ensuring ultimately a solid basis for the work, it is inevitably often hampered by drawbacks which, without the historical explanation of their origin, must seem anomalous to strangers.

The development of the religious missionary into the probation officer has been noted, and out of 792 probation officers working in the courts, 248 are the servants of religious societies. These officers are nominated and paid by the society, appointed and supervised by the Probation Committee, approved but liable to be dismissed at the end of the first year by the Home Office and under the direction of the particular justices in the court which they serve. The British tendency to accept compromise rather than pursue logic has enabled the system to work fairly smoothly, but the more advanced reformers, voiced by the Howard League of Penal Reform, are striving for a uniform state service under which all probation officers would be appointed by the Home Office and paid directly by the Treasury.

Desire for local economy is very strong amongst local authorities and there is a tendency which must be recognized for the justices in some districts, who are often members of the local authorities, to cast their burdens rather upon the Treasury than upon the rates.

All prisons and Borstal Institutions are now paid for and under the control of the central government, whereas the certified schools for children under 16 and the probation services fall largely upon the local rates. It is to be feared that this state of things militates in some districts against the appointment of a sufficient number of efficient and well-paid, full-time probation officers and against the committal of children to schools where they could be reformed at an earlier age than in a Borstal Institution. It is significant that while in 1913, 18,916 juvenile adults (i.e. boys and girls between 16 and 21) were committed to certified schools, only 466 were committed to Borstal Institutions. In 1927, 6,550 children under 16 were committed to certified schools, while 602 juvenile adults were committed to Borstal Institutions. No one who has had much experience of delinquent children can doubt that in the vast majority of cases delinquent, juvenile adults were in fact addicted to criminality before attaining the age of 16. From whatever cause, therefore, this increase of numbers sent to Borstal arises, it is of vital importance that it should be considered and dealt with, the more so as the certified schools, almost of necessity, produce better results than the Borstal Institutions. The remedy already suggested of dealing with young offenders at the earliest possible age cannot be too strongly emphasized, and also the securing of greater efficiency and interest in the children's courts.

IX. Essentials of success

The essentials of success in probation work may be briefly summarized:

1.   *The right choice of a probation officer.* This should be the paramount consideration, for upon him everything depends. If he is strong and brave and earnest he can carry on his work in spite of difficulties of organization and administration, important as these may be. He should possess:

    a.   Distinctive personality. Upon this his power of influence depends.

    b.   A real profession. Probation can never, and should never be, a mere untrained vocation.

    c.   A good general education. The want of this tends to produce a narrowness of view inconsistent with the best work.

    d.   Special study in sociology and economics and some knowledge of psychology and of criminal law and practice.

    e.   A very careful training in the best courts and under the most efficient probation officers.

2.   *A genuine interest on the part of the Justices.* However efficient the probation officer may be in his work, he must depend upon the action of the justices and their right selection of cases for probation. Two factors have tended largely of late to increase this interest.

    a.   The existence of the Magistrates' Association. This body came into being in 1920. Its function is to promote a knowledge amongst justices of the best means of treating delinquency and particularly of the probation system. It has the Lord Chancellor as its President.

    b.   The appointment of women justices. These have shown an extraordinary interest in their duties, not perhaps so much because of their sex, as because they have been more carefully selected for their social work and activities than their male colleagues.

3.   *A careful selection of cases for probation.* Two mistakes are frequently made in this selection. Some justices seem to think that the mere fact that the case is that of a first offender is sufficient reason in itself for placing him on probation. The acceptance of this principle is disastrous, since it tends to become a direct encouragement to crime and is treated by the offender as his right. Other justices hold that probation is only properly applicable to first offenders. This has been shown to be an erroneous view. In order to justify the making of a probation order, there should always be:

    a.   A full inquiry into the character, circumstances, mentality and environment of the offender. For such an inquiry a remand is in most cases necessary, either in custody or on bail.

    b.   The proposed probation officer should either make, or be a party to the making of, these inquiries.

    c.   No case should be put on probation unless the proposed probation officer believes that the case is a suitable one and that he has a reasonable chance of succeeding with it.

    d.   Where there are any abnormal symptoms in the offender, expert medical opinion should be obtained.

    e.   Where the present environmental conditions are hopeless, a change of residence should be insisted on as part of the order.

    f.   A definite scheme of treatment, e.g. the obtaining of work, the abstention from alcoholic liquor or gambling, etc., should be devised.

    g.   In many cases a long remand on bail is desirable, thus giving an opportunity to the offender of showing his desire to reform, his efforts to obtain work and his fitness for probation before the order is actually made.

4.   *The enforcement of the order.* A probation order should *always* be either enforced or cancelled. Nothing does more harm than the breaking of a recognizance

with impunity. It is a temptation to a careless probation officer to let minor breaches pass, since he can then proclaim the case a 'success'. The probation committee should therefore exercise, as they are bound by the law to do, the most careful supervision. Conditions which cannot be enforced should not be put in a probation order. In England, breaches of probation orders may be punished:

a.   By a fine not exceeding £10. The infliction of this penalty does not of itself put an end to the probation order.

b.   By the forfeiture of the recognizances. This automatically puts an end to the order.

c.   By conviction and sentence for the original offence. This in general practice puts an end to the order, though it does not do so necessarily and the order may continue in effect after the completion of the sentence.

X. Psychological examination

The desirability for a medico-psychological examination of offenders showing symptoms of abnormality has not been realized in England to at all the same extent as in many of the United States. None the less, the idea is gaining ground. Birmingham (a city which has so often led in the path of progress) has recently appointed that well-known and eminent psychologist, Dr. C.L.C. Burns, to superintend a child guidance clinic and his services will be available to the courts.

Two of the London juvenile courts have in regular attendance at their sittings, doctors belonging to the Tavistock Clinic, the Child Guidance Clinic and the Jewish Free Clinic. The attendances are quite voluntary and there are at present no funds available for paying for these services. The two courts in question owe therefore a great debt of gratitude to these distinguished experts who make no small personal sacrifice in their desire to help.

The doctors of the Tavistock Clinic, whose President is Dr. Crichton Miller, most generously assist the adult courts when requested to do so in special cases.

Experience is proving more and more in England, as in America, that there are many offences committed owing to physical and psychological causes which are curable by the right method of treatment. In the cases of such offenders as 'exhibitionists' this treatment has proved particularly effective. The branch of psychiatry dealing with such problems deserves far more attention and needs greater opportunities for observation than have yet been afforded to it in this country.

The establishment of an 'Observation Home' for young offenders, somewhat on the lines of those at Molle and Namur, is now under consideration by the Home Office. The London County Council is fortunate in having for some years past been able to retain the services of the well-known psychologist, Professor Cyril Burt. His book, *The Young Offender*, gives the result of his experiences and is the principal English text-book on the subject. His services are, however, available only for the children actually in the London Remand Home, which is maintained by the London County Council as the Education Authority for the Metropolis, and these services are unfortunately too seldom requisitioned.

The Child Guidance Clinic presided over by Dr. William Moodie, owes its origin and support to the splendid generosity of the great American philanthropist, Mr.

Harkness, who has given an impetus to the study of the subject for which this country cannot be too grateful.

As neither this, nor the other clinics named have as yet any official recognition, their services are purely voluntary and given at the request of the court in cases either remanded on bail or under the care of a probation officer. Greater systematization and coordination are urgently needed and these should eventually secure state recognition and support.

XI. Need for greater Anglo-American cooperation

It will be seen that England owes much to the United States, not only for giving the lead in study, investigation and example, but in direct financial assistance from two of its leading citizens.

Would not a closer cooperation between the English National Association of Probation Officers and the American societies formed with similar aims give valuable results? An interchange of ideas and experience should be of assistance to both countries in the path of development. We venture in this country to hope that the study of our methods may be not without value in the United States, since while we give the fullest recognition to the value of the work done there, we believe none the less that our experience, different as it is in many ways, is by no means without value to America.

From Sir William Clarke Hall, 'The extent and practice of probation in England',
in S. Glueck (ed.), Probation and Criminal Justice: essays in honour of Herbert C
Parsons *(New York: The Macmillan Company), 1933, pp. 276–295.*

19 Working with offenders (1937)

Jo Harris

Under the Probation System the offender is placed on probation for a certain period of time with certain conditions to be observed and rules to be kept. All this is entered on a form called a recognizance form which is given to the offender before he leaves Court. From that time he is under the care of the Probation Officer.

And so the Probation Officer goes to his work, not as a super-policeman, but as a friend who understands and sympathizes and who is ready and able to help the offender back on to the right path.

He must be capable of listening to the outpourings of all his charges, of dealing with each individual case according to its special need. No two cases are alike, and to get the best out of an offender it is necessary to hear his side of the story. This is always necessary before remedial measures can even begin to take effect.

It has always been my practice in every case that came under my care to make friends with the offender in my own study and to appeal to him, 'Now we are going to have one good talk about the whole thing, and then we will put it behind us for ever and start afresh'.

It is usually a very solemn half hour, but I have always found that it makes all the difference to the probation period.

By this method one discovers the offender's friendships, his habits, his use of leisure, his attitude to life in general, his likes and dislikes, and one is able to start him off having obtained a fair diagnosis of his characteristics.

At this first interview one also goes through each point in his recognizance form, and then gives it into the keeping of the offender who now understands that it is a reminder of what he has to do during his period of probation. This is the surgical part of the interview; next comes the advisory talk, in which the offender is shown how to fight his special temptation; and perhaps for the first time he starts to have rules for his life, and to be responsible on his honour to keep them.

To many this new method does not appeal at all. The offender is on probation for a year, or perhaps longer. Why, it seems an eternity to him! As one boy said to me, 'I'd rather have been birched and finished with it'. But at the end of his two years, when we shook hands, and said our official good-bye, the same boy said, 'I'm glad I've been on probation. I found a new friend, and you have made a new chap of me'.

I can quite understand the attitude and feeling of a new probationer. To have to report at a given time and place every week over a lengthy period is no joke, but this is a rule never to be played with, or slackened. It is the action which kneads the character, just as the rule of getting in at a certain hour tests the character.

Sometimes other rules are added, viz.

- Must not frequent the fish-market.
- Must not attend the cinema.
- Must avoid certain companions.

Often they are ordered to link up with some organization.

Whatever condition is imposed, they are always for the good of the individual case. Sometimes there is a condition of restitution.

A broken rule is broken faith; I never tolerated it. If a boy failed to report, he always got a postcard summoning him at a certain hour. The boys hated being defaulters in this way, and I had very little trouble once they understood.

It was the same with their curfew rule. Very few broke faith because they knew they were being trusted, and they also knew that on very special occasions I would grant them a permit to stay out later.

Occasionally it was necessary to change the school in order to bring new influences to bear, or perhaps to break up a gang.

It is extraordinary how differently various types of character accept the position of being on probation, and the responsibility it entails.

Looking back to the days when the only remedy for wrong-doing seemed to be Punishment with a capital P, one realizes what a brave, bold venture it was to start the new method of curing the offender, or rather helping him to cure himself in his own environment amongst his own people.

Knowing the results after these many years, I can truly say the venture has more than justified itself.

In those early days before the War, scorn and ridicule often dogged the footsteps of the new Act. But pioneers could see in it the dawn of a new era in legislation. To them it was a proclamation of progress in dealing with offenders. To them it was a vision of the years to come when punishment would part company with revenge, and link itself with reform not only of the law, but of human character.

Redemptive work is of necessity slow, and the offender often proves most difficult material, but the Probation System does provide the authoritative atmosphere and possibility of redemption of every offender who responds.

… The ending of a probation period should be as impressive as the beginning. And so one can divide this personal work into three sections.

1.   The surgical or heart-searching section when the offender tells out the story of his wrong-doing.
2.   The advisory section, when the Probation Officer gives him advice, rules to observe, and a line of life to which to adhere during his period of probation.
3.   The result of this treatment is revealed at the last interview. Once more a heart-to-heart talk in my study, this time not to a scared, nervous offender, but to a lad, or a man who, through the period of probation, has grown to realize the strength of friendship and also to know that he really counts as a citizen who has responsibilities to shoulder and a character to keep.

Just as in that first interview I handed him his recognizance form as a reminder, so at the last one he usually handed it back to me, and together we watched it burn to ashes. Just a little bit of ritual perhaps, but to us a sign that his probation was ended satisfactorily. He had wiped out his offence and it would be remembered against him no more.

A friendly talk, kindly advice and a handshake – this is the official good-bye, but it is not the end.

One of the happiest experiences of my life is the aftermath of probation. The steady stream of letters from all parts of the world prove that the writers remember and are grateful – and the greatest of my Christmas joys is when, year after year, men and boys come voluntarily to my house to wish me a Merry Christmas. They are probationers of the past. Home on furlough from the Army and Navy, on holiday from Reformatory and school, they come like a big family.

It is this aftermath that reveals more than anything else the power, the wonder, and the success of this great system. Aftercare is the part of probation work that never ceases, for when probation time is over and the official visits ended, the friendship still goes on. Those who were once a charge are always welcomed as friends. Their confidences, and the letters from every part of the Empire, prove beyond doubt that the Probation System has indeed established an extra relationship in the great human family.

From Jo Harris, Probation: A Sheaf of Memories *(Lowestoft: M.F. Robinson and Co.),*
1937, pp. 22–27.

20 Probation officers (1950)

Sewell Stokes

Probation officers are on sight unrecognizable, except perhaps to one another. Even then recognition is doubtful, so nondescript in every way is their appearance. Unlike clergymen, scurrying about like black beetles, and made familiar by their collars, court missionaries remain shrouded in anonymity. A caricaturist cannot typify them, since outwardly they present no striking feature for him to seize upon. To describe them in words is difficult enough; and after four years in their company I find myself unable to do them justice. Indeed the nearest I can get to giving some impression of them as a whole, is to say that when I attended a largely representative gathering of my colleagues at the Zoo, the spot chosen for the event seemed exactly the right one. I mean no disrespect. A breed apart is not to be despised for its isolation from the common run of mortals. In its very uniqueness lies the fascination that all rare specimens have for the inquiring student of human nature. ...

Every profession, I suppose, attracts those who, for one reason or another, feel themselves likely to succeed in it. Men not predominantly imaginative join the services; those who like making an exhibition of themselves become actors. And so on. But what decides anybody to become a probation officer is a question impossible to answer satisfactorily. Some I came across appeared to have made the choice out of sheer capriciousness. Others looked upon it as a serious mission. (The trouble with them was they took themselves too seriously.) And there were those who made no pretence about its being a job which, since no special qualifications were needed for it, came to them as a God-send. It is true that every now and then there arrived upon the scene earnest young things, blessed by the Home Office, with a course of psychiatric training to their credit that was supposed to put them streets ahead of the rest of us. But in my experience they were not an asset. Square pegs in round holes are bad enough, but match-sticks in the cannon's mouth invite disaster. Miss Baneystock invited it at every turn.

Miss Baneystock I met at a court I was sent to in one of the more remote districts of London ... I noticed [her] on my first morning in court and was aware of how intensely interested she appeared to be in my one case, having none of her own. She fitted exactly the description Mr Weddup [the male probation officer] had given me of her: 'Too bright and too eager. A bit of a crackpot, if you ask me.' Not that it would have been wise to depend upon Mr Weddup's opinion, since far from being bright and eager himself, he was likely to be prejudiced against anybody who showed even a spark of life. Nor in any assembly of crackpots would he himself have looked in the least out of place. The only difference I could see between the two of them, was that they were cracked in different places.

'A peculiarly interesting case, the one you had in court this morning', observed Miss Baneystock, wandering uninvited into my office … She sighed. And in that sigh was deep pity (mixed with a hearty contempt) for those unfortunates in The Work who had not come to it, as she had done, straight from a course of lectures on the psychiatric treatment of delinquents.

'Might I', she said, taking up the record of Badger's case from the desk, 'have a peep at the boy's antecedents?' She read it in a silence which she punctuated with a number of revelational utterances – 'Ah! … As I thought! … Naturally!' and so complacently self-assured was her manner that I was hard put to it not to descend to the level of mimicking her. 'Well', she said, finally, looking me straight in the eye, 'it's crystal-clear to me'.

'What is ?' I asked.

'The reason why Badger did what he did.'

'So it is to me. And so it was to the magistrate. That's why he gave him three months.'

'Three months!' Miss Baneystock repeated the words as if they were the most loathsome in the language; as if they horribly offended her ears. 'He ought to be ashamed of himself', she added.

'I agree', I said. 'To steal money from offertory-boxes in churches is one of the meanest forms of petty larceny. He was lucky to get only three months.'

'I was not', said Miss Baneystock, 'referring to the boy, but to the magistrate. He is the culprit, not poor Badger. Though I suppose it's too much to expect such an ignorant old fossil to realize what harm he does by sending an innocent man to prison.'

'I'm afraid', I said, 'I don't see what you are getting at.' I had a pretty good idea, though not good enough to prepare me for what was coming. The effect of that magical word 'psychiatry' upon the fledgling's mind is often quite unpredictable.

'But it's crystal-clear to me', said Miss Baneystock, 'that all Badger's troubles result from his never having had a mother. Surely it is to you too?' (How sweet of her to include me, even tentatively, in the charmed circle of her medical intelligentsia.)

'No, it's not clear to me', I said. 'Besides, Badger *must* have had a mother, mustn't he?' Miss Baneystock had the grace to let this pass, for which I was thankful. I had slipped. I should have known that she was not one to suffer fools gladly, that facetiousness was out of place in this earnest discussion.

'Badger, from an early age', said Miss Baneystock, quoting from the report, 'was brought up by an aunt in the country until he was 16, when he came to London to live with his father, a *widower*. Suddenly he takes in into his head to steal. Several times he is charged with stealing. But always from church offertory-boxes, and usually in the country.' She paused that the facts (with which I was already familiar) might sink in. Then she continued: 'Doesn't the similarity of all these cases strike you as oddly significant?' Judging from my dead-pan expression that it did not, she asked pointedly: '*Why* do you suppose the boy constantly ran away to the *country* and invariably went into *churches* to commit his offences? Might he not just as well and with greater profit to himself have robbed a *bank*, in *London?*'

With extraordinary calm, I replied to her challenging questions in the order in which she had put them to me. I said that I saw nothing odd or significant about the similarity of all Badger's thefts. It was the common practice of criminals to specialize in a particular type of work and stick to it. Obviously he went to the country because his aunt lived there, and she being an over-indulgent person, whereas his father was exactly the reverse – a fact made plain in the report – he naturally preferred his aunt's home to his father's. The reason he chose a church as the field for his operations was that offertory-boxes are customarily found there and not elsewhere. I concluded with the suggestion that to rob a bank in London required far more skill and guts than Badger at present possessed.

Whilst I spoke Miss Baneystock endured my words – no more – and for some seconds after I had finished, she clearly doubted the use of imparting to me the wisdom of her years – all 25 of them. The satisfaction of doing so, however, proved too strong for her to resist.

'The boy Badger', she said, and I instantly pictured a boy with a badger's face, 'is subconsciously searching for his lost maternal parent. That explains why he finds himself drawn by an irresistible impulse towards Mother Earth and Mother Church. It's obvious.'

'Oh, crystal-clear!' I agreed. I had to. So irresistible was my own impulse to resort to violence, that I felt the interview must be brought to an end at any cost. An argument was sure to result in disaster. And fortunately for both of us, the fool left the room. Really, I could not even respect Miss Baneystock's intentions. For all the good that she, and others like her, did in the courts, the lectures she had attended might as well have been on art needlework, or tap-dancing. No; the students of psychiatry whom I greatly admired, for the attitude of humility and practical sense with which they approached their subject, were the young foreigners who, with Home Office permission, occasionally sat in courts to watch our methods of work. These intelligent enthusiasts, without meaning to, showed some of us up pretty badly, I felt. For instance, whenever a magistrate benignly informed a prisoner that where he was sending him he would receive the psychiatric treatment recommended in his case, the student asked eagerly; 'I may see over one such of these clinics, yes?' and on being told that the prisoner wasn't going to a clinic, but to a prison where he'd be lucky if he got anything even resembling treatment, would observe: 'But the judge then has said wrong, yes?' after which there was nothing for it but to admit that the judge had said wrong; since he knew nothing of what went on inside of a prison, and had never troubled to find out.

I don't know how Mrs Gage, a comfortable old body, self-educated and unable quite to pronounce the word 'psychiatric', put up with Miss Baneystock as an assistant. (She didn't have to for long, because the magistrate, exasperated one day by her attributing a girl's behaviour to influences which she considered pre-natal, but which he knew were post-whisky, had her removed elsewhere.) Or rather I did know, for Mrs Gage was one of those rare women with an instinctive gift for The Work. She had come into it in the early days, and the amount of good she must have done her fellow creatures is beyond calculation. She accepted life, making the best of what it sent her. Even of a Baneystock. 'Poor thing', she used to say shaking a head of grey hair that struggled to escape from its net, 'you have to laugh, don't you? You'd never believe some of the rubbish she talks. Mind, it's not all her fault. She's been too highly educated, I think. I could have done with a bit of education myself, I dare say; but I've managed without it somehow. You know, Mr Stokes, I was asked once how I stuck it here, year in and year out, trying to help people who mostly don't say thank-you when you have. To tell you the truth I'd never thought about it. And when I did, I decided that with me it was just a case of liking everybody – good or bad. Terrible, isn't it', she said with a laugh, 'liking people as much as all that? Doesn't seem natural, does it? You must think I'm a funny one. Though I warn you, what others think of me doesn't bother me a lot!'

Mrs Gage had that heart of gold all right: but she had something else besides. She was no sentimentalist, and when the situation seemed to her to demand it, could call down the wrath of God upon somebody she believed had not played fair with her. Coming into her room once, I saw her bearing down on a young woman who had called to see her on being released from Holloway. A poor creature she looked, and her chastiser had reduced her to tears of anguish, which appeared to me to be perfectly genuine. Seeing she was thus engaged, I made to leave, but Mrs Gage bade me stay. I firmly believe she hoped my presence might add to the girl's embarrassment, which it may have done. But I think nobody in the world can have been as embarrassed as I was, at being suddenly included in this wretched scene.

'What is to be done, Mr Stokes, with a girl who refuses to take the advice that's given her?' Thereafter I heard a story of how ungrateful this girl had been in spite of the chances she had had; how when on probation to Mrs Gage she had frequently deceived her, how because she had got herself into further trouble, the magistrate had finally no alternative but to send her to prison.

'You're not my responsibility now', stormed Mrs Gage, wagging a threatening finger at her victim. 'You had your chance, my girl, and threw it away. I've no time for your sort, so stop that snivelling now and get out. Do you hear me?'

The girl said something about wanting a job.

'A job! I like that', cried Mrs Gage. 'And who, pray, do you think is going to give a good-for-nothing slut like you a job? Answer me that if you can.'

Was this the woman, I asked myself, with whom it was just a case of liking everybody – good or bad? It was. As the girl reached the door, Mrs Gage reached for her bag, and taking a pound note from it, called out, 'Here you are, Elsie. Dry your eyes, do; have a perm, and buy yourself a lipstick. For heaven's sake make yourself look like something. With all the competition there is about you'll never get a decent job if you don't – off with you now! And mind you pay me back when you're earning.' Turning to me after Elsie had gone, she said, 'I can't tell you how happy that girl coming here to-day has made me. I like Elsie. Always have. I keep telling myself that there must be *some* good in her. And there's no telling that I won't find it one of these fine days.'

From Sewell Stokes, Court Circular *(London: Michael Joseph), 1950, pp. 223–230.*

21 The English probation system and the diagnostic ideal (1986)

William McWilliams

Between the late 1930s and the 1960s the probation system in England was transformed from a service devoted to the saving of souls through divine grace to an agency concerned with the scientific assessment and treatment of offenders. So crucial was the diagnostic ideal to the change which took place that the period as a whole aptly may be dubbed as the 'phase of diagnosis'. Nowhere was that ideal more central and publicly visible than in the practice of social enquiry for the criminal courts, and hence this paper ... pays particular attention to probation officers' social enquiry reports during the period in which the diagnostic ideal held sway.

In terms of conceptual understanding of the social enquiry report, the movement from the missionary phase of special pleading to the phase of diagnosis required fundamental philosophical changes (McWilliams 1983, 1985). Those changes were profound inasmuch as their effects were spread over three crucial aspects of the practice of social enquiry. First, the ontological status of the offender changed radically; in the phase of special pleading he was, ultimately, to be understood and depicted as a 'sinner' susceptible to grace through moral reform; whereas in the phase of diagnosis his ultimate status was that of a 'patient' susceptible to cure through scientific treatment.

Secondly, there came a basic shift in the understanding of the knowledge of man itself. The epistemology of the phase of special pleading was founded in metaphysics; whereas in the phase of diagnosis the basis of knowledge was seen to lie in science, and especially in an incomplete version of empiricism. Thirdly, it was these changes, which had sprung from the methodology of 'scientific charity' or 'case work', which enabled probation officers to become diagnosticians in their own right, and supported the claim that the social enquiry report had been transformed from a special plea for mercy to an instrument of objective professional appraisal.

The changes outlined above are closely interrelated. My purpose in this paper is to explore the processes involved through an examination of the rise and elaboration of the diagnostic ideal in social casework, and to relate this to social enquiry practice in probation. In what follows I argue that the essence of 'social diagnosis' is *imposed meaning*. It is the *worker* who defines the *real* meaning of the facts of the client's person and social circumstances; by extension, what should be done in the light of the meaning. Assessments are diagnostic *only* to the extent that they involve the imposition of meaning on the client by the worker.

The rise of casework and the elaboration of diagnosis

The origins of modern casework can be traced back to the organisation of charity in Britain during the nineteenth century, and in particular to the philosophy of 'scientific charity' espoused, developed, and stoutly maintained over a considerable period of time by the Charity Organisation Society (COS). The Society, founded in April 1869 under the formal title of the London Society for Organising Charitable Relief and Repressing Mendacity, proclaimed its purpose in its first annual report as being to provide 'machinery for systematizing, without unduly controlling, the benevolence of the public' (Owen 1964: 221), and its idea of charity:

> ... claimed to reconcile the divisions in society, to remove poverty and to produce a happy, self-reliant community. It believed that the most serious aspect of poverty was the degradation of the character of the poor man or woman. Indiscriminate charity only made things worse ... True charity demanded friendship, thought, the sort of help that would restore a man's self-respect and his ability to support himself and his family ... It offered an alternative to socialism as a means of realising a better society.
>
> (Mowat 1961: 102)

Charity was defined by the secretary to the Council of the COS, Charles Loch (1883), as being 'the work of the social physician' (p. 10), and he believed firmly that this work should be kept separate from religion. He said that intrusion 'into the houses of the poor ... if combined with religious ministration, tends to hypocrisy ... The separation of religious teaching and almsgiving is therefore, in the interests of morality, most necessary' (p. 16). Loch also believed that religion tended to make thorough investigation and objective assessment difficult, and on this he said:

> ... men who are intent on doing spiritual good, whose mood for the time must of necessity be one of hopeful and intent earnestness, and who are unable for the moment in their absorption in their object to take notice of details, are quite unfit then to judge of evidence, and quite liable to deception by those who are callous to their earnestness and in no way scrupulous of acting a part.
>
> (p. 16)

The history of the COS has been extensively studied (Mowat 1961; Owen 1964; Rooff 1972; Steadman-Jones 1971; Young and Ashton 1956), and an outline is not appropriate here, but it will be useful to our subsequent discussion to record one or two historical points, and to identify the main principles by which the work of the COS was guided; the latter constitute the methodology of 'scientific charity' which later became casework. The method of 'charity' or 'case work' as it came to be called from about 1885 (Young and Ashton 1956: 98) was founded on careful investigation of each applicant for assistance, and in the Society's annual report for 1885, this investigative basis of action was said to have a four-fold value:

> It enables us to decide whether a case is one for help or not. It helps us to decide the form that assistance should take to give the most permanent results. It enables

us to find means of assistance apart from cash, and it helps us to give the best advice for the future welfare of the client.

(Young and Ashton 1956: 103)

This method of 'case work' is usually cited as the forerunner of modern social work practice, and generally in positive terms. To take an example of this, we find Mowat (1961: 38–39) saying:

The approach to each 'case' as that of a man or woman in need, in circumstances unique to each, seems very modern, the essence of contemporary casework … The COS … began to employ a salaried staff to supplement the work of … volunteers. In this and in its later provision for training it helped to found the profession of casework.

It does seem that Mowat and other scholars are correct in seeing the method of the COS as the precursor of modern casework, and in particular of the diagnosis–treatment model of social work intervention. That this method *did*, from the beginning, entail the imposition of meaning is made clear by Charles Loch, the most eminent of the Society's secretaries. Specifically, in respect of 'investigation' and 'assistance', Loch said (1883: 129) that when

… the case has been investigated, the facts are laid before the Committee … in order that … they may decide how the case is to be treated … If they determine to assist, they may have to decide … *irrespective of the special form of relief asked for by the applicant*, what kinds of charity are best calculated to make the applicant independent of charity and the Poor Law. (Italics added)

I wish to focus on the *methodology* of the COS, not simply the methods themselves; because it is this methodology which persists unchanged into aspects of modern practice.

The methodology of social diagnosis

Professor William Brewer of Yale University, in a paper given to the National Conference of Charities and Corrections in 1895, confidently asserted that:

The universe is governed by law. Science investigates the ways of nature and deduces the laws governing her work … and man's work, to be successful, must be in accordance with them … The efficient and economic management of charity and correction on the scale we now have to deal with must be conducted as an applied science … directed along the lines marked by the fixed laws of nature.

(Germain 1970: 11)

Echoing these sentiments, James Jackson, the Chairman of the Conference Committee on Needy Families in their Homes, said in 1905:

... the painstaking inquiry into, and the recording of, as many facts as possible bearing on the problem at hand, are precisely the methods by which modern inductive science has achieved its astonishing results.

(Germain 1970: 14)

This inductivist methodology was to have its finest and most elaborate social work exposition in the scholarly work of the American social diagnostician, Mary Richmond.

Mary Richmond, who was granted an honorary masters degree by Smith College for her work in 'establishing the scientific basis of ... [the] new profession' of social work (Germain 1970: 12), published her substantial and definitive book 'Social Diagnosis' in 1917. This book, reprinted three times in its year of publication and a further 16 times between then and 1964, had a profound influence on social work practitioners and on subsequent theorists. The book is a thorough and highly detailed account of the methods of social diagnosis, illustrated by numerous examples.

The originality and breadth of Richmond's work cannot be captured in short compass, but her central message about the diagnostic process may be stated simply enough. The first task for the worker was the diligent collection of facts. These might take the form of 'real evidence ... the very fact at issue ... presented to our senses' (Richmond 1917: 56); 'testimonial evidence ... the assertions of human beings' (p. 57); or 'circumstantial evidence ... everything which is not the direct assertion of a human being' (p. 59). The second task for the worker was to draw inferences from the facts, 'passing from known to unknown facts' (p. 81); and the third was the interpretation of facts and 'this last is diagnosis' (p. 363).

Up to this point the process described by Richmond identifies clearly an empiricist methodology: the movement is from 'objective matters of fact' (p. 345), through inductive inferences, to the empirical generalisations which form the diagnosis. A good deal of social work at the time, and certainly at least part of the missionaries' work, consisted of straightforward moralising, and Richmond's exposition was intended to move social work as a whole towards a more factually-based process of assessment. However, there were substantial flaws in the methodology of social diagnosis, which she exemplified in her work.

Flaws in diagnostic methodology

A crucial flaw in diagnostic methodology is the assumption which it makes that facts are neutral in respect of theory. The modern contra-assumption that facts are actually theory-dependent has profound implications for the social diagnostician. It means, for example, that even the simplest fact-gathering exercise rests upon theoretical definitions and choices; this central problem in empiricist epistemology is not the only incorrect element in the methodology of social diagnosis. A careful examination of the methodology reveals a difficulty which apparently has claimed little attention. It will help to elucidate this problem if we show the diagnostic process described so far in diagrammatic form, thus:

Facts→Inductive Inferences→Diagnosis

A central purpose of Richmond's book was to work out the elements of this process, but additionally she envisaged a further step in the logic; namely the movement from diagnosis to treatment. Hence, more completely, the diagram should take the form:

Facts→Inductive Inferences→Diagnosis→Treatment

Richmond did not believe diagnosis to be *prescriptive* of treatment, and, importantly, that *treatment arose from the facts*. She teaches that a 'good social diagnosis is at once full and clear, with emphasis placed upon the features which indicate the social treatment to be followed' (Richmond 1917: 364). Hence the massive proportion of attention Richmond devoted to the variety of fact-finding process (four-fifths of the book) and her great emphasis on getting the facts right.

At the point of movement from diagnosis to treatment there is a sharp break with empiricist methodology. Under the inductivist 'method of science' which Richmond pursues, the empirical generalisations of the diagnosis can legitimately 'emerge from the facts', but the treatment, which is a moral prescription of what *ought* to be done, cannot. This is so because under empiricist epistemology a clear distinction is made between facts and values.

It follows from the foregoing that we must conclude that the reality of the methodology which Richmond espoused is not that which she suggests, and can actually be portrayed diagrammatically thus

Facts→Inductive Inferences→Diagnosis→Moral Goal→Treatment

This is the medical model. In medicine the break in the logic between diagnosis and treatment is not usually noticeable because it seems 'obvious' that a patient diagnosed as suffering from condition 'x', which is known to be curable by treatment 'y', should be given treatment 'y', on the basis of the diagnosis. The fact that the treatment is actually given on the basis of a moral goal rather than the facts of the diagnosis is not noticed, or is not seen to be important, because the moral goal of the cure of the disease is an *agreed* moral goal in most instances.

In contrast, the moral goal in social work is *not* so readily agreed. The model certainly is not 'scientific' in the way in which Richmond intended, nor, in empiricist terms, can its validity be rescued by any suggestion that the moral goal of treatment can be verified and shown to be true empirically. In empiricist epistemology factual statements can be shown to be true or false, at least in principle, through sense-experience, but moral statements cannot be verified at all.

To summarise, we may say that treatment does not arise directly from the facts; rather diagnosis is an interaction between social facts and moral evaluations, and treatment is a moral prescription of what *ought* to be done in the light of the moral evaluations made. Further, as facts are not the theory-free entities envisaged in empiricist epistemology, and as the *selection* of facts in diagnostic practice is influenced not only by theory, but also by *values*, it must be concluded that this methodology of social work diagnosis is gravely flawed.

The persistence of a flawed methodology

In support of my earlier claim that this pseudo-empiricist methodology, born of the 'case work' of the COS, persists in the modern era of social diagnosis, let us look at some of the formulations of a number of well-known social work theorists who have written on the topic of social diagnosis after Mary Richmond.

Gordon Hamilton, who was Professor of Social Work at the New York School of Social Work, Columbia University, contributed to the social work literature for many years from the 1920s, and probably her best-known work is the book *Theory and Practice of Social Casework*, which was first published in 1940. Hamilton's work is of particular interest not only because of its influence, but also because she wrote from a point of view which embraced Freudian insights denied to Mary Richmond and earlier theorists. The predominance of psychoanalysis is apparent throughout the book; thus, in respect of the client's history, for example, Hamilton (1951: 185) remarks that there are:

> ... two aspects or phases in history: (a) initial history for diagnosis and focus, which is readily obtained in the first contacts, and (b) history as abreaction or reliving certain emotional experiences, which comes much more slowly and should be regarded as within the treatment process.

The Freudian emphasis in Hamilton's work seems to make no difference to the methodology which she relies upon. She is somewhat less explicit than Richmond, but the essence appears the same; thus:

> In the diagnostic approach there is always a phase of fact gathering appropriate to the problem and the request initially presented. Out of this information understanding is gained as to the nature of the difficulty (diagnosis) and the evaluation of the person's functioning in terms of the service or treatment asked for.
> (Hamilton 1951: 148)

Again, in Hamilton's work, the relationship between diagnosis and treatment in which the latter 'emerges' from the former appears to accord with Richmond's vision. Hamilton (1951: 148) says that whilst the steps of study, diagnosis and treatment are intellectually distinguishable, in practice the:

> ... casework process flows along in one single, comprehensive movement or unity. We make a tentative diagnosis at the outset; we 'treat' in some fashion right away ... and as long as the treatment continues there are recurrent phases of study, diagnosis and evaluation.

Another American theorist who has been very influential in the elaboration of casework diagnosis is Helen Harris Perlman. In her book *Social Casework: a problem-solving process*, she develops a problem-focused approach wherein diagnosis is a continuous process of appraisal and reappraisal, but again the methodology follows that of Richmond, whose work Perlman (1957: vii) cites as 'brilliant', and 'the outstanding single effort to order the process of casework help'. Perlman's formulation of the process is as follows:

> The facts that constitute and bear upon the problem must be ascertained and grasped ... The facts must be thought about. That is to say, they must be turned over, probed into, and reorganised in the mind ... Some choice or decision must be made that is the end result of the consideration of the particular facts, and that affects or has the intent of resolving the problem.
> (Perlman 1957: 60–61)

Perlman saw difficulties with this prescription, however, and remarks that 'the study-diagnosis-treatment formula has presented a persistent stumbling-block in casework' (p. 61). This is because the model:

> ... tended in practice to produce more problem-solving activity on the caseworker's part than on the client's. What seems to happen is that the client becomes subject to the caseworker's efforts, and this despite valiant efforts to conceive of the client as a participant from the first.

> (p. 61)

The problem-solving approach which Perlman advocates seeks to overcome this difficulty by means of a 'difference of emphasis and dynamics' (p. 61), but, as Perlman rightly says, this is 'not a fundamental change in the *structure* of the casework process' (p. 61, italics added). The *methodology* is the same as Richmond's, and thus the potential for imposed meaning is retained, and as a consequence the client, as subordinate to the worker, is 'subject to the caseworker's efforts' rather than being a prime mover in the achievement of his or her self-defined purposes. This is a persistent by-product of the diagnostic methodology.

The unity of professional casework and science

When casework was re-imported to Britain the methodological legacy of the COS which had travelled to the New World at the end of the nineteenth century was returned intact, and casework was warmly welcomed home again. It brought with it renewed ideas, and the diversity of activities and agencies pursuing the social work task came to be seen as having a fresh and inspiring unity. Thus, according to the new insight, probation work *was* casework in essence, and precisely the same applied to all the others. Writing in 1950, in an edited book which brought together contributions from a number of branches of social work, Una Cormack and Kay McDougall (1950: 19) say that specialist groups of social workers:

> ... embody, each in their own way, the different applications of the principles of one fundamental method of doing social work, that is, the method of case-work, and all are members of one main class of professional social workers; that is, they are all case-workers.

The Home Office inspector in charge of probation officers' training at that time, William Minn (1950), who also contributed to the book, certainly seemed happy with the formulation cited above.

Social enquiry and diagnosis: some examples

So far our discussion has been of a fairly general nature in relation to the methodology of social diagnosis. The question naturally arises as to the extent to which probation officers were influenced by the methodological precepts of scientific diagnosis. Certainly, within my own experience the books provided by Richmond, Hamilton and Perlman were standard texts for the training courses for probation officers in the late 1950s and early 1960s; but did the precepts of teaching and training extend into practice, and how, if at all, was this manifest in social enquiry reports prepared for the criminal courts? ... [In] what follows we will examine [examples of reports from the 1930s and the 1960s] prepared by probation officers and consider the implications of the changes to be found in them.

Example 1 – A report from the 1930s

Report to Deanside Magistrates' Court 10 June 1938
Billy Joseph Paulson, aged 17, C of E Lane School
Charge – Larceny of shoes and cigarettes at school

This lad has never had any real home life or parental affection. He was brought up by his Grandmother, up to five years of age, his Father having deserted his Mohher (sic) before the boy was born, making it necessary for the Mother to go to work. The Waifs and Strays Society took him in and from the age of five years, until 14 he lived in several of their Homes, with the exception of a brief period with a Foster-Mother. Upon leaving the Home at Brecton, he went to work on a farm near Daleby and after about a year, he left there to come to Lane School, where he has been ever since. He has never had the advantages of (family) (sic) life and the control and training of parents.

The Steward at Lane School informs me that Paulson is a boy who can work hard when he likes the job and at present he is in control of other boys, but he sometimes gets himself into trouble through sheer thoughtlessness and sky-larking. He needs constant supervision.

Since he has been on Probation, I have had frequent contacts with him and have tried to persuade him to take life more seriously. Until these offences came to light, he had behaved very satisfactorily. He appears to me to be a lad who is weak-willed and weak in moral principles in one or two directions and, consequently, he finds it very difficult to resist certain temptations. He agrees that he knows that it is wrong to steal, but finds himself unable to resist the temptation to take something he wants badly when the opportunity presents itself sometimes. I have had a long talk with him and tried to impress him with the folly of this course of life and I believe he sees it and is sorry.

His great aim in life is to get into the mechanised side of the Army and as he is 17 years, he is of an age to join. Such a life would make a man of him. I feel that his chief need is understanding and friendship, which will help him find himself. I do not think he is a vicious lad, in fact, he is a very likeable lad. If the Court would help him to realise his ambition and get into the Army, I do not think he will offend again. He has promised me, voluntarily, that he will go straight in future and I believe he means it.

Comment

In my view this report typifies pre-diagnostic social enquiry practice in many respects. Perhaps the first thing to note about it is that it is relatively short compared with later reports ... In its original form it occupied less than one sheet of foolscap paper, and this is the case with all the reports which I have from the 1930s. Also, by modern standards, these reports were rather poorly presented, with additions to the typescript made by hand and numerous corrections made in the same manner.

Each of the 1930s reports in my sample begins with some factual information and then moves on to a section which is undisguised moral evaluation. This is true in the case of Billy Paulson where the moral evaluation is connected in a commonsensical way to the explanation of the offending. He is said to be 'weak-willed and weak in moral principles' and this is linked directly (by the word 'consequently') to his difficulty in resisting 'certain temptations'. In ontological terms Paulson is depicted as partly determined by forces beyond his control: he 'knows that it is wrong to steal', but because of his weak moral principles, he 'finds it very difficult to resist certain temptations'. At the same time in the conclusion of the report, Paulson is clearly depicted as having freewill: 'He has promised me, voluntarily, that he will go straight in the future'; and the probation officer accepts this and believes 'he means it'. It seems to me that the overarching ontology here would claim freewill for Paulson.

The whole tone of the reports from the 1930s is that of lay documents written for a lay audience. There is no hint at all of psychological explanations of action; the explanations appeal to common sense and a consensual view of morality. In the illustrative report which we have used here, for example, the advantages of a 'normal' family life go without saying, and it is obvious that the army would 'make a man' of Paulson. Other reports from the period contain similar language and understanding. ...

Example 4 – A report from the 1960s

Report to Pengwern Magistrates' Court 12 June 1964
Peter Henry Goodman, age 20, Church of England (nominal)
Charge – Unlawful sexual intercourse

The following social enquiry report has been made with the consent of the accused person and/or the concurrence of the defending Solicitor, and such consent has not to my knowledge been withdrawn.

Goodman lives with his widowed mother in a three-bedroomed council house situated on a pleasant housing estate. During my visits, I have always found the house clean and tidy and with adequate comfort. There is no family history of any serious illness, and Goodman appears to be a strong and healthy young man.

At the local Secondary Modern School he was said to be of good average ability, and in his earlier years he presented a stable and happy outlook. In 1959 Goodman left school and commenced employment as an apprentice carpenter with a local firm. He says that he felt that he was not making progress, explaining that he was making joints on his first day at work and three and a half years later he was doing exactly the same job. He was able to have the apprenticeship transferred to another firm but his feelings of frustration and dissatisfaction continued, resulting in an unsatisfactory work record. He was also at this time making complaints of the low wage he was receiving in his apprenticeship.

In 1963 Goodman's mother sought the advice of the Probation Service regarding her son, the main complaint being that he was idle and had not paid his board and lodging for many weeks. It would seem that this pattern of behaviour has continued, although his mother says that people outside of the home always speak well of him. Goodman was being maintained by his mother as he was not registering for employment and consequently he was ineligible for National Assistance aid. Within the past month, however, he has commenced employment in a local factory where his wage is 5/1d per hour.

In his leisure time, Goodman likes an occasional drink of beer, and since the present alleged offences came to light he has commenced smoking cigarettes. He has a motorcycle which appears to be his main absorbing interest.

Goodman says that he met the young lady about 15 months ago and has been in love with her. He does not offer any excuses for himself or his actions. He says that at the time of the intercourse he knew that he was doing wrong and that it was against the code taught to him by his parents. He goes so far as to say that he did not enjoy his sexual experiences, probably because of his guilt feelings, and now says that he does feel ashamed of his actions. He tells me that he has agreed not to contact the girl until she is over 16 years of age, but adds that if it had been possible he would have married her.

Goodman has a background of security which has been fractured by the death of his father. This psychologically traumatic experience occurred at the time he was due to leave school and he found himself unable to face the responsibility of being the male figure in the home. Concurrently his mother became dependent upon him but also rather over-indulgent. His feelings of emotional insecurity and inadequacy became apparent and his immature reaction to the home and economic pressures caused anxieties to himself and others.

I feel that Goodman is very worried and anxious about his pending court appearance. There is the promise that he will keep his word regarding contacting the girl and also his working regularly, but I am not confident that he is sufficiently stable or mature as a personality to keep these promises without some additional support and guidance. Although he has not been very co-operative in the past with the Probation Service, a period of supervision could be useful.

Comment

A glance back at the report for the 1930s shows the enormous difference between the report and this example from the 1960s reproduced above. The language of the 1960s' report is strikingly different, as is the underlying philosophy which it reveals. In the 1960s' report the psycho-social diagnosis has swept aside many (although not all) of the earlier understandings, and 'explanations' based on causal concepts hold sway. Also the language has gained a new professional mode, the common understanding of 'a happy childhood', for example, is translated into 'in his earlier years he presented a stable and happy outlook'.

In Example 4 (in sharp contrast with Example 1) the accused offers a promise to the probation officer, but it is rejected on the determinist grounds that the officer is 'not confident that he is sufficiently stable or mature as a personality' to keep a promise. Common understandings of human motivation have been replaced by professional appraisal based upon particular conceptions of the nature of man. Consider the penultimate paragraph of the report, it is the epitome of the psycho-social diagnosis, the young man has lost his security through the death of his father which was 'psychologically traumatic', and he becomes the 'male figure', but he cannot cope because of his 'emotional insecurity and inadequacy'. Of course, the officer in Example 4 might well have been right about these matters, but that is not the point at issue here.

At the heart of all social enquiry practice there lie attempts to comprehend at least aspects of the human condition, which entail the imposition of meaning even under the most favourable circumstances. The phase of diagnosis amplified these attributes of social enquiry to a very considerable extent, as we have seen from the example given above which is quite typical in this respect of the sample of reports which I have for this decade. In the 1960s, however, the diagnostic phase was reaching its end; ultimately, the 'explanations' which it offered failed to satisfy the practitioners and they turned in other directions.

The decline of overt diagnosis

It seems that the apogee of the phase of diagnosis was reached in the mid-1960s, and this had been preceded by much writing on the topic. One of the most influential books was published in the late 1950s. This was the post-war handbook of probation, edited by Joan King (1958) which was, like its predecessor (LeMesurier 1935), published by the National Association of Probation Officers. The central message, so far as diagnosis in social enquiry reports was concerned, took the following form:

> Probation, like all other forms of casework, should begin with social diagnosis. In many instances the first stage of such diagnosis occurs when the probation officer is required to prepare a report for a court on a child or an adult appearing before it. Whereas many caseworkers can take two or three interviews before attempting to formulate a diagnosis the probation officer often has to come to conclusions about an offender after one brief interview, conducted against time and great difficulties, in the precincts of the court, in a police cell or in the offender's overcrowded living room.
>
> (King 1958: 81)

Thus probation *should* begin with diagnosis. Later editions of the Handbook, including the last (King 1969), continued to advocate the 'scientific methodology', but from the start it had been fairly clear that there were snags in the way to fulfilment, and over time the magnitude of these became apparent. First, as Weston (1978: 11) has remarked, under the diagnostic model the probationer was placed 'in the position of a co-operative recipient of expert treatment rather than being a prime agent in his own rehabilitation'. This echoes precisely the previously cited concern of Perlman (1957: 61) about 'more problem-solving activity on the caseworker's part than on the client's'; but this was not the only difficulty.

In many instances probationers were *not* co-operative recipients but, on occasion, downright antagonistic. There were, of course, apologists for the coercive model. Hunt (1964: 251, italics added), for example, in a much-cited paper, avowed that 'in many respects the probation casework process is *enriched by enforcement*'. The problems of imposed meaning would not go away, however, and doubts about the ethics and practicality of enforced treatment by the probation service continued to grow.

Secondly, in the much-used *Probation Officers' Manual*, Jarvis (1980: 114, italics added) says of the modern probation officer that:

> Since his purpose is not necessarily to get the offender on probation but to help the court towards the best sentence possible, his report is intended as *an essay in objectivity*. The purpose is to provide the impartial professional appraisal of the offender and his situation *which is vital to effective sentencing* as now understood.

Here again there is the worm in the bud: if the major justification for objective diagnosis is an increase in the effectiveness of sentencing, then objective diagnosis appears to fail. Jarvis does not enlarge upon what he means by 'effective sentencing', but as Martin Davies (1974: 21) has pointed out:

> There is no evidence that the growth in the use of social inquiry reports has occurred with any significant improvement in the 'effectiveness' of sentencing as measured by its success in reducing the level of crime … Nor does it appear that the growth in the use of social inquiry reports has occurred simultaneously with any lessening in the range of sentencing disparities.

Three concluding remarks

Before we end our review of the diagnostic phase of understanding in the English probation system, there are three final matters to be considered. The first of these takes the form of a crucial question which was posed by Eric Sainsbury (1970: 7) in his book *Social Diagnosis in Casework*; he asked that:

> … we should consider how far the worker's intuitions, emotions and value-judgements may appropriately find a place in diagnosis, and whether the worker should seek to be (even if he could) wholly objective and unemotional … is diagnosis a value-free conclusion, built on known facts, or is it a process in which the value judgements and feelings of both worker and client play a part?

We must conclude that the latter of Sainsbury's alternatives is correct. We must also conclude that the endless preoccupation with the techniques of fact-gathering, inductive inference and interpretation, which figured so large in the phase of diagnosis, had the highly undesirable effect of diverting attention away from, and reducing the importance of, vital debate about the moral bases of *any* professional social work intervention in people's lives. This is not to suggest that social workers should not act, but rather that continuous critical debate should focus upon the justifications of action much more than on the techniques of bringing it about (on this point see Whan 1986).

The second matter concerns the effects of diagnostic thinking on the relationships between the court, the offender and the probation officer. In the phase of special pleading (McWilliams 1983) these were characterised by a form of reciprocity. The offender gave an earnest of reform and received the plea of the missionary or officer and the mercy of the sentencer. The officer gave a pledge to look after and supervise the offender in pursuit of his moral reform and received an enhancement of his own grace; and the sentencer extended mercy and, like the officer, engraced his own soul.

In the diagnostic phase this three-way relationship was radically altered. Under the diagnostic methodology the offender, ideally, should be 'motivated' to co-operate in the expert treatment. Coercion may be applied to those who are initially unmotivated; but the logic of anticipating a motivated offender or coercing him to be so is suspect in a determinist perception of man; hence the offender does not necessarily give anything except, in certain circumstances, his consent. For his part the officer gives the court a social diagnosis and invites the sentencer to share his 'scientific' vision of the appropriate treatment. If this happens and the sentencer passes the sentence recommended, it might be said that the relationship between the officer and the sentencer retains elements of reciprocity; but it is subtly altered. In appropriate cases the missionary officer and the sentencer shared a common perception of the moral good, and although the missionary was undoubtedly trying to tell the sentencer what to do, he did so from the subordinate position of one advancing *a plea*. The diagnostic officer, in contrast, is also trying to tell the sentencer what to do but, as an expert, his stance is much more that of an equal or even a superior. The catch-phrase of the diagnostic era, 'educating the magistrates', nicely captures the arrogance involved.

The third and final matter concerns the current status of social diagnosis within the probation system. We may see that the *language* of diagnosis is still widespread; thus one social work teacher, Robert Harris (1977: 440, italics added), complains that if the probation officer:

> ... sees his primary function as being to persuade his clients to desist from delinquent activity, the other factors in a *social work diagnosis* may tend to be subordinated to this. The best decision, having regard to the global picture of the client's developmental needs may not, therefore, be made.

But, despite the language, this does not necessarily imply that the 'best decision' to which Harris refers will be based on full-blown diagnostic methodology. This is so because despite the persistence of diagnostic phraseology, recent years have witnessed an acknowledgement that the edifice of diagnostic and treatment thinking within the probation service is beginning to crumble. As one chief probation officer, Colin Thomas (1978: 30), points out, 'critical findings about the general outcome of treatment cannot be ignored – the evidence is too strong'; and he concludes that the 'certainties of our traditional knowledge-base have gone'.

The loss of certainty has had profound effects upon the probation service as a whole; the mission which began in the 1870s has twice been transformed in the century. I hope to address the second transformation and the nature of the modern mission in the final essay in this quartet.

From William McWilliams, 'The English probation system and the diagnostic ideal',
Howard Journal, *25(4), 1986, pp. 241–260.*

References

Cormack, U.M. and McDougall, K. (1950) 'Case-work in practice', in C. Morris (ed.) *Social Casework in Britain.* London: Faber and Faber.

Curran, J.H. and Chambers, G.A. (1982) *Social Enquiry Reports in Scotland.* Edinburgh: HMSO.

Davies, M. (1974) 'Social inquiry for the courts', *British Journal of Criminology* 14: 18–33.

Germain, C. (1970) 'Casework and science: an historical encounter', in R.W. Roberts and R.H. Nee (eds.) *Theories of Social Casework.* Chicago: Chicago University Press.

Hamilton, G. (1951) *Theory and Practice of Social Casework.* 2nd ed. New York: Columbia University Press.

Harris, R.J. (1977) 'The probation officer as social worker', *British Journal of Social Work* 7: 433–42.

Hunt, A.W. (1964) 'Enforcement in probation casework', *British Journal of Criminology* 4: 239–52.

Jarvis, F.V. (1980) *Probation Officers' Manual.* 3rd ed. London: Butterworth.

King, J.F.S. (ed.) (1958) *The Probation Service.* London: Butterworth.

——(1969) *The Probation Service.* 3rd ed. London: Butterworth.

LeMesurier, L. (ed.) (1935) *A Handbook of Probation and Social Work of the Courts.* London: National Association of Probation Officers.

Loch, C.S. (1883) *How to Help Cases of Distress: a handy reference book for almoners, almsgivers and others.* London: Longman Green.

McWilliams, W. (1983) 'The mission to the English police courts 1876–1936', *Howard Journal* 22: 129–47.

——(1985) 'The mission transformed: professionalization of probation between the wars', *Howard Journal* 24: 257–74.

Marshall, T.H. (1981) *The Right to Welfare.* London: Heinemann.

Minn, W.G. (1950) 'Probation work', in C.Morris (ed.) *Social Casework in Great Britain.* London: Faber and Faber.

Mowat, C.L. (1961) *The Charity Organisation Society 1869–1913.* London: Methuen.

Owen, D. (1964) *English Philanthropy 1660–1960.* Cambridge, Mass.: Harvard University Press.

Perlman, H.H. (1957) *Social Casework: a problem-solving process.* Chicago: Chicago University Press.

Richmond, M.E. (1917) *Social Diagnosis.* New York: Russell Sage Foundation.

Rooff, M. (1972) *A Hundred Years of Family Welfare.* London: Michael Joseph.

Sainsbury, E. (1970) *Social Diagnosis in Casework.* London: Routledge and Kegan Paul.

Steadman-Jones, G. (1971) *Outcast London: a study in the relationships between the classes in Victorian society.* Oxford: Oxford University Press.

Thomas, C. (1978) 'Supervision in the community', *Howard Journal* 17: 23–31.

Weston, W.R. (1978) 'Probation in penal philosophy: evolutionary perspectives', *Howard Journal* 17: 7–22.

Whan, M. (1986) 'On the nature of practice', *British Journal of Social Work* 16: 243–50.

Young, A.F. and Ashton, E.T. (1956) *British Social Work in the Nineteenth Century.* London: Routledge and Kegan Paul.

22 Probation as treatment (1956)

Elizabeth R. Glover

Probation has now been available to the English courts for half a century, so it is possible to draw some conclusions from experience as to the value of the various interpretations given to it, and its potentialities.

It was undoubtedly first devised as a means of saving people from the degradation of a prison sentence. (Even yet a prison sentence is rarely regarded as anything other than disastrous from the point of view of the prisoner.) That is to say, it was a 'let off'. It was assumed that the more decent type of offender would naturally realize that he had merited punishment, and be deeply moved by gratitude and penitence if instead of condemning him to this, society gave him the chance to make amends. It was assumed, too, that he could do this, if he wanted to. Nearly fifty years experience of probation have now shown us that these assumptions may be in some respects over-confident.

First, offenders cannot be classed into black and white, depraved and decent. Offenders, like everybody else, are a mixture of good and bad qualities. They can be generous and unreliable, loyal and unscrupulous, competent and self-seeking, well-intentioned and impulsive, all at one and the same time, making them admirable people in some respects, unsatisfactory in others.

Secondly, experience has shown that very few offenders are humble enough to believe that they have merited the humiliation and exposure of arrest and charge, and the condemnation of public opinion. Very few people take this view of other disastrous happenings, such as being dismissed from a job, failing in business, losing a friend. Offenders are no exception. 'I'm no worse than anyone else. Why pick on me?' 'Stealing a rotten old pair of shoes is not so bad as stealing somebody's husband. Why don't they run after Mrs So-and-So and arrest her for stealing my husband?' 'They ought to look after their stuff better.' Most people, they think, are out for Number One; most people placed as they were would have done the same; life has always been hard; it's unfair; some people have all the luck. The new probationer leaves the court relieved – yes, certainly relieved – but neither penitent nor grateful; full of self-pity, angry humiliation and suspicious apprehension about the supervision he has let himself in for.

Thirdly, we have come to see that for the very reason that people are such a mixture of conflicting traits of good and ill they are not always – on the contrary they are rarely – able to change their nature by an act of will. Human nature is not as simple as this. Though we all like to think we act by our own freely determined choice, we do not. What we choose to do today depends upon the disposition of our minds, and that depends on our past habits of living and thinking. A person habitually attuned to thinking in terms of his own exclusive pleasure or profit, or fear of being thought ridiculous, or alternatively to never thinking at all, cannot overnight, simply by deciding to, become altruistic, independent, reflective; he has not developed the necessary mental and moral muscles. We react to the present situation, in short, with our present mental and emotional apparatus, the only one we have.

There followed another phase in the interpretation of the probation method. In certain schools of thought and practice probation was believed to hold possibilities of punishment. Too great a measure of leniency was thought to be ill-advised. These people, it was argued, though one hesitated to ruin them by a prison sentence, yet needed a wholesome reminder that they could not offend with impunity. So some magistrates and probation officers deliberately made probation as unpleasant as possible. Probationers were asked to report at the most inconvenient hours, a Saturday afternoon for instance, thus preventing industrial workers from their only chance of outdoor recreation. They were expected to travel long distances to see their officer and to pay their own fares. They were subjected to military discipline at the office, told to stand at attention and take their hands out of their pockets, to come with clean fingernails and collars, and to answer deferentially when spoken to.

This kind of thing is now seen to have little remedial effect on character. The selfish, unstable or unscrupulous person does not become generous steady and upright because he has been humiliated in this fashion. He merely hates it: hates the authority that imposed it; is more than ever convinced that life is hard and he is unlucky; and makes up his mind not to get caught again, but to get his own back if he can.

Probation officers have now come to see that the law governing probation permits of another interpretation – treatment. A year or two of close personal contact between the offenders and the probation officer may be an opportunity to improve the former's health, to enlarge his legitimate interests and scope, to redirect his feeling and emotions along healthier channels, so that his outlook on life and attitude of mind are altered, and new mental and moral muscles developed. Instead of having a negative function saving the offender from a worse fate, or teaching him not to do this again, probation has assumed a positive one, introducing him to a better way of life.

A new factor has come into the situation since 1907, which has greatly contributed to this interpretation of the probation provisions. This is psychiatry.

The lay public do not always distinguish the many modern developments connected with psychological research. The two sciences which concern behaviour problems are psychology, the science of human behaviour, and psychiatry, the science of healing the mind. A psychologist is one who has made a study of the way the mind works, and a psychiatrist is one qualified to treat mental diseases, that is to say, a fully qualified medical practitioner with additional qualifications in psychology. Further, psychological treatment is not synonymous with psycho-analytical treatment, as is commonly supposed. Psycho-analysis is one method of treatment only, by which a psycho-analyst helps people to analyse themselves and see their motives as they really are, and so to understand and manage themselves better. This is always a long process, and often a painful one, for the picture so revealed is usually less flattering than had been imagined. Because it takes a long time it is expensive; and because it is painful not everyone can face it; because it requires a degree of insight and reasoning ability not everyone is a good subject for it. Psycho-analytic treatment is analogous to surgery. Most doctors hesitate to recommend anything so drastic as a surgical operation unless there seems absolutely no alternative. Even then, some patients are so ill that the risk of surgical treatment is a greater one than the risk of letting things take their course. And some patients are so horrified at the thought that they will not give their consent. So it is with psycho-analysis. There are other and more common methods of bringing relief to sick minds, and this applies as much to delinquent as to non-delinquent patients.

The psychiatrists established themselves in public opinion in Great Britain first during and after the 1914–18 war, in treating shellshocked soldiers and sailors. Their reputation and sphere were vastly enlarged during the last war, when every reception area in the country clamoured for their immediate assistance in dealing with children who before evacuation had been regarded as normal. Between the two wars Child Guidance Clinics began to be set up, and to establish a reputation for giving sound advice and help in the handling of difficult children. Many of the bigger hospitals also opened psychiatric clinics where similar advice and help was given to adults labouring under distress of mind.

The great contribution which psychology has made from the point of view of probation is that it has led us away from the purely legal or moral approach to delinquency to the scientific or curative one. It has taught us that all conduct, good or bad, has a reason, and that if the conduct is bad, one must first look for and find the reason before one can hope to correct it. The scientist, when his experiments take an unexpected turn, does not pass judgement, 'This powder *ought* not to have turned green'. He says, 'Good heavens, it has turned green; now I wonder *why?*' In seeking an answer to this why, his knowledge of the matter is greatly increased. Similarly, the probation officer's attitude should be not 'That man ought not to beat his wife, or that girl to tell lies', but rather *why* do they do so? Unless he can discover why they do these things, he cannot hope to help them, for he will be working blind.

Looked at in this way all delinquency takes on a highly individual aspect. For instance, what might be the reasons for stealing? Some steal for the excitement it brings them. The small boys who compete with each other up and down the street markets to see who can pinch from most stalls without getting caught are an example of this. Older boys who steal motor cars and plan burglaries also sometimes come under this category. Some steal to impress. The child, for instance, who feels despised by teachers and fellows alike for his ineptitude in school may win a dare-devil name for himself and so considerable esteem at any rate from a circle, by his thieving exploits out of school. It is the applause he is after, not the things he steals. Some steal out of a genuine desire to help somebody. A child might steal coal to help his mother, for instance. Some steal because they badly need affection, and by stealing pretty little articles and giving them away as presents they hope to win it. Some steal out of funk. A youngster is dismissed from his job, and not daring to return home without his wages, steals the money to make up. Some steal out of sheer irresponsibility. This is called 'borrowing'. It seems quite clear that in some cases the offender never meant to take, much less to keep, what did not belong to him. Some steal from a deliberate wish to hurt someone. A girl, for instance, may have been jilted by her lover or reproved by her employer, and steals to spite them. Some steal because they cannot help doing so. This is called pathological stealing, or kleptomania, and is a recognizable disease. The symptoms of pathological stealing are that the offender has no use for what he steals, and takes none of the usual precautions against detection.

This list is not, of course, by any means exhaustive, but is sufficient to serve the purpose of the argument here. The point is that, to be effective, treatment must be related to the cause of the trouble, and therefore it will in all cases be highly individual, individually planned, to meet individual needs. Whatever else may form part of the plan of treatment, the child who steals for excitement must be provided with legitimate outlets for his high spirits and wits; the child who steals to win approbation must be given more approbation in the normal way, and his self-respect built up by those who have care of him; those who steal because they want to help someone must be shown better ways of helping; the child who needs affection must be given it, and, if he is unwanted or unloved, possibly found other more affectionate people to live with; those who steal out of funk must have their self-confidence built up, so that they can face their difficulties courageously. For the malignant or pathological thief it is well to seek the guidance and help of a psychiatrist. The reasons for these reactions are harder to find for the lay, and therefore treatment without expert advice is likely to be ineffective.

In short, to mete out the same treatment to all offenders is as ineffective as to dose all out-patients in a hospital with cough mixture. There must be individual treatment to meet individual needs and conditions.

But a good doctor does more than treat the immediate symptoms of any illness; he also has an eye on how his patient's general resistance can be built up so that he does not so easily fall prey to infection again. That is to say, he not only studies factors conducive to illness, he must also have regard to those that build up health. Similarly, good probation treatment must seek not only to alleviate the immediate problems which may have contributed to or arisen from the offence, but also to develop factors which conduce to moral health.

We must therefore consider what attributes go to the making of moral health. The actual circumstances of life, wealth or poverty, good or bad health, success or failure, are not the factors which exclusively determine our happiness or mould our natures. Some people brought up in abject poverty and want, in the midst of friction, frustration, anxiety and ill health, grow into the saints of the earth, strong, true, generous and courageous folk; while others born into easy affluent circumstances, who have never been crossed, sometimes grow up into lazy, selfish, irresponsible, good-for-nothings. It is not only what happens to us, but how we react to what happens, that affects our characters and peace of mind. So that material circumstances, though no doubt they contribute, are not alone decisive in forming character.

There are four factors which it is here suggested are important constituents of sound moral health: affection, friends, interests, and faith or philosophy of life.

By affection is meant love; not the hot, passionate emotion of love affairs, but the deep, strong, abiding ties of concern and regard that bind one person to another or to others. Psychologists tell us that it is absolutely essential to the human spirit both to love and to be loved (Suttie 1935: 50). Our own observation tells us as much. One has only to compare a completely independent person, who is bound to nobody by any bonds of affection, with an ordinary individual who loves those near and dear to him. The one is wrapped up in himself and views everything that happens as it affects himself only; the other is concerned for the welfare and happiness of those he loves, and takes a wider view. It is when we begin to love another that we learn naturally and spontaneously, not by effort of will, generosity, tolerance, responsibility and courage. When we love another we do not lightly destroy his peace of mind or his belief in us by doing what would horrify or disappoint him, and thus we learn to modify our own inclinations and wishes. A person who loves no one has neither the same incentive to moral qualities, nor the same restraining force. Love is the baṣis of our moral standard.

Similarly friends or the lack of them have a profound effect upon character. A person who has no friends loses his sense of proportion and judges everything from his own exclusive point of view, thus becoming narrow in his outlook and egocentric in his interests. If he loves those in his intimate circle, then without friends the love becomes exclusive and possessive and therefore loses some of its potency for good. Good fellowship leads to large-heartedness and large-mindedness within the group. Social approval is a great restraining force on behaviour. Indeed, it sometimes seems too much so, as if we bowed to the dictates of public opinion, rather than exercising our own discrimination. The child at school and the man in his profession alike are sensitive to what is and what is not 'done', and take trouble to conform to it. This is not to say that adults as well as children do not frequently try to assess how far they can go without evoking the displeasure of the group and sometimes assess it wrongly. But a person who keeps his own company and shuns the society of his fellows has less opportunity of sensing public opinion and less incentive to conform to it.

Interests have considerable power to shape character. People who have hobbies or purposes of their own to pursue develop powers of imagination and initiative, judgement and self-discipline, persistence and skill in carrying them out. Further, these interests often lead them to seek the advice and therefore the company of others of like interests, so that interests often lead to friendships. Those, on the other hand, who have no interests and have never found anything they think worth pursuing lose the sense of enjoyment and purpose which others have, and tend in consequence to become restless and unsatisfied. Those who know they have abilities but feel unable through circumstances or temperament to use them, tend to become irritable or cynical. Unsatisfied people are apt to become unsatisfactory people.

By faith is meant faith in a living God, by philosophy a sufficient answer for the time being to life's enigmas. Without some belief in an ultimate purpose or scheme of things, people begin to feel just so much flotsam and jetsam, meaningless, purposeless, worthless. People who are able by reason of their faith or philosophy to feel there is something worth living for, have an ideal to live by, and a scale of values whereby to develop judgement. These things give the ability to see things in better perspective and to take a long view. Such people are not so prone to hasty judgement or action or to the hopelessness of despair or bitterness as others, and hence have a staying power or a resilience in adversity which sees them through.

All these things are what the psychologists mean when they tell us that we are motivated by our emotions rather than by our reason. Emotion in psychology means not hysterics but feeling.

'All the motives which govern and drive our lives are emotional. Love and hate, anger and fear, curiosity and joy, are the springs of all that is most noble and most detestable in the history of men and nations', says John Macmurray (1945: 146). It is what we care about and the extent to which we care that the psychologists mean when they say our lives are governed by emotional factors. And it is this, what we care about and the extent to which we care, that makes our characters. We are beginning to realize that our emotions exercise terrific power over our bodies. We turn sick with fear; or an invalid like Elizabeth Barrett Browning leaves her sick bed when she falls in love; worry is recognized as a potent cause of illness. It is true also of the mind. We like to think we are rational beings, who govern our lives by reason, but most of us feel first and think afterwards. We think and act according as we feel. A man feels angry, and hits somebody, metaphorically or actually; then he thinks, and he thinks he finds very good reasons for justifying his actions.

If this is true, then if we seek to reform a man's character we must look to his emotions; engage his interests and inclinations; awaken, mend and redirect his capacity for feeling. Punishment is an appeal to reason; it is most effective when the emotions are concerned in it too. A boy is distressed and concerned when someone whom he loves and admires reproves or punishes him. But if he has no regard for the punisher, he simply dislikes the man and the system more than before, and justifies or excuses himself in his own mind for what he did. Love is the basis of our moral standard. He may decide not to venture that way again if he has been punished, but if so it may merely indicate a surrender to 'Safety First' or self-defence, rather than a moral preference.

Insofar, then, as probation is considered to have the positive function of introducing the offender to a better way of life, the art of the probation officer lies in arousing and redirecting his emotions.

The extent to which the emotional factors here mentioned are at present operative or deficient varies of course very greatly, from one offender to another, just as factors conducive to physical health are operative in varying degrees with different patients. The contention here is that these things profoundly affect character, and therefore must be considered by anyone seeking to reform character. Effective probation must begin with careful enquiry into these matters …

> *From Elizabeth R. Glover,* Probation and Re-education, *2nd ed. (London: Routledge and Kegan Paul), 1956, pp. 15–25.*

References

Macmurray, J. (1945) *Freedom in the Modern World.* London: Faber and Faber.
Suttie, D.I. (1935) *The Origins of Love and Hate.* London: Kegan Paul.

23 Whither probation? (1958)

Frank Dawtry

After fifty years, the Probation Service may well look back with pride on its achievements, but it is more concerned to look forward. It does so in the knowledge that it must keep itself up to date, equipped and able to turn modern knowledge to the advantage of those for whom it is called upon to work, while not losing the basic belief, on which the Service was founded, in the value of every human person.

Fears are sometimes expressed that, as in other fields, science seems likely to replace the arts and humanities, so in the field of delinquency and its treatment the modern uses of psychiatry and the scientific analysis of human conduct may conflict with and replace what is regarded as the human and personal approach to behaviour problems. The Probation Service stands in this situation as one in which the daily contact with delinquents and others in trouble obviates any possibility of purely human relationships being abandoned, though the awareness that intuitive responses are not sufficient leads it to turn increasingly to the expert for assistance and to search for greater knowledge for its own use.

The Probation Service itself came into being because of the efforts of those who were in their own day in advance of their time. They saw, or felt, that the long chapter of violence and repression in the treatment of crime should come to an end; that the centuries of torture and violence, banishment, execution and imprisonment had succeeded only in separating the offender from the community, whereas it should be possible to regard the offender as still being a member of the community and to remind the community of its responsibility for him. This idea, developed by the early penal reformers, was built on by those who thought that many offenders need not go to penal institutions at all. These were the pioneer missionaries who met offenders in the police courts and offered them advice and friendship, and their work was recognized in the Probation of Offenders Act, 1907 which established the Probation Service.

The early organization was loose, the probation officers were paid by fees for each case undertaken, and their efforts may now be regarded as being elementary. They worked largely in a belief that human beings could be helped by example and exhortation or that practical work involved only an adjustment of circumstances. It was disappointing when apparent failure showed that it was not enough to change a man's conditions when he was in any case unable to cope with life, or to set an example he could not comprehend.

Nevertheless the early probation officers achieved remarkable success, and from its earliest days the Service has groped its way forward, its wiser members ever seeking greater knowledge, more information, and a proper understanding of problems with which they had to deal. It is an endless search. But the urge to know where it is going, the desire to improve its work, are manifestations of what might be called divine discontent amongst probation officers, and in modern days the urge is more insistent than ever. Can the Service cope with all the demands on it, can it man all the posts where it is needed, is its training on the right lines, does its organization need modernizing? These and a dozen other matters are of urgent concern today, and the knowledge of its own limitations becomes at times a source of anxiety and discontent which expresses itself in distrust of authority and anger about inadequate recognition of the difficulties of the work or reward for its labours. Probation officers are familiar with the tributes paid to them by magistrates, judges and even Home Secretaries, but the pat on the back for doing a good job is sadly reminiscent of the days of underpaid patronage in which the Police Court Missionaries lived. Probation officers know that their work is of tremendous importance to the community (or they could not go on with it) but they feel that the tangible recognition of this by the community shows little real knowledge of its value. They are, however, not concerned only about material rewards. They are aware of the still inadequate public understanding of what probation is seeking to do, they know that in recent years the Service has grown on an old foundation without time or opportunity to sit back and think, and they are sadly conscious of many shortcomings. They feel, in fact, that after fifty years of endeavour it would be a most useful thing for their progress to be examined and for a public assessment to be made of both the work and the organization of the Probation Service.

Such an assessment would not be a new experience. Although the first probation officers did not start their work until January 1908, a Departmental Committee was appointed in March 1909 to examine the workings of the 1907 Act. This Committee noted considerable variations in the use of probation by the courts, and suggested that magistrates should be educated in the meaning of probation. It also expressed the opinion that a case-load of sixty was a desirable maximum for a probation officer dealing with people on probation for short periods.

The first world war threw up many social problems with which the new Service had to cope and in 1920 another Departmental Committee was appointed. It reported in January 1922 that there were 784 probation officers but that most of these were voluntary workers, each with few cases and occupied in a large variety of other employments. Only a small number were permanent full-time officers. The main recommendations of this Committee were that wherever possible probation officers should be employed only on probation or similar work, that remuneration should be improved and should be by salary and not by fees, that every court should have a probation officer at its disposal, and that a Government grant should be made towards the cost of probation. It also recommended that an Advisory Council should assist the Home Office, as the central authority, and that this should be responsible for some form of training for probation officers. But the standing of probation at the time may be measured by the Committee's comment on a suggestion that University training should be available for probation officers; it pointed out that men and women who went to Universities usually did so to fit themselves for a professional career and it was doubtful whether probation would attract candidates with University training.

The main recommendations of this Committee were embodied in the Criminal Justice Act of 1925, and from that time onwards the Service has been gradually transformed into one almost entirely of full-time officers, paid from public funds, though recruitment for long remained local and haphazard, while only a tentative beginning was made with training. A further and more important Departmental Committee was appointed in October, 1934 and this recognized probation as a modem social service. Its Report recommended that there should be a Training Board allied to the Advisory Council; it suggested that probation officers should have knowledge of public administration, and that they should have sufficient knowledge of psychiatric method to enable them to detect who would benefit from expert diagnosis and to follow up any line of treatment recommended by the specialists. This Committee regarded a University training, to be followed by a specialized probation training course, as desirable and urged that no time should be lost in launching a comprehensive training scheme. It also laid down for the first time a national scale of salaries. Its Report has been the basis for many subsequent developments in the field of probation.

It is interesting to note that in the first twenty-eight years of the Probation Service, when its basic nature and duties altered little, there were thus three enquiries into its work, whereas during the last twenty-two years, while its work has undergone tremendous changes, no impartial assessment of these or of their impact has been made.

It may be useful to summarize some of these changes.

The basic work of the Probation Service has always been with offenders placed on probation, and this remains so. Its work in this field has continued in a period of extreme pressure, largely due to the increase of crime during and since the war, but it has continued also in a period of subtle change. Case-loads are heavy, but they tell an inadequate story, for the nature of the loads has altered. Probation, once used for the simple or youthful offence, is now regarded as a form of treatment for serious social problems where the work of well trained caseworkers is required. Many of those placed on probation by the courts today are seriously disturbed people who need a long period of supervision and intensive casework, rather than simple friendship and guidance. This in its turn has contributed to the demand by probation officers for more knowledge and greater understanding of their own motives and a parallel increase in their understanding of the motives and needs of those with whom they are called upon to deal. The elementary and intuitive approach of the pioneers has been replaced, and the probation officer of today is a qualified caseworker who sees his task as that of establishing with each individual in his care a relationship within which that individual can achieve greater understanding of himself and be assisted to make the necessary adjustments which will enable him to lead a happy and socially acceptable life.

In addition, however, to a change in the intensity and depth of its work, the Probation Service has accepted many responsibilities in the wider field of delinquency or of the social work of the courts. The Report of the 1936 Departmental Committee suggested that probation officers should not be recommended to undertake the aftercare of discharged prisoners, and should only undertake the aftercare of those leaving Borstal Institutions or approved schools where other arrangements could not be made. Nevertheless the 1948 Criminal Justice Act led to the establishment of the Central After-Care Association and the acceptance by probation officers of a statutory duty to undertake the aftercare of prisoners discharged from corrective training and preventive detention, certain young prisoners, all those discharged from Borstal training, and those coming from approved schools where the managers so require. Subsequent Probation Rules have added to this list certain groups of prisoners from ordinary imprisonment, and today 7,000 persons discharged from penal or training institutions are under the care of probation officers.

In the field of matrimonial conciliation the 1936 Committee made recommendations to regularize the considerable amount of voluntary work undertaken by probation officers. The recommendations were embodied in the Summary Procedure (Domestic Proceedings) Act of 1937.

Matrimonial conciliation and enquiry work grew rapidly when the war provided its excess of hasty and unsatisfactory marriages and the calls on the probation officers in this field have remained high – in any given year approximately 75,000 actual or potential breakdowns of marriages are dealt with by probation officers and in many of these cases prolonged casework is required. In recent years, on the recommendation of the Denning Committee the work of probation officers has been extended to the Divorce Courts, by the experimental appointment of court welfare officers to deal in particular with the welfare of the children of parties seeking divorce. The success and value of the experiment was recognized by the Royal Commission on Marriage and Divorce, which recommended that such officers should be available to all Divorce Courts, a recommendation now being implemented. The officers undertaking this highly skilled work are also finding themselves called on from time to time by the judges to try to effect reconciliation even in marriages which have reached the Divorce Court.

The position of the Probation Service is now so readily recognized in some circles that it is almost automatically relied upon when new duties are required in the courts; in matters of adoption, for instance, the 1936 Committee had suggested that probation officers should be employed only in exceptional circumstances, but officers are increasingly used to act as guardian *ad litem,* particularly in cases where the local authority's own officer is an interested party. In recent months the Committee on Alternatives to Short Sentences of Imprisonment was quite clear that probation officers should be used more widely in social enquiries by the courts and that the demand for such enquiries might increase if its own recommendations were adopted that no first offender should be sent to prison unless the courts saw no reasonable alternative. Similarly the Wolfenden Committee suggested greater use of the Probation Service for social enquiries in the case of homosexual offenders and of those prostitutes appearing in court for the first or second time, and regarded its suggestion of prison sentences for persistent prostitutes as a measure likely to lead them more readily to accept the help of probation officers. It is significant that these reports assume that probation officers will be available and presuppose their ability to undertake the work involved. The Service can be proud of the confidence in it displayed by such recommendations, but would like to be properly equipped to meet such demands.

As the 1936 Committee recommended, there is now a Probation Advisory and Training Board which supervises the general policy of the Service and organizes the training. Almost three-quarters of the probation officers now serving have been trained, a growing proportion of them at a University, but officers may still be appointed without training. Moreover, there is still no certainty that training is on the right lines. Many students entering the Service discover a wide gap between theory and practice, while the training appears to lack a central direction and apparently fails to give the student a feeling that he is entering a dynamic service which is ready to welcome him.

The recent development of supervised casework is welcomed and accepted by probation officers, but this too demands re-adjustment, further training for some of the older officers and a reconsideration of the relationship between leadership in administration and leadership in casework. The growth of knowledge, the improvement of training and the introduction of supervised casework also brings into question the value of duties now performed by Probation Case Committees and the probation inspectors. The former, composed of magistrates, are required to exercise a general supervision, over the work of probation officers, but they can hardly expect to become experts in casework and it is interesting to note that in a recent article an eminent Clerk to the Justices suggests that, with the growth of supervised casework, Probation Case Committees may need to concern themselves only with broad issues of policy (Wilson 1957).

Similarly the place of the inspectorate may need reconsidering. Where public funds are involved central inspection is of course necessary and the inspectors must continue to satisfy themselves that the work is being properly carried out. Their opportunities, or need, to offer advice should, however, become less as the quality of the service and of its local organization improves, and it is not unreasonable to suggest that less frequent inspections could now release some inspectors for more urgent duties in the field of training, in contact with the Universities, and for activities concerned with propaganda and particularly with recruitment.

The latter is a most serious matter in which the Service as a whole shares the concern which the Probation Advisory and Training Board must feel about the failure to provide adequate staff to meet current demands, let alone the desire of many Probation Committees to increase their staff to meet the increased demands made upon it. It was recently suggested (Report of Industrial Court Proceedings 1957) that the shortage of probation officers was only about 2–3% and therefore not so serious as, e.g. the shortage of policemen or teachers. But in probation every officer missing means that another officer is carrying an excessive case-load, and it may also mean that courts will hesitate to use probation where this is eminently desirable. Furthermore the estimated shortage is based on current establishment but this is in many areas below the desirable number, while the undermanning of the Service is disguised by the appointment of untrained officers or the filling of vacancies by temporary appointments. In some areas officers have preferred to work longer hours with heavier loads rather than to see the standard of their work lowered by such appointments.

The Committee of 1936 stated that 'there is obvious danger in the appointment of unqualified persons and the effect of such appointments would be felt for many years'. Yet twenty years later the appointment of unqualified persons remains a lamentable necessity, with damaging effects on the work and possibly on the lives of those placed on probation. The Service would like to know why the recruits are not forthcoming.

On matters of policy and organization it is true that the establishment of the Probation Advisory and Training Board makes possible some assessment in the Home Office of developments in the Service and its work. But the Probation Division of the Home Office is not a remote civil service department – it is closely associated with the daily work of the Service it administers. This is a condition much appreciated by probation officers, but one which means that the administrators may not be able to see the total situation or to see this as objectively as might be desirable. The work of the Division itself may not have kept pace with the times and could usefully be reviewed.

So could the payment and conditions of service of probation officers. Provision has been made for dealing with these through the establishment of a Joint Negotiating

Committee, but that Committee's interpretation of the term 'conditions of service' is an extremely limited one, and it deals with salaries only by comparisons with other services which come within the knowledge of its members. It is heavily weighted with local government representation and is not able to take a completely objective view of the Probation Service and its current value to the country as a whole.

These and many other considerations lead to the belief that the time has come for a new departmental committee or royal commission to examine all aspects of the Probation Service. Its current problems, its local difficulties, the problems of recruitment, the training of a modern service, the best use of the inspectorate, the organization of the Probation Division, are matters of concern to every probation officer. There are also many matters in the daily work of the Service to which no one has the time to sit back and give disinterested thought. Should the organization of aftercare or of matrimonial conciliation work involve specialization by certain officers? Can the newly developing prison welfare service be integrated and interchangeable with the Probation Service? Is the organization of approved probation homes and hostels on the best lines? Can the demand for more internal training be met? Is it satisfactory for the organization of the London Probation Service to be under direct Home Office control? Can a Government Department effectively administer a local and personal service? Is a principal probation officer to be a departmental head with somewhat remote control of a local service or to retain his present unique position in local services of knowing and partaking in the daily work of his staff? In a growing service seeking to keep pace with modern demands and modern skills, the list of matters now pressing for answer could be extended indefinitely.

The probation officer stands in court today, and in the public service, with a responsibility for the welfare of other individuals equal to that of the magistrate, the clerk or the doctor, and he feels that his place in that group should be recognized and his work organized to enable him to do justice to it. His purpose is unchanged from that of his predecessor of fifty years ago though his ideas may be sounder and his equipment better. He suffers no sense of complacency about his work and his wish to keep pace with the modern scientific age springs only from a desire to use the advances of today for the better benefit of those in his care.

When the Probation of Offenders Act was passed, sixty miles an hour was considered to be the limit of speedy travel; today an aeroplane can travel at a thousand miles an hour. But its only legitimate purpose is still that of getting from one place to another, and it is useless if the direction is wrong. The Probation Service, seeking to work by better and more scientific means, carries on, with changing methods, but it too would like to be sure about the direction in which it is going. It would welcome a new impartial assessment of its position, its direction, its organization and its work, and it would be happy to abide by the result.

From Frank Dawtry, 'Whither probation?', British Journal of Delinquency, 8(3), 1958,
pp. 180–187.

References

Report of Industrial Court Proceedings (2648) (1957) Probation Service.

Report of the Departmental Committee on the Social Services in Courts of Summary Jurisdiction (1936) Cmnd. 5122. London, HMSO.

Wilson, J.P. (1957) 'The Work of the Probation Case Committee', *The Magistrate* 13(8): 95–97.

24 Magistrates and probation officers (1964)

Marjory Todd

London probation officers have been heard to say that they have too many bosses. They have their own seniors, they have their headquarters, the London Probation service, they have the Home Office (since, in London, they work directly under the Secretary of State), and they have their magistrates. They are paid, incidentally, by Scotland Yard. Since I became a relief officer, liable to draw pay of varying amounts at irregular intervals, it has often amused me to watch bank clerks look up from the money order I pay in. What sort of nark can this woman be, to what snips of information do such differing sums relate?

When I was a probation officer in training I was once involved in a difference of opinion with those who sought to examine what I did. My senior voiced no adverse criticism. An official of the London Probation Service arrived and we discussed my work intelligently and on a friendly note, showing nothing but approval. Next came an Inspector from the Home Office, from whom I learned a lot. Skimming through one of the files – the record of a little girl under supervision after having been found in need of care and attention – she evinced a quick, warm interest in my handling of the case. Three weeks later another Inspector came and, by an awkward chance, picked up the same record. *Nothing* was right; everything I had done was inadequate or wrong. I am sure I behaved disgracefully on that day. I sat in a stubborn, silent, almost delinquent mood and let her talk. She may well have been right: the first Inspector may have been mistaken, though I do not honestly think this was the case. What was disturbing me, at that stage, was the need to encounter so many individual and subjective opinions, one following so quickly on the last and differing so widely from it.

That episode blew over. There were still the magistrates. The relationship of magistrate and probation officer is unique in my experience. They are not in fact one's employers, though they can, I gather, especially during one's own probation year, play a considerable part in influencing one's future in their court, or any other court.

They come in two kinds: lay magistrates, who are Justices of the Peace and who deal throughout the country with the vast majority of all offences and with all cases of juveniles, and stipendiaries, who in large boroughs and in the Metropolitan area have to be lawyers of at least seven years standing and who sit alone.

All my first years were spent in juvenile courts, so I worked with justices from the special juvenile court panel. I have encountered many: I have liked most; I have despised a few. Why do they do it? The work is unpaid. You must feel an urgent impulse towards social service, I assume – or else you love publicity and power. In some magistrates I have met the impulses are merged, I am sure. Standing silent before them, I may be impressed one minute by a moving display of understanding and compassion: outraged by silly exhibitionism the next. I would be prepared to swear that some phrases I have heard, enunciated carefully from a juvenile bench, have been thought out and memorised beforehand. They make the evening papers. Perhaps that is what they were meant to do. I have seen noisy outbreaks of temper which may impress some listeners, may even terrify a few; they have failed to impress me. They have a hollow manufactured ring. If only magistrates could hear the comments made outside swing doors by parents, probation officers, police.

On the whole – and I do not say this entirely out of feminist bias – women magistrates are better than men, I have found. They are more reasonable, more ready to judge each case on its own merits; they have less interest in making everything conform to theories they have already publicised in the press or on television. They are less sentimental. They seem to lack the instinct for personal publicity and are none the worse for that.

All the same, one day in the week in a juvenile court is a day out, a non-professional day out for many, a day on which to pronounce on manners and morals, a day of authority. You can watch the weak give in to all the temptations such an opportunity offers and you can watch the strong, the ones you respect, use it for what it ought to be.

My first real encounter with stipendiary magistrates was at Bow Street and nowhere could I have been more fortunate. There is a something – an undefined standard of behaviour – which always came down from the top – anywhere. I have noticed it when I have been a patient lying in hospitals. If the Matron is a good administrator, efficient but humane, her concept of the duties of her office, her pressure on those who serve below her, from sisters, staff nurses, young probationers, right down to the humble orderlies, will prevail. And the patient, supine and with scarcely a voice to raise even in her own interests, will benefit accordingly. It is best, perhaps, to forget those institutions where the Matrons lacked this all-pervading influence.

Stipendiary magistrates are more remote; administration is largely in the hands of chief clerks, warrant officers, gaolers, but I think that something does come down from above – even from them. Difficult to define perhaps; if I had to sum up the qualities which go to make a good stipendiary magistrate I should have to list intelligence first, I suppose; he must be quick and learned, both at once. He must be compassionate and humane even while he wields authority on behalf of us all. Courtesy counts for a good deal, I am convinced. A happy court (if that is not in itself a contradiction!) can only rest on a foundation of mutual consideration and respect.

There have been times when, working with justices, I have felt myself blush hot and red; I have been almost ashamed to meet, outside, the parents of a child who has just left the court. There is that great yawn, for instance, not even stifled, when a father, twisting his cloth cap in his hands, says:

‘Can I say something, sir?’

‘Yes, *what?*’

There is that crass insensitivity which can allow a magistrate to read out a probation officer’s report which *has* to mention matrimonial troubles if a boy’s problems are to be understood, in front of other parents who are present because their boys, too, are charged, but who are the *neighbours*, who may delight in such a bit of gossip. The magistrate goes home at the end of his day; the probation officer is left to cope with all the raw, hurt feelings he has left behind. Yet some are able to create an atmosphere of sympathy and understanding which does not preclude authority.

'Thank you, officer ...' to the police.

'Thank you, you have been most helpful ...' to the probation officer.

'Yes, Mother, what would you like to say? ... Thank you very much. Do sit down, Mrs–'

It costs nothing; its value is immense.

A probation officer's role in court is a peculiar one. He is the servant of the court, but, as I have already quoted, he has many bosses. He is responsible to more than one authority. He has a responsibility, a very great one, for the reports he makes, reports which may help to shape a human life; he has a responsibility to his magistrates, for, without his services, they may only see one face succeed another in the dock; they cannot know, at any depth, the circumstances which lie behind the offence.

There is a great deal of 'Sir-ing' – 'Yes, Sir. No, Sir ... As Your Worship pleases ...' in courts. I do not mind this; it oils the wheels. My judgement of my magistrates is sharp and critical only at the point where they fail to catch the ball in the air, to take up a point with speed and exactness, or to deliberate justly without sentimentality or caprice.

So, since now I have left them all and some, even, are dead, I look back on those whose holding of their office I remember. Some do not seem to bother much about the law. There is always the Clerk to put them right, though the ill-educated parents must often find this odd.

'Behave yourself!' one magistrate roared at a proud, difficult, stubborn sixteen-year-old girl who was to be placed under my supervision after she had run away from home. 'You do what Mrs– tells you!' (He got my name wrong for a start, something which could only help to confuse the girl even if, to him, the mistake seemed unimportant.) 'If you don't, she'll bring you back on a breach! Yes, that's what she'll do – bring you back on a *breach!*'

Apart from the fact that there can be no *breach* of a supervision order – the word belongs to probation – what meaning could the unhappy child extract from this? I wondered if she might perhaps have been given a mental image of a stretcher, and me trundling her back to court on it! Fortunately she said nothing while she still stood, rubbing one foot against another, tall and contemptuous, looking down on the man who spoke these incomprehensible words. But outside, as soon as the swing doors had closed behind us, she hissed, 'Bloody parrot!' She had my unvoiced sympathy.

I can recall one magistrate who would insist that a probation officer say in open court what should be done about a child – as a judgement rather than as a tentative recommendation, because he feared, and did not hesitate to make it clear he feared, an appeal and a reversal which might destroy his *amour propre*. One might be forced to follow his instructions – one cannot have an open row in court – but one obeyed, I found, with inner reservations of a damaging kind. If the executive is to give judgement, if justices are to be no more than rubber stamps on the decisions of salaried probation officers or others, then one is bound to wonder what they are doing on the Bench at all; why the whole business is not transacted in the office.

In general, how high class they often were!

'Now you will be going to a nice Home in the country. You'll live amongst fields. You'll like that, won't you, Jimmy?'

The child looks puzzled. The country – fields? He may even be quite terrified by the strange breadth of such a prospect.

It is hard to sell East Enders an idea of country pleasures – mercifully, so it has often seemed to me. If you are condemned, really condemned by birth and circumstance, to spend your life in streets like some that I have known, surely it is better in the long run that you should find your happiness there? It seems absurd, even pointless, to foster discontent by trying to impose alien and illusory standards.

'It's boring, the country. There isn't anything to do, what I've seen of it,' a young girl once remarked to me, in sullen rebellion against a magistrate's view of where, perhaps, he might like to see his own girls grow up. She much preferred the Kingsland Road.

'You will be well looked after by the authorities,' another magistrate says, kindly, to a pair of little boys. 'But you can't go home yet. Your sister is much too young to look after you.'

'She *isn't* young!' The boys begin to sniff.

'Now now, don't cry ! Of *course* she is too young. Why, she's only fourteen, isn't she? She can't cook for you yet.'

'She *can* ! She cooks *smashing*!'

A touching championship and, given their standards, which are not necessarily the magistrates', a valuable one.

The children are led out weeping. I who was cook and house-keeper and everything to my own family at the age of twelve, stand stiffly to one side, torn apart by understanding for the children *and* by the genuine, kindly interest of those who hold the children's future in their hands.

From Marjory Todd, Ever Such a Nice Lady *(London: Victor Gollancz), 1964,*
pp. 159–164.

25 A history of the use of groups in probation work (2003)

Maurice Vanstone

This article ... traces the development of work with groups of probationers from the very early years of the probation service to the heyday of the treatment model, and in so doing sets out to demonstrate, firstly that this story is an important part of the epistemological history of the supervision of offenders in the community, and secondly that it provides a relevant context for understanding current developments within the Effective Practice Initiative. Moreover, it contends that groupwork, which for most of its life has existed on the margins of practice, latterly has moved to a position of dominant influence in the development of policy, research and practice; and that this shift has taken place against the backdrop of a change from a relatively benign to a challenging social and penal environment.

Pro-social moralising

The beginning of probation officers' engagement with groups of offenders is discernible during a period of probation history that can be characterised as the pro-social moralising phase. As Barr (1966) claims, there is a long history of probation officers employing groups such as youth groups as part of the helping process, and indeed, the practice was recognised and encouraged in the 1926 Probation Rules. Early on, prime sites for this activity were camps and probation homes, and an early example of what Barr terms 'a form of residential group work' can be seen in a description of Robin House in Croydon (Moore 1921). Moore describes an ordered regime premised on interdependence, mutual responsibility, practical activities and sport, coupled with an evening club held twice a week for former residents with the purpose of 'upraising and supporting' them upon their return to 'their miserable surroundings' (p. 281). It is stretching a point to describe this as groupwork in the sense that it is understood today, but the use of a group living together was clearly normative in intent. One historian (King 1969) touches upon this aspect of residential care. She describes the probation home as a 'controlled setting' in which the probationer in contact with other young people with similar problems 'can be helped to face the necessity and possibility of a change in his attitudes' (p. 112). Moreover, she argues that because of the close working relationship between wardens and liaison probation officers, homes and hostels 'provide an excellent setting for intensive group and individual therapy' (p. 113). However, the place of homes and hostels in the history of groupwork is a tenuous one because as Bochel (1976) points out, few wardens had any training let alone in group therapy. Moreover, the Morison Committee highlighted how this led to a lack of appreciation by wardens of the objectives of officers (p. 219): a point reinforced by Le Mesurier (1935), who makes no reference to group therapy. Rather she describes probation homes as places 'of training in citizenship where a boy or girl can receive guidance from an experienced house-father or house-mother during the difficult period of breaking from parental control and while self-discipline is still insufficient to ensure right use of liberty' (p. 172). According to her, Padcroft, probably the most high-profile home of its time, provided 'some training, good food, mild discipline and regular hours' (p. 192).

Until the 1950s, there is scant evidence of officers working therapeutically with groups, but the fact that there was an awareness of the power of group situations is evidenced by the club for the 'unclubbables' established by Miss Croker-King during the First World War (Page 1992). She used her Bethnal Green flat each Monday evening as a 'social reporting centre'. In her own description, the boys played games so that she could 'get to know the boys very much better' (Croker-King 1915). While there is no indication from her account that she used the group with any therapeutic intent, she was aware, nevertheless, of the value of observing and engaging with the boys in a more realistic milieu, and was therefore involved in working with groups. Another female officer also used the concept of a social club, this time for girls (Cary 1915). Her method with girls convicted of theft, soliciting, drunkenness and attempted suicide, was to put them into a shelter for two weeks where they would be cleaned up, fitted with clothes and found employment in service 'in a good class neighbourhood' (p. 102). She then used hired rooms at a local Church Institute in Chelsea where for two evenings a week the girls could 'gossip', play table tennis and dance, and she would 'try and lift their conversation, teach them to play fairly' and involve them in prayers and hymn singing, communion and confirmation, and talks from the vicar. She began with 15 and at the time of her journal article 30 attended. The whole tenor of her portrayal of this work is imbued with the moral guidance and religious persuasion so typical of early probation work, but it is placed within the context of a club, a well-acknowledged method of instilling normative values:

> Then in the club gatherings it is possible to get to know these girls in their relationships to others. To tone down the horseplay to which some are prone when excited, to try and lift conversation from silly innuendo and spiteful back-biting to a higher level. To teach them to play fairly and without loss of temper. Then, too, we never close without our little prayer gathering and hymn singing. It has been quite easy to trace the growth of reverence and self-control among members during these months.
>
> (p. 103)

An early version of Intermediate Treatment?

Some 35 years later, an officer in North London was using a similar approach to influence unclubbable boys 'to join the youth club, cadets or other clubs' (McLean 1951, p. 135). The Service, therefore, has long recognised the normative potential of groups, if only in terms of referral to the scouts, the boys brigade and such like. As early as early as 1914, Leeson (1914) had highlighted membership of the scouts or boys' clubs or Settlements as an important concern at the initial inquiry stage (p. 74). In discussing the issue of inappropriate compulsion, Le Mesurier (1935) refers to the case of a boy being ordered to attend the scouts as a condition of a probation order in the face of the fact that his father objected to it on principle. She throws doubt on such conditions, arguing 'a child who joins an association voluntarily is likely to become a better member of it than one compelled by an Order' (p. 116). Later, in 1947 Basil Henriques is said to have set up the Highdown Camp for boys from London's East End to encourage 'natural' relationships between probationers and officers (Page 1992, p. 201). In fact, Henriques's part in it was to offer the use of the camp site, and it was established by probation officers attached to the East London juvenile court (Pearce 1951). The first attempt was not particularly successful, and the only 'unifying experience [was] that of delinquency' (p. 15); moreover, according to Pearce, there were considerable problems in maintaining discipline amongst the 30 boys who attended. In subsequent camps, a programme of activities plus the division of the boys into small groups each with an experienced leader appears to have ensured a more constructive experience. The full programme is described as a mixture of sports, fishing, boating and daily prayers selected from the National Association of Boys' Clubs and the Boy Scouts' Camp books (p. 16).

In 1949, the Barge Boys' Club was set up using a sailing barge called the Normanhurst that was berthed at Wapping. Aimed at unclubbable boys it was run by Merfyn Turner as warden and it won several sailing cups (Page 1992, p. 214). It seems highly probable that such an initiative required support at a policy level, and Page provides some evidence of this. According to him, by this time 'group therapy and camps for probationers were perceived as new techniques in probation work, worthy of consideration' (p. 222). However, such support was not consistent. One of the respondents to a survey by Rimmer (1995) reported experimentation with groups in 1945. This involved eight girls aged ten and eleven years who lived in the same street and in a first offence had broken into their school. Because of pressure of work the female officer had them reporting together, and the group made dolls and talked 'about their home life and their plans for the future' (p. 183). According to this officer's recollection, groupwork was relatively unknown and her principal probation officer and a Home Office inspector reprimanded her for 'not carrying out her duties in the customary way' (p. 183).

As these examples suggest, groupwork was predominantly practical in its orientation; nevertheless, it was on the threshold of absorption into the 'science' of casework. The quest for professional status through the incorporation of psychological theories by some probation officers is evident in relation to one-to-one work from the late 1920s onwards, and in the 1930s in particular, the *Probation Journal* is full of contributions from psychiatrists and psychologists. This dimension to probation work occurs significantly later in work with groups because it is connected to developments in the application of group psychotherapy to offenders. However, it is an important part of the story of the treatment paradigm.

The treatment paradigm

By 1948 trainee probation officers were being taught social psychology, and a component of the course at the University of London's diploma course was 'Recent Advances in the Study of Groups'. This involved life in groups; the influence of groups on individuals; group therapy and training; leadership dominance; and the leaderless group. Furthermore, Home Office trainees in 1953 and 1954 were involved in the Arethusa Camp set up on the sports ground of the training ship Arethusa at Upton,

Rochester, Kent (Pratt and Ratcliffe 1954). That camp was 'an experiment in helping the individual to self-discipline and identification with society' (p. 61).

Combined with contact students had with the Tavistock Clinic, the Henderson Hospital and experimentation in borstals and prisons, some officers were beginning to be influenced by the group psychotherapy developed by psychiatrists during the Second World War (Barr 1966; Landers 1957). In his description of group therapy in Wormwood Scrubs, Landers (the Chief Medical Officer there) (1957) maintains that until the Second World War psychiatric treatment in the English prison medical service had concentrated on individual treatment, and that the end of the war 'ushered in an enthusiasm for reconstruction and expansion in the psychiatric field' (p. 328). The work of Doctor Moreno in New York on how dynamic interpersonal influences impact on individuals was, according to his historical account, widely read; and it 'stimulated the existing work of British army psychiatrists and psychoanalysts, in particular Bion, Foulkes, Main, Wilson and several others' (p. 328). Dr J. C. Mackwood pioneered group therapy in British prisons, and subsequently Maxwell Jones adopted Moreno's therapeutic community ideas in Belmont. The significance of this for probation practice lies in the fact that there is evidence (see below) that officers were directly involved in such work, and that work by Bion, for instance, was referred to in training. Landers claims that the group therapy at Wormwood Scrubs was unusual as far as it was 'an attempt to include modern methods of analytical psychology in group treatment'. Specifically, those methods were based on Jungian therapy and were deemed apposite because they 'blended well with early social attitudes and religious teaching of the majority of prisoners who form[ed] the groups' (p. 328).

While there was influence, it did not appear to have had any major impact on the service: groupwork remained 'a scarce commodity' (Brown 1992, p. 1), and there is a dearth of written material by officers until the 1960s, exceptions being papers on group reporting and hostel groupwork. Indeed, it is at the beginning of the 1960s that the first significant indications of the influence of psychotherapy emerge. In one of the first attempts to deal with the ideological and practical problems of, and reservations about, this new enterprise, Hawkins (1952) set down some principles applicable to working with groups. She defines the aims of group therapy as getting to know probationers better, providing the opportunity for alternative communication to words, and to 'help them adjust'. In her estimation, groups provide a more natural situation in which reaction and behaviour can be observed particularly for younger people and people of below average intelligence; adjustment can be 'regaining self-confidence' (p. 184). She counters the *contamination* criticism by arguing that it is preferable for the officer to be able to counter bad influence through 'his treatment of the group'; the *rewards for offending* criticism by suggesting that the group need not have 'tea parties, camps or outings'; and the *neglect of individuals in the group* danger by exhorting officers to keep the individual in focus. For her, however, the greatest danger is approaching groupwork with preconceived ideas, and she makes the interesting point that officers should allow the group to develop its own code of ethics in order to be able to see the probationers in their true light. While her motivation appears to retain a treatment orientation, nevertheless it suggests an accession to the power of the recipients of treatment less likely in one-to-one work of that period.

A further example of a different perspective on the potentially collaborative nature of the probation officer–probationer relationship is provided by Parker and Bilston (1959) who relate their experience of working with groups in the Social Rehabilitation

Unit at Belmont Hospital. According to their account, it gave them a rare opportunity to 'gain experience in group work with all types of people suffering from character disorders' (p. 36). Presumably, it was also one of the earliest examples of probation officers being involved in a therapeutic community in which approximately 30% of patients were probation clients some of whom were under treatment via s.4 Criminal Justice Act 1948. Their paper casts very little light on what the probation officers actually did; rather they inform the reader that probationers were not seen individually as far as possible but only in the daily groups. Those daily meetings were chaired by a patient and followed by groups of 25 facilitated by one doctor in which problems were openly and frankly discussed. In a way that was typical of the therapeutic community model the group had its own internal discipline system. Usually the probationers stayed for between four and six months before returning to the supervision of their home probation officers.

Although it is lacking in the detail of practice, this paper is of significance because it reveals an instance of officers working directly with other professionals in a high skill situation, it involves a treatment model premised on an early form of empowerment, and it begins an increase in attention to groupwork in the *Probation Journal*. As will be seen in Barr's survey, this does not reflect a large amount of groupwork activity but it is safe to assume that it does mark a significant increase.

Unsurprisingly, the articulation of probation officers' involvement in groups is couched in the social scientific language of therapeutic intervention, and in this sense, groupwork of this period adds to our understanding of the history of the treatment model. Thus, work with 14 to 15-year-old boys is 'a small experimental therapeutic group' (Bilston 1961, p. 150), and its justifications are the provision of mutual support; the opportunity to relate to peers as opposed to a single authority figure; the 'dilution of transference'; insight development; group interpretations; observation and study of personal relationships; and the formation of new diagnoses. Redolent of the descriptions of individual supervision, the jargon of psychoanalysis permeates Bilston's description; and this is no surprise because he draws on work by Maxwell Jones on community therapy, and Foulkes and Anthony on group psychotherapy. This time, elements of practice are detailed: each session lasts 45 minutes; the aim is to achieve 'some modification in social attitudes' rather than 'deep-rooted personality trait' changes (p. 151); the sessions are based on an accepting ethos and equality; role play is used, and the group members are described as participating in their own treatment. The latter dimension is a significant variation on the treatment model dominant in individual treatment at this time, and reflects, perhaps, the influence of the therapeutic community model. How far this was acknowledgement of the probationer as the expert on her or his problems is a moot point. The paper hit a nerve of sorts, and might be seen to prefigure one element of the later non-treatment paradigm (Bottoms and McWilliams 1979).

Two people were moved to write to the journal in response to the paper. The first letter by Bissel, who later was to contribute papers on the subject himself, raises concerns about groupwork being embarked upon to save time. He argues that it is a version of casework that demands high levels of skill and knowledge to be applied when a probationer's problems are not being addressed effectively by one-to-one supervision, and he concurs with Bilston's view that the work is rewarding and stimulating. The second by Bagshaw asserts that there is a 'lot of experimenting going on in the Service', and adds weight to the previous correspondent's concerns about using groups to save time. But, in the light of the fact that probation work 'is focused mainly on socialising the unsocial', he questions the appropriateness of group therapy, and expresses concern that group therapy will become a kind of indiscriminate treatment regardless of the needs of the client. Then he outlines briefly his own work with a group of boys aged 15 to 18 years: 'I experimented first and developed later such theory as I now have. On the whole, I think, the experiment worked, but it has led me to seek further knowledge about group dynamics', and it drew him also to the conclusion that 'group treatment' is appropriate for 'character-disordered clients'. He backs this by reference to Slavson, but puts in a plea for probation related research to help 'the process of creating effective groups'.

A mixture of encouragement and doubts about the adequacy of training characterises a view from the medical world (Waycott 1961). Alongside fulsome assessments of public confidence in probation, probation effectiveness and improved training and techniques, Waycott places less confidence in the adequacy of training for groupwork. He states that more and more work of this kind is being undertaken in borstals and prisons; and probation officers need to be skilful enough 'to permit and encourage uninhibited communication and, wherever necessary, to interpret to the group the unconscious origins of attitudes and feelings' (p. 167). Such abilities in giving insight, the key to rehabilitation and 'recovery', in Dr Waycott's opinion requires officers to undergo analysis.

Some accounts, however, suggest less ambitious aspirations, and perhaps more accurately reflect the reality of practice. Ashley (1962) professes the simple aim of encouraging a small group of adolescents to discuss any topics that they care to raise, alongside the hope that under his tutelage 'their various points of view [can] be brought together and clarified and common ground thereby discovered' (p. 6). The group of young men aged from 17 to 25 years (most being 17 to 19) had been convicted of theft, burglary, taking and driving and in one case buggery and gross indecency; on the face of it they appear an incongruous group with first offenders mixing with more persistent offenders, and with one sex offender amidst them. Significantly, they were all employed. Ashley reports the criterion for membership as a problem with making meaningful relationships with others of their own age. His database, and the fact that he kept it, is of interest: it encompasses age; offence; number of previous convictions; nature of employment; estimated intelligence; health; position in family; parents' marital status; clubs or groups attended; and supervision status. His function as leader is collating viewpoints and verbalising their feelings; and the focus of the discussions is initially topics such as the cinema and girlfriends, and later more personal matters, 'sex, parents, friendship, marriage, the significance of clothes, politics, swearing, Lady Chatterley, personal responsibility and a host of related topics' (p. 6). Devoid of any knowledge of groupwork techniques, Ashley nevertheless shows some insight into scapegoating, leadership and the roles people play in groups; and he does discuss the dangers of contamination, the discussion becoming 'too deep' for him to cope with, and the informality of the group undermining the authority of the probation setting. He does not present any concrete evidence of success, but instead reports that several members indicated that the experience was valuable; another's work record improved; and '[r]ather withdrawn boys came out of their shells, and two rather superficially extroverted boys listened to other people' (p. 7). There is no overt concern about reduction in offending.

Later he provides a very clear account of practice and its theoretical rationale and influences (Ashley 1965). The discussion groups held in Plymouth were used both as an alternative and supplement to one-to-one supervision. Initially for boys only, topics included, for example, offending and offenders, parents, politics, religion, films, work and 'women'. Insight into the style of leadership is provided in Ashley's description:

> My role was, as before, rather like that of a catalyst in a chemical process, in that I believe I enabled the reactions to go on between the group members without becoming directly involved in them, though I cannot press this analogy too far since a catalyst, at the end of the reaction, remains unchanged, and this was certainly not so in any case. I did, from time to time, attempt to bring together their viewpoints and verbalise their feelings when these seemed to be becoming obscure.
>
> (p. 7)

However, he was not averse to interpretation: in explaining their motives for wanting girls in the group, he suggests that one boy needed to confirm his heterosexuality and virility and had mother problems.

Unlike that of others, Ashley's practice was informed by theory and accounts of groupwork undertaken by psychiatrists with neurotic patients. He refers to Bion's theories about the basic assumption group, self-preservation and fight and flight; and he delineates Slavson's list of qualities in a leader that precludes the 'compulsive, the paranoid, the rigid or moralistic' (p. 8). His own theoretical premise for entering into what he describes as an experiment is the need in the adolescent to develop an identity in a peer group, and the opportunity the situation provides for the modification of personality and environment. He hopes that the group 'might act as a sounding board or testing-out area for both sexes in their attempts to establish their own sexuality and identity' (p. 8).

Interestingly, it is in descriptions of groupwork in the journal that work with females finds most (albeit still limited) expression. McCullough (1962) had been running discussion groups for five years when she described her work with a group of seven to nine girls in a hostel. She states specifically that her approach is the application of casework theory to groupwork, and she demonstrates knowledge about group dynamics and group process. The theoretical texture of her approach is more evident than Ashley's, in for instance, her description of closure:

> The meetings last from an hour to an hour and a half and I begin to close them after an hour. This piece of 'structure' I have introduced deliberately – in the delinquent authority situation people tend to want to prolong a meeting you are trying to close whereas faced with an indefinite period of time they seem more likely to resist with silence. (p. 36)

Initially, she attempts to be 'the passive, silent, enigmatic leader', her 'interpretations are rare and simple', but later the groups become 'leader-centred' (p. 37). She exploits tension within the group, and encourages the development of self-understanding through interactions with others; she deals with anti-authority feelings; she observes non-verbal communication; notes seating positions; and helps the group members to come to terms with authority through her to resolve feelings about their parents. While acknowledging the strain the work puts on the leader, she advocates the use of groups because it facilitates an enhanced relationship between worker and client in a situation that 'stimulates real life more closely than the one-to-one' relationship (p. 37). McCullough (1963) provides an illustration of a technical approach to working with groups that belies the description 'discussion group': it seems much closer to a psychotherapeutic model. In another description she refers to basic requirements, namely seven or eight group members, chairs placed in a circle, a constant position for the group leader and choice for the other group members. In work with five young female shoplifters another officer explains how she maintained the passive role despite anxiety, and that it was paramount to her main aim in running the group which was 'internalization of authority' (Freeguard 1964, p. 18).

The belief of both officers in the potency of the group situation is clear, and in an overview, Jones (1962), an academic outside the Service, endorses this aspect of groupwork. He questions the viability of the individual approach because of the fact that current trends in delinquent behaviour show the importance of the 'group-life of the young offender', and expose the inadequacy of the individual model's capacity to counter the pressures of the social environment. In his view, the current developments in group therapy suggest that it can be used in rehabilitation. Jones then delineates some of the conditions for effective treatment: delinquents must be placed in a cohesive group with 'law abiding' pressures so that there is sufficient stress for them 'to rub the rough corners off each other' (p. 60); the leader (as a modern caseworker) must work with the 'anxieties and guilt' of the client; there must be positive 'intra-group conflict'; and properly designed the group should be a 'kind of autonomous social system' that provides social experiences from which the group members can learn (p. 61). The leader's role is one of facilitator, interventionist and protector, and provider of insight; but Jones's sights are firmly fixed on correction with the officer 'helping a group of essentially normal young people to find satisfaction in law-abiding rather than law-breaking activity' (p. 62). The paper ends with a clarion call for officers to accept the need for training such as that being provided by the Tavistock Clinic and Leicester University. Three years later Jones (1965) reinforced his exhortations in a description of groupwork in Leicester. He confirms that the advantages evident for so long in group psychotherapy are also clear in the counselling, but he acknowledges the problems:

> [it] is this potency of the group as an arena for intense personal interchange which makes groupwork so stressful for both probation officer and probationer. Silence and depression in a group, and even absenteeism, are as often caused by a desire on the part of group members to escape from this forcing-house.
>
> (p. 91)

For Jones, the group situation presents a more realistic setting within which to impact on offending behaviour because it approximates to a real-life situation, and clearly, he provided encouragement to those of like mind within the Service.

Bissell (1964), for example, adds his support to these arguments. He confronts the uncertainties surrounding groupwork and challenges the notion that it is 'a scientific undertaking' exclusive to those who have been through analysis. Arguing from within the conceptual framework of the casework model, he juxtaposes the problems of individual work to the advantages of groupwork. Caseworkers, he asserts, are deeply involved in issues of authority, communication and conformity, and the one-to-one approach compounds problems surrounding those issues. The client is reacting to the officer on the basis of previous experience with authority figures; confusion about technical terms such as transference, clinical and therapeutic are exacerbated in one-to-one encounters; and 'each probation order passes from the challenging freshness of its early confrontations into the habitual and conforming to the tos and fros of normal supervision' (p. 179). Groupwork on the other hand offers the opportunity for clients to compare problems; safer, less threatening encounters; opportunities for observation of real-life situations; the experience for the client of 'a true experience of relating to others'; and exposure to a greater range of skills and experience (p. 180). It should, he continues, be used with those clients who do not relate well; groups who have committed offences together; the emotionally damaged; those needing practical advice about money and work; parents; and in matrimonial work. Two years earlier, in an account of a series of 'gang-group' meetings with eight boys aged 15 to 18 years who had been convicted of 'sexual orgies' with four girls on a recreation ground, he refers to a 'widespread interest' in groupwork (Bissell 1962). This appears to have been a form of sex education, and although he echoes tenets of psychoanalysis by stating that the primary function of groupwork is to reveal 'hostility and conflict' he alludes to a more client-centred approach:

> The P.O. deliberately refrained from pronouncing judgement, simply restating the facts and allowing them, from their own reconsiderations, to draw conclusions [...] at no time did the P.O. attempt to interpret to the individual concerned the issues involved in the problem he had introduced.
>
> (pp. 234–35)

Not all groupwork was aimed at probationers. In work that acknowledges the systems within which probationers live, Stanley and McCarthy (1965) focused on parents. Led by a senior probation officer who unlike his coworkers had experience of working with groups, the groups explored the problems of parenting. The value of the groups seemed to lie in the opportunity they presented to officers 'to discuss and make interpretations, to hypothesize in a safe and acceptable way under supervision'; and to increase their skills and understanding (p. 100).

These groups are typical of the groups described in the *Probation Journal* in the 1960s and into the 1970s, and they vary in conceptualisation from psychoanalysis and psychotherapy to more straightforward practical applications. Whitehouse (1965), for example, tells the story of his work with a group who committed offences together; it lacks aims, and is seen as an alternative to the artificiality of individual interviews. Each of the 24 sessions focused on a topic: the disparate list includes the law, leisure, churchgoing, the Kennedy assassination, girls, parents, the commercialisation of Christmas, and taxes and rates. A clue to his psychotherapeutic agenda lies in his comments that the content of the discussions often 'pointed towards personal problems and relationships' (p. 106), and that the group members 'want people with time to share with them the task of finding themselves' (p. 107). Coker and Sands (1970) use the 'therapeutic potential' of the group of men in their early 20s in a prison setting to address three areas of difficulty: motivation for offending; the problems of serving a sentence; and the difficulties of rehabilitation. The sessions focus mainly on individual personal problems, and it is judged that the members derived some 'therapeutic value'. A theoretical model is implied rather than stated overtly; thus, expressions of anger can be testing out or projection of guilt; and having no problems is interpreted as 'defensive denial'. Members are encouraged to focus on personal problems by the life story of the youngest; a shy man is helped to talk about his marital and gambling problems; another is helped with anxiety about release; and a withdrawn man is helped to see that he is carrying his anger with his father into other aspects of his life ...

Conclusion

By the mid-1970s a growing number of CQSW [Certificate of Qualification in Social Work] courses within which probation officers were trained, included some theoretical input on working with groups (Brown *et al.* 1982). In a half century, then, the practice of working with groups of probationers had been transformed from the use of activity as a vehicle for moral influence to a kind of collective casework treatment. As early as 1948 group therapy and the use of camps were seen by at least one service as new methods to be explored (Page 1992, p. 222), and in 1963 the Home Office invited Dr Pierre Turquet from the Tavistock Clinic to be chairman of a working party set up to explore the potential of groupwork in probation (Page 1992). So there was some official support for the approach, but its emergence as a viable form of intervention was primarily the result of individual innovation. This is not surprising because this part of its story occurred during a period when probation enjoyed relative immunity from critical scrutiny, innovative practice was unencumbered by demands to demonstrate effectiveness and officers enjoyed considerable autonomy. What the first part of this history also shows is that, albeit slower in its development, groupwork was as much a part of the history of the treatment model and the Service's aspiration to professional status within the criminal justice system as individual work. Moreover, the individual was as much the focus of the effort to influence and change, psychology was also the theoretical source for that effort, evaluation was as scarce, the needs of females were as much neglected, and probationers from ethnic minorities were as invisible.

However, there is reason to believe that within aspects of groupwork practice there were the seeds of the new paradigm to be advocated by Bottoms and McWilliams (1979). They argued that under the treatment model the concepts of 'choice' and 'client-self determination' become redundant, and that of 'respect for persons' is implicitly diminished. The post pro-social moralising groupwork described in this article undoubtedly embraced that treatment model and is vulnerable, therefore, to the same criticisms. However, the setting up of groups inevitably had an impact on the power relationship between probation officer(s) and group members; whether wittingly or not officers were involving themselves in much more complex power structures than is evident in one-to-one transactions. As Forsyth (1990) puts it: '[g]roups tend to be powerful rather than weak, active rather than passive, fluid rather than static, and catalysing rather than reifying' (p. 12). Whether intended or not, groups would at least have loosened constraints on choice and self-determination. Of course, simultaneously they would have opened the door to some group members constraining the choices, and inhibiting the degree of self-determination of other group members. The point is, however, that the control of the group leader(s) would have been diffused to some extent. More importantly, perhaps, those groups influenced by the therapeutic community model and its adherence to shared decision making, group consensus, trust and social learning made some tentative steps towards the model advocated by Bottoms and McWilliams. Indeed, it may be no coincidence that some of the early sites of the implementation of that model were social skills groups and day centres.

> From Maurice Vanstone, *'A history of the use of groups in probation work: Part 1 – from "clubbing the unclubbables" to therapeutic intervention'*, Howard Journal, *42(1), 2003, pp. 69–86.*

References

Ashley, P. D. (1962) 'Group work in the probation setting', *Probation* 10(1): 6–8.

Ashley, P. D. (1965) 'The development of a mixed group', *Probation* 11(3): 94–99.

Barr, H. (1966) *A Survey of Group Work in the Probation Service.* Home Office Research Study No. 9. London: HMSO.

Bilston, W. G. (1961) 'Group therapy in a probation setting', *Probation* 9: 150–51.

Bissell, D. (1962) 'Group work in the probation setting', *British Journal of Criminology* 2: 229–50.

Bissell, D. (1964) 'Group work in the probation setting', *Probation* 10(12): 178–81.

Bochel, D. (1976) *Probation and After-Care: Its Development in England & Wales.* Edinburgh: Scottish Academic Press.

Bottoms, A. E. and McWilliams, W. (1979) 'A non-treatment paradigm for probation practice', *British Journal of Social Work* 9(2): 159–202.

Brown, A. (1992) *Groupwork.* Aldershot: Ashgate.

Brown, A., Caddick, B., Gardner, M. and Sleeman, S. (1982) 'Towards a British model of groupwork', *British Journal of Social Work* 12: 587–603.

Cary, Mrs (1915) 'Social clubs for probationers; their needs and objects', *The National Association of Probation Officers* 6: 102–3.

Coker, J. D. and Sands, D. (1970) 'The use of small groups in prison', *Probation* 16(1): 71–75.

Croker-King, E. (1915) 'Juvenile probation', *The National Association of Probation Officers* 5: 66–67.

Forsyth, D. R. (1990) *Group Dynamics.* 2nd ed. Pacific Grove: Brooks/Cole.

Freeguard, M. (1964) 'Five girls against authority', *New Society* 72, 13 February, 18–20.

Hawkins, E. (1952) 'Some thoughts on the principles of group reporting', *Probation* 6(16): 184–85.

Jones, H. (1962) 'The group approach to treatment', *Howard Journal* 11: 58–63.

Jones, H. (1965) 'Groupwork: some general considerations', *Probation* 11(3): 91–94.

King, J. (1969) *The Probation and After-Care Service.* 3rd ed. London: Butterworth.

Landers, J. J. (1957) 'Group therapy in H M Prison, Wormwood Scrubs', *Howard Journal* 9: 328–42.

Le Mesurier, L. (1935) *A Handbook of Probation.* London: National Association of Probation Officers.

Leeson, C. (1914) *The Probation System.* London: P. S. King and Son.

McCullough, M. K. (1962) 'The practice of groupwork in a hostel', *Probation* 10(3): 36–37.

McCullough, M. K. (1963) 'Groupwork in probation', *New Society* 21, 9–11.

McLean, D. S. (1951) 'Club training: an experiment', *Probation* 6(12): 135.

Moore, H. K. (1921) 'Robin House Croydon', *National Association of Probation Officers* 15: 277–81.

Page, M. (1992) *Crime Fighters of London: A History of the Origins and Development of the London Probation Service 1876–1965.* London: Inner London Probation Service Development Trust.

Parker, K. and Bilston, W. G. (1959) 'Belmont: a therapeutic opportunity', *Probation* 9(3): 36–37.

Pearce, W. H. (1951) 'Probationers in camp', *Probation* 6(2): 15–16.

Pratt, E. G. and Ratcliffe, S. (1954) 'Arethusa Camp: notes and criticisms', *British Journal of Delinquency* 6(1): 53–61.

Rimmer, J. (1995) 'How social workers and probation officers in England conceived their roles and responsibilities in the 1930s and 1940s', in J. Schwieson and P. Pettit (Eds.) *Aspects of the History of British Social Work.* Reading: University of Reading.

Stanley, R. and McCarthy, J. (1965) 'Working with parents', *Probation* 11(3): 99–101.

Waycott, J. A. (1961) 'Probation officers and group therapy', *Probation* 9(11): 166–67.

Whitehouse, S. J. (1965) 'An educational process', *Probation* 11(3): 102–7.

26 The emergence of community service (1980)

Ken Pease

The specific origins of community service

... the intention here is to record briefly the reasons why community service orders emerged as an attractive penal option when they did, and the process by which community service orders were translated from an idea to a sentence.

Young (1978) has most interestingly analysed the immediate background to the community service innovation. He argues that the received wisdom of the late 1960s was that prison was intrinsically harmful to the individual and of dubious value in deterring the convicted criminal from repeating his crimes. Young writes:

> By the time of the Criminal Justice Act 1972, a majority of Parliament seemed to have fully rejected imprisonment, certainly as a reformative tool and to a lesser extent as an individual deterrent.
>
> (p. 41)

This recognition combined with humanitarian motives to look with distaste upon the overcrowding of prisons and the drain on the public purse which these prisons represented. However, all this does not suggest why new alternatives to prison should be developed in preference to the greater use of existing alternatives. Young suggests that in the late 1940s and early 1950s:

> the apparatus of the Welfare State was directed towards those features of society which formed the basis of popular theories of crime causation: poverty, poor housing conditions, lack of educational and employment opportunities and class conflict. Thus it was not unreasonable to expect a reduction in the crime rate.
>
> (pp. 48–49)

The crime statistics of the era flattered only to deceive later, and by consequence of the increase in recorded crime, dissatisfaction with extant non-custodial sentences increased.

Given an underlying desire to reduce the use of imprisonment, and given also the desire to introduce new, rather than to develop existing non-custodial sentences, it was predictable that the new non-custodial sentences be harsh rather than lenient. Other bandwagons on the roll at the time were concern for the needs of the victim and the desire for penal sanctions to serve to reconcile victim and offender. Community service orders, as recommended and introduced were the result of the confluence of these factors.

The process whereby community service developed into an available sentence has six distinct stages, which are as follows:

- The Wootton Report
- The Home Office Working Group Report on Community Service by Offenders
- The Criminal Justice Bill
- Passage of the Bill through Parliament
- The Criminal Justice Act
- Preparations in individual areas

The rest of this chapter will be subdivided in this way.

The Wootton Report

In general the Sub-Committee of the Advisory Council on the Penal System which produced this report (Home Office 1970) was concerned with 'the average run of minor offenders' and besides the primary task of devising alternatives to custodial sentences, it considered the need for a wider range of non-custodial powers for dealing with those offenders who would not, in any case, be deprived of liberty. Some of the proposals, including community service, were recommendations for experiment. Chapter Three of the Report outlines the ideas and recommendations of the Sub-Committee on Community Service by offenders, and the scheme is described as 'the most ambitious proposal of this Report'. The most attractive feature of community service to the Sub-Committee was the opportunity it gave for constructive activity in the form of personal service to the community and the possibility of a changed outlook on the part of the offender. It was hoped that offenders would come to see it in this light, and not as wholly negative and punitive. To be maximally reformative, it was argued, community service should be done with volunteer non-offenders although the Report does not rule out offender-only groups. The Sub-Committee envisaged the scheme as being dependent upon voluntary agencies and local authorities supplying tasks. Community service tasks would be such that if they were not done by unpaid labour, they would not be done at all (for the naïveté of this position see Pease and West 1977).

The type of offender suitable for community service was not detailed in the Report, although the Sub-Committee held the view that it might be good for young offenders as volunteers are often young people. It expressed the view that community service would be inappropriate for trivial offences and should not be restricted to offences punishable by imprisonment, being suitable for some cases of theft, taking away of vehicles, serious traffic offences, malicious damage and minor assault. Besides being seen as an alternative to a short custodial sentence, it should be considered as an alternative to a fine and for fine default, or to stiffen probation where an additional obligation other than a fine is desired. The probation and after-care service was recommended as appropriate to administer the scheme. The reasons for this given by the Sub-Committee were that the service is locally based, with an extensive network of local offices. It exists to serve the court and it carries out a wide range of duties connected with the tradition of working through the use of general community resources. Representatives of the probation service giving evidence to the Sub-Committee agreed that it would be the appropriate organisation to administer the community service scheme.

Much thought was given to the kind of court order suitable for this type of penalty. The choice was between the extension and/or modification of the existing probation order or a new separate order for community service alone. The Sub-Committee considered that there were arguments in favour of either alternative and decided that courts could exercise their discretion in a choice between the alternatives.

It recognised that new legislation was essential for the implementation of its proposals on community service and added that there should be pilot schemes to test the feasibility of the whole idea of community service. The status of the schemes and standardisation between areas could be achieved by allowing courts to make orders for community service only when they were notified that appropriate facilities were available, thus ensuring control appropriate for each local scheme.

The Home Office Working Group Report on Community Service by Offenders

The terms of reference of the Home Office Working Group (1971) were:

> To consider in the light of the recommendations of the Advisory Council on the Penal System, the practical issues raised by a scheme of community service by offenders and what form of arrangements seems best suited to give effect to it.

The Group contacted certain voluntary organisations and local authorities who indicated that a wide range of tasks might be made available. The Group endorsed the Wootton Report's view of the probation service as the appropriate agency to administer the community service scheme. It further thought that only one kind of court order, a community service order, should be available to courts rather than the two types recommended by the Wootton Report. Justification for this was that community service was a new and independent concept in the treatment of offenders and as such warranted an independent position in the court's sanctions. The Group also endorsed the view that community service as a sanction for fine default would be difficult to combine with community service as conceived for other offenders.

The Working Group took the view that the court should not have power to make a community service order without first consulting a social inquiry report. It further emphasised that the order should be consensual, i.e. that the offender's consent to it would be necessary. Community service should be limited to those offences which were imprisonable for adults and that the number of hours to be worked should lie between a maximum of 120 and a minimum of 40, at least during the experimental period. The time allowed for completion of an order might vary between six months for an order of 40 hours and one year for an order of 120 hours. The Group's suggestions about breach procedures and administration of the scheme through a sub-committee of the probation and after-care committee led directly to legislation.

What is perhaps particularly interesting about the Working Group's deliberations was its conviction that probation casework and community service should be separate and distinct forms of treatment and that any casework deemed necessary should be given on a voluntary basis.

To sum up, the Working Group made suggestions for the implementation of the proposal of community service by the Wootton Report and amended the recommendations of the Wootton Report in the following ways:

- Offenders should only be eligible for community service if they were convicted of an offence punishable by imprisonment.
- The imposition of community service for fine defaulters was not endorsed.
- The Working Group favoured a community service order but not a probation order with a condition to perform community service work.
- The Group was more specific than Wootton about the length of time which should be allowed for completion of a community service order, suggesting orders between 40 and 120 hours in length.

The Criminal Justice Bill

In the Criminal Justice Bill of 1971 the Working Group's conclusions formed the basis for the provisions on community service. The major differences between the Group's conclusions and the provisions of the Bill were as follows:

- The maximum number of hours which the courts could impose was increased from 120 to 240. The 40 hours minimum was not changed. The time allowed for completion of an order of any length was set at one year.
- The Bill empowers community service for fine default. The Government expressed the view that community service has a part to play in the search for effective alternatives to imprisonment in such cases. (This provision has not to date been activated. See West (1978) for a powerful statement of why it never should be.)
- The financial arrangement for the administration of the scheme was to be the same as for probation and after-care committees and therefore attract the same 50 per cent (now 80 per cent) Home Office grant. The Government however accepted the suggestion that the scheme should be wholly financed by the central authority during the experimental period and an amendment to that effect was tabled later.
- The Bill allows community service to be ordered as a penalty for breach of a probation order. (This clause has not to date been activated.)

Passage of the Bill through Parliament

The Bill was introduced in the now familiar context of rising crime and overcrowded prisons. Community service was seen as an alternative to imprisonment for minor, non-violent offences, the overall aim being that offenders whose crimes did not include violence should, as far as possible, be punished by means other than imprisonment. The Home Secretary said, with what Young (1978) regards as political rhetoric:

> Those who need not be sent to prison, those who are not guilty of violent crimes, should be punished in other ways in the interests of relieving the strain on the prison service and in the interests of the community. We propose a number of new ideas, some of them experimental, which will, I hope, be fruitful in the long run. The first is community service. I was attracted from the start to the idea that people who have committed minor offences would be better occupied doing a service to their fellow citizens than sitting alongside others in a crowded jail.
>
> (H.C.Deb. Vol.826 col.972)

The Opposition gave approval to community service with the proviso that reparation to the community did not involve ignoring the individuality of offenders, that menial tasks be not given to offenders, and that offenders have contact with non-offenders while carrying out their sentences. Debates on the community service provision were marked by general good-will and enthusiasm. The general view appeared to be that community service was a means of giving self-respect to the offender and breeding a sense of social responsibility, as well as providing work which is of value to the community at large.

In Committee, many questions were asked about the scheme. It was revealed that probation and after-care committees in five areas had been asked to implement the scheme during the experimental period: Durham, Inner London, Kent, Nottingham and South-West Lancashire. It was said that those areas represent a wide geographical spread, comprised both urban and rural areas and contained varying numbers of existing voluntary bodies. Two divisions occurred in Committee. The first involved an amendment whereby the work an offender is instructed to perform should be suitable having regard to his training, experience, capabilities and mental condition. It was argued that such an addition to the Bill was unnecessary since the designated probation officer would consider these things anyway. Moreover, it provided an excellent means for offenders to argue themselves out of doing the work assigned to them. The amendment was defeated. The second division concerned financing arrangements. Amendments were proposed which had the effect of transferring financial responsibility for the new provisions of the Bill, including community service, onto central government permanently rather than for the period of the experiment. The amendment was defeated.

During the Third Reading of the Bill, some discussion centred upon the maximum and minimum number of hours available to courts. An amendment was proposed specifying no lower limit and a maximum of 120 hours. It was argued that a 40 hour minimum may be too much for some crimes and a high maximum might encourage a high drop-out rate. The amendment was not carried.

In the House of Lords, Baroness Wootton said she was glad that it was intended that offenders should work alongside volunteers. She had no strong views on the 240 hours upper limit but hoped that this longer sentence might involve some kind of weekend residential treatment. In Committee she proposed an amendment which was supported. This ensured that offenders were given an explanation in court of what community service entailed and what was expected from them, what would be the consequences of breach and that the court had power to review the order at the request of the designated probation officer or the offender himself.

As a result of its passage through both Houses, the Act differed from the Bill in ways relevant to community service as follows:

- Baroness Wootton's amendment had the effect of requiring the court to explain to the offender the purpose, effect and requirements of the order; also the consequences of breach, and the possibility of reviewing the order on application of either the designated probation officer or the offender.
- The probation and after-care committee was given the responsibility of appointing members of the community service committee, and the number of co-opted members was required to be no more than half the committee membership.

- A Government amendment allowed the Crown Court to impose a fine for breach of a community service order without prejudice to the continuation of the order. Such power had already been given to magistrates' courts in the Bill.
- Two financial provisions were made: the first gave members of the community service committees the same status for travelling and subsistence allowances as members of the probation and after-committee to lay the burden of expenses on an offender's original community service committee if he does community service in that committee's area.
- A small but important amendment removed the 50 per cent limit of government grant for probation committees' expenditure under the Act. This ensured total government provision for community service for the experimental period.

The Criminal Justice Act 1972

The Act received the Royal Assent on 26 October 1972. In December letters were sent by the Home Office to the relevant courts in Inner London, Nottinghamshire and Shropshire, notifying them that community service orders would be available to those courts from 1 January 1973.

Preparations in individual areas

As early as April 1972, the chief probation officers of the experimental areas were discussing working arrangements for community service with the Home Office. Besides the five areas mentioned originally, the Shropshire Probation and After-Care Service also became involved because of the possibility that Shropshire might be added to the experiment in order to take advantage of the special work opportunities at the Ironbridge Gorge Museum.

Preparatory work in all the experimental areas had remarkably similar characteristics. Firstly and obviously, the appointment of a senior probation officer to oversee the scheme was put in hand, with the exception of Inner London, where the appropriate rank was thought to be assistant chief probation officer. In all areas there were preliminary contacts with agencies which could provide work and the establishment of the community service committee. Areas also felt the need to do studies of the likely uptake of community service orders in their areas. The final enterprise shared by all areas was the dissemination, by document and by word of mouth, to courts and probation officers, of information about the way in which the scheme would operate.

Besides the common features of preparation, individual areas took distinctive lines. For example, in Nottingham the Assistant Secretary of the Nottingham Council of Social Service was appointed to work part-time with the senior probation officer responsible for community service with the intention of providing contacts with community agencies in the area. It is perhaps fair to say that Nottingham came to be well known among the experimental community service areas for its emphasis on individual placements hopefully leading to offender change, and Young (1978) suggests this emphasis had influence on areas introducing schemes after the experimental period. Inner London, on the other hand, appears at the very early stage of the scheme to give much more accent to impersonal tasks, usually of a manual nature, than any of the other experimental areas. This led to fierce criticism of the scheme by Radical Alternatives to Prison (Uglow 1973). However, what should be borne in mind when considering the 'chain-gang' image of the Inner London service is that this area stressed community service as an alternative to custody more clearly and consistently than any other of the areas. For example, this is evident in the Inner London attempt to estimate the number of offenders who might be sentenced to community service. It was found that from the Metropolitan Police District, roughly 5,000 men and women aged 17 and over were sentenced to imprisonment for indictable offences in 1970. The inclusion of non-indictable offences, excluding drunkenness, would raise the figure to over 6,000. A rough estimate of the number of those people living in Inner London was between 2,000 and 3,500. Of these, 1,500 to 2,500 would have sentences of up to one year. The Working Group believed that the number sentenced to community service *from among this group* would depend on the readiness of the courts to use the new measure.

Perhaps the most distinctive characteristic of the Kent scheme was its emphasis from the earliest days on an administrative centre for the scheme where offenders in the early stages of their orders would be assessed while at work. Further, while the area is a relatively small one, one cannot fail to be impressed at the speed and efficiency with which Kent proceeded in the early days. The document entitled *Guidelines to the Community Service Section of the Criminal Justice Act 1972* produced by Kent Probation and After-Care Service (1972) is perhaps the most exhaustive description of policy, practice, accountability, supervision, social inquiry reports and research existing at that time. It also contained an appendix listing confirmed and possible tasks and refusals of work. The trade union experience of the second organiser of the scheme also proved particularly valuable.

Perhaps the greatest difficulty facing the organiser in South-West Lancashire was the characteristically high rate of unemployment in that area. The organiser had to be very circumspect about the work to be performed on community service. Any project involving work for local authorities where there was a possibility of paid employment would come under particularly close scrutiny from local trade union representatives. As the community service organiser expressed it to the writer, 'If you tell anybody in Liverpool that the snowdrops are out, they want to know whether the dockers will be out next'.

The Durham community service organiser found himself in a particularly difficult position because he was in the latter part of 1972 being phased out of work as a welfare officer in Durham prison. Thus a good deal of the preparatory work in that area was and had to be undertaken by the assistant chief probation officer. Even when in December 1972 the community service organiser was able to devote the whole of his time to community service, he was in temporary accommodation until February 1973. It is perhaps fair to say that the distinctive characteristics of the Durham scheme were less obvious in the preparatory stages than the distinctive characteristics of any other area. However, in the early stages of the experimental period, perhaps the most remarkable feature of the scheme was the uniquely high proportion of individual offenders placed with work groups of non-offender volunteers (see Pease *et al.* 1975).

Shropshire was unique among the experimental areas in that it had a single work placement, with the Ironbridge Gorge Museum. It was this which led Shropshire to be interested in being included in the experimental phase of the scheme. It was not initially one of the areas which the Home Office had contacted with a view to supplying a scheme. A full-time supervisor was employed to supervise offenders on community service at the Ironbridge Gorge Museum. The post was financed by the Cadbury Trust.

With hindsight it is evident that the single placement model operating in Shropshire was not a success. Subsequently the Shropshire scheme has diversified to include many placements outside the Museum. In fact, at the time of writing, I understand that no work is being done by community service offenders in the Ironbridge Gorge Museum. However, it should be stressed that the experiment was well worth trying. The model operated by Shropshire, and their initiative in establishing a scheme at all, contributed greatly to the lessons learned during the experimental period.

The first orders

The first community service orders were made in January 1973 in Nottingham, London and Shropshire; in February in South-West Lancashire; in March in County Durham, and in April in Kent. These orders represent a landmark in English penal history. They concluded hectic months of preparation and triggered hectic months of operation. They were first examples of an order whose popularity quickly proved itself and which on present trends may constitute the bulk of the work of the probation service coming through the courts in the 1990s (Pease 1978). The writer and his colleagues in the Home Office Research Unit at that time were uniquely well placed to witness the translation of the scheme from the broad outlines of the Wootton Committee to the practical details involved in getting numbers of men to specified places to be supervised by named people at the right time and in full knowledge of the consequences of what would happen if they failed to appear. The early community service organisers can be counted among the most able people in the probation and after-care service whose success as innovators is attested by the rate of development of the order. The notion that the wages of sin is work may be as old as the hills, but its successful translation to a viable penal alternative by the first generation of community service organisers stands to their credit. Doubts about the order may now, entirely justifiably, be raised. Nonetheless, given the context in which the experimental scheme organisers were working, theirs is an achievement worth recording.

From Ken Pease, 'A brief history of community service', in K. Pease and W. McWilliams (eds.), Community Service By Order *(Edinburgh: Scottish Academic Press), 1980, pp. 5–13.*

References

Home Office (1970) *Non-Custodial and Semi-Custodial Penalties* (Report of the Advisory Council on the Penal System, chairman: Baroness Wootton). London: HMSO.

Home Office Working Group on Community Service by Offenders (1971) *Report*. London: Home Office.

Kent Probation and After-Care Service (1972) *Guidelines to the Community Service Section of the Criminal Justice Act 1972*. Maidstone: Kent Probation and After-Care Service.

Pease, K. (1978) 'Community service and the tariff', *Criminal Law Review*, May, 269–75.

Pease, K., Durkin, P., Earnshaw, I., Payne, D. and Thorpe, J. (1975) *Community Service Orders*. Home Office Research Studies 29. London: HMSO.

Pease, K. and West, J.S.M. (1977) 'Community service orders: the way ahead'. *Home Office Research Bulletin* No.4. London: Home Office Research Unit.

Uglow, S. (1973) *Community Service Orders in Inner London – An Exercise in Illusion*. London: Radical Alternatives to Prison.

West, J.S.M. (1978) 'Community service for fine defaulters', *Justice of the Peace*, 142: 425–28.

Young, W. (1978) *Community Service Orders: the development of a new penal measure.* University of Cambridge, unpublished PhD thesis.

27 The future of the probation service

A view from government (1989)

David Faulkner

1. This talk is about the job which the probation service has to do; how that job is changing, and how the pressures, expectations, and demands on the probation service are changing with it; and the issues which the probation service has to face in doing its job as we approach the 1990s.

2. I would like to make three preliminary points about the context of probation work and about the nature of the probation service itself. First, the probation service is a criminal justice service. It is one of the five criminal justice services, the others being the police, the courts (perhaps more an institution than a service), the Prison Service and, a newcomer to the scene, the Crown Prosecution Service. All five services are about crime and what to do about it – preventing or reducing it, dealing with its consequences and with those who commit it, and mitigating its effect. The different tasks fall on different services in different ways, and at the operational level they are fairly clearly and rightly distinguished; but at a more general level the services all share or ought to share a common purpose and common objectives, even though their character is very different. Each can frustrate any of the others, and action or lack of action by any of them can affect the workload and success of each of the others, so they must understand one another and they must work together. The point is obvious, but it does not easily happen.

3. Second, crime is a serious matter. It can cause serious distress and sometimes injury to its victims, and bring fear to many others who may never experience crime or even be seriously at risk. It fills the postbags of Ministers and Members of Parliament, the newspapers and news bulletins. It causes many people to live restricted and sometimes unhappy lives. It contributes to economic decline and hinders economic revival. It destroys trust. Suspicion and fear can begin to undermine our concern for the freedom of the individual, the protection of suspects and the humane treatment of offenders, and to give undue emphasis to the more repressive aspects of criminal justice. The probation service itself can be undervalued or even appear irrelevant.

4. Third, the probation service is acknowledged to be a service having its roots in social work, as having a social work base. It has rightly moved on from the days when it saw itself as a social work agency: it is much more than that today. But it is not always clear what a social work base does and does not mean. Professor Bottoms has referred to five key social work values. These are respect for persons, care for persons, hope for the future, community cohesion and social justice. Having a social work base certainly implies that all these are important

elements in the work which the probation service has to do, and in the service's approach to it. But these values are not unique to the probation service: policemen, and even civil servants, can subscribe to them as well. We may hear more of what a social work base means for the probation service later in the conference. What I hope it does not mean is an exclusive commitment to the interests of the so-called 'client'; an assumption that the individual social worker/offender relationship is so much at the centre of the service's work that everything else is secondary to it; or worst of all a belief that probation officers are somehow the 'nice guys' of the system, balancing or even correcting the repressive work of the other services.

5. This brings me to the nature of the job the probation service has to do, and the specific tasks which it has to perform. The service's job is set out in the 1984 Statement of National Objectives and Priorities. Basically it is to supervise offenders in the community, both under direct court orders and after release from custody; to provide reports to courts with a view, but not exclusively with a view, to the making of such orders; the work which the service does in prisons (still not all that clearly defined); and largely self-contained but certainly not to be overlooked, the service's civil work. In tackling this job I would say that the service needs to do, and be equipped to do, the following things:

    i.   To influence human behaviour, either directly through counselling and supervision, and increasingly, by opening up opportunities for offenders and situations in which they are motivated to take advantage of those opportunities – to see that there can be more to life than thieving;

    ii. To analyse offenders' circumstances and situations in ways which indicate the sort of influences and opportunities which are likely to have the most positive effect; and

    iii. To mobilise resources and construct programmes through which these influences and opportunities can be realised.

6. The service must also be able to persuade the courts to use these programmes; and to convince the wider public that they are effective and worthwhile in reducing the likelihood of future offending, in providing adequate protection to the public, and as a proportionate response to the gravity of the offence.

7. It is at this point that we come to questions mainly of control, to which I believe the service is now largely reconciled, and punishment, where I know there are still problems. But the service cannot escape the fact that people expect offenders to be punished, that that is what they expect the courts to do and what the courts expect to do themselves. But it is important to be clear what punishment means for this purpose. We are not talking about punishment as a separate activity or a set of measures which are somehow added on to the elements of a statutory order and which are intended to be degrading or humiliating for their own sake. That is not the intention of community sentences either. Punishment in this context is based on the proposition that any restriction falls to be determined by a court taking into account what is required by the nature and seriousness of the offence and the interests of the public. For those restrictions on liberty which are applied in the community, the probation service will be called upon, as it does now, to administer which is in effect a form of punishment.

8.   But there is another point about punishment which must not be overlooked. Punishment must not mean rejection. When it takes the form of imprisonment it may mean temporary or sometimes prolonged removal, but even with imprisonment the offender should again become a full member of the community with all its resources and opportunities available to him on release – although we know only too well how difficult that can be. When it takes place in the community the links if they exist need not be broken, and if they do not, or if they are faulty – as too often happens – the task of constructing them can begin at once. Punishment in the community has been criticised as likely to reinforce society's instincts for repression and rejection, and I share the implied concern that we must not create an isolated, criminalised and potentially hostile underclass: but I would hope that these instincts are driven more by crime and fear of crime – as I said earlier – than they are by hatred for individual offenders. There is research evidence to support this view. If properly applied, the notion of punishment in the community should help to reinforce the community's sense of responsibility for its misfits and failures.

9.   What is expected of the service has been building up steadily over the last 25 years, and there is no need to repeat here the growth in the range of activities with which it has been involved. Our perception of what this meant, or what it should have meant, for the service has unfortunately been confused by practical, political and intellectual preoccupations with subjects like prison overcrowding, and the development and status of so-called 'alternatives to custody'; disillusion with the treatment model and the IMPACT [Intensive Matched Probation and After Care Treatment] project; and the service's own internal arguments about care and control. Questions of management and internal organisation, performance, output and service delivery were not seriously addressed during the 70s and early 80s.

10.   The service has worked at these matters since then, but the transformation from a social work agency to a criminal justice service with a social work base must be completed if the service is to do what is now expected of it, especially in the context of the Green Paper on Punishment, Custody and the Community and the Action Plan, and in the Carlisle report on Parole. It may be surprising, but it is very significant, and I hope for the probation service encouraging, that expectations of the service have reached this point at a time of rising crime and fear of crime, of increasing politicisation of the crime problem, and when pressures to move in a more repressive direction might have been strongest. These pressures do, however, make it all the more important for the service to demonstrate its credibility and commitment to dealing with the crime problem, and not to undermine its credibility with too much abstract argument about care and control, or about the nature of punishment.

11.   Three conclusions so far. First, a social work base is a valuable part of the equipment which enables the probation service to do the job which is expected of it, but it is not by itself sufficient for that purpose. It is no longer enough, if it ever was, to think of the probation officer's job simply, or even mainly, in terms of advising, assisting and befriending, and of a casework relationship with an individual offender. If that ever was an adequate description, it has changed out of all recognition today. Second, the service must operate as a service with the leadership, organisation, communications and loyalties which

that implies. It is professional but not a profession. It exists to perform a range of specific functions, with specified objectives and targets for the courts, the public and offenders, in that order. And third, the service – and behind the service the Home Office and the rest of this system – must set ourselves the explicit task of reducing reoffending. I know success cannot be guaranteed and I acknowledge the service's concern that it should not be 'set up to fail'. But if the service and the Home Office are to be taken seriously, we must commit ourselves to the attempt, however difficult it may be.

12.   This brings me to the range of issues with which the probation service has to deal in the late 1980s and with which it will have to deal in the 1990s. Several of them have been raised by recent reports of the Audit Commission and the National Audit Office.

13.   I would mention first leadership, and the relationship between leadership and management. I pay tribute both to the progress which ACOP [Association of Chief Officers of Probation] have made in recent years in developing a national forum and national policies for chief officers, and to NAPO's [National Association of Probation Officers] contribution to the development of professional practice. But I am not clear where in the service one should look for an authoritative vision of its future, or an ability to say with confidence what makes a good probation officer or a good probation service. ACOP? Central Council [of Probation Committees]? Individual respected chief officers? Individual probation committees? NAPO? The Inspectorate? The courts? Or Home Office Ministers and civil servants? Perhaps all of them in different ways, but the messages they give are fragmented, confused, and sometimes contradictory. The service still needs a more coherent sense of its own objectives and purpose, which are not the same as its identity and values with which it has perhaps been too preoccupied in the past. How to achieve it – individual example, reorganisation, or internal arguments and dialogue – is one of the questions which I hope this conference will discuss.

14.   Next, management. The service has come a long way fast, and is in some ways feeling the strain, but there is still more to be done in developing coherent management systems which include the setting of both corporate and individual objectives, measuring their achievement, identifying target groups, guaranteeing the delivery of services and maintaining their quality, holding individuals to account, and handling the service's increasingly complicated external relationships. There are questions about the size and structure of senior management teams; and perhaps even more importantly, but so far still often neglected, about the functions, tasks and accountability of Senior Probation Officers. Their managerial role is crucial – not so much in terms of exercising authority or giving detailed instructions to their teams, but in the sense of fixing priorities and arranging dispositions so as to achieve the maximum results from a team's collective effort, and the maximum contribution to the service's overall objectives.

15.   Effective management needs information: research and statistics are crucial. Reasonable information now exists on activity – numbers of reports, caseload and so forth – but still not much on effectiveness and use of resources. The Inspectorate has made a great deal of progress over the last year in using the available statistics to prepare performance indicators. Important tasks are now

to seek measures of value for money and effectiveness in social inquiry reports; to measure the use of manpower on different activities through a re-run of the national activity recording survey, and the wider costings involved in FMIS [Financial Management Information System]; research and monitoring of the use and effectiveness of hostels and day centres; and to put ethnic monitoring in place.

16.   On research there is a general problem which is partly a reflection of the service's own history: lack of consistency and too much reliance on individual initiative. Many area services are doing very good work in this area, but many seem still not to have any clear focus for the work of their research and information officers. There is a great deal of scope for comparative work by local services, but for this purpose they need uniform and consistent aims and methods. And the quality of the research itself is not always good enough to support the results – promising or disappointing – which are sometimes drawn from it. I would like to see a more systematic programme for commissioning research, for publishing the results and for identifying and applying the lessons to be drawn from it.

17.   My next point is about internal structure and organisation. The typical pattern of court-based teams, area teams, special teams for hostels, community service and day centres, and a scatter of specialists for drugs, alcohol and other problems, often looks fragmented and confusing to an outsider. Martin Davies' research at the University of East Anglia shows that almost half of all probation officers are now employed in specialist functions. You hear of day centre teams being out-of-touch with officers holding probation orders, and both being out-of-touch with opportunities and facilities available in the wider community, and about court teams being out-of-touch with everything. Offenders are passed from hand to hand according to the situation or the problem of the moment. And it seems to be left very much to the almost random judgement of individual probation officers to decide how much of the range of service facilities is considered for individual offenders. Some offenders, especially if they are black or female, or worse still both, get neglected altogether. A central message of the Green Paper is that an offender must be thought of as a whole person, both at the stage of the social inquiry report and during the period of the order, and not as a collection of needs and characteristics to be fitted into whatever facilities or activities the service thinks it would like to provide.

18.   Next, and related to that point – the social inquiry report itself. I think we all recognise that the 1986 circular has resulted in a lot of people, including a disproportionate number of young blacks, going into prison without social inquiry reports, often after pleading not guilty. There are continuing complaints from judges and sometimes magistrates about what they call unrealistic recommendations, and the language in which reports are written. This is a big subject which I do not have time to explore in detail in this talk, but it urgently needs attention and perhaps radical fresh thought. I am glad that ACOP have it in hand.

19.   There are also questions not just about the organisation or structure of particular services, but also about what I will call the professional structure of the service as a whole. They are about the significance and need for the CQSW [Certificate of Qualification in Social Work] qualification in its present form,

and about the service's flexibility or lack of it in making use of staff with different qualifications or with none. Professor Davies' work in the University of East Anglia has some important things to say to us here; Dr Coleman's report on sponsored training, probably to be published later this month, will start to open up further debate on some of these issues. Training for senior management is already being developed, for example with the new course at the London Business School. But there are many important questions still to be addressed.

20. A point related to that is the range of tasks and services which the probation service should perform or provide itself, and those which it should coordinate but leave to be provided by others. There are some which are unquestionably for the probation service itself – reports to court and the actual supervision of orders, including judgements about breach proceedings. The service exercises coercive powers affecting the liberty of individuals, and they must be exercised by a statutory service within a proper structure of public accountability. There are other functions which are clearly not for the probation service – providing education classes or running industrial workshops are examples. But between these there are facilities like accommodation schemes, employment services, drug or alcohol groups, or even day centres and community service, where it is not obvious that the probation service should be the direct or only provider, and others perhaps in the voluntary or commercial sectors may have better skills and more experience. The probation service must resist the temptation to think because a task is there to be done, it has to do it itself: there is a danger of dissipating its skills and overloading its management, and a more relevant skill and a higher priority for the probation service may be in assembling packages, co-ordinating services provided by others and seeing that collectively they achieve the right results.

21. The final point in this list is about the service's external relationships. The importance of these relationships – with the courts, the Crown Prosecution Service, the voluntary sector, the legal profession, the prison service, the police, local authorities, the media and even the Home Office – is well recognised and often discussed, together with questions about the role of probation committees and liaison committees, and the demands which they make on senior management. What we do not yet have is a collective sense of how these relationships are best organised and managed – what is best done nationally, at regional or circuit level, at service or at local level, by whom, with whom and in what structure of working relationships. We do not want to set up elaborate new bureaucratic procedures, but we do need a better understanding between those involved of what each service, or institution requires and can legitimately expect of others, and better structures and patterns of communication for establishing that understanding. The regular circuit liaison meetings, and the meetings between judges and chief officers to discuss social inquiry reports and the Green Paper have provided a good start. And of course, the issue arises just as much for the other services and the voluntary sector as it does for the probation service itself.

22. These are some of the issues which I see as important for the probation service as we prepare to enter the 1990s. Questions about cash limits, 100 per cent funding, relationships with local authorities, and the role of probation

committees are in a sense secondary to them. The answers will all depend on what view we take of the service's job and its performance, and changes should only be made if they can be expected to improve that performance. Changes of this kind will certainly be on the agenda for the future legislation when the time comes, but I see the immediate agenda as the issues I have indicated in this talk. Some of them are already the subject of discussion within the service, and between the service and the Home Office, and important changes have already been made or are already in hand; in other instances the discussion is only just beginning.

23.   But we have an interesting and exciting time ahead of us.

From David Faulkner, 'The future of the probation service: a view from government', in R. Shaw and K. Haines (eds.), The Criminal Justice System: a central role for the probation service *(Cambridge: Institute of Criminology), 1989, pp. 1–8.*

Part C

Theoretical models

Introduction

As the probation service evolved from its beginnings as a court missionary service towards its role as a primary criminal justice agency, various attempts were made to theorise its fundamental nature. These models and their implications for practice were of interest both for their similarities as well as for their differences. This section explores the variety of models that have been proposed.

We begin, a little provocatively, with Geoffrey Parkinson's infamous article (Reading 28) in which he avows the essential significance of simple, practical help. His claim, 'I give them money', unleashed a storm of protest which culminated in his suspension pending the result of an inspection of his records for evidence of profligate generosity towards the individuals on his caseload. He was reinstated when inappropriate recourse to the public purse (in those days, the probation service's aptly named 'poor box' was precisely that – poor) was not discovered.

What had Parkinson, a long-serving probation officer, done to attract such controversy? In his article, describing himself cheerfully as 'a shallow caseworker', he complains of contemporary 'contempt for money' within the social work profession. He defends his professed practice of giving money, not merely because of the poverty which dogs probationers' lives, but on the pragmatic grounds that, unlike the psychological language of social casework, this is a form of communication which offenders find accessible, meaningful and helpful. Although it was his claim to provide material inducements for his probationers' co-operation that aroused managerial interest in his case files, Parkinson was in fact offering a carefully considered critique of the casework practice of the time. Thus, he offended not only administrators and managers, but also practitioners whose faith in social casework (by which was usually understood intervention rooted in psychodynamic theory) held firm. Moreover, he caused professional outrage by undermining a claim to professional status based on possession of skills unique in the criminal justice system. Ultimately, he wreaked a happy revenge for his treatment: he subsequently became known for his 'Tailgunner Parkinson' series of short, sardonic anecdotes and commentaries on the foibles of the probation and other welfare services, together with their colourful clientele, which appeared, as did his original inflammatory article, in *New Society*.

The radical school of social work enjoyed a following in the probation service during the late 1970s and early 1980s, in the collective subgroup of the professional association commonly known as NAG (NAPO Action Group). Within the service, NAG members were generally admired for their ideals, commitment to clients and their parties at the annual professional conference, which were approved as by far the liveliest. This is not to say that their views and approach met with universal endorsement, although probation officers were generally united by concern for the social plight of many offenders. Stan Cohen's examination of the radical school (Reading 29) is an impressive publication, not only for the acuity of his critique, but for the naked honesty of his exposure of the theoretical and practical weaknesses of a movement with which he himself was associated. It is also of interest today, because we can now review his observations in the light of Hilary Walker and Bill Beaumont's exposition of the radical model applied to probation (Reading 34), which was published six years later.

Although Walker and Beaumont attempt to offer a socialist model that recognises the realities of probation officers' position within an agency of the state, it is questionable whether they are able to address the root concerns expressed by Cohen. Insofar as they achieve the realism to which they lay claim, this is perhaps bought at the expense of any truly distinctive feature of a socialist practice. Walker and Beaumont's efforts illuminate the backdrop to the sympathies of many politically conventional probation officers: their 'real world' socialist practice bears a close resemblance to the principles of good social work. Nevertheless, theirs is a brave attempt to map out a future for the probation service that seeks to challenge and improve the social exclusion endured by offenders and many of their victims. Even as they wrote, the tide was already turning against such a quest as the probation service struggled to reassert its authority as a professional agency in the aftermath of the collapse of the rehabilitative ideal. Walker and Beaumont correctly foresee the approach and impact of a 'coercive tilt' – a climate in which social change seems less viable as a way forward than social control.

Prior to Walker and Beaumont's radical vision, during the late 1970s, there was a flurry of attempts to devise a role for the probation service – some more theoretically sophisticated than others. Taken together, all share certain characteristics: an acceptance of the death of rehabilitation as the probation service's *raison d'être*; an attempt to preserve probation's social work identity; and a proposal to separate an offender's consent to supervision from his or her acceptance of help. Authors take different approaches to the conundrum of preserving rehabilitation while simultaneously admitting its defeat at the hands of penal evaluators. Robert Harris, from an academic viewpoint (Reading 30), and Malcolm Bryant and his colleagues from the perspective of practitioners (Reading 31), argue for the separation of social work from the punishment and control aspects of probation, focusing on organisational arrangements for providing informal access to support within a formal framework of punishment. Tony Bottoms and Bill McWilliams make a similar case (Reading 33), but further propose re-defining the rehabilitative ingredient in the relationship between probation officers and offenders in terms of collaborative help rather than diagnosis and treatment. Presciently, they also develop arguments for probation service involvement in diversion from custodial sentences and social crime prevention, although these elements of their model attracted little interest at the time.

David Haxby (Reading 32) adopts a different approach to the problem. His vision of the probation service as a community correctional service was greeted with alarm by many officers who saw their agency being defined as a prison without walls. Yet, the collation of an extract from his lengthy book has posed a surprising challenge since, although it is well remembered as a confrontation with the orthodoxy of the probation service as a social work agency, the theoretical argument for community corrections is in fact relatively undeveloped. Indeed, reviewed with hindsight, Haxby's exposition seems little more than an extensive analysis of the range of social work interventions already available to the courts, combined with encouragement for their wider and more imaginative use.

The remaining readings in this section are somewhat different. Dating from the late 1980s, by which time the probation service had, for better or worse, adapted to the loss of rehabilitation, the writers present further attempts to model probation, based on the results of this endeavour. Bill McWilliams' final article in his quartet of essays on the history of change in the probation service (Reading 35) summarises the key elements in the theoretical models it had embraced over time. From the phase of special pleading by court missionaries, through the period in which a medical approach of diagnosis and treatment was favoured by an emergent profession, McWilliams arrives at a more fragmented organisational ideology framed by pragmatic expedience. Here, in the late 1980s, he sees the relegation of recognition of the individual offender as the primary focus of activity in favour of a policy drive to reduce custodial sentencing. Notably, McWilliams seems disappointed with the results of this move in the direction of a key element of the non-treatment paradigm that he had earlier devised with Tony Bottoms.

In fact, a vein of disillusionment with the alternatives to custody movement was emerging during the late 1980s. In his article (Reading 36), Rob Canton complains that a movement entitled 'alternatives to custody' essentially accepts custody as the penal norm; moreover, the justice model that superseded the rehabilitation ideal, while successful in constraining the excesses of the treatment model, achieves little in assuaging sentencers' thirst for punishment. Canton argues that the probation service should not be shy in acknowledging the relatively slight impact on crime achieved by any of the conventional penal measures, while emphasising that non-custodial measures avoid the harms of custody. Two years later, Judith Rumgay (Reading 37) seeks to reaffirm the necessity of explicitly embracing rehabilitation as the probation service's overarching goal.

By the mid-1990s, however, debate had moved on again. Mike Nellis (Reading 38) explores the implications of redefining the probation service as a community justice agency. Again, dissatisfaction with the service's adjustments to its predicament spurs Nellis to develop his proposals. However, the result in this case is the first open rejection of social work as the professional base for the service's work and an attempt to locate its ideology within the framework of contemporary criminal justice concerns: anti-custodialism; restorative justice; and community safety.

The article by Ken Pease (Reading 39) is unique in this section, since it constituted the first Bill McWilliams Memorial Lecture. It therefore alludes to and builds upon McWilliams' body of work in an attempt to illuminate a conceptualisation of probation based upon his ideas. In this sense, it is less driven by the urgency of the probation service's perceived predicament than by the author's intellectual curiosity. Nevertheless, Pease's argument for a service dedicated to the reduction of the harm caused by crime offers an attractive route out of debates which had become entrenched in the balance between care and control, rehabilitation and punishment in the service's interactions with offenders. Moreover, it provides a theoretical justification for an involvement with the victims of crime which harmonises, rather than competes with its concern for offenders.

Finally, Judith Rumgay's examination of partnership (Reading 40) is included here because it attempts to theorise the relationship between the probation service and its partners, in particular by contrasting this with the contemporaneous emphasis on effective practice through cognitive behavioural treatment programmes. The current and increasing extent of involvement of non-statutory agencies in the delivery of supervision suggests that this should be a vital element in any future effort to model the probation service's activity.

Readers might remark on the absence of a contribution that posits a model of the probation service as an agency of public protection. This is simply because this recent innovation in the evolution of the probation service's identity has not to date been adequately theorised. Indeed, its suitability and capacity for such a role has been assumed in policy far more than it has been tested in theory. But theorising has not disappeared although it is more likely to be confined to academics than practitioners these days. The main approach seems to be a neo-rehabilitationism that is related to desistance theories (see, for example, McNeill 2006; Raynor and Robinson 2009; Ward and Maruna 2007). However, it is not at all obvious that such a theoretical approach, in developing implications for practice, would distinguish the probation service as a unique agency in offender supervision. And given the current plans for contestability, this may be what is needed.

The nature of the probation service's enterprise that emanates from assertions by government is, it seems, now taken as given, even though this varies with the political mood. A profession that previously sought pro-actively to define itself and to sustain debate about its unique enterprise currently responds reactively to the prescriptions of the centre.

References

McNeill, F. (2006) 'A desistance paradigm for offender management', *Criminology and Criminal Justice* 6(1): 39–62.

Raynor, P. and Robinson, G. (2009) *Rehabilitation, Crime and Justice*. Basingstoke: Palgrave Macmillan.

Ward, T. and Maruna, S. (2007) *Rehabilitation: beyond the risk paradigm.* London: Routledge.

28 I give them money (1970)

Geoffrey Parkinson

While I was visiting Pentonville prison, Ronald White, aged 24, with twelve court appearances behind him, called at the probation office and asked to see me. I have known him for a number of years and watched him grope his way from gas meter theft to the impressive delinquent heights of robbery with violence. He was now a voluntary after-care case and my aim was to maintain some sort of coarse, casual contact until perhaps age and an overdose of prison made him more benign.

On being told I was away Ronald asked to see somebody else, which meant the duty officer. That day the duty officer was an experienced worker, specially trained in psychoanalytically orientated casework and familiar with Ronald White and his history. What went on between them is not clear but my colleague left me a brief note giving his impression of the interview: 'Ronald White called at the office today. I remembered him because he was under my supervision once in Hampshire. The interview started by his asking for financial help but it soon became apparent that he had more fundamental worries; his marriage has just recently broken down after only six months and I felt he had quite deep feelings about this. I am sure he would welcome seeing you again and you may be able to help him work through his difficulties in this area.'

A week later I saw Ronald. 'What's all this about your marriage?' I asked. 'Oh that ain't much. I didn't want to marry her anyway', he answered casually. 'When you saw my colleague he felt you were pretty fed up.' 'Yeah well, it was like this, I was a bit short of money and I thought you might loan me a dollar or two. When they told me you were out I saw Mr T. I was once under his supervision. I told him what I wanted and he started to ask me some questions about myself and when I told him about my marriage he got very interested and wanted to know all about it. I really didn't want to go into it but he seemed pretty keen. He is a nice bloke and after all the interest he was taking, I didn't feel I could end our talk by saying "I have not come here about my marriage, I want some money", because it might have seemed ungrateful for all the trouble he was taking with my problems. So anyway, I decided I would have to get the money from somewhere else and I thanked him and pushed off.'

There is nothing very momentous about these two interviews. I told Ronald that I felt he could cope with his marriage breakdown, that he would be a bloody fool if he allowed it to lead him into more crime, and I then gave him ten shillings, a letter to the Ministry of Social Security, and asked him to keep in contact. I think it is highly likely that he will, while I give him cash and boost his fragile ego.

This little incident is too fragmentary for any deep analysis but it illustrates two methods of approach towards clients that arise quite frequently in the probation service and in other casework agencies. My colleague, in classical style, got past the 'presenting problem' to a fundamental area of Ronald's life – his broken marriage. Ronald at an earlier interview had assessed me as 'a hard sod, good for a soft touch'. I am, as one of my colleagues aptly described it, a shallow caseworker.

In the late 1950s and early 1960s deep casework appeared to offer almost magical possibilities for the treatment of clients. Crude assumptions about human motivation were being swept away in our social services. When I had entered the probation service in 1954, reports to courts were little better than police antecedents with a dash of Patience Strong sentimentality. They were mostly based on the 'pull yourself together lad' theory of life. Many advanced voluntary social work agencies looked unhappily at the work of the probation officer. The good Family Welfare Association supervisor of these days could almost be induced into a fit if one said one had given a client money without an analysis in depth of his personality and problems. There was a biblical zeal about the contempt for money shown by those early caseworkers of the New School. Old charity organisations like the Family Welfare Association were particularly vigorous in the pursuit of the pure air of casework, since their histories were usually stained with chronic almsgiving. They had decided money solved nothing, it was merely the symptom of the disease. What was needed was an understanding of the fundamental problems. Giving money made the client dependent on the social worker; giving insights into the cause of his moneyless state, on the other hand, gave the client independence. The tradition nostalgically lingers on. Good casework is associated with insight, limited casework with giving money.

I gave Ronald money. I give most of my clients money. I give it because it is the one thing they all accept joyfully; it makes them feel valuable; it breaks down, if only for a moment, their sense of isolation. It makes them believe that I may solve their problems, it buys their cooperation and their friendship which invariably they would not sell for any other price. It shows my concern in the only way they understand. I give money with all the difficulties and dangers of dependence it can produce because I feel I have precious little choice within the context of the situation my clients offer me. There is one further reason: 'conning' money out of the probation officer is perhaps a continuation of the client's delinquent activities, but performed within an accepting environment; it is one of the first steps away from actual stealing and as such is to be welcomed.

My clients cannot accept insight; even if they understood what I was trying to get at, the experience would be too claustrophobic for them. They have no 'reasonable ego', they are emotionally frozen, non-verbal and unmotivated towards change, except perhaps when afraid of the punishments the court may impose on them. Helping my clients with cash is like giving a frozen man brandy before asking him to recount the adventures that caused his condition. The sum does not have to be large. I hand out perhaps £2 a week. But the fund available to the Inner London Probation Service, from which I draw this money, can be vital in opening up relations with a client.

On all this there would, I think, be relatively little disagreement nowadays, just some mild regrets and the hope expressed that gradually the client would be able to use the casework situation more constructively. At one time, however, it was the subject of great and terrible casework war, with all the theorists cursing cash.

The theorists in social work have been a great worry to practising caseworkers. Whilst initially helping, they thereafter probably delayed many agencies in delineating their function, except perhaps by means of protest. For its part, probation had a love affair with psychoanalysis. Many of the noted social theorists of recent times have plagiarised their insights from the works of Freud and Melanie Klein and hoped that we would match our methods with their ideas. Carmelite casework, its nods and grunts and germ-free insights, was offered to clients in mouldy little offices all over England. We weren't too worried if the clients didn't like it. The theorists had explained that quite easily as 'resistance'. What mattered was the technique, radiating from its centre, the Tavistock Clinic. It took us years to realise that 'the truth' did not always set our clients free.

The probation service is crammed full of dedicated officers who have an accumulation of complex, though partial and half-digested, psychoanalytic theories and insights into human behaviour. Well-meaningly they blunder their way through their caseloads, hoping it all makes some sort of sense. Some may even abandon native intelligence to will-o'-the-wisp theorisings about unconscious motivation. It may even make sense when read in their records and receive high commendation from supervising officers who share the same culture of half-formed theorisings. Yet the central question is, 'What does it mean to the client?' There are a large number of Ronald Whites on our caseload, not so eloquent but probably more shrewd. Time and time again the situation repeats itself. The caseworker, desperately looking for a client who will talk about problems, finds one who is willing to meet the demand. Then off goes the client, followed in hot pursuit by the caseworker, feathers fly in hours of deepening insight until at last the probation officer returns to his case conference exhausted but happy and the client returns unaffected to his crimes. Caseworkers are continually bewildered by the continuing delinquencies of their best clients!

Visiting a prisoner at Springhill some years ago I noticed that he had once been on probation. I asked him how he got on. 'Fine', he said, 'it was very helpful. We used to talk all about my problems, I was going through a difficult time with my wife.' I said it couldn't have been all that helpful since he had ended up doing more bird. 'No, no', he replied without showing any signs of regret, 'it was valuable, but you see my probation officer never told me that if I ever got into trouble again I would end up in a place like this.' His remark may have been naive, but its message for treatment is profound.

Marriage problems, for example, may excite and interest a caseworker, but if the client is before him for criminal activity the focus ought to be on the effect a broken marriage may have on the possibilities of further delinquent breakdowns rather than on the marriage as such. There can be no assumption that the client will make the necessary links between matrimonial disharmony and criminality, if links there are. He must be told and told again.

In so far as they have a theoretical knowledge about life, our clients resort to old saws and maxims of the 'it takes two to make a quarrel' variety. These sayings are the client's intellectual contribution to the casework situation and are patronisingly, though not necessarily unsympathetically, assessed by the worker. What the worker may not realise is that invariably he is offering the same sort of patterned stereotyped material back to the client, only it is middle class, more 'psychological' and better presented. The client has learnt a fragmented philosophy which hasn't much bearing on his behaviour. The social worker has a psychology more sophisticated but often almost as rigid, which has little to do with the client's real life, or indeed the social worker's real life, in many cases.

In the future we may have to face in our society not the ignorant inflexibility of much social welfare, but a new insightful inflexibility that comes from knowing 'the truth'. Local welfare authorities, members of the clergy, marriage guidance councillors and a variety of social work agencies, are already frequently offering, with rigid hygienic zeal, something of the medicine that has been so ardently advocated in the name of insight, progress and reform. ...

An ex-colleague of mine, back from the United States, said social workers are more and more leaving their clients to their secretaries to deal with and devoting themselves to case conferences about clients. The joke, I think, is serious. The flight from the client is probably on the increase; the gap between casework theory and practice is not as great now as it once was, but it is still leaving students ill-prepared for what they have to meet in the field and encourages some to withdraw to the shelter of administration, social work training or research.

This situation has revealed itself most clearly in the super-ego, middle class preoccupations of many social inquiry reports and casework records, and a curious idealisation of clients' problems and attitudes. With amazing speed, feelings of guilt are discovered in clients and trifling gestures are interpreted as the hallmarks of subtle reparation: 'His father was once a criminal; now he feels a bad side in himself and is ashamed', one recent report said of a young man who was clearly going through a mild attack of remand-home remorse.

Middle class assumptions are legion. Descriptions of home surroundings frequently convey more about the social worker's emotional background than about that of his client. This is particularly true in assessments of the delinquent's mother. Officers are always discovering that she is 'over-protective' and 'over-anxious' and while these descriptions may be justified at the time of the court appearance, the way the mother has dealt with her anxieties in her day-to-day life by behaviour may be far more damaging to her children: her arid emotional life and self-preoccupation, her extended absences to enjoy the social life of the pub or the launderette, her obsession with bingo or, more frequent than is generally believed, her promiscuous sexuality.

The idealisation of clients' motives is seen in assumptions about their preoccupation with relationships, most characteristically illustrated by my colleague's contact with Ronald White. This particular client's anxiety about his wrecked marriage was a luxury that only the caseworker could really afford. Ronald's narcissism put forward his real priorities. He could stand a broken marriage, but not half an hour without cigarettes. The Family Welfare Association was, I felt at one time, the most pathetic example of the tug of war that can exist between the client's narcissistic preoccupations and the worker's relationship preoccupations. Clients tried to talk about the gas bill, workers tried to talk about the client's mother. Perceptive clients got the gas bill paid by talking about mother.

A great danger in the field of social work is the rigidity of established concepts among those who see themselves as belonging to the casework elite. In their ranks there are many with that curious instinct which allows life to be seen only through a filter of words and concepts. It is understandable that many social scientists and social workers, having gained new knowledge at great personal sacrifice, will not relinquish or amend it willingly. Flexibility seems a thin return for deserting impressive theoretical superstructures, particularly as it leaves a great gulf of uncertainty which feels, even though it is not, unprofessional.

From Geoffrey Parkinson, 'I give them money', New Society,
February 1970, pp. 220–221.

29 It's all right for you to talk

Political and sociological manifestos for social work action (1975)

Stanley Cohen

I would like in this essay to deal with certain aspects of the relationship between sociology (the sociology of deviance in particular) and social-work practice. The aspects I have chosen have been suggested quite specifically by my personal experience and that of my colleagues in our contacts with various groups of social workers, especially those in probation, community work, youth work and residential institutions. In these contacts – as we trail around the country, serving on study groups, examining on training courses, or simply talking to captive audiences at the inevitable weekend conference by the sea – the most familiar reaction we encounter is encapsulated in the phrase (often quite explicitly used): 'it's all right for you to talk'. The implication is that, however interesting, amusing, correct and even morally uplifting our message might be, it is ultimately a self-indulgent intellectual exercise, a luxury which cannot be afforded by anyone tied down by the day-to-day demands of a social-work job. This reaction is especially pronounced when our message is supposed to be 'radical' and our audience includes self-professed 'radical social workers'.

I am still surprised, even on occasion hurt, by this reaction because I continue to think that those areas of sociology which interest me should be relevant to social workers and also because I self-consciously avoid presenting ideas in a style that could be pejoratively termed 'academic'. Yet the negative reaction still comes up, either in an extreme form which is accompanied by manifest hostility and defensiveness ('we've got to do your dirty work', 'what right have you got to stand up there and judge us?', 'you've got no idea about our problems'), or in a weaker version which allows the validity of the sociologist's claims but is genuinely perplexed about their practical implications.

Our responses to such attacks are invariably feeble. We either resort to a simple-minded role theory – poor social workers are trapped in their professional roles and cannot detach themselves enough to see what is to be done – or else the only slightly less simple-minded political variant of this theory couched in the rhetoric of 'working in the system', 'tools of the state', 'bourgeois individualism'. Such responses are not only patronizing, not only intellectually inadequate but also downright useless to most social workers. They only serve as self-fulfilling prophecies for the 'it's all right for you to talk' position and further reinforce the social worker's feeling that we don't take their problems seriously ...

The promise of deviancy theory

In the last decade or so a liberal view of deviancy percolated through into social work under such rubrics as interactionism or labelling theory. The basic premises of this perspective are simple enough and involve little more than recognizing the deviants' right to present their own definition of the situation, a humanization of their supposed process of becoming deviant and a sensitivity to the undesirable and stigmatizing effects of intervention by control agents. ...

It is of course true that labelling theory doesn't get directly at the roots of inequality and human misery, but it seems absurd to write off all the many reforms that are consequent on its position. We find the following in *Case Con*, the 'revolutionary magazine for social workers' which has enjoyed such a wide success and which I will take as representing the radical position in the United Kingdom: 'This means that labelling theory really goes no further than being able to reform the ways we deal with deviance, so that we don't create deviant "careers" and don't amplify social problems' (Cannan, 1970). As radicals we would obviously want to go much further, but would it really not be a significant social change if we could reform our 'ways of dealing with deviants'? The indictment of labelling theory is not so much that it goes no further than this, but that it hasn't been clear about how to get this far ...

... The worker in a residential institution who reads Goffman wants to know how institutionalization can be dealt with; the community worker hearing about deviancy amplification is interested in how this spiral can be checked; the caseworker wants to operate without further stigmatizing his clients. The reason why these matters have not been spelt out ... is because of the laissez-faire, hands-off attitude behind the new theories. As Young (1975) correctly states: 'New deviancy theorists have been stridently non-interventionist.' They have often done little more than ask the middle-level managers of the control apparatus to leave deviants alone.

That this defect is not simply an oversight which will eventually be dealt with is shown by the recent attempt by Edwin Schur (1973), a successful apologist for the theory, to dignify non-interventionism as a preferred solution to certain policy matters. ...

Radical non-intervention: the liberal answer?

... [Radical non-intervention's] assumptions are clearly based on the new deviancy theory, incorporating concepts derived from labelling and interactionism. The stress is on stigma, stereotyping and societal reaction, together with a somewhat more radical reformist position than in the older liberal version. Delinquents are seen not as having special personality characteristics nor even being subject to socio-economic constraints. They suffer, rather, from contingencies: they are the ones who have been processed through the juvenile justice system. ...

The focal point of attention thus switches from the individual delinquent to his interaction with the social-control system, and policy is directed towards changing the system: there should be voluntary treatment, decriminalization (particularly in regard to crime without victims), a narrowing of the scope of juvenile court jurisdiction and its increased formalization rather than relaxation towards a welfare model. There should also be an unmasking of euphemism: an end to the use of rhetoric of treatment and rehabilitation in juvenile courts and correctional institutions to negate or disguise the reality of punishment. ...

... [T]he non-intervention model implies a policy to increase societal accommodation to youthful diversity, with the basic injunction: leave the kids alone wherever possible. Even further in the background, lies a vague commitment to radical social change in structure and values rather than piecemeal social reform. It must be said that model is very appealing ... Social workers should endorse any programme which would take them away from the seductive powers of the treatment model. They would also be well advised to support non-interventionist tactics particularly in those areas where the legal system has extended too far and conversely where the legal model has been eroded by moralistic busybodies under the banner of welfare. They should certainly take up Schur's call for an end to euphemism and should stop trying to resolve the contradictions between their dual commitment to welfare and control by pretending that the control element does not exist. But beyond this, the non-interventionist argument peters out: it is painfully weak theoretically and it offers very few prescriptions to resolve day-to-day problems. Specifically:

1. Schur correctly notes how the sociological model has undermined the notion of individual pathology, but he suggests an alternative which rejects all notions of constraints. He complains, for example, that '... the reform outlook to a large extent rests on the notion of structured variations in the freedom of individuals to shape their own destinies' (1973, 83). Now no social worker can get through an hour of his round without being aware of precisely such 'structured variations' and it would be absurd to expect him to be convinced of a policy which suggests otherwise. ... but again the defect of 'neo-antideterminism' is not so much that it is incorrect – it has been a crucial antidote to the over-determinist legacy of positivist criminology – but that its implications for practice have not been spelt out. It matters a great deal theoretically to show, say, that a female shoplifter acted intentionally and with some degree of choice rather than from some obscure condition called kleptomania or menopausal depression, but *how* this may matter to the probation officer dealing with her is not at all apparent.

2. When it comes to the argument about the over-reach of criminal law the non-interventionist case rests primarily on the pragmatic grounds of the law's sheer inefficiency in controlling certain areas of undesirable behaviour. When principles are cited, they tend to be little more than a restatement of traditional Wolfenden-report rhetoric about the existence of realms of private morality which are not the business of the law. Now both pragmatic and principled arguments are all very well in areas of normative dissensus and crime without victims. It is clearly desirable for any self-respecting social worker to devote energy – through pressure-group politics and campaigns – to change certain laws in such areas as drugs, abortion, homosexuality, prostitution rather than simply to mop up the casualties of the law. But there are two inbuilt limitations to the decriminalization argument: the first is a self-admitted one that only a small proportion of offences are suitable candidates for this treatment. The vast bulk of offences – property crime – plus other obvious areas such as personal violence will remain criminal. This is not to say anything of the other areas of social work activity – in regard to poverty, homelessness, mental health – where the criminal law has little significance.

    The second limitation is less often admitted. Once an area of deviance stops being criminalized, it still has to be policed by some other form of social control. ... Now it might be preferable for all sorts of reasons to treat, say, drug-taking within a medical or welfare rather than a criminal model, but someone still has to man the control machine.

3.   This leads to the third problem with non-interventionism from a social worker's point of view. … It may be quite in order to talk of organizations producing deviants and to say that 'from an organizational standpoint the problem of delinquency is to some extent one of management' (Schur, 1973, 130). … But … my concern is that the preferred system of management … remains obscure.

4.   Finally, there is a more disturbing aspect of the non-interventionist case to be considered: its argument against treatment and reform rests, quite correctly, on a fundamental questioning of the taken-for-granted assumption that delinquency is a problem about which something must be done. But to combine this question with the actual evidence that current delinquent policies are unworkable and even harmful, in order to justify a theory of accommodation to diversity, is empty without some guidelines for establishing just how this accommodation is to take place. Moreover, although some aspects of delinquency problem – and indeed many other social problems as defined by the powerful for social workers to deal with – can wither away, the structural features of society which both create real problems for certain members and then exacerbate them unfairly, will not. Non-intervention can become a euphemism for benign neglect, for simply doing nothing.

… What [the new deviancy theory] implied – although not perhaps as unambiguously as some critics suggest – was an image of the naturally good man who was interfered with by state busybodies. If he was left alone, his problems would disappear. … [C]learly, this picture cannot be held against the day-to-day experience of social workers. The man threatening to drop his baby from a window ledge, the alcoholic suffering from withdrawal symptoms, the pregnant schoolgirl kicked out of her home, are all doing things which call for help. The help (or control) hasn't yet come to interfere with them or change their natures. …

… With the rise of militant and aggressive deviant groups, some of the new theorists … started (and some have never stopped) celebrating such deviance and claiming it as evidence of a new found political consciousness. Virtually any anti-social activity became elevated in this way. …

Client co-option: a revolutionary manifesto?

Social workers themselves were correct in suspecting that uncomfortably mixed up with the liberalism of deviancy theory was a degree of romanticism. They saw the deviant co-opted as hero in a series of revolutionary struggles as deviancy theorists rushed around to find in the actions and – with greater difficulty – the words of football hooligans, vandals, rapists, bank robbers and kidnappers signs of militancy and class consciousness. In some quarters prisoners were seen as being in the vanguard of the revolutionary struggle, homosexuals as precursors of the destruction of the bourgeois capitalist family, and schizophrenics as visionary prophets of man's alienation. …

… Having rejected the legacy of positivism, having conveniently (or so they thought) disposed of the notion of deviant as victim, ['hip Marxists'] now urged sociologists to join hands with their subjects and social workers with their clients in a joyous storming of the Bastille of social control. The hip Marxists could sit in their universities and conferences while the social workers … would spread the message to the people. Deviants of the world unite, you have nothing to lose but your stigmas.

Unfortunately not only was this approach excessively romantic in conception but – like the radical non-intervention model – carried remarkably few prescriptions that could actually be followed by social workers in any practical sense. Indeed this supposed radical alternative to traditional social work was often extremely evasive about what sort of gains the clients could expect from their new social workers. ...

... The *Case Con* type of programme seems to consist of three separate strands which I will call *theory, self-help* and *client-co-option*. The first strand stresses the need for a total socio-political theory (obviously Marxism, but some are a little coy about the label) which would inform action. It is continually emphasized that part of being a radical social worker is to have such an ongoing analysis to provide a critique of the welfare state and a guard against not being conned by the system. ... This strand of the programme ... is backed up by the standard polemic about a world in which international capitalism is always on the edge of a crisis and in which every government measure ... is an attack on the working class.

The second strand ... stresses the social worker's own internal organization ... the forging of alliances with the relevant unions, rank-and-file involvement in NALGO [the National and Local Government Officers Association], militancy about pay and conditions, protecting victimized colleagues.

The third strand ... is to find a work role for the social worker as something other than an agent of control, buttressing up the system. ... Th[e] forging of links with various militant groups of deviants and dependants, together with general support for anything identified as the 'working-class struggle' is the main basis of radical social-work activity.

... Working outwards from what most social workers actually do, though, [these elements] represent something less than a guideline for action. Not only do they leave out those very groups which because of their lack of organization, grass roots activity, and militancy make up the bulk of social workers' clients, but ... they can be incompatible.

... [I]t seems to me an inescapable conclusion ... that ... the radical social worker will not only be able to derive very little from [Marxist] theory, but in fact will also encounter a line of argument that mere practical help is in fact undesirable. He will end up – like the Freudian caseworker – doing very little in the way of immediate help or more long-term community action. Such help by improving the client's material condition is seen as dangerous because it blunts the contradictions in the system. ...

... [W]hat if these clients refuse to see themselves in this way? ... Not only are we back to the elitism of the psychoanalytically derived casework – whatever you say, we really know best what your problem is – but we end up with another form of non-intervention or benign neglect: only this time, one reserved for the unfortunate few who refuse to see themselves as the social worker's political allies. What if the client actually wants something looking like casework? A case of false consciousness, no doubt. One can only hope that social workers who take this strategy literally will also respect a client's refusal to have anything to do with them.

... [E]ven the likeliest candidates for co-option can be refused support on the grounds that this would be counter revolutionary. The argument is that the working class are not yet equipped to lead a radical movement ... Working with tenants and claimants (and one shudders to think what this orthodoxy makes of the freaks, the lonely, the misfits), so the line goes, is alienated from the needs of the genuine working class. ...

'The unfinished'

Here, cryptically, would be some of my suggestions for a radical social work programme:

1.   Tell those sociologists who urge you to be theoretically more sophisticated to get off your backs. ...
2.   Refuse the ideology of casework, but always think of cases: your constituency is not just claimants' unions, tenants' associations, but also mothers of autistic children, suicidal housewives in council tower blocks, derelict old vagrants ... You don't have to be sentimental about these people but neither should you write them off.
3.   Take the insights of deviancy theory ... seriously. Think very concretely about how to aviod stigmatizing your clients, unwittingly facilitating their drift into further troubles, trapping them in cycles of rejection.
4.   Stay in your agency or institution, but don't let it seduce you. Take every opportunity to unmask its pretensions and euphemisms, use its resources in a defensive way for your clients, work for abolition.
5.   In practice and in theory, stay 'unfinished'. Don't be ashamed of working for short-term humanitarian or libertarian goals, but always keep in mind the long-term political process. This might mean living with the uncomfortable ambiguity that your most radical work will be outside your day-to-day job.
6.   Most important: don't sell out your clients' interests for the sake of ideological purity or theoretical neatness.

And keep telling sociologists and political theorists 'it's all right for you to talk'.

From Stanley Cohen, 'It's all right for you to talk: political and sociological manifestos for social work action', in R. Bailey and M. Brake (eds.), Radical Social Work *(London: Edward Arnold), 1975, pp. 76–95.*

References

Cannan, C. (1970) 'Deviants – victims or rebels?' *Case Con* 1 (January).

Schur, E. M. (1973) *Radical Non-intervention: rethinking the delinquency problem.* Englewood Cliffs, New Jersey, Prentice-Hall.

Young, J. (1975) 'Working-class criminology.' In Taylor, I. R., Walton, P. and Young, J. (eds) *Critical Criminology.* London, Routledge and Kegan Paul, pp. 63–94.

30 The probation officer as social worker (1977)

Robert J. Harris

The changing nature of the relationship between the probation service and other penal agencies has been the subject of a number of papers in recent years. This article, written from the standpoint of a practising probation officer and social work teacher, explores some of the elements in this relationship which combine with other factors to diminish the effectiveness of the probation service as a social work agency. The article suggests that some radical philosophical and practical modifications are needed for the probation service to take its place at the centre of national penal policy.

The centenary in 1976 of the police court mission highlighted a number of facts about the probation service. Most obviously, it is surprisingly recent; it was conceived at a time of penological desperation, born of philanthropic and religious concern and nurtured in the spirit of individualism heralded by the Gladstone Report.[1] Of religious beginnings, therefore, the service had few crises of conscience and it aimed from the first to reform. (The original surety system under which it operated made that explicit.) The Freudian concept of ego-strengthening through identification gave credence to the assumption that reform through relationships was possible, and, in spite of modifications, the assumption is still today the basis of most probation practice, despite the consistently gloomy research findings which assess probation's deterrent efficacy as either marginal or illusory. ...

The probation service has not kept pace with the developing roles demanded of the main social service agency operating in the penal field, while the expectation of courts and public alike that it will continue to provide a rather odd mixture of discipline for its own sake and treatment has rendered innovations of limited value and has reduced the extent to which probation officers can use their considerable training for the benefit of their clients. ...

Let us look at some examples of this dysfunction, reflected as it is both in the internal organization of the service and in its relationships with the court. As I enumerate some of the inherent conflicts which currently exist I shall suggest some ways in which the conflicts can be resolved so that the work in which probation officers are involved can come to involve a greater number of the skills which they will have learned as part of their training.

Professional autonomy versus public accountability

The years 1958–71 saw an increase in full-time probation officers of over 150%, and the extension of the service's role to include supervision on licence of the hard core of young offenders and of parolees. The period saw, too, a reducing responsibility ... for supervision of marginally delinquent juveniles.

The effect of these changes was to make the probation service less involved with clients whose offences were trivial, and more involved with criminals whose actions posed a real or potential threat to society. Sentencing policy for young offenders meant also an increase in supervision, so that statutory after-care clients, for whom the probation service became responsible, were highly likely to be persons who had *already failed on supervision,* and who were certainly people who had not agreed to be supervised.

... [C]an anyone doubt that it is only a matter of time before a probation officer, entrusted with the supervision of a dangerous or persistently serious offender is publicly berated as a result of the way in which he carried out his duty? But what is the nature of the supervision which courts and public expect? What safeguards exist, for officer and client, to prevent public acrimony and retribution? What do courts and the public require of their probation officers, and is there a gap between what they are getting, and what they think they are getting?

These are awkward questions, and hence all too seldom asked. When they are asked, they are often answered by such phrases as 'experience', 'professional judgment' and 'professional opinion'. Indeed, the skill to make such judgments, and to make assessments of clients' strengths and weaknesses, needs and wishes is an integral part of any social work course, and probation officers will accordingly be anxious to use their judgments in their professional work. Unfortunately, however, so far as crime specifically is concerned, irrespective of the undoubted ability of social workers in many situations to assess their clients, there is considerable evidence of probation officers' poor track records in either predicting or preventing crime. Whatever social work training does do, it does not give any expertise whatsoever in stopping people getting into trouble, and only when probation officers accept this, and only when the public know and accept this will the probation service be freed from a notional 'policing' activity, at which it persistently fails, and enabled to use the very considerable skills which it does have, and which all social workers should have, to the benefit of the client.

I am suggesting that the present situation is one of extreme dishonesty. The probation service is widely assumed to have, and does not deny that it has, some sort of magical power to prevent crime. That in reality it has no such power is indisputable, but what it is in a position to do is to provide a highly trained, caring and effective social work service to a disadvantaged section of the community: the offender. ...

Once the assumption of penal responsibility is taken away from the probation officer he will be able to function better as a social worker. At present, the disciplinary aspects of the probation relationship collude with a desire to punish as well as help. Yet there is no reason to believe that a reluctant client is a workable client and if he does not want help then perhaps he should have the right to refuse it. ... To those who say that those most in need of help may be slowest to seek it, we may ask, first, on what one bases the assumption that a man who rejects help does in fact need it; and secondly we may ask for evidence that help offered to the unwilling recipient is at all effective. ...

I am not arguing that offenders in the community should not be forced to do anything. I am, however, suggesting that what they are forced to do should be punishment with any therapeutic gains merely fortuitous spin-offs. The social work treatment should be kept distinct from this punishment rather than being a rather philosophically confused part of it. Only when this clear-cut division between treatment and punishment is made can the former, which is the task of the social worker, involve maximally the skills which that social worker will have learned and hence will be qualified and competent to practise.

Professional autonomy versus submission to the courts

It may well be that there should exist a court officer to ensure that former defendants are fulfilling the terms of any order to live in a certain place, or to work. There is, after all, a court officer to see that orders to pay fines are carried out. … But the training which probation officers now receive, combined with the different sort of person who becomes a probation officer, render them singularly ill-equipped to carry out this sort of function. The consequence is that these conditions are frequently ignored: in other words a client who is not trying to find work, or who moves house without permission, is highly unlikely to be brought back to court. This is because the probation officer, trained in social work techniques, aware of the value of a client contract which is individually tailored to the needs of that client, will ignore any externally imposed condition which he considers irrelevant or damaging to that client's development. …

So the implication of the present situation is that neither justice nor probation officer is able to feel satisfied with what is happening. If a justice wants a close and disciplinary eye kept on a specific defendant he has only the probation service at his disposal, and he has every reason to feel it unlikely that his wishes will be carried out. If a probation officer feels, as a social worker, that a client needs to be given a bit of rope he is able to do this only by ignoring the externally imposed conditions which bind both him and his client. …

… Accordingly, a far wider range of task-centred orders (such as community service) is required, with a minimum of discretion in reporting failures given to people who are not social workers. Redeployed prison officers, for example, would seem to be potentially well qualified and politically acceptable work supervisors. The probation officer would then be freed to operate his own voluntary referral system for defendants in court. He would be able to choose the way he worked and the length of time he worked with a given client. … The probation officer could intervene, with maximum impact, in the lives of clients at a crisis point to a far greater extent than is open to him today. Liaison with police and solicitors, for example, could put him in touch with clients who badly needed help at a time when they needed it, not for the two years after they may well have ceased to need it.

Professional autonomy versus organizational expectations

On my first day as a qualified probation officer I was approached by a senior colleague and asked which day of the week would be my 'report night' so that it could be entered on the office rota. Now I had, and still have, no objection to committing myself to be available to callers on a given evening each week, and there are obvious practical and professional reasons for doing so. But those reasons are, or should be, a means to an end and that end, I would suggest, should be the provision of an effective and efficient social work service. But means in organizations which are not constantly aware of the need for dynamic reconsiderations of their roles and functions are often in danger of becoming ritualized as ends. So it is with report nights. For our 'old style' probation officer, weekly reporting was first a discipline for the client, and second a way of vetting that client's situation in a way economical of time. ... [T]he backcloth of punitive-cum-therapeutic reporting remains basic to the expectations of the service.

So we can add to the argument of earlier sections that the relationship between probation officers and the magistracy has not changed, the further argument that the probation service itself has done relatively little to adapt its expectations and practices to the needs of a professionally and generically trained staff. I do not for one moment decry the efforts of individual offices where imaginative innovations have taken place, nor do I decry the efforts and hard work of probation officers who have taken justified pride in fulfilling their more traditional tasks. Rather, the sheer volume of work which results from lengthy probation orders, statutory after-care, and the various other tasks which are the staple diet of the probation officer have made it virtually impossible to set aside time to innovate in the busier of our offices. So the problem is an organizational one rather than the fault of individual officers. ...

The second and associated problem is one of skills. I have argued in this paper that probation officers spend a considerable proportion of their time doing tasks which do not necessitate the use of social work skills. The corollary of this is that they spend a relatively small proportion of their time actually being social workers. ... Skills, like metal, can turn rusty, and while no realistic person can sensibly expect to be able to use the whole gamut of his skills all the time, we can legitimately suggest that the organization, by using singularly few of those skills, is stultifying the development of its officers, and hence of itself.

Conclusion

Above all, I have argued in this article for the dissociation of the probation service from the court's sentences. The present system is ineffective in that compulsory supervision apparently makes no difference whatsoever to the likelihood of a client reoffending; it is also inappropriate for a trained social worker to have his avenues of client referral controlled by a non-social worker magistrate; it is damaging to the many defendants who are deprived of short-term assistance by the fact that probation officers' functions do not embrace their needs, no court order having been made; it is damaging to the court, whose intentions are liable to be thwarted by the ever-widening gap between their expectations and those of the probation officers to whose care the defendants are entrusted; it is damaging to the officers themselves who, by spending a high proportion of their time fulfilling a function for which they are not qualified, spend an accordingly smaller proportion of time practising and developing their professional skills.

I have suggested that only by making explicit the dissociation of treatment from punishment can the courts and clients get the best out of the probation service. The existence of the blanket probation order has concealed the need to devise and implement a full programme of imaginative community punishments for offenders; these punishments should *be* punishments, but the services of a probation officer should be available to offenders undergoing the punishments as much as to other offenders.

I can foresee a number of objections to these proposals. How, for example, can I justify resource allocation to offenders rather than to other needy groups within the community, unless those resources are benefiting that community by controlling deviance? But the resources are *already* allocated and are making no difference at all to the extent of crime. ... The principle that offenders, coming as many of them do from deprived backgrounds, and failing as many of them do to adjust to society's expectations, need help is well established. But to gear that help to discipline and overt persuasion to desist from crime is a somewhat unsophisticated approach given the training which probation officers now have.

This training, the more advanced sociological and psychological understanding about deviance and deviants, and the greater professional social work skills which exist to cope with all client categories all combine to emphasize the need for a new relationship between the probation service and the other parts of the penal process. Probation officers do a lot of work which is of great value to their clients, and it is from a recognition of this, not from any desire to carp or to belittle the service that this article springs. Probation officers can no longer seek to justify their existence by illusory fluctuations in reconviction rates: few criminologists take that criterion very seriously anyway. But they can justify themselves by proving beyond doubt that the service they provide is of intrinsic value to the client, and that it has brought about some real benefit to a person whose own situation may have previously been intolerable. If probation officers do not accept the challenge which this task implies, which is to educate public opinion away from a utilitarian approach to caring for deviants and towards a truer understanding of the situations which those deviants frequently have to face in their day-to-day existences, they will be less than true to themselves. They will be perpetuating the credibility gap which already exists between themselves, the magistracy and many members of the public. They have played the game by the rules of utilitarianism for too long already: under those rules they are doomed to lose. Let them, therefore, start playing a new game, by the rules of caring, and start persuading other players to join them. In doing so they will at least be giving their skills a chance to blossom and, who knows, those skills may even, as an incidental bonus, start reducing crime.

From Robert J. Harris, 'The probation officer as social worker',
British Journal of Social Work, *7(4), 1977, pp. 433–443.*

Note

1 The Committee reported in 1895 and argued for greater elasticity in dealing with prisoners and for a more sensitive response to their individual needs.

31 Sentenced to social work? (1978)

Malcolm Bryant, John Coker, Barry Estlea, Sheila Himmel and Ted Knapp

The present time is one of declining use of the probation order in favour of other penalties. It is a time of pressure to find alternatives to imprisonment for the petty recidivist offender who finds himself ultimately being sentenced to successive terms of imprisonment. It is a time of acclamation for the community service order and of proliferation of social inquiry reports and growing domestic work. But it is also a time of doubt about the competence of the Probation and After-Care Service and the efficacy of probation methods.

The belief that social work with offenders would itself make an impact on reconviction rates (the 'treatment model') has been shown by a whole series of research studies to be only very marginally valid, if at all. This has enormous implications for the future development of the Service and the way in which current resources are managed. The traditional social work dimension of the agency is likely to be increasingly identified as just one part (albeit an important part) of what should be available to community, courts and offenders. This process is already under way and is evidenced by the use of ancillaries and the development of community service.

Thus the concept of differential treatment, once used to describe a range of social work skills, is now taking on a much broader meaning, since it is gradually encompassing provision based on justice, reparation and punishment, where social work in the traditional sense may have a limited place.

The purpose of this article is to examine the nature and function of a redefined probation order which, we believe, might have an important part to play in a broadly based Probation and After-Care Service devoted to the provision of publicly credible non-custodial alternatives to imprisonment.

The present position

The current political and economic climate should not be ignored when considering the trends referred to earlier and some might think our ideas are linked too much to a state of affairs which will prove temporary and of little significance. Nevertheless we consider that the declining use of the probation order by the courts reflects a declining credibility about the philosophy of the Service and the way it operates. Probation officers, trained as social workers, often appear confused about such fundamental questions as 'who is the client?' Is it the court, the offender, the agency or a subjectively defined mixture of the three?

Furthermore they experience considerable frustration over the amount of their time spent in routine administration related to the oversight of offenders as distinct from pure social work activity. The nature of their relationship with offenders and courts, coupled with the one-to-one methods of work which still predominate, can so easily lead to the offender's responsibility for his own behaviour being transferred to the probation officer to the point where the officer feels culpable when further offences are committed. Thus once again the implication would seem to be of a service which works on a medical model where the officer is expected to cure the offender's criminality rather than an acknowledgement that some offenders could benefit from social work help because of the people they are and the problems they face.

The redefined probation order

We suggest a system which would operate as follows. If, in the view of the court, an offender could be dealt with appropriately by a probation order the court would define the length of the order *and the frequency of reporting to the Probation and After-Care Service* (e.g. you are required to report to ... office weekly for 12 months at a time convenient to the ... office). Standard conditions would also include the avoidance of further offences and the notification of changes in address or employment. Special conditions, relating for example to residence at a hostel or medical treatment could be included as at present.

The key differences would thus be that the level of contact with the agency would be defined in open court and that a brief statement would be included about the various resources and opportunities which would be available to the offender through the Probation and After-Care Service. The offender's consent to the order being made would be necessary, and thus the *primary contract* would be between the offender and the court. By reporting as required to the appropriate office and observing the other conditions the probationer would be honouring the order. On his first visit to the probation office, the offender would be interviewed by a probation officer and the purpose of this induction interview would be to ensure that all probationers were aware of the way in which the order would operate thereafter. The subsequent system would involve the probationer simply reporting to the reception desk where he would sign a reporting record sheet and would give information about any change of address or employment. On each visit he would be asked by the receptionist if he would like to see a probation officer, and could opt into the other resources of the agency if he chose, but would not be required to do so under the primary contract already referred to.

If he did choose to see a probation officer, a *subsidiary contract* might well be negotiated based on a joint assessment of his problems and the opportunities to be provided, but a failure to comply with this subsidiary contract would never in itself represent a breach of the primary 'reporting' contract with the court. This particular aspect of the system would have been emphasised strongly by the probation officer in the induction interview. As a result of work undertaken through the subsidiary contract, however, a probation officer might make application to the court for early termination of the order or a reduction in the frequency of reporting. The reporting record sheet maintained at the reception desk would act as documentary evidence in the event of proceedings being taken in connection with a breach of the primary contract through failing to report.

Reception area

It is obvious that the reception area of the probation office would be very important, since it would act as a shop window for the service. It would be bright and colourful with a welcoming atmosphere and would offer a visual presentation of the various types of social work and welfare opportunities available. These would include such things as personal counselling, assistance with family problems, membership of groups, special education, assistance with welfare rights, development of work skills, information about employment and accommodation, day training centres, hostel placements, etc. The intention would be to encourage the motivation in clients to deal with problems, and ultimately external professional assistance in design of the reception area might be helpful. The receptionist would be in a key role, and would need to be both sensitive and skilled in dealing with clients who may find it difficult on occasions to articulate their requests for assistance, whilst allowing those who simply wanted to report to do so without difficulty.

The objective for the probation team would therefore be the creation of a wide range of opportunities for offenders and the effective development and management of its resources in order that a local service relevant to clients' needs would be provided. We believe that such a system would offer considerable advantages over current practice. The offender would be treated as a more responsible individual, and by allowing him to choose social work help, the dignity inherent in self-determination would be recognised. Courts would surely have more faith in an order where the level of supervision was defined in court, and where breach of this primary contract would lead to the offender's re-appearance unless the failure to report was unavoidable. The skills and time of probation officers as professional social workers would be given recognition as valuable resources and where subsidiary contracts were made these would be with motivated people who would thus be clients in the true sense.

As the system developed, a range of other people with relevant training and skills might be employed, such as accommodation and employment officers, psychotherapists, legal advisers, specialist teachers, welfare rights officers, etc. The services provided for clients could be monitored in terms of the successful resolution of personal and social problems, and if a positive impact should happen to be made in terms of reduced criminality this would be a welcome bonus. The redefined probation order would therefore be an expression of the community's belief that some offenders may be dealt with appropriately through supervision in the community and that by virtue of the people they are and the problems they have it is reasonable that social service resources should be made available to them.

Philosophy and objections

The underlying philosophy of these ideas is by no means new. In *Social Casework for the State,* published in 1962, Beatrice Pollard wrote '... whatever the impact of society on the individual's situation, no help can be offered effectively, no solution be evolved which the client is unable or unwilling to make his own. The whole history of casework, however, is a lesson on the futility, sometimes disastrous, of offering help which the individual client cannot wholeheartedly use.' [Pollard 1962]

More recently, Robert Harris writing on 'The Probation Officer as Social Worker' (1977) suggests that 'Probation officers can no longer seek to justify their existence by illusory fluctuations in reconviction rates: few criminologists take that criterion very seriously anyway. But they can justify themselves by proving beyond doubt that the service they provide is of intrinsic value to the client, and that it has brought about some real benefit to a person whose own situation may have previously been intolerable.'

It may be thought that, however attractive in theory it is, our redefined probation order would not work in practice. 'Why not ask the offender to report to a police station?' Because reporting to a probation office would ensure that the probationer at least has contact with the agency where the resources are located, and where the induction and reception procedures outlined above could be operated carefully. The intention of the proposed system is that the supervisory and helping aspects of the service should run parallel to but separately from each other. A police station could not meet these different but concurrent objectives.

'What about the large rural areas with poor public transport?' Courts in such areas would be well aware of the problems and the frequency of reporting could be reduced to take account of the transport situation. 'Why would a court make a probation order rather than imposing a conditional discharge?' Because a probation order enables the offender's behaviour to be monitored; it also inconveniences and to that extent punishes him whilst putting him in contact with resources if he chooses to make use of them. 'What if very few probationers asked for the help of a probation officer?' This would ensure that those clients who did ask would receive more intensive help and would provide opportunities for checking why the existing provision was not attracting clients. 'But surely the clients who reported and did not take advantage of the other opportunities would in effect be simply receiving a punishment?' This may be true but their consent to the order would be necessary, and it should be remembered that they may prefer this level of inconvenience to the possibility of a custodial sentence.

The relationship of the service with the courts

We consider that the advantages of separating social work provision from the routine oversight of offenders in the community far outweigh the disadvantages. The Probation and After-Care Service would be available as a resource to any person facing court proceedings who sought assistance on a voluntary basis: our role in this respect would become more active than at present, with attractive advertising in court waiting areas describing the services available from the local probation office, and there may even be a duty officer available at the court to deal with immediate problems. Social inquiry reports would still be prepared in cases where the court considered that they would be helpful. These reports would be addressed primarily to the question of custodial or non-custodial penalties rather than the need for social work assistance, though information about the offender's personal and social situation would be included. The work undertaken at this point by the probation officer concerned might, of course, form the basis for a subsidiary contract at a later stage in the event of a probation order being made. The officer would bear in mind, however, that a failure to identify a social work task at the social inquiry stage would not preclude a probation order being recommended. A primary contract could still be made with the court and might be appropriate.

In many cases the court might consider that the nature of the offence and previous convictions were such that a probation order could be made without a social inquiry report. Such orders would be welcomed by the Service which, while monitoring the probationer's reporting and compliance with the other conditions of his order, would provide opportunities for a subsidiary contract in the normal way. Where social inquiry reports were prepared their changed focus would encourage the use of more objective information, such as reconviction tables.

Conclusion

We believe that the proposals for a probation order as described in this article would be of benefit to courts, offenders, probation officers and the community. Practical problems emerging could be overcome in the light of experience, and the values implicit in the revised system take account of current penological and social work thinking. It seems likely that more probation orders would be made, fewer social inquiry reports written, and more time devoted to the provision and organisation of the appropriate resources for motivated probationers. In short, offenders would be supervised in the community with opportunities for personal development rather than being 'sentenced to social work' as at present.

> *From Malcolm Bryant, John Coker, Barry Estlea, Sheila Himmel and Ted Knapp,*
> *'Sentenced to social work?',* Probation Journal, *25(4), 1978, pp. 110–114.*

References

Harris, R.J. (1978) 'The Probation Officer as Social Worker', *British Journal of Social Work,* 7(4): 433–442.

Pollard, B. (1962) *Social Casework for the State,* London, Pall Mall Press.

32 Probation as a correctional service (1978)

David Haxby

There is a need to reaffirm the relevance of probation to the present-day task of finding alternatives to custodial methods, and to develop policies for encouraging the use of probation. Within an expanded correctional service in the community, probation must be maintained as the keystone of the edifice. If present trends continue, probation will eventually be regarded by the courts as irrelevant to their major problems, and the correctional service will be mainly concerned with the administration of other kinds of penal measure and the provision of after-care. ... [T]he case for retaining a separate probation and after-care service must rest on the advantages to be gained from having a service which is focused on crime and delinquency and on the development of methods for dealing with offenders...

The following ... will try to identify certain major themes around which a community correctional service can be structured ... I ... attempt to sketch the outlines of a service dealing with offenders in the community which has a range and variety of provision going well beyond the scope of the present probation and after-care service. We are no longer talking about a specialised kind of social-work service. We are talking about a unified administration for a variety of penal provisions in the community. Social workers, in the guise of probation officers, will remain probably the major professional group in this service, but it will employ other skills and inter-disciplinary approaches, and will make provisions which do not use social workers...

Alternatives to custody

It is a cliché of contemporary discussion amongst those interested in the penal field, to say that we need to develop alternatives to imprisonment. The arguments for this policy vary. Concern is usually at its height when overcrowding in the prisons is at its worst, and the call for reform is then related as much to the economics and organisation of the prison system as to the welfare of offenders. Other arguments are concerned with the characteristics of many of the offenders in our prisons. ...

One of the problems at the moment which is widely recognised is that many inadequate offenders are committed to prison over and over again; they literally fill up the prisons and it has little result on the offender himself. By and large they go into prison for very minor offences. A lot of these individuals are inadequate, quite a number of them are homeless and rootless, and a not insignificant number have very poor work records, or very bad relationships or no relationship at all with families, and we believe that experiments already started in the provision of hostels for some adult offenders should be substantially extended. This would provide the courts with alternatives to imprisonment for inadequate offenders.

(House of Commons 1971: Q728)

This argument is a mixture of humanitarian concern for the offender and lack of faith in the effectiveness of prisons. But the majority of offenders who are in prison are not inadequates, and we should be asking whether we can develop effective methods outside prison for dealing with more serious offenders. Arguments based on the effectiveness of non-custodial methods, when contrasted with custodial methods, are of course based on the premise that it is not the primary aim of a penal measure to be punitive, but rather to ensure that the offender does not offend again; if comparisons show that certain non-custodial methods produce fewer reconvictions than custodial methods, they are to be preferred. Further, it is argued that even when the evidence merely shows that the non-custodial methods are no less effective than the custodial, they are still to be preferred on both economic and humanitarian grounds.

The arguments for developing non-custodial methods have recently been given considerable support by the Advisory Council on the Penal System in its report on *Young Adult Offenders*. The Advisory Council (1974: 55–56) state:

> Neither practical experience nor the results of research in recent years have established the superiority of custodial over non-custodial methods in their effect upon renewed offending: this is still an open question ... While the research results do not indicate that the general effect of detention in a custodial establishment must be deleterious, they do show that there is a significant number of young adult offenders whose behaviour seems to be little improved as a result of serving custodial sentences. Research and experimentation on this question in California have pointed in the same direction and have taken the argument a stage further by suggesting that many types of offender who have in the past been sentenced to custody might well be supervised in the community without any increase in the rates of re-offending at the conclusion of the sentence ... [W]e believe that the goal of helping, assisting and influencing the offender to live his life and manage his affairs without committing offences has a better chance of being achieved in the community than by committing him to custody.

The first priority of the new service, then, must be a commitment to develop non-custodial methods and to reduce the use of prisons, borstals and other custodial methods to a minimum. Just how far it is possible to go in this direction must depend on public opinion and political opinion, and it has to be accepted that within the foreseeable future there will always be a need for some form of imprisonment to deal with those offenders who represent a real threat to the safety of the public. However, the fact that within western Europe there are wide variations in rates of imprisonment gives ground for thinking that much more could be done in Britain. The Netherlands now has an imprisonment rate of 20 persons per 100,000 compared with 72 in England and Wales, 83 in West Germany and 94.3 in Scotland.

The development of alternatives to custodial measures is, of course, the main *raison d'être* of the probation service. When the Probation of Offenders Bill, later to become an Act, was having its second reading in the Lords, the Earl of Meath made the following statement, which now strikes a curious note: 'This Bill can hardly be called a first-class measure in the ordinary sense of the term ... It is not one which creates a great deal of popular excitement ... There can be no doubt whatsoever that the Bill will prevent crime and to a large extent empty our jails'.

The problem now presented is different from that in 1907. Then, the urgent need was to demonstrate that some offenders could be helped to re-establish themselves as law-abiding members of the community through reformative and supportive methods, and that this was better both for the offender and the community than imprisonment or other custodial methods. The probation service largely succeeded in that task. This, however, has made it more difficult to persuade courts that there is still scope for the further development of non-custodial methods. The high reconviction rates which follow imprisonment and borstal training, especially of offenders who have been 'inside' before, convince courts that the inmates of these institutions are already a 'hard core' and it is difficult to convince sentencers that the results might be no less effective if the use of probation were extended, or other non-custodial methods were introduced. ...

Community involvement

Having established that the service must have a primary commitment to the development of alternatives to custody, we can examine certain other themes which should permeate its work and determine its ethos.

First is the need for the service to command a broader base in the community. Crime and delinquency represent on one view a failure of the community's systems of social control, both informal and formal. Different kinds of community or neighbourhood may take different views about law-breaking, but whatever view is taken, the attitude of the public to law enforcement and law-breaking must be a crucial element in determining both the incidence of law-breaking, the rate of detection of offences, and the success of official agencies such as the correctional services in restoring the offender to the community and preventing further crime. Involvement with the community is clearly an important area of policy for a community-based correctional service.

A related issue, but one which needs separate exploration, is the future role of the service in the prevention of crime. This is a major issue for the service to face, and will require a decision by government.

Whether in prevention or in treatment and rehabilitation, the service will have to go on developing and supporting voluntary effort, and this is clearly another aspect of community involvement. It represents, however, another theme to consider, since it is clear that the service of the future will have to depend heavily on voluntary support.

New methods and new approaches must be a regular part of a service which is trying to keep in tune with a changing social and cultural environment, in which attitudes to crime and criminals do not remain fixed. But innovation also requires evaluation. Not all new ideas are good ones. We must look, therefore, at the place in the service of innovation and research.

Finally, the extension of the work of the service, embracing a greater involvement with the community, with preventive work, and with voluntary effort, implies a shift away from the traditional preoccupation with casework. There are other developments in social work which may have relevance to the future service ... [and there is a] need for the service to embrace a wide range of methods, and to consider some of the implications of this diversity...

Diversification of methods

In the period from about 1955, perhaps even earlier, through to the late 1960s, probation officers generally saw themselves as social caseworkers, attempting to influence the behaviour of their clients through the skilled use of a professional relationship.

The Morison Committee set out clearly the views which were widely held in the service at the beginning of the 1960s, and in so doing helped to add the weight of their authority to this particular approach to the probation officer's task. They spotlighted the importance, within social work generally, of a 'new and highly professional approach described by the term "social casework"', and went on to say that 'the probation officer must be seen, essentially, as a professional caseworker, employing, in a specialised field, skill which he holds in common with other social workers' (Home Office 1962: 23).

The Committee made it clear that they did not envisage 'intensive casework' as being appropriate in all cases. Nevertheless, they went on to describe at length the steps the caseworker must take to appraise the position of his client and build a relationship which would be itself the means of helping him. It was recognised that there might be some scope for altering the external influences which bore on an individual, but 'fundamentally the caseworker's purpose is more profound than any environmental alteration he can achieve. He seeks to establish a relationship which will, itself, be a positive influence, counteracting and modifying the ill-effects of past experiences and of irremovable factors in the present' (Home Office 1962: 25). Later, the Committee noted that 'It is the appreciation of, and concentration upon, the probationer's ability to benefit from a developing personal relationship with the probation officer that principally distinguishes probation supervision today from that of a quarter of a century ago'; and with the kind of assurance which only fifteen years later seems quite amazing, they comment that 'if the welfare state has freed the probation officer from preoccupation with the material needs of offenders, it has also shown with startling clarity that crime is not primarily the product of economic hardship (Home Office 1962: 25). ...

Many of the assumptions which lay behind the Morison view of probation casework must now be re-examined. In work with individuals under supervision, the supervisor must ask himself in each case whether a 'treatment' model provides an appropriate framework for offering help. Casework may still be a legitimate activity, but its boundaries and content must be redefined. ...

The community corrections service of the future must take as one of its principles a diversification of methods. This diversification must apply both to assessment and to methods of intervention. The service must be willing to use the contributions of a number of different professions, including teaching, medicine, psychology and law. It must also look again at the social-work activity of the service, and move from its traditional reliance on social casework (often itself viewed as a kind of relationship therapy) towards vision of the social worker's repertoire of methods of intervention [e.g. advocacy, short-term contracts, group work, community work]. The social work staff of the service must develop a range of skills which will match the extended role of the service, and will enable its clients to be offered social work help which is appropriate to their situation. The service should also be prepared to develop ancillary services through which the social workers can support and help their clients.

The fact that the future service may be responsible for administering penal services which do not rely on supervision (such as Community Service) or which utilise a number of professions in a multi-disciplinary situation (as in Day Training Centres and assessment centres) makes it even more important that probation officers should be clear about their own professional identity as social workers within a service for offenders.

Institutions and after-care

In its origins the probation service was concerned with keeping men out of prison, and we have seen how recent developments, and legislation, have given a new impetus to the search for effective alternatives to imprisonment.

However, the service has also in recent years become more involved in after-care, helping the ex-prisoner to return to society. The service has always had some responsibilities in relation to statutory after-care – i.e. the supervision of persons released on licence following sentences of special kinds such as borstal training, preventive detention or corrective training, and more recently detention centre sentences. However, a substantial change came about following the report in 1963 of the Advisory Council on the Treatment of Offenders on *The Organisation of After-Care.* The service then became responsible for making available after-care help to all ex-prisoners on request, and also for staffing the prison welfare officer posts in prisons.

Probation officers thus became directly involved in the work of the penal institutions towards which they had in the past shown such antipathy. At a later date the service also took responsibility for social-work posts in detention centres, borstal allocation centres, and in some borstals. The introduction of parole in 1967 has brought probation officers into an even closer relationship with prisons, involving some senior officers in the work of the local review committees (as well as the main Parole Board).

During the same period of a decade or so the neat division between treatment in the open and custodial methods has become more and more difficult to maintain. In the juvenile field there has been a substantial investment of time, and rather less of resources, in establishing forms of intermediate treatment. In the adult range (i.e. 17 and over) the probation and after-care service is becoming involved with, and even directly responsible for, a growing range of different types of institution based in the community. Probation hostels and homes, for persons under 21, were a long-standing but small commitment, involving the appointment of liaison officers but no management responsibility; voluntary after-care hostels began to appear during the 1960s, and the grant system required the involvement of a probation officer in the hostel committee; special hostels and units were established for alcoholics and drug-takers; and more recently, through the 1972 Criminal Justice Act, the probation and after-care service has been empowered to provide probation hostels, day training centres, bail hostels, and 'other establishments for use in connection with the rehabilitation of offenders'. The boundary between custody and non-custodial treatment is also blurred to some extent by the prison service, with its open institutions and hostels attached to prisons and borstals, and the Wootton Report (Advisory Council on the Penal System 1970) discussed such ideas as week-end imprisonment.

In the future, if an offender cannot be dealt with by the courts through the use of a purely non-custodial measure such as a fine, probation, or community service, the courts will be able to consider an increasing range of semi-custodial provisions or open institutions before finally resorting to imprisonment. It seems likely also that within the period of a sentence there will be much more executive flexibility about whether the sentence is served behind walls, or whether the offender can be moved to conditions of greater freedom.

The Younger Report, though primarily concerned with young adult offenders, has introduced ideas which are equally applicable to older groups. The report questions the efficacy of custodial forms of treatment. In recognising that some offenders will nevertheless have to be held in custody, the report notes that 'the doctrine has been gaining ground that, while reformation should indeed be the main objective of a custodial regime, it is wrong to send an offender to custody, or to decide how long he should be kept in custody, purely on reformative grounds, since it is only in a relatively small proportion of cases that custody is a condition of constructive treatment, and indeed it may often be an obstacle to it' (Advisory Council on the Penal System 1974: 7).

The alternative must be to view the period in custody as only one part of a continuous process which includes supervision and control in the community. Younger suggests that the total sentence should be determinate and designed to reflect the gravity of the offence, but how much of this period should be spent in the community rather than in custody would be a matter for the exercise of judgement, and the arrangements for transfer would be by executive decision.

We have already considered the community correctional service as the administrative base for establishing alternatives to custodial treatment. However, it remains ... to consider the part it must play in relation to custodial methods. The penal system shows two trends which can be seen operating in other social services, and which are complementary in their operation. The first is for the institution to be brought into the community; the second is for the community-based service to be brought into the institution.

At one time the prisoner was, for the period of his sentence, totally removed from free society. However, the prison department has developed open prisons and borstals; hostels operating both within the prison boundary and on a satellite basis; opportunities for inmates and trainees to contribute to local community projects in organised groups; and schemes under which those serving long sentences can take up employment outside the prison for a period before release.

It would be easy to over-estimate the extent to which the experience of imprisonment has been ameliorated by such developments. Nevertheless, it is true that the prison is not the totally segregated community which it once was. Moreover, the introduction of parole has meant that many prisoners now serve a part of their sentence under supervision in the community.

There is, however, a further sense in which the institution is being brought into the community. The development of hostels in recent years has come about not only as a response to the accommodation problems of offenders, but also out of recognition of the fact that they can often be adequately helped in small institutions which enable them to remain in employment, to have freedom of movement in the community, and to avoid the dependency and institutionalisation which can come from frequent imprisonment. There is a growing range of residential provision in the community, offering different degrees of support and control.

This movement away from the large, isolated, 'total' institution has its parallels in other parts of the social services. Services for the mentally ill, the mentally handicapped, the elderly, and children, have all been trying to develop new forms of supportive environment which would emphasise the self-respect and independence of the residents – hostels, family group homes, sheltered housing and so on.

In these other services there is also an increasing use of day care provisions, which enable the 'client' to continue living in his own home, but provide a semi-institutional regime on certain days of the week. The day training centre is the first development of this kind in the penal field.

The contrary trend is for the community to have more involvement with the penal institution. In the social services there is an increasing part played in institutions by both voluntary workers and statutory services based outside the institution, and it is important to remember that probation officers are not the only 'outsiders' involved in prisons. Prison visiting, for example, has a long history as a form of voluntary service, and statutory agencies such as education and the Department of Employment provide services inside prison-service establishments.

The probation and after-care service is now represented inside the prisons by prison welfare officers. Probation officers outside the prisons are increasingly concerned with the need for contact with a prisoner *during* his sentence, and with helping wives and families of men 'inside'. The parole system even involves officers in the process which leads to release.

There is no contradiction in discussing penal institutions in an outline for a community correctional service. As Margaret Shaw says in her report on *Social Work in Prison*, 'The prison can no longer be regarded as an institution cut off from the normal life of the community' (Shaw 1974: 90). This may be regarded as an aspiration rather than a statement of fact, but at least the walls do not look so high these days.

From David Haxby, Probation: a changing service *(London: Constable), 1978, pp. 148–152, 186–187, 211–212, 240–245.*

References

Advisory Council on the Penal System (1970) *Non-Custodial and Semi-Custodial Penalties*. London: HMSO.

——(1974) *Young Adult Offenders*. London: HMSO.

Advisory Council on the Treatment of Offenders (1963) *The Organisation of After-Care*. London: HMSO.

Home Office (1962) *Report of the Departmental Committee on the Probation Service*. London: HMSO.

House of Commons Expenditure Committee (1971) *First Report from the Expenditure Committee (Session 1971–72): Probation and After-Care*. London: HMSO.

Shaw, M. (1974) *Social Work in Prisons*. Home Office Research Study 22. London: HMSO.

33 A non-treatment paradigm for probation practice (1979)

Anthony E. Bottoms and William McWilliams

'If I were asked what was the most significant contribution made by this country to the new penological theory and practice which struck root in the twentieth century – the *measure which will endure,* while so many of the other methods of treatment might well fall into limbo ... – my answer would be probation ... *Probation is fundamentally a form of social service preventing further crime* by a readjustment of the culprit under encouraging supervision of a social worker guided by the courts of justice.'

(Radzinowicz 1958; italics added)

'The reformation of the criminal ... has been central to the English approach to criminal justice since the end of the nineteenth century. ... But penological research carried out in the course of the last twenty years or so suggests that penal 'treatments', as we significantly describe them, do not have any reformative effect, whatever other effects they may have. The dilemma is that a considerable investment has been made in various measures and services, of which the most obvious examples are custodial institutions for young adult offenders and probation and after-care services in the community for a wide variety of offender. *Are these services simply to be abandoned on the basis of the accumulated research evidence? ...*'

(Croft 1978: italics added)

These two quotations, respectively by the first Director of the Cambridge Institute of Criminology and the present Head of the Home Office Research Unit, are separated in time by only 20 years; but they seem poles apart in orientation. Radzinowicz, reflecting the accepted wisdom of the time, accords to probation the coveted prize of being the jewel in the crown of the 'new penology'. Croft, in the unassertive tone of the English civil service, quietly but starkly poses the possibility of the disappearance of this once-priceless gem.

In the light of what has happened in those 20 years, we believe that Croft is entirely right to pose this question. The research results do indeed cast major doubts on Radzinowicz's confident assertion that probation is 'a form of social service *preventing further crime*'.

This is not the appropriate place to discuss the various research studies in detail; suffice it to say that all those who have responsibly reviewed the relevant literature (Lipton, Martinson and Wilks 1975; Greenberg 1977; Brody 1976) have reached the same broad conclusion – that dramatic reformative results are hard to discover and are usually absent. ...

Against results like these, some will argue that the probation service is not, and never has been, a crime-preventing agency. The task of the service is, they will say, limited to the classic statutory duty to 'advise, assist and befriend'. But we do not think that this objection cuts much ice. Most probation officers, and certainly almost all policymakers, have always tacitly assumed that the advice and assistance offered did have an effect in steering at least a proportion of their charges away from criminal acts. It is precisely because this assumption is now seen to be very doubtful that the crisis of confidence implied by Croft has arisen.

Yet in one sense Croft, radical though his stance may seem, poses only one-half of the possible critique of probation's traditional rehabilitative practice. His critique is empirical: probation treatment does not seem to reduce recidivism. But, especially in the USA, a theoretical critique of treatment has also developed. As the American Friends Service Committee (1971: 21) neatly put it, this criticism provides:

> compelling evidence that the individualised-treatment model, the ideal towards which reformers have been urging us for at least a century, is theoretically faulty, systematically discriminatory in application, and inconsistent with some of our most basic concepts of justice.

For present purposes, the most important of these three charges are the first and the third – that the treatment model is theoretically faulty, and capable of injustice. Why theoretically faulty? ... [E]ssentially the fault lies in the persistent yet inappropriate analogy made with individual medical treatment. This analogy is doubtful on a number of grounds. First, in the understanding of ordinary language, most crime is voluntary and most disease is involuntary. ... Second (and closely related), the assumption of the medical model is that crime is pathological, but this notion is difficult to sustain, at any rate for most crime, in the light of sociological critiques (Durkheim 1895; Taylor, Walton and Young 1973). Third, the treatment model applied is one of individual treatment, while many of the assumed causes of crime are social: treatment-orientated criminology has never learned the lesson of social medicine that better drains may be worth scores of doctors. ...

In the heyday of the 'rehabilitative ideal', as Allen (1959) has aptly dubbed it, no one raised these kinds of empirical or theoretical doubts about treatment. And this led to treaters taking upon themselves the right to coerce offenders into accepting what was going to be 'for their own good in the long run'. ...

It is precisely this ready acceptance by treatment agents of the need for coercion which raises the possibility of injustice referred to by the American Friends Service Committee. For if a probation officer ineluctably believes in his powers of treatment, and in his right to force others to submit to them, then eventually he will almost certainly reach two conclusions. First, he will decide that he has a right to take compulsory power over people's lives additional to that which is justified by the offence, in order to make the treatment 'work'. Second, he will tend to ignore the so-called 'client's' view of the situation, and to define the situation entirely in his (the treater's) terms. It is the results of these pieces of implicit arrogance (which, to set the record straight, the authors have themselves subscribed to in the past as practising probation officers) that may be criticized as unjust. ...

A new paradigm for probation practice

... Our paradigm stems from the preliminary observation that, in relation to the criminal side of probation practice, there have been four basic aims of the service, under which all other objectives could be subsumed as second order ones. These four primary aims are and have been:

1.   The provision of appropriate help for offenders
2.   The statutory supervision of offenders
3.   Diverting appropriate offenders from custodial sentences
4.   The reduction of crime. ...

Aim 1: the provision of appropriate help for offenders

We have already mentioned in passing the classic official aim of probation practice: 'to advise, assist and befriend'. This phrase, which first appeared in the Probation of Offenders Act 1907, has remained unchanged in successive legislation, and still stands on the statute book of today (e.g. Criminal Justice Act 1948, Schedule V, para. 3(5); Powers of Criminal Courts Act 1973, Schedule III, para. 8(1)).

The original practice of the early probation service was probably to stress, in particular, advice and practical assistance. Within the context of a strongly moralistic relationship, the offender was steered into better paths by exhortation, the arrangement of employment, and so on. ...

With the advent of casework, things changed. ... [F]riendship did not mean quite what the man in the street might think it meant; rather:

> all clients are best helped by a special type *of friendship, viz, the professional casework relationship* in which the probation officer's warm and sincere concern fertilizes the probationer's capacity for growth and change.
>
> (NAPO, in King 1958: 73–6, italics added).

But the clients themselves have not been much impressed by this 'special type of friendship'. ...

> Most parolees define *help* in terms of achieving a solution to practical problems; matters which relate to feelings are not usually thought to fall within the framework of a 'helping' relationship and so are not expressed. Yet these are the very issues the officers themselves are often seeking to discuss. ... The most overwhelming impressions to emerge from the interviews with parolees were of the irrelevance and superficiality of supervision ...
>
> (Morris and Beverly 1975: 131, italics in original)

... Morris and Beverly report that 'constructive relationships developed only where parolees felt their probation officer understood them and was concerned about them *as people*' (1975: 132, italics added). And this, in a very real sense, is precisely what the casework relationship, as classically conceived, fails to do – for all the lip-service it pays to this principle. Let the reader consider, for example, that NAPO definition of 'a special type of friendship', and then let him try to imagine telling anyone with whom he has a real reciprocal relationship that he is going to offer him some 'warm and sincere concern' which is going to 'fertilize his capacity for growth'. ...

We turn, then, to the second main idea for future practice, that of *help*. And we may usefully begin once more with a comment from Morris and Beverly:

> In establishing a relationship with their client it seems crucial for the probation officer to begin from a point that has meaning for the parolee, yet ... it seems that it is usually the officer who defines the situation (and the problem) and then proceeds to try and put things right.
>
> (1975: 132)

... Clients want help from social workers; aspiring social workers apply for training because they want to help people. This simple idea should not be lost to sight in all the complexities of modern social work. Indeed, we would agree with Carol Meyer (1972) that ultimately the central business of social work is not with achieving changes defined without regard to clients' opinions of their needs, nor with effecting cures for professionally diagnosed pathologies, but with giving help, and, very importantly, that: 'if we choose the helping rather than the socialising goal, then we will be freer to attend to the improvement of services – to socialise *them*, if you will'. ...

What exactly are the implications of adopting a 'help' rather than a 'treatment' model? ... The caseworker does not begin with an assumption of client-malfunctioning; rather, he offers his unconditional help with client-defined tasks, this offer having certain definite and defined boundaries (we shall return to the 'boundaries' later). If the offer is accepted, this leads to a collaborative effort between worker and client to define the problem requiring help, and to work out jointly a set of possible alternative strategies; the worker is also absolutely explicit about what kinds of help his agency can and cannot offer. The client is then left to make the choices for himself. Hence, schematically:

(a)	Treatment	*becomes*	Help
(b)	Diagnosis	*becomes*	Shared assessment
(c)	Client's dependent need as the basis for social work action	*becomes*	Collaboratively defined task as the basis for social work action

... [T]hree interim comments may be made. First, nothing that we have said should be interpreted to mean that 'help' means only material help. ...

Secondly, we are aware that many probation officers currently do offer 'help', in client-defined terms, in a range of situations. ... But at present they have no adequate conceptual apparatus with which to theorize these activities; so that the moment they begin to talk about them the language of treatment tends to be brought in and distorts what they are really offering to clients. We see it as a major task for social work theorists to provide an adequate conceptual understanding of 'help' for the benefit of social workers in their daily practice. ...

Thirdly, it is worth noting that various modern theoretical developments in social work may be interpreted as generally consistent with the switch from treatment to help – this would apply to 'task-centred casework' (Reid and Epstein 1972), welfare rights work, radical social work and community work, for example, and possibly also to 'Systems theory' (Davies 1977). Yet, ... all these new techniques are potentially translatable still into the old officer-centred wisdoms of traditional social work. It is therefore of prime importance to emphasize that the ultimate test of the new model is that of client help – not 'task-centredness', or whatever. ...

As we have made clear, the 'help' model has been adopted in this paper because it is considered more likely than 'treatment' to facilitate a response to the expressed needs of clients. No expectation has been raised that the help model will be beneficial in the reduction of crime, and it is central to our argument to insist that this is not the purpose of shifting the focus from treatment to help. Nevertheless it must be pointed out that there is, ironically, at least a tiny shred of research evidence to suggest that, after all, help may be more crime-reducing than treatment.

The evidence comes from two sources – one indirect and one direct. The indirect source is a study of compulsory after care in a group of young adults released from a closed borstal institution (Bottoms and McClintock 1973). The application of intensive casework methods was found to have no impact on reconviction rates, even when allowance was made (through a prediction instrument) for the previous history of the offender. On the other hand, and using the same statistical control for previous history, placement in certain sorts of post-institutional social situations did have a significant impact on reconviction rates – this included marriages, jobs, and so on. It is not suggested that probation officers become marriage brokers, but an implication of this study is that if offenders are genuinely seeking to 'settle down', and if probation officers are able to help them by collaborating in getting them into stable social situations, this will be more beneficial than intensive casework on the treatment model.

The more direct evidence comes from a Danish study of through-care work with short term prisoners (Berntsen and Christiansen 1965). This is one of the very few studies to produce a significantly lower reconviction rate in an experimental 'treatment' group as against a control group *(P<0·01)*; and, though its favourable result is not wholly unambiguous (Brody 1978), it is worth serious attention. This is particularly so in the present context, since we are told that 'normally help was only given when the prisoners themselves asked for it' (Berntsen and Christiansen 1965: 53), and that the help given was overwhelmingly of a very practical kind. ...

Aim 2: the statutory supervision of offenders

... In our view nothing is gained by a refusal to face squarely the fact that probation officers are and always have been law enforcement agents, and that this part of the role cannot be shuffled off without far-reaching consequences. ... [O]ne of the 'boundaries' of the help offered has to be that the help must be consistent with the agency function of law enforcement. ...

Thus, offenders placed on probation or other compulsory supervision would still be obliged to submit to the formal requirements of the order, the authority-base for which derives quite clearly from the *court*; but the authority-base for the 'help' would reside unambiguously in the *client*. Probation officers would have to stop operating, as they often do now, on the assumption that either the authority to treat or the authority to compel attendance derived from professional expertise. ...

This discussion helps to clarify that both the pure treatment model and our model involve an element of pressure, but in different ways. The compulsory treatment model imposes coercion as to either 'co-operating in expert treatment' or implicit rejection by the worker. The help model obliges the client to make a series of moral and behavioural choices, but the worker does not reject the client whatever choices are made. There have to be definite boundaries to the help available: probation officers cannot provide help outside the scope of their agency function; nor can they collude with the client to evade the formal requirements of the probation order; nor can they help clients in certain ways, for example in procuring drugs or housebreaking implements. But within the limits of these clear boundaries, unconditional help is offered, though the client must make the choices: this gives the client greater responsibility, and also means that in certain contexts he must carry the consequences of wrong choices – for example in further court appearances. The worker cannot help the client to avoid those consequences; but equally, the worker will not make the consequences worse for the client by an implied or actual rejection in the social inquiry report. ...

Lastly, we may make two final points about this second aim of 'surveillance'.

The first is to draw attention to some recent research which perhaps shows, in different contexts, that surveillance may (for as long as it lasts) be beneficial in 'holding' clients from reconviction (Berg *et al.* 1978; Home Office 1977). ... Secondly, we should note that this second aim provides the essential answer to the obvious question: 'if we substitute help for treatment, why should any court ever put anyone on probation?' ... [I]f courts can be persuaded to see that probation meets the community's wish for surveillance, whilst also allowing the client to select appropriate assistance if desired, then indeed there are sound reasons to make such orders. ...

Aim 3: *diverting appropriate offenders from custodial sentences*

... [T]here are available within the probation service a number of resources – probation itself, community service, day training centres, probation hostels, day centres, and so on – which might well 'hold' many offenders as successfully in the community as in prison, and more cheaply. The deliberate use of such facilities irrespective of offenders' suitability for treatment and irrespective of social need should, therefore, allow a considerable expansion of non-custodial possibilities. It would also meet sentencers' anxieties about alternatives in a responsible and realistic manner, without making any false assumptions about the treatment efficacy of such alternatives.

... It is our contention that if these measures were reconceptualized in non-treatment terms it would allow them to be used more fully in the middle range of seriousness because they could be considered in cases of low social need. ...

... We believe [that a further substantial reduction in custodial sentences] can be achieved – but only if:

(i)   probation officers abandon treatment concepts in making recommendations;
(ii)   they cease to recommend custodial or suspended sentence disposals;
(iii)   they think imaginatively but realistically about alternatives within the range of existing facilities, and develop appropriate recommendations in suitable cases.

We do not consider that present practice comes near to these specifications, and we are therefore not impressed by the counter argument that 'the probation service is already doing all it can do by way of diversion'. ...

Aim 4: the reduction of crime

… If treatment or 'help' will not reduce crime, what will? There is only one realistic answer: crime prevention. But 'prevention' can mean many different things to different people – it can mean, for example, applying extraversion tests to small children, picking out those 'difficult to condition', and giving them 'a much more rigorous and efficient system of conditioning than the normal person' (Eysenck 1977: 184); it can mean the redesigning of urban architecture, especially in residential buildings (Newman 1973); it can mean advice to the public about locking houses and cars, and buying burglar alarms … ; or it can mean a complete revolution in society, since 'it must be possible via social transformations to create social and productive arrangements that would abolish crime' (Taylor, Walton and Young 1975: 20).

We do not propose to discuss such prescriptions here, though all of them can be heavily criticized in different ways. The point simply is that none of the skills required to construct these alleged Utopias exist within the probation service, so they are not worth considering in depth in this context.

Rather, we shall argue here that crime is predominantly social, so that any serious crime reduction strategy must be of a socially (rather than an individually) based character; that 'treatment' strategies as applied to communities are as inappropriate for crime prevention as they are for individual 'help' for offenders; that nevertheless there are some plausible clues which might be followed in a crime reduction strategy by the probation service; that these clues essentially consist of possible microstructural and socially integrative ameliorations within communities; but that these ameliorations can take place only if significant power in their implementation is given to the residents of high crime rate communities, with the professional probation officer restricting his role to that of helper and catalyst. …

Hence we believe that the probation service should not engage in crime prevention work except in communities which actively wish it, and that, throughout the work, the authority base for the social workers' actions should remain with the residents and their wish for assistance. This is, of course, fully congruent with the 'help' concept which has flowed throughout this paper. …

Conclusions

We began this paper with a quotation from the present Head of the Home Office Research Unit in which he raised the possibility of the demise of the probation service. We have argued that this possibility, remote though it might seem, must now be taken seriously. We have therefore attempted to specify some of the central issues which confront the service and to create a new paradigm for practice which tries to meet and overcome them in the inevitable confusion which must follow the death of treatment. …

From Anthony E. Bottoms and William McWilliams, 'A non-treatment paradigm for probation practice', British Journal of Social Work, 9(2), 1979, pp. 159–202.

References

Allen, F. A. (1959) 'Legal Values and the Rehabilitative, Ideal'. *Journal of Criminal Law, Criminology and Political Science*, 50: 226–32.

American Friends Service Committee (1971) *Struggle for Justice*. New York, Hill and Wang.

Berg, I., Consterdine, M., Hullin, R., McGuire, R. and Tyrer, S. (1978) 'The Effect of Two Randomly Allocated Court Procedures on Truancy'. *British Journal of Criminology*, 18(3): 232–244.

Berntsen, K. and Christiansen, K. O. (1965) 'A Resocialisation Experiment with Short-Term Offenders', in K. O. Christiansen (ed.), *Scandinavian Studies in Criminology, Vol. I*. London, Tavistock, pp. 35–54.

Bottoms, A. E. and McClintock, F. H. (1973) *Criminals Coming of Age: a study of institutional adaptation in the treatment of young and adolescent offenders*. London, Heinemann Educational.

Brody, S. R. (1976) *The Effectiveness of Sentencing: A review of the literature*. Home Office Research Study 35. London, HMSO.

Brody, S. (1978) 'Research into the Aims and Effectiveness of Sentencing'. *Howard Journal* 17(3): 133–148.

Croft, J. (1978) *Research in Criminal Justice*. Home Office Research Study 44. London, HMSO.

Davies, M. (1977) *Support Systems in Social Work*. London, Routledge and Kegan Paul

Durkheim, E. (1895) (English translation 1964) *The Rules of Sociological Method*. New York, Free Press.

Eysenck, H. J. (1977) *Crime and Personality*. Third Edition. St. Albans, Paladin.

Greenberg, D. F. (1977) 'The Correctional Effects of Corrections: a survey of evaluations', in D. F. Greenberg (ed.), *Corrections and Punishment*. Sage Criminal Justice System Annuals Vol. 8. Beverly Hills, Sage, pp. 111–148.

Home Office (1977) *Prison Statistics*. London, HMSO.

King, J. F. S. (ed.) (1958) *The Probation Service*. First Edition. London, Butterworth.

Lipton, D., Martinson, R. and Wilks, J. (1975) *The Effectiveness of Correctional Treatment*. New York, Praeger.

Meyer, C. H. (1972) 'Practice on Microsystem Level', in E. J. Mullen and J. R. Dumpson (eds), *Evaluation of Social Intervention*. San Francisco, Jossey-Bass, pp. 158–190.

Morris, P. and Beverly, F. (1975) *On Licence: a study of parole*. London, Wiley.

Newman, O. (1973) *Defensible Space: crime prevention through urban design*. New York, Macmillan.

Radzinowicz, L. (1958) Preface to *The Results of Probation*, a Report of the Cambridge Department of Criminal Science. London, Macmillan, pp. x–xii.

Reid, W. J. and Epstein, L. (1972) *Task-Centred Casework*. New York, Columbia University Press.

Taylor, I., Walton, P. and Young, J. (1973) *The New Criminology*. London, Routledge and Kegan Paul.

—(1975) 'Critical Criminology in Britain', in I. Taylor, P. Walton and J. Young (eds), *Critical Criminology*. London, Routledge and Kegan Paul, pp. 6–62.

34 Socialist probation work (1981)

Hilary Walker and Bill Beaumont

Towards understanding

In this section we turn from the level of theory and analysis to the more practical and immediate level of day-to-day probation work, addressing the question, 'But what can we do in the job?' ...

We have attempted to draw prescriptions from our analysis. We do not see the development of a distinct 'radical probation work' as a realistic aim, instead we emphasise the importance of a clear understanding of the issues faced in practice as the basis for determining appropriate action. ...

Limitations

A fundamental conclusion of our analysis is that probation officers are paid to do a particular job for the state and that this role is generally supportive of capitalism. ... This position of state employee limits the oppositional action possible in the job. There is room for manoeuvre and the limits are often unclear but some actions may simply be unacceptable. ...

As a consequence of their role, socialist probation officers will often find themselves at odds with their agency and should not expect to enlist official support. We need to be guarded about management supervision and cautious of agency initiatives and promises. Although sometimes we will be in agreement with the agency, and such alliances can be useful, they are likely to be short term and limited. Many aspects of the job, such as the conditions in probation orders and parole licences, are 'structured in'. These act as a constraint which tends to define the nature of contact with clients and may restrict flexibility in ways of working. ...

It is important to bear in mind the relatively weak position of the probation service within the powerful criminal justice system and the coercive base of that system. This marginal status means that the probation service is rarely in a position to initiate change but rather follows developments in the criminal justice system. In a tilt towards coercion it is even conceivable that the consent-securing role of probation work might become redundant. ... In a coercive tilt opportunities for positive innovation will be limited but a defensive, oppositional stance is of great importance. ...

Contradictions

Our analysis suggests that there can be no absolute solutions or clear ways ahead in the job. All the possibilities and opportunities for socialist probation officers will also contain problems and dilemmas. We suggest that the Marxist concept of the contradiction is helpful to understanding here. ...

A primary contradiction arises because we work within definitions, with which we disagree, imposed by powerful institutions of the state. For example, working with laws we consider unjust and prisons we abhor places us immediately in a difficult and contradictory position. Such definitions cannot be escaped and we need to decide whether we can work positively despite them, living with the discomfort arising from this position. It may be helpful to be able to recognize the source of this discomfort.

Another major contradiction faced is that the aspects of the job which give both clients and probation officers room to manoeuvre – flexibility, discretion, autonomy and the brief to help – also produce other consequences. The exercise of discretion and mercy serves to legitimate the criminal justice system. The humane, welfare aspects of probation work represent a cost to the capitalist state but are also functional in securing consent. Another contradiction arises from the flexibility in the job which gives socialists the opportunity to work in humane and less oppressive ways. Equally it allows others to work in more authoritarian ways, for example by readily breaching or recommending recall. This use of flexibility can result in a lack of uniformity in dealings with clients – and thus potential injustices. ... [W]e might oppose the possibility of such inequity of treatment but attempts at standardization may well produce a more oppressive system.

... [C]ontradictions will also arise in day-to-day contact with clients. First, clients will tend to see us as authority figures and therefore keep some distance and censor their comments, despite our wish to encourage an open relationship and to 'get alongside' them. Second, our analysis identifies crime as a social and political construct which is unlikely to respond to individual attention. Thus probation work seems unable to attain the goal of helping individuals stay out of trouble. ... Third, there are contradictions related to providing material benefits for clients. The benefits we can obtain will usually be delivered in the state form and therefore be reinforcing capitalist social relations. Often they will prove woefully inadequate and so cannot be a fully satisfactory solution. Helping clients with practical problems in this way poses the familiar contradiction that such individual assistance ignores the communality of problems and cannot attack the source of need.

Crime and the working class

... We have noted that the probation service deals mainly with working-class clients, as a direct result of the way in which the law demarcates certain forms of activity as illegal. Working-class experience and attitudes towards crime are contradictory. Working people are concerned about crime and threats to their safety and property posed by offenders. Their experience of the damage and hurt caused by criminal activity is often real (although the extent to which people's lives are directly affected by crime remains unclear). However, their fears are fed by the media's sensational reporting of, and intense concentration on, crime and by the way in which the state consistently presents it as a major problem faced by working people. This misleading representation, with the false 'fetishized' form of the law, leads working people to believe that the law can and will offer them the protection they need. So calls for 'law and order' can attract substantial working-class support. At the same time, this surface appearance of neutrality is often penetrated. Working people recognize that the law and its enforcement are not impartial and bear down disproportionately on them. Frequently they recognize that some of those labelled as criminal are not an alien threat but ordinary people much like themselves. Support for harsh punishment of 'criminals' can contrast sharply with a tolerant and sympathetic concern for offenders personally known.

... Not surprisingly there have been few working-class struggles in the area of crime and the law. The major exception to this occurs when traditional trade union rights and activities are criminalized or are threatened with criminalization, as with the opposition to the Industrial Relations Act 1971 or current resistance to changes in picketing law. Even when this happens, the connections between such 'political' crime and other crime are not made. The law is rarely dealt with as an issue for working-class struggle in politics. A recent exception to this has been the 'Sus' campaign, which succeeded in enlisting support from the labour movement.

Probation officers' orientation in their work and focus of concern has traditionally been almost exclusively with the offender. This has often been taken to the extreme of unreservedly championing the interests of the client and ignoring the impact of offences and the damage sometimes resulting for other working people. These attitudes arise from humane concern for the client, reinforced by the role specification (the brief to be concerned) and the social work emphasis of the job. There are dangers in this orientation because a total concern for the client is held at the expense of a more balanced approach, acknowledging the realities and problems of crime. It is consistent with our analysis to adopt a more even-handed approach. This would involve a shift away from the position of unqualified support for clients towards a more rounded concern with crime in so far as it is a problem for the working class. We need, however, to keep crime in perspective as a problem. It is by no means the greatest threat faced by the working class and we should refute that view by counterposing the greater threats – exploitation, low wages, injustice and inadequate welfare services.

Potential

... We think that many conventional accounts of probation and social work are hopelessly ambitious, overstating the potential of social work for transforming both individuals and society. To present a more realistic base of expectation may seem an anti-climax but it is likely to equip people better to face the difficulties of practice.

... In our view, a continuing emphasis on the search for positive and initiating strategies has led to an undervaluing of the importance of defensive and oppositional action. Socialist probation officers find themselves working within a criminal justice system, much of which they oppose. Whatever the scope for other action, they will find themselves seeking to protect people from the worst consequences of the system, resisting its values and opposing the way it works. ... Here we wish to stress the positive nature of opposition within an antagonistic criminal justice system. In a period of coercive tilt, an oppositional stance will be particularly important: changes in the job will need to be resisted and the opportunities for progressive development are likely to be limited.

We have argued that the juridical system plays a crucial role in legitimizing the capitalist state. ... Equally though, the fact that the criminal justice system underpins the capitalist state makes it a vital arena for struggle. ... It matters that there are *probation officers* prepared to state publicly that prison is destructive, that there are unjust laws, that law enforcement is discriminatory and even that the probation service cannot cope with the poverty and hardship our work uncovers. It could be even more effective if magistrates, police officers and prison staff were also prepared to dissent: their silence places even more responsibility on probation officers. The whole burden of opposition and exposure otherwise falls on those processed by the system, offenders whose credibility is easily undermined. ...

Here we are identifying potential for probation officers to contribute to 'struggle within the state'. ... As well as posing challenges within the criminal justice system probation officers gain knowledge and experience relevant to struggles in the welfare state. They can contribute to struggles being waged over housing, education and poverty. Again, what probation officers do and say gains significance from their position of employment within the state, and gains credibility because it is based on knowledge drawn from experience in the job.

... The stereotype of social workers who put all their energy into campaigning at the expense of their clients is a cheap and cruel caricature. The pressures of the job too often take people to the opposite extreme. Socialist probation officers must find time and use opportunities to take their knowledge and experience beyond individual probation practice.

It will remain the case that most of us spend most of our time in direct probation work with clients. ... Defensive and oppositional action will also have an important place in individual practice. Social enquiry reports can seek to lessen the oppressive effect of the criminal justice system. In probation work we can seek to minimize the negative and repressive aspects of the job. The results of such action may not appear as a dramatic new practice, but they will be experienced and appreciated by clients. ...

Our perception and understanding of the state, the criminal justice system and issues in the welfare state can be brought into work with clients. This will affect both the way we view and talk about the difficulties facing them and the action taken in response to those difficulties. The 'space' available in the job also allows us to act humanely and with consideration towards clients, qualities rare in the criminal justice system. Opportunities exist to take account of and respect clients' views and attitudes. Finally we can use our position to provide and devise services which are genuinely useful and helpful to clients. Within the limitations and constraints we have outlined, the emphasis on autonomy of judgement and decision in the probation role provides considerable potential in which to develop a socialist practice.

Framework for understanding

... We are concerned to leave readers in a position to apply our analysis to a range of situations they will face in the job. We therefore conclude this chapter with an outline framework for understanding, which we hope will prove a useful analytical tool. We have set out some questions based on our general analysis which we suggest can be specifically applied to problems faced. ...

The state

Placing a particular issue within the wider context of the role and function of the state under capitalism helps us to understand the often conflicting and contradictory aspects of the job, the relative significance of this aspect of probation work, how it connects with and contributes to the state's function. It helps to place the issue in a broader perspective and may identify relevant areas of struggle. So we suggest asking:

- What connections can be identified with the functions of the state?
- What values does it promote?
- Does it contribute to the securing of consent? To which part of the state apparatus and in what way?
- What other parts of the state apparatus are particularly relevant here? What role do they play? Do their definitions predominate? Does it support/strengthen/adopt/oppose those definitions?
- Does it relate to changes within the state?
- What potentially oppositional features can be identified?
- What connections are there with struggles in the state?

Clients

Having located the issue within the structure of the state we need to assess its impact on clients. We need to identify what it will mean to them and what their response will be. So we suggest asking:

- What is the impact on clients and their families? Are benefits provided/won? If so, under what conditions and in what form?
- What restrictions does it impose?
- What messages and values does it convey to clients?
- How much real consent can clients exercise?
- What do clients say about it? What is their reaction?

The working class

Our understanding should extend to the impact on working people and consider connections with issues relevant to the working class as a whole. So we suggest asking:

- What impact will it have on the working class?
- Does it relate to problems faced by the working class as a whole?
- Can connections be made with working-class struggles?

The probation role

Finally, we need to appreciate the significance of issues for the way they affect our work and whether they involve changes in the role of probation officers.

- What are the main features of the role here with clients and with other state institutions?
- What does this role mean for the way probation officers work?
- What opportunities are there for individual discretion and autonomy?
- Does it imply a change in the probation role and in what direction?
- What are the major contradictions and dilemmas it involves?

From Hilary Walker and Bill Beaumont, Probation work: critical theory and socialist practice *(Oxford: Basil Blackwell), 1981, pp. 159–173.*

35 Probation, pragmatism and policy (1987)

William McWilliams

This is the final paper in a quartet of essays in which I attempt to trace the history of ideas sustaining the English probation system since its beginnings in the late nineteenth century (McWilliams 1983, 1985, 1986). The understandings of the probation service which I have tackled so far embrace two periods which I have called the phase of special pleading, dominant from the mid-1870s to the 1930s, and the phase of diagnosis which held sway from the 1930s to the early 1970s. The current understanding of the service had its roots in the 1960s and developed in the 1970s, and because of its characteristics it may most appropriately be identified as the phase of pragmatism. Table 1 shows that modern phase in the context of the history of ideas, and the conceptual changes which have taken place since the latter part of the nineteenth century. ...

Table 1 shows the phase of pragmatism as being very different from the earlier phases; the commonality of understandings which held in the phases of special pleading and diagnosis have broken down, and three distinct 'schools of thought' have emerged; but despite this the consensus can still be seen to hold in certain respects. First, there is agreement that the modern probation service is characterised by its diversity of operation, and few challenge the popular wisdom that this is as it should be. Secondly, although they have different reasons for doing so, each of the schools of thought shares the opinion that the probation officer's task in court is to offer realistic disposals with a view to reducing custodial sentences. Thirdly, and most importantly in gaining a grasp of the nature of the changes which have occurred between the phases of diagnosis and pragmatism, we should note that the ontological view of the offender is the same for each school. To expand that point: the individual is still of great importance to the probation service, and in practice offenders are, for the most part, still dealt with one by one; but at the same time the uniqueness of the person's soul, or his mind and the nexus of his social circumstances, can now be viewed *only* within a framework of policy. Of course, the schools differ in the degree to which they cleave to this ontological vision but, as I will attempt to show in subsequent sections, none escapes completely from this modem denotation of the offender. ...

Table 1 Understandings

PHASES	Ontological view of offenders	Main source of knowledge guiding action	Ultimate objective of action	Justification of action	Means to objective	Operational mode in court	Defining characteristic of probation service
1. Special pleading (1876–1930)	Individual: unique in the sight of God	Faith	State of grace	Morals	Moral reform	Plead for mercy	Idealism
2. Diagnosis (1930–1970)	Individual: unique psycho-social traits and behaviour	Psychological science	Cure	Facts	Scientific treatment	Give diagnosis and treatment plan	Professionalism
3. Pragmatism (1970–)	Individual in a framework of policy					Offer realistic disposals with overarching aim of reducing custodial sentencing	Diversification
Managerial School		Management science	Social conformity	Rational efficiency	Social control mechanisms		
Radical School		Marxism	Social change	Egalitarianism	Consciousness raising		
Personalist School		Modified Kantianism	Enhancement of person in existing society	Individual rights	Helping individuals		

Diversification and changes

... The diversification and expansion of the work of the probation service was accompanied by substantial increases in the levels of staffing. ... [T]he levels of staffing more than kept pace with the increase in work as far as criminal supervision was concerned. At the same time the proportion of the staff who undertook the actual supervision of offenders (that is, basic grade probation officers) declined. ...

The diversification and increase in tasks of the probation service, the growth in its size and, in particular, the alteration in its organisational structure in terms of the percentage distribution of officers as between the different grades all had profound implications for the culture of the agency. In the 1950s and early 1960s the service was a small enterprise; its major preoccupation was the supervision of offenders who were on probation and for whom probation officers were personally and directly accountable to the courts. An individual officer was, in many crucial ways, *the* manifestation of the service in his particular locale. ...

This intimate, almost cosy service, composed in large part of staunch individualists, was to be transformed through the changes which took place in the late 1960s and early 1970s. The effects of these changes were substantial: among the most important was a movement of the service away from the judicial towards the executive arm of the state, the bureaucratisation of the probation system, and the rise of managerialism (McWilliams 1981). ...

The retreat of treatment and the rise of policy

... (A)t the time when the organisational machine for the rehabilitation of offenders was being created, doubts about the efficacy of rehabilitation were growing and, in the 1970s, the belief that penal 'treatments' could cure offenders was officially abandoned. By then, of course, the service machine existed, and although the question might be raised of whether it too should be abandoned, it was hardly seen as realistic. Rather the machine could be directed towards another purpose, to satisfy the pragmatic need to relieve the pressure on custodial institutions by dealing with a greater proportion of offenders than hitherto via community-based disposals. It is important to observe that there was no conflict here; probation officers held a long tradition of helping offenders, and attempting to keep them out of custody could be seen precisely in those terms; but the creation of the policy-serving organisational machine was a very different matter.

... The 'new', policy-pursuing probation service was no longer missionary, no longer scientific, and, no longer unified. The ultimate reaction of individuals to change within the service was to divide into three distinct schools of thought; and these I have called 'the managerial', 'the radical', and 'the personalist'. ...

The managerial school

Currently the extant literature on management and the control of organisations is vast and much of it is highly specialised and technical. It is also the case that a great deal of the work on the topic and most of the available models for the conduct of management continue to derive from industry and commerce, and there is comparatively little which might be seen as directly relevant to the conduct of professional organisations whose end-products are less easy to specify than those of the commercial. Nevertheless, as the probation service moved towards administrative understandings of the nature of efficiency and goal-achievement, the models derived from industry came to be seen as appropriate, at least by members of the managerial school.

... [T]here can be little doubt that this modern ubiquity of 'management' is of an extent sufficient to entail that many people would find it difficult to conduct substantial parts of their lives were they unexpectedly to find themselves without access to the framework of thought which the management construct provides in myriad social institutions. Within the probation service the concept of management is now firmly ensconced, but its rise and development has been far from unproblematic. Numerous commentators, including those drawn from the ranks of those now deemed to be managers, have questioned the relevance, validity, and even the propriety of importing into the agency the ideas and insights gained in, say, the running of General Motors or the marketing, distribution and sale of Coca Cola (see, for example, Weston 1973).

... Twenty-five years ago ... the probation service was based on a professional–supervisory–administrative model of organisation, geared to the treatment of individual offenders. Under that model the professional skills of the probation officers were seen as being enhanced by enabling administrative provision, and the quality of their work ensured by a specific type of casework supervision. It would probably be agreed generally that some parts of that model persist to the present day, but also there can be little doubt that the model has been substantially changed by the introduction of management control over the professional conduct of probation officers. ...

... It is this which gives us the key to understanding the managerial school: it is the managers who define the policies and the objectives, and as a consequence perhaps the members of the managerial school have come to believe that they have now taken the role of embodying the service *in propria persona* which, in the 'old' probation service, was held by the probation officers. This is not a view which would win universal acclaim outside management circles. ...

The radical school

Recent years have seen the publication of a number of texts on social work which have avowed a radical intent (see, for example, Bailey and Brake 1975; Pritchard and Taylor 1978; Brake and Bailey 1980; Walker and Beaumont 1985). ...

Interestingly enough there are similarities here between this 'radical' approach and the position of the managerial school. Both, it seems, involve a decisive ontological shift in the perceived status of the offender who is no longer the 'individual with unique psycho-social traits and behaviour' of the diagnostic phase, but rather a unit within a defining system of policy considerations. ...

In essence, then, the radical school is not as radical *in practice* as its theories might imply, and, as I have suggested already, it shares with the managerial school an ontology which gives precedence to systems over persons. Ultimately, for both the radicals and the managers, persons are *means* to be used in the pursuit of transcendent policies rather than *ends* in themselves. ...

The personalist school

In Table 1 I identify the ontology of the personalist school as being a form of 'modified Kantianism'. By this I intend to imply that all personalists cleave to Kant's view when he says that:

> man, and in general every rational being, *exists* as an end in himself, *not merely as a means* for arbitrary use by this or that will. ...
>
> (Paton 1964, p. 95, italics in original)

The Kantianism of the personalist school is modified in so far as personalists would agree with Kant without reservation that men must be viewed as *ends*, but they would be less inclined to agree that the grounds for doing so depend on man's rationality. ...

... [T]he fundamental reason for eschewing the touchstone of rationality in determining the status of a person as an end is that empirically not all human beings appear to be rational, but nevertheless the personalists would insist that they are *persons to be treated at all times as ends rather than means*.

Because *all* the members of the personalist school share only this essential ontology and may vary considerably in other respects, the school is marked by its diversity of attitudes and views and, ontological understanding apart, it is not possible to cite *typical* personalists. On the ontological ground, however, it is probably accurate to identify as members of the personalist school such writers on the probation service as Hugman (1977), Millard (1979), Bailey (1980), Stelman (1980) and Raynor (1985). ...

In the future of the probation service, Millard sees ... the development of 'a range of strategies related to need and opportunity provision as well as counselling' (p. 87). All of which is far removed from the views of both the managers and the radicals; but, as I suggest in Table 1, all three schools of thought come together in three crucial respects: each of the schools is pragmatic, each sees the offender as bounded by a framework of policy, and each says that the service should be providing alternatives to custody. ...

Unifying ideological features of the three schools

So far as the managerial school is concerned, I think we may take it as inevitable that their understanding of the offender is that of a unit to be processed within a framework of policy. After all, the proclaimed primary task of managers is to create the very policy through which offenders are to be dealt with by probation officers as efficiently and economically as possible. The pragmatism of the managerial school, however, requires further elucidation.

One of the problems of the managerial pursuit of rational efficiency is that it tends to blur the distinction between ends and means. Thus we can find a sub-committee of the Conference of Chief Probation Officers (1979) reaching the conclusion that 'it is reasonable to define the role of the service by reference to the nature and extent of its duties' (p. 5), and saying nothing whatsoever about the *aims* of the probation service.

... For the radical school the individual falls naturally into a framework of policy, but for the members of this school the ideal would be *socialist* policy. As radical probation officers remain employees of the capitalist state they are obliged either to leave the service or to acknowledge that offenders are currently contained in a policy framework defined by the managers. Thus in the radical philosophy the offender is to be rescued from one policy framework, but only to be placed in another. The pragmatism of the radicals is contained in the fact that many of them do not depart from the service of a capitalist state which they deeply despise, but rather trim their vision constantly in order to survive. ...

The school for which the idea of the offender within a framework of policy creates the greatest difficulty is the personalist. Members of this school would actually prefer *not* to conceive of persons in this way at all, but (and in this they are like the radicals) it is precisely by their efforts *against* the policy orientation that they acknowledge its existence. Of the three schools the personalist is the one with the longest tradition in the probation service, and because of its specific ontology of man it is the one which is the least pragmatic. At the same time ... personalists, because they are within a service now dominated by policies relating to classes of offenders, cannot escape from some compromises which are essentially pragmatic. ...

... [A]ll three schools of thought agree that the modern probation service should be in the business of providing alternatives to custody in its court-based work, but each cleaves to this precept for different reasons. First, for the managerial school, the policy 'to provide acceptable alternatives to custodial sentences within the criminal justice system', as the Management Structure Review put it (Joint Negotiating Committee 1980), is *the managers'* policy, to be carried out by probation officers through the medium of their social enquiry work. ...

Secondly, members of the radical school of thought also bear allegiance to the policy of providing alternatives to custody but, unsurprisingly, for reasons very different from those of the managers. The managers believe in the rational efficiency of the organisation; the radicals believe in working class struggle against the capitalist state. ...

Thirdly, the policy of providing alternatives to custody is dear to the hearts of the members of the personalist school, but their reasons for this differ from those of both the managers and the radicals. For the personalists, social enquiry practice is about working jointly with offenders. ...

The stress on the *person* of the offender ... marks out the personalist approach from that of the managers and the radicals. The personalist is not dealing with *classes* of persons within a transcendental policy as, in their different ways, are the managers and the radicals. Rather he is dealing with unique individuals who are free to make choices of their own and who are to be helped in those choices. ...

The justification of mission

... In the post-diagnostic era the probation service has not actually lost its sense of mission (although it must be noted that the conception of that mission now varies as between the different schools of thought); rather it is that the loss which the service has suffered is that of any satisfying transcendent *justification* for its present concerns with providing realistic alternatives to imprisonment. ... The contemporary claim that one can deal with offenders somewhat more cheaply and more humanely than might otherwise be the case may appeal to economists with a soft spot for their fellow men, but it hardly has the cachet, or indeed the rectitude, of a claim to save men's souls or change their psyches.

For those in the higher ranks of the service the collapse of confidence in the diagnostic-treatment model was a severe blow ..., but at least for them there was the growth in the management ideal into which they could retreat, and the fast-developing notions of policy towards which they could direct their energies and idealism. For those at the basic level of the service, however, those continuing to be involved in the daily business of practice, no such escape was possible; and, if anything, the new managerialism in the upper reaches of the organisation was felt to be more of a burden than a helpfully liberating force. ...

Small wonder that the practitioners retreated somewhat, and that practice failed to meet the ideals of policy even on points of consensus. ...

From *William McWilliams, 'Probation, pragmatism and policy',*
Howard Journal, *26(2), 1987, pp. 97–121.*

References

Bailey, R. (1980) 'Social workers: pawns, police or agitators?', in M. Brake and R. Bailey (Eds.), *Radical Social Work and Practice*, London: Edward Arnold.

Bailey, R. and Brake, M. (Eds.) (1975) *Radical Social Work*, London: Edward Arnold.

Brake, M. and Bailey, R. (Eds.) (1980) *Radical Social Work and Practice*, London: Edward Arnold.

Conference of Chief Probation Officers (1979) 'Future prospects for the probation service: some options' (unpublished).

Hugman, B. (1977) *Act Natural*, London: Bedford Square Press.

Joint Negotiating Committee (1980) *Report of the Working Party on Management Structure in the Probation and After-Care Service*, London: Joint Negotiation Committee for the Probation Service.

McWilliams, W. (1981) 'The probation officer at court: from friend to acquaintance', *Howard Journal*, 20, 97–116.

——(1983) 'The mission to the English police courts 1876–1936', *Howard Journal*, 22, 129–47.

——(1985) 'The mission transformed: professionalisation of probation between the wars', *Howard Journal*, 24: 257–74.

——(1986) 'The English probation system and the diagnostic ideal', *Howard Journal*, 25: 241–60.

Millard, D. (1979) 'Broader approaches to probation practice', in J. F. S. King (Ed.), *Pressures and Change in the Probation Service* (Cropwood Conference Series 11), Cambridge: Institute of Criminology, University of Cambridge.

Paton, H. (Trans and Ed.) (1964) *Kant's Groundwork of the Metaphysic of Morals*, New York: Harper Torchbooks.

Pritchard, C. and Taylor, R. (1978) *Social Work: Reform or Revolution?* London: Routledge and Kegan Paul.

Raynor, P. (1985) *Social Work, Justice and Control*, Oxford: Basil Blackwell.

Stelman, A. (1980) 'Social work relationships: an exploration', *Probation Journal*, 27, 85–94.

Walker, H. and Beaumont, B. (Eds.) (1985) *Working with Offenders*, London: Macmillan.

Weston, W. R. (1973) '"Style of management" in the probation service', *Probation Journal*, 20, 69–73.

36 Working at the margin, campaigning at the centre (1987)

Rob Canton

What does the Probation Service stand for? Time was when the answer to that question was seen as straightforward. The Probation Service affirmed the value of a particular strategy – casework treatment – to effect a reduction in crime by the rehabilitation of individual offenders. It may have been acknowledged that the practice often fell short of the theory, but treating is what most probation officers would have said they were trying to do.

The concept of treatment has been thoroughly discredited (see particularly Allen 1964; Flew 1973; Bean 1976); ideas of rehabilitation attract scepticism and even reduction meets suspicion. Yet there is a reluctance to re-open the question, to ask what the Service is to value, if not treatment. This diffidence has its strengths: it permits a wide and flexible interpretation of the Service's tasks. But the Service needs a philosophy to inform and shape its practice and to defend that practice against those politicians and sentencers who may be less shy about stating their own penal philosophy.

'Alternatives to custody': negative thinking

An influential idea has been that it is the Service's task to provide and extend 'alternatives to custody'. Yet this does not affirm what the Service stands for: it is what it is against. Saying what one is against is rarely enough. Fragile and peculiar alliances are formed in opposition, but do not survive the first attempt to frame a positive policy. It is possible to join with the Prison Officers' Association in denouncing the intolerable overcrowded state of our prisons, but there should be neither surprise nor indignation to learn that their solution involves the building of more prisons. Similarly, the Service's preoccupation with 'alternatives to custody' harmonises with Government policy, but the identity of interest is superficial. The Service does not (or should not) oppose custody because it is expensive or because existing conditions are squalid. There is a need to articulate a principled and reasoned opposition to custody that is grounded in a coherent penal philosophy.

'Alternatives to custody' has a pragmatic appeal, but it has outlived its usefulness and always conceded too much. Fitzmaurice and Pease (1986) have recently shown that the increased use of alternatives would have no more than a slight impact on the prison population.

Sentencing all 14,254 adult males who currently get sentences of six months or less to non-custodial measures instead would reduce the prison population by less than 2,000 – and this is an over-estimate. ...

They conclude that 'such slight diversion as has been achieved has been achieved at the cost of confusion and attendant injustice'.

Spurious pragmatism

Thus, even the pragmatic appeal is spurious. Conceptually, 'alternatives to custody' acknowledges penal custody as normal and established, the disposal by which all others are to be tested. Yet it is precisely this assumption, central to our sentencing culture, that needs to be challenged, not conceded at the outset. As it is, it is the alternatives that are having to be justified to sentencers. Report writers will be familiar with the circumstances in which a case has to be made for probation: unconvinced, the sentencer decides upon imprisonment, for which there is commonly no case at all.

Sterile debates begin about whether or not a particular penalty is or is not (to be regarded as) an alternative to custody. Sentencers are required to pose to themselves tortuous hypothetical questions about what they would have done, but for the power to do something else. The probation order, in particular, is challenged to demonstrate a level of success (as measured by reconviction) which no one expects prison to meet.

The Probation Service's dependence on the theme of alternatives to custody would have been less serious had it been set in the context of a penal philosophy. Instead, the Service has been left dangerously vulnerable to intrusive and punitive definitions of its task. It has been felt that most non-custodial schemes can be accommodated. It is for this reason that the extension of parole, control units, coercive conditions of a probation order and even tracking schemes have found some support within a Service that has persuaded itself to think of 'alternatives to custody' as its fulfilment.

It is not a coincidence that these schemes try to approximate to the custodial experience: it is an inevitable result of the adoption of a principle which accepts the wrong definition of the problem and immediately places the Probation Service on the defensive. When the Service is encouraged to devise credible alternatives to custody, it is a mistake to shuffle apologetically in that direction. The first response is to insist that there is nothing remotely credible about custody.

Discrediting of treatment

The Probation Service's philosophical uncertainty – and its consequent defensiveness – begins with the discrediting of treatment. This was nothing less than the rejection of the central principle of probation practice. Its abandonment would be deeply demoralising for probation officers aspiring to the status (and salary) of a profession and claiming precisely this as their distinctive professional skill.

It was for only a very short time, however, that the idea of treatment posed a threat to the dominant sentencing culture (Rutherford 1986), although matters appear to have gone further in America (Allen 1964; Milford 1975). The sentencing culture has been shaped and characterised by principles of punishment. Individualised treatment may be appropriate, but needs to be justified in as much as it is a departure from the normal standard or tariff of penalties (Thomas 1979). This tariff is shaped by many factors, but principally by considerations of retribution and deterrence.

The tariff as habit

Thus the theory. In reality, the single most important determinant of the tariff is habit: defendants are sentenced as they are because that is the sort of penalty which that offence tends to attract. It is only rarely that the tariff looks out at the world. When it does, it is almost always a need for increased penalties that is inferred. This offence is now seen to be more harmful than had been appreciated: retribution requires a greater penalty. That offence is becoming much too common: more severe punishment is needed to deter. It is worth remarking how rare it is to hear defenders of punishment urge a reduction in penalty because it has been identified as retributively excessive or ineffective or extravagant as a deterrent. It is in this way, incidentally, that the combination of retribution and deterrence has a much greater inflationary impact on the penal tariff than would the application of either principle on its own: if not one principle, then the other can always be cited to oppose a reduction of penalty.

Normally, though, the tariff is simply unreflective and disposes under the influence of habit. Whether its general scale is retributively appropriate or effectively deterrent is not usually allowed to arise as a question. Habit can sometimes be challenged simply by the recognition that it is habit. It may be that the sentencing culture could be shaken by an insistence that sentences reflect critically upon their practice. This is not something they often do at the moment: the training that most sentencers now receive is nothing much more than an acclimatisation to the culture of their Court. In the longer term, training should enable careful scrutiny of sentencing practice. Meanwhile, the challenge must come from the outside.

Instead of defending 'alternatives' against custody, the Probation Service should strive to change the terms of the debate. It is the assumptions of the sentencing culture that must be challenged. For example, the imagined harmony between retribution and deterrence must be questioned: reference to 'punishment' obscures the point that these principles are inherently in conflict (Acton 1969). In practice, the main retributive penalty – imprisonment – is neither deterrent nor, usually, otherwise reductive of crime. There could be a systematic reduction of all penalties with incalculable benefit to the penal system and without violation of any philosophy of punishment: retributive proportionality could be preserved and there would be no reason to anticipate an increase in crime.

Marginal impact of penal system

There is one element of our sentencing culture in particular that seems to me to be the single most intractable obstacle to penal reform. It is a belief asserted by politicians and by journalists, frequently alluded to by judges and magistrates and almost always implicit in public debate. It is that the penal system is the main determinant of levels of crime: whatever the origins of crime, it is the task of the penal system to control it and that system can be manipulated in response to changes in patterns of offending. Thus any proposal to reduce sentences evokes a fear that increases in crime will follow. Yet the history of the penal system this century shows clearly that the system is altogether marginal to the social phenomenon of crime (Ryan 1983). Theories and policies have shifted. Less often practice has varied. Throughout, crime levels have continued in their own direction.

The view that the penal system is marginal to crime can be expressed in a strong or a weak form. The stronger thesis would have it that the penal system is structurally incapable of influencing offending in a significant way: behaviour is guided by attitudes, by values, abilities and opportunities and on these the penal system has no bearing. A weaker statement would allow the possibility that the penal system may have an important influence, but insist that the extent to which that influence operates is not known. There is therefore no way of manipulating this system towards any particular impact on crime. On either account, there is no convincing reason to suppose that increases in crime would follow upon an extensive and systematic reduction in the scale of penalties.

The manipulation of the penal system to reduce overall levels of offending remains a part of the thinking of all political parties and is a central tenet of our sentencing culture. It hinders considered debate about crime. Its influence on the penal system has been pernicious. The Probation Service has normally colluded, sometimes by choice, more often by default. Instead it must affirm the marginal relevance of the penal system to the incidence of crime.

The Probation Service, then, can campaign at the centre. By challenging the conventional understanding of the relationship between crime and the penal system, it can enable a more considered debate about crime. It can also contribute positively to that debate because probation officers may be uniquely placed to hear and to take seriously the accounts that offenders give of their behaviour and so to help to identify those considerations that have had a real influence.

The limits of the justice model

But what are the implications of this analysis for the penal system and for the Probation Service in particular? One possible response would be to disavow reductive considerations altogether. The Justice Model urges a response of that kind: it is not the purpose of the penal system to control crime, but to administer just penalties for wrongs done. Though the Justice Model may have been successful in limiting the excesses of treatment, it has had worse fortune in its attempt to challenge deterrence theory. It has therefore left the sentencing culture unthreatened and, indeed, has been called upon to justify increases in punishment. Although its origins were liberal, it has certainly now been appropriated by the punishers. The radical potential of a sentencing theory which emphasises desert always seemed to have been overstated. It is also unclear how the Justice Model could accommodate probation practice in anything like its present form (Bean 1981).

A statement of practice

What seems to be required is a statement of probation practice, set in the context of a philosophy of the penal system, which escapes the sterility of retribution, but also avoids any ambitiously reductive pretensions which would collude with the sentencing culture. An indication of what such a penal philosophy would look like is offered by Andrew Rutherford (1986). He suggests that most young offenders mature out of crime, but points out that this process is retarded by institutional detention. Rutherford is concerned with juveniles, but his thesis can be generalised: it is life opportunities that are associated with rehabilitation, whether it be a relationship or a home or employment. Custody necessarily denies these opportunities and undermines the capacity to take advantage if they do occur. The penal system, then, can destroy these opportunities, although it cannot create them.

That the penal system is structurally marginal to crime does not entail that its impact on individual offenders is insignificant. On the contrary, its influence can be profound and life-changing and, as concerns custodial sentences, is normally negative and productive of further offending. Non-custodial sentences, although unlikely to be sufficient to ensure a reduction in an individual's offending, do not normally destroy the opportunities that lead to stability.

This argument sets up a strong presumption in favour of non-custodial penalties, which makes use of reductive considerations without colluding with the sentencing culture. The distinctive contribution of the Probation Service which this analysis suggests consists of the creation of opportunities, or the enabling of access to such opportunities or the assistance to take advantage of them. The implied philosophy of probation is characterised by:

1.   Limited reduction of offending. The reduction of an individual's offending should be re-affirmed as a legitimate and plausible objective of probation practice.
2.   Opposition to penal measures which promote crime or inhibit its reduction. This primarily involves the rejection of custody, explicitly on the grounds that, of its nature, it promotes further offending or at least delays 'growing out of crime'.
3.   Rejection of intrusive schemes which try to approximate to custody. The approximation will never satisfy the expectations of the sentencing culture. It is the culture itself that needs to be challenged.
4.   This conception of probation is closer to an educational than a treatment model.

In conclusion

To work at the margin is to acknowledge that probation practice is seldom the most influential consideration in an individual's rehabilitation, although its contribution can be significant. It is also to acknowledge that the Service is a small part of a large system which is itself marginal to the social phenomenon of crime.

Campaigning at the centre may involve taking a view about the connection between crime and political and economic strategies. It must insist that manipulation of the penal system is largely irrelevant to crime and likely to be harmful to the system itself. It may suggest that only the mythology of the sentencing culture argues against a substantial overall lowering of the tariff. This is not a case that needs to be expressed apologetically or defensively. The punishers in all political parties have stolen this issue (Downes 1983) and it is time it was taken back.

From Rob Canton, 'Working at the margin, campaigning at the centre',
Probation Journal, *34(3), 1987, pp. 97–100.*

References

Acton, H.B. (ed.) (1969) *The Philosophy of Punishment: a collection of papers.* London, Macmillan.

Allen, F.A. (1964) *The Borderland of Criminal Justice: essays in law and criminology.* Chicago, University of Chicago Press.

Bean, P. (1976) *Rehabilitation and Deviance.* London, Routledge and Kegan Paul.

——(1981) *Punishment.* Oxford, Martin Robertson.

Downes, D. (1983) *Law and Order: Theft of an Issue.* London, Fabian Society.

Fitzmaurice, C. and Pease, K. (1986) *The Psychology of Judicial Sentencing.* Manchester, Manchester University Press.

Flew, A. (1973) *Crime or Disease?* London, Macmillan.

Milford, J. (1975) *The American Prison Business,* Penguin.

Rutherford, A. (1986) *Growing out of Crime.* Harmondsworth, Penguin.

Ryan, M. (1983) *The Politics of Penal Reform.* London, Longman.

Thomas, D.A. (1979) *Principles of Sentencing: the sentencing policy of the Court of Appeal Criminal Division.* Second Edition. London, Heinemann.

37 Talking tough

Empty threats in probation practice (1989)

Judith Rumgay

The probation service, traditionally the most quiet and unassuming branch of the criminal justice system, currently finds itself at centre stage in the noisy debate about penal policy. Thrust into the limelight by the demand, encapsulated in the recent Green Paper (Home Office 1988), for alternatives to custody, rather than sentencing reform, as the means of reducing the burgeoning prison population, the service is watching this debate with considerable unease, yet appears uncertain how actually to assert a role as a main, and authoritative protagonist.

A major source of the probation service's disquiet is the language being invoked to describe its potential role in the provision of alternatives to custody. 'Punishment' and 'control' are the central tenets in the development of 'tough' and 'demanding' programmes of probation and community service. In his address to the Association of Chief Officers of Probation (ACOP), the Home Office Minister, John Patten, roundly chastised probation officers for their squeamishness over the use of such words, urging that 'it is bizarre to scratch around to find polite euphemisms for what is going on' (Patten 1988: 12). But whatever one's personal or professional, moral or political beliefs about the appropriate treatment of offenders, such words carry a strong message about the purpose of community-based sentencing by explicitly linking the concept of punishment – that is, the infliction of pain – to the non-custodial disposals operated by the probation service.

It is not hard to grasp that the service's alarm stems from the belief that the adoption of the language of punishment would herald a fundamental change in its traditional rehabilitative function. But how real is this fear? Patten argues reassuringly that 'practice will prove that underlying tension (between rehabilitation and punishment) to be more theoretical than real' (Patten 1988: 14). The purpose of this paper is to examine the foundations of the probation service's discomfort, not only with the language of punishment, but in devising its own professional response, and to consider the implications for probation practice of this development in the language of non-custodial sentencing.

A language problem

…The thrust of the arguments in the Green Paper and Patten's speech are intended to demonstrate the compatibility of the language of punishment with a rehabilitative goal. The Green Paper links punishments in which 'offenders are confronted with their offending behaviour and have to recognise the effects of their behaviour on the victims' to the development of a moral responsibility in which 'self-control', 'self-reliance' and 'respect for others' are the key themes (Home Office 1988: 1). Patten argues that the discipline and inconvenience of reporting to specified places at specified times are accurately described as punishment and control and that the notion of control further embraces such activities as 'the counselling which attempts to set limits to particular forms of conduct' (Patten 1988: 13). Nevertheless, the probation service appears unconvinced of these attempts to demonstrate the hitherto unrecognised harmony of punishment and rehabilitation, fearing rather that acquiescence in this semantic exercise will herald the erasure of rehabilitation from its endeavours and its replacement by punishment, pure and simple.

It is ironic that the Green Paper's remarks just noted claim to represent many current practice trends. The probation service is indeed no stranger to this very debate and in some respects has been its own worst enemy in contributing to the present anxious state of affairs. Examples may be drawn from both the practical and the theoretical levels of its contribution. At the practice level, the Kent Probation Control Unit explicitly emphasised control and containment within a disciplinary structure of supervision (Kent Probation and After-Care Service 1980). Despite its unequivocal espousal of the language of punishment, the acrimonious condemnation of the wider service to the venture seemed to dismay and puzzle its proponents, who apparently saw no contradiction between this forceful statement of intent and a rehabilitative function (Hills 1981). At the theoretical level, Martin Davies, speaking from a base in social work education, urged the provision of a non-custodial disposal 'that will be seen as a punitive, retributive and controlling facility in its own right' (1984: 4), placing his faith in the strong social work tradition of the service to counter overly punitive programmes in community control centres which would 'become the focus of those traditional penological objectives: vengeance, retribution and deterrence; rehabilitation will be an integral part of the sentence' (p. 5). Davies's punctuation is instructive, discounting rehabilitation as a 'traditional penological objective', yet assuming its presence in the content of programmes.

These practical and theoretical initiatives seemed unconcerned about the possible conflict between punishment and rehabilitation sheltering under one umbrella simply because this was not the focus of their attention. They held at their heart, neither rehabilitation nor punishment *per se*, but the reduction of custodial sentencing as their primary aim, with the guiding belief that this could be achieved by the provision of alternative, community-based programmes. Alternatives to custody would become credible and attractive to sentencers when they embraced the functions of custody – control, containment and retribution – at least as much as they embraced rehabilitation. The formulation of these initiatives thus contained an ambiguity. They did not own rehabilitation as their primary goal; they invoked the language of punishment to describe their structure; yet they did not intend to abandon rehabilitative methods in the content of their programmes. ... But why should committed rehabilitationists assume that the language of punishment will speak their cause more loudly to sentencers than the language of rehabilitation?

Rehabilitation lost

Over the past 15 years, the probation service's worthy cause has attracted considerable criticism. The rehabilitative ideal as a goal of penal policy has been attacked at a number of levels. Repeatedly disappointing evaluations of programmes led inexorably to the conclusion that 'nothing works' (Martinson 1974) and further critiques advanced evidence that not only did rehabilitation not do any good, it actually did harm by extending the network of social control and possibly even accelerating the use of custody (Cohen 1985; Schur 1973). Social workers and probation officers thus found themselves apparently guilty of unwarranted and damaging interventions in people's lives in the name of an infeasible objective. ...

The rise of justice

With the loss of rehabilitation as either an achievable, or a justifiable goal of penal policy, and the consequent loss of confidence in its own practice, the search was on in the probation service for a new direction for, or at least an acceptable language in which to describe, its activities with offenders. Instead of rehabilitation, the service's stated aims have become associated more with the (seemingly) less ambitious and more attainable idea of harm reduction. The harm perpetrated by imprisonment might be alleviated by the provision of alternatives to custody. Furthermore, the harm done by rehabilitationists themselves through over-zealous interventions into individuals' lives might be mitigated by the protection of offenders from such misguided extensions of social control. The combination of these efforts has led to a concern with issues of 'tariff', 'gatekeeping' and 'targetting', diverting offenders from probation until such time as that disposal would represent a corresponding diversion from custody. Probation officers can sometimes be heard remarking disparagingly on orders made on 'welfare' grounds, as if there is nothing odd about the implication that the probation service may have no interest in the welfare of its clients.

This re-orientation of the probation service reflects not only the loss of rehabilitation, but the rise of the justice ideology in penal policy (von Hirsch 1976), which prescribes that a penal response should be proportionate to the seriousness of the crime. This provides a theoretical justification for the aforementioned developments in probation practice, since the notion of proportionality pointed the way to the protection of offenders both from the excessive use of custody and from the harmful effects of the rehabilitative approach.

However, a further central tenet of the justice model is that 'only a combined notion of deterrence and desert can yield a foundation both necessary and sufficient to justify the existence of penal sanctions, and the application of these sanctions to particular individuals' (Hudson 1987: 39). Thus, the theoretical linking of punishment, the infliction of pain, to the structure of penal sanctions, lies at the heart of the justice model.

The problem for the probation service has arisen in the impossibility of accepting the first ingredient of the justice model whilst dissociating itself from the second. The distancing of the service from the explicit ideology of rehabilitation and the attractions of elements of the justice ideology effectively weakened its hold on a clear formula linking goals to methods. The phrase 'alternative to custody' holds no intrinsic prescription for the content of practice, and without the explicit ownership of rehabilitation as the service's goal, there is no inherent justification for the use of rehabilitative methods. Flogging and hanging, after all, are alternatives to custody! ...

The probation service, then, has been caught in an impossible paradox, and the significance of the language it uses has become abundantly clear. In accepting and responding to the criticisms levelled at rehabilitation, even to the extent of fighting shy of invoking its name, the service never intended to relinquish its methods. Yet no other statement of purpose carries with it the intrinsic prescription for a practice drawing on rehabilitative methods. Probation officers cannot have it both ways. They cannot be covert rehabilitationists, separating their averred aims from the methods they use in their day to day practice. The Green Paper is forcing this issue into the open, effectively calling their bluff.

Thought disorders

The difficulty for the probation service in extricating itself from this linguistic, and thereby theoretical, quagmire is clearly to be seen in a recent ACOP (1988) paper, published, in pre-emptive strike fashion, just before the Green Paper. Entitled *More demanding than prison: a discussion paper*, its language from the outset appeals to the punishment lobby, yet its arguments are intended also to reassure probation officers that their traditional rehabilitative methods will suffice to implement its proposals. ...

Perhaps the most startling recommendation, however, is for a Community Restitution Board, comprising members of the local judiciary, voluntary and statutory agencies to oversee the sentence and decide on alterations to and breaches of individual orders. This would reinstate executive discretion, not only a key principle in the rehabilitative model but the very one on which was focused the criticisms of the excesses of practitioners!

ACOP's paper, then, invokes the worst of both rehabilitation and justice worlds. But it is not alone in the confusion wrought by the attempt to prove that punishment and rehabilitation are reconcilable. Patten calls for 'a flexible approach geared to the needs and circumstances of the individual offender' (1988: 13) within a punishment framework, yet the tailoring of punishments to fit the offender rather than the offence would be an absurdity in both rehabilitative and justice terms. ... The Green Paper also floats the idea of judicial supervision of orders, whereby executive discretion for variations would be devolved to magistrates outside the courtroom.

Rehabilitation rediscovered

It has been argued that the loss of rehabilitation and the rise of the justice ideology in penal policy has led to a position in which potentially there is no intrinsic prescription for the use of rehabilitative methods in the community-based supervision of offenders. The current vogue for the language of punishment is significant in that it highlights this theoretical gap by offering an agenda for the content of practice in which rehabilitative methods cannot be assumed. Furthermore, the probation service has left itself vulnerable to co-option into the punishment movement by its own retreat from the explicit embrace of the rehabilitative goal and adoption of a language which, at worst, invokes punishment in misguided pursuit of credibility with sentencers and, at best, is empty of a clear prescription for the content of practice.

That this dislocation of goals from methods provides good cause for anxiety about the future of rehabilitative practice may be found in the emerging critiques of the justice model of sentencing. Reviewing the evidence from a range of American and British studies, Hudson concludes:

We have come to a fundamental paradox – or deceit – in the justice model. Although it purports to imprison people only for serious crimes, although it purports to deal with people on the basis of individual culpability, although it purports to protect equally the rights of all people to fair limitations on punishment, not having extra intervention in their lives because of membership of deviant subcultures, racial groups, criminogenic families and the like, it is in fact bound to do exactly the opposite.

(1987: 113)

She echoes the earlier astonishment of Cullen and Gilbert 'that those who mistrust the state to administer criminal justice rehabilitation in a just and humane manner are now placing their total faith in the state (the legislature in particular) to punish justly and humanely' (1982: 19).

The lesson to be learned from the evidence on the operational effects of the justice ideology is that the way forward from the problems associated with rehabilitation is not to abandon that goal but to temper its application in order to strip it of its harmful by-products. Indeed, only the rehabilitative approach seems flexible enough to develop in accordance with research findings on its effects, precisely because of the prescriptive relationship between its goals and methods. Within the justice ideology, the emphasis on deterrence and desert leads only to debate about the due severity of punishments, in which evidence of ineffectiveness of punishments to reduce crime will attract calls for increased harshness.

This may be all very well in principle, but necessitates re-examination of the poor record of rehabilitation shown in evaluative research. The overall finding of ineffectiveness in studies of social work with offenders has been tempered for some time with evidence within them of differential effects related to different types of offender, in terms of personality and criminal history (Shaw 1974; Folkard, Smith and Smith 1976), yet the general despair engendered by the research results distracted attention from this detail. Whilst it appears trite to suggest that different people respond to different approaches, it nevertheless has taken some time for the message that 'structured approaches addressed to specific problems, behaviours or social skills appear able to effect constructive changes' (Reid and Hanrahan 1981: 17) to be grasped in the development of social work practice. ...

The observations of the evaluative studies just mentioned identify the flexibility required in rehabilitative practice in order to provide programmes which are relevant to the characteristics and problems of different offenders. This is not the kind of flexibility which can easily be envisaged within community punishments, where individualisation concerns itself mainly with the degree of restraint to be imposed on offenders' freedom of movement. If executive discretion is instituted in the operation of punishments in the community, it will probably be necessitated by the inflexibility of punishments, creating frequent demands for variations in the context of movement and change in probationers' lives. Flexibility in rehabilitative practice, however, need not entail intrusiveness and widening of the social control network. The development by probation services of rigorous internal self-monitoring procedures to regulate against unnecessary interventions and unjustifiably discriminatory practices should be incorporated into explicitly rehabilitative practice, rather than allied to the adoption of the justice ideology.

... Within studies of sentencing recommendations, there is less evidence of the lack of credibility of probation among sentencers than of the need for probation officers themselves to be confident and positive in making recommendations for it (Bottoms and McWilliams 1986; Harraway *et al.* 1985; Stanley and Murphy 1984)...

Rehabilitative practice, therefore, is capable of developing in response to critical evaluations of its outcomes in order to contain its excesses and to discriminate between different offenders in terms of their criminal histories and social and personal circumstances. This is not to suggest that rehabilitation is on course to becoming an infallible approach to the prevention of offending, but that energies would more properly be directed to the development of rehabilitative practice, rather than to a change in the goal of community-based supervision. ... It is perhaps unlikely that anyone else will assert confidence in the rehabilitative work of the probation service if probation officers themselves display uncertainty about its worth in the language invoked to describe policy and practice.

From Judith Rumgay, 'Talking tough: empty threats in probation practice',
Howard Journal, 28(3), 1989, pp. 177–186.

References

Association of Chief Officers of Probation (1988) *More Demanding than Prison: a discussion paper.* London: Association of Chief Officers of Probation.

Bottoms, A. E. and McWilliams, W. (1986) 'Social enquiry reports twenty-five years after the Streatfeild Report', in P. Bean and D. Whynes (Eds.), *Barbara Wootton. Social Science and Public Policy. Essays in her Honour.* London: Tavistock.

Cohen, S. (1985) *Visions of Social Control.* London: Polity Press.

Cullen, F. T. and Gilbert, K. E. (1982) *Reaffirming Rehabilitation.* Cincinnati: Anderson.

Davies, M. (1984) 'Community-based alternatives to custody: the right place for the probation service', *Prison Journal,* 53 (New Series): 2–5.

Folkard, M. S., Smith, D. E. and Smith, D. D. (1976) *IMPACT Volume 2: the results of the experiment.* Home Office Research Study 36. London: HMSO.

Harraway, P. C. *et al.* (1985) *The Demonstration Unit 1981–1985.* London: Inner London Probation Service.

Hills, A. (1981) 'Controversy on the Medway', *Probation Journal,* 28: 80–85.

Home Office (1988) *Punishment, Custody and the Community.* Cm. 424. London: Home Office.

Hudson, B. (1987) *Justice Through Punishment. A Critique of the 'Justice' Model of Corrections.* Basingstoke: Macmillan (Croom Helm).

Kent Probation and After-Care Service (1980) *Probation Control Unit: A Community Based Experiment in Intensive Supervision.* Maidstone: Kent Probation and Aftercare Service.

Martinson, R. (1974) 'What works? Questions and answers about prison reform', *The Public Interest,* 35 (Spring): 22–54.

Patten, J. (1988) *Punishment, the Probation Service and the Community.* London: Home Office.

Reid, W. J. and Hanrahan, P. (1981) 'The effectiveness of social work: recent evidence', in E. M. Goldberg and N. Connelly (Eds.), *Evaluative Research in Social Care.* London: Heinemann Educational Books.

Schur, E. (1973) *Radical Nonintervention: Rethinking the Delinquency Problem.* Englewood Cliffs: Prentice-Hall.

Shaw, M. (1974) *Social Work in Prison.* Home Office Research Study 22. London: HMSO.

Stanley, S. J. and Murphy, M. B. (1984) *Survey of Social Enquiry Reports.* London: Inner London Probation Service.

von Hirsch, A. (1976) *Doing Justice.* New York: Hill and Wang.

38 Probation values for the 1990s (1995)

Mike Nellis

For a number of years now there has been great confusion about the nature of probation values, epitomised by the chief probation officer who wrote, quite rightly, that 'the probation service has always been fiercely proud of its values and has fought to protect them in an often hostile "law and order" climate', and then added: 'Curiously, there is no probation service statement of values ...' (Matheson 1992: 146). This undoubted absence has meant that in its more fierce and protective moments the service has repeatedly fallen back on 'the social work ideal', for which the phrase 'advise, assist and befriend' was once a kind of moral shorthand. From 1988 onwards, in particular, the service stridently proclaimed this ideal, drawn from a *generic* understanding of 'social work', to ward off the threat of the government's 'punishment in the community' strategy (Allan 1990). ... Among basic grade officers in the service there was a widespread belief that these developments entailed a diminution of 'social work', but among some managers, *pace* Matheson, there was a greater preparedness to ask if talk of 'social work values' had not, in fact, become something of a political liability. ...

... [A]lthough opinion varied among probation managers as to how tough 'punishment in the community' was going to be, ... almost all concluded that generic values could and should be reaffirmed within the new policy framework. This paper will take a different view, and argue that in the aftermath of 'punishment in the community', and of the managerial culture which it has helped to set in place, a more fundamental reconceptualisation of probation values is needed.

'Modernising' the Probation Service

... Because of its insistence that community penalties be tough and demanding the [Criminal Justice Act 1991] was perceived by many probation officers as the ultimate expression of the 'controlism' (Raynor 1985) and 'coercive tilt' (Walker and Beaumont 1981) that they had repeatedly warned against, although to the police, magistrates, judges and eventually the media it was seen – precisely because of its restrictions on sentencing and its focus on community penalties – as liberal and lenient, almost a 'criminals' charter'.

Although from a probation standpoint, the most drastic proposals in the 'punishment in the community' strategy were not immediately implemented – a fully nationalised service and electronic monitoring, for example – the ethos and organisation of the service nevertheless underwent rapid change, and led to a marked lowering of morale among basic grade officers (May 1991: 182). The worst may not have happened but there was a feeling among many that what they did was no longer 'social work' as traditionally understood, and angry cries of 'give us our jobs back' (Watson 1993).

Such discontent was inevitable, for behind a veil of 'modernising' rhetoric, government ministers and officials had made no secret ... of their view that while social work skills and values have a part to play in what the probation service does, it has, firstly, no monopoly on caring skills and values, and, secondly, that it should have 'moved on from the days' (Faulkner 1989: 1) when such skills and values embodied its sole purpose. ...

... Throughout 1992 and 1993 a variety of factors – inexorably rising crime figures (which ministers reluctantly agreed reflected economic deprivation), an initially falling prison population, public and police concern about youth crime, car crime and offending while on bail, a backlash from sentencers and the arrival of harder-line ministers at the Home Office – coalesced into a 'new' law and order crisis. The government conceded the inadequacy of the CJA 1991, and blamed it on the influence of liberal penal reformers! Within six months of its implementation crucial restrictions on custodial sentencing were being diluted, and within a year prison governors were warning the Home Office that prison overcrowding had again reached crisis proportions. The Home Secretary's response was to revise the 1991 legislation, to insist that 'prison works' (to incapacitate), to expand private prisons and to talk (at least) of tougher regimes. ...

... A third strategy, neither punishment nor 'social work' (though its mission statements are frequently flavoured with social work language), was becoming apparent in the Three Year Plan [for the probation service; Home Office 1992], a strategy which Pratt (1989) calls 'corporatism' and Rutherford (1993) 'expedient managerialism'. These terms describe a form of political control in which 'the capacity for conflict and disruption is reduced by means of the centralisation of policy, increased government intervention and the co-opting of various professional and interest groups into a collective whole with homogeneous alms and objectives' (Pratt 1989: 245). ...

In moving 'centre stage' the probation service is being more closely drawn into these corporate forms of social regulation, and (at least at management level) is adapting more quickly to these developments than other agencies caught up in the same modernising process, particularly the police and the courts. But, according to Rutherford (1993), and also Peters (1986: 32), the process means in practice that 'many of the earlier humanitarian ideals have been lost in a drift towards business-like, centralised, bureaucratised and efficiency-oriented policies in which financial and quantitative considerations loom larger than the philosophy of resocialisation'. ...

The limits of genericism

Quite apart from the fact that it played supremely well into the hands of Home Office critics who believed that it 'is not always clear what a social work base does and does not mean' (Faulkner 1989: 1) the service's retreat into its social work identity as a means of resisting 'punishment in the community' ignored the limited contribution which generic social work had made, historically, to innovation in probation practice, or to the 'successful revolution' (Jones 1993) in juvenile justice which had occurred in the 1980s. ...

The most that genericism has contributed to probation values has been a debate on the respective merits of welfare and control, and while this debate remains important ... it no longer has pride of place. It is nonetheless possible to argue that those issues which have displaced it in recent values debate – desert theory, rehabilitation and anti-discriminatory practice – still fail to exhaust all that could be said about specifically probation values. Even within a 'humanist' (liberal and humanitarian) framework, reflection on what these values might be does not lead inexorably back to genericism, nor to the view that the only way to preserve a 'social work' (that is, respectful, caring and decent) ethos is by making rehabilitation, once again, into the cornerstone of probation practice. The liberal and humanitarian tradition need not be departed from, for it contains within it ... an imperative to resist injustice and oppression. But the managerial culture which is steadily tightening its grip on the service does not square easily with this tradition. ...

The rise of benevolent corporatism

McWilliams (1987) recognised immediately that the growth of corporate management within the probation service represented as strong a challenge to the nature of probation practice – defined in terms of 'personalism' – as the toughening-up of community penalties. ... Essentially the service has been compelled to adopt a rather idealised version of private sector management techniques (Stewart 1992), which are arguably more authoritarian than those now used in industry itself (Lewis 1991). The effect has been the creation of a regulatory culture in the probation service which imprisons practitioners, and indeed managers themselves, in a hierarchy of policies, guidelines and monitoring arrangements which rob lower level staff of the last remnants of discretion, turning them ... into 'competent functionaries' (Howe 1991).

Much effort has been expended by probation managers and also by those whom Chomsky (1989: 46) calls 'technocratic and policy-oriented intellectuals' to portray this not only as a necessary development, but also as a progressive one. A variety of discourses (for example, about enterprise, consumerism, equal opportunities, quality assurance etc.) have combined to create an image of *benevolent corporatism* as ... a new organisational form in which 'the basic values of the Service will hold good and not be lost' (Statham 1992: 74). ... Fellowes (1992) boldly suggests that the loss of personal discretion, coupled with the feeling of security attendant on following a clear policy, will actually constitute a form of staff empowerment, although staff themselves seem not to experience it this way (Watson 1993). Only Saiger (1992), among recent writers, honestly admits that managerialism, with its essential emphasis on hierarchy and on encouraging and enforcing obedience to policy and procedure, is at heart coercive, but she fails to see that strategies of authorisation (orders from the top), routinisation (standardised techniques of working) and surveillance (monitoring) lead inexorably to the depersonalisation of those on the receiving end (see Milgram 1974; Bauman 1989), whether basic grade officers or offenders to whom the regulatory ethos is inevitably passed on.

... No discourse has in fact done more to legitimise a managerial culture in the probation service than that of anti-discriminatory practice, and, as McWilliams (1987) anticipated, a close affinity has now developed between the radical and managerialist positions. There are steep ironies here, for while claiming always to recognise and resist the 'risk of incorporation' (Senior 1989: 316) and to be 'in and against the state' radicals seem not to have noticed how effortlessly government officials have, however, disingenuously, used the crisis of discrimination against black people in the criminal justice system to augment their own case for greater oversight and regulation of practice (Faulkner 1989; Flescher 1992).

For all its oppositional pretentions, and its confrontational ethos, much contemporary radical thinking in social work and probation ... has helped to widen and strengthen the regulatory net within welfare organisations by suggesting, for example, in respect of anti-racism, that 'management needs to be encouraged to develop effective policies that check on individual practice' (Senior 1989: 314) and by supporting the case for National Standards on the grounds that 'we cannot demand tough sanctions ... over racist practice if we do not accept the need for standards over other aspects of our daily practice' (Senior 1990: 31). Pressure for the dispersal of finely calibrated forms of regulation throughout the probation service has come, in the name of anti-discriminatory practice, as much from NAPO as from government. ... The surveillance of speech (euphemistically called 'monitoring') which NAPO (undated) has introduced at its conferences and in its branches has made its own insidious contribution to the culture of fear and obedience (Watson 1993) which government agencies and probation managers, using more straightforwardly economic arguments for regulation, may not have been able to create on their own. ...

Thus, drawing on ideas from criminology, the rest of this paper will suggest that a new probation value-base could be constructed around the three elements of anti-custodialism, restorative justice and community safety. ...

Anti-custodialism as a value

Despite Hugman's demand that 'diversion from custody must be a priority aim' (1980: 151), Senior's (1989: 298) recognition of widespread probation 'support for decarceration' and the observable fact that there are 'no probation officers who like to see their clients being sent into custody' (Millard 1991) an explicit anti-custodial stance has never been incorporated in statements of 'social work' values. ...

The strategies of resistance outlined in Mathiesen's (1990) later work involve counter-functional work, counter denial-work, victim work and offender work. Counter-functional work consists of making visible, by argument, imagery and research, the oppressive functions which the prison serves, questioning the value of segregating offenders and the false reassurance that something is being done by building more prisons and by increased custodial sentencing. The need for counter-denial work ... arises because governments invariably deny the harm that prison does, and consistently seek new justifications for its use – whether it is conceived in rehabilitative, preventive or deterrent terms. ...

Restorative justice as a value

The concept of restorative justice is associated with two kinds of project: one concerned with victim-offender mediation, the other with neighbourhood dispute settlement. Over the past decade, the probation service has been involved with both types, recognising, in the case of the former, that meeting a victim can sometimes foster increased personal responsibility in offenders, and in the case of the latter, that the settlement of disputes between neighbours may prevent escalation into criminal activity (Kennedy 1990). The Home Office intention was to fit such projects into existing philosophies of diversion from prosecution and crime prevention, but the discourse which actually developed around them was also permeated by more radical ideas from a semi-independent mediation movement. This promotes and envisages a move towards informal processes of community justice and away from state administered systems, which, in some formulations, converges with later developments in abolitionist thinking (Christie 1982; de Haan 1990).

... The more radical versions treat crime as a species of interpersonal conflict, or as a civil tort, discourage the appropriation of such conflicts by state-based professionals and seek to avoid the compounding of one harm (the crime) by another (the punishment) (de Haan 1990). All but the most conservative versions accept that so long as most of the victim's needs are met, and their rights respected, a broadly rehabilitative and socially integrative approach can be pursued with offenders. This draws on existing practice and is compatible with the 'offender work' required by Mathiesen's abolitionist strategy.

... [D]espite the obvious affinity between the principles of restorative justice and the (supposed) principles of good 'social work' practice – 'a focus on problem-solving rather than blame-fixing, on the future rather than the past, on empowering participants to find a solution rather than on coercive intervention by the state, on meeting both parties' needs, on the total context of the offence, and on "right" relationships rather than "right" rules' (Zehr 1990: 211–14) – mediation and reparation were once looked upon by NAPO as being 'outside the Service's mainstream activities' (Gretton 1988: 78). ... [T]he service has in my view no real choice as to whether it promotes restorative values, for it is only in the context of genuine concern for the needs and experiences of crime victims that concern for offenders (expressed as rehabilitation) will have any political plausibility. ...

Community safety as a value

... Using whatever purchasing power they have, the comfortable, affluent and wealthy within 'the culture of contentment' (Galbraith 1992) can become consumers of security, locking, lighting and zoning themselves out of harm's way. Poorer people are more vulnerable and it is their need for protection and safety which the probation service, if it is to be anti-oppressive, cannot ignore either in its own work, or in the partnerships it makes with other statutory and voluntary agencies.

For those most at risk of crime tend to be the already disadvantaged members of society, poor women, long-term unemployed young men, and ethnic minorities; for some their experience of crime compounds, and in some analyses (Campbell 1993) constitutes, their sense of oppression. ...

... [I]n view of 'social work's' acknowledged role in protecting victims of child abuse (and latterly domestic violence), it is again rather strange that within debate on generic 'social work' values the notion of safety has not been enlarged and expanded to cover crime victimisation generally. If safety had been more clearly understood as a 'social work' value then sections of the probation service may have been less ambivalent than they have been towards crime prevention strategies ... and more aware of how these strategies could become, and be understood as, anti-oppressive work. ...

Conclusion

... It is ... time for the probation service to ask what it gains from continuing to think of itself as a 'social work' agency, and whether more might be gained from thinking of itself as a 'community justice' agency or even as a broadly conceived penal reform body. It does not need – and in the past it has not benefited from – the false protection of genericism in order to express or defend progressive values. These exist independently of genericism (Rutherford 1993; Garland 1990) and can be – and are – expressed in settings outside 'social work'. Such old probation values as need to be preserved can be contained in the new framework. ...

There are large political issues here, not merely penal ones, and it is only in the resolution of the latter that an organisation as small as the probation service can reasonably be expected to play a part. ... The values sketched here ... may still be insufficient to prevent the worst from coming to the worst but unless they are adopted in some shape or form ... the probation service will be alarmingly unprepared for the seasons of fury which lie ahead.

From Mike Nellis, 'Probation values for the 1990s',
Howard Journal, *34(1), 1995, pp. 19–44.*

References

Allan, R. (1990) 'Punishment in the community', in: P. Carter, T. Jeffs and M. Smith (Eds.), *Social Work and Social Welfare Yearbook* 2, Milton Keynes: Open University Press.

Bauman, Z. (1989) *Modernity and the Holocaust*, Cambridge: Polity Press.

Campbell, B. (1993) *Goliath: Britain's Dangerous Places*, London: Methuen.

Chomsky, N. (1989) *Necessary Illusions: Thought Control in Democratic Societies*, Montreal: CBC Enterprises.

Christie, N. (1982) *Limits to Pain*, London: Martin Robertson.

de Haan, W. (1990) *The Politics of Redress: Crime, Punishment and Penal Abolition*, London: Unwin Hyman.

Faulkner, D. E. R. (1989) 'The future of the probation service: a view from government', in: R. Shaw and K. Haines (Eds.), *The Criminal Justice System: A Central Role for the Probation Service*, Cambridge: University of Cambridge Institute of Criminology.

Fellowes, B. (1992) 'Management and empowerment: the paradox of professional practice', in: R. Statham and P. Whitehead (Eds.), *Managing the Probation Service: Issues for the 1990s*, Harlow: Longman.

Flescher, T. (1992) 'Initial thoughts of the head of probation at the Home Office', *NAPO News*, 40, 6–7.

Galbraith, J. K. (1992) *The Culture of Contentment*, Harmondsworth: Penguin.

Garland, D. (1990) *Punishment and Modem Society*, Oxford: Clarendon Press.

Gretton, J. (1988) 'Can victim-offender mediation change the face of criminal justice?', in: A. Harrison and J. Gretton (Eds.), *Crime UK: An Economic, Social and Policy Audit*, Newbury: Policy journals.

Home Office (1992) *Three Year Plan for the Probation Service 1993–96*, London: HMSO.

Howe, D. (1991) 'Knowledge, power and the shape of social work practice', in: M. Davies (Ed.), *The Sociology of Social Work*, London: Routledge.

Hugman, B. (1980) 'Radical practice in probation', in: M. Brake and R. Bailey (Eds.), *Radical Social Work and Practice*, London: Edward Arnold.

Jones, D. (1993) 'The successful revolution continues', *Justice of the Peace*, 8 May, 297–8.

Kennedy, L. W. (1990) *On the Borders of Crime: Conflict Management and Criminology*, New York: Longman.

Lewis, P. (1991) 'Learning from industry: macho management or collaborative culture?', *Probation Journal*, 38, 81–5.

Matheson, D. (1992) 'The probation service', in: E. Stockdale and S. Casale (Eds.), *Criminal Justice under Stress*, London: Blackstone Press.

Mathiesen, T. (1990) *Prison on Trial*, London: Sage.

May, T. (1991) *Probation: Politics, Policy and Practice*, Milton Keynes: Open University Press.

McWilliams, W. (1987) 'Probation, pragmatism and policy', *Howard Journal*, 26, 97–121.

Milgram, S. (1974) *Obedience to Authority: An Experimental View*, London: Tavistock.

Millard, D. (1991) 'Letters', *Probation Journal*, 38, 218.

NAPO (undated) *Monitoring, Advice and Guidelines*, London: NAPO.

Peters, A. (1986) 'Main currents in criminal law theory', in: J. van Dijk *et al.* (Eds.), *Criminal Law in Action*, Arnhem: Gouda Quint.

Pratt, J. (1989) 'Corporatism: the third model of juvenile justice', *British Journal of Criminology*, 29, 236–54.

Raynor, P. (1985) *Social Work, Justice and Control*, Oxford: Basil Blackwell.

Rutherford, A. (1993) *Criminal Justice and the Pursuit of Decency*, Oxford: Oxford University Press.

Saiger, L. (1992) 'Probation management structures and partnerships in America: lessons for England', in: R. Statham and P. Whitehead (Eds.), *Managing the Probation Service: Issues for the 1990s*, Harlow: Longman.

Senior, P. (1989) 'Radical probation: surviving in a hostile climate', in: M. Langan and P. Lee (Eds.), *Radical Social Work Now*, London: Unwin Hyman.

——(1990) 'Standardisation: assessing the consequences for probation practice', in: D. Woodhill and P. Senior (Eds.), *Criminal Justice in the 1990s: What Future(s) for the Probation Service?*, Sheffield: PAVIC Publications, Sheffield City Polytechnic.

Statham, R. (1992) 'The strategic dimension', in: R. Statham and P. Whitehead (Eds.), *Managing the Probation Service: Issues for the 1990s*, Harlow: Longman.

Stewart, J. (1992) 'Guidelines for public services management: lessons not to be learned from the private sector', in: P. Carter, T. Jeffs and M. Smith (Eds.), *Changing Social Work and Welfare*, Milton Keynes: Open University Press.

Walker, H. and Beaumont, B. (1981) *Probation Work: Critical Theory and Socialist Practice*, Oxford: Blackwell.

Watson, W. (1993) 'Letter', *Guardian*, 24 September.

Zehr, H. (1990) *Changing Lenses: A New Focus for Crime and Justice*, Scottdale, Pennsylvania: Herald Press.

39 The probation career of Al Truism (1999)

Ken Pease

Altruism is defined in Chambers Dictionary as the principle of living and acting for others. The career of altruism can be considered in relation to the individual probation practitioner and the probation service, albeit in different ways. The purpose of this paper is to rehearse some of the ideas of the late Bill McWilliams, to suggest their continuing relevance to probation, and to argue how his thinking might have developed had his active life been longer. Altruism in its appeal to selflessness, and its lack of discrimination between the categories of other to be served, offers a reasonable organising principle in probation, of which Bill would have approved, and which will be elaborated somewhat in the final section of the paper. ...

... Bill described the main strands in probation thinking as being from special pleading, through diagnosis to managerial pragmatism. The view of the offender which underpinned these were respectively as: a unique individual in God's sight, a unique collection of psycho-social attributes, and as a unit for policy processing. The justifying knowledge framework was respectively faith, psychology and management science. The justification for action was moral, then factual, then efficiency-driven. The means through which the aim was to be achieved was respectively moral reform, scientific treatment, and social control. This was operationalised in court as, respectively, a plea for mercy, a diagnosis and associated treatment plan, and finally the specification of a realistic disposal within the overarching policy aim of reducing the use of custody.

Why was Bill's perspective on probation history influential and compelling to many people? First, it was based on impressive scholarship. Second, it resonated with the ambivalence which many experienced probation officers felt about the development of their service, and where it rubbed uncomfortably against the personal values which had led them into probation work. Finally, it was palpably the work of someone who cared passionately for the service of which he wrote. As Mike Nellis pointed out in his *Howard Journal* obituary, Bill was at heart a police court missionary:

> but never in a naive or nostalgic sense; he simply insisted that the Service, as it turned to face new challenges, should not discard the moral and spiritual traditions on which it had originally drawn.
>
> (1997: 226) ...

The vulnerability of current probation justifications

To sustain its claim to be an efficient means of processing offenders, the probation service requires the demonstration that treatment by community sanctions is at worst not criminogenic relative to custody. Yet this can only be demonstrated by methodological sleight of hand. ...

What gets counted in penal effectiveness seems odd (or worse) relative to the real world of public protection. Measures of reconviction are conventionally used as indicators of the relative success of different penal sanctions. These measures are typically of the proportion of those given different sanctions (prison, probation and so on) who are reconvicted within a two-year risk period, that is, two years at liberty. When reconviction rates are compared in this way, the differences between sanctions are typically slight. However, what this neglects is the point at which the risk period starts. For probation, it is immediate. For those given custodial sentences, it only starts after release from custody. ... The statistics as presented look as though probation is as good as prison in conferring public protection simply because reconvictions only start being counted after the incapacitation effect of prison has done its bit. The comparison should be from the point of sentence, that is, that two-year reconviction rates for probation should be calculated from the same point as two-year conviction rates for imprisonment, dating from sentence. Only thus is relative public protection clear. Why is this not done?

(i)   Because of cost and sentiments of mercy, there is a continuing wish to reduce the use of custody. To clarify its advantage in public protection would not be regarded as helpful.

(ii)   The extent of measured effectiveness required would demoralise the probation service. ...

Incorporating the incapacitation effect means that, after any time period, the proportion of those reconvicted after a custodial sentence is lower than the proportion reconvicted after a community sentence, given that the effect of sentence is vanishingly small in both cases. ... By the time a prisoner having served an average sentence length is released, some 28% of those given a community sentence will have offended again, at least once. ...

... Any defensible benchmark comparison with custody leaves community sanctions a lot further behind in terms of public protection than has typically been acknowledged.

Another tactic which has been used to promote alternatives to custody has been the attempt to shame Britain by representing it as almost uniquely punitive. Cross-national comparisons of prison population typically place the UK at or near the top of the league of number of prisoners per 100k population. The mental leap is then made to the conclusion that the UK is punitive. This is like saying that the higher the number of people in hospital, the more caring the society. The amount of disease may in large part determine the number of people in hospital. Likewise, the amount of crime and the activity of the criminal justice agencies may have something to do with the number of people in prison. Looking at the prison population *per conviction* places England and Wales among the least punitive countries in respect of rape, robbery, assaultive crime, theft and fraud (see Pease 1994). Shame induced by the assertion that we are given to punitiveness is almost certainly misconceived.

In short, reliance on efficiency and cost arguments will pay dividends only so long as people do not notice the methodological shortcomings of the relevant comparisons. ... The purpose here is not to decry the work of the probation service, any more than that was the intention of Bill McWilliams's critiques of the service, but rather to reassert Bill's point that the original justification for the police court missionary was a moral one, and the moral force of the aim to help remains the primary one. If one moves from this to a more utilitarian conception of appropriate sentencing, one is on difficult ground indeed, reliant on criminologists not to mention the probation Emperor's nakedness, and on politicians to place economic considerations before public protection.

What might yet be

... [C]ounterfactual history ... is the informed speculation about how history might have played itself out if decisions had been made differently or events had turned out differently. ...

... [O]ne historical outcome does not extinguish the strands of thought temporarily defeated. ... There remain in probation strands of missionary thinking. The understandings offered by a virtual history of probation would allow the recognition of how police court missionary thinking may have developed, and hence how those strands could be stressed in prescriptions for modern probation practice which would revive missionary zeal. ...

The route of the vanquished missionary

What would the probation service have been like had the missionary ideal not been overtaken by the pseudo-science of casework? The central purpose of the missionary's work was communicating social disapproval, and reconciliation with God. ...

... Bill remained centrally concerned with the justification for giving such help. In a joint paper with the writer of this article, Bill contended that:

> The cost-effective-cum-humanitarian justifications put forward for the present policy of 'alternatives' lack the cachet, and indeed the rectitude, of earlier claims to save souls or to change psyches. Lack of over-arching purpose makes probation particularly vulnerable to political pressure. The probation service's response to overt and covert attack over the last decade has been conceptually spineless, and in consequence unpersuasive. The probation service stands in need of a transcendent justification for its activities.
>
> (McWilliams and Pease 1990: 16)

Bill thought he had found a route to the answer in the philosopher Alan Gewirth's (1978) Principle of Generic Consistency. This is too complex to describe here, but the lesson which Bill drew from it was that the purpose of punishment was to restore membership in the community by an offender's unforced choice, a theme consistent with recent emphases on restorative justice.

The central advantage of such a perspective is that it does not neglect distributive justice while considering punishment, contending that distributive justice must be departed from only in such a way as to reinstate an equality which has been disrupted. In short, Bill would have seen:

- a central concern for distributive justice
- the provision of help

as the themes to which the police court missionary would resonate, and which are of sufficient contemporary interest to fuel a resurrection of missionary thinking. ...

Lures for missionary thinking to resurface

If a concern for distributive justice and the provision of help were the modern concerns of the reborn and secular police court missionary, what are the issues which would act as lures to induce the missionary part of most officers to resurface? In more modern terms, what the court missionary addressed was social exclusion. ...

... Social exclusion as it concerns offenders is located at the nexus of distributive and retributive justice. Retributive justice concerns the restoration of the balance of effort and advantage between an offender and society. Distributive justice concerns the range and limiting conditions which humans should be allowed to experience, notably as regards pain and poverty. It is the intersection between these where the most pressing problems of probation and other penal sanctions lie. At the crudest level, what is the justification of 'goodies for baddies', like driver training for motoring offenders and after-care for prisoners? The justification can't lie in retribution. It must concern the restoration of the state of citizenship which would have applied in the absence of the penalty, or at least a state which does not hamper the resumption of citizenship. Difficult questions arise about distributive justice as it applies to the families of prisoners, and to those whose previous life has so damaged them that they will never resume citizenship in any meaningful way. Does distributive justice allow goodies for baddies to restore a state which never existed before, and where many will believe that it never existed because of the offender's badness? In any event, the social concerns of the missionary societies were about exclusion (including exclusion from a state of grace), and recent concerns with social exclusion provide a means for the revival of police court missionary thought. ...

The second lure inducing missionary thinking to resurface is the contemporary role of the victim movement. The work of the police court mission took the missionary to many places. ...

One missionary in the year [1877/78] visited courts, prisons, fire and railway stations, and cab stands. Visits to cab stands outnumbered visits to court by more than two to one. ... It was pressure from courts which led to the increase of missionary involvement therein, not the demands of the vocation. In other words, missionary work took its exponent to wherever useful work was to be done. ...

Institutional concern with offenders pre-dated *institutional* concern with victims. Obviously this is not to say that sympathy for and charity to victims of crime was not evident before. ... The victim *movement,* however, is a product of the mid-20th century, and the attempt to reclaim offenders was active a century earlier. ...

... The important question concerns what the probation service would have looked like had the victim movement been active at its inception. If the need for help had not been seen to begin and end with the person in the dock, what would the service have done? It would have ministered to all those caught up in and hurt by criminal justice process, rather than merely those punished by it. Victim support and witness protection would have been part of a generic service available to all those at need. The separate existence of an organisation such as Victim Support would surely have astonished and affronted the police court missionary. If the cab rank was fair game, why not the witness stand?

The counter-argument is that the mission involved bringing sinners to repentance, and victims weren't sinners, or at least no more than the rest of us. But does the cab stand host a bigger population of sinners than the witness box? Does not the experience of crime victimisation lead to hatreds which separate one from God? The aspiration that took the missionary to the cab stand should not have kept him from the witness box.

... The question remains as to whether it is now too late to re-invent the probation service as a generic helping service for the courts. ... The notion of altruism is passé in the service. ... Yet to revive probation as a service which gives help where there is a need for help to alleviate the secondary victimisation which criminal justice entails, would chime precisely with the impulses and practice of the police court missionary. That the police court missionary did not specifically minister to victims is surely just an accident of history. ...

Stand up, Al Truism

The point has arrived at which to explain the title of this paper more fully. The first reason is that Bill McWilliams would have liked it. The second is that altruism has two kinds of career in probation. The first is the individual altruism of officers joining the service. Bill never wavered in his view that the motives of new officers were noble, and that their central motive was the selfless provision of help. However, personal altruism survives intact only in organisations conducive to it, and I think Bill saw the career trajectory of probation officers' altruism as being the manifest justification for their work as being too short, being replaced by cynicism and the politicking to which frustrated idealists are prone. The second altruism career is that of the service as a whole. In its first manifestation, imperfect as it was, the tone of the service was moral. Its later manifestations were not overtly moral. The consequence was the career trajectory for individual officers described above. Bill's attempt was to reintroduce a central moral justification for the service. That can most readily be done by transforming the probation service into a generic helping service for all those whose experience of criminal justice impoverishes them, materially, emotionally or spiritually. It would de-emphasise and become honest about the cost in crime which such an approach incurs, and seek over time to lessen that cost, without justification by partial data compiled using odd conventions. The pity is that Bill McWilliams will not be here to argue the case.

From Ken Pease, 'The probation career of Al Truism',
Howard Journal *38(1), 1999, pp. 2–16.*

References

Gewirth, A. (1978) *Reason and Morality.* Chicago: University of Chicago Press.

McWilliams, W.W. and Pease, K. (1990) 'Probation practice and an end to punishment', *Howard Journal* 29(1): 14–24.

Nellis, M. (1997) 'Bill McWilliams 1932–1997', *Howard Journal* 36: 225–6.

Pease, K (1994) 'Cross-national imprisonment rates: limitations of method and possible conclusions', in R.D. King and M. Maguire (Eds.) *Prisons in Context.* Oxford: Oxford University Press.

40 The barking dog? Partnership and effective practice (2004)

Judith Rumgay

Introduction

The 'curious incident' of the dog that 'did nothing in the night-time' (Doyle 1894) has been a popular metaphor for our human fallibility in problem perception for many years. The failure of the dog in the Sherlock Holmes tale to bark, and thereby to rouse people from their slumbering insensitivity to a perilous intruder, told the mastermind of crime detection that the danger had in fact emanated from within the household. Outside of that story, crime fiction has many times offered alternative reasons for the unlikely silence of dogs at crucial moments: perhaps the intruder was a trusted friend; or the malign stranger fed the (oddly unsuspecting at this point) animal meat impregnated with tranquillisers.

The argument that I wish to develop here invokes a very different account of human failure to hear a warning. In this account, the players have not been, and, indeed, still are not listening. Moreover, their deafness is not the result of physiological misfortune or environmental conditions beyond their power to resist or correct. Rather, it is rooted in a wilful disregard of obvious signals that all is not well. In this version of the legend, the members of the household simply do not want to hear the barking dog.

The household of this narrative is the probation service, currently caught up in a drama of challenge and change that is shaking the foundations of the family home, and placing its faith for salvation in the drive for effectiveness that has become commonly known as the 'What Works' agenda. ... The argument explores an alternative pathway to the household's survival: to call on the neighbours and seek their help ...

The scale of the partnership enterprise

Throughout the 1990s, and continuing to the present day, the probation service has been enmeshed in an increasing and diversifying range of partnership activities. Whilst the service has generally been keen to proclaim its traditions of inter-agency co-operation, the past decade of partnership expansion has derived more noticeably from central policy and legislative mandate than from any particular intrinsic driving enthusiasm for the enterprise. ...

The service's involvement in partnerships during this period of rapid, centrally mandated growth has been remarkable for the diversity of forms that it has taken. It has been required to develop mechanisms for contracting for elements of its provision for offenders; to participate in multi-agency collaborations for community crime prevention (Crime and Disorder Reduction Partnerships); to join multi-agency groups targeting specific groups of individuals involved in, or at risk of involvement in crime (Drug Action Teams, Youth Offending Teams, and Multi-agency Public Protection Panels); and to contribute to inter-agency implementation of social policies for support of society's most vulnerable groups (Rumgay 2003). ...

In the face of such upheaval, it can hardly surprise us to learn that the service's response to the demands of partnership has been often reluctant, uneven and based selectively on a mixture of perceived political imperatives and territorial preferences (Rumgay 2000; Mair and Jamel 2002). Nevertheless, as the mandates for partnerships to tackle a broad range of social problems increase, it is the argument of this chapter that the probation service should not squander the opportunity that they present to assert its unique identity as keystone of the bridge between the criminal and social policy worlds. Since the probation service is obliged to enter into partnerships in diverse fields of policy and practice, it should turn the endeavour to the purpose that will best serve its future interests for the preservation of its mission and organisational integrity.

Defining the crime problem and its solution

The expanding demand for partnership activity reflects a growing appreciation of the complexity of a broad range of social problems, including crime, and the consequently poor prospects of resolving them through the typically uncoordinated efforts of organisations working in comparative isolation (Annie E. Casey Foundation 1995; Glisson 1994; Johnson *et al.* 1990; Lowndes and Skelcher 1998; Mattessich, Murray-Close and Monsey 2001; Orians, Liebow and Branch 1995; Rosenbaum 2002). Policy makers' recognition of this, and of the inertia of organisations that continue to operate autonomously in the face of exhortations to do otherwise, is demonstrated in the extent to which they have been willing to subject collaborative participation to statutory mandate. Indeed, it is fair to remark that Mattessich, Murray-Close and Monsey caution against '"collaboration mania" among some people who set policy and offer funding' (2001: 34), raising the prospect that we might achieve the denigration of a good idea through indiscriminate application, that has been the fate of a number of penal innovations. Those who most welcome the collaborative mood that has characterised much contemporary criminal and social policy making are also those who strongly counsel its judicious implementation (Annie E. Casey Foundation 1995; Huxham 1996; Mattessich, Murray-Close and Monsey 2001). ...

The ways in which social problems become defined, and redefined over time, has been the object of much study. Moreover, that such definitions may reflect strategic, political and attitudinal positions more than the fruits of dispassionate research in empirical realities, and that their subsequent redefinitions do not always advance in the manner of progressive enlightenment, has been observed many times. ...

From the perspective of partnership engagement, however, the variable relationships of individuals and organisations to research-based definitions of the problem which they are charged collectively to tackle are to be *expected, accommodated and used* to advance the collaborative enterprise. One reason for this integral flexibility derives from the frequently observed problems of communication and conflict that arise when different professions invoke specialised theories of, descriptive vocabularies for and intervention approaches to the problems with which they deal (Armstrong 1997; Bennett and Lawson 1994; Minicucci 1997; Rosenbaum 2002). Equally, not all partners are specialists in crime, experiencing it only as an occasional issue in their work. ... The fact that potential partners have been brought to the collaborating table by statutory mandate, the prospect of new funding, or even altruism is no guarantee of rapid or sustained agreement between them on project objectives and strategies (Sutton and Cherney 2002). Indeed, Mackintosh describes partnerships as 'sites of *continuing* political and economic renegotiation' (1993: 211, emphasis added). Thus, where crime reduction policies are not understood by alternative agencies to complement other policies with which they are more directly concerned, partners may drift away from the table through loss of interest (Sutton and Cherney 2002). ...

Another reason for accommodating flexible – and not entirely accurate by research standards – definitions of the problems at stake stems from the trend for inclusion of lay members of the public in consultations and projects targeting crime prevention and offender management. There is, to my knowledge at least, scant evidence of communities (or partner organisations for that matter) demanding programmes for the correction of the cognitive deficits of their offending members as their preferred solution to their pervasive problems of poverty, disadvantage and social disorder. A number of studies have remarked on the disappointing failure of local community residents to appreciate either social scientific knowledge of crime problems or the priorities for their resolution that are set at central policy making level. Of particular interest, here, is the tendency for community residents to conflate specific crime problems with broader quality of life concerns (Clear and Cadora 2003; Hausman 2002; Mair and Jamel 2002).

The wise collaborator is advised to adapt crime prevention planning to include these expectations of broader social opportunities and neighbourhood improvement in order to keep partners at the table and to retain local goodwill towards the project (Hausman 2002; Mackintosh 1993; Mattessich, Murray-Close and Monsey 2001). Such accommodation of organisations and individuals with alternative perspectives on crime and its resolution appears as a distraction from the real task of crime prevention when viewed from the perspective of a restrictive definition of the problem, particularly one that is couched in offenders' unique deviance from normality. Yet, we know that crime clusters with multiple social problems of poverty, environmental decay, unemployment and sickness (Social Exclusion Unit 1998). ... [T]o treat criminal behaviour in isolation from the social and economic contexts in which it disproportionately arises wastes the potential resources of co-operative effort for community improvement, notwithstanding the compromises that may be necessary along the way (Rumgay 2001). ...

Such a contextual approach recognises the importance of the relationships between offenders and their communities in seeking partnership arrangements that protect the public, hold offenders accountable for their behaviour and offer them a pathway towards reintegration (Karp and Clear 2002). Moreover, it explains and justifies the probation service's resource expenditure in the partnership enterprise, and joins it to the contemporary mood for collaboration at central policy making and local practice levels.

Implementing the solution

No writer in the field of partnerships pretends to underestimate the difficulty of the enterprise, for 'comprehensive system reform is the path of most resistance' (Annie E.

Casey Foundation 1995: 9). The partnership focus on systems as the targets for change challenges the inertia of organisations that have been long accustomed to discrete, categorical, rather than integrated, cross-disciplinary approaches to the social problems that concern them. ...

The partnership approach *expects* projects to vary across locations, to change over time and to develop unique adaptations of 'model' programmes in light of local conditions. Thus, effective innovations in community provision actively attend to the history, culture and contemporary attributes of the specific neighbourhoods in which they are developed, as does the process of their successful transfer to alternative settings (Dalton, Elias and Wandersman 2001). When supporting mechanisms of clear leadership, objective setting and lines of communication are in place to prevent project drift and 'collaborative inertia' (Huxham 1996), review and adaptation of specific goals and methods in light of progress and altered contingencies is regarded as positive and beneficial to the collaborative process and its outcomes (Annie E. Casey Foundation 1995; Dalton, Elias and Wandersman 2001; Mattessich, Murray-Close and Monsey 2001; Rosenbaum 2002). Moreover, such creativity, rather than standardised replication, is regarded as crucial to the local ownership, vitality and endurance of the enterprise (Dalton, Elias and Wandersman 2001).

The most successful partnership ventures undertaken by the probation service exemplify creative adaptations to unique variations in constraints and opportunities, and, moreover, would make little sense if they did not reflect local conditions in this way (Rumgay 2000). Moreover, it is arguably indefensible for community support services to be skewed towards special provision for offenders while their law-abiding neighbours suffer continuing disadvantage (Rumgay 2001). Thus, recent explorations of the dimensions of partnership approaches to community safety and offender supervision emphasise 'place' as a determining influence, not only on the nature of the crime problems experienced within a neighbourhood but also on the formulation of locally relevant and valued responses (Clear and Cadora 2003; Karp and Clear 2002).

This observation does not imply a demand for a *laissez-faire* approach to practice development at central level, nor is it a licence for indiscriminate or atheoretical local innovation. Rather it points to the need to strike a balance between 'top down' direction and 'grass roots' initiative. Indeed, commentary on multi-agency collaborations reveals a strong consensus that the issue at stake is not a choice between one or other approach, but the means to establishing such a balance between central policy making and implementation guidance and local flexibility (Dalton, Elias and Wandersman 2001; Hassett and Austin 1997; O'Looney 1997; Provan and Milward 1995). If anything, top-down directions to develop multi-agency partnerships have been remiss, not in pursuing the advantages of the collaborative approach in principle, but in their failure to provide the supportive infrastructure that is needed in terms of preparation time for the complex challenges of implementation, training in the skills needed for effectiveness and dissemination of good practice examples (Rumgay 2000; Mair and Jamel 2002).

Exclusivity and exclusion

... The partnership perspective observes that offenders share in the problems of non-offending disadvantaged groups. From this point of view, provision of support services to those groups can be improved by integrated multi-agency practice. Thus, the partnership approach looks to inclusion of offenders in mainstream provision, alongside other disadvantaged groups, rather than exclusion from narrowly targeted programmes when they are expected to fail. In so far as offenders require special assistance, it is to enhance their access to, and ability to utilise mainstream services ...

Effectiveness, evaluation, and accountability

... Evaluation of the partnership approach in action recognises that its effectiveness is likely to derive from interaction effects accruing from multi-dimensional programmes (Klitzner 1993; Provan and Milward 1995; Rosenbaum 2002; Sanderson 2002). Moreover, the partnership literature acknowledges, far more than the currently favoured effective practice evidence appears to, the difficulty of attributing cause for any changes that occur to the effects of a single intervention, when social welfare and criminal justice agencies are in constant states of flux and a range of community-wide programmes are being introduced over the same time period (Klitzner 1993; Martin and Sanderson 1999). Thus, outcome evaluation of multi-faceted partnership programmes would consider the summative impact of the different contributing projects on broad level measures of community well-being (Murphy-Berman, Schnoes and Chambers 2000). ...

Summary

The 'What Works' initiative has been remarkable for the extent to which it has been driven from the top. Partnership, however, even when statutorily mandated, relies on grass roots support for its accomplishments. The accompanying table expresses some of the tensions between 'top down' and 'grass roots' approaches to community provision for offenders exposed by this comparison of the effective practice initiative, as it has been understood and implemented thus far, and a partnership perspective.

Table 1 Two models of integrated provision

	Top down	*Grass roots*
Policy	Crime reduction	Social exclusion
Direction	Central government	Local agreements
Funding	Secure	Insecure
Provision	Standardised	Diverse
Access	Equal	Uneven
Mandate	What works	What's needed
Partnership	Contractual	Collaborative
Programmes	Standardised Accredited Targeted Coerced	Local adaptations Inclusive Mixed voluntary/coerced
Success	Reduced reconvictions	Reduced need

While central policy tends to emanate from a specific primary objective such as crime reduction, local collaborations, as we have seen, thrive when there is a broader stated aim capable of accommodating diverse interests. It is precisely this accommodation that keeps partners at the 'negotiating table' (Hausman 2002; Mackintosh 1993). Indeed, the whole point of partnership, in contrast to specialist isolation, is to pool diversity of expertise and resources (Chavis 2001). Thus, collaborative grass roots projects targeting social exclusion might more readily offer the flexibility of purpose required to sustain motivation and effort among partners with different perspectives and priorities. Top down approaches take their direction from central policy making level, while grass roots operate on the basis of local agreements that reflect unique conditions in terms of the particular set of statutory and voluntary sector partners, opportunities and constraints. Funding for an enterprise mandated by central authority is generally more secure, at least in the early stages of the project, while grass roots initiatives often struggle to find funding from multiple and impermanent sources.

Where the top down agenda strives for standardisation of provision, grass roots partnerships embrace local diversity. In the partnership context, effective leadership may be seen in management of a fluid, and sometimes volatile external environment to enhance staff capacity to cope, rather than control of the behaviour of front-line practitioners (Menefee 1997). A theoretical advantage of standardisation is equality of access to the service, while opportunities are notoriously unevenly distributed when left to the discretion of local areas. This would hopefully be true in terms of geographical availability, although ... access to programmes accredited through the 'What Works' initiative is restricted to those who meet their entry criteria.

The mandate for service type in the top down approach is what works in terms of its specific primary objective, while the broader remit of grass roots initiatives requires a local perspective on what is needed to resolve a community's problems. Within the top down 'What Works' agenda there is little acknowledgement of, or scope for inter-organisational relationships other than those based on contracts for provision of elements of accredited programmes. A grass roots approach aspires to a collaborative style of multi-agency relationships that will address issues in negotiation, power sharing and resource interdependence. Top down practice development directs the implementation of programmes that are centrally accredited, targeted on specific offender populations and coerced. Collaborative grass roots initiatives, however, will include intervention strategies that are adapted to local contingencies, are accessible to a broad range of community residents with common problems and thus capable of mixing voluntary and coerced clientele. Finally, while success in the top down approach is measured narrowly in terms of reduced convictions, the broader remit of grass roots collaborations will look to reduced levels of need in local communities.

In so far as the top down approach yields an integrated structure of provision, it is a relatively limited form of integration in the sense of coherence between a focused policy objective and its implementation in respect of a narrow target group. The grass roots approach aspires to integration of services across disciplines and client groups, which is altogether a broader, more multi-faceted and more inclusive conceptualisation of a policy goal and the pathways to its achievement. While there is undoubtedly a place for the former approach, particularly for the most challenging groups of offenders with specific needs relating to their rehabilitation and community safety, it is the argument of this chapter that this limited project should not overwhelm the capacity of the probation service to invest vigorously in the latter enterprise. Moreover, while central guidance is needed for policy direction and good practice dissemination (Foster-Fishman *et al.* 2001; O'Looney 1997), it should not suppress the vitality of local flexibility and creativity.

Conclusion

Unlike the silent hound in the Sherlock Holmes tale, the partnership dog is barking furiously. Were we to listen, we would hear its message clearly: the probation service's commitment to mandatory partnerships is increasing in depth and breadth; the time, effort and resources being committed to partnerships demands a defensible return; and the partnership enterprise offers an alternative, more realistic and more palatable vision of the service's mission, grounded in its own traditions, than one founded on delivery of narrowly defined offending behaviour programmes. Yet, few, if any, are listening to the valiant hound's attempts to attract attention. ...

... [T]he search for another organisation capable of 'brokerage' (Lowndes and Skelcher 1998) between the worlds of criminal justice and social welfare, with equal appreciation of both and without prejudice towards either, would be long, hard, and certainly fruitless. The success of the contemporary partnership enterprise requires just such an organisation, with '(c)redibility and legitimacy ... to speak with authority and candor, to be taken seriously ... and to become a respected source of information ... ' (Annie E. Casey Foundation 1995). Indeed, it has been remarked that examples of the probation service's practice excellence and strongest commitment derive from those projects in which it contributes collaboratively to the overall health of its local communities (Rumgay 2000). Thus, the partnership approach, properly presented, holds the promise of securing professional support through its appeal to the service's established traditions (Dalton, Elias and Wandersman 2001).

... In many respects, the service has not chosen the partnership pathway for itself. Rather, policy and statutory mandate have thrust that path upon it. The expenditure of resources thus to be committed could be put to good use in securing the service's future role in the community. It is not an effort to be wasted, but an opportunity to be exploited.

From Judith Rumgay, 'The barking dog? Partnership and effective practice', in G. Mair (ed.), What Matters in Probation *(Cullompton: Willan), 2004, pp. 122–145.*

References

Annie E. Casey Foundation (1995) *The Path of Most Resistance: Reflections on Lessons Learned from New Futures.* Baltimore, MD, Annie E. Casey Foundation.

Armstrong, K. L. (1997) 'Launching a Family-centered, Neighbourhood-based Human Services System: Lessons from Working the Hallways and Street Corners.' *Administration in Social Work,* 21(3/4): 109–26.

Bennett, L. and Lawson, M. (1994) 'Barriers to Cooperation Between Domestic-violence and Substance-abuse Programs.' *Families in Society: The Journal of Contemporary Human Services,* May, 277–86.

Chavis, D. M. (2001) 'The Paradoxes and Promise of Community Coalitions.' *American Journal of Community Psychology,* 29(2): 309–20.

Clear, T. R. and Cadora, E. (2003) *Community Justice*. Belmont, CA, Wadsworth/Thompson Learning.

Dalton, J. H., Elias, M. J. and Wandersman, A. (2001) *Community Psychology: Linking Individuals and Communities*. Belmont, CA, Wadsworth/Thompson Learning.

Doyle, A. C. (1894) 'The Memoirs of Sherlock Holmes: The Adventure of Silver Blaze'. Reprinted in A. C. Doyle *Sherlock Holmes: The Complete Illustrated Short Stories*. London, Chancellor Press, 1985, pp. 235–56.

Foster-Fishman, P. G., Salem, D. A., Allen, N. A. and Fahrbach, K. (2001) 'Facilitating Interorganizational Collaboration: The Contributions of Interorganizational Alliances.' *American Journal of Psychology*, 29(6): 875–905.

Glisson, C. (1994) 'The Effect of Services Coordination Teams on Outcomes for Children in State Custody.' *Administration in Social Work*, 18(4): 1–23.

Hassett, S. and Austin, M. J. (1997) 'Service Integration: Something Old and Something New.' *Administration in Social Work*, 21(3/4): 9–29.

Hausman, A. J. (2002) 'Implications of Evidence-based Practice for Community Health.' *American Journal of Community Psychology*, 30(3): 453–67.

Huxham, C. (1996) 'Collaboration and Collaborative Advantage.' In C. Huxham (ed) *Creating Collaborative Advantage*. London, Sage, pp. 1–18.

Johnson, C. A., Pentz, M. A., Weber, M. D., Dwyer, J. H., Baer, N., MacKinnon, D. P., Hansen, W. B. and Flay, B. R. (1990) 'Relative Effectiveness of Comprehensive Community Programming for Drug Abuse Prevention with High-risk and Low-risk Adolescents.' *Journal of Consulting and Clinical Psychology*, 58(4): 447–56.

Karp, D. R. and Clear, T. R. (2002) 'Preface. The Community Justice Frontier: An Introduction.' In D. R. Karp and T. R. Clear (eds) *What is Community Justice? Case Studies of Restorative Justice and Community Supervision*. Thousand Oaks, CA, Sage, pp. ix–xvi.

Klitzner, M. (1993) 'A Public Health/Dynamic Systems Approach to Community-Wide Alcohol and Other Drug Initiatives.' In R. C. Davis, A. J. Lurigio, D. P. Rosenbaum (eds) *Drugs and the Community: Involving Community Residents in Combatting the Sale of Illegal Drugs*. Springfield, IL, Charles C. Thomas, pp. 201–24.

Lowndes, V. and Skelcher, C. (1998) 'The Dynamics of Multi-organizational Partnerships: An Analysis of Changing Modes of Governance.' *Public Administration*, 76, Summer: 313–33.

Mackintosh, M. (1993) 'Partnership: Issues of Policy and Negotiation.' *Local Economy*, 7(3): 210–24.

Mair, G. and Jamel, J. (2002) 'Crime and Disorder Partnerships in Liverpool.' Paper presented at the European Society of Criminology Conference, Toledo, 5–7 September.

Martin, S. and Sanderson, I. (1999) 'Evaluating Public Policy Experiments: Measuring Outcomes, Monitoring Processes or Managing Pilots?' *Evaluation*, 5(3): 245–58.

Mattessich, P. W., Murray-Close, M. and Monsey, B. R. (2001) *Collaboration: What Makes it Work*. 2nd Edition. Saint Paul, MN, Amherst H. Wilder Foundation.

Menefee, D. (1997) 'Strategic Administration of Nonprofit Human Service Organizations: A Model for Executive Success in Turbulent Times.' *Administration in Social Work*, 21(2): 1–19.

Minicucci, C. (1997) 'Assessing a Family-centered Neighbourhood Service Agency: The Del Paso Heights Model.' *Administration in Social Work*, 21(¾): 127–43.

Murphy-Berman, V., Schnoes, C. and Chambers, J. M. (2000) 'An Early Stage Evaluation Model for Assessing the Effectiveness of Comprehensive Community Initiatives: Three Case Studies in Nebraska.' *Evaluation and Program Planning*, 23: 157–63.

O'Looney, J. (1997) 'Marking Progress Toward Service Integration: Learning to Use Evaluation to Overcome Barriers.' *Administration in Social Work*, 21(3/4): 31–65.

Orians, C. E., Liebow, E.B. and Branch, K. M. (1995) 'Community-based Organizations and HIV Prevention Among Seattle's Inner-city Teens.' *Urban Anthropology*, 24(1–2): 36–58.

Provan, K. G. and Milward, H. B. (1995) 'A Preliminary Theory of Interorganizational Network Effectiveness: A Comparative Study of Four Community Mental Health Systems.' *Administrative Science Quarterly*, 40: 1–33.

Rosenbaum, D. P. (2002) 'Evaluating Multi-agency Anti-crime Partnerships: Theory, Design and Measurement Issues.' In N. Tilley (ed) *Evaluation for Crime Prevention*. Crime Prevention Studies Vol. 14. Monsey, NY, Criminal Justice Press, pp. 171–225.

Rumgay, J. (2000) *The Addicted Offender: Developments in British Policy and Practice*. Basingstoke, Palgrave.

——(2001) 'Accountability in the Delivery of Community Penalties: To Whom, For What and Why?' In A. Bottoms, L. Gesthorpe and S. Rex (eds) *Community Penalties: Change and Challenges*. Cullompton, Willan, pp. 126–45.

——(2003) 'Partnerships in the Probation Service.' In M. Nellis and W. H. Chui (eds) *Moving Probation Forward: Evidence and Arguments*. Harlow, Longman/Pearson Education.

Sanderson, I. (2002) 'Evaluation, Policy Learning and Evidence-based Policy Making.' *Public Administration*, 80(1): 1–22.

Social Exclusion Unit (1998) *Bringing Britain Together: A National Strategy for Neighbourhood Renewal*. Cm 4045. London, HMSO.

Sutton, A. and Cherney, A. (2002) 'Prevention without politics? The cyclical progress of crime prevention in an Australian state.' *Criminal Justice*, 2(3): 325–44.

Part D

Supervision: practice and programmes

Introduction

This section explores 'real world' practice down the years of probation history. We have been keen to record the lived experience of probation officers attempting to implement their goals and principles in the day-to-day world of offender supervision. While there are a few contributions from academics, these have been selected for their close relationship to practice. For the most part, rather than the objective commentaries of observers, we attempt to capture the raw experience and passions of probation officers as well as their observations on practice. In this section we see the rich, imaginative and bold diversity of practice in the history of the service. Moreover, the shared passion of probation officers for their agency's significance and development within the criminal justice system shines through their differing approaches.

One of us recalls, as an untrained probation officer in the early 1970s, being advised to read Florence Hollis' (1964) book on psychosocial casework and, desperate to understand the mysterious nature of the work into which she had stumbled, doing so with diligence. Yet, while impressed by the author's sincerity and commitment, she was quite unable, throughout the many anecdotes illustrating the theory outlined within its pages, to discern what precisely brought social worker and client together. Clare Winnicott's article, 'Casework and agency function' (Reading 41), therefore offers a welcome examination of a theoretical approach that seems generally to ignore its organisational setting; it explores in detail the relationship between institutional constraints and practice. Winnicott points out that, notwithstanding the prevailing view of the social caseworker as possessing generic professional skills geared to the amelioration of social and personal problems, the ways in which those problems manifest themselves and the tools with which they might be tackled are shaped by the agency tasked to address them. While chastising social work for its neglect of agency function, Winnicott displays the characteristic confidence of her time in the ability of the developing social sciences to refine the casework approach.

A.W. Hunt's exploration of enforcement (Reading 42) similarly addresses an area of practice that the then prevailing theoretical ethos in social casework often overlooked, or perhaps hoped would quietly disappear (see Foren and Bailey 1968 for an exception). Hunt, an experienced practitioner, points out that generic casework fails to provide a clear grounding for the obvious fact that, for probation officers, their clientele's cooperation in the assessment and treatment of their problems is generally not readily forthcoming. Like Winnicott, however, he does not respond to this problem by questioning the relevance of psychosocial theory to probation practice but by attempting to fill the gap left by an approach that tends to disregard the significance of agency. Also like Winnicott, he sees the enforcement role of the probation officer as a tool and even an asset in, rather than an impediment to, engagement with the offender under supervision.

J.R. Mott's contribution (Reading 43), reflecting on personal experience at around the same time as the foregoing articles appeared, offers a very different illumination of probation casework. Here we see the bluff, pragmatic approach, laced with a smattering of common-sense psychology that characterised the practice of many officers (see Part B Introduction and Readings 20, 21), often coming to the service from diverse backgrounds in alternative careers. Mott explores practice largely through the vehicle of anecdote rather than theory. His *ad hoc*, problem-solving approach might startle a contemporary audience for its disregard of certain social and professional niceties. Nevertheless, his cheerful humanity and staunch defence of offenders' interests (albeit that today these might seem somewhat arbitrarily perceived) is irrepressible. Moreover, he appears to have good reason for his optimism, apparently enjoying an impressive measure of success!

As we move through the 1970s, we begin to see an expanding diversity of approaches. Bruce Hugman's account of his work as a detached probation officer (Reading 44), electing to live and work in the very neighbourhood in which many offenders and their families lived, is fascinating for several reasons. First, and very importantly, this unusual and bold project is approved and supported by his senior managers over a substantial period of time; it is even preserved when Hugman himself withdraws. Second, Hugman embraces and exemplifies what McWilliams would later term the 'personalist' school of thought. Indeed, although the extract here has drawn upon his account of raw experience, elsewhere in the book Hugman develops a passionate conceptual argument for his adventurous approach, starting from a critique of the large, institutional setting of the generic social services in the 1970s, geographically and personally removed from the realities of survival in socially deprived urban areas. Third, the approach to problem solving is, both necessarily and intentionally, immediate, practical and humanistic. Finally, and notably, despite his immersion in unconventional lifestyles, Hugman at no point forgets, ignores or conceals his agency of origin but rather sees this as the essential framework for his own, idiosyncratic practice.

The Berkeley sex offender group (Reading 45), which began in the late 1970s, is reviewed by the probation officers who developed it after running for seven years. This, in itself, is an impressive achievement in a service in which attempts at innovative practice have been frequently short lived, dying when their pioneers move on or with changes in fashion, fortune and policy (see Readings 56 and 63). The group was notable for certain strong attributes: it did not demand serious commitment to change prior to joining the programme; it allowed for group membership over a substantial period of time; it combined personal support with exploration of individual offending behaviour. The programme successfully engaged a group of recidivist offenders.

Many innovations in probation attempted to adapt themes emerging in contemporary social work. Thus, the 'Going Local' projects described in Scott *et al.*'s series of accounts, while appealing to a history of probation activity at community level, reflect renewed interest consequent upon the proposals of the Barclay Report (1982) for social services to focus on local 'patch' work. The selected contribution from Huddersfield (Reading 46) describes difficulties common to many of the projects in making a clear impact in neighbourhoods: neither local agencies nor inhabitants were easily recruited; officers in the field felt unsupported by senior management; and initiatives were fragile and often unsustained. Nevertheless, and particularly following clarification of management investment in the enterprise, some opportunities were created and a degree of organisation by local people was galvanised.

In a similar vein of following developments in social work, Goldberg *et al.*'s study of the adoption of task-centred casework by a probation team (Reading 47) illustrates the challenge of adapting a generic theoretical model to the formal constraints of probation supervision. A number of positive developments in relationships with offenders emerge in this project, although limitations to the model's applicability are also evident. Unfortunately, space allows only for the inclusion here of the project summary; the much lengthier full account shows close involvement of the evaluators in the development of a shift in conventional practice and thus captures the probation officers' experiences of curiosity, caution, learning and encouragement by results.

Probation officers during the 1970s and 1980s grappled with difficult questions. Tim Chapman's scrutiny of NAPO's policy against probation service involvement with politically motivated offenders (Reading 48) confronts important ethical choices. Chapman identifies the discrepancy between NAPO's view, that political motivation was not an attitudinal or behavioural problem amenable to correction, and the perception of offenders and their families that opportunities for personal assistance were being denied them. While illustrating the differences between Northern Ireland and the mainland in the application of the policy, Chapman reveals the great respect in which a politically neutral probation service was held in the province. Ultimately, however, he questions the underlying motivation of probation officers themselves to protect their professional autonomy by avoiding politically sensitive work.

John Smith (1983) attracted the fury of many probation officers when he published an article in support of supervised antabuse therapy: he succeeded in offending the social work precept of client self-determination while invoking the spectre of a service based on behavioural control rather than personal change. Perhaps in an attempt to moderate first impressions, he subsequently published this account (Reading 49) of supervision of an individual offender in which antabuse therapy is shown to provide a gateway to personal development through more conventional social work methods. But, no doubt further to his chagrin, probation officers continued to disagree with him.

In 1981, the number of probation orders made by the courts reached an all-time low. The collapse of faith in rehabilitation, sometimes viewed as an academic debate about which probation officers cared little, could now be seen to have penetrated the professional consciousness. The consequent loss of direction, combined with the growth in emphases on control through parole and punishment through community service, now threatened to overwhelm the service's defining activity. The Demonstration Unit of the Inner London Probation Service, experimenting with increasing recommendations for probation (Reading 50), shows that clear proposals for supervision could influence sentencing. Notably, no changes in the basic conduct of supervision were offered, although reports explored how conventional methods could help to expand the range of choices made by individual offenders. This report points to the need for probation officers to show confidence in their product.

Soon afterwards, however, David Bale developed a Risk of Custody Scale (Reading 51), designed to enable probation officers to make defensible proposals for probation targeting high-tariff offenders. Bale argues that the advantages of his scale include the capacity for restraining net widening – the use of intensive programmes for lower-tariff offenders who would not have been at risk of a custodial sentence. Bale was initially criticised for his efforts to develop accountable practice (for which read constrain professional autonomy); yet his initiative rapidly became commonplace in the service. Although 'gatekeeping' tended to disappear as an issue when the 1991 Criminal Justice Act made community penalties sentences in their own right, rigorous gatekeeping remains desperately needed; in 2003, Rod Morgan, the Chief Inspector of Probation, complained about the 'silting up' of the probation caseload with low-tariff offenders, and today almost half of all community orders are made for summary offences.

The tide of opinion was turning fast towards the potential for enhanced probation orders to offer alternatives to custody that would be attractive to sentencers. The Home Office's experiment with Day Training Centres in the early 1980s provided a spur to imagination. The fact that the Home Office's initiative was directed at petty persistent offenders did not deter the service from adapting this template to the pursuit of more serious, custody-bound offenders. The service was rapidly becoming caught in the mesh of its different ambitions: to diversify its social work methods; to attract high-tariff offenders; and to avoid further recruitment to the cause of social control. The tension is aptly revealed in two articles reprinted here: David Millard's retrospective analysis of team-based social work supervision (Reading 52), which attracted much positive interest within the service; and Nigel Spencer and Pat Edwards' reflections on the Kent Control Unit (Reading 53), which raised a storm of protest. Ironically, the successful appeal against an order requiring attendance at an intensive programme, which reached the House of Lords in the case of *Cullen v. Rogers*, was not directed at the Kent Control Unit but an alternative project. However, the result was to close down all such schemes until the Home Office produced new legislation in the Criminal Justice Act 1982, enabling the probation service to resume the development of tougher regimes.

Despite these pre-occupations, Jeff Bowe *et al.*'s review of policy and practice in the wake of inner-city disturbances in 1985 (Reading 54) provides a helpful reminder that the probation service in the mid-1980s was still responsive to immediate local events. The commentary, however, points to a divergence of opinion between field staff and senior managers as to the form that the response should take. Here, we can see the emergence of a managerial approach to prescribing probation officers' duties that was later subject to the caustic criticism of Bill McWilliams (1992).

Michael Sheath's complaint about the trend in confrontative work with sex offenders (Reading 55) targets a very different approach from that described in the Berkeley project five years earlier. Sheath (who later left the probation service to specialise in sex offender work) highlights the service's shift towards punitive practice in its efforts to prove itself capable of interventions with high-risk offenders. In this article, the doubts of many probation officers about the direction in which their ambition was taking them, particularly in terms of distorting social work methods, are encapsulated.

We conclude this section with George Mair's critique of the proliferation of specialist activities in probation (Reading 56). Mair's complaint about the uncoordinated development of special programmes, dependent on the imagination of individual officers, makes interesting contemporary reading as we contemplate an era of much more standardised, regulated practice delivered through centrally accredited programmes. A Home Office researcher at the time of writing, Mair's frustration with the inability of the centre to keep up with the inventions of the field seems incongruous when viewed from today's perspective of centrally prescribed practice.

Collectively, these accounts of practice raise challenging questions for the academic debate on evaluation (Part F this volume). How many of these initiatives would meet the standards required by an external researcher? Is it only the engaging passion of the practitioners that induces us to see them as accounts of good practice? Is good day-to-day practice necessarily the same as the successful practice that leads to positive evaluation results? And how can the successes of these initiatives be formally recorded? Thus, Hugman's (Reading 44) distraction of a violent offender by taking him to a pub out of town might, arguably, represent an inspired piece of crime prevention or risk reduction, yet is unlikely to be found in any statistical analysis of effective practice: it is an example of qualitatively good practice that is almost impossible to define quantitatively. 'Going local' in Huddersfield enabled some residents to become active in trying to ameliorate their community's problems, yet it would be difficult to attribute any local crime reduction directly to the probation service's enterprise. These, and other examples within this section, challenge us to accept certain interventions as good in themselves; they are recognisable as qualitatively and intrinsically meritorious in ways that defy conventional evaluative methods (see Reading 71).

It was not our specific intention to halt this exploration of practice in the mid-1990s, but there are several reasons for this outcome. First, we have not included writings on the topic of cognitive behavioural programmes. This certainly does not reflect any particular antipathy on our part. Consistent with our original stated aims for this collection, we did not wish to use space for a topic that has in recent years been the subject of wide discussion and research in a body of readily accessible literature, collectively known by the rubric 'What Works'. We have preferred to highlight examples of practice that are less well known and less easily discovered, yet which illustrate the breadth of the probation service's imaginative endeavour over many years.

Second, although the accredited cognitive behavioural programmes have become well known within the service, accounts of delivering contemporary cognitive behavioural programmes written by probation officers themselves are rare. Indeed, this notable absence of the practitioner's voice in the case of cognitive behavioural programmes is part of a wider silence of probation officers about their day-to-day practice.

The reasons for the disappearance of the autobiographical voice are unclear. One important factor might be the remodelling of the *Probation Journal* which, since the early 2000s, has sought to appeal more clearly to an academic audience, with consequent implications for its content. It might possibly be the case that probation officers are so preoccupied with the pace and scale of organisational change that they no longer have the time to write about their experience. Perhaps, in a world of prescribed delivery of accredited programmes, they no longer feel any particular ownership of their own endeavours. Whatever the reasons, we consider this disappearance of the raw material of experience to be a loss to the body of probation service literature and hope that officers might soon resume lending their voices to the illumination of real-world practice.

References

Barclay Report (1982) *Social Workers: Their Role and Tasks – Working Party Report.* London: Bedford Square Press.

Foren, R. and Bailey, R. (1968) *Authority in Social Casework.* Oxford: Pergamon.

Hollis, F. (1964) *Casework: A Psychosocial Therapy.* New York: Random House.

McWilliams, W. (1992) 'The rise and development of management thought, in the English Probation Service', in R. Statham and P. Whitehead (eds.), *Managing the Probation Service: Issues for the 1990s,* Harlow: Longman.

Morgan, R. (2003) 'Thinking about the demand for probation services', *Probation Journal,* 50(1): 7–19.

Smith, J. (1983) 'Supervised Antabuse Therapy', *Probation Journal,* 30(4): 130–132.

41 Casework and agency function (1962)

Clare Winnicott

For a long time now I have wanted to try to explore further this question of agency function and its effect on the casework process. The subject has intrigued me. It is a very vital subject, and at the same time a practical one in view of the fact that caseworkers function within agencies.

It seems to me especially important that as we move away from specialisation both in training and in our professional life, we should try to understand more fully than ever the essential nature of the functions of each agency and the effect that these have on the caseworkers who give them meaning for the client.

Recently in the Younghusband Report (Ministry of Health, Department of Health for Scotland 1959) ... we have had convincingly put before us evidence which shows that one factor contributing to the lack of co-ordination of the social services is the social worker's lack of clarity about the functions of other social services, and the lack of clarity about his or her own functions within a particular service. The Ingleby Committee (Home Office 1960) summarised and endorsed these findings.

The problem of defining functions within a social service and between the social services is, of course, one which must be tackled at all levels throughout the services, and must be seen from many different points of view. There is no doubt that only by effective co-operation can we make full use of the social provisions which we have been fortunate enough to achieve in this country. But as the Younghusband Report reminds us, the basis of co-operation is each one's confidence in his or her own function.

In what I shall say about casework and agency function I shall be focusing on one bit of this complex problem of defining functions, in my view a vital bit, because it concerns the integration of casework function and agency function. I shall try to state the dynamics of agency function in casework terms.

Surprisingly enough this problem was seen and refreshingly stated as long ago as 1903 by Professor Urwick writing in *The Charity Organization Review* for that year. He said then in 1903, of the practitioner of social work, that 'his methods must be made scientific, his practice must be founded on a true knowledge of principles of law: and he, the practitioner, must himself acquire that knowledge and be trained in these methods'. He goes on to say (and this is the important part) '[The social worker] must learn to realise the slow growth that lies behind each condition and fact; to see in the social structure whole or part, of state, or of institution, the expression of a vital meaning; to feel beneath the seemingly plastic relationships of social life, the framework of economic necessities; and to find in each causal tendency and habit the effect of slowly changing mental processes. Not the training of the man of science, but the scientific attitude, must be his; that at least is necessary if experience is to be used aright' (quoted in King 1958).

It is inspired creative thinking such as this that has led to our emergence as a profession. More recently we have been profoundly influenced in our development by the writings of American Social Workers who were able to see more quickly than we were that, in particular, the findings of dynamic psychology could and must be applied to social work if it were to move forward towards a greater understanding of individual social maladjustment. The work done by our American colleagues in refining our social work concepts from the application of theory to practice has given us the basic requirement of a profession, that is, a language in which to communicate essential ideas, and this we have taken over from them. We shall Anglicise it and alter it in the light of our own thinking and experience, but without it we should have had to start from scratch.

During recent years Social Caseworkers in all fields have been especially concerned with establishing themselves as a group of people bound together by common professional aims, standards, techniques and attitudes, a group whose entity can be recognised by others. We are at the present time engaged in exploring and understanding the common ground between us. We find that out of the confusion of human predicaments with which social workers are confronted there emerge certain essential truths about the people behind the predicaments and the ways in which help can be made available to them without loss of human dignity.

It is on these essential matters, which have been extracted from knowledge and experience, and that are the concern of all social caseworkers, that the principles and techniques of casework practice are based. It is not my purpose here to discuss these principles in detail but I should like to say that from my point of view their validity is unquestioned because they reach down and give practical expression to the human rights which belong to us all, caseworkers and clients alike.

Having said this, I now want to take up my main theme, the question of agency function and its effect on the casework process. What does the agency do to the caseworker by putting him or her in a certain position in relation to the client, and how does this position affect the actual work done? These are, of course, complicated questions, and I want to try to formulate some preliminary ideas about them which may pave the way for further discussion. I shall make some general comments and then go on to discuss the work of three agencies: Probation, Child Care, and Medical Social Work.

I want to make it clear that I am not confusing agency function with agency policy or methods. I am concerned with the basic function of the agencies to meet social needs. We all know that policy and methods can distort and obscure function and that only as all concerned can get a firm grip on function can this danger be avoided.

First of all I should like to say that I am aware that the casework principles which I have been referring to have been worked out and arrived at by workers in all kinds of agency settings and they are therefore not divorced from the influence of agency function on casework practice. They represent the common denominator of casework in all agencies whatever their function. As I have already implied, it seems to me important that we should not be so concerned with establishing our common casework skills based on commonly held principles that our view of the particular form in which problems are presented in our particular agency is obscured, otherwise we might fail to make full use of the function of our agency and of other agencies to meet the needs of clients. We must be confident enough in our common casework skills to be able to look at differences which exist between the agencies because of the particular function each has in relation to the client. In other words, although our function will be different according to the agency we are working in, our attitude to our clients and the ways in which we work with them will be the same whatever the agency.

Sometimes social workers talk as if the social services exist in order to provide a setting in which they can practice their casework skills. I can appreciate this keenness to establish professional skill – it must be present in every caseworker otherwise he or she will never achieve anything and moreover the drive to achieve means that the chosen profession gives scope for satisfactions in the individual. But the question of emphasis arises. Is the caseworker aiming at practising a professional skill, or at serving the community? We know that in the interests of all, these aims must be complementary and integrated into the professional life of each individual worker.

However, I do know that there are agencies which for all kinds of reasons do not give caseworkers the opportunity to develop their professional skills in the service of the agency. This may be a matter for adjustment between worker and agency. Such adjustment will take time, and it presents a challenge; or it may be, of course, that the agency needs structural alterations which will allow for the better deployment of staff resources as suggested for the Health and Welfare Services in the Younghusband Report. But whatever the situation, I suggest that as we increasingly lay stress on the value of casework skill, it is important to remind ourselves that casework skill is not an end in itself, but is a means whereby we serve the community and find our place in it. I often wish that we were called *Social Servants*, because I think that this would describe our function today in a way that the term *Social Worker* does not. There is something dignified about being a servant, and moreover the word implies a relationship to the community whereas the word *worker* simply implies that work is being done.

At this point I should like to remind you of something that Professor Titmuss (1954) has said: 'the worker, the client, and the setting are the basic components of action and must be viewed as a whole'. This statement seems to me to sum up so much that is important for social workers. A sense of wholeness implies integration. If this sense of wholeness which is necessary for maximum productivity is missing we shall not be in a position to further the integration of our clients into the community, because at some point we ourselves have failed to achieve such an integration.

As social workers how do we become integrated into the community? Of course the ability to do this involves the achievement of maturity in the individual, a process which we know starts in the earliest years of life. It has been said that the hallmark of maturity is an individual's capacity to identify with the community without loss of identity and sense of self. I do not propose to trace the steps which lead to this state of affairs now, because they are very complex. But roughly speaking, if the needs of the individual are sufficiently well met at the various stages of development, then he or she comes to be able to identify with the people in the environment who meet his or her needs. Her own capacity to identify with her child is of course the basis of the mother's knowing what the child's needs are. This meeting of needs is a two-way process, a matter of giving and taking. The infant and child takes from his mother and at the same time gives to her her capacity to be a mother through her function as one, just as anyone who takes a present gives at the same time to the giver his capacity to give, to be a giver. This is what clients do for the social worker. By using our services they give us a function in relation to themselves and at the same time they give us a place in society which wants this function performed and has created the agency to perform it. Agency function therefore is not simply a meeting point for worker, client, and community, but a dynamic force which welds them together. It represents the creative urge in the community towards the client, and a creative urge in the client towards integration. These creative urges are embodied in the social worker who gives them 'vital meaning' in Professor Urwick's words. How vital the meaning will be will depend on the professional skill of the caseworker and on his or her own creativity. In my view therefore agency function is the central dynamic of the whole casework process. It is not something that is tacked on to casework and which is sometimes regarded as hampering to the practice of casework principles. It is the very crux of casework, and to lose touch with it would be to lose touch with the needs of our clients, and the forces in society which tend to meet these needs.

At this point I can imagine that some people may say this is all very well, but what about our difficult clients, those who seem beyond our scope and take and give nothing, and in whom the integrative urge is negligible? I think that this question does not really affect my argument, because the fact that they are our clients means that they are still within the scope of society's concern although we have as yet insufficient knowledge or provision to be able to help them. The less responsible the client can be the more actively responsible must society become in relation to him through the function of its various social work agencies and their personnel. Obviously the majority of clients in any one agency are able to make use of the agency's function otherwise the agency would have died a natural death.

We all know that social work agencies can become obsolete. I like to remember that when I first started social work in what was then called a 'distressed area' I was concerned with something called 'The Mayor's Boot Fund' for unemployed miners. This agency obviously died long ago, for although presumably miners still need boots, they are no longer unemployed; and if they were, they come within the more effective national insurance policy which now exists.

As social conditions change, the social needs of our clients express themselves in new forms which have to be recognised and understood in the light of new knowledge if the function of the agency in meeting needs is to be maintained. We recognise it as the special responsibility of the professionally trained social workers to keep under constant review, and to adjust to, the social needs of their clients, but the social workers are in a position to do this only because society employs them and in so doing takes the over-all responsibility for client and for worker alike.

How long society will go on taking this overall responsibility depends on many factors, one of them undoubtedly being the social worker's ability not only to meet the needs of clients, but to contribute to the creating of a social climate in which the work will be maintained.

I should now like to apply what I have said about agency function in relation to casework by reference to the work of particular agencies.

First of all Probation. I was stimulated in my thinking about casework in this setting by a paper given by Arthur Hunt (1961), Principal Probation Officer for Southampton at the A.P.S.W. Refresher Course, April 1960. He raised the problem of the application of casework techniques to Probation work and particularly mentioned the important question of the compulsory nature of the relationship of the Probation Officer to his client. I should like to quote one sentence: 'The fact of enforcement has emerged as a much more positive feature than I would have believed at one time, and certainly more so than people are taught to expect, and is far from being an impediment to the application of casework techniques.' I am sorry that Mr. Hunt was unable to elaborate this point in the particular paper I am referring to, but it was not his main subject.

In view of what I have said about agency function it does not surprise me to find that Mr. Hunt sees the enforced relationship as a positive factor in his work. In fact are there not theories which teach us that the delinquent is unconsciously looking for just this, for a human being to become a respected and controlling authority, because this is what he has been deprived of in his family relationships?

The clientele of the Probation Service mainly consists of boys and girls, men and women, who show a periodic exacerbation of an anti-social tendency which has become part of their lives. This tendency belongs to a deprivation and repeats an urge (mainly unconscious), to reinstate what is lost. The individual steals in a claim over objects and satisfactions, or acts destructively expressing the unconscious need for a reinstatement of parental controls that have been absent at some crucial point or over a period of time.

When a child or an adult commits an offence of a certain degree and kind, he brings into action the machinery of the law. The Probation Officer who is then asked to do casework with the client feels he ought to apply techniques implying the casework principle of self-determination, but he loses everything if he forgets his relationship to his agency and the court, since symptoms of this kind of illness are unconsciously designed to bring authority into the picture. The Probation Officer can humanise the machinery of the law but he cannot sidestep it without missing the whole point of the symptom and the needs of the client. If he does miss the point the client either gives up hope or commits another offence to ensure the re-instatement of legal machinery.

In a book on the Probation Service edited by Joan King (1958) there is a story of a 9-year-old boy who after a few months surprised his Officer by saying: 'It isn't reporting that matters'; and when asked what did matter, he replied: 'Yer promise to the Court'. Was not this child reaching out through the individual Probation Officer to feel the reality of the authority which the Officer represented?

The principle of the client's right to self-determination is still implicit in the Probation Officer's work with his client, but the client will only be capable of becoming a self-determining individual if he finds a strongly backed environment in which he can safely live and discover his own true personal impulses.

There is then something deep down in the delinquent that comes to meet the Probation Officer, and this is why enforced relationships can work. It seems too that this is why the Probation Officer can often offer more to the delinquent than, for instance, the Psychiatric or Child Guidance Clinic. The delinquent may in fact need psychiatric treatment as well, but it cannot replace his primary need for a human being who is the embodiment of the legal machinery of society's reaction to him – a human being who is in a strong position in relation to himself and with whom he can gradually come to terms.

I suggest therefore that the Probation Officer finds that his agency's function reflects both the client's needs and society's reaction to these needs, and it also sets the basic pattern for the relationship. The effectiveness of the relationship will of course depend on the Probation Officer's ability to give vital meaning to the function, and in so doing his professional casework skills are fully needed. ...

It seems to me that what I have been saying about agency function *implies* something which needs to be *explicit* in our thinking. In functioning within an agency, a social caseworker as well as being a trained professional person who uses her knowledge and skill to help people, also *becomes* something in relation to her clients on behalf of the whole community. The Probation Officer becomes an authority figure, the Child Care Officer becomes a parental figure, and the Medical Social Worker as part of the medical team becomes a healing person on whom the patient's health depends.

If we fail to embody these roles in our work with our clients something very vital will be lost. We shall in fact fail our clients at the point of their deepest need, which is to reintegrate through the services of the agency into the life of the community as independent self-determining people. ...

From Clare Winnicott, 'Casework and agency function',
Case Conference, 8(7), 1962, pp. 178–184.

References

Home Office (1960) *Report of the Committee on Children and Young Persons.* Cmnd 1191. Chair: the Right Honourable the Viscount Ingleby. London, HMSO.

Hunt, A. (1961) *Ventures in Professional Co-operation.* Association of Psychiatric Social Workers.

King, J. F. S. (ed.) (1958) *The Probation Service.* First Edition. London, Butterworth.

Ministry of Health, Department of Health for Scotland (1959) *Report of the Working Party on Social Workers in the Local Authority Health and Welfare Services.* Chair: Dame Eileen Younghusband. London, HMSO.

Titmuss, R. (1954) 'The Administrative Setting of Social Service.' *Case Conference,* May, 1(1).

42 Enforcement in probation casework (1963)

A.W. Hunt

Developments in social casework practice and training have been exceptionally pronounced in the last two decades, and of overriding importance in these developments has been the provision, mostly during professional training, of a rationale for casework practice. Emphasis has tended towards the insight-giving processes, acknowledgment of the individual's right to self-determination, and to the importance of a non-directive and accepting approach by the caseworker. Much contemporary literature and general teaching reflect experience in casework where need is overt or openly acknowledged by the subject, and in consequence a dilemma is presented to probation officers and others employed in the correctional field who are called upon to reconcile the concepts of generic casework teaching with the fact that they work in a clearly authoritarian setting in which many of their professional relationships contain the element of enforcement. ...

Denial of the reality of the probation situation is often aided by the superficial fact that the probationer acknowledges need by virtue of the voluntary acceptance of a period of supervision, but there are few who would fail to recognise the naïvety of a suggestion that such an undertaking in itself implies recognition of need in any form.

Moreover, there appears little doubt that, if the probation officer attempts to approach the probationer without careful reference to the fact that in many instances co-operation may be grudgingly given, he may not only fail to develop an approach which can honestly reconcile the fundamentals of casework with the approach necessary in many correctional settings, but he will also find his capacity to help a number of deprived and maladapted people seriously impaired.

A relationship which is enforced by the full sanction of the law is clearly open to abuse and it is recognised that the insights developed in relation to the motivation of the practitioner have been invaluable in pointing to the dangers of dominating and pontifical control. However, a cause for increasing concern over the years has been the frequency with which the probation officer's special position in relation to his probationers and others under supervision has been described in relatively negative terms. Experience shows that the negative aspects of enforcement have been referred to much more frequently than the positive elements, and many occasions have arisen when, because of uneasiness about the coercive factor in their relationships, probation officers have tried to deny the facts of the situation and have exaggerated the positive quality of their relationships to a highly unrealistic degree. It would seem that one of the most important reasons for such a situation rests on the fact that so much of our dynamic casework practice is based on psychotherapeutic techniques developed within clinical settings where voluntary co-operation is assured and where such co-operation is deemed to be indispensable. Probation officers share with others the common experience of cases where a seriously disturbed person is considered unsuitable for treatment merely because he is not prepared to undertake treatment of his own volition or because of aggressive elements in the personality which conflict with special institutional or agency requirements. The basis of case selection of this type can be understood, but it is of very little assistance to the probation officer, many of whose cases would fall into such a category, and it would be a very great pity indeed if he concluded from such experience that lack of initial co-operation eliminated therapeutic opportunity or that maturation could not be encouraged.

With such problems as emotional disorder, personality defect or severe neurosis the relevance of the psychotherapeutic approach may be perceived. To see the relevance of such an approach is not easy when one deals with the many under-achieved, egocentric and extroverted delinquents where the primary problem appears to be one of defective character development, or encounters professionally the range of spontaneous antisocial behaviour normally apparent in the growing child who has clearly not developed a pattern of delinquent behaviour.

The concept of delinquency as a neurotic manifestation has received considerable attention in recent years, but it does seem that this attention is disproportionate when a broad view is taken of criminality and antisocial behaviour as a whole. Personal experience of a wide range of delinquents suggests that much antisocial behaviour arises from the failure of a socialisation process and that the compulsive, neurotic, affectionless or seriously unbalanced person is in the minority. Moreover, recognisable in much relatively casual delinquency is the presence of poorly sublimated aggression in which the failure of primary or social institutions of control is in evidence. ...

A rational development of a social or individual therapeutic approach in conditions of full enforcement has not yet matured, but there is convincing evidence to show that, contrary to the opinion of some clinicians, probationers and other offenders can make some adjustment even when compelled to relate to authority. In support of this view it is held that the most important and influential relationships in any person's life are those which are, in their very nature, enforced. A child is born into a family whether he or she likes it or not, and with very few exceptions there are no opportunities for the child to evade the necessity to make some adaptation to the demands made by the parents, and vice versa. Similarly in school, adjustment between child and teacher is necessary, even although in the first instance adjustment is unwillingly made. ...

In everyday life opportunities for withdrawal from trying situations are limited, and it seems that it is because of this fact that we develop our capacity to tolerate demands which ordinary living places upon us. For the majority of people with relatively normal personality and character development, marriage imposes similar disciplines; quarrels between husband and wife tend to resolve themselves much more rapidly because of the fact that opportunity to flee from an emotionally disturbing situation is not available, and because the fact of simple, urgent, sexual drive will force a compromise in order that straightforward satisfactions may be achieved. Such adaptations are frequently made and often fail to occur in an atmosphere of quiet acceptance or forgiveness. Indeed, it would seem that in the developmental pattern of human beings concern is often expressed in vigorous and active terms and often in the guise of punishment. I would personally regard this as very important, because within our present sphere of practice the possibilities of active and positively expressed concern do not receive very much attention. ...

[An] example is the following letter from an 18-year-old Borstal boy to a probation officer known to him before committal:

> I am writing this letter to thank you for helping me out in court. I am sorry I have not written before, as I could not remember your name. I am hoping that when I come out of here that I will be under your supervision. I'm sorry if I seemed to be rude to you when we were outside of the court, but as you may already know, no-one could hardly expect me to be happy about going to court. ...
>
> Please tell Mr. S ... if you see him that I'm sorry I let him down so much because I always did like him visiting my mother's house. And those little talks we had used to knock a bit of sense into me. Really what I needed when I was little was a good hiding but I always knew I would not get one, but this is just as good as one although it has taken me a long time to bring me to my senses.

... Such examples are far from uncommon in work with delinquents, and from such incidents it may be concluded that lack of criticism or annoyance may be interpreted by the emotionally deprived as indicating a lack of basic concern and by the delinquent with weak ego as emasculated control. It is of significance that on many occasions an entirely unexpected response is encountered in a probationer or client who has become involved in further trouble. In spite of the fact that the probation officer does not feel resentful or annoyed, letters are received showing quite clearly that it is assumed that he will experience such feelings, and that such feelings will arise from basic feelings of regard and concern for the probationer. ...

Before referring to ways in which probation casework techniques should acknowledge the special needs of the probation setting, it is necessary to return briefly to one other consideration arising from the original observations about enforcement in primary social situations. In everyday life anxiety may express itself in simple ways, such as in procrastination and evasion, but within the ambit of the court these features are encountered more frequently and in such degree that people are found who are prevented from taking even the most simple step which might remedy the source and cause of anxiety. Given a chance, most people will tend to take the superficially easy way out of their difficulties, and it is only when they are faced with a situation from which they cannot extricate themselves, or faced with a person they cannot avoid, that they are helped to overcome inertia sometimes produced by quite intense anxiety. This, it is felt, is one of the special strengths of the enforced relationship, and it can be seen why it is that probation officers are often the recipients of information which could more appropriately be disclosed, for example, to a psychiatrist or family doctor. The following example is used to illustrate the argument. A short time ago a probation officer completed supervision of a boy in his early teens whose behaviour was being adversely affected by excessively indulgent and over-protective handling by the mother. He was petulant and selfish and his thefts were not of a compulsive nature but more of the 'what I want I have' variety. Initially the Child Guidance Clinic had offered some assistance, but no treatment was possible because the mother repeatedly failed to keep the appointments. During the course of supervision it became increasingly obvious that the mother's attitude towards her son was coloured by feelings previously experienced in a very uneasy and ambivalent relationship with her younger brother. Her brother had, long before the boy's behaviour became increasingly troublesome at home, died tragically as the result of a rapid malignant illness. It appeared, and was subsequently admitted by the mother, that she felt very guilty for the many real and imagined unkindnesses shown to her brother, and her indulgent handling of her son was related to her need to make reparation in some way for her past hostility. By the end of supervision the mother was accustomed to talk quite freely about these considerable anxieties, the nature of which she had previously kept secret. On her own admission, she benefited from these interviews, but when it was suggested to her that, even although official contact would have ended, she could call and see the probation officer at his office, which was quite close to the home, she found this quite impossible to do. Her superficial reason was simply that if she came to see him he might think her reason for anxiety silly, and she would have difficulty in explaining her presence. If the probation officer called on her, however, under the provision of an Order which made it necessary for him to see her and her to see him, then the matters which caused her anxiety could be touched upon in the general course of interview. However, it seemed equally implicit that the fact of enforcement provided reassurance for the mother that relationship was finite and that the demands she made could be contained by this situation.

Probation casework is rich in examples showing how people may be helped in an enforced situation and how even the very dull are able to perceive the positive implications which may in the first instance appear to be against their interests. Simple examples can illustrate the point.

The first case is of a young man in his early twenties who had drifted away from what was a relatively settled home, but one in which control and guidance were limited. During his independent life he encountered difficulties over employment, found himself in financial trouble and committed what was a relatively simple offence to solve his immediate problem. The early phases of supervision were marked by a general air of discouragement which did not amount to seriously morbid depression, and the young man was becoming deterred from energetic pursuit of necessary employment because of very real difficulties due to some prevailing unemployment.

The probation officer concerned took practical and active measures to secure employment for this young man and they spent many hours together in this search. At one stage shortly before it proved fruitful the probationer was seen in the absence of his officer by a colleague. This colleague was surprised to encounter very positive warmth after what was a short period of supervision, and after some difficulty in describing the quality of his relationship the probationer eventually said 'I wish my father had been like Mr. Blank because when I am with him he makes me feel that things are going to get better for me at last'. Although a simple example it shows how much reassurance can be given by the competent management of the situation by a caseworker, and obvious parallels can be seen between this type of situation and the type of encouragement and reassurance which is given to children by the untroubled action of parents. ...

The last of the examples concerns a man in his middle thirties who had a long record and was placed on probation with certain knowledge that failure would result in a long prison sentence. It was evident that the fear of such a sentence acted as an additional external discipline and the man succeeded in keeping free from actual criminal behaviour. However, he broke contact after taking some seasonal employment and the probation officer recognised the set of circumstances which had preceded earlier criminal behaviour. A warrant was issued, the man was arrested and was eventually brought before the original sentencing court. In his behaviour towards the probation officer the man showed little obvious resentment and appeared to acknowledge and accept the reason given for the action taken. During the period of remand the man received news that attempts had been made to retain his employment for him and he saw that the report on his conduct was without obvious bias. A fresh Order was made, but for several days it was not possible for the probationer to commence residential employment. The probation officer shared with him the difficulties of finding temporary accommodation and it was noticeable that the officer was asked repeatedly not to 'worry' about the man. Subsequent discussion with this man at a much later date revealed that he had been impressed by a feeling that his further criminal behaviour and his material circumstances were of direct personal concern to the probation officer, and this theme emerged repeatedly during a phase of supervision lasting some eighteen months.

The examples given are quite ordinary ones but they are representative and valuable in providing a focus for some general conclusions.

1. Probation is inescapably identified with punishment as well as reform and reclamation. If emphasis is given to the deterrent and revengeful element then this must create difficulties for the caseworker who is motivated by reparative feeling. If, however, it is seen that there are directly positive features of punishment, notably an explicit expression of concern for the offender, it is possible to draw on experience of primary family and social situations to provide a conceptual basis for casework activity.

2. Some external control of the individual can assist in the process of maturation because it provides real and promised stability, and again by implication can contain the unconscious and sometimes near-conscious anxieties about aggressive and destructive impulse.

3. Enforcement goes some way to counter superficial evasion and avoidance behaviour which prevents appropriate social action on the part of the individual.

4. The enforced relationship and casework are not mutually exclusive. Indeed, in many respects the probation casework process is enriched by enforcement, and the explanation appears to centre on the fact that enforcement is an essential component of all early socialising processes. If there is anything distinctive about casework in enforcement, it is that the caseworker needs more often to show himself as concerned through positive action, even although it is found that such activity does not prevent the coincidental use of interpretive techniques or the relatively inactive processes of casework in the clinical setting.

From A.W. Hunt 'Enforcement in probation casework',
British Journal of Criminology, *4, 1963–64, pp. 239–252.*

43 Working with problem clients

Alcohol, sex and mental health
(1992)

J.R. Mott

At the South Western [magistrates' court] I was fortunate to be sharing an office with Barry Swinney, MBE. ... [T]his extraordinary Probation Officer eventually became so honoured because of his work with alcoholics. You will never find his methods of dealing with those unfortunate people in any textbook nor could most Social Workers put such methods into operation. His personality was accepted by his superior officers as being part of his approach, and all his clients loved him. Time meant nothing to him and he cheerfully accepted the immense amount of pressure put on him by his clients. I remember him walking into the office at about 9.30 one morning, with about six pairs of trousers. He bounded in and said: 'That bugger won't be going to the pub this morning – I've got all his trousers!' Apparently, it was Social Security day and Barry had called at the flat early to give the man's wife the opportunity of getting her shopping before her husband blew the lot at the pub. This was typical of him and his clients never thought any the less of him because of these activities. ...

Even though there was never a dull moment when Barry was around, he was, nonetheless, extremely caring and probably very much underrated when it came to the deeper understanding of the problems of both his clients and their families. His unfailing maxim: 'Never – ever – trust an alcoholic' was conveyed not only to those involved with the alcoholic, such as family, friends, etc., but to the man or woman in such a way as to give them a much better understanding of their own problems and the subsequent practical and emotional problems that they created for those around them.

Some months after I first met him, in conjunction with Lord Soper, he got several of us involved in the opening of a clinic for alcoholics in Regent Street. ... [W]e ran the clinic more or less on the lines of a pub, with tables and bar, but only tea or coffee was available. It caught on at once, and after a few months we were always crowded. We had a side room where clients could consult a doctor in private. ...

One of our patients was told one day that his wife had only twelve months to live. From that moment he stopped drinking. He and his wife came each week to the clinic and we gave them all the support that we could. He got a job, and during the next twelve months they were probably happier than they had been for a long time. Barry ... kept very close to them until eventually the unfortunate lady died.

After the funeral, her husband went missing – we knew what he was doing but we didn't know where he was. Then – three weeks later – he appeared in court charged with being drunk and disorderly. We got him home and were able to get him back on his feet – and back to the clinic. But while he was missing Barry Swinney had gone to his house every day and fed the cat! Sharing an office with a man like this was an education in itself. And he did give me one invaluable tip. If you wish to make an initial appointment with a person with a drink problem – meet them in the pub. One more drink won't make that much difference, and at least they'll turn up!

... One of the cases that perhaps gave me the most satisfaction was the case of a man, aged 43, who had been indecently exposing himself for nearly 30 years. He had been on probation before, had been to prison and had been in a mental hospital. No form of treatment had yet had any effect upon his behaviour, and no form of punishment had yet acted as a sufficient deterrent. Now, he had done it again, and almost out of despair, the Court placed him on probation for a period of three years. ...

Something, about 30 years ago, had triggered off the first of a long series of indecent exposures which had continued ever since. Why had this started at all?

... He could not account for the repeated offences of indecent exposure. He said that it always worried him and particularly his wife because she never knew when the police might be knocking at the door. He said he had tried to stop but could not understand how or why this sudden urge would take over. He would like to be able to stop for good – but how?

... He told me that he first exposed himself at the age of 14, and we looked at the existing circumstances at the time. It was here I got my first clue.

His mother had died several years earlier and ... his father had remarried. She was, he recalled, a very attractive woman and he liked her very much. She was 13 years older than he was, and his father was 13 years older than her. He admitted he was sexually attracted to her, but her attitude towards him, he thought, was over-authoritarian, and in fact she kept him in his place. Why do you prefer my father to me, he thought? Am I not just as much a man as he is – look everybody – I am a man. Could this be the situation which had triggered off a lifetime of offences? ...

Can it be, then, that the sexual overtones had now become secondary to stepmother's dominant personality? The need to stand up to her and be a man, still manifesting itself in exposure? ...

He had been going to work in his car when he saw a workmate whose car had broken down. He stopped but went on to work after agreeing to clock his mate on. He was doing this when he was spotted by the foreman, who gave him a dressing down in front of the other man. Result: indecent exposure.

... When the correct set of emotions clicked into place – exactly fitting those aroused in him by stepmother – he resorted to the same reaction.

> 'But you must know you're going to do it – why not take some evasive action, or control it yourself?'
>
> 'I never linked it with my stepmother after all these years.'
>
> 'Can you see it now? Enough to recognize the symptoms and take evasive action?'
>
> 'I'll certainly try.'
>
> 'OK. Here's what we'll do. You know enough about the background now to be on your guard if you are worried or upset in a manner that may trigger it off. Get to a telephone as soon as possible and phone me at my office. If I am not here speak to my secretary for as long as you like – all about Chelsea Football Club!'
>
> 'Chelsea – why Chelsea?'
>
> 'Because you are unlikely to phone and say that you feel like indecently exposing yourself.'

'Oh – right.'

'You go to Chelsea quite a lot with your wife don't you? And I follow football too, so there's nothing to feel self-conscious about. I'm hoping, assuming we've got it right, that it will let down the tension and get your feelings back to normal. Anyway, we've nothing to lose, and it might work.'

For the next 18 months we carried out this plan, the calls getting fewer and fewer because he began to feel less need to rely upon the call. I was feeling that it was actually beginning to work, when an incident occurred that really seemed to indicate a measure of success. I received a phone call from the local police inspector who told me: 'We've had a complaint about one of your clients, from a bus conductress. She had a row with him on the bus and he started to masturbate a rolled up magazine on the bus.'

'Ha, ha,' said the police inspector. 'That's an improvement isn't it?' – But it was!

I was delighted. Eighteen months ago there was no way he could have used a rolled-up magazine. Later, when I saw him in my office he told me that the conductress had had a go at him for pushing and made him feel very upset. 'But I was on the bus, Mr Mott, and couldn't get to a phone, so I had to do something else.'

Towards the end of three years probation I involved his wife in the phone calls, because I wished to ease myself out of the case altogether. …

At the end of three years probation there had been no actual incidents of indecent exposures, and as far as I am aware there have been none since. …

There are times when decisions have to be made for and on behalf of both the client and the general public as a whole. Sometimes such decisions are not easy to make and even involve a degree of uncertainty. When this situation arises I would rely on my own maxim – do what you believe to be right. … [O]n such occasions one sometimes had to stick to one's guns in the face of adversity. …

I was working at Sutton magistrates' court at the time when I met Mark. He was just 17 … came from a nice family and was always clean and tidy and presentable. He was also quite nice looking and polite, which was later to contribute to his problems. …

Mark was, to say the least, of low mentality and totally unable to fend for himself in society. While his parents were alive, he was looked after properly, fed and clothed, but alas, both parents died within a short time of each other, and this left Mark homeless.

… I managed to get him a place in a special hostel, because he had attended a special school for low IQ pupils. It was a good hostel and Mark settled well at first, but he could not accept the fact that he could survive for only a short time if he had no support and guidance. He wanted a job, and as I have said, he was presentable and polite, but he completely lacked powers of concentration or a sense of responsibility. With the best intentions in the world, he would set off for work, but fail to arrive there. I would find him in a local café or on a street corner with no feelings of guilt or shame for letting people down.

It was, of course, not his fault. His was an inadequate personality, and he would always, in my opinion, need support.

… [A]lthough he lived on social security and grants for his lodgings, he would constantly find himself out of benefit because he was deemed to have left his job of his own volition. I had many discussions with the DHSS about him but his general appearance gave no indication of his personality problems, and I found it almost impossible to convince them. When he once again became homeless I had the greatest difficulty in finding yet another place for him. I had further psychiatric reports, and managed to get him into another special hostel where he stayed for a time, but he would disappear for several days and would tell me he had stayed the night with a male friend. I was deeply suspicious about this relationship, but as far as Mark was concerned, it was a means to an end – a bed for the night.

... I was acutely aware that he was fast becoming a cross I had to bear – how could I let him down when he always came back to me when all else failed?

I got him into a hostel at Richmond and I begged the warden – PLEASE *don't* get him a job. Three days later the warden phoned me triumphantly. 'I've got him a job – he's a road sweeper – he has a handcart and is sweeping the road up in the High Street.'

It was in the High Street the next day that they found the handcart abandoned – and no sign of Mark. Several weeks went by, and then a phone call from the police in London. Mark had been told, by an older man, to go into a jewellers shop and bring out a tray of rings. When he did so, the man snatched the rings and ran, leaving Mark outside the shop where he was arrested. The man was caught later and the rings recovered.

... Mark, now homeless, was sentenced to Borstal Training. Now although this seemed to be tragic at the time, it did serve as a respite and was in fact just what Mark needed. ... He was living in a structured society similar to a hospital. He had to keep to the rules, as did the other lads – and he was one of them. At last, he actually belonged with others. He worked in the kitchen, washing up, etc., and was never any trouble. I gave it a lot of thought.

It seemed that he needed this sort of environment after his release, for his own sake, and at the present time there were no existing plans for his future. One thing was certain, I was not going to allow him to go back to London on his own. I telephoned a doctor at a hospital at Epsom. He had seen Mark on a previous occasion and knew about his background and personality. He thought that he could find a place for him. ... Before I could make any further arrangements, I received a request to attend a case conference at Feltham, to be chaired by the resident psychiatrist. ...

I was expecting a general discussion about Mark's welfare, and his future, but I was certainly not expecting the method adopted by the psychiatrist. There was a ring of chairs around the room with one chair in the middle for Mark. Various people were to sit around him in a ring and discuss him, while he sat in the middle. One of the prison officers in charge of a wing was present, as was a junior doctor who was also on the borstal staff. I discovered that a probation officer from Inner London was also in attendance, having been invited to attend by the psychiatrist. ... [I]t became clear that none of them knew very much about his background or behaviour outside borstal.

I was appalled at the setting in which I found myself, and particularly upset at the thought of Mark being made the subject of this embarrassing situation. I told the group that there was no way that I would take part in this meeting. I also pointed out that, as Mark's probation officer, I would be making all the arrangements about his after-care and that completely excluded any return to Inner London, which would be sure to have disastrous results. ...

Do what you believe to be right! Well, I had certainly done that, but now I was on my own with Mark, once again. Or was I?

The next day, still feeling indignant, I received a phone call from the senior prison officer who had been in the group.

'Mr. Mott?'

'Yes.'

'I just want you to know that I agree with everything you said yesterday – that boy needs treatment – he is a very nice lad, and if I can help you in any way, please let me know.'

I thanked him very much. I told him that I had been in touch with a doctor at an Epsom hospital but the doctor wanted to see Mark prior to release.

'OK – look, you fix up the appointment with the doctor, then let me know the time and date and I'll bring Mark to the hospital and then bring him back here.'

'That's terrific.'

I couldn't really believe my ears. The next day I received a letter from the junior doctor at Feltham. It simply said: 'Good luck with Mark – if I can help in any way please let me know.'

The officer duly brought Mark out of Feltham where he was interviewed by a specialist doctor. He felt that Mark should be admitted to hospital on his release, provided that he agreed. It was hoped that, with treatment, he might become much more self-sufficient. My officer friend arranged to bring Mark himself to the hospital on the day of release, and this he did. ...

At that time, borstal licence was for a period of 12 months, and I kept in touch with Mark for the whole of that time. The hospital welfare officer made arrangements about his discharge after his licence had terminated. I was told that he had matured considerably, and they knew of no other offences involving him. I do know that he went to live with a family in Scotland and I think he's married now.

From J.R .Mott, Probation, Prison and Parole: a true story of the work of a
Probation Officer *(Lewes, Sussex: Temple House Books)*, 1992,
pp. 19–21, 63–66, 70–74.

44 Act Natural

The Sheffield detached probation project (1977)

Bruce Hugman

It should not have been necessary to write this book.

It is a plea for helpers of all sorts – social workers, priests, probation officers, doctors, psychiatrists, teachers – to drop pretentious images of themselves and 'act natural'. One of the stark facts about many people, and about the deprived and underprivileged in particular, is that they have never been helped to discover and enjoy their true talents nor their portion of happiness. One of the clear facts about many 'professionals' is that they willingly accept codes of behaviour which smother and stultify their natural talents. 'Professionalism' in those jobs most demanding of warmth and sensitivity has come to mean distance, coolness, efficiency and ritual. The broad principles of professional practice are of next to no value if the individuals subscribing to them are not relatively happy, liberated people willing to share their happiness with others. It is with the achievement of internal, personal liberty that most can be offered to others and without which no procedures of codes of practice have any use except as cover-stories for failure.

Public attention has been drawn to disquieting, isolated incidents of failure in the social services but, other than the generalised protests of senior policemen few people have expressed concern about the basic assumptions and practices of the services as a whole.

Social work in general, and post-Seebohm social work in particular, has become obsessively concerned with huge and expensive distractions from the immediate and sensitive reality of human need: the mechanical reorganisation of services; the erection of great buildings; the establishment of elaborate hierarchies; the thoughtless perpetuation of procedures and practices (which may or may not be valuable); the pursuit of high pay, status and professional elitism; the (irrational) acts of faith in particular theories of human behaviour and 'professional' training; all of which must seem to an outsider to imply the growth and development of a self-critical, self-conscious, and potentially effective service. And yet the truth is, that the new system is moving ahead at such a frenzied gallop, and at such a level of sophistication, that it is beyond even questioning, let alone changing. As with most galloping monsters, this one does not seem to have much time to notice fragile creatures and human needs as it careers along. …

The business of being a good helper is essentially bound up with being a good person, that is to say, thoughtful, generous, sensitive, relatively unselfish, relatively accepting of self, liberated in spirit, tolerant, reliable, acquainted with weakness and inconsistency, caring, committed, purposeful, capable of joy and sadness, and faithful to a belief in the creative humanity of all people. An ideal? Certainly. But whoever achieved anything but in the pursuit of an ideal? And who can give much to others who is lacking substantially or apparently lacking in these qualities?

... The Sheffield 'detached' probation project was started by me in 1971. Through five extraordinary years it has continued, now in new premises with more and different staff.

The project had its origins in the work of Ian Chisholm, a priest on the Bishop of Sheffield's staff. ... Ian frequently came in contact with probation officers and he and they both found the role of the conventional PO very limited in offering help to [a] sizeable group of young people. In discussion with Probation the idea of a 'detached' PO was born. This was to be an officer freed from the burden of a large caseload and from normal office ties and duties. ... Fortunately, no one had any very clear idea of what the job was, and there was an admirable willingness to wait and see what developed – a situation remarkably without prejudice or preconception.

Shortly after starting, I acquired the tenancy of a ground-floor flat in a decaying area near the city centre. ... This area was chosen because of its reputation ... both as an area of disproportionately high delinquency, and as an area familiar and homely to deviant groups. ...

Peter and the angels

Peter ... had established the habit of visiting daily at least. He was a dilettante Hell's Angel who, though he didn't have a bike at the time and was not totally involved, felt bound by the fierce loyalties of the chapter. One day there was talk of a motorised invasion from another area, and prospects of a large-scale fight. Peter had not long been out of custody and was under a suspended sentence for theft and violence.

He had been going through a quiet period, making real efforts to control his desperate temper and to stay out of trouble. The break-up of his marriage a year earlier had precipitated a period of offences and the consequent emotional turmoil had left him little in control of his great anger and despair. At this time things were better and he was beginning to find some new relationship satisfactions and was desperately torn between the life he had glimpsed, and the compulsion towards the standards and expectations he had seized upon to provide the solid outer context of his identity and which had given him his only hope of survival. By those standards he had no choice and could see no escape, though all he had been struggling for was threatened.

No amount of talk could give him the strength of will to resist. Instead, I casually suggested that he and his girl-friend might like to drive out of the city for a drink that evening. Not a chance, they said. I repeated the time I would be going, and dropped the subject.

... They both came early, smartly dressed and justifiably pleased with their decision. I was very aware of the responsibility I had undertaken: I was daring to relieve a man of his principal patterns of social behaviour, loyalty and feeling. I was implying that through me he could achieve something better. He sensed that I was right but knew even less than I did about the new directions we might take. ...

What was possible here was the offering of genuine alternatives which were not merely theoretical. 'Don't get involved in the fight: go out for a drink or something', is so different from saying 'Come out for a drink with me.' Again and again, that realistic, personal intervention was crucial to the bringing about of change. ...

One night Peter invited me to drink with his fellow Angels in their pub. ... I was sufficiently self-conscious of my role to feel that in such a setting no amount of goodwill or social competence on my part would make me generally acceptable. But clearly, I couldn't refuse. ...

As it was, I was bought so much beer that I had to slip out leaving several pints on the table, only narrowly anticipating passing out. ... The real significance of the evening was in its meaning to the Angels – a meaning quite hidden to me and revealed only months after the event. It was seen to show 'class' to walk alone and unprotected into the chapter's pub, something of a compliment from a group of self-consciously heroic young men. What it achieved, which very rapidly became clear, was to open lines of communication with a group otherwise exclusive and isolated. Those lines were used at a number of crisis points, as well as for purely social purposes. There were a number of occasions when muscular, leather-clad, stud-belted groups drank coffee with gentle, pot-smoking philosophers in the flat, and I marvelled that such meetings could take place. ...

Caseworkers in tower-block corridors

What struck me day by day, with startling clarity, was the absence from the scene of those many others with statutory or other responsibilities for those I met. I did not underestimate the absurdity of the size of caseloads, nor the natural anxieties and conscious limitations of many social workers and POs, nor demand that all should work as I have, *but*, again and again I asked: where were these people?

Frequently, and quite casually, I bumped into people who were in need of advice, or helpful action, for whom others had a clear responsibility. Here, now, at this moment, this man is being arrested; here, now, at this moment, this woman is supposed to be at the other end of town for a job interview; here, now, at this moment, this man is stoned and depressed and is not safe wandering the streets; here, now, at this moment, there is need, and there is one who is responsible, and where is he? Who knows? Least of all he or she in need. But the charade does not end there. Even if the responsible person's location were known, would the needy person make his way (for a real example) to the posh, multi-storey block in the city centre (supposing he were needy between nine and five, of course), run the gamut of fitted carpets, commissionaires, lifts and (if by this time he were not utterly put off or actually lost) apply at the reception desk, expose his need, and wait (how long?) in a potted-plant-lined waiting room with a crowd of other applicants? Could he go through that with any confidence that he would receive help; could he go through that without feeling absurd, vulnerable and lost? I doubt if I'd go through that if I were at death's door. But of course these provisions are not made for the strong and self-reliant.

It is necessary to hold on to the clarity and intensity of the issues exposed in that paragraph, lest we lose all sense of reality and purpose in a sea of prevarication and expedience. Obviously there will be a compromise of ideals, but not, please not, a compromise which belongs only to the world of the ludicrous.

I [write] of being in the right place at the right time. That is possible for many who are not placed as I was. But by being office-based we shall miss out on many events, sometimes spectacular, sometimes minor. It is only after such events, always unexpected, that their value can sometimes be seen. One must move out knowing that every interaction is significant and knowing that often the most unexpected are the most valuable. This means tolerating periods of apparent purposelessness, or absence of specific purpose, and understanding that planned purposefulness may miss the whole point. ...

Such closeness is not always easy or comfortable. The events of [one] Saturday night ... indicate one area of real difficulty. Here my unwillingness to have blood let on my front doorstep, the blood of a wanted man in my flat, caused me to offend a number of basic local standards. I called the police for advice and used them, while they were on the phone, as a threat, and Peter, the potentially violent man, went away. But he was enraged at a minor assault on his woman, and by local standards physical retribution was totally permissible. Had the fight taken place, the avenger might well have had his suspended sentence imposed, and there might well have been some serious injuries to boot ... [S]ome could not understand my action, and some could not forgive it.

A conflict such as that, and the destructive, negative emotions it aroused in some people towards me, I found hard to take. But I found it equally hard to deal with the local loyalty which at one point promised to beat up someone who had done me a supposed injury.

At such times – and at many, many more – it was essential to know exactly what one's standards were. That was also true in situations of dubious legality. One was accountable both formally and informally to so many people, that unless there was integrity and coherence in all one said and did, which could be perceived and accepted, if not necessarily approved of, one was in a perilous situation.

Compromise is not the wholly disgraceful thing I once thought it to be, except in a few instances where the issues are so vital as to require a clear, unambiguous stand. At the simplest level I felt no scruples at all at dressing up in my dark suit and looking 'respectable' in court, even if that was colluding with a system I didn't entirely approve of. I wasn't there to make political points on my own behalf and thereby risk prejudicing attitudes to someone in the dock. But equally if things went wrong in court, I pursued what remedy I could. (On one occasion the prosecuting solicitor presented the evidence from two quite different cannabis cases as the evidence against one man. There I intervened. On another it was clear that the magistrate thought that four hundred milligrams of cannabis was something like a sackful. On both these occasions I wrote up these incidents and circulated them. They led to what I think was a very useful round-table conference with magistrates and officers covering a wide range of issues.)

The question was often asked of me as to whether or not in the open, detached situation, I was not likely to be in possession of more than average information about offenders. It was partly a realistic question, but also partly one arising from fantasy fears, that is to say that I was hiding information about murder and rape, probably. This, of course, was untrue, and such information as I did have from time to time was usually of offences of the more minor kind – most frequently about someone who had taken some sort of drug, or a girl who was soliciting.

The whole question was answered clearly and maturely by members of the project sub-committee: the issue, they said, was not whether or not I had discretion to withhold information, but how the discretion was used. I was accountable for my decisions. That was a heartening position of trust to be permitted.

From Bruce Hugman, Act Natural: a new sensibility for the professional helper
(London: Bedford Square Press), 1977, pp. 1–2, 4–5, 44–46, 61–63.

45 The Berkeley sex offenders group

A seven year evaluation (1984)

Christine Weaver and Charles Fox

The Berkeley Group for non-violent male sex offenders has been operating since February 1977.

Facts and figures

The group, run by two officers for up to ten men at any time, meets fortnightly. By July 1983, 38 men had attended more than three group sessions and were therefore included in the study. The legal definitions of their offences were indecent assault, indecent exposure, gross indecency and USI [unlawful sexual intercourse] with children under 16 or 13 years old. The majority of men had committed offences of exposing (16) or indecent assault against children (17). Three of the latter had been with children in the family. It is difficult to assign a very specific set of characteristics to each category of offender, but over the years we have been able to arrive at some broad generalisations.

Indecent exposure

There are two broad types of exposer:

1. Isolated lonely men who have little or no sexual experience. Exposing is their only, and childlike, means of sexual expression and they rarely offend in other ways.
2. Men who are socially quite well integrated. They often have regular relationships with women, including marriage, and normal friendships with both sexes. They experience a need to expose at times of depression or when they feel under stress.

Indecent assault on women

This behaviour can vary from the touching of a knee in the cinema to violent assault falling little short of rape. The men usually lack self confidence in their relationships with women, have difficulty treating them as individuals rather than sex objects, but yearn for a normal heterosexual relationship. We have not been able to make generalisations about other personal or social characteristics.

Indecent assault on children

This ranges from genital touching, to masturbation in private or public places, is usually non-violent and sometimes mutual. The relationship has often been built up over a period of time, although some men initiate one-off sexual encounters with children they do not know. We have no real experience of men who commit violent assaults on children.

True paedophiles become 'lovingly' involved with pubertal or pre-pubertal boys or girls. They experience a mixture of parental or childlike love and sexual feelings and enjoy the sense of power. They are unable to enter into an 'equal' relationship and many never experience sexual attraction to adults of either sex. Although often normally competent at work and in some social relationships, their behaviour, and the long prison sentences it attracts, quickly lead to social ostracism and isolation.

The men in the group have ranged in age from 22 to 61 years, with the paedophilic offender inclined towards the older end of the scale and exposers and assaulters of women towards the lower ages. The majority of men (26) were single, five divorced and the remainder (8) were married. None changed marital status during his time in the group. All the 17 child molesters were single.

The majority of the men attended the group for between 6 months and 2 years (21 men). Six attended for less than 6 months and 11 for over 2 years. We could find no correlation between type of offence and period spent in the group. Average weekly attendance has been relatively consistent at about 70 % of the potential complement, eight men travelling distances of between 10 and 20 miles each way.

Selection

There are two firm criteria for selection: that men should be over 21 and that they have been convicted of more than one sexual offence. This is to avoid the danger of confirming people in a sexual identity or behaviour when it may be a passing phase or 'one off' event. In fact only six men have had less than three previous convictions and the average overall is four.

Most referrals come from Avon probation officers although two local psychiatrists have referred four men. Eventual selection depends on men first attending an interview with the leaders, the purpose of which is: 1. assess feelings about their problem and motivation to change; 2. provide information about the group; 3. allay the men's anxieties; 4. make ourselves, the leaders, known. Almost without exception, anyone who expresses even a glimmer of motivation to attend is offered a place with the suggestion that they commit themselves to six sessions to start with. Only three men have failed to take up this offer since the group started. In our view this demonstrates a very 'unselective' selection process, although we are unable to be precise about the criteria used by probation officers when they make the initial referrals.

Objectives

In 1977 our objectives were:

1.   Provide a forum for discussion of mutual problems.
2.   Help reduce isolation and feelings of abnormality.
3.   Attempt to reduce offending in a high risk offender category.

By 1983 we also hoped to:

4.   Provide long term support and continuity.
5.   Encourage the development of wider social contacts.
6.   Provide strategies for the management of sexual feelings now and in the future.

Much of the discussion which follows provides evidence of the degree to which these objectives are being met for the men who attend the group.

What happens?

Meetings start with about 15 minutes of informal socialising followed by discussion. Some of the topics are: how men feel about being labelled as a sex offender; how they can recognise when they are at risk of offending; whether they want to stop and how they can set about it. This includes building on other positive areas of their personalities and broadening their social activities and personal supports. Discussion therefore varies widely and may arise spontaneously. It may also be initiated by asking each man in turn to comment on how he is coping, or by the leaders introducing a previously agreed topic. Occasional use is made of other simple techniques – pairing, brainstorms, 'hot seat' and pencil and paper exercises. With the help of the members we have devised a short checklist covering five important areas which can be used to review progress or initiate discussion:

1.   Acknowledgement of the problem.
2.   Understanding of the build up to offences.
3.   Development of alternative strategies.
4.   Implementation of these strategies.
5.   Development of supports outside the group.

The presence of men with different offences involving different types of victim has encouraged rather than inhibited discussion. People don't automatically understand one another, they question and challenge and avoid the tendency to sink into a cosy exchange of anecdotes about similar offences. Although most of the group see the child molesters as perhaps the most serious offenders (reflecting views in the wider community) they are aware of the similarities in needs and loss of control amongst them all.

In the seven years the group has been running it has become very apparent that most of the men we deal with require long term support if they are to manage their sexual feelings without reoffending. This makes the development of other relationships crucial if we are to move them on safely. Some men cling to the group and pose a problem for the provision of places for new members.

However, there is also no doubt that many men can develop controls or alternative means of expression, and this has encouraged us to become less accepting of the compulsive 'I can't help it' explanations. Group discussions have become more focused and positive as a result.

Consultancy

Access to some form of consultancy is highly desirable even in a short-running, fixed-life group, but with an on-going group is essential in order that the leaders do not become jaded or too set in their ways. We have had regular sessions with a local consultant psychiatrist throughout the time we have been operating. However, it is also true that in a group where the members may stay for up to 2 years, they take on some leadership functions very efficiently – welcoming new members, initiating new topics for discussion, challenging their colleagues, supporting people in distress etc.

Unlike some short life groups, there has always been a strong feeling of commitment and purpose, transcending membership changes.

Evaluation

Information was gathered from those members of the Berkeley Group, past and present, who had attended more than three sessions, yielding a potential total of 38 subjects. The information comprised:

1. Criminal Records Office check to establish the existence of convictions post-dating the man's appearance in the group.
2. A questionnaire which was posted to all former group members and given to current members to complete.

Results

CRO Check: Of the 38 full members of the group 30 had not reoffended sexually when the check was made in July 1983. Eight men had further convictions and of these, two returned to the group, staying another 18 months without further trouble.

Three reoffended after leaving and have not returned, and three continued to offend during the time they were attending.

Amongst these 8 men it was not possible to find any common factors which were related to attendance or time spent in the group. However, seven of the eight were indecent exposers rather than any of the other categories of sexual offender and all these had more than three convictions before starting the group. Three had very long lists indeed – one clocking up an impressive total of 127 convictions.

Although we do not have figures relating to a control group, the fact that 30 men have not reoffended at all is very encouraging indeed, particularly since the average number of preconvictions for all group members was four and eight had six offences or more.

The Questionnaire: This was designed in conjunction with Mr. E. Brazier, psychologist, Bristol Polytechnic with the objective of exploring:

1. Expectations of the participants.
2. Therapeutic value of the group sessions.
3. Learning of control mechanisms.
4. Aspects of the social development of the members.
5. Weaknesses and strengths of group organisation.

The results of the postal enquiry were regarded as probably more reliable than those completed by current members owing to the absence of inhibitions about upsetting the group leaders or their own social position in the group. However, inspection revealed a close similarity between the two sets of responses. We received 14 completed questionnaires, 36% of the potential total, so the results overall must be treated with some caution.

1. Expectations

The expectations of participants are obviously important in determining subsequent attitudes to the group and motivation. The questionnaires revealed that men in a high state of anxiety before they started the group also had unrealistic expectations of a cure and perceived the leaders as 'distant and different'. Those participants with a clear understanding of group aims and methods before joining have more realistic expectations and lower anxiety levels. This confirmed our impression that contact by the leaders with new members before they start in the group, to achieve such understanding, is of paramount importance.

2. Therapeutic value of group sessions

There was a very strong expression of feelings of relief at being able to talk about difficulties in a supportive, non-judgemental atmosphere, by all respondents. For many the group remained their only outlet for the expression of their problems, but some men were able to talk to others outside the group once they had achieved initial release and support. This may be related to length of stay in the group, which varies considerably.

3. Control mechanisms

The general view was that these 'worked sometimes'. Unfortunately, we don't know whether this means that people are occasionally reoffending or whether they are referring to an urge rather than its expression in actual behaviour. However, the notions of control and personal responsibility were clearly reflected in the responses and the majority had attempted to use their group learning since moving on.

4. Social development

Although spare time interests remain limited and sometimes solitary e.g. fishing, the majority indicated that they had been able to make friends since leaving the group. There was strong evidence of attempts to make wider social contacts, often successfully, which is a very encouraging finding given the previous extreme loneliness and isolation of many group members. We have witnessed considerable change in some men over the years, as their increase in confidence and self respect has enabled them to make friends and develop social activities.

5. Group organisation

Most people either felt satisfied with the fortnightly frequency of group meetings or would have liked to meet more often. There was a tentative feeling expressed that meetings should change format occasionally to make them more interesting, perhaps not surprising in an open-ended group which people attend over a long period. Time spent with the members during group sessions in planning ahead, can be very productive in keeping interest maintained and in encouraging members themselves to take responsibility for the format of meetings.

Conclusions

As the group does not cater for first sexual offenders at all, and most of the men could be described as recidivists, i.e. well established in the commission of sexual offences in certain circumstances, the results of the CRO check were very encouraging. A comparison with people supervised in different ways would be needed to confirm conclusively that the group experience is a safeguard against future offending, but it can certainly be claimed that the general public is not being put at risk by these people being supervised in the community rather than being sent to prison.

The responses to the questionnaire clearly reflect the value of discussion in a supportive group, and given the isolation of this type of offender and their inability to discuss their difficulties in other circumstances, it seems to provide a sufficient rationale for the group's existence.

Control methods

However, much of the discussion in the group centres on methods of controlling or redirecting sexual behaviour and what is less clear from the responses is the lasting value of the control methods learnt. The process involves a gradual acceptance by the men that their desires will not magically disappear, an understanding of their own positive as well as negative feelings about their behaviour and why it has been functional for them to continue it in the past. They can then move on to a detailed investigation of the circumstances when they are most likely to offend, and the points (during what is often quite a long build up) at which they can make choices to change the outcome. Methods by which this process could be more effectively tackled would obviously merit further investigation, but as most men arrive at the group wanting to believe that their actions are compulsive, it is encouraging that notions of control and personal responsibility are being taken up in some measure.

Length of stay

As already mentioned, the length of time men spend in the group varies considerably. It would be useful to know whether an optimum length of stay could be worked out for each individual using agreed criteria under the kinds of headings we have been investigating, rather than the present more arbitrary factors – length of probation order, move from the area, etc. Monitoring of progress would then be more precise. There could also be an argument for working more closely with the families of men who are in this position, but that is a new and untried area to date.

Our experience as leaders of this group over a long period has encouraged probation colleagues and some others in related professions to seek advice in the management of cases they have found difficult. The group could, therefore, be seen as the focal point for this type of offender in the county. But perhaps the best indicator of the need for this facility (leaving aside the effects it may or may not produce) is the fact that there have been fortnightly meetings for over seven years, all of which have been well attended, and that there is never a shortage of men struggling with this problem who feel that joining the group might provide them with a means of tackling it.

From Christine Weaver and Charles Fox, 'The Berkeley sex offenders group: a seven year evaluation', Probation Journal, *31(4), 1984, pp. 143–146.*

46 'Going Local' in Huddersfield

Group and community work issues (1985)

Paul Falkingham

Introduction

The Community Group Scheme attempted to examine the relevance of community work theory and practice to the Probation Service. It resulted from a critical concern about the relevance of the traditional service offered to individuals and individual families. It sought to examine the Service's ability to engage with structural problems at a community level. To some degree, it represented an attempt at innovative practice. It would assess the impact of such a scheme on levels of work generated for the Service, and hence contained a preventative element. The Scheme was explicitly experimental and of fixed duration. The major theoretical inspiration was Paulo Freire's *Cultural Action for Freedom* and *Pedagogy of the Oppressed*.

The Scheme began in September 1977 and ended in September 1982. It can be described in terms of four phases.

1. Negotiations

Negotiations and a 'feasibility study' took place, within the Huddersfield Probation Office but also involving the Divisional ACPO and with reference to the CPO, from September to December 1977. They were initiated by a main grade officer. They took place within the context of average office caseloads in the mid-thirties, and staff discussions about a radical restructuring of office staff into three bands of workers (intensive, middle, and volunteer supervisors), which eventually came to nothing.

The proposal was that the main grade officer should substitute for an orthodox caseload an attempt to set up and then work with self-help community groups on specific council estates in Huddersfield which were perceived as generating the largest proportion of the office's workload.

Initially, the Scheme was seen as a resource for the office, working across the three team's geographical boundaries. The central argument was that the Service was poorly equipped to deal with structural problems like bad housing, low income/ unemployment, absence of local amenities, etc.; yet the majority of clients either referred to these as significant problems or frequently lived in communities where they were present. The community group might provide a framework within which such problems could be examined. Residents would be responsible for identifying and dealing with problems with the probation officer/Service supporting this process.

The Service ought to be able to 'enter' specific communities through its contact with present and former 'clients', although group membership would be open to all residents, not restricted to probation clients.

The idea for the Scheme was initially floated with colleagues via an introductory 'discussion starter' paper, considered at a staff meeting. There, permission was obtained by the main grade officer to carry out a feasibility study to test the Scheme's practicality. There were two quite separate phases to the feasibility study, each one geared to a report-back to a staff meeting, and permission was obtained from colleagues at each stage through the mechanism of a staff meeting. The whole process was deliberately structured and lasted from September to December 1977, with permission to go ahead being obtained at a December staff meeting.

The first part of the feasibility study consisted of identifying numbers of clients from specific estates; and the proportion of those whom Huddersfield staff felt might be interested in and could benefit from a community group. The second part consisted of direct contact with clients to establish how many were actually interested in trying to form such a group. At the end of the first part, it appeared four groups might be viable on estates in each of the three teams' areas. At the end of the second part, it seemed two groups might be viable totalling 19 clients in two areas, covered by two teams. The two areas were the Walpole estate and the Sheepridge–Deighton area.

The majority of staff favoured proceeding with the Scheme. However, the three senior officers were concerned about how much resourcing the Scheme would require, and included a requirement that the main grade officer should build up to an involvement with thirty statutory clients. The Scheme was to be set up initially for twelve months. It would then be reviewed, involving the Service's Research Unit. The main grade officer obtained agreement that the minimum age for Scheme clients would be sixteen.

In December 1977 meetings took place in the Probation office with clients from the two areas to clarify how the Scheme should start and where the groups could meet. In January 1978 the first community group meetings were held within the two respective areas.

Walpole

It is necessary to describe the two areas. The Walpole estate consisted of approximately 350 council houses, built in the late 1930s, predominantly in short terraces of four, of pebble-dashed brick which had turned grey and peeled off over the years. The estate was two miles from the town centre, and was physically demarcated by private houses on two sides, and open land on the other two sides. In early 1978, the estate's amenities were a pub; a working men's club; and six shops. Walpole had no history of any community work projects.

Sheepridge and Deighton

In contrast, Sheepridge and Deighton's 'boundary' was unclear. Most of the 1,750 council dwellings had been built immediately after the Second World War, with a later phase in the 1950s. In the mid-1970s, one part had been modernised; but most property was in the same condition as the Walpole estate. The area also contained 'pockets' of privately owned property of variable age and value. Within the area were four churches or chapels (two supporting a scout troop and Boys' Brigade respectively); four schools (primary and secondary); a civic youth club; a number of shops dotted about the area; a doctor's surgery; and a couple of expanses of ground described as 'playing fields'. Four major road routes broke up the area. In the past, there had been three, short-lived, community work initiatives in Sheepridge, one of which had involved a local authority social worker.

2. The first stage

... The first months were naturally a period of uncertainty – would the groups expand their membership and survive; what was their purpose; what roles were available to group members; and what levels of commitment existed from individual residents? The main grade officer was also exposed to new experiences. Although his role was explicitly facilitative and supportive (rather than didactic or directive), there were constant negotiations about what tasks he should take on.

Apart from its first meeting in a pub, the Walpole Group met in members' houses on an informal rota basis. The only variation was experimentation with daytime and evening meetings. The Sheepridge–Deighton Group met in the evening – until April in a local school (open for adult education classes); from April to June in the civic youth club (until the youth leader left); and thereafter in Group members' homes.

Quite independently, the two Groups decided early in their existence that a major problem was juvenile delinquency – especially vandalism – and that this was largely attributable to a lack of constructive leisure facilities locally. The question has to be asked whether the Groups would have identified the same problem if their worker had been a community worker rather than a probation officer? The 'solutions' identified by the two Groups were not dissimilar. The Walpole Group decided to look for a building which could be used as a community youth club. The Sheepridge–Deighton Group decided that an adventure playground was needed.

Both solutions were to prove over-ambitious in the short term, although the demoralising realisation of this came at different times. For example the Walpole Group rapidly discovered that few suitable buildings existed nearby, and those which did were unobtainable. The Sheepridge–Deighton Group delayed their disappointment by deciding that the first step was to raise money for material. Nonetheless, what emerged, to counter the demoralisation, were the classic small scale community events aimed at raising money, or providing a community benefit, or sometimes both simultaneously. Below is a summary of the two Groups' activities during that first year.

The most ambitious development was the second-hand furniture scheme. Furniture, freely donated, was collected from around Huddersfield, stored in the Sheepridge–Deighton area, and sold at low cost to residents. The Group's major 'coup' was to be recognised by the DHSS as a supplier with regard to furniture grants.

Lack of premises or resources obliged both Groups to contact other organisations and agencies. The first jumble sales took place in a school and a youth club – thanks to the support of the Head and the youth leader. From October onwards, the Sheepridge–Deighton Group became increasingly involved with the local United Reformed Church whose members were anxious to see their hall more widely used by the local community. The youth leader for the civic youth club nearest to Walpole, motivated by concern at the low numbers of Walpole children using his club, offered

Table 1

	Walpole	Sheepridge–Deighton
April		Jumble sale
May	Coffee mornings	
June	Jumble sale	Day trip to Leeds gala
August	Sponsored walk	
	Day coach trip to Filey	
September	Sponsored jog	Start of furniture scheme
	Day coach trip to Morecambe	
October	Sponsored slim	Jumble sale
November	Start of craft and drama groups for children	Sheepridge Fair
December	Jumble sale	Furniture auction
	Children's Christmas party	
January	Trip to pantomime in Bradford	

his premises for the craft and drama groups. Equally, there were the failures. For example, the Walpole Group failed to interest the Housing Department in providing a house or houses for use as a community centre. It is not surprising that both Groups, planning for 1979, attached such a high priority to securing premises.

Some of the Group's contacts with other organisations reflected their growing status. Thus, Walpole Group members joined the youth club Management Committee; they helped form a steering group seeking to establish a community centre for the larger area which contained Walpole. Sheepridge–Deighton Group members joined a working party, chaired by the Community Relations Officer, concerned with community provision and the involvement of the large proportion of black people living in the Sheepridge area. This working party later liaised with a local councillor and obtained £40,000 towards community centre provision.

3. Review and re-negotiation

In January 1979, the Scheme's main grade officer produced a report, describing these events and identifying problems. The report represented the first stage in a protracted review process which ended with a meeting of all staff involved in November 1979. It would be difficult to separate 're-negotiation' from 'review' in this process.

The process was protracted primarily because it was unclear how far the Scheme was understood and 'owned' by the Service. The main grade officer and his team supported the Scheme's continuation, subject to certain amendments. The team responsible for the Sheepridge–Deighton area were far more ambivalent, to say the least. The research staff were supportive and enthusiastic. The ACPO was initially unsure about the Scheme, whether to resource it further, and, if so, how. The review process helped increase the ACPO's understanding; but it is fair to say that he and the other staff involved were relieved when the DCPO put his seal of approval on the Scheme's continuation.

During the review, developments naturally continued within both Groups, of which account had to be taken. On occasions, staff were reviewing '*faits accomplis*'. A successful bid for Group leadership by one member of the Sheepridge–Deighton Group, coupled with suspicion about that member's involvement with the furniture scheme's finances, prompted the Scheme's officer to resign from the Group in May, publicly severing connections between the Group and the Service. In June, the Walpole Group learned that two houses would be made available for a community centre. In addition, extraneous and unforeseeable factors were introduced into the process. The DCPO proposed in July that there should be an assessment of whether a youth employment scheme, run in conjunction with the MSC [Manpower Services Commission] and NACRO [National Association for the Care and Resettlement of Offenders], could be set up on and for Walpole. Delays also arose from the decision to rewrite the original report, adding contributions from the SPO, ACPO, and DCPO, and a 'future developments' section from the main grade officer and Research Unit.

By September 1979, the review had identified difficulties present during the Scheme's first twelve months and set out the terms of the Scheme's continuation. A major area of difficulty was that the Community Groups were substitutes for an ordinary caseload. Research had shown that the latter occupied less than 30% of a probation officer's time. The officer had insufficient time to carry out appropriate tasks on behalf of the Groups. The preoccupation with thirty statutory clients in part explained this. It also explained Sheepridge and Deighton being lumped together when they were not one community, making a nonsense of creating one Group for the whole area. It had resulted in the Scheme being resourced and operationalised outside one team's area, and at office level, resulting in problems of 'ownership' for the two teams to which the Scheme's officer did not belong. The preoccupation with numbers had tended to make the Scheme appear synonymous with patch work, obscuring or diminishing its primary community work/development element. Finally, some objectives had clearly been inappropriate – perhaps over-ambitious – within the time scale up to September 1979.

Consequently, it was decided that the Scheme should continue exclusively on the Walpole estate, within the organisational structure of one team. The officer would be freed from court and office duties, and be based in the new community centre. The preoccupation with statutory client numbers would end. However, the officer would be responsible for statutory clients and court report preparation on Walpole residents. Future plans – the formation of Junior and IT groups – should allow the Scheme to cater for juvenile residents. An original objective of increasing people's welfare rights knowledge should be met by creating an advice service on Walpole, run by residents. The creation of a youth employment scheme would be investigated. Involvement in the Scheme of Social Service staff should be sought. The Scheme would operate for a fixed period of three years. The Research Unit would be involved, in a 'research auditor' role.

4. Final Phase

As stated above, events to some extent overtook the review stage. Most important of these for Walpole was the local authority's decision to opt for comprehensive modernisation of the estate (another option had been demolition). The first part of a three stage programme started in August 1979, involving almost half the houses on the estate.

The modernisation programme

The modernisation programme involved the Group in three types of work. Firstly, it operated as a pressure group from early 1979. Later when the local authority had to decide about stages two and three of the programme, it took up this role again to try and ensure completion of the programme. Stage three was completed in October 1982.

Secondly, starting in March 1980, as residents moved back to their modernised houses, the Group surveyed resident views, compiled lists of faults, and negotiated (in the main successfully) with the local authority (and the contractors) to get these rectified.

Thirdly, the Group took up residents' complaints about the open plan front gardens, and successfully negotiated with the local authority the provision of fencing 'kits' to provide boundary fencing. Unfortunately, the local authority said money was not available for fence erection, and the Group undertook to distribute the kits, and help any resident unable to erect it for him or herself. The major problem was the slow process. The local authority acknowledged its mistake in August 1981, agreed to provide fencing in November, but did not deliver the first batch of fencing until April, 1982. The Group was still involved with distributing fencing in September 1982, and was heartily sick of the whole business. Ironically, when the Group applied for charitable status in March 1982, this was rejected on the grounds that its housing campaigns rendered it 'too political'.

The community centre

Delay dogged the development of the Community Centre. Planning permission to convert the two houses was obtained in September 1979, but the Group did not obtain the keys to start work until May 1980. Partly due to the Housing Department's lack of experience in handling community centres, partly due to the Group's shoestring resources, the Centre was not opened until March 1981. Thereafter practical problems continued – the Electricity Board disconnected the supply twice without notice (as inappropriately wired for a Centre!); and burst pipes, flood damage, lack of money and insurance company delays closed the Centre from December to April 1982. These problems may help explain the limited use by residents of the Centre. Acquisition of the Centre resulted in its running costs dominating the Group's meetings

One consequence was that the main grade officer, instead of being based on the Walpole estate for most of the three years, was only there from May to December 1981 and June to September 1982. This affected his availability to Group members, clients and residents in general. A second related consequence was the delay in developing an Advice Service. As soon as the Centre opened, residents interested in a welfare rights course were identified and this was run – via Adult Education – from September to December in the Centre. A community work student on a ten week placement from January 1982 surveyed resident opinion and confirmed that a resident staffed service would be acceptable. Residents suitable to staff the office were identified and in May the local authority made a grant towards training costs. However, by September 1982, no resident had been placed on a CAB training course in Leeds due to the pressure for places. From March 1981, a 'temporary' advice solution was the inclusion in the Group's community newspaper of a welfare rights supplement; and this supplement continued virtually without a break until the Scheme's end.

The 'Walpole World'

This monthly community newspaper was started in 1979, and represented the Group's desire to keep residents informed of its work. It was distributed free to every home, funded by the Probation Service. The intention was that the Group should become as self-sufficient in producing the newspaper as everything else. After buying a duplicator, the Group produced the November and December 1981 issues at the Centre: but the flood damage put an end to this until May. In August the Group started to have the newspaper produced at a fast-print shop, seeking advertising from local shopkeepers to help pay production costs.

The Junior Group

The Junior Group's existence was also partly affected by community centre delays. However, it suffered mainly from a lack of adult helpers. It was set up as a 'community youth club' in October 1979, thanks to the local authority IT officer making his unused IT Centre (situated ten minutes walk from Walpole) available until June 1980. It was anticipated that Walpole's own Centre would be open by then; and when it was not, the Junior Group ceased until March 1981. Helpers continued to be hard to find and the Centre was really too small for a youth club. In July 1981, the Junior Group members staged a '*coup d'état*', demanding their own committee, under which they had operated in 1979 at the IT Centre. However, this also failed as they were still unable to recruit enough committed adult committee members. From December 1981 to May 1982 the Centre was closed to the Junior Group; but after it reopened, lack of help continued to undermine it.

To some extent, the Group was over extended with other work. There was some recognition that paid youth workers were necessary, but the youth service would not have been able to fund such staff for Walpole. Ironically, in principle, the Group had always ascribed a high priority to young residents on the grounds that they were 'the citizens of the future'. In practice, they – adolescents especially – proved too demanding. Nonetheless, whether formally or informally, young residents were the greatest users of the Centre, identifying it as theirs, helping to repair it when it was burgled and later flood damaged.

Work with young residents and Social Services Department involvement came about through the formation of a community based IT group in 1980. The staff consisted of two local authority social workers, the probation officer, and a student on placement with him. A twelve week programme was devised, around the theme 'surviving on Walpole', and nine juvenile residents were recruited. Unfortunately, at the end of the programme the social workers dropped out, and the student placement had ended. The probation officer agreed to the young residents' request to go on meeting. They adjusted group membership to make it co-terminous with a natural gang on the estate. Over the next two years, group members offended – some more than once – but it proved possible to divert them from custody and, in most cases, formal supervision. Unfortunately, no further Social Services involvement proved possible despite several formal and informal approaches – perhaps not surprising for a department which drew two teams' boundary line down the centre of the estate!

The youth employment scheme also came to nothing. Virtually all the investigation work was done by the Scheme's officer, with some Research Unit involvement. The

DCPO's ideas had been to engage unemployed young residents in refurbishing the estate, but the modernisation programme put paid to that. Further, the MSC would not contemplate a scheme exclusively for Walpole's unemployed. Any employment scheme would have to be based on the Huddersfield Probation office. The Scheme's officer saw it as appropriate to hand over the project at that stage to middle management.

The officer's major role continued to be support for the Community Group. In August 1979 the Group progressed significantly by arranging its election at a public meeting on the estate; and followed this up at the 1980 AGM by the adoption of a written constitution. In adopting an orthodox elected committee structure, with officers, for the first time in 1979, it was seeking status/legitimacy, a mandate from the estate, and to demonstrate that it was not a clique. It also now had representation from the Housing Department & Education Welfare, local clergy, and the community constables attending its meetings.

Group dynamics

There is insufficient space here to explore the dynamics of the Group over the three years. At times, its membership was committed and active; at times, it struggled to obtain members and carry out its business. Personality was more important than constitutions or structure in influencing the Group's success; and gender was as important as personality. During the three years the Group was dominated first by women (Vice-Chair, later to become Chair; Secretary; and Treasurer); and then from May 1981 by a male Chair. Where an emphasis could be identified, the first period was characterised by community care events, and the second by community action and residents' interests. Race was not an influential factor. Although 20% of residents were of Caribbean origin, racial tension on the estate was virtually non-existent. Racism towards Asians, who did not reside on the estate (apart from one Asian shopkeeper from 1980) was present. Only one black resident briefly joined the Group (elected in 1979); and the Group failed to pursue the 'positive discrimination' necessary to secure representation.

Impact on practice

The table below indicates court report numbers, the proportion of defendants who became 'clients', and the subgroup with whom 'innovatory' work under the Scheme was possible. For reference, Walpole had traditionally produced a caseload of around twenty clients. At the end of the Scheme, the officer had nine clients, of whom seven were Walpole residents.

The officer's involvement with the Walpole estate modified his role as a probation officer. Court report was characterised more by reference to a defendant's contacts and opportunities (or lack of them) on the estate, rather than psycho-emotional factors; and by description of what was happening on the estate. 'Innovatory work' was the officer's attempts to involve statutory clients in the work of the Group. Thus, a single parent shoplifter was placed on probation specifically to involve her in setting up and running the Junior Group in 1979. Two young adults worked on the Centre under community service orders. The IT group constituted work with a natural gang. During the three years, fifteen clients were worked with innovatively. Their involvement

Table 2

	Total SIRs	No. of Clients	Type of Client			Innovatory Work
			Cust.	Sup.	CSO	
1979	29	14	5	6	3	6
1980	23	10	1	4	5	3
1981	30	14	5	6	3	6
1982	21	9	2	3	4	3

frequently led to family or friends also participating. The officer's accessibility and role also resulted in him being involved in reparation and mediation prior to any police or court involvement. The officer was frequently told that he was 'not like a probation officer'. Research conducted by a colleague into client perceptions revealed that he was perceived as an amalgam of 'friend', 'teacher' and 'social worker'.

Community work

There were three major community work elements within the Scheme:

(i)   The officer supported residents in the initiation of 'community care' activities – like day trips to the coast and children's Christmas parties – and the formation of groups (like the Junior Group).

(ii)   There were the instances of 'community development' and 'community action', primarily around the modernisation programme, where residents were demanding a voice in what happened to their community, and some shift in the balance of power from elected and appointed local authority representatives to themselves.

(iii)   The officer attempted to share and transfer what knowledge, expertise and skill he possessed to enable residents to operate and negotiate more self-confidently and successfully on their own account, without needing or being dependent on professional support and advocacy.

Above all, the officer was determined to avoid a leadership or 'banking' approach to his work, whereby he identified problems and determined strategies. Rather, the approach was to facilitate and understand residents' definitions of their problems and how to tackle them; and to develop his own and residents' 'consciousness' by a process of constant dialogue. Research generally failed to materialise – partly because the Research Unit was small and its staff changed, but mainly due to the Scheme's 'ownership' remaining unclear. Staff changes and increased caseloads meant that the Huddersfield office was relieved to see the Scheme, and its resource demands, end in September 1982. Ironically, the office would a few months later become involved in a scheme on the Sheepridge estate, initiated by the local authority and based in converted council houses.

Conclusions

It would be easy to emphasise the Scheme's difficulties and failures. It would be easy to point to the massive good luck of the modernisation programme, which converted one of the two least desirable Huddersfield estates into one for which there was a waiting list. It can be argued that this good luck resulted from a Labour-controlled local authority seeking loopholes in the Conservative Government's policies.

Yet it can also legitimately be asked if modernisation would have come to Walpole without the Community Group's existence. None of the other activities, trips, Galas, and Groups would have existed without the Scheme. Nor would the exposure to new experience, for resident, client, and probation officer alike. The Scheme also provides experience of a limited investment of resources.

The Service is at present attempting to interpret 'community involvement'. Clearly, community work, like social work, has no inherent ideology – both are capable of producing social control. The crucial question is: whose will be the dominant voice in arriving at the interpretation, residents or the Home Office? The interpretation will need to take account of limited available resources, but will also need to locate work in the community in the mainstream of Service operation, even if staff numbers involved continue to be small. The spectre at the moment is of neighbourhood watch schemes combined with volunteer-run tracking schemes, with a token probation presence to lend an air of respectability, whilst effectively colluding with neighbourhood prejudices and fears about crime.

So the black youth, even under the neighbourhood watch scheme, still gets reported because he is *suspected* of being about to offend. Or the pro-reparation probation officer inadvertently lands the offender with the double punishment of court sentence and voluntary reparation. Or the juvenile on a tracking or intensive IT Scheme ends up subject to more surveillance than if he had been sent to Detention Centre. As much as the need to patrol the boundary between custody and non-custody, the Probation Service needs to patrol the boundary between broad-based community support and help, and an illegitimate extension of surveillance which seeks to satisfy the narrow demands of 'respectable' subgroups within a neighbourhood.

Commentary

This work ... began after a feasibility study, and some negotiation at local level. The worker had clear notions of what different community approaches could offer and attempted to apply these in practice. In particular he wished to 'de-skill' himself in an explicit way by seeking guidance from residents about both problem definition and resolution.

The Probation Service worked out clear supportive and facilitative arrangements for the key worker and resourced the scheme to its end.

Despite these instances of agency commitment, a number of critical points must still be made about the feasibility study, initial entry, worker support, overall project objectives and the key worker's role.

(i)   Feasibility – it did not concentrate on the currently advocated community profile but emerged from a mix of supposed client interest (probation officer determined) in forming a group, more generalised client interest and middle management notions of workload contributions.

(ii)   Entry – this was primarily via present and ex-Probation clients. Non-offender contacts were not used initially despite the view of the key worker that the offender/non-offender distinction was not such a crucial divide as was supposed. He argued that both categories shared a common social, political and economic context, and that this was more relevant as a focus for entry.

(iii)   Support – commitment to the particular support needs of the worker seemed to give way to a 'general management' of the project as a whole.

(iv)   Overall objectives – the scheme was always envisaged as of a fixed duration with no provision however tentative for developmental possibilities. Its life was not defined by resident or neighbourhood needs but by the Probation Service's finite commitment of resources.

(v)   Worker role – despite the formal application of agency resources to this work, the ultimate style of work depended on the individual entrepreneurial skills, personal morality and ideology of the key worker. There was a 'gap' between the formal framework and the actual work processes. This 'gap' begs major questions of Probation investment in similar schemes. If these are to continue, more attention must be paid to the implications of the contradictions between the formal objectives and the work on the ground.

From Paul Falkingham, 'Huddersfield: group and community work issues', in D. Scott, N. Stone, P. Simpson and P. Falkingham (eds), Going Local in Probation? Case Studies in Community Practice (University of East Anglia Social Work Programme, Norwich and University of Manchester Department of Social Administration, Manchester), 1985, pp. 65–77.

47 Task-centred casework in a probation setting (1985)

E. Matilda Goldberg, Stephen Stanley and Jenny Kenrick

Summary

This exploratory study sought to describe and evaluate task-centred casework in a probation setting. In particular the project aimed (1) to explore whether the task-centred model, originating from work with 'voluntary' clients who want to do something about acknowledged problems, can be used in the context of a judicial order; (2) to find out how effective the method is as judged by the clients themselves, by the probation officers and by reconviction rates.

The design of the study was a simple before-and-after one which compared the state of the problem(s) and aims of probation at the beginning of the probation order with the situation at the end of the order and with reconviction rates three years later. The project was carried out under the joint auspices of the National Institute for Social Work (supported by a DHSS grant) and the Inner London Probation and After-Care Service in an experimental probation office – the Differential Treatment Unit (DTU) located in the Borough of Islington. The officers in this unit carried reduced caseloads and devoted most of their time to the exploration and application of task-centred methods to their probation work.

After a pilot phase in which task-centred methods were studied and tried out and recording instruments adapted to the probation setting, all the offenders referred for a social enquiry report (SER) from the courts served by the DTU were approached within the framework of the task-centred model.

The probation officers used the remand period for a thorough problem exploration; if a problem area and a task could be agreed with the offender and the case was considered suitable for probation, the officer would recommend a short-term probation order in his or her report to the court, which would normally terminate after six months. Contrary to expectations it took over two years to assemble a sample of 100 completed short-term probation orders, since only 23 per cent of the court referrals resulted in short-term probation orders – a percentage which is in accordance with the general norm in Inner London.

The 100 offenders who were placed on probation with a view to discharge after six months were broadly similar in their social and demographic characteristics to those who received other sentences. The main reason why three out of four clients were not recommended for probation was an inability to locate or agree on a target problem or to formulate feasible tasks. In some situations no problems, or only trivial ones, could be detected; in others, problems appeared to exist but were not acknowledged by the offenders, or problems were so pervasive and chronic that short-term probation could not hope to alleviate them.

Almost two-thirds (64) of the 100 short-term orders were terminated at the end of six months and were considered to be task-centred as they fulfilled the following criteria: a target problem or problems and tasks were agreed between worker and probationer, there was evidence that work on the task(s) had been carried out, and the order was converted to a conditional discharge after six months. In most of the remaining orders further delinquency or adverse circumstances either led to the probation period running for a full year or to the clients' disappearance or to custodial sentences. These thirty-six offenders for whom the task-centred method did not work out differed in some socio-demographic respects from those who successfully completed a short-term task-centred probation order. There were more persistent delinquents among them, they were younger, far fewer lived in families, more belonged to ethnic minorities and more were unemployed.

The majority of the sixty-four task-centred clients were under the age of 35; three-fifths were men. Practically half were unemployed at the beginning of the order; over two-thirds had at least one previous conviction, and half had two or more previous convictions. Most had committed some form of theft.

Dissatisfaction in social relations and difficulties in role performance, mostly related to work, were identified as target problems in over half the cases. Tasks were aimed at gaining some insight into the clients' behaviour and working out a strategy with them for bringing about some small and specific changes in their activities and relationships. Tasks in connection with the work role were mainly of a practical kind, such as work search sessions, literacy classes for those who could neither read nor write, and social skills training of various kinds.

The social work was carried out by nine experienced probation officers, only three of whom (including the senior) remained at the DTU throughout the project period. Some students also participated in the project. The officers, who had been used to an exploratory stance with the aim of achieving insight as the central concern, found the task-centred goal-setting and the 'shift from what is wrong to what is needed' difficult to incorporate into their skills. They discovered that they had to help clients to scale down ambitious and global targets to small, achievable aims; they experienced some initial discomfort in 'letting go' rather than to fish for further problems when their clients had in fact achieved the agreed tasks. Although they differed in their use of task-centred methods, all officers acknowledged that this model had helped them to become clearer about what they were trying to do, to share their thinking and feelings more openly with their clients, and to encourage more self-help and problem-solving in the clients themselves.

Certain features of the task-centred method stood out clearly:

(1)   The more sharply the problem(s) and the task(s) were specified, the more clearly the clients were able to describe their task-centred efforts at the follow-up interview.

(2)   Although clients stressed their own effort and initiative in achieving their tasks, they also emphasised the probation officers' participation and their encouragement. The reciprocity and equality experienced in the relationship were often commented on.

(3)   The probation officers evolved a successful device for dealing with emotional obstacles to task achievement by setting aside a finite number of sessions for exploration and ventilation of these difficulties.
(4)   The process of listing and ranking problems in order of urgency seemed to protect both workers and clients from being overwhelmed and to encourage hope and initiative.
(5)   The idea of being kept to the tasks seemed to appeal particularly to the less articulate and intelligent clients, though a minority resented the focused task orientation.
(6)   The well-prepared ending of the order and the final review of progress (or lack of it) in relation to initial problems and objectives of probation were generally experienced as helpful by both client and worker.
(7)   The great majority of the forty-four clients who were followed up commented with satisfaction on their feelings of achieving an objective, however small, and on their increase in self-confidence.

The main outcome measures were based on two ratings – one by the practitioners in their final interviews with the clients on how far the task(s) had been achieved, and the other by the independent assessor in the follow-up interview with the client in which the answer to the key question 'How is the problem(s) now compared with how it was when you first saw the probation officer?' was rated. These two measures were only available for forty-four of the sixty-four task-centred cases as twenty failed to keep their appointments with the independent assessor. An additional independent outcome criterion was the proportion of offenders in the whole sample who were reconvicted up to three years after the offence for which the probation order was made.

There was a high degree of congruence between task achievement scores and problem reduction scores in the forty-four cases which were followed up. Any discrepancies (eight cases) were largely explained either by circumstances unrelated to the tasks undertaken, bringing about a temporary alleviation of the problem, or by different problem areas being rated in the two interviews in which outcomes were assessed.

Half (twenty-two) of those clients whose order was converted after six months and who were followed up had high ratings on both task achievement and problem reduction. The other twenty-two had lower scores, but only six clients had the lowest possible scores on both task achievement and problem reduction. The results were mirrored in the reconviction rates which were considerably lower for the twenty-two who had come out well on both task achievement and problem reduction than for the rest, although this is partly explained by the larger number of low-risk clients among the former group.

It was difficult to establish any clear relationships between backgrounds, type and amount of input and successful or unsuccessful outcome. There was a hint that those who obtained high scores on task achievement and problem reduction were somewhat better risks from the point of view of living circumstances and delinquent behaviour before and during the probation period. Full agreement between offender and probation officer on both problem area and tasks to be undertaken seemed to be associated with successful outcome, while there appeared to be no connection between type of problem tackled and outcome.

There were few indications that amount of input, methods used, concentration on the task and worker style were directly associated with outcome. However, some officers achieved better results in relation to both project outcome and subsequent reconvictions than other officers. Numbers were unfortunately too small to clarify these issues further; carefully designed experimental studies may throw some light on them.

Not unexpectedly, those who achieved their tasks and felt that their problems were much reduced displayed more positive attitudes towards task-centred, short-term probation than those who had done less well. Thus almost all of the twenty-two high scorers felt that probation had worked out well, compared with only half among the rest. The satisfaction of having achieved a great deal oneself went hand in hand with the recognition that the probation officer, too, had contributed much to the success, which highlights the part reciprocity and partnership played in working out problems and achieving aims. The importance of congruence between client and worker perspectives was underlined by the fact that practically all the high scorers felt that their probation officer had understood their problems, compared with less than half among the rest. In stark contrast none of the six lowest scorers felt that they had achieved much, or that their probation officer had helped them or had understood their problems, and none liked the task-centred approach.

A study of reconvictions in this sample over a three-year period suggests that this time-limited method is at least as effective in preventing further convictions as are long-term probation orders. There are strong indications that favourable outcomes of task-centred probation are associated with an avoidance of reconvictions and that this effect is mainly evident in a middle-risk group of younger probationers who are first or second offenders. Clearly, these hypotheses need extensive experimental testing.

From E. Matilda Goldberg, Stephen Stanley and Jenny Kenrick, 'Task-centred casework in a probation setting', in E. Matilda Goldberg, J. Gibbons and Ian Sinclair (eds.), Problems, Tasks and Outcomes: the evaluation of task-centered casework in three settings (London: George Allen and Unwin), 1985, pp. 89–166.

48 Political motivation and probation practice (1986)

Tim Chapman

Existing policy

At the 1975 NAPO AGM it was resolved that: 'This Association deplores the involvement of its members on a statutory basis, with those offenders whose actions are determined by motives of a patently political nature. Consequently, we call upon the National Executive Committee to issue instructions to all members of the association to refuse to conduct any SER on any such person charged under the conspiracy laws, and in Northern Ireland, those dealt with under the schedules of the *Emergency Provisions Act 1974*, and further to refuse to carry out statutory supervision of any person convicted in similar circumstances'.

At the National Executive Committee on 18th July 1975, the following amendment to this resolution was passed:

> That this NEC welcomes the policy passed by the Newcastle AGM, deploring the statutory involvement of NAPO members with offenders whose actions are determined by motives of a patently political nature. It thinks it illogical to limit the practical implementation of this policy to only those charged under the conspiracy laws, and broadens the instructions to the membership to include all offenders, whose motives are of a patently political nature, whatever charges they face.

This effectively broadened the boundaries to include all politically motivated offenders and remains national NAPO policy.

The policy had its origins in the practical experiences of members in Northern Ireland and was proposed at the AGM by the Northern Ireland branch. However, it was understood that the difficulties which faced members in Northern Ireland were qualitatively the same as those in England & Wales even though they were likely to be both more frequent and more intense. The principles underpinning the policy were the same whenever a probation officer was faced with working with a politically motivated offender.

The rationale

What were these principles? Every citizen has the right freely to hold political opinions even if such opinions result in criminal actions. The state has the right to punish criminal actions but not to use its authority to change the political motivation leading to the offences. Probation officers are given statutory authority to collect information on and assess the motivation of offenders through social enquiry reports, with a view to advising sentencers on how criminal behaviour might be changed. Statutory duties such as probation orders, parole and other forms of licence involve the use of social work methods aimed at assisting offenders in changing their ways and attitudes to avoid further offences. Given this contradiction between the citizen's rights and the probation officers duties, NAPO believes it to be an unethical and inappropriate use of professional skills to try to change an offender's political views and motivation.

Implementation in England & Wales

Although the policy had its origins in the political crisis in Northern Ireland, the mid seventies in England & Wales were quite turbulent politically. Both Loyalist and Republican organisations were active in Great Britain, as were militant Welsh and Scottish nationalists. Most of the 'Angry Brigade' had been imprisoned for causing explosions, conspiracy, etc, and were coming up for parole. Trade Unionists such as the Shrewsbury building workers were in court for offences arising out of picketing. Police were making many arrests at anti-apartheid, CND and Socialist Workers Party demonstrations.

Between 1975 and 1978 the national panel set up to advise members of the implementation of the policy received nine referrals. Each of these cases was settled in such a way that reports were eventually prepared or supervision was undertaken. A way was always found to get round the policy and this, perhaps, reflected the rather cautious style of leadership in NAPO at the time. A case was being developed that the policy was not relevant to probation practice in England & Wales. At the 1978 AGM a motion was proposed by the Professional Committee to rescind it in England & Wales and make Northern Ireland an exceptional case. Northern Ireland branch was anxious not to be isolated and mounted strong opposition to the motion on the basis that the same principles applied wherever probation officers worked. The motion was overwhelmingly lost.

Anti-racist activity

In 1979 probation officers in Middlesex refused to do reports on Asian and Anti-Nazi league activists arrested during demonstrations in Southall if they claimed their motivation was political. This action received publicity and was interpreted by Magistrates and the Police Federation as probation officers having political sympathy for those charged. The chair of the Police Federation at the time went so far as to say publicly that it was an attempt to 'manipulate the criminal law to suit ... political beliefs'! The local Labour MP commented that if it was, he would applaud it.

In 1980 several serious offences were committed in the Midlands by Pakistanis protesting against events in their homeland. Local NAPO members saw these offences as politically motivated. Local management disagreed and undertook to do the reports themselves. NAPO responded through an NEC resolution that it was inappropriate for management to interfere with the professional judgement of a probation officer.

For a couple of years the panel had few cases to deal with; a demonstrator charged with assault on the police, an ex-member of Sinn Fein on parole, students arrested for picketing a factory.

Miners' strike

In 1984 the national panel decided that offences of public disorder arising out of picketing in the course of the miners' strike were politically motivated. Local branches of the NUM disagreed, seeing such offences as industrially or economically motivated, and welcomed reports as a means of keeping their members out of prison. Some courts on the other hand perceived the policy and its implementation as a confirmation of their opinions that the miners were not ordinary strikers but subversives. Many members were keen to have reports prepared to mitigate the harsh sentences meted out. They saw community service orders as viable alternatives to custody. Furthermore, some miners admitted that they had been drinking heavily prior to the offences, or that they had lost their heads and now regretted their actions. The notion that NAPO policy guaranteed probation's neutrality was being challenged.

During this period the panel was also receiving referrals concerning animal rights protestors and peace campaigners. CND made it known that they believed NAPO's policy to be unhelpful and repressive. The panel sought opinions on the policy from branches. The majority felt that a review was necessary.

Northern Ireland

The outbreak of violent political conflict in Northern Ireland in 1969 had two effects which particularly concerned local probation officers. Firstly, the criminal justice system became one of the primary means of dealing with this conflict. The Special Powers Act gave the Government the power to intern without trial. The police were increasingly employed in dealing with civil disturbances. Secondly, and as a consequence of this politicisation of the criminal justice system attention and resources were directed away from the ordinary offender. Thus, local NAPO members feared that probation practice would become focused upon politically motivated offenders to the extent that other offenders would be neglected.

In 1970 concern was expressed about the Service's ability to supervise after-care licences on young prisoners and borstal licences due to the volume of young people being arrested in the course of riots. This problem was exacerbated by the Temporary Provisions Act which provided for mandatory sentences of imprisonment for offences arising from riots. This highlighted to many officers the irrelevance of providing Social Enquiry Reports as required by the Juvenile Court. It also increased the number of after-care licences. At this stage local officers perceived a real danger of the Service being seen as part of a particular political or sectarian system and not as a politically neutral social work service. Partly as a result of the disquiet expressed by probation officers, mandatory sentencing was soon abolished and in 1974 statutory after-care for young prisoners was suspended. Borstal after-care remained.

In 1973 the Emergency Provisions Act replaced the Special Powers Act. This Act listed a number of offences which it considered to be terrorist acts and these came to be known as scheduled offences. It also introduced a new Court (the 'Diplock' court), which entailed less rigorous rules of evidence and no jury for the trial of scheduled offenders.

Juveniles

At this stage the main dilemma facing probation officers concerned the preparation of reports for the juvenile court. It was apparent to report writers that the determining factor in many offences was involvement in political or paramilitary groups and not family background. There was a growing conviction that it was not the job of a probation officer to assess such an involvement and that social work intervention could not influence such attitudes and behaviour.

Consequently the Northern Ireland branch of NAPO proposed the motion quoted above at the 1975 AGM. This resolution was timely as a year later the Government changed its approach of seeing politically motivated offenders as a 'special category' and treating them differently in custody. They introduced the policy of criminalisation which resulted in bitter resistance both outside and within the penal system.

During the past 10 years the criminal justice system has become one of the main arenas in which the political conflict in Northern Ireland has been fought. The ending of internment meant that it was more difficult to secure the conviction of serious politically motivated offenders. The difficulty in finding evidence and witnesses resulted in abuses in police interrogation methods. There was a period in which some paramilitary offenders refused to recognise the court. A protest within the prisons against the ending of special category privileges culminated in the hunger strike in which ten republican prisoners died. Most recently controversies have concerned the 'supergrass' system of securing conviction, the use of plastic bullets by police in controlling riots, the 'shoot to kill' policy by the police and the strip search of prisoners in Armagh women's prison. These struggles have taken their toll in loss of life and liberty and in human misery. Many police officers, prison officers and several magistrates and judges have lost their lives.

Gaining space under pressure

In the meantime probation officers have used the NAPO policy to gain the space necessary to demonstrate their commitment to working effectively and humanely with ordinary offenders. No probation officer has been seriously injured or killed in the course of their duties. The Service operates freely throughout the province.

It has not been easy to sustain the policy. Officers have had to withstand pressure from judges while standing in the witness box explaining the policy.

There was an attempt by the Northern Ireland Office in the mid-seventies to encourage the Service to become more closely involved in working with the welfare groups of paramilitary organisations. This was successfully resisted. Management have never accepted the principles although it has been prepared to negotiate procedures to ensure consistency of implementation. In 1982 management became determined to develop 'an overall proactive strategy' attacking the 'reactivism' and 'neutralism' of NAPO's position. NAPO successfully mobilised middle management to resist the initiative. Fear of personal safety became an issue at this juncture for the first time.

Lifer Home Circumstances Reports

Most recently a controversy has occurred which has placed severe strains on the policy. There are several hundred men and women serving life sentences for politically motivated offences, many of whom are now being reviewed by the Life Sentence Review Board (the equivalent of a Parole Board). The Board has asked for home circumstances reports from probation officers. Northern Ireland Branch is opposed to preparing these reports on the grounds that they will be used to assess the likelihood of further offending. Management insists on them being done.

Prisoners divided

What has complicated matters is that the prisoners are divided over the issue. Republican prisoners on the whole reject or at best are indifferent to these reports, recognising their irrelevance to what is essentially a political decision. The majority of Loyalist prisoners on the other hand wish to participate in the reviews and are willing to use their political power to remove any obstacles to this end. Consequently, whatever course NAPO takes it will not be seen as neutral. However an arrangement has been made in which volunteers will prepare reports under strict guidelines. This arrangement is to be monitored and reviewed.

Contrasting experience

Whilst the NAPO policy has been applied throughout England, Wales and Northern Ireland, there are obvious differences between the circumstances of its application between Northern Ireland and the mainland. Whilst there has been a steady flow of referrals in England & Wales, they have tended to be scattered throughout the country, come in waves as a specific issue gains a high profile and then is submerged once again, and have ranged in intensity and gravity from minor disorderly offences on demonstration to serious, violent offences. They have involved a wide variety of groups including political parties, pressure groups and trade unions each having different aims and attitudes towards breaking the law to achieve their objectives. Each case has been examined on its own merits and almost in every case some arrangement has been made through which a report could be prepared or supervision be undertaken. The policy has been seen as a matter of principle and little concern has been expressed regarding personal safety or its relevance to the Service's general relations to the local community.

In Northern Ireland politically motivated offences have been a daily occurrence throughout most of the province since 1969. They are usually serious offences resulting in major physical damage or personal injury, and are planned and executed by recognised paramilitary organisations. Their effects pervade the social, political and economic life of the people living in Northern Ireland. It is accepted in the vast majority of cases that the probation officer's role is limited. No pretrial reports are prepared for the Crown Courts on those charged with scheduled offences. Probation orders and community service orders are rarely considered options for such serious offences. A panel has been set up jointly between the Service and NAPO to assess post-trial referral for reports. The majority of these are passed as having no political motivation. A few cases are fudged but generally the system is effective. The one exception to this situation is the provision of reports to life sentences Review Board.

NAPO's policy, in my opinion, fits the circumstances in Northern Ireland more appropriately than those in England & Wales. Many of the cases referred in England would not have been considered serious enough to fall within the policy in Northern

Ireland. The policy is effective in dealing with an organised political campaign in which serious offences are committed as a strategy. It preserves professional integrity, personal safety and political neutrality in a society which is experiencing violent and fundamental conflict. It is, however, a blunt, inflexible method of guiding probation officers during a politically turbulent though not yet critical situation.

Preserving professional autonomy

So, one reason for the decision to review the policy was its decreasing usefulness as a guide to officers in England & Wales. I do not, however, believe it to be the underlying reason which, in my opinion, lies in the contradiction between probation officers' over-riding desire to preserve their professional autonomy and the pressure of change within the criminal justice system, and more specifically in probation practice.

For most main-grade officers the great advantage to the job is the ability to do their work with the minimum of interference. NAPO is the main weapon in the main-grade's struggle to preserve this autonomy and almost every probation practice policy (which is observed) is based upon this notion (though it is rarely spelt out). Officers instinctively know that involvement with politically motivated offenders will limit their autonomy. Such offenders are aware of their own power and are willing to use it. Officers' autonomy depends to a great extent on the powerlessness of most clients.

Contrary to the fears of magistrates and the police, the politically motivated offenders policy is in fact motivated by a desire to avoid political activity and remain politically neutral (or more accurately irrelevant). This contradiction creates a curious paradox whenever there is conflict between main-grade and management over this issue. What actually happens is that the main-grade adopt a pragmatic position but argue it in ideological/ethical terms whilst management argue in a pragmatic fashion a position which reflects the changing political reality outside the service.

Change

NAPO's policy on politically motivated offenders is over 10 years old. What has changed during that time and how have these changes affected probation practice?

As political conflict replaces consensus, the political neutrality and independence of the criminal justice system become luxuries which can no longer be afforded. This is clear in Northern Ireland where the practices of the police, the courts and prisons are adapted to deal with organised and militant opposition to the State. While not so developed, the politicisation of the criminal justice system is apparent in England & Wales. The police have changed their methods of organisation in the face of mass picketing. Police leaders are more prepared to make blatantly political statements. Local authorities seek to make the police more accountable. The Government increasingly uses the courts against its perceived 'enemies', whether they are striking miners or civil servants who leak information to the press.

In sum, the criminal justice system is increasingly becoming a political arena in which people are faced with political choices. To choose to do nothing, to be neutral, may be correct in some cases; in others it may be to avoid responsibility. To assume responsibility on the other hand is to invite public accountability and in so doing to reduce one's autonomy.

Ten years ago there was still a consensus about probation practice; it was directed at the prevention of re-offending through diagnosis and attitude change. A social enquiry report was an objective assessment of the personal and social circumstances and attitudes leading to the offence. A probation order provided the treatment and/or help necessary for the offender's rehabilitation.

Since then we have seen the development of community service orders which are more about punishment than treatment or help. The dominance of the need to provide alternatives to custody has resulted in Social Enquiry Reports becoming strategic documents intended to reduce the number of people locked up and probation orders assuming all sorts of forms to convince sentencers that they are credible alternatives. Bottoms and McWilliams, amongst others, have suggested that the probation order can have several purposes other than attitude change. With increasing opposition to imprisonment, after-care is seen more in terms of reducing the detrimental effects of incarceration and aiding resettlement than in finishing off a rehabilitation process. These developments must lead one to question whether the offender's motivation in committing an offence is still so central to probation practice.

In conclusion

Changing political and economic conditions have affected both the criminal justice and probation practice. The space in which probation officers can both sustain their autonomy and remain relevant to the realities of crime and the criminal justice system is contracting on all sides. To a certain extent the choice that faces any probation practice policy is whether to defend this autonomy or to become more relevant to the real conflicts of present day society.

Community based practice, clients' rights and democratic accountability all threaten the comfortable security of probation practice. Working with politically motivated offenders presents, perhaps, the greatest threat and such a step must be taken with great care. I believe that the original principle underlying the policy is as relevant now as it was in 1975. However, much probation practice no longer depends upon attitude change and may, therefore, no longer apply to the policy.

Furthermore, there are different levels of politically motivated offences in terms of seriousness and organisation. I have no doubt that probation officers are largely irrelevant in situations of polarised political conflict in which serious acts of violence to persons or property are a regular feature. Our role then is limited to one of first aid e.g. prison welfare.

However, other levels of political action such as demonstrations and picketing may offer opportunities for officers to mediate within the criminal justice system and to mitigate the full force of the state's reaction. Guidelines for such positive action need to be established for such practice. By limiting the application of the current policy, NAPO will have a clear position on serious politically motivated offences and free itself to develop a positive strategy for probation in the face of increasingly turbulent political conditions.

From Tim Chapman, 'Political motivation and probation practice',
Probation Journal, *33(1), 1986, pp. 8–12.*

49 Antabuse of probation

An example in practice (1986)

John Smith

Contrary to impressions that may be drawn from Dr Colin Brewer's paper (1982), significantly more time is needed in counselling the previously homeless vagrant drinker whose medication is being supervised at the office, which cannot and should not be delegated to unskilled staff. In the case of the drinker who is still tenuously hanging on to a wife and family, and is involved in the treatment programme, the counselling time may become less more quickly.

Taking people out of circulation, drying them out, and launching them back is not the answer. It is easy to sober someone up. The difficulty is to keep them sober. The trauma of returning to all the previous tensions of daily life without alcohol is too much for many people, and the temptation to drink too great. These pressures on top of a sense of failure ultimately lead to worse problems.

A case illustration

Breaking the old pattern

Brian appeared before a Magistrates' Court for a shoplifting offence to which he pleaded guilty. This was his 42nd conviction. He was homeless, and had been out of prison six days, and obviously in a state of alcohol withdrawal. I had previously spoken to Brian and the duty solicitor that morning, and agreed that we should ask for a remand to prepare a SER to find a way of putting a wedge in his revolving door. The question of bail was considered briefly but, as there were no beds available for detoxification – there never is in London – he was remanded in custody for three weeks. When I visited ten days later, he showed a marked recovery. We discussed his drinking history of the past twenty years, his previous treatments and accidents, the breakdown of his marriage, and his social decline. At 51 years of age he felt his life was finished and he was doomed to spend the most of his remaining years in prison. I am trying to identify whether this is ambivalence about further treatment, or an acute sense of failure and depression. In discussing with him the proposal of supervised antabuse therapy as a condition of a two year probation order he was thinking 'This is a way to avoid another sentence'; 'I don't want to drink again but I can get it when I need it'; 'It sounds better than those hospital groups'.

Bail assessment

The Court granted a further four week remand on bail. This is desirable in most cases to assess his medical suitability, and to enable him to make a valid and informed consent to treatment when the probation order is made. Experience has shown that it is imperative to commence antabuse therapy that day and an appointment with a doctor was prearranged. The doctor examined Brian, prescribed antabuse, and gave him his first dose, at the clinic. The consequential reaction of taking alcohol is reinforced by the doctor (far more relevant than it is from me) and he is given a medical warning card to carry, advising against any administration of alcohol. Vitamin pills and a mild sleeping tablet were also prescribed. These were lodged at the hostel as they needed to be taken daily. Antabuse can also be taken daily, but there is a need to establish a pattern, and initially incorporate the medication into the behavioural modification programme. Antabuse is the first coping response to the craving, and to alleviate the problem by direct intervention is an initial behavioural approach.

Brian was seen three times a week at my office (Mondays, Wednesdays, and Fridays). His antabuse was seen to be taken (dispensed in water). He needed a lot of reassurance during those first few critical weeks. He was frustrated by long waits at the DHSS Office. He was under pressure from previous drinking acquaintances to buy them a bottle, or share the bottle they had. Every other shop was an off-licence, or a licensed supermarket, and the money in his pocket still added up in cans of Special Brew, or half bottles of whisky.

Early progress

Brian was seen twice further by the doctor during the remand period for a blood test; liver function test; brain scan, and assessment of antabuse dosage. The change was quite remarkable. He became alert, energetic and eager, the depression had gone. He was eating heartily, sleeping well and looking for work. The medications were playing their part. The antabuse necessitated his abstention, and enabled him to avoid the trigger spots to drinking. He was beginning to learn in a real life situation. The frustrations and anxieties are not so easily dealt with, hence the need of frequent contact, a positive approach to maximise objectivity and minimise assumption and speculation.

By the fourth week Brian had exceeded his previous longest period of sobriety in the community during the past five years and there was no hesitation in his desire that this should continue. The conditions of the order to be asked for at Court were spelt out quite clearly and that any breach may mean a return to Court. For example, should he fail to take his antabuse as prescribed at any time, he will be sought within 24 hours, and we will discuss his 'slip-up'. There may be a valid reason; it is more likely to be an intention to resume drinking and he will need at least 48 hours free of antabuse to do this or possibly longer. The doctor's part of the contract is to retain medical oversight for at least 12 months and to examine any complaints of suspected adverse effects, which are normally very few. My part of the contract will be to retain a diminishing degree of control to enable him to become an integrated, functioning man capable of accepting responsibility for himself and those around him.

I deliberately avoid referring to ultimate goals in more positive terms. To discuss with him – even at this stage – total sobriety for the rest of his life would seem unattainable and meaningless. Recovery consists of a chain of responses: coping with cravings; gaining self-respect; overcoming inhibitions; learning to relax; being more assertive; communicating; learning new skills; finding better accommodation; finding a job. All are prerequisites to the final step and each, as learned, must be directly and continually reinforced. At the end he will make his own decision about total abstention. Until then, and to enable us to work towards that end, I will endeavour to see he keeps to his part of the contract.

A new pattern

The probation order was made and Brian settled to a routine of visiting the office three times a week. He still needed time to quietly adjust to a new way of life. After a further month, supervision of antabuse was transferred to the hostel, and would in future be taken daily. This is administratively more convenient to the hostel and reduces the dose. It also freed him from coming to the office so frequently. We had a firm appointment weekly, and an optional appointment when I would be available on another day. Transferring the antabuse supervision brings in another person to care about his recovery and well-being. It is agreed with the hostel nurse in Brian's presence that, should he miss at any time, I or the doctor will be informed within 24 hours.

Positive depression

A month later – month three of sobriety – came the depression. Nothing was going right. Brian was fed up with the hostel, the weather was miserable, he had lost £10 – I later learned this was gambling. He was bored and felt there was little point in going on. We were able to look at his depression in a positive way. It is good that he is feeling depressed! It's an indication that he is ready and wanting to change his present life style, and has been seeking alternatives to drinking, although perhaps gambling – now revealed – was not appropriate.

We set about registration with the local housing authority, and applying to a local single homeless project. We considered work, and the attributes he has to offer an employer. He is clean and tidy, mature, reliable, and a good time-keeper. His previous experience has been mainly in the catering and retail food trade. The problem will be references from previous employers – none over the past seven years. So it may be better to start off on a casual basis, as a kitchen porter or something similar, which may lead to something more regular.

I am now getting Brian actively involved in thinking about and arranging his future. He chose the time to do this, not me. He needed a little prodding, as his lethargy inhibited motivation.

Maintaining momentum

The next few months progressed steadily. There was a noticeable growth in his confidence and ability to negotiate with other agencies. Through this, an offer of a one bedroomed council flat came quickly. Local voluntary services were able to help with furnishing and transport, and Brian moved into his own home, the first in twenty years. The transition was not easy. His home was many miles away, housing benefit had to be organised, and supplementary benefit changed. He had to re-learn self-catering and budgeting, sit alone of an evening listening to a small transistor radio, instead of watching television and being with many other people. There was now a change in his coping responses, and continuity of antabuse supervision is again paramount during this transition. Brian coped extremely well, but the journey to my office again three times weekly was a drain upon his time and finances. The doctor had previously reduced the antabuse dosage so after a month, when Brian felt far more settled, we agreed that he should administer his own medication twice weekly Mondays and Wednesday, and I would see him each Friday.

I am now shifting the responsibility for self determination to Brian. He appears to have the right attitude. He is very conscious of his good fortune, and is anxious not to lose his home.

Setback

It was Christmas time when Brian relapsed. He had telephoned to say he was ill with flu and could not see me on the Friday, and we rearranged the appointment for Monday. On that day I was informed by other clients that Brian has been seen in the West End very much the worse for drink and in a filthy state. Tomorrow is Christmas Day! One of his friends still living in the hostel offered to visit Brian over Christmas to which I agreed. Brian turned up after Christmas dejected, remorseful but sober. He had been helping an elderly neighbour with moving her furniture, who then offered him a brandy. He thought 'I've had no antabuse for the last few days because of my cold'; 'It's alright now I can handle one small drink'. He did have a mild reaction – sweating and facial reddening – but this faded fairly quickly. Within hours he had bought and consumed a half bottle of brandy, and remembers little else until his friend called on Christmas Day.

Brian experienced a difficult withdrawal, and came back to the hostel for the rest of the holiday. He was determined not to lose what had been gained. I enquired as to whether he had been picked up by the police. He said 'I know I could be in trouble with you already, but to break the probation order as well would mean the end'. Despite his state, he said 'I never once forgot I was on probation'. Brian was congratulated, he had acknowledged a relapse, and for the first time ever had stopped of his own accord. We have been able to use the experience of that relapse quite positively and he has identified his own ultimate goal of total abstention.

Relapse is always a difficult situation, and needs careful and tolerant handling. Detoxification is sometimes necessary. A return to Court for breach is not necessarily the end. A further remand on bail for reassessment and a fresh start sometimes works. It is essential not to abandon him at the time of his greatest need.

Brian still attends my office regularly; there was no need to alter the pattern. His own response to the relapse was positive and encouraging and perhaps in this case it was necessary for him to test himself. He is now working regularly, expanding his social life, and finding it very easy to say 'I don't take alcohol, thank you, it doesn't agree with me'!

An ethical adjunct to social work?

Brian's case is not typical, but just one example of sixty individuals whose own initial common need is sobriety in the community long enough to learn other ways of living without alcohol which to them is poison. The effectiveness of the treatment is systematically monitored with respect to his compliance, use of alcohol or other drugs, improvement in social relations, and employment status. The duration of antabuse therapy is individualised and is determined by the client's response to treatment as well as by the development of any adverse clinical effects. The goal of treatment is to allow him to establish resources necessary for maintenance of control after antabuse has stopped. Supervised antabuse therapy does not have a primary role in the rehabilitation of the chronic alcoholics, but rather as an adjunct to behavioural and social therapies directed at the correction of alcohol related problems.

In April 1984 the Standing Committee of the General Medical Council considered the use of Disulfiram (Antabuse) in treating patients who are subject to probation orders. The Committee stated:

> They appreciate the difficulties faced by a doctor who finds himself treating a patient who has been required by a Court to undergo a certain regime of treatment, especially where the doctor himself has reservations about the use of the particular drug in question. The Committee nevertheless took the view that it would not be unethical for a doctor to go ahead with such treatment provided he could be satisfied that the prospective patient's valid and informed consent had been obtained before the probation order had been made. It was pointed out by a member of the Committee, who is himself a magistrate, that he would expect discussion to have taken place between the offender, the Probation Service, and the doctor concerned before the probation order was made, so that the offender could give the undertakings requested of him in the full knowledge of what they would involve.

> From John Smith 'Antabuse of probation: an example in practice', Probation Journal, *33(1), 1986, pp. 13–16.*

References

Brewer, C. (1982) 'Probation with Antabuse: a new chance for alcoholic offenders?' *Probation Journal* 29(1): 10–14.

50 Increasing the use of probation (1986)

Members of the Demonstration Unit, Inner London Probation Service, 1981–84

It is often difficult to pinpoint precisely when a mood or atmosphere changes in the development of any social policy, but that such changes occur is well illustrated by contrasting discussion of the use of the probation order in the Morison Report (Home Office, Scottish Home Department 1962), and the Statement issued by the Central Council of Probation & After-Care Committees in November 1978. From comparative equanimity, the mood had altered to one of grave anxiety. Perhaps the most immediate cause was the publication of figures for use of probation in 1976 and 1977. It certainly appears to have been these that gave rise to the General Council's alarm. However, also of importance was the ending of the IMPACT experiment (Folkard *et al.* 1976) with results which appeared to chime with the mood of the time. Martinson (1974) in the USA, and Brody (1976) in this country, had raised serious questions as to the efficacy of 'treatment' when considering reconviction rates. The expansion of the Service over the period, with a steady influx of younger officers, often with university backgrounds, seems, additionally, to have played its part, to judge from the frequent disparaging references to them in the literature.

Today, following the work of McWilliams (1981), Roberts and Roberts (1982), and particularly Bottoms (1983), it is clearer how the probation order may have suffered a decline for reasons that had little to do directly with the youth and education of its practitioners. Even in 1981, it was apparent that much of the alarm ran counter to our experience as ordinary field officers. What was conspicuously lacking in all the proposals for new kinds of order and officer was any genuine test of the utility and popularity of the probation order based on something more than inference from criminal statistics, or the odd dyspeptic remark of a disgruntled judge. What might provide more convincing evidence would be an attempt to increase the recommendation made for probation orders with specified groups of offenders and measure the concordance rate.

Finding the new orders

When the Demonstration Unit opened, the opportunity to mount such an exercise was uniquely available. In the previous year, ILPS (Inner London Probation Service) had undertaken the largest survey of SERs (Social Enquiry Reports) (Stanley and Murphy 1984) to date. From the assembled data, it was possible to see which types of offender attracted requests for reports by the type of offence they had committed, and the number of previous convictions they had amassed, at each of the three Magistrates Courts covered by the unit: Thames, Old Street, and Highbury Corner. The survey also gave information on the concordance rate for recommendations for probation, as well as other outcomes. It was, therefore, possible to select groups of offenders who either had a low recommendation rate for probation, or low concordance rate for such recommendations as were made. Following further survey work of our own to confirm these initial findings, we selected offenders charged with burglary and TDA (Take and Drive Away), who had two or more previous convictions, as our target groups.

Over an eighteen-month period, the officers at the unit took all reports requested on these offenders appearing at the three Magistrates Courts, living in the London Boroughs of Islington, Hackney and Tower Hamlets, who were not currently the subject of supervision by the Service. In each case, working within normal professional boundaries, we attempted to make a recommendation for probation wherever possible. No special conditions were asked for, nor did we lobby magistrates, except in one particular respect to explain why disqualification would be a hindrance in the case of TDA offenders.

The principal strategy employed was to place more emphasis than we believe we had done formerly in our SERs on discussion of the offence, and how it was hoped the probation order could be employed to widen the range of choice about offending for the client. The result of these efforts can be seen by comparing the tables. An increased recommendation rate for TDA offenders results in some fall in concordance, but a large increase in actual orders. For burglary offenders, an increase in recommendations brought about both an increase in orders and in concordance rate.

The importance of recommendations

The figures suggest that there has been no loss of confidence in the probation order by magistrates. Nevertheless, not every offender attracted a probation recommendation, *nor* was every recommendation accepted. We were keen to explore whether there were any constant patterns in the factors that appeared to be associated with the recommendation of probation and its acceptance. A major part of our preliminary work had, therefore, involved establishing a data collection format that offered the possibility of standardising the information we acquired on each offender so that a large number of variables could be handled in computer analysis. The data handling is a story in its own right, which is detailed in a separate section of our final report. The procedures adopted allowed us to employ predictive attribute analysis (Simon 1971) to examine the patterns of recommendation and sentencing.

Perhaps the most important finding to emerge from this stage of the investigation was the power of the recommendation for probation. While few others are made these days without a recommendation, what is perhaps less well recognised is that a recommendation for probation can override regularly and consistently any combination of adverse criminal record variables. Given that power, it was naturally intriguing to explore further what led the probation officer to make the recommendation initially. The officer's overall impression of the offender proved the most compelling factor. Where a favourable impression was formed, this apparently subjective assessment was revealed in further analysis to be composed of the defendant possessing a concerned attitude to the offence, and being perceived as having little likelihood of re-offending. By contrast, an unfavourable impression and, hence, low recommendation rate, was most likely to follow the defendant having a negative attitude to the offence, and making only one contact with their probation officer during the remand period.

Space only allows for a brief synopsis of the analytical work undertaken on the decision-making of both officers and the court, and a full account appears in the final report. Also covered in the document is a lengthy descriptive account of the burglary and TDA offenders from which a picture emerges that, we believe, most officers would find consistent with their own younger persistent offenders.

Working with offenders

We worked with the offenders we had on probation in basically traditional ways through the medium of individual counselling and focused group work. A driver retraining scheme was the group work format developed for the TDA clients. It concentrated on encouraging them to take the steps towards passing their driving test. A full account of the approach is to be published shortly (Harraway 1986).

For the burglary offenders, group work was not so prominently employed, but where it was, we drew heavily upon the inspiration of Priestley *et al.* (1978), with modifications and developments of our own.

How effective were the orders?

During the final part of the project, we concentrated on giving an account of how those on probation had progressed during the course of their orders, and the manner in which the orders ended. We attempted two broad types of evaluation, one concentrating on changes in the social circumstances of the probationers, and the other, to which we devoted the most time, on re-offending. We had collected as full a picture as we could of our clients' previous offending histories, as well as of their present offence. We were, in consequence, able to consider the length of time between convictions, the seriousness of any reconvictions, *vis-à-vis* the original offence, as well as whether reconviction brought the case to an end.

Table 1 ILPS SER Survey 1980 (N.E. Division Magistrates' Courts only)

Offence Type	Total SERs	Total Prob. Recom.	Rec. Rate	Total POs Made	Concordance Rate
TDA	70	17	24%	17	100%
Burglary	76	20	26%	10	50%

Table 2 Demonstration Unit Referrals 1982–1983

Offence Type	Total SERs	Total Prob. Recom.	Rec. Rate	Total POs Made	Concordance Rate
TDA	104	75	72%	58	77%
Burglary	137	79	58%	58	73%

(A further 28 TDA referrals, resulting in 22 Probation Orders, were seen at the unit, but are excluded from these figures as they possessed less than two previous convictions.)

As one of our objectives was to illustrate the holding effects of the probation order, there was natural concern to see on how many occasions reconviction ended the order. In remarkably few cases where reconviction occurred once, or more than once, were the orders terminated, suggesting that sentencers are not expecting miracles from the probation order. Rather, it appeared that magistrates were willing to support a serious effort to develop an understanding in the probationer of his offending behaviour, and how he might begin to change it for himself.

The principal difficulty, however, with the final stage of our project, was that of finding a true comparison group against which to judge the performance of our clients. In the end, we had to be content with a series of best estimates drawn from existing prison statistics, and the work of Phillpotts and Lancucki (1979) and Farrington and Morris (1983). A further procedure we were able to adopt was that of using the probationers as their own reference group. The technical difficulty of finding these comparisons must cast doubt on the validity of past attempts to estimate the effectiveness of probation, and reinforces once more how easily we have allowed ourselves as a Service to be deluded into believing that we make no contribution to the prevention of offending.

Our analysis suggested that positive improvements in accommodation and employment were associated strongly with not re-offending, while those who did re-offend had more factors associated with the disruption of their family in their backgrounds. These outcomes will not be surprising, we suspect, to most colleagues. The rate of reconviction for our 16 probationers with two or more previous convictions during the two years following the making of their orders was 59%, or 69 clients. Our best estimate of the expected rate of reconviction for this period had been 65% to 70%. When we adopted the procedure of using the probationers as their own controls, we found 100 of them had re-offended in the two years prior to their order. In the succeeding two years, 60 or 55% of them re-offended, a figure that compares favourably with 65% in the Farrington and Morris study. A much fuller account of our findings is to be found in the final report.

Conclusion

We feel that our work goes some way towards reaffirming that the traditional probation order can yield results that are no worse, and are often rather better, than those to be expected from other disposals. Of course, it will be argued that we worked in special circumstances, but perhaps the privilege of being allowed to concentrate on probation orders is one that should be demanded by more officers, if we wish to see the ordinary order continue to make a significant contribution to reducing the prison population.

From Members of the Demonstration Unit, 1981–84, Inner London Probation Service, 'Increasing the use of probation', Probation Journal, *33(3), 1986, pp. 87–90.*

References

Bottoms, A.E. (1983) 'Neglected features of contemporary penal systems', in D. Garland and P. Young (eds.) *The Power to Punish*. London, Heineman Educational, pp. 166–202.

Brody, S.R. (1976) *The Effectiveness of Sentencing: a review of the literature*. Home Office Research Study 35. London, HMSO.

Central Council of Probation and After-Care Committees (1978) 'The diminished use of the Probation Order.' *NAPO Newsletter* 164.

Farrington, D.R. and Morris, A.M. (1983) 'Sex, Sentencing and Reconviction.' *British Journal of Criminology, 23*(3): 229–248.

Folkard, M.S., Smith, D.E. and Smith, D.D. (1976) *IMPACT Volume 2: the results of the experiment.* Home Office Research Study 36. London, HMSO.

Harraway, P. (1986) 'The Driver Retraining Scheme: towards managing autocrime', in J. Pointing (ed.) *Alternatives to Custody.* Oxford, Blackwell, pp. 55–70.

Home Office, Scottish Home Department (1962) *Report of the Departmental Committee on the Probation Service* Cmnd. 1650. Chair: R. P. Morison, QC. London, HMSO.

Martinson, R. (1974) 'What Works? Questions and answers about prison reform.' *The Public Interest* 35 (Spring): 22–54.

McWilliams, W. (1981) 'The Probation Officer at Court: from friend to acquaintance.' *Howard Journal* 20(2): 97–116.

Phillpotts, G.J. and Lancucki, L.B. (1979) *Previous Convictions, Sentence and Reconviction: a statistical sample of 5,000 offenders convicted in January 1971.* Home Office Research Study 53. London, HMSO.

Priestley, P., McGuire, J., Flegg, D., Hemsley, V. and Welham, D. (1978) *Social Skills and Personal Problem Solving: a handbook of methods.* London, Tavistock.

Roberts, J. and Roberts, C. (1982) 'Social Enquiry Reports and Sentencing.' *Howard Journal* 21(2): 76–93.

Simon, F.H. (1971) *Prediction Methods in Criminology.* Home Office Research Study 7. London, HMSO.

Stanley, S.J. and Murphy, M.B. (1984) *Survey of Social Enquiry Reports.* London, Inner London Probation Service.

51 Using a 'Risk of Custody' scale (1987)

David Bale

A recent development within the Probation Service has been the use in some Areas of risk scales to illuminate and inform probation practice. For several years a routine assessment of the risk of custody (ROC) has been made by Cheshire Probation whenever a SIR has been prepared. This ROC score is based partly on the reporting probation officer's assessment of the gravity and emotive nature of the offence, and partly on basic facts concerning the offender's criminal history. Calculating the ROC score is thought to have increased awareness of custodial risk in Cheshire and to have encouraged suitable recommendations for non-custodial alternatives.

Other places where risk scales have been used in the Probation Service include Leicestershire, where interesting work has been done by Steve Heygate and others in relating probation intervention to the risks and the needs associated with particular groups of offenders, and throughout the Midlands RSD area, where tariff scores devised by Colin Roberts have been used in training exercises that relate probation officer recommendations to court sentencing.

Simplistic techniques

There is an evident need for some revision of the indices of quality control used within the Probation Service. The only criteria employed by the Home Office in statistical returns are *previous custody* and *no previous convictions*. Neither criterion is a very effective predictor of custody. A survey of recent Social Inquiry Reports (SIRs) in Cambridgeshire showed that for 44% of those receiving custody, it was a first sentence of imprisonment. Previous custody can therefore hardly be regarded as a very useful criterion for prediction. Similarly although only 8.4% of those with no previous convictions were imprisoned, only a minority of those with previous convictions (35.2%) received custody anyway. In other words, if *no previous convictions* were to be used as the sole criterion for predicting custody (i.e. *no previous convictions* is taken to indicate a non-custodial sentence and *some previous convictions* to indicate a custodial sentence), the predictions would be wrong more often than they would be right.

Nevertheless, simple indices of this kind have quite frequently been used to evaluate or justify the effectiveness of Probation schemes. Even a cursory glance at the statistics involved will show that considerable caution must therefore be exercised if extravagant claims are not to be made about the effectiveness and quality of alternative to custody schemes. What has been lacking is an effective tool of measurement by which schemes can be assessed. However, to the extent that even with crude and inadequate tools an attempt has been made to base good practice on consistent and objective criteria, it seems to me that gate-keeping and evaluation of this kind is an improvement on a totally intuitive approach to probation practice – if only because there is a visible basis on which our work can be assessed and appreciated by others, including the sentencers and politicians whose co-operation we ultimately require if we are to work effectively with large numbers of high tariff offenders. The drawback in using any simple evaluative technique is that it simply will not work very well. Consideration of either the offence or the offender in isolation will give a distorted indication of the genuine risk of custody faced. Combining data related to the offence with data related to the offender normally gives a much more reliable indication but it can also give rise to practical and statistical difficulties. These can easily dissuade probation officers from diving too deeply into what are still largely uncharted waters.

Probation Officer intuition

By a fortunate coincidence of my own personal interests and those of my local probation management team, I have recently been able to spend a substantial amount of time tackling the problem of developing a reliable risk of custody scale. In a survey of 862 cases (all the cases in which an SIR was prepared in Cambridgeshire over a six month period), probation officers' predictions about the likelihood of custody were compared with predictions based on three risk scales or tariffs. Contrary to the expectations of some academics I have spoken to, probation officers proved to be good predictors of custody, especially when asked simply to say whether or not they thought a case would result in custody. They were right in respect of 75% of the cases examined. Predictions based upon their estimate of the percentage risk of custody apparent in each case proved to be slightly less accurate with 72% predicted correctly.

Of the three risk scales or tariffs tested only one matched the performance of the probation officers' predictions. This scale (which was 73% accurate) incorporated as a feature a gravity of offence table which placed offences into five categories of seriousness. The full table gives a fairly comprehensive breakdown of offences of varying degrees of seriousness, but [Table 1] gives a sample.

For each case, this scale gave an overall risk of custody assessment based both on the gravity of the offence table and on a criminal history score. The criminal history score was derived largely from information obtained from the list of previous convictions.

Table 1

Gravity Category	Examples of Typical Offences
1	Drunk/Disorderly, Theft under £50
2	ABH, Theft under £200, TWOC
3	Burglary (less £1,000), GBH
4	Burglary of dwelling house, Arson
5	Rape, Robbery, Manslaughter

A fresh start

I analysed the factors that made up the criminal history score and it was apparent that although this scale performed better than the other scales tested, the association between some of the variables included in the scale and the incidence of custody was not found to be especially strong. For this reason, I retained the basic structure of the scale that incorporated the gravity of offence table and, employing a fairly sophisticated log linear model under the guidance of an expert statistician, worked out not only the best variables and the optimum number of variables to include in a new scale but also the best cut-off levels at which to allocate scoring points in relation to the chosen variables.

The accuracy of this newly developed scale – The Cambridgeshire Risk of Custody Scale Version 2 – worked out at 81%. This represents a significant advance on the 72–75% level of accuracy achieved by probation officers' predictions about their own cases and I feel this justifies consideration of the uses to which this scale can be put. I should say at this point that the Cambridge Risk of Custody Scale gives each offender a score between 0% and 100% which represents the risk of custody to the nearest 5%.

It gives two sets of readings: a basic score that gives an indication of an equitable sentence in each case and an adjusted score which takes into account various prejudicial factors that also seem to affect sentencing decisions.

The Scale in action

Thus, a client with no custodial experience but with five previous convictions, three of which had been in the past two years, would have a basic risk score of 5% if he appeared in court on only a gravity category 1 charge. If, however, he appeared in court on more serious charges, his basic risk score would increase to 20% (gravity 2), 55% (gravity 3) or 95% (gravity 4 or 5). The prejudicial factors included in the adjusted score, relate to the type of sentencing court and the client's sex and remand status. Therefore, should the defendant described above be male and appearing on bail before the Crown rather than the Magistrates Court, his risk of custody would increase to 50% (gravity 1), 55% (gravity 2), 80% (gravity 3) and 100% (gravity 4 or 5). The risk scores for women work out about 10% lower than those for men. Finally, defendants of either sex who are remanded in custody are considered to be about 20% more likely to be sentenced to imprisonment by virtue of their remand status alone.

I would suggest that there are at least eight ways in which either a basic or an adjusted version of the Cambridgeshire Risk of Custody Scale might be usefully employed in the Probation Service, although I can see that it is possible to think of other more controversial uses to which the scale might also be put. It could for example be used by managers within the Service to evaluate officers' performance, or else by sentencers to enforce a policy of tariff sentencing on the lines already established in places such as California and Minnesota.

1. Expose and quantify discrimination within the Criminal Justice System

There are some sections of the population who appear to receive rough justice in court and to be more frequently imprisoned than others in the community. Examples could possibly include ethnic minorities, homeless persons, the financially disadvantaged, the unemployed and in some situations, women. Instead of looking simply at the number or proportion of disadvantaged groups within society who are being imprisoned, attempts to match a group of these subjects with a standard control group by means of basic risk score readings can ensure that criticisms that are often

Table 2 Cambridgeshire Risk of Custody Scale – Version 2

---

1. Look up principal offence on GRAVITY TABLE overleaf, circle, and enter **GRAVITY SCORE**_____

2. Calculate CRIMINAL HISTORY SCORE

Circle relevant scores

1–3 previous convictions	1
4–7 previous convictions	2
8 or more previous convictions	3
1–2 convictions in past 2 years	1
3 or more convictions in past 2 years	2
1–6 previous custodial sentences	1
7 or more previous custodial sentences	2
Currently on suspended sentence for a similar type of offence	3
Currently on suspended sentence for a dissimilar type of offence	1
CS imposed in past 12 months	1
1–3 additional imprisonable offences (not TICs)	1
4 or more additional imprisonable offences (not TICs)	3

CRIMINAL HISTORY SCORE_____
(add circled scores)

3. Look up GRAVITY SCORE and CRIMINAL HISTORY SCORE on the table below and read off **BASIC RISK SCORE**

CRIMINAL HISTORY SCORE

	0	1	2	3	4	5	6	7	8	9	10+
1	0%	0%	5%	5%	5%	10%	25%	25%	65%	65%	75%
2	0%	10%	10%	15%	20%	40%	40%	60%	85%	85%	85%
3	0%	15%	35%	35%	55%	75%	75%	75%	85%	85%	85%
4	45%	45%	60%	75%	95%	95%	100%	100%	100%	100%	100%
5	80%	80%	95%	95%	95%	95%	100%	100%	100%	100%	100%

Enter **BASIC RISK SCORE**_____%

4. Calculate ADJUSTED SCORE

If Crown Court, add 45 or
If Juvenile Court subtract 10_____
If female, subtract 20

If on bail throughout, subtract 10_____
If in custody, add 30 or
If bailed following custody, add 10____
Enter **ADJUSTED SCORE**_____

5. Look up ADJUSTED SCORE on the table below and read off final **RISK SCORE**

ADJUSTED SCORE

minus						10–	20–			40–	50–			70–	80–	90–	100–	110–	120–	130+
20	15	10	5	0	5	15	25	30	35	45	55	60	65	75	85	95	105	115	125	
0	5	10	15	20	25	30	35	40	45	50	55	60	65	70	75	80	85	90	95	100

RISK SCORE

Enter final **RISK SCORE**_____

6. If RISK SCORE is 70% or more, there is a high risk of custody of 6 months or more. Consider the offender for Probation 48 assessment.

levelled at unmatched comparison studies can no longer be made. For example, if the examples are matched for comparability, it could no longer be alleged that blacks have a disproportionately large representation in our prisons solely because they commit a disproportionate share of the more serious offences. Similar matching exercises may reveal incontrovertible evidence of injustice in relation to other disadvantaged groups.

2. Offer a second opinion to probation officers preparing Social Inquiry Reports

Since prediction about court decisions based upon adjusted risk of custody scores have been shown to be rather more accurate than those based on probation officers' judgements, it would seem sensible for probation officers to look at the risk of custody scale for a second opinion when making recommendations to the court. Calculation of the risk of custody score may therefore perform much the same function as consulting with a colleague about the likely outcome of a particular case – with the added advantage that the risk scale is always available for immediate consultation and has, I believe now, established a good track record for reliability and accuracy in its predictions.

In advocating use of the scale in this way, I would in no way wish to detract from probation officers' autonomy or to undermine their right to put forward their own recommendations to the court regardless of what the risk scale may say. Indeed I suspect that the *best* probation officers will always out-perform a fixed scale, even if I have demonstrated that the fixed scale can outperform the *average* officer.

3. Act as a gate-keeping device and to monitor the quality of orders

A frequent complaint about so called 'alternative to custody' schemes is that they simply move offenders up tariff and make little real impact on the numbers being imprisoned. The use of adjusted risk scores to measure the realistic likelihood of custody could do much to put alternatives to custody schemes on a sound footing. Moreover the scores can be used as fixed units of measurement whereby schemes can be compared and monitored effectively.

In Cambridgeshire, introduction of a probation order with a Section 4B requirement has coincided with the routine assessment of risk of custody scores for all cases on which an SIR is prepared. As a result, entrance to the 4B Unit has generally been restricted at present to those scoring 70% or more on the adjusted risk scale. My research showed that a substantial majority of cases that scored over 70% received sentences of imprisonment of six months or more.

4. Use as a marketing device to 'sell' the Probation Service to sentencers, politicians and the public

If the Probation Service is to have an important role in providing custodial sentencing options that can enable more offenders to be diverted from custody, it is necessary to convince those outside the Service of the contribution we can make. Clearly our case will seem more convincing if we can produce quantifiable evidence of the work we are doing. If we are increasingly working with higher tariff offenders, it would be helpful to be able to demonstrate this reality. Reference to basic or adjusted risk of custody scores could assist in this task. It could also provide some hard evidence in support of claims for better funding in the Probation Service and to improve pay, status and conditions of service for probation officers.

5. Provide a sound basis for the fairer allocation of resources within the Probation Service

Although risk of custody is only one of the yardsticks by which the Service can measure the appropriateness and quality of its work, used in conjunction with other yardsticks, such as the rates of successful order completion, a fair assessment may be made of the effectiveness of different aspects of the Service's work. More resources may need to be channelled to disadvantaged areas, teams or projects or else to those who have demonstrated an ability to work effectively with the resources allocated to them. Further local adjustments can be made to the adjusted risk scores to allow for harsher than average local sentencing practices. Additional resources might then be allocated to those working in such areas.

6. Monitor sentencing practice and trends

Using average risk of custody scores for different sentencing outcomes, it is possible to make comparisons between the relative harshness or leniency of particular courts. By sharing this information with the Probation Liaison Committees of 'harsh' courts, or with a 'tough' Crown Court judge, it may be possible to persuade sentencers to adopt a more enlightened approach to sentencing. Similarly by making comparisons of sentencing practice over a period of time, long-term sentencing trends may be clearly detected.

Establishing the existence of long-term trends could encourage the formulation of an appropriate sentencing policy for the future. Similarly, there could be early detection of increased use of custody, not by counting the number of custodial sentences given (usually a year or two after the sentences have actually been imposed), but by checking the adjusted risk score whenever custody is given. In this way a sentencing trend can be detected early enough to react to it in a positive way and long before local or national statistics are published.

7. Inform case discussion, supervision and training

Reference to a fixed scale of measurement could add a new dimension to training exercises and considerably assist the discussion of cases or other aspects of probation work at all levels within the Service.

8. Use in working directly with clients

Last but by no means least of the suggested uses to which a risk of custody scale might be put is to share risk scale assessments with clients. Often our clients have a very good understanding of the odds against their retaining their liberty when they appear in court. At other times they display a totally unrealistic understanding of the risk of custody that they may face when appearing in court. The risk scale offers an objective assessment that could form the basis of what might be termed 'reality training'. This could not only encourage clients to become more realistic about the risk of custody associated with their own pattern of offending behaviour, but it could also lead them to a better appreciation of situations in which a non-custodial sentence has clearly been imposed only as a genuine alternative to custody and this might lead to better appreciation also of the serious consequences that breaching that sentence might have.

From David Bale 'Using a "Risk of custody" scale', Probation Journal, 34(4), 1987, pp. 127–131.

52 Looking backwards to the future?

Teamwork innovation (1989)

David Millard

First and foremost, I remember sharing – sharing space, sharing clients, sharing work, sharing responsibility, sharing authority. I was the senior, of course, so I have to acknowledge that my memories may be somewhat fanciful, but I don't remember being much of a senior. I didn't really have to be. Shared professionalism, and the respect that we had for each others' ability and commitment, meant that questions of authority could be resolved through argument and debate without being stymied by the kind of personal antipathies that have to be contained by authoritarian decision making.

The sharing itself grew naturally from this mutual respect for each others' work. Moreover, we got on well together; we enjoyed meeting each other at work (!) and although we did not socialise a great deal together away from the office, we were nevertheless interested and caring about each other's lives. This kind of climate within a team cannot be created artificially, and no amount of managerial head scratching can bring it into being. But it does sometimes emerge through the natural chemistry of human beings interacting with each other, and if it is recognised and nurtured, then creativity and enthusiasm will blossom.

Escaping the strait-jacket

If that sounds nebulous and intangible, I have mentioned it first, because without it I don't think that anything would have happened at Shelton at all. But because it did exist, we were able to use it as a foundation on which to build. At Shelton we were a single team office with a clearly defined geographical patch, and we served one court. We had moved to a single team office from a city centre multi-team office, and we took with us a well defined traditional pattern of one to one working. In retrospect, I think that many of us were beginning to be dissatisfied with the rigid, strait-jacketing effects of working in this way, but at the time we had no clearly thought out alternatives.

These alternatives began to emerge over a period, and it is the way in which this happened that illustrates the importance of the relationships that we had with each other. For example, it began to become apparent that one colleague was persistently seeing all of his clients in the staff room! Whenever any of us went in for a quick brew, there he was with yet another client – or maybe two – drinking tea and rattling away as though they were friends! When challenged, he said he thought they *were* friends, and in any case he was fed up with all this intensity behind closed doors; it wasn't getting us anywhere, and it wasn't relevant to the practical problems that his clients faced. In my memory this lives on as an important moment, and it is because we were able to discuss the implications of what he was doing in an open and undefended way, that we were able to learn from that example and adapt it to all our needs.

We discovered that we'd got a whole building that wasn't being used for most of the time, and a high proportion of clients who hadn't got anything to do or anywhere to go for most of the day; we discovered that we didn't actually need all that sacrosanct private office space very much at all; and we certainly didn't need a sacrosanct staff room. And as a result of these small beginnings we began to develop a notion of the probation office as a resource building which could be used in a variety of ways for most of the day; and a notion of the probation team as the providers and facilitators of a network of groups and other facilities. At various times there were client groups of every kind, and throughout the day there were groups at work in the building, creating within the environment of the office itself the sense of a little community of people (albeit often shifting and shiftless), discovering together some sense of common purpose and solidarity.

Coping with chaos

None of this meant the end of traditional probation work. Every client was allocated to an officer in just the same way as had always been the case, but no longer was this the end of the story. As a consequence of the various activities that were going on, each client would in due course have the opportunity of joining in one of the constellation of group activities that were being developed within the team. At various times there were drop-in groups; a pre-school playgroup; a formal discussion group; a group that worked on the production of an office news sheet; an art group; a group of officers and users which met and discussed office rules and shared tasks. From time to time there were outings, projects of various kinds and continually the clients had the opportunity of getting to know each other and the officers in (at that time) radically new and unexpected ways.

This could be very exhausting of course. Often we were surrounded by clients, sharing all our facilities with them, from the moment when we opened in the morning to the moment when we closed at night. This placed a very high premium on internal group discipline and commitment in relation to duty rotas, and the responsibility for different groups, and the recording of what was going on. And I could not pretend that we solved all our problems. Often the experience was one of being in the middle of unstructured chaos. But unstructured chaos is the nature of many people's lives and I believe that if we are to understand it all, we must sometimes be ready to live it a bit as well.

Principles of service

Since working at Shelton, I've attended any number of meetings and seminars about the more efficient organisation and targeting of the Service's work. All sorts of ideas are tried and experimented with, they last for a while and are discarded. But I think that there are some important things that we learnt which do need to be restated. The first of these is the important principle of 'continuity of care'. Over the years I have been dismayed by the number of re-structuring schemes which have depended for their success on the endless transferability of clients from officer to officer in the interests of a more 'efficient' service. And yet one thing that I believe that we learnt at

Shelton is that however many additional facilities are created, most clients want and need to have one particular personal officer whom they can identify as 'theirs'. Indeed, if they don't have such an officer in whom they can place real confidence and trust, the likelihood is that they will not take real advantage of the other services on offer anyway.

The second principle has got to be 'simplicity of administration'. Sometimes it seems as though the Probation Service is unable to resist the temptation to over-complicate things and to introduce systems of work allocation which demand so much time to monitor and review that the clients themselves become invisible beneath the vast machinery required to keep the miniscule engine running. My own recommendation would be that any proposal for innovation in client supervision in the Service should be tested against these two questions – Does it provide for continuity of care? Is it administratively simple? If the answer to either of these questions is 'no', the chances are it won't work.

Relevance today

Finally, is there anything that we learnt and tested out during those days in the seventies which is relevant to us now? Yes, I think there is. When we opened the doors to our office, and encouraged people to make ever-increasing use of it, we discovered that the people who came most frequently and enthusiastically were the poorest, least able, and least articulate people, frequently lost and bereft with no sense of community and no sense of real aspiration for the future. They used us and each other, sometimes as a haven and refuge, sometimes as a testing out place for the most disturbing aspects of their own personalities, sometimes as a jumping off point for a new foray into a world which all too often (even then) they found harsh, oppressive, and incomprehensible. They did not come as a consequence of 'conditions', but because of what was offered, and sometimes they began to discover the possibility of a voice and a quality of life, at least temporarily, which maybe they had not known before.

I do not wish to romanticise the poor and the alienated, for to do so is to be guilty of patronage that is no better than oppression; but I believe that at a time when the Service is in fact being asked to *manage* the poor, it is worth remembering that the real task is to *empower* them. In retrospect, the work we did at Shelton wasn't that much. Lots of things have happened since then, and been done with much greater professionalism. But I do believe that our work contained some clues as to how probation officers can sometimes become the allies of the weak, rather than their managers. And if ever we needed to know how to do that, we need to know it now.

David Millard 'Looking backwards to the future?', Probation Journal, *36(1), 1989,*
pp. 18–21.

53 The rise and fall of the Kent Control Unit

A local perspective (1986)

Nigel Spencer and Pat Edwards

Perhaps it is a pity that the creation of Kent's Probation Control Unit came a little before the tabloids picked 'Laura Norder' up from the present administration and began promoting it. We leave you to devise the headlines, but certainly a field day was there to be had, with liberal, lefty probation officers condemning a way of keeping their clients out of prison. An own goal here, surely. Even the new wave, right wing social commentators just missed this – Roger Scruton, Digby Anderson, *et al.*, what could you have written! As it was, the nearest we came was also the furthest – Bruce Hugman's new look *Probation Journal* opened with a commissioned article from a *Guardian* journalist. Ann Hills went, saw, and smiled: her uncritical account of life at the centre was hardly the article NAPO wanted, nor the fanfare the *Journal* deserved.

But this was no 90 day wonder. Throughout its life the Control Unit remained at the heart of the care/control debate within the Service, a clear cut example of one way to provide alternatives to custody. From its inception, local branch members were puzzled by Kent's espousal of this controversial unit, the very name of which sounded out a challenge to the Service's traditions. It remains an enigma that the unit should have been established in a county known for its generous conditions of service, managed by a chief respected by many as liberal, sensitive and shrewd. The existence of the unit seems to contradict these qualities.

Why did it happen?

First, the unit did not just 'appear'. It was not a completely new venture – it developed out of the Close Support Unit, a joint Probation/Social Services venture akin to some of today's more intensive IT schemes. What's in a name? Quite a bit, it seems. Initially, the notion of 'close support' for juveniles did not attract the censure of local NAPO members, individually or as a branch, even though the close oversight of truanters – frequent contact with schools through the day, etc. – changed the traditional style of intervention. However, the tolerance extended was not so forthcoming when 'close support' became translated into 'control'.

Secondly, it was one of many responses to the perception that probation orders were no longer instrumental in bringing clients to the Service. Whether Home Office studies pre-empted the internal and external criticisms of the Service or the Conservative Government's stance of tougher attitudes towards law and order had more sway is difficult to determine. It seems there was a complex process of change. The introduction of day centres and community service in the early '70s resulted in an expansion of the latter at the expense of the former. Research on day centres was allowed to peter out whilst inconclusive findings regarding the original purpose of community service as an alternative to a custodial penalty led to the extension of the scheme across the country. A straightforward interpretation of this is that the day centres (as originally envisaged) represented treatment and community service punishment in the community. The 'collapse' of treatment may be acceptable to both left and right for good reasons but the ideology of rehabilitation has never flourished in a favourable climate; it came and went without real commitment from society as a whole.

In Kent, one of the original experimental counties for the development of community service, the Medway Centre first evolved as a community service enterprise for the three Medway towns. The Control Unit was developed as part of this centre and would seem to reflect a combination of the strands of influence on the Service described above. Community service provided a model of working with offenders – based on the work ethic – which was extended into the unit.

Thirdly, attention should be drawn to the considerable emphasis on innovation with which the unit was heralded. Initially, this appeared to be the most significant impetus for those developing and supporting the unit within Kent. In fact, it is our perception that innovation which led to publicity and interest was felt to be inherently good. In some respects this had the unintended effect of attracting more criticism than other, equally dubious, practices. This was clearly not the intention, but it was not the only implication that was overlooked in the initial enthusiasm.

NAPO's contribution

NAPO's first October conference was held in Bridlington, in 1981. The crisp, clear air of the North East coast contrasted with the emotionally charged atmosphere within the hall, as the association wrestled with a number of challenges, including a breakaway movement from Seniors and what many saw as a challenge to the very principle and ethos of the Service. National debate had been initiated earlier through the NEC who had instructed the Professional Committee to report back on the regime. Their paper, *Kent's Challenge to the Probation Service*, criticised both the regime at each unit – 'essentially based on a programme through which offenders are processed not because it is directly related to the personal needs or their offending, but because they are at risk of being locked up' – and rationale for the units which were 'mainly justified by a desperate search for (cheap) alternatives to ... imprisonment'. The paper also stressed the need for NAPO to develop an alternative, 'rigorous theory of probation practice'.

The AGM concurred with these sentiments and stated opposition to the units in a lengthy motion:

> This AGM opposes practices which increase the control and surveillance role of the Probation Service, and calls for changes in the law to prevent such developments. In particular, the close support probation and control unit in Kent are examples of developments which necessitate clients degrading themselves by relinquishing normal rights as citizens. This AGM believes that existing alternatives such as Day Training Centres and voluntary Day Centres have already begun the task of diverting offenders from custody. Therefore, this Association calls for the provision of extra resources for Day Centres and other alternatives at attempting to promote change for the benefit of both clients and society through willing

co-operation. Accordingly, it calls upon members not to co-operate with such practices as the close support and control unit and to inform the Association of developments in this area throughout the country.

David Sawtell's comments in a recent NAPO Newsletter express a continuing uncertainty amongst members in their attitudes to statutory conditions. Some of the arguments first heard most clearly in 1981 have become well established cornerstones. At the heart of the debate, NAPO argued that alternatives to custody should not be based on the ideas of deterrence, containment or surveillance, but on those offering offenders opportunities to develop self-control and independence.

This statement was taken by some opponents to mean a denial of those aspects of control inherent in the role of probation officer. Acknowledgement by all concerned of both the elements of care and control vested in the role has led to a more productive and sensitive debate about the way in which probation officers work with offenders. Some of this knowledge, it seems to us, is not containable within a 'rigorous theory', but the substantial contributions NAPO's policies have made bring out the structural implications of the philosophy of imprisonment and highlight methods of negotiating the power relationship between probation officers and their clients.

Meanwhile, the Unit flourished

With a steady rate of referrals, many of them direct from court, the unit grew. The strategy of 'selling' the unit hard to courts first, soft to probation officers second, seemed to have been vindicated. The unit enjoyed then, as it has done since, the backing of the local Clerk to the Court and influential judges on the local circuit. Unit staff could, and did, argue that NAPO's opposition was meaningless since most NAPO members had not been there anyway. Moreover, they said, it did not make any difference if NAPO was in favour or not, as there were only a minority in NAPO against it, and NAPO's opposition was ineffective.

Why did the Unit eventually change?

The writing was on the wall for the Control Unit from the time the Close Support Unit closed. Many had seen the later unit as something of a success – but in the end it failed on three crucial counts: it was not particularly successful at keeping people out of trouble, it cost more than Detention Centres, and thirdly, the success of the cautioning system in Medway meant there were very few referrals.

One of the most articulate champions of the unit was the Magistrates Association but they carried a sting in the tail of their arguments. They supported the unit but saw it as an inappropriate task for the Probation Service.

Professor Martin Davies set out his stall when addressing a Kent Probation Conference in April, 1982. He referred back to the years of Morison, Streatfield and Wootton, and described the emergence of two separate strands in the Service – the correctional and anti-correctional lobbies. Davies left few doubts as to where he placed Kent's brave new experiments on this map. He thought they would be the forerunners of a radical new venture to open up and empty out local prisons by providing a 'punitive, retributive and controlling facility within the community'. This Davies saw as 'the only way in the end of bringing about radical reduction in the size of the prison population', but he accepted that this proposed strategy went beyond the brief of the Probation Service. It was seen by many as a template for weekend imprisonment – then in vogue but shortly to be ditched by the Home Office.

We find it difficult to assess the impact of the *Rogers* v. *Cullen* judgement – which led to the shutdown of the Control Unit as such – and the subsequent amending legislation of the 1982 *Criminal Justice Act* which enabled the Unit to be reopened. The swift introduction of Schedule 11 orders seemed then to negate the spirit of *Rogers* v. *Cullen*. With its delineation of the need to segregate probation from imprisonment, and the introduction of a maximum order from 90 to 60 days, the Act lent credence to the notion enshrined in the judgement. It is now accepted practice that probation orders should not impose conditions alien to a non-custodial sentence.

In the unit, staffing proved problematic as it was unpopular with main grade officers. This was seen by staff within the unit as an unwillingness to work the long hours. However, more significantly, in the teams locally the unit was seen as offering a method of working with clients that was inconsistent with officers' own practice.

Finally, the unit was hoisted with its own petard. The arguments had been simple – probation orders had been dropping – courts no longer found them credible – new more controlling sentencing options would reverse the decision and cut prison numbers. Ultimately, probation officers would accept the need to change to a more controlling role because they would deflect more clients from custody.

During 1985, a Kent Probation working party, which included a NAPO representative, reviewed the function of the Medway Centre. It submitted a majority report to the Chief Officer, arguing for the retention of the centre with the abolition of the control unit, and the development of a single Day Centre programme. In examining the differences between the types of offender passing through the two units in the centre, from the statistics gathered by Kent's Research Officer, and by working party members from their own teams, confusion was apparent over different purposes and target groups in the two units. The statistics were particularly damning. They revealed no significant difference in the criminality (measured by seriousness of current offence, recent previous offences and frequency of offending) of clients sent to the control unit and day centre over a given period. On two of the three counts (excluding frequency of offending) the Day Centre clients appeared to be the more serious offenders. The essential justification for the control unit – that it was more effective than day centre provision at diverting from custody – was thus removed.

On a more positive note, during the deliberations of the working party it was noticed that the programme had slowly changed in response to comments and criticisms. Constructive relationships between clients and staff were apparent. Some of the activities (in the community) were chosen by clients. These were aspects of the unit that the working party hoped to reinforce by an emphasis on working in groups around offending behaviour.

The core of the programme was activity groups which had a philosophy in common with groupwork in the Service as practised throughout the country. This type of work needs careful scrutiny but the Medway Centre is in this respect undergoing a change in emphasis that reflects the training and resources which are now put into groupwork generally, rather than in isolation.

The present position

The control unit as such no longer exists but changing the name has not changed its character altogether. Some recommendations of the working party have been implemented, but in some cases, in a half-hearted fashion. The local branch is concerned about use of curfew, no longer an integral part of the programme but nonetheless individuals have experienced pressure to consider curfew when making referrals to the day centre. There is resistance to this from teams and some dismay at the length of the day for the first month of the programme. In effect, there are indications that it remains a more controlling programme than is generally acceptable in the county. However, the significance of these criteria has diminished and we feel that the tide has turned.

Ironically, Kent Service's current policy echoes NAPO's affirmation of the '81 AGM motion, of its belief in day training centres and voluntary day centres. Kent is now committed to developing a dual approach, with day centres offering a programme for clients subject to conditions (Section 4B) and probation centres providing a more informal regime for clients across the caseload.

In some respects, the message of the Control Unit has been the need to clarify and identify methods of working with clients in a climate of punishment/containment. The original manager of the Medway Centre was able to do this and in addition he practised the methods he preached despite criticism. Strength of purpose is needed in a Service in which liberalism frequently leads to loss of direction and purpose. NAPO and Chief Officers (reinforced by Home Office directives in the form of SNOP and currently FMI) have taken up this challenge. It remains to be seen whether it is taken seriously by middle management. The success of any coherent strategy for improving probation practice is dependent on senior probation officers' understanding and capacity to motivate teams by securing cooperation of individuals.

Day centres have had a chequered career. Kent's current policy is an attempt to achieve a balance. Across the county the Inner London DTC has had more influence than Medway. Philosophically, the unit was originally posed as being a debate between the 'middle of the road' and a small minority on the extreme left. Down, if not quite out, the Medway Centre has remained isolated, espoused by a small vociferous minority.

From Nigel Spencer and Pat Edwards, 'The rise and fall of the Kent Control Unit:
a local perspective', Probation Journal, 33(3), 1986, pp. 91–94.

54 Inner city disturbances

Lessons from Liverpool 1985 (1987)

Jeff Bowe, Linda Crawley and John Morris

Escalating tension

Although it was the events of early October 1985 in Liverpool which once again focused media attention upon 'Inner-City Riots', these events were the culmination of a gradual escalation of tensions in the Liverpool 8 area, stemming back to the summer of 1985. Probation staff working in the area were aware of this either by witnessing, or hearing of, intensive police activity, or through contact with clients/families who cited examples of what was perceived as provocative policing. Local councillors responded to this situation by convening a series of meetings at which individuals and community groups raised a variety of concerns including:

1.   The activities of unmarked OSD (operational supportive division) vehicles.
2.   Aggressive and racist behaviour by police officers.
3.   Complaints regarding victimisation following crime in the area.
4.   A lack of faith in the existing police complaints procedure.

When Merseyside CC Police Committee's Liaison Sub-Committee raised these issues with the Chief Constable, Kenneth Oxford, in June 1985, he declined to make any specific comment and instead questioned the representativeness of those who had raised the initial concerns, implying that these were minority views, not widely held in the community at large. Events in the area further escalated when, during the course of the annual summer Caribbean Carnival, a black Londoner was stabbed and later died. Intensive police enquiries led to the arrest of a local man who was subsequently released without charge. However, in an already volatile atmosphere, his detention prompted a demonstration at a local police station which at its height involved a partial occupation of the building. Later, in August four local men were arrested for affray in the fatal incident; and their weekly appearances in court attracted considerable community attention, drawing consistently large crowds from the Liverpool 8 community.

October disturbances

When the four defendants appeared at Liverpool Magistrates Court on October 1st, a large crowd assembled, and after the hearing was over a number of incidents occurred as the crowds moved away from the City Centre. Between 5 pm and 4 am the following day, disturbances occurred in the Liverpool 8 area, including the smashing of windows at a local police station, the setting alight of parked vehicles and passing traffic being forced to stop.

Policing of the area, during this period fell into two distinct phases:

1.   Between 5 pm and 6 pm, when the local superintendent dispersed gathering groups in a way broadly supported by local people.
2.   Between 6 pm and 4 am when the OSD were deployed.

It was from this phase of policing that serious allegations were later to arise from local people. These submissions were later presented by the local law centre to the Police Committee and serve to illustrate the state of tension at the time. Examples include:

'A dozen officers fighting with each other to find part of a man to hit.' (Local Vicar)
   Constant use of racist language in a goading manner by police officers.
   Police vehicles driving along pavements indiscriminately knocking people down.
   'He [the officer], put it [camera] down and began hitting the zoom lens with his baton.' (Freelance Journalist)

Clearly, such allegations are always difficult to prove beyond doubt. However, *The Observer* (7.10.85) gave some clues as to the problems that had arisen when reporting that the local superintendent had told Merseyside Police HQ that 'members of the OSD had contributed to the unrest on the streets'. When a sub-committee of the Police Committee later investigated the disturbances, it suggested that throughout the latter policing phase it would be fair to ask 'Who was in charge of operations?'

Probation issues

Both before and after the 1981 civil disturbances in Liverpool, the local Probation Team had worked in a manner which broadly conformed to the areas addressed in NAPO's 1982 *Report of the Inner-Cities Working Party*, with an emphasis on community orientation in Probation practice, as opposed to the individualisation of wide-spread structural problems. Detached work, on a community-based model, had been practised in various forms since the late 1970's, attempting to deliver a relevant social work service from an informed understanding of what were the crucial issues to the local community. Without doubt, police behaviour and racism have been two constant themes throughout this period.

Accumulated experience of working in this manner had led workers to believe that, firstly, such is the sensitivity of the Police–Community relationship, extreme caution needs to be exercised by both the Service as an organisation, and individuals working within it, in adopting strategic positions of alliance with the Police and, secondly, that to believe that working in a community-based way can have any 'pay-off' in terms of preventing civil disturbances is erroneous; such a view grossly over-estimates the influence which Probation staff can have in such matters.

In summary, the team view of Probation practice in the area was that a community-orientated social work service was the most appropriate medium by which a service could be provided to the courts and local community. Experience has further led to the conclusion that, such was the level of suspicion of the Police by local people, that to consider forming organisational links with the Police pragmatically made work tangibly more difficult, quite apart from the fact that, in such a setting, it was often impossible to justify or condone, activities of the Police force.

Management's view

Merseyside Probation Management's view of interagency links with the Police force was and remains very different from the field workers' view. Between the 1981 and 1985 disturbances, their broad stance had been that all statutory agencies had a brief to work closely together in attempting to prevent further civil disturbances and that, by greater liaison and co-ordination of services, it was possible to develop activities in the area which would divert people away from considering such behaviour. In practice, this view took a variety of forms, the key elements being:

1. Use of MSC staff in working co-operatively with the Police to generate leisure and activity interests.
2. Urging staff to participate in Police community liaison forums.
3. In the summer of 1985, the securing of special funding for a temporary project, the aim of which the CPO outlined as 'That the Probation Service would step up its efforts to assist Police in containing problems and preventing serious trouble'.

Clearly, a considerable gap in perception exists between field and management on these issues. Firstly, management's easy acceptance that the Service had a role to play in preventing disturbances was not universally shared and understood. Secondly, knowledge of the area led the field to be sceptical about forums in which management invested great importance; for example, the majority of black-community groups in Liverpool 8 boycott Police community forums due to their irrelevance. Thirdly, management's preparedness to adopt a preventative mantle entailed that, in October 1985, a mixture of permanent and MSC staff were requested to be physically deployed at the point of the disturbances, in a soft policing role.

In conclusion

As a result of these events, in July 1986 Merseyside NAPO Branch considered the evidence and concluded that neither the Service nor NAPO had developed sufficiently sensitive policy towards Police–Community relations since 1981 and that, as a result, in 1985 management had made executive decisions as to the deployment of staff, followed by statements in the media, which could only serve to alienate the Service from its community.

The Branch adopted as policy specific proposals which are currently being considered by local management:

1. While the Service will continue to have a working relationship with the Police, that should not extend to the attempted prevention or containment of civil disturbances.
2. The specific deployment of staff at the point of disorder is wholly inappropriate.

3.   The *ad hoc* allocation of resources, with a brief to prevent disorders, should be viewed with caution, and that NAPO Branch officers should be fully consulted in advance of such proposals.

4.   Consideration should be given to how staff can advise and assist those members of the community affected by such disorders.

5.   The Service should urgently develop its role in the courts in order to cater for such events.

6.   As a trade union, NAPO should campaign with others for greater police accountability to the public.

These issues are still being considered on Merseyside by management and NAPO. It is hoped that, in some small part, this article will inform practitioners facing similar dilemmas throughout the country, to assist in initiating a debate which seems likely to be with the Probation Service for the foreseeable future.

From Jeff Bowe, Linda Crawley and John Morris, 'Inner city disturbances: lessons from Liverpool 1985', Probation Journal, 34(1) 1987, pp. 10–12.

55 'Confrontative' work with sex offenders

Legitimised nonce bashing? (1990)

Michael Sheath

Over the last five years the Probation Service has made great strides in its willingness to work with sex offenders, so much so that it would seem churlish to question any of the fundamental assumptions which officers make about the nature of the problem faced and the way in which it ought to be tackled. Much of the work currently being undertaken by probation officers in this field appears to rely upon the use of structured confrontational interviews, where sex offenders are required to give an account of their offending and to have that account challenged as to its veracity. Elements of victim blaming, distorted thinking, denial and the minimising of responsibility are identified, confronted and, ultimately, changed.

The purpose of this article is to set out the short-comings of this approach and to suggest an alternative perspective. The attractions of overtly confrontational interviews, especially for male workers are manifold, and probably explain why the approach has gained in popularity so quickly. Given the often repellent nature of sexual offences and the frequently repellent nature of sexual offenders, the gut reaction of most male probation officers is to want to kick their teeth in. Sexual offenders in prison attract the 'nonce' label and perform a vital function as scapegoats. Male prisoners are able to affirm their own healthy heterosexuality by 'giving the beasts a hard time'.

There's no point in writing articles which might be seen as critical of others if you can't be critical of yourself, and I have to admit that my initial work with sex offenders was designed to give them as hard a time as possible. Since nonce bashing was denied to me, I learned the technique of the confrontational interview.

The limitations of the approach became self-evident fairly quickly, although early attempts by colleagues to suggest that there might be other ways of working were met with great anger and cries of 'you're being collusive'. I pressed on regardless.

Three scenarios

From my fairly extensive use of the confrontational interview there would appear to be fairly common routes down which such interviews might progress:

The Seduction: This is, at least overtly, the most successful. Using a variety of assumptions about how sexual offenders operate – pre-planning, masturbation, coercion and so on, we lull the offender into a belief that we know exactly what he did without him even having to tell us. The use of the seductive, hypnotic, calming voice merely requires the client to nod his assent and to wonder at our insight into his behaviour which he thought was a secret known only to himself and his victim.

The Pantomime: This occurs when the client fights back! This is a relatively rare occurrence, but leads to the most unproductive interactions along the lines of 'Oh yes you did' – 'Oh no I didn't'. At the end of the pantomime interview we consign the client to the 'unmotivated' bin or, after time, he is transformed into:

The Brainwash: The successfully brainwashed interviewee is one who can successfully repeat key phrases provided, at least initially, by his interviewers. Favourites include 'It's all my fault', 'I planned it' and 'I hurt my victim'. The brainwash interview is a tricky one for the interviewer because it is absolutely impossible to tell whether the guy is just trying to give you what he thinks you want, or whether there has been some real movement.

Each approach has its own limitations, the problem with the seduction interview being that at the end of it the worker realises that all of the effort has come from himself, the presence of the client being only of peripheral interest. If sex offenders are to change their behaviour the effort must ultimately come from them, and that process of change is inevitably going to be slow, painful and almost imperceptible. Pantomime style interviews usually end with great and unproductive anger on both sides, with the client prematurely written off as being impossible to work with.

Brainwashing interviews are potentially the most dangerous. From what we know about the personalities of convicted sex offenders, the prevalence of submissive (at least to adults) personalities is quite marked. Given this, it is entirely consistent that these clients will be anxious to confirm and to express views and sentiments which are designed to win approval. Hence, they will quickly learn to substitute their genuinely held beliefs about the world for ones which lead to that approval being given. That change will often persist for the duration of individual sessions – with a reversion to the core, deviant value system as soon as the client leaves the office.

The function of denial

Each scenario is a depressing one to contemplate unless one focuses upon the function of denial in sex offenders, and perceives it as part of a dynamic process rather than as a door which has to be kicked down.

In a paradoxical sense, the manifestation of denial in sex offenders is a good thing, in that it suggests one of two possibilities – either that the perpetrator has an internal view that what he did is wrong and that he is attempting to distance himself from it, or that he is aware of the cultural disapproval of his activities and is attempting to protect himself from that. In the first case the client will have an enormous investment in presenting a consistent image of himself as a caring, non-abusive and harmless party. Although this stance is patently false, to attempt to dismantle that image over the course of a single interview, or a series of interviews, is to risk the destruction of that perpetrator's whole personality. ('Hooray' I can hear people cry – if he tops himself then good riddance!) Unfortunately, what we know about sexual offenders is that their offending often provides an escape route, a compensatory activity in times of stress, depression and rejection. By stripping away defences so quickly and brutally we may actually recreate the conditions and life experiences which have led to the commission of offences previously.

In the second case – the 'external shame' – offenders may actually lack any internal boundaries which would prevent them from offending. By engaging with these men before their own values and views have been adequately explored we court disaster by providing them with all the right answers. Probation officers who work with men who commit offences against children are going to be asked to express views about the desirability of those men returning to homes where children are present. It is entirely conceivable that men could present themselves as 'cured' by adopting the 'correct' values of probation officers with whom they have worked.

Providing space

The difficulties I got into by operating on an overtly confrontational basis stemmed from a failure to differentiate between assessment and treatment. The flawed beauty of an approach which makes great assumptions about sex offenders and the way they operate is that it fails to recognise that every single sexual offender is unique in the way that he perceives the world, his sexuality, his victims and his responsibility. Unless we provide the offender with some space, some opportunity to set out his beliefs without immediately hammering them then we will never be able to construct a treatment programme which fits his circumstances.

By concentrating too heavily upon the offending behaviour, and by viewing a completely honest account of a deviant sexual act as a mark of success, we sidestep those issues which lie at the heart of the client's problems – their sexual orientation, self-image, sexual fantasies and belief system. An attempt to intervene in sexual offenders' behaviour whilst they are still in a state of defensiveness, and before their motivations for committing sexual offences have been adequately mapped out is at best a frustrating and nihilistic exercise and at worst a counter-productive one: we should be more concerned with concentrating upon the significance and function of denial than with attempting to prevent its manifestations. Once clients are aware that our acceptance of them is not incompatible with our abhorrence at their activities then their need to deny as a means of shoring up their self image becomes less necessary.

If a client is to make any progress in coming to terms with the fact of their having been sexually abusive, that work is likely to be stressful and painful for them to undertake; that pain is an anticipated side effect of the client's internal struggle rather than something to be applied by an outside agent.

In conclusion

The intention of this article is not to demoralise those officers who are already working with sexual offenders, nor is it to suggest that the basis upon which much of the work of sexual offenders is being undertaken is flawed. The work of Finkelhor and Wolfe and the work of feminist writers has informed the work of Hereford & Worcester officers in the same way that it has informed the work of others, but it need not be overlain by a set of values which have more to do with the needs of the workers than those of the clients.

In the current political climate the whole Service is having to present its work in ways which might curry favour from those who pay the wages, and our vocabulary has begun routinely to include the words 'confront', 'tackle' and 'challenge'. The outcome for all our clients of such an approach may be less therapeutic than we realise; with sexual offenders the stakes are so much higher. If we are to protect women and children from sexual assault then nonce-bashing will have to take a back seat.

From Michael Sheath, '"Confrontative" work with sex offenders: legitimised nonce bashing?', Probation Journal, *37(4), 1990, pp. 159–162.*

56 Specialist activities in probation

'Confusion worse confounded'?
(1995)

George Mair

Introduction

Traditionally, probation officers have had a considerable degree of autonomy in how they go about their work. While there have been fashions in working which have come and gone, historically probation officers have been only marginally and loosely controlled within a non-bureaucratic management structure; they have never been fully incorporated into a formal bureaucratic system. This situation has been progressively changing and some of the implications of this will be touched upon below, but it remains the case that probation officers still enjoy a considerable degree of independence and discretion in what they do and how they do it despite ten years of governmental initiatives which began with the *Statement of National Objectives and Priorities* (Home Office 1984, [Reading 9 this volume]).

One criticism which has been made often of probation work, and which derives at least partially from the independence and discretion of probation officers, is its inconsistency: offenders are dealt with rather differently depending upon the probation area in which they are located. Community service has been particularly criticized in this respect, although straightforward probation supervision has not been immune. In this chapter I want to consider the case of specialist activities run by the probation service within the context of autonomy, independence and wide discretion. How do these impact upon specialist activities and what are the implications of this for effective, efficient, economic and equal service for offenders?

A fairly loose definition of specialist activities will be adopted which can include the obvious, such as work with sex offenders or drug misusers, employment schemes or help with accommodation, but which also covers probation centres (or day centres as they used to be), money payment supervision orders, bail information schemes and the like. Excluded are straight probation, community service and the combination order.

The remainder of the paper is divided into three sections. First, a brief assessment of the nature of the problem. Second, some possible explanations of why the situation is as it has been described. And third, a discussion of what the future might hold for specialist activities in the probation service.

The nature of the problem

In a research project carried out for the Home Office towards the end of the 1980s, Martin Davies and Andrew Wright found that half of the probation officers they surveyed (n=785) described themselves as employed in specialist duties (for example civil work, day centre, hostels, prison-based, etc.) and more than half claimed to have a specialist area of knowledge or expertise which either led to them being allocated special cases or being used in a consultative capacity by colleagues. Specialist knowledge covered such diverse subjects as drugs, welfare rights, sex offending, psychodynamic casework, adult literacy, debt counselling, outdoor pursuits and HIV/AIDS (Davies and Wright 1989). It was rather surprising to find such a large proportion of probation officers who defined themselves as specialists. In the context of the research, Martin Davies argued that this finding had implications for the training of probation officers, but it also raises profound questions about the effectiveness of probation work generally.

One of the consistent findings of research which has been carried out into specialist probation activities is that there is wide variation in the approaches taken. The research carried out into day centres in the second half of the 1980s (Mair 1988) found that: the centres were unevenly distributed around the country; they had varying numbers and types of staffing; they accepted different kinds of offenders (and non-offenders); they opened for different periods of time each week and for different numbers of days; an order could be for 30, 40, 45, 50 or 60 days (and some centres operated two levels of order); programmes of activities varied widely, as did the numbers attending centres and their offence. The report's major conclusion was 'to emphasise the great differences which exist amongst day centres. It is clear that such disparities do not lead to equitable treatment for offenders; and they also raise serious issues concerning the efficiency, effectiveness and economy of day centres.' (Home Office Research Study, p. 31). A later study looking at the reconviction rates associated with day centres found some with rates of lower than 45 per cent while others had rates in excess of 80 per cent (Mair and Nee 1992). ...

The same kind of picture is to be found again and again in reports on specialist activities. Paul Henderson, then of the National Institute for Social Work, in his study of community probation work found a situation characterized by uncertainty about what community probation work was and by diversity in the models being used by those who claimed to practise it (Henderson and del Tufo 1991). HM Probation Inspectorate in a thematic inspection on offender employment and the work of the probation service concluded that 'there is considerable room for those involved at an operational level to develop a more managed and co-ordinated response to the subject' (HMIP 1992). And David Downes too has noted a lack of coherent policy and practice with regard to employment schemes for offenders (Downes 1993). ...

Even in an area where there has been a good deal of centralized planning and development – bail information schemes – there remain differences between schemes, although these are not considerable and may diminish over time (Lloyd 1992; HMIP 1993). Finally, evidence from three other recent research projects suggests that variation remains a key characteristic of probation work with sex offenders (Barker and Morgan 1993), with drug-related offenders (Nee and Sibbitt 1993), and in the area of probation motor projects (Martin and Webster 1994).

Overall, then, the evidence shows that specialist activities in probation are neither uniformly distributed nor consistently organized and operated. They tend to be developed on an *ad hoc* basis and, as a result, are fragmented and widely varying. An argument can be made that this demonstrates local flexibility and innovation – and this is certainly not a point which should be dismissed out of hand. But it can also be argued that it shows uncontrolled discretion, lack of accountability, reinvention of the wheel, 'flavour-of-the-monthism', and that it results in inefficiency and ineffectiveness and provides a poor service to courts and offenders.

Explaining the situation

Why has this situation come about? One key factor, as has been noted, is the autonomy and independence which have been granted – possibly by default – to probation officers. Because of the nature of their work and the traditional one-to-one casework approach, it is difficult to keep a close watch on probation work and to insist that it be carried out in certain ways. Unfortunately, this tends to lead towards an extreme whereby there are as many approaches to dealing with offenders as there are probation officers; a situation which is viewed positively by officers and exemplified by such clichés as 'there's no such thing as a normal probation order'. The solution to this extreme is pictured as closing down all of these options and forcing probation officers to utilize only one approach; this, of course, is anathema to officers. The fact that neither of these two extremes is ever likely to happen is irrelevant.

Specialist activities tend to be a 'bottom-up' development and as such lack rational planning and co-ordination. A frivolous example will illustrate what is meant. A probation officer wakes up one morning and decides that she is rather bored by mundane, straightforward probation work. She remembers that there have been a few cases of garden gnome theft recently in her area which seemed to rouse some interest and she decides to become an expert in dealing with garden gnome thieves. She sets up a little programme with the tacit consent of her senior probation officer, talks about it at various conferences, a few other probation officers in different parts of the country realize that this is an interesting area or notice a rash of such thefts and set up programmes of their own. Relatively quickly, there are more than a dozen specialist programmes for garden gnome thieves and numbers are growing. By the time the Home Office, the Association of Chief Officers of Probation, or the Central Probation Council has realized that there are such programmes, it is too late to co-ordinate them easily. Various approaches have been developed and are held as sacrosanct by their disciples, although there is no research evidence to suggest success. Imposing some form of order or guidelines by this stage is rather like closing the stable door after the horse (or perhaps the gnome) has bolted.

This caricature uncovers the essential elements which – to a greater or lesser extent – lie behind the way in which specialist probation activities are developed and organized. At best, probation officers perceive a new problem which demands a response, but it may be boredom or a desire to get on and be noticed. How often are trends in garden gnome theft monitored in order to assess whether there are enough offenders to keep a programme going for years? If there are not enough offenders then a programme will stumble along, changing its target group in order to justify its existence, watering down its original intentions, and then presumably wondering why it does not work.

There is, too, an element of competition amongst probation services, whereby if Upshire has a garden gnome programme then Downshire must have one. From a good number of years of personal experience of probation research it is clear to me that probation officers who wish to set up a specialist programme rarely know where to get information about previous efforts, or fail to consult widely with colleagues in other areas. Indeed, locally available resources may be ignored in the desire for probation services to provide their own programmes (it should be noted that in some cases, of course, there may be no locally available resources or they may be inappropriate). Thus, programmes are set up on an *ad hoc* basis, they are not fully contextualized within the local probation service, and they lack a clear rationale or theoretical foundation.

Local management must take some of the blame for all of this, and so too must the Home Office. There is no reliable mechanism whereby a new initiative can be brought to the attention either of the Home Office or the professional probation associations. In the late 1980s when risk of custody scales were spreading rapidly, the Home Office only found out about this development when many areas had already introduced scales. Far too often such scales were not well designed, had not been properly validated and were transferred to other areas without any revalidation. This kind of situation could have had serious consequences for prediction scales generally, for the reputation of the local probation service and for the sentencing of offenders.

When the day centre study which was carried out in the mid-1980s was being planned, it came as a considerable surprise to find that there was no list of day centres held in the Home Office. There is still no list of specialist activities held by the Home Office, and this lack of knowledge is at least partly responsible for the uncoordinated development of specialist activities. It also makes life a little harder for research as in at least four recent cases a census of all probation areas has had to be conducted prior to the research proper.

The future

There are already underway several developments which should help to impose some order upon this confused situation. The introduction of national standards, although not directly related to specialist activities, should have a general – though perhaps not immediate – impact in terms of encouraging more consistent approaches (a review of the standards is underway). Similarly, the new 'partnership' policy should encourage probation services to take a closer look at the specialist activities they offer and decide whether these can be more effectively and appropriately delivered by other agencies. It is unfortunate that neither of these developments is being accompanied by research to determine the nature and level of their impact. There is also the example of the model followed for the development of bail information schemes where a National Steering Group has tried – fairly successfully – to control such schemes by providing official endorsement. On the subject of employment there is now a National Offender Employment Forum and work is underway to develop guidance on employment issues for the probation service. And a paper setting out guidance for the service on addressing problems of drug and alcohol misuse among offenders is due to be issued in 1995. While these latter two developments are positive responses, they are entering the game late in the day when trying to impose a coherent structure will be much more difficult.

The Home Office Research and Planning Unit (RPU) has put forward plans for an annual register of specialist activities, which would be made available to the probation policy division and HMIP as well as all probation services. This would help the Home Office keep abreast of specialist developments, and help probation services see what other areas are doing. It is hoped that we might be able to begin collaborative work on this in the near future.

Ideally, one might envisage a system whereby any novel specialist programmes could be identified at a very early stage – preferably before they had begun operating, at the planning/design stage. Monitoring should have been carried out to ensure that there would be an adequate throughput of appropriate offenders, and the proposed programme should be based upon some coherent theory. The programme could be brought to the attention of HMIP who, perhaps with the RPU, could ensure that some form of basic 'natural history' of it all was prepared. After a minimum of 12 months, decisions could be made as to whether or not such a programme was necessary or desirable in other areas. At this point a number of programmes utilizing different models of organization and operation could be set up and a research/evaluation exercise designed. On completion of the research, good practice guidelines for such a programme would be issued and a uniform monitoring system for all specialist programmes of the specific type put in place. A system such as this would not eliminate the flexibility of local probation services or inhibit the desire or need to be innovative; it would control and channel discretion and lead to greater consistency.

The approach to specialist activities up to now has been one of 'let a thousand flowers bloom' and then benign neglect. Individual specialist activities may only account for a small proportion of probation work but taken together they probably now take up more than half of such work. A more co-ordinated and structured approach can only be to the advantage of all concerned, and particularly offenders.

From George Mair, 'Specialist activities in probation: "confusion worse confounded"?', in L. Noakes, M. Levi and M. Maguire (eds.) Contemporary Issues in Criminology *(Cardiff: University of Wales Press), 1995, pp. 251–258.*

References

Barker, M. and Morgan, R. (1993) *Sex Offenders: a framework for the evaluation of community-based treatment.* London: Home Office.

Davies, M. and Wright, A. (1989) *The Changing Face of Probation.* Norwich: University of East Anglia.

Downes, D. (1993) *Employment Schemes for Ex-offenders.* London: Home Office.

Henderson, P. and del Tufo, S. (1991) *Community Work and the Probation Service.* London: HMSO.

HMIP (1992) *Offenders into Work: report of a thematic inspection.* London: Home Office.

——(1993) *Bail Information: report of a thematic inspection.* London: Home Office.

Home Office (1984) *Probation Service in England and Wales: Statement of National Objectives and Priorities.* London: Home Office.

Lloyd, C. (1992) *Bail Information Schemes: practice and effect.* RPU Paper 69. London: Home Office.

Mair, G. (1988) *Probation Day Centres.* HORS 100. London: HMSO.

Mair, G. and Nee, C. (1992) 'Day centre reconviction rates', *British Journal of Criminology* 32 (3).

Martin, J. and Webster, D. (1994) *Probation Motor Projects in England and Wales.* London: Home Office.

Nee, C. and Sibbitt, R. (1993) *The Probation Response to Drug Misuse.* RPU Paper 78. London: Home Office.

Part E

Diversity

Introduction

This section was planned as an extension of the previous; we intended to capture initiatives in supervision focused on ethnic minorities and women, these being the two groups within the broad heading of diversity about which most concern has been expressed and most has been written. However, a problem immediately arose: much has indeed been written in the way of overviews of issues concerning these groups in the criminal justice system and of general critiques of policy and practice, but remarkably little has been written that exposes the raw material of practice.

We decided to stay with our original plan as far as possible, even though this would reduce the number of contributions in this section. Our reasons for this were similar to those guiding previous selections. It became very clear to us, as we trawled for practice examples, that general overviews and critiques are readily accessible in journals and other collections. Yet the very scarcity of detailed accounts of real world practice examples, despite the repetitive voices of concern, seems to us to highlight the importance of bringing them to the attention of an audience apparently thirsty for inspiration. We do not ourselves present the following selection as exemplars; we leave it for readers to draw their own conclusions about their merits or otherwise.

The reasons for the comparative scarcity of accounts of practice are not very clear. Moreover, it cannot be assumed that reasons are the same for ethnic minorities and women. For example, absence of programmes for female offenders are often, at local level, attributed to insufficient numbers to fill places cost effectively; it is not clear that this has regularly been used to account for lack of special programmes for ethnic minority offenders.

It is striking to note the publication dates of the first three contributions in particular, clustering at the beginning of the 1980s. This suggests a spurt of interest and the will to attempt innovative practice with ethnic minority offenders. The following two readings also appeared later in that decade and, taken in conjunction with the articles on politically motivated offenders and inner-city disturbances from the previous section (Readings 48 and 54), indicate, tentatively, that during the 1980s there was particular interest in practice development for specific socially excluded groups (although, as we have seen and will again see, this could include refining the arguments *against* supervision). If this was indeed the case, however, the question why this enthusiasm did not consolidate remains unanswered.

Two of our authors, Pat Carlen (Reading 61) and Jim Lawson (Reading 59) refer to the difficulty in exposing practice to public gaze in a highly sensitive area of work, both because criticism can almost always be found from some perspective and because good ideas may become distorted in their implementation. Indeed, Bruce Carrington and David Denney (Reading 57) begin by throwing down the gauntlet in their examination of the mutual lack of effective communication and understanding between probation officers and Rastafarian offenders. The authors appear to view probation officers' lack of appreciation, whether wilful or unconscious, of their clients' experience of racism as largely at the root of this predicament. Their approach, however, while illuminating probation officers' diffidence in the face of cultural difference, like a number of more general critiques makes few clear suggestions for improving practice generally, although it does highlight the innovative Handsworth Alternative Scheme.

Richard Pinder (Reading 58) explores a project that rose to the challenge. Making opportunistic use of premises for black youth in Chapeltown, Leeds, one probation officer developed an informal reporting session which, essentially, took the probation service out to the offenders rather than requiring them to come to a formal office. Although this probation officer did not, it seems, go so far as to move into the neighbourhood, this project is reminiscent of Hugman's detached work (Reading 44), embracing similar goals and principles. Jim Lawson's account of a probation team's scrutiny of its practice after inner-city riots in St Pauls (Reading 59) follows a similar path to an extent, by capitalising on the enthusiasm of one probation officer for becoming involved with a black community, particularly young males, on its own terms. Results emerged not only in terms of individual responsiveness to probation intervention but on an inter-agency and community level. These initiatives bear some comparison with the models explored in the previous sections; for example, the non-treatment paradigm (Reading 33) expressly proposes developing help in terms defined by the client. These projects begin from the idea that the process of discovering what constitutes valid help as perceived by the client must start from meeting in the client's geographical and psychological space.

Mary Davies and Gillian Stewart examine NAPO's 1986 resolution to consider good practice in the light of its support for decriminalisation of prostitution (Reading 60). Their argument is interesting to re-evaluate in the light of Ken Pease's later proposal for a model of the probation service as a harm mitigation agency (Reading 39). In their examination of sentencing alternatives, they conclude that all penal measures apart from the Absolute Discharge are potentially or actually harm *increasing*, given the constraints of lifestyle choices that have propelled women into prostitution. Here again, although from a very different starting point, we find strong encouragement to probation officers to formulate confident proposals in line with their professional principles.

Carlen (Reading 61) explores the potential risks of moving towards policies and practices designed specifically for women but, with this in mind, takes the further step of contemplating what such measures would contain. This article, while not dealing with a particular programme, became well known within the service for setting out a challenge to examine current practice critically. Moreover, it contains concrete recommendations for practice development. Nevertheless, innovations have not proliferated. Judith Rumgay (Reading 62) considers reasons for this, moving on to an account of one programme that, championed by a Chief Probation Officer, not only came into being but survived and eventually evolved into an independent, voluntary sector organisation. This programme was later identified as a Pathfinder in the Home Office's Effective Practice initiative, but failed to gain accreditation. This historical note is worthy of attention here, since the failure of practitioners to communicate their aims and methods in ways accessible to the panel of accreditation was repeated in the following contribution which describes a similarly frustrating experience.

Patrick Williams offers a welcome recent account of innovative practice with ethnic minority offenders (Reading 63). The Black Offender Groupwork Programme in Greater Manchester grew from examination of existing practice supported by a theoretical framework emphasising, in particular, empowerment as essential to relevant rehabilitation. The approach bears comparison with the tenets of the radical social work model (Reading 34). A programme devised and delivered with considerable dedication by probation officers appears to have been welcomed by participants. Nevertheless, in the process of pursuing accreditation, its essential aims became distorted, reflecting the earlier warnings of Carlen in relation to interventions for women. With its preoccupation on effectiveness through the vehicle of cognitive behavioural programmes, the accreditation process weakened the aim of empowerment to a definition of the project's purpose in terms of preparation for participation in other groups. Williams' commentary also introduces us to the jungle of acronyms, programmes and projects that has come to characterise contemporary probation.

We conclude this section with Loraine Gelsthorpe's exploration of dealing with diversity (Reading 64). While it kicks against our aim of revealing real-world practice by presenting a review of issues, this contribution provides a timely reminder that those groups falling into the category of 'diversity' should not then be regarded as homogenous. Gelsthorpe shows that broadly similar starting points have led to very different responses in relation to ethnicity and gender.

Collectively, the readings in this section amount to a three-fold exhortation to probation officers: to be bold in developing their work; to establish and protect ethical principles; and to 'get real' (or, as Hugman argues in Reading 44, to 'act natural') in practice with offenders whose social worlds are very different from those who seek to interact with them as sales representatives for conventionality.

57 Young Rastafarians and the probation service (1981)

Bruce Carrington and David Denney

The response of Britain's West Indian community to the recent tragedies in South East London highlights the growing feelings of anger and frustration felt by many racial minorities in this country. Continued racialist attacks and, demonstrations, alleged police harassments and the persistence of discriminatory practices in the labour market and elsewhere have prompted the growth of forms of black resistance of which Rastafarianism is the most publicised.

As this movement gathers momentum social workers must confront the issues raised by this group.

CCETSW [the Central Council for Education and Training in Social Work] on a number of occasions has recommended that courses give more adequate attention to social work with racial minorities, but the evidence available suggests that relatively little effort has been made by social work educators in this area (Barker and Husband 1979).

Who are the Rastafarians?

The Rastafarian Movement first emerged in Jamaica in 1930, following the coronation of Haile Selassie I (Rastafari) in Ethiopia as the 'King of Kings, Lord of Lords and Conquering Lion of Judah'. This event was of considerable significance to black nationalists, for it confirmed the prophecies of their leader Marcus Garvey that there would eventually be an independent black nation in Africa, ruled by a black king. Moreover, the Ethiopian theocracy was also looked upon by the Garveyites as a symbol of African resistance against racial and colonial oppression. By 1934 Rastafarianism was well established, due mainly to the efforts of Leonard Howell. Under Howell the early Rastafarians (the Brethren) formed a rural commune (the Pinnacle) cultivating yams as a subsistence crop, and Ganja (Marijuana), as a cash crop. It was the latter activity which brought them into conflict with the Jamaican authorities. A series of police raids led to the dissolution of the Pinnacle in 1941. Although the Rastafarians re-established their commune in 1953, further police raids caused them to disperse. Many fled to the ghettos of Kingston. These experiences described above served to heighten their political awareness. By 1963 the Rastafarians were acting as a pressure group, campaigning vigorously against colour-class gradations in the social structure, and racial segregation in the tourist playground in the north of the island. At first the Jamaican state used repressive measures to silence the Brethren. When these failed, the state attempted to contain the movement by sponsoring an image of the Rastafarians as 'a fringe millenarian group bereft of political significance'. Despite the various attempts to control Rastafarianism, its popularity has steadily increased, both in the West Indies and elsewhere. Haile Selassie's visit to Jamaica in 1966 served to stimulate its growth. Since then the influence of Rastafarianism has extended to metropolitan countries such as Britain, where among West Indian youth it constitutes 'a culture of resistance to white society and white values' (Campbell 1980).

At the risk of oversimplification, the following tenets form the basis of the Rastafarian belief system:

(1)   Rastafari (i.e. Haile Selassie) is the Living God.
(2)   Ethiopia is the true name of Africa and is the home of the black man.
(3)   Repatriation to Ethiopia is the way of redemption for the black people of the West.
(4)   The ways of the white man are malevolent, in particular, in relation to the black man.
(5)   The black races are the true Israelites and Haile Selassie I is the direct descendant of Solomon and Sheba. The exile and enslavement of the Israelites in Babylon is viewed as comparable to the exile and enslavement of black people in the American colonies. Moreover the white man has held the black man in 'slavery', under various guises, from 1655 to the present. Capitalism is seen as the system of Babylon and (black) wage labour under capitalism as a perpetuation of slavery.
(6)   Ganja is sacred.
(7)   Legitimate marriage is condemned.
(8)   Gambling and the use of alcohol are forbidden.

The belief system described above gives rise to a wide range of cultural and political practices among West Indian youth in British society. For example, although there are some West Indians who stress the spiritual aspects of Rastafarianism – particularly its concern with the understanding of God through black eyes – others give less emphasis to its religious dimension: some contemporary Rastafarians do not believe in the deity of Haile Selassie I, for example. In general terms, this group rejects the notion of wage labour. It is stressed that the response of Rastafarians to official agencies and to those in authority (police, teachers, probation officers, etc.) is highly variable and differentiated. Whereas some refuse to engage in any form of discourse with the authorities, others reveal a willingness to compromise and, in some instances, to co-operate. It will be apparent that Rastafarianism is a highly complex phenomenon and is certainly something that is more than a form of religious proclivity. It embodies a clearly articulated political position and may be regarded as a culture of resistance both to capitalism and racism. The wearing of Dreadlocks and woollen caps in the Ethiopian national colours *symbolise,* on the one hand, the cultural links of the Rastafarians with Africa, and their rejection of Western culture and values, on the other. For a growing section of West Indian youth, the Rastafarian world view provides a 'theoretical framework' with which to make sense of a racially structured society. It also offers black youth a number of strategies with which to *contest* their *caste-like structural position.* It is these strategies which inevitably bring the Rastafari into conflict with the authorities.

The study

A small study was undertaken in an urban centre with a high Afro-Caribbean population which sought to examine:

(1)   Probation officers' perceptions of Rastafarianism.
(2)   Methods of intervention currently employed by the probation officers in relation to Rastafarians.
(3)   The personal responses of a group of Rastafarian offenders to probation.

The sample consisted of a cross-section of thirty probation officers, including men and women, from basic grade to assistant chief probation officer. With the exception of one West Indian male, the members of this group were white. A qualitative methodology was employed, based upon loosely structured interviews. Antagonism on the part of the Rastafarians meant that it was only possible for us to interview fifteen of the offenders. Of these, seven allowed us to tape record the interviews. The content of fifteen SIRs on Rastafarians was also examined.

The Probation Officers' response

Given that all of the probation officers we interviewed found Rastafarians to be a problematic group, how did they make sense of the latter's behaviour? Most of the interviewees suggested that two major categories of Rastafari could be distinguished. These they referred to as: *'the true Rasta'* and *'the untrue Rasta'*. They held that the 'true Rasta' based his (or her) lifestyle upon a system of religious beliefs, involving a number of rituals including the smoking of ganja. This group was apparently more amenable to probation intervention than the 'untrue Rasta'. The probation officers divided the latter group into two further sub-categories. One sub-category was often referred to as 'the Bandwagon Rastas', i.e. West Indians of school age, who adopted the outward appearance of the Rastafarian but who allegedly lacked any real cognisance of the Rastafarian world view. The 'Bandwagon Rastas' were seen as especially vulnerable to manipulation by a second sub-category of 'untrue Rastas', who were perceived by the probation officers as a politically (rather than religiously) motivated group, with Marxist leanings.

Various causal explanations of Rastafarianism were offered by the probation officers. Seventeen viewed it as an individual, psychologically determined phenomenon. Of these, some depicted the Rastafarians as facing 'an identity crisis' as the result of living in an 'alien' and 'hostile' society. Unable 'to cope' and 'incapable of adjusting' to life in Britain, the West Indian youth, in a state of desperation and ontological insecurity turned to Rastafarianism as a means of achieving a sense of self. Others advanced explanations which were reminiscent of Adorno's (Adorno *et al.* 1950) account of the authoritarian personality. For example, probation officers alluded to the 'generation gap', to present a view of the Rastafari as an individual who, during adolescence, revolts against the strictures of an authoritarian father figure, and a rigid upbringing based upon the ascetic values of the Pentecostal Church. Paradoxically, other probation officers attributed the Rastafarians' rejection of the work ethic and values of the parent culture, to the matriarchal structure of the West Indian family, by claiming that Rastafarianism stemmed directly from the absence of a strong father-figure in primary socialisation!

The remainder of our interviewees proposed 'sociological' rather than 'psychological' explanations of Rastafarianism. Eight saw it as a reaction by black youth against the suppression – i.e. 'unintentional stifling' – of West Indian culture in British society. This suppression, however, was not associated with racism. In fact, only two of the probation officers we interviewed perceived Rastafarianism as a sub-cultural response to racism. Although the three remaining interviewees did suggest that Rastafarianism may be construed as a reaction on the part of black youth to their unequal position in employment, housing and education, none seemed willing to attribute these inequalities to racial discrimination.

Few of the social inquiry reports made any reference to the Rastafarian client's beliefs. Although the reasons for this omission were never intimated, it was assumed that such omissions were deliberate and were intended to protect the client from the magistrate who may be unsympathetic to Rastafarianism. In such cases the probation officer is placed in a Catch 22 position, for the social inquiry report is meant to provide an unbiased account of both the social background of the offender and the background to the offence. If these reports are intended to provide the court with an understanding of the motives underlying an individual criminal act, then the failure of the probation officers to make any reference to the Rastafari clients' beliefs, must necessarily involve a failure on the part of the court to understand the offender's motives.

All of the probation officers interviewed had encountered problems when dealing with Rastafarians. Those most frequently mentioned were lack of punctuality, unco-operative and sometimes aggressive behaviour and the use of Creole Dialect, which was seen as an obstacle to effective communication. The reaction of the Rastafarian to probation left many of our interviewees feeling cold and despondent. They saw their position as untenable and expressed surprise that so many Rastafarians were placed on probation. Most expressed pessimistic views when the issue of casework was raised, although some thought that this was an area where 'bridges might be built'. About a third of the probation officers felt that the problem might be alleviated by using black volunteers. Some interviewees reported that they had tried working with volunteers, but without success. In many instances the respondents considered it to be more difficult for the black volunteer to intervene than the white probation officer. Moreover, some of our interviewees also mentioned that they had made abortive attempts to use groupwork techniques with Rastafarians.

Table 1 represents the age, sex, offence, and kinds of supervision offered to Rastas in the fifteen social inquiry reports which were analysed.

The Rasta response

It was in this area that most difficulty was experienced in attempting to interview respondents. Understandably the Rastafarians expressed resentment to the researcher, some believing the research to be a police operation. Reference has previously been made to a differentiated Rastafarian response. Some six of the respondents had to some extent accepted the conditions of the probation order. They were prepared to acknowledge that they had broken the law and considered themselves lucky not to be serving a custodial sentence. In these cases little comment was made to suggest a rejection of dominant political and social structures, although the existence of racist practices, particularly in the fields of employment, was mentioned by all the respondents. The remaining clients were doing probation on sufferance, and in these

Table 1

Age	Sex	Previous supervision	Offence	Recommendation made by PO
18	M	Supervision	B	'Supervision impractical'; expectation of Borstal
18	M	Supervision	B	Supervision response minimal; recommended Borstal
18	M	Supervision	B & TMV	Recommended Borstal
18	M	No previous	R & B	Recommended supervision
17	M	Supervision	B	Continue supervision
17	M	Care order/DC	TMV	Defer sentence for 3 months
19	M	DC licence	R	Defer sentence
18	M	Supervision & DC	TMV	No recommendation; prepared without consultation with defendant
17	M	Supervision	R	Borstal
18	M	Supervision & DC	TMV	No recommendation; prepared without consultation with defendant
19	F	None	T	Probation
18	M	Care order/DC	B	Fine
18	M	Care order/DC	R	Continue supervision
23	M	Probation	UW, AP & R	'Probation of little value'
22	M	Borstal/Comm. service	UW	Custody; / 'no alternative'

R – Robbery; B – Burglary; TMV – Taking a Motor Vehicle; T – Theft; AP – Assaulting Policeman; DC – Detention Centre; UW – Unlawful Wounding

cases little distinction was made between the police and the probation service. Only three of the respondents could see any constructive results from probation, and in these cases it was difficult to gauge the effect that the interview situation was having on the response. Perhaps these respondents felt it necessary to play along with the interviewer in the same way that they played along with the probation officer.

The implications for social work practice

It appears from our limited efforts that probation officers lack an adequate understanding of Rastafarianism, viewing it either in psychological terms as a form of deviance which stems from an inadequate socialisation, or in sociological terms as an ethnic solution to an identity crisis.

Furthermore, the two categories employed by our respondents to make the phenomenon intelligible do not take account of the diversity of practices (religious, political, social) deriving from the Rastafarian world view.

It would be imprudent to single out any one of these responses as being authentically Rastafarian (e.g. religious responses).

The realisation that all groups of clients, particularly young black people, are not amenable to social work intervention and cannot be treated in the same manner has been slow to dawn on social workers, and even more slowly on social work teachers.

Methods based upon individual pathology, although acceptable to the courts, are totally inappropriate when applied to multi-racial Britain. Many young blacks, and particularly Rastafarians, have penetrated the assumptions lying behind these methods and find them to be irrelevant to the experience of living in what is often a hostile and racist society. In many cases these methods serve to divert attention from structural inequalities towards so called inadequacies in the family or the individual.

Social work needs to shift from an assimilationist position which underlies the explanations outlined here. The argument seems to run, if Rastafarians could overcome their personal problems, which are preventing them from accepting the dominant value system, then life would be easier for everyone. Such an orientation may understate the depth and extent of racist sentiment. Some critics of current social work practice have argued that such notions impede the practitioner's comprehension of the context in which the black client must exist. Lena Dominelli (1979) has suggested that a non-racist practice must observe the full acceptance of a multi-racial Britain, the affirmation of the cultural specificity of different ethnic minority groups, the examination of traditional work methods and their appropriateness in working with ethnic minorities, and the development of client centred community strategies for change. Slowly, due mainly to the developing resistance of the black community, and the efforts of imaginative social workers working in the field, there is a movement towards such a practice. Particularly relevant to this study is the work being done in Birmingham at the Handsworth Alternative Scheme. The project, backed financially by the Home Office and administered jointly by NACRO and the Probation Service aims to offer a wider range of social work approaches to black offenders in the 17–25 age group. The scheme, staffed by black workers, concentrates its efforts in the areas of education, employment and housing. Attention is directed particularly at resource development in these areas. Although the scheme came into operation only in April 1979, successful efforts have been made to generate work opportunities from the Careers Service and Manpower Services, and to improve access to YOP and STEP schemes. Substantial headway has also been made in the area of accommodation, for the young black homeless. Much has also been achieved in the area of education with much emphasis being placed on basic numeracy and literacy and black studies. Rastafarians are particularly likely to benefit from such forms of intervention which concentrates on the needs of black people, and appears to be aiming for a client-centred, community-based form of work.

Since this approach is at present in its early stages, it would be unwise to make anything resembling a prescriptive statement in relation to social work methods with this group. The Rastafarians represent one of many forms of growing black resistance to the differential allocation of scarce resources and to racial violence. The Rastafarians have been instrumental however, in making some probation officers reappraise their methods. This has led to an exploration of the contradictions implicit in attempting to impose the will of the court whilst instigating both a client-centred and community-based form of intervention. How long will it be before social work educators begin to tread this path?

From Bruce Carrington and David Denney, 'Young Rastafarians and the probation service', Probation Journal, 28(4), 1981, pp. 111–117.

References

Adorno T.W., Frenkel-Brunswick, E., Levinson, D.J. and Sanford, R.N. (1950) *The Authoritarian Personality*. The American Jewish Committee Social Studies Series 3. New York, Harper.

Barker, L. and Husband, C. (1979) 'How has Social Work Education responded?' *Social Work Today* 10(25): 24–26.

Campbell, H. (1980) 'Rastafari: Culture of Resistance.' *Race* and *Class* 22(1): 1–22.

Dominelli, L. (1979) 'The Challenge for Social Work Education.' *Social Work Today* 10(25): 27–29.

58 On what grounds?

Negotiating justice with black clients (1982)

Richard Pinder

We started having this thing on a Monday night ... What used to happen was, we used to have shouting and jumping up and down sessions, people just being exhibitionist or awkward, then you would get a period of serious conversation, when an issue would arise and people would seize on it and we would try to seize on it and try and push it forward a bit, but obviously the group dictated what they wanted to talk about in the end.

(Martin Austwick)

'This thing' was an informal reporting session run by Martin Austwick, a Leeds probation officer, at the Palace Hostel in Chapeltown from 1979 to 1981. The Hostel served not only as home for up to a dozen lads but also as focal point for the other activities – youth club, work schemes, play schemes undertaken over several years by the Palace Youth Project with and for young black people in trouble. In its time, the Palace has aroused suspicion and hostility. It has also developed a critical role within Chapeltown, best demonstrated in its success in organising peaceful bonfire night celebrations in 1980 and 1981, bringing to an end what had become a tradition of violent confrontations between black lads and the police on that night. The Palace is thus caught up in various ways in issues of justice in Chapeltown.

Lads subject to various kinds of order were to be found at the Palace. As they would report to a probation office only intermittently, Martin promoted the idea of a reporting session at the Palace. He later summed up the logic: "I don't think the probation officer is that significant: you've got to make yourself significant ... by getting to see them on their own ground."

This article is about 'getting to see them on their own ground'. It is based on a far from extensive research investigation. During April and May, 1981, I made six visits to the Palace: on five of them I observed Martin's work at the two-hour reporting session; the sixth was to a management committee meeting. I also studied files on seven of the lads supervised at the Palace and, finally, tape-recorded an interview with Martin. The question throughout was: What form does probation practice take in such a context?

Style, jokes and dignity

The more recent sessions follow the pattern of the original ones, with rapid shifts in mood and content. Much of the time is given over to displays of style on the lads' part. Such displays give way to 'serious conversations' – about the police, the National Front, the riots; about housing and (un)employment; about fines; about family, girlfriends, children. An ability to tolerate the 'shifty' nature of the event is crucial, as is an ability to judge when to pursue a 'serious' subject with an individual, and when to let be. The location makes such judgments problematic. At home in the Palace office, clients can achieve a position of dominance by behaving as they normally do – only more so! As hosts, they bring out their best behaviour.

There is thus a strong 'joking' element in Martin's relationships with the lads. They seek to knock Martin off-balance with verbal sallies (accompanied by sudden shifts in physical position). One asks: "Are you questioning me – or am I questioning you?" Their aim is not (I think) to destroy Martin's credibility, but simply to enable themselves to talk with him on more or less equal terms – to counter the potential and (on occasions) actual power an officer has at his/her disposal. If he treats this – and himself – seriously, his position is jeopardised:

> If you want to stand on your dignity, you're just not going to get through to anybody, because these people are not dignified … well, they're dignified, as human beings, but they've not got false dignity about them. … Once or twice it did get entirely out of control. But it always used to swing back to something important … As for dignity, I don't know quite what that means. I think they've got dignity when it comes to it, they will stand together. I think that's probably dignity. Dignity for a probation officer is to try and do the job the best way you can, and, [the Palace] seemed to be the best way to do it for me.

On the surface, the Palace is one of the last places one would expect to find dignity: the place is in a state of gross disrepair, and the lads themselves, if not the 'wretched of the earth', certainly face the worst modern hardships. In such circumstances, it is easy not to respect people – or to fall back on an abstract respect for them as 'human beings', and not work through to an understanding of what constitutes these particular people's dignity. Martin's statement indicates that that further understanding has to be achieved – not as a moral, but as a professional imperative. To complete any professional task with the lads, to get them to demonstrate what the courts would consider responsible behaviour, it is necessary to acknowledge the dignity they create through their collective identity – to see them 'standing together', for all that this increases their negotiating strength. To be a probation officer 'on their ground' is a matter, not of imposing terms on them, but of coming to terms with them.

Shifting ground

Episodes from Martin's dealings with one lad, Ben, reveal the implications of this shifting ground:

> 13.4.81: Ben reported to the Palace. In a bit of a funny mood. Tried to steal one or two small items lying around. We had a rather light-hearted argument about this sort of petty criminality and Ben backed down, much to my surprise.

Ben taking drawing pins, pocketing a table-tennis ball, using the Palace phone without payment – these are the actions that lead to the 'argument', one of a series of confrontations between Ben and Martin. The character of the confrontation illustrates the process of negotiating justice at the Palace:

This is an interesting thing for probation officers, because you do represent very unrealistic standards. On the other hand, if you let somebody get away with nicking, say, a packet of drawing pins when he's on probation he's going to get really ambivalent ideas about it. I think to some extent you have to indicate limits.

But this is no abstract exercise in ethics. The feedback is real and immediate: what is at stake is Martin's personal and professional credibility. Ben, moreover, has a strong case. His first point, the simplest, is: 'The Palace is for me, not for you'. His second is that, because the items involved are common property, his behaviour does not constitute theft. His third: 'I'll tell you your trouble, you whites think you know what's good for everybody else'. His fourth is that Martin has no basis for judging a black lad's behaviour, because their worlds are so different. Martin is able to respond to each of these points, precisely because of his long term involvement with the Palace and his familiarity with other black lads and with Ben's own family. It is through his response on these terms that he is able to demonstrate a recognition of and a respect for Ben's position. Ben's dignity remains intact – he is enabled to back down.

As Ben's arguments imply, wider issues, to do with the predicament of black people, come to the surface: prejudice, discrimination, conflict and (on 13 April) the Brixton riots. The confrontation at the Palace is always given a sharp edge by being a local symbol of a more general black–white divide. 'This guy is pressuring me ... this white guy ... this probation officer', as Ben says, during his phone call.

Here Martin has a difficult path to tread – one that recognises the legitimacy of protest but does not confuse this issue with that of 'petty criminality'. This is perhaps the key to the negotiations. By accepting that Ben is demonstrating responsibility in his concern for civil rights, Martin is able to insist on a similar responsibility in the case of Ben's 'petty criminality'. If the various issues get collapsed, not only is Ben likely to lose the confidence of other parts of the criminal justice system, notably magistrates and the police. Either consequence is potentially damaging.

This practical and comprehensive respect for Ben's responsibleness makes possible the continuation of a supervision that was from the outset problematic:

> Ben, I didn't want him to be on probation in the first place, he's a great big lad, he's difficult and he's awkward. But I've seen him at the Palace, and we do talk about things that have got some relevance like race and attitudes towards each other, and work ... I felt Ben had got his life sorted out the way he wanted it. He played basketball and he trained ... although he wasn't working, he was doing things with his time, which is all I could encourage anybody to do these days.

It also underpins the following transfer summary:

> This is a question of keeping in touch and trying to respond to Ben: if only I could think of some way of getting him to see the way his 'bull in a china shop' manner affects other people. On the other hand, being a bit intimidating can be useful at times ... Ben's way of life has not changed. He reports regularly and has paid his fine. I recommend he be seen at the Palace.

'Appreciation' and justice

Martin's work at the Palace indicates that shifting on to other people's territory has serious consequences. Firstly, where power has evidently shifted towards the client it is not surprising that 'At times I used to wonder, what am I doing? This is awful!' It is often difficult to discern any kind of structure to the proceedings, or sense any control over them. In consequence, a feeling frequently emerges that the work lacks depth – particularly in contrast to affairs in an office, where interviews are less susceptible to distraction, disruption and sabotage.

Secondly, in a setting where one is constantly exposed to the concerns of black people – unemployment, homelessness, racist violence (and counterviolence), official racism – one is forced to appreciate these factors in a particular light. In court, they appear as background features, which may help to explain a particular offence. At the Palace they are in no sense background features: to treat them simply in relation to the criminal justice system is to trivialise them. Here they inhabit the foreground, and determine many of the specific helping tasks an officer has to carry out.

Thirdly, to survive, one has to recognise that one is not a passive administrator of justice. One has rather to construct justice, fashion it in the midst of conflicting interests. This at times implies being 'less objective' than in some other circumstances:

MA: You have to side with people on the issues that they're concerned about.
RP: As a probation officer?
MA: Yes. And saying [to government] this is not right, this is not right, this is what people feel …
RP: This political perspective is something that a lot of officers would disagree with.
MA: Yes, it's something that I would probably have disagreed with two or three years ago.

All three points – the apparent breakdown of order and control, the change in perceptions, the 'siding' with clients indicate the vulnerability to which one is exposed when working away from home, and the possibility of compromising, as opposed to developing, the Probation tradition. And yet, it must be acknowledged that a variety of difficulties hinder – or even prevent – orthodox forms of supervision for black clients; that there is a crisis in relationships between black citizens and white authority; that black people see more of a threat in the establishment's behaviour than in the behaviour of the National Front. It may be that if the Probation Service is to develop and keep a black 'market', the danger associated with shifting on to other ground has to be written explicitly into normal practice.

That such a development can occur is evident in some of Martin's case notes – commenting, for example, on the lads' reactions to bonfire night, 1980:

> 6.11.80: They seem to have enjoyed themselves and though I think it was realised that the dance and afterwards were planned to divert them from trouble, no-one seems to resent that.

A little later in that year:

12.12.80: Persuaded Elliot to give himself up from the Palace. Was surprised other residents didn't resent me doing this and felt I'd no other choice and were obviously worried about police in the building looking for Elliot.

This latter note demonstrates Martin's role at the Palace admirably. There is no suggestion of hiding his identity as a probation officer, his identification with the criminal justice system. But the specific item of justice – Elliot's giving himself up – is negotiated rather than dictated. In the process, the other residents recognise not only their own interests but also the logic of Martin's behaviour. There is thus the basis for a mutually acceptable deal.

Success in carrying off such a deal depends (as traditionally it has done) on painstaking attention being paid to the interests of the lads. Had Martin not offered obvious practical services – spending much of any session dusting, sweeping, taking note of the repairs that most urgently required attention; arranging employment opportunities; securing accommodation – 'this thing' would not have continued. The lads recognised Martin's authority in return for tangible benefits. But success depends on an officer exploiting the resources of places such as the Palace, not just by being there, but by gaining access to a network of people (including the residents themselves) who also are motivated by a concern for justice for black lads, even if they express their concern in a different way. Sensitive, authoritative dealings – knowing how to judge the mood of an individual, when it is appropriate to grab somebody by the coat lapels to make a point, when it is sensible to 'breach' a lad, how to assess tolerable levels of noise, cleanliness, morality – are only possible in such places and through such people.

From Richard Pinder, 'On what grounds? Negotiating justice with black clients',
Probation Journal, 29(1), 1982, pp. 19–23.

59 Probation in St. Pauls

Teamwork in a multi-racial, inner-city area (1984)

Jim Lawson

Much has been said and written on the subjects of race and ethnicity, prejudice, discrimination and disadvantage, topics which, for the Probation Service, took on a special meaning following the riots and disturbances which occurred in a number of inner-city areas in England in the early eighties. Whilst acknowledging that simple remedies do not exist to overcome the massive political, social, economic and, arguably, moral problems which were fundamental to those disturbances, it was felt appropriate here in St. Pauls, as doubtless it was elsewhere, for probation officers, individually and as team members, to take a long, hard look at themselves and their operations, with a view to seeing if steps might not be taken to deliver a more relevant service for persons and groups, living in the community and, especially, in the vanguard of those troubles.

Characteristics of the area

It was during the Spring of 1980 that the 'St. Pauls riots' took place, a year before the disturbances which occurred in other parts of the country and which quickly seemed to relegate what had happened here to a back seat in people's consciousness. Yet, despite being a part of Bristol, a city which, if the absence of special status in terms of government eligibility for 'special grants' is anything to go by, is seen as non-problematic, St. Pauls as an area has, I would suggest, many characteristics in common with the other inner-city areas where riots occurred.

Housing in St. Pauls typically consists of a mixture of Victorian terraces and blocks of council accommodation; half of the area has for some years been the subject of 'housing action', the human result being one of movement and change, the visual result being one of urban chaos and contrast; considerable industrial wasteland exists on the fringes and a predominance of the hostel and short term lodging accommodation to be found in the city. The population is predominantly working class and very mixed in terms of race, nationality, age and mobility. Contained in the community are significant numbers of Bristol Street prostitutes, petty criminals and rootless alcoholics and those people who tend to congregate and survive in the decaying parts of inner-cities. Unemployment is high, above the average for most other parts of Bristol. There is also a core of black residents, mainly of Afro-Caribbean descent, and a number of cafés and 'blues' which provide social centres for many of them to go to, including a significant number of people who do not live in St. Pauls. There is a sense of depression around, with few opportunities for advancement, and 'hustung', a term which includes burglaries, muggings, drug dealing and pimping, tends to figure prominently in a significant number of people's lives.

It is to one particular group of offenders, disadvantaged young blacks, and the Probation team's response to them, which this article addresses itself; this is not to suggest that the St. Pauls 'riots' were simply about race; this was not the case but they did have their roots in fundamental social problems, which include unemployment and racism, triggered off by a police raid on a café which caters predominantly for black people, in the heart of the area.

Complacent probation practice

The St. Pauls Probation Team has, over the years, worked in a fairly traditional way from a community-based office. It consists of a small team, a senior and five probation officers, and its work style has involved a predominance of one-to-one work together with occasional groups arranged on an *ad hoc* basis, when the need has arisen; quite good community contacts have always existed. Regular team reviews going back to the early 70's had, until three years ago, indicated that the number of black clients within the team's caseload had consistently remained around the thirty mark (about 15% of the team's caseload). Now, whilst this figure has little meaning itself, it was always somehow felt to be 'smallish' or on the 'low side', particularly in the knowledge of there being significantly high numbers of black inmates in penal establishments, especially those for young prisoners.

The team began to ask itself questions although it is perhaps only now, three years later, that some possible explanations can be postulated. I think now we can look back and acknowledge the institutional racism which existed in our team – and maybe, on occasions, still does. Yet, at the time, we were completely unaware of this, happy sometimes to criticise police activity or the courts' misinterpretation of some black emotional responses (both appropriately) but smug in our thinking that we were all right and providing a 'fair and professional' service. A fatalistic acceptance of the status quo had developed and no strategies or plans to improve this state of affairs had ever been successfully devised.

A new specialism

The change began by chance, one cold afternoon, some four years ago when four young black men arrived together at the office to see four different probation officers; it was subsequently suggested by one of those officers that there might be some value in the young men being seen together; the next week, that officer, John Carver, had increased his caseload by three and the seeds of the 'ethnic minority specialism', as it has come to be known, were sown within the team.

The situation, as at the beginning of 1984, was that the team's total caseload included 97 black clients, of which 63 were part of John Carver's caseload. This number represented some 36% of the team's caseload, and nearer 41% if one excluded those 'non-community-based' clients who came under the team's responsibility, on behalf of the wider PSD, for residents at a local Probation Hostel and prisoners in a training prison in Dorset. How has a three-fold increase in the number of black clients been achieved?

The right person

Most important has been the personality and commitment of John Carver and the acceptance he has gained, in what has traditionally been a fairly indifferent – and, at worst, hostile – community, by his personal concern, investment and interest in his clientele, and others in the community, over the last few years. There are, I believe, three important points to be made here all of which to some extent overlap. Firstly, it is manifestly clear that probation officers are not always best managed as jack of all trades; there are officers who have particular skills and work best in particular settings, and the potency of the services provided by the Agency is maximised if these qualities can be identified and capitalised upon. Secondly, the importance of team stability cannot be overemphasised. Thirdly, probation officers cannot expect to enter such communities and to be respected or accepted simply by virtue of their position or status; this can only be earned and cannot happen overnight. These points, though simple and in some ways obvious, are crucial and have as much validity, I would argue, for all organisations, and especially those associated with statutory authority, working in inner-city, multiracial areas.

John has offered a robust and hard-working approach coupled with the development of a real empathy, not only with his clientele, but also with the community, its ethos and its problems. This point is demonstrated not only by John's knowledge of and relationships with a large number of black individuals in the community (all of whom he is able to recognise instantaneously – a serious point!) but, and this is partly about dealing with one's own racist awareness, his growing love and understanding of the Afro-Caribbean culture.

Relevant service

A second theme is that, in our experience, many young black, male offenders do not, on the whole, welcome probation involvement in their lives, do not fit into traditional models of Probation or social work and require a more relevant and flexible style of intervention. This has resulted in an approach which can be loosely described as community-based and detached, involving, as it does, the vast majority of work being undertaken on the streets, in cafés and in pursuit of recreational activities.

Two aspects of this style of work need particular emphasis. Firstly, the use of sport, and especially football, as a medium through which to engage many of the young black clients. Thus, continuously, for the last three years, John has run a five-a-side football league one evening a week, pulling in young men, promoting competitions, arranging tournaments. Contacts made here have inevitably had their spin-offs in terms of new contacts, best illustrated now by John's position as Deputy Chairman of St. Pauls City, a club which now runs two eleven-a-side teams in a local Bristol league and consists entirely of 'front-line' black players. Sport, at a time when the opportunities for achievement everywhere are extremely limited, provides a creative outlet where much energy can usefully be channelled and a sense of belonging reinforced. The same applies for other sports such as cricket, basketball and netball.

Secondly, the importance of working in and with the community on a variety of levels; from involvement with the more formal groups and organisations, such as the CRE and the Police Crime Prevention panels, through membership of management committees for local hostels, youth workers and community centres to informal contacts with cafés and 'important' individuals. Inevitably, there are both political and economic dimensions to community involvement reflecting the dynamic and in-built reciprocity of transactions required when operating in this way, and an input of resources is required, either from the Agency or from elsewhere, in order to develop and sustain the activities. This itself necessitates a level of entrepreneurial prowess!

Team support

A third aspect is the importance of team support. There is a popular myth that unless a team is working in the same way or according to a universally accepted model, it is not operating as a team. I would argue that a team which, consciously and explicitly, frees members to take on particular responsibilities and ways of working, so long as it conducts itself on the basis of mutual respect and trust, is functioning very much as an integral unit. In consequence, whilst much has been spoken of John Carver and his particular style, equal credit must go to the rest of the team members – who, in terms of the work they have undertaken individually and together, have contributed to the development of John's specialism. A further payoff has been that, whilst John has had the major involvement in working with the black community, this has inevitably 'rubbed off' on his colleagues, in terms of contact, interest etc., and a number of black clients are in fact supervised by all team members.

Weighing success

Where does the success lie? I have mentioned the 'numbers' angle, which, notwithstanding the games people can play with statistics, does carry a valid message. I can point to the increased status and respect the Service has in the community, through varied and unsolicited feedback. I can provide examples of young men who, through the Service's intervention and notwithstanding a level of re-offending in some cases, are still at liberty, are reaching the end of their adolescence and are beginning to demonstrate a sense of newly-found maturity and self-respect. I can identify young black men who have voluntarily requested help or asked that a social enquiry report be written on them in a way which never happened in the past. I can claim with justification that local Courts are now more prepared to place such offenders on Probation. I can talk about the bedsitter project currently under way. I can mention the police who, when faced with delicate situations, have requested John Carver to take on the role of go-between, for example, encouraging youngsters to attend the police station voluntarily, or leave a house where they had been squatting, thereby diffusing potentially volatile incidents. All of this amounts, in my opinion, to the provision of a more relevant Probation Service for the black community in St. Pauls, a Service which, I need hardly say, is constantly evolving.

I am conscious that any article which talks about racial issues in a fairly explicit way is open to criticism from a number of angles, ranging from the philosophical to the pragmatic. Debates about the justice or paternalism inherent in topics such as positive discrimination tend to be both absorbing and endless. I have chosen not to enter this debate here, nor am I wanting to provide a blueprint of what is the right way for a probation team to operate in a multi-racial, inner-city area. Certainly, no extravagant claims can be made to say that crime has dramatically reduced in St. Pauls – the prevailing sub-culture of 'hustle and survive' makes that an impossible and unattainable objective. But I believe that our team, in a small way, has succeeded in providing a more relevant service for a number of offenders in a multi-racial community.

From Jim Lawson, 'Probation in St. Pauls: teamwork in a multi-racial, inner-city area',
Probation Journal, *31(3), 1984, pp. 93–95.*

60 Prostitution and the Absolute Discharge strategy (1987)

Mary Davies and Gillian Stewart

Further to NAPO's support for the decriminalisation of prostitution, this AGM calls upon Probation Practice Committee to provide guidelines to aid the preparation of SERs in cases of loitering for the purposes of prostitution and soliciting.

Resolution 21, 1986 AGM

We remain convinced that the Absolute Discharge is the only viable disposal for two reasons. Firstly, it is the only disposal which neither punishes nor extracts promises from women to cease an activity they either wish to, or feel they have to, continue. Secondly, this is the only disposal which does not contradict the existing NAPO policy calling for the decriminalisation of prostitution-related offences.

Prostitution is ideologically a difficult area. It clearly represents an exploitative relationship between persons of different status. As probation officers, we are uncomfortable with the negative effects that working as a prostitute can have on women's mental and physical well-being but recognise that predominantly they take a rational decision to do so, in the light of their restricted access to other means of improving their standard of living. The role of the probation officer – in acknowledging the paradox of punishing those who supply a service while condoning those who demand it – must be to mitigate the harmful effects of the criminal justice system on women working as prostitutes and not to compound the difficulties of their situation. Surely the Probation Service would not seek to support the hypocrisy of the law relating to this offence or deny that the origins of prostitution lie in a society which oppresses women.

Other disposals?

What is wrong with all the other disposals then? The 1982 Criminal Justice Act precludes imprisonment for loitering for the purposes of prostitution, likewise suspended sentences. Community Service operates as an alternative to custody and is thus inappropriate.

Probation orders

A probation order is not warranted from either a welfare or a justice perspective. On a welfare level, it seems more practical to make women aware of the agencies they can approach voluntarily for assistance if they feel they need it than to compel them to report to a probation officer. The Probation Service does not have a monopoly on counselling, advice and advocacy and may indeed be more restricted in what it can offer – faced with the anomaly of working with offenders whom NAPO feels should not be treated as such – than other agencies in the community. In respect of justice issues, the offence is a very low-tariff one for which to impose oversight in the community and intervention in the home. If the woman has decided to stop working as a prostitute, there is no pattern of 'offending behaviour' to work with. If she has decided to continue, and it is unlikely that being subject to a probation order could have changed her material circumstances to the extent that she feels no need of further money, then a breach of a probation order will be added to the list of offences at the next court appearance with a tariff-escalation effect. Probation orders are, therefore, really only viable in the event of other offences additional to loitering where there is the possibility of an immediate custodial sentence.

Fines

Financial penalties represent another particularly dysfunctional disposal. Paying a fine reduces income, increases the need to find customers to pay for services and raises the possibility of an eventual prison sentence for non-payment of fines. Ironically, research by NAPO has shown that, following the 1982 Criminal Justice Act, which removed imprisonment for soliciting, higher levels of fines have been imposed and have resulted in more women being imprisoned than was the case before the Act. Some courts have compounded this injustice by perceiving themselves almost as an extension of the Inland Revenue, assuming that they know the amount earned by prostitution and deducting what they estimate to be a high proportion of such earnings by way of fines. The court thereby simultaneously punishes the prostitute and benefits from her actions.

Conditional discharges

Conditional Discharges differ from Absolute Discharges insofar as they are conditional on the women not re-offending during a given time and can thus have a tariff-escalation effect, possibly resulting in the fines that would not otherwise have ensued.

Reasons for doubt

Logically there would seem to be no alternative to recommending Absolute Discharges. The doubts raised at conference fell into three main categories. The major preoccupation by far was with maintaining credibility in the court setting. The point was made that if courts became aware that the Probation Service was operating a 'blanket recommendation' policy of Absolute Discharges for such offences, then it would cease to request SERs for those offences and the woman may be dealt with inappropriately, this would then represent a loss of face for the Probation Service. This has not been our experience. Carefully written reports, tailored to the individual circumstances of each woman but with the same recommendation, have convinced magistrates in a number of areas, as will be discussed later, that the Absolute Discharge is a sensible disposal.

The issue could also be discussed at Magistrates Liaison meetings to prepare Magistrates for the arguments that are likely to be put forward in reports. As members of Probation Management Committees, many Magistrates would realise that this is consistent with the objectives and priorities of our work, as set by the Home Office, in concentrating our resources in work with high tariff offenders.

Attack on autonomy?

A second concern was with the individual probation officer's discretion in making recommendations; it was felt that autonomy was under attack. The failure of our original motion means that NAPO members are not being directed to follow this course of action but it does seem the only rational one to choose. We hope that those who may have had such reservations are now convinced, by our earlier argument, that there really is no other reasonable disposal.

Finally, concern was expressed that the welfare needs of women working as prostitutes may cease to be met if probation orders were no longer recommended. In this respect we would only add to what has already been stated in this article that we are probably the least welcome welfare agency available, in view of the controlling aspect of the probation task, and welfare needs could be better met if we were to refer women to appropriate local voluntary agencies at the SER stage.

Points of practice

The type of report we are suggesting should be presented in these cases does not differ significantly from what is generally accepted as good practice. However, we do feel that the following points should be included and that reports should:

- describe the social conditions leading to the offence and any personal consideration compounding the need for additional finances.
- give a detailed breakdown of the finances of the individual or family involved, including outstanding fines, debts, special needs, etc. but not including possible earnings through prostitution.
- describe the nature of the choice of work as a prostitute and call attention to the paradox of punishing one of two consenting partners.
- detail counselling services available in the community.
- detail the disposals available and their possible consequences.
- recommend the use of Absolute Discharges and the remitting of previously imposed financial penalties.

Lessons of experience

Following the Bournemouth Conference, we have liaised with the Probation Practice Committee and have received many requests for advice from probation officers throughout the country who are preparing such reports. The points above form the basis of the advice we have passed on and we are pleased to report that we have received feedback to the effect that this strategy has proved successful in many areas. Even where the recommendation for an Absolute Discharge has not been followed, the fines imposed have been substantially smaller than was hitherto the norm. What has been pleasantly surprising is the extent to which some courts will go along with recommendations for Absolute Discharges. In two notable cases where the women were facing five and ten charges of loitering for the purpose of prostitution five and ten Absolute Discharges were given respectively. We have also heard of courts remitting previously imposed fines in the region of £300.

Conversely, we know of cases where recommendations for probation orders for prostitution-related offences have been followed by the court, with the women then receiving custodial sentences shortly afterwards for relatively minor dishonesty offences committed, in one case, prior to the loitering offence. The women were viewed, it seems, as having been 'given the chance' of probation supervision, only to have 'reoffended', so they were dealt with more harshly than the dishonesty offences might otherwise have merited. This shows how a well-meaning welfare disposal can in reality have a very damaging effect. It is also important that previous convictions of loitering for the purpose of prostitution are not seen as representing 'a pattern of offending behaviour', so that subsequent unrelated offences are not viewed as an extension of offending, otherwise women with such convictions will be dealt with more punitively.

The recommendation for Absolute Discharges is not the end of the story. In some courts where such recommendations have already been followed, the women in question have received further Absolute Discharges on subsequent appearances without further reports being requested. It is not inconceivable that the development of such a pattern in sentencing may lead to decisions not to prosecute in these cases, which could ultimately pave the way for the eventual decriminalisation of prostitution-related offences. This would then be compatible with existing NAPO policy.

From Mary Davies and Gillian Stewart, 'Prostitution and the Absolute Discharge strategy',
Probation Journal, 34(2), 1987, pp. 51–53.

61 Feminist jurisprudence – or women-wise penology? (1989)

Pat Carlen

I am often asked whether I think it is possible (and/or desirable) to develop a distinct and different way of thinking about female lawbreakers and state punishment, whether a 'feminist jurisprudence' can or should be developed to inform the management of women's prisons, the writing of social enquiry reports for women, and the running of female offenders' hostels or probation groups etc. The question is an important one. For as Carol Smart (1989) has recently observed:

> The search for a feminist jurisprudence signals the shift away from a concentration on law reform and 'adding women' into legal considerations to a concern with fundamental issues like legal logic, legal values, justice, neutrality and objectivity.

Yet although Smart argues that we do indeed need to theorise women's oppression she expresses many reservations about the quest for a 'feminist jurisprudence'; not the least among them relating to the knowledge that 'once enacted, legislation is in the hands of individuals and agencies far removed from the values and politics of the women's movement'. For this and several other reasons she sounds a 'warning to feminism to avoid the siren call of law'. Avoidance of law, however, is not an option open to those women who stand before it not voluntarily seeking remedy but involuntarily awaiting punishment.

A feminist penology?

The question of how to think about women lawbreakers has been a thorny one for feminists. It is one thing to search for a 'feminist jurisprudence' ... but who wants a feminist penology? Well, people involved in the criminal justice and penal systems might, for a start. Concerned women (and men) working in the courts, prisons and non-custodial agencies might find it helpful to have some general feminist guidelines on penal policy, while lawbreaking women might find themselves to be less frequently written out of the judicial and penal scripts if a programme of criminal justice for women were to be among other (jurisprudential) paradigms informing the administration of criminal and penal justice.

I take Carol Smart's point that a 'feminist jurisprudence' might merely replace one closed and global system of 'Truth' with another and that, consequently, application of some principles of a feminist jurisprudence (e.g. 'equality', the appeal to 'rights') might merely result in advancing certain feminist claims to the detriment of others.

But, at the same time, I would argue that use of the indefinite article can put *any* jurisprudence in its place.

For although I myself can conceive of the possibility of several feminist jurisprudences – i.e. perspectives on the interpretation and administration of laws which are informed by the knowledge that women's life experiences are different to men's, I can think, too, of several other jurisprudential and political considerations which might also rightly inform decision-making and assessments in criminal cases involving women.

Dilemmas in practice

For instance, probation officers might sometimes correctly calculate that if they argue for equality of provision for their women clients, their claims will be answered by withdrawal of the existing facilities in question from their male clients. Likewise, a competent probation officer might know both that her client will gain advantage if it can be demonstrated that she is a good housewife and mother (Eaton 1986) *and* that by privileging that woman's housewifely and mothering performances she will also be colluding in, and promoting the stereotype of the *criminal* woman who is NOT a wife and mother, and thereby possibly disadvantaging single, divorced, childless and lesbian female offenders.

That such dilemmas exist should not be surprising. The varied constellations of political, ideological and economic conditions in which penal philosophies are realised mean it is seldom that we can expect to 'read-off' a penal policy from a jurisprudence – whatever it is called. Nonetheless, because of the 'involuntary' relationship between lawbreakers and the criminal law, and because, too, women have traditionally been so invisible in the criminal justice and penal systems, I do think that in relation to this branch of law, feminists should seek principled ways in which the criminal justice and penal systems might become more women-wise. Nowhere, in recent times has this need been more apparent than in the Chief Inspector of Prisons Report (1989) on Drake Hall, the Staffordshire Open Prison for women.

Drake Hall report

This is a sensitive and interesting Report with comprehensive coverage of most aspects of prison life and over a hundred recommendations to the Governor. My concern here, however, will be with just one of its revelations: the (at least threefold) difficulty which prison administrators appear to have in conceptualising women prisoners and women's prisons. First, it becomes apparent that masculinist culture is seen as an essential element of a *real* prison. Second, bereft of the masculinist yardstick, the Inspectors have no consistent criteria for assessing the regime's relevance to women's needs. Third, once they have accepted that women prisoners' needs may be different to men's, the Report's authors still find it difficult to 'make sense' of either Drake Hall or its inmates. Thus we learn that even 'the allocation of women to open conditions still owes much to immediate expediency and little to any reasoned system' (p.32).

Patriarchal

But a 'reasoned system' of allocation can hardly be expected of an administration which evidently has no consistent criteria for assessing either lawbreaking women or the penal regimes to which they are subject. Certainly at the time of the Autumn 1988 Inspection, its Governor did not see Drake Hall as a prison. Rather he explicitly described it as being an 'extended family' or a 'boarding school' (p.34), a blatantly patriarchal attitude heavily criticised by the Inspectors. Yet, apart from suggesting that inmate committees be formed (as in male prisons), the Inspectorate repeatedly admits to its inability to explain some of the already well-known features of women's imprisonment.

At the end of it all we are again left with the stereotypes of 'women' who 'naturally' care and who have a greater 'need' than men for 'familiar' relationships and more support, and *therefore* a higher staff-to-prisoner ratio than their male counterparts. At the same time we are reminded, 'Drake Hall is bound by the same policies and rules as the rest of the Prison Service' (p.85). So much for the possibility of developing a women-wise institution! On the other hand, the Inspectorate's repeated attempts to theorise the 'as-yet-untheorised' – the implications for penal policy of the recognition that women's experiences are different to men's – demonstrate the need for the development of a feminist jurisprudence *and* a women-wise penology (see Carlen 1989 for one account).

Let us now, therefore, discuss briefly what form a woman-wise penology might take and how it is already influencing (or might in the future influence): the writing of women's social enquiry reports; all-female hostels and housing schemes; and all-women lawbreakers and ex-prisoners' self support or agency-run groups.

A women-wise penology

Two fundamental aims of a women-wise penology might be to ensure: (1) that the penal regulation of female lawbreakers does not increase their oppression *as women* still further; (2) that the penal regulation of lawbreaking men is not such that it brutalises them and makes them even more physically or ideologically oppressive towards women in the future.

Three strategic principles informing policy might be: *remedial action* to redress the present wrongs of women in the criminal justice and penal systems; *resistance* to penal or other regulatory measures based on essentialised stereotypes of gender; *democratic exploration* of the many different possible modes of living in a variety of all-female (and for women who prefer them, mixed) schemes and groups.

SERS and sentencing

This is an area where concerned probation officers have already deployed innovative strategies informed both by research findings and professional experience. Strategies include: resistance to pushing women 'up tariff' by recommending a disposal aimed ostensibly at 'help' with her problems; instead, offering the help required (on a nonstatutory basis) at the Report writing stage and then, where appropriate, recommending a conditional discharge; discussing reports with other officers in order to detect and reject sexist language, stereotyping and assumptions; and reviewing the operation of Community Service Orders and the type of work done by women under CSOs.

Accommodation schemes

Until criminal justice policy is subordinated to and co-ordinated with, a strategy for social justice in general, we can expect homeless and destitute recidivist offenders to continue to go to gaol. In the meantime, housing policy for women in trouble and ex-prisoners could be informed (and often is) by women-wise strategies which would at least be supportive (rather than destructive) of ex-offenders' attempts to fashion for themselves a satisfying but non-criminal life-style. For example:

- Places reserved for women in trouble whether in mixed or women-only hostels should be retained as such, even if the result is occasional under-occupancy:
- Except in the very few hostels with a preponderance of extremely disturbed or mentally-incapacitated women, housing schemes and hostels should be run on democratic lines with all participants invited to be involved in decisions which affect their day-to-day living conditions;
- The 'dependency/independency' ideological couplet (so often invoked to justify completely contradictory approaches to women's needs) should be displaced by 'move on but come back' schemes which would allow women to 'move back' in at times of crisis and in any case regularly visit to partake of communal facilities and collective activities;
- Schemes should allow for as many different household-forms and life-styles as possible and even women in hostels should have their own keys and front door bells;
- Administrators of accommodation for mothers and children should not enact administrative policies designed either to regulate female sexuality or to police parenting.

All-women

Many co-ordinators of all-women probation-run or other groups for women in trouble have already theorised their own and group members' reported experiences in order to fashion spaces where troubled women can remedy (by assertiveness sessions, legal rights information/action, and co-operative enterprise) some of the oppression they regularly suffer in their daily lives. It is therefore very important that women-wise probation (and other) women's groups continue to exist – and for the following specific reasons:

- They provide a space for the remedy and assistance of women's oppression;
- They provide a forum in which women can collectively, democratically and responsibly fashion principles for the future (self) governance of their lives;
- Offence-focused groups, whilst recognising that there are no essentially 'female' causes of women's law breaking (only historically-specific economic political and ideological conditions) can slowly gain knowledge of the combinations of circumstances in which women most frequently choose to break the law and subsequently develop 'behaviour-changing' therapies which women recognise as relevant to their needs;
- The very existence (and popularity) of probation-run women's groups in neighbourhoods bereft of most other social amenities calls into question what the

criminal justice system and its agents are really for … and ensuing analysis demonstrates that far from being concerned primarily with serious lawbreakers, the CJS and its officers are more frequently providing support services for people who might not have been in trouble at all if they had been in employment and in receipt of decent provision from the education, housing, health and welfare services.

I have not tried to draw up a blueprint for a 'women-wise' penology but have merely outlined some guiding principles and existing good practice. Strategies must vary to meet changes in economy, politics, ideology and patterns of lawbreaking and law enforcement. The main purpose of this article has been to argue that in order to right some of the wrongs presently suffered by women in a criminal justice system that has persistently discriminated against them 'women-wise' penal strategies should be fashioned from overall policy calculations based (at least in part) upon a 'feminist jurisprudence'.

From Pat Carlen, 'Feminist jurisprudence – or women-wise penology?',
Probation Journal, *36(3), 1989, pp. 110–114.*

References

Carlen, P. (1989) *Women's Imprisonment: A Strategy for Abolition.* Occasional Paper 3. Keele, University of Keele Centre for Criminology.

Eaton, M. (1986) *Justice for Women? Family, court and social control.* Milton Keynes, Open University Press.

HM Chief Inspector of Prisons (1989) *Report on HM Prison and Young Offenders Institution Drake Hall.* London, Home Office.

Smart, C. (1989) *Feminism and the Power of Law.* London, Routledge.

62 Policies of neglect

Female offenders and the probation service (2000)

Judith Rumgay

... Exploratory practice in one Probation Service

In 1993, Hereford and Worcester Probation Service took a policy decision to create separate provision for female offenders under supervision, establishing a particular structure for service delivery. A groupwork programme was designed to introduce women to topics relevant to their offending and lifestyles, incorporating sessions on female crime, relationships, stress management, assertiveness, anger management, substance use, health and employment/training. Led by two female probation officers whose time was dedicated to developmental practice with women on probation, the programme was scheduled on one day per week, when transport, lunch and a crèche managed by volunteers were provided. It was enhanced by a serendipitous opportunity to use some redundant council premises as a centre for the exclusive purpose of delivering services to women. Female link officers, located in field teams, undertook the majority of direct individual work, liaised with the centre and advised their colleagues on provision. Focused staff investment, however, led in the longer term to recognition of issues which illuminated the predicament of women offenders in relation to their access to probation service provision. These issues, and their implications for service quality, will be explored in the following account of the project's experience. ...

... Staff felt that their groupwork programme was well received by the women who attended it; the evaluative feedback collected from participants from every group was consistently positive. They thought, however, that the programme was underused owing to field officers' failure to refer and encourage women to attend. Moreover, recurrent challenges to the justification for separate provision arose within the service through the perception that it targeted low-tariff offenders, whose supervising officers became enmeshed in a tangle of personal distress rather than focused on criminality. ...

The targeting controversy

To examine the probation service's dissatisfaction with its targeting of women for probation, a survey of ... pre-sentence reports (hereafter PSRs) in female cases and their outcomes was carried out, involving 180 reports prepared in 1994. ...

... [T]he frequency with which particular disposals were imposed by sentencers [was compared with] the frequency with which they were proposed by report writers. ... [P]referred proposals coincided with their popularity as sentences in the courts, with standard probation (i.e. probation without additional requirements) being the most frequent proposal and outcome, followed by conditional discharge and community service. Nevertheless, officers proposed conditional discharge considerably more often than the courts imposed it; they also worked to a shorter tariff in that they never proposed custodial sanctions and only one proposal for a combination order was made in the entire year. ...

[T]he 'concordance' between PSR proposals and the outcomes at court, i.e. the number of occasions on which the outcome in a particular case agreed with the report writer's proposal [was also examined]. Probation officers were more successful than otherwise in all categories of the proposals which they used, except for the combination order.

The enthusiasm for the conditional discharge suggested that officers were exercising tariff vigilance, seeking to push women down the scale where possible. These proposals included some adventurous successful arguments for conditional discharge, for example, in a case of deception involving £3,500 and in two cases of drunk driving. The fact that officers appealed sparingly to extra requirements in probation orders also suggested active tariff attention, and reflected both the service's policy against forcing women onto programmes dominated by male interests, and preference for encouraging voluntary attendance at the women's groupwork programme. Overall, probation officers restricted appeals to extra requirements to cases in which they perceived little alternative.

... [O]nly eight first offenders were recommended for probation: four were convicted of deception involving large sums of money over appreciable periods of time; two had committed drink-driving offences involving both high alcohol readings and aggravating features; one was convicted of a substantial theft from an employer; and one of perverting the course of justice. Moreover, what appeared as relatively trivial or first offences in the statistical information collected within the service, often involved complex issues of seriousness. For example, benefit fraud is commonly brought to court on the basis of one or two 'specimen' charges. Thus, statistical data recorded minor offences with a small total value. Yet, probation officers' proposals reflected appreciation that the court was dealing with repeated offences, sometimes sustained over a substantial time, amounting to large sums in total. Accumulation of such 'typical' female cases contributed to the perception that the women targeted for probation were first, minor and low-risk offenders, and should be disqualified from probation, while obscuring problematic sentencing issues. ...

Offending

... [D]ishonesty accounted for over half of the offences for which the women were sentenced. The predominance of deception, the most common variety being benefit fraud, and shoplifting reflects research evidence that these are 'typical' female crimes (Hedderman and Hough 1994; Morris *et al.* 1994; Simon and Landis 1991). Probation officers related such offences to poverty and responsibility for family care in most cases. However, as we have seen, a connection with social deprivation does not prevent such offences from appearing serious to the courts.

Needs

After the almost universal poverty, five areas of need received particular attention in PSRs: psychological problems (38 cases, 21%); current or previous involvement in abusive partnerships (36 cases, 20%); child abuse survival (22 cases, 12%); alcohol problems (20 cases, 11%); and drug problems (18 cases, 10%). Since only explicit reference to abuse was counted, and non-specific accounts of 'difficult' or 'unhappy' childhoods or partnerships were rejected, these are probably underestimates of abuse histories.

Offence narratives frequently linked these areas of personal distress directly or indirectly to the women's criminality. For example, an excess alcohol and dangerous driving offence was committed in an attempt to escape from immediate domestic violence; seemingly uncontrolled aggression was displayed after a woman discovered her partner's abuse of her children, in an effort to prevent him from re-entering the house. In ten cases ..., the offence was linked to a pressurised relationship with a male which was not said to include violence. For example, a partner's refusal of financial support or unpredictable absences often underlay benefit fraud; all [five] cases of perverting justice were linked to intimidation by males.

Chronic psychological damage from abuse was also connected to offending. For example, in two cases, childhood trauma was linked to the development of obsessive-compulsive disorders which included shoplifting. Several women were rape victims; one woman's violence was an attempt to ward off further attack. Rare offences, such as arson and conspiracy, involved unique circumstances, usually compounded by complex psychological disturbance: a woman set fire to her flat in a suicide attempt, after first ensuring her child's safety.

Probation officers' proposals responded to these aspects of female offenders' lives. In two cases, community service was excluded because of the danger of exacerbating an abusive relationship. In two cases, an officer assisted the woman to a place of safety following an attack during the report preparation period. As implied by much research on female offenders (e.g. Baskin and Sommers 1998; Maher 1994), therefore, probation officers found themselves, in a very real sense, working with high-risk victims. This perspective challenges the common assumption that risk concerns only the degree to which predatory offenders threaten the safety of an innocent public.

The PSR survey thus revealed, first, that repetition, seriousness and risk were all observable in the offending of women, but were obscured by the application of measures of their presence derived from assumptions about typically male offences. Second, probation officers' involvement in areas of personal distress, commonly viewed as irrelevant to an offence focus, reflected connections drawn in the women's offence narratives. Third, the offences, needs and their interconnections characterising this group of women reflected research findings. Probation officers thus appeared not so much transgressors of articulated policy as practitioners whose intensified exposure through the introduction of gender-separated provision sensitised them to these issues. ...

A model for practice

The problem for practice development had been constructed as one of poor targeting and inappropriate focus, defined by the criteria applied to typically male offending.

If, however, probation officers were neither inappropriately targeting minor offenders, nor involving themselves irrelevantly in personal distress, then the real challenge was to sensitise practice to the features of typically *female* offending. Assimilation of the PSR survey was followed by a shift from defensive to pro-active practice. This involved developing strategies to enhance women's access to the service, particularly the groupwork programme, and articulating a rationale for gender-sensitive provision.

Enhancement of access

... Specialist staff believed they lacked influence over women's access to the centre. Two strategies in particular altered this predicament.

First, specialist staff reached out pro-actively to field teams, monitoring the imposition of probation orders, enquiring about supervision plans and exploring the potential contribution of groupwork participation. Regular meetings of specialist and link officers promoted open case discussion. Officers referring women accompanied them to the centre for a preliminary meeting with specialist staff, thereby engaging the women's interest and confidence.

Second, complementing the service's approach to its intensive programmes for male probationers, a book was produced to articulate its strategy for females. ... This initiative raised the visibility of a practice model which explicitly embraced separate provision, integration of individual and groupwork methods, and gender-sensitive responsivity.

Integration of services

The existence of an exclusive centre for the delivery of the groupwork programme facilitated investment in collaborative multi-agency effort. The overarching goal of 'normalisation' underpinned this aspect of practice: it enhanced female offenders' access to community-based networks of support; and decreased emphasis on the probation service as a focal resource for women whose social and personal problems were shared by many non-offenders. Reducing emphasis on the criminal justice base of the women's centre included, therefore, developing its use as a community centre.

A specialist officer described three elements in the centre's development as a community resource: provision of a space exclusively for women which was safe, comfortable and enhanced their social and learning opportunities; development of a focal point of networking and a forum for groups working with women; and the offer of direct services for users, which included education, advice and the probation groupwork programme. In pursuit of these themes, the centre accommodated a variety of community groups. ...

While this is a very different approach from that of the conventional probation centre offering offence-focused programmes exclusively for offenders, and therefore could appear peripheral to core provision, this integrative approach resolved difficulties of locating women within the mainstream of the service's opportunities. Because of their typical offending patterns, women offenders were not attractive candidates for conventional tariff-based provision. Because of their distinctive histories, it was inappropriate to force them onto programmes designed for and dominated by males. Because of their particular needs, enhanced access to community support networks represented empowerment. Precisely because of the probation service's difficulty in locating these women in its core provision, it became vital to connect them to their communities.

Introducing the user's voice

... Most women had embarked on the programme with few expectations, at the behest of their probation officer or the court. Evaluations, however, were overwhelmingly positive. Women almost unanimously applauded the group's gender exclusivity, recording freedom of expression, mutuality of perspective and absence of discomfort and denigration which was associated with male presence. ...

Women predominantly identified relationship as both the best and the most influential aspect of the programme. ... Many comments identified influential programme features, almost invariably deriving from the relational group process: reduced stigma and isolation; increased confidence and self-esteem; enhanced self-identity and self-assertion; improved social skills and help-giving; altered criminal attitudes and behaviour; reduced stereotyping and greater appreciation of women's diversity; stimulation and learning; and increased readiness to seek help. ...

Hard lessons to learn

... Letting voiceless clients speak

[The probation service] is not well known for direct involvement of offenders in development of provision. It is more likely to test its programme recipients for evidence that they have changed in prescribed ways than to open its service to the critical scrutiny of offenders. ...

Yet how *should* the wider agency receive the news that dedicated resources had produced positive relational experiences for over 100 offenders? Women's emphasis on the significance of relationship in the group process reflects the importance of relational involvement for female psychological development, learning and rehabilitation (Bandura 1997; Covington 1998; Gilligan 1988). Their attributions of liberation to the group's gender-exclusivity are supported in research (Tannen 1992). Nevertheless, how powerful is a defence of practice based on appeals to the subtleties of gender psychology, when advanced within an organisation under strong contemporary pressure to effect individual change by challenge, confrontation and control? ...

'Feeling more able?'[1]

The decision to establish separate provision ... forced into the open the difficulties of responding creatively to female offenders within the context of the probation service's modern sense of mission. These difficulties remain muted and unfocused where the predominance of male offenders swamps the client population and drives the forms of policy and practice which develop. Their deepest irony lies in the evolution of a policy framework in which the female offender, by the very nature of her less serious offending and lower public risk, has come to be regarded as undeserving of opportunities for rehabilitation. Equally, her status as offender disqualifies her from recognition as the victim with whom the probation service is most regularly and directly brought into contact. It is a distressing paradox that a service which has been engaged for some time in an effort to enhance its support for victims of crime, and which currently presents its mission in terms of public protection, should have come to perceive responsiveness to the real danger of victimisation experienced by many female offenders as an unwarranted reaction to a welfare problem. Poignantly, the female offender's isolation within local communities creates a situation in which the probation service may offer her only gateway to appropriate support networks.

Within a powerful organisational tradition of prescriptive practice, strengthened further by contemporary penal pressures, the user's voice is muted. The minority user's voice is weaker still, since to recognise its message demands the effort to engage with an alternative personal world, to locate need within a fully articulated organisational mission, to respond creatively and to sustain the vigour of that response.

From Judith Rumgay, 'Policies of neglect: female offenders and the probation service', in
H. Kemshall and R. Littlechild (eds.) User Involvement and Participation in Social
Care: Research Informing Practice *(London: Jessica Kingsley), 2000, pp. 193–213.*

Note

1 A woman wrote 'Feeling more able?' on her programme evaluation questionnaire when invited to comment on the assertiveness and anger management sessions.

References

Bandura, A. (1997) *Self-efficacy: The Exercise of Control.* New York: W.H. Freeman and Company.

Baskin, D.R. and Sommers, I.B. (1998) *Casualties of Community Disorder: women's careers in violent crime.* Boulder, CO: Westview.

Covington, S. (1998) 'The relational theory of women's psychological development: implications for the criminal justice system', in R. Zaplin (ed.) *Female Offenders: critical perspectives and effective intervention.* Gaithersburg, MD: Aspen Publishers.

Gilligan, C. (1988) 'Prologue: adolescent development reconsidered', in C. Gilligan, J.V. Ward and J.M. Taylor (eds.) *Mapping the Moral Domain.* Cambridge, MA: Harvard University Press.

Hedderman, C. and Hough, M. (1994) *Does the Criminal Justice System Treat Men and Women Differently?* Research Findings No. 10. London: Home Office.

Maher, L. (1994) *Sexed Work: Gender, Race and Resistance in a Brooklyn Drug Market.* Oxford: Oxford University Press.

Morris, A., Wilkinson, C., Tisi, A., Woodrow, J. and Rockley, A. (1994) *Managing the Needs of Female Prisoners.* London: Home Office.

Simon, R.J. and Landis, J. (1991) *The Crimes Women Commit, the Punishments They Receive.* Lexington, MA: Lexington Books.

Tannen, D. (1992) *You Just Don't Understand: Women and Men in Conversation.* London: Virago Press.

63 Designing and delivering programmes for minority ethnic offenders (2006)

Patrick Williams

Introduction

In June 1999 a group of probation practitioners, voluntary sector managers, teaching consultants and research staff were commissioned to design, develop and implement a groupwork programme specifically for minority ethnic offenders being supervised by the Greater Manchester Probation Area (GMPA). ... The development and implementation process came to fruition in the Spring of 2000 with the pilot of the Black Offender Groupwork Programme. Simultaneously, national developments were apace to provide evidence of What Works for Black and Asian offenders resulting in the development and piloting of four Pathfinder groupwork models. The practice and cultural interplay between the local probation area and the National Probation Directorate (NPD) introduced an additional set of variables, which significantly 'influenced' the delivery of services within the local area. ...

This chapter will return to the sequence of events that gave rise to the development of the Black Offender Groupwork programme. In addition, it will examine the relationship between the 'local' and the 'centre' to highlight the complexities and difficulties that arise in the provision of 'guidance' from the centre to inform practice and interventions within the local context. ...

Probation programmes for Black offenders

There were a number of drivers behind the development of Black offender groupwork programmes. First, there was growing evidence of a differential in the delivery of services to Black and Asian offenders. Official statistics showed a disproportionate increase in the numbers of Black offenders receiving custodial sentences (Home Office 2003). In addition, studies found a disparity in the quality of pre-sentence reports prepared on Black and Asian offenders and highlighted the concerns of practitioners about the types of interventions available (HMIP 2000, 2004). Second, the absence of 'diversionary' interventions for Black and Asian offenders, which had been implemented for a generic caseload, made the organisation susceptible to a charge of discriminatory practice. Third, there emerged 'dissenting voices' that questioned the legitimacy of the application of 'effective practice principles' for Black and Asian offenders which were as yet largely unproven.

Groupwork – traditional goals versus modern concerns

The use of groupwork as a mode of intervention for addressing the related needs of offenders has a long history within probation practice. ... I would like to focus on the seminal period of 1972 through to 1984. ...

It is during this period that groupwork was utilised as a tool for participant empowerment, reflecting the socio-political value base of the Probation Service. Within this construct, the offender was deemed a product of wider societal inequality and oppression and thus the intervention was developed to recognise and redress the social status of the client (Mitchell-Clarke 1998).

... Moreover, the advancement of practice to be 'anti-discriminatory', 'anti-oppressive' and 'anti-sexist' provided the subtext for this political shift (Nellis and Gelsthorpe 2003). ... Increasingly, the design and development of groupwork reflected the 'strategies' employed to 'reduce, eliminate, combat and reverse negative valuations by powerful groups in society affecting certain individuals and social groups', by challenging institutional and social oppression (Payne 1991: 229).

The mid-1980s through to the 1990s saw a move away from the use of groupwork programmes to 'empower' the individual, towards its re-employment as a mechanism for the 'control' of the offender within the community. ... This saw the isolation of the individual from their social environment towards explanations of causality based solely on individual characteristics and rejecting considerations around social, political and economic justice. ... The emphasis upon 'control' was embraced by the [NPD] as a means through which the organisation could exert a claim of effectiveness in the management of offenders within the community. ...

Difference – the experience of Black people in British society

... The work of Calverley *et al.* (2004) provides an invaluable insight into the experience and 'needs' of Black and Asian offenders. ... Notably, what is reiterated within this study is that the perception and experience of social and economic inequality is as a result of wider racism and discrimination. This perception is learned and internalised within a criminogenic environment, devoid of legitimate opportunities, 'successful talk' or stories, and where the benefits afforded to the majority of society members become perceived as the preserve of 'others'. ... [T]he onset of offending behaviour is facilitated by a lack of pro-social strategies to manage the 'strain' that accompanies these negative life experiences. Crucially, strategies for working with Black and Asian offenders must therefore be located within the social, economic and personal constructs of the individual and be able to engage and address [this] multiplicity of factors. ...

Groupwork for Black offenders – towards empowerment

There is little the Probation Service can do to change the social environments within which offenders live, but it can assist them through the exploration of self-identity and self-conceptualisation to change their views about the choices available within those environments....

Though variations existed, empowerment programmes for Black and Asian offenders tended to be multi-faceted, with explorations of racism, social exclusion and discrimination providing the springboard from which discussions around personal responsibility to the self and other within the community could be explored. In this respect, far from allowing offenders to abnegate responsibility, the process encouraged them to take responsibility for their actions, to be less of a victim and more of an agent. ...

Specifically, a model of empowerment developed within GMPA consisted of five programme sessions with the aim to 'explore the levels and types of internal, external and institutional racism', and how these attitudes may 'impact' upon the offenders' social and criminogenic attitude'. In addition, session content ranged from discussions around the historical context of Black people within Greater Manchester, focusing on 'how we came to be here', to sessions in relation to 'self definition' and 'how we see ourselves'. Other sessions facilitated discussion around 'survival strategies from slavery to the present' and sought to highlight the process and features of decision-making taken by significant figures throughout history. Importantly, empowerment sought to present the historical context of racism and discrimination within a modern framework relevant to programme participants, leading to an examination of the nature and role of citizenship in the present. ...

... [W]ithin the Greater Manchester area offenders were assessed and given the 'informed' choice of attendance at either a specific Black offender groupwork programme or at the 'generic' offending behaviour programmes delivered within local probation offices. During the period January to December 2003, 177 Black and Asian offenders who met the eligibility criteria were referred to offending behaviour programmes and of these 35 (19.7 per cent) opted to attend the generic programme within local probation offices instead of the empowerment programme (Williams 2003). ...

The evaluation of local programmes highlight that the completion rates for Black empowerment groups compare favourably with those currently achieved for general offending behaviour programmes. ... [C]ompletion rates of between 50 per cent and 70 per cent were realised for groups run in the West Midlands and Greater Manchester probation areas (Dunn 2000; Williams 2003). These comparable completion rates appear to reflect the positive comments made by the participants of Black empowerment groups. In many cases, this is the first opportunity offenders have ever had to discuss issues around race, being Black, and their needs in relation to offending and race within a safe, supportive environment (ILPS 1993: Williams 2001; Durrance *et al.* 2001). Equally, programme participants are able to relate the issues covered in the programme to their offending. ...

Local and national drivers – different song sheets

In the absence of a national strategy and with the voicing of practitioner concerns ..., local probation areas began a process of developing groupwork interventions for Black offenders. ... [T]he features and needs that gave rise to the development of specific groupwork programmes for Black and Asian offenders from local probation areas represented a genuine drive and concern that sought to redress the experiential inequalities of the offender as a means through which to empower the individual and to develop strategies to reduce future involvement in offending behaviour. ...

... [T]he Home Office decided to take the agenda forward by developing and testing out a number of Pathfinder models (Stephens *et al.* 2004). ... [A] core component of the Pathfinder programmes was the inclusion of Black self-development models in the wider context of standard general offending behaviour programmes currently running within the Probation Service. Within the general offending behaviour programmes, criminal behaviour is deemed symptomatic of 'cognitive deficits' that have resulted from a deficient socialisation process and learned behaviour. These cognitive deficits lead to a lack of well-developed problem-solving techniques and social skills. ...

Concurrently, there had been a significant change in the theory base underpinning the delivery of probation practice to offenders. The emergence of the What Works theory base isolated a number of key principles upon which all probation interventions were to be built. The acceptance of these principles by the National Probation Service (NPS) resigned many 'locally developed' initiatives, or 'legacy' programmes, as they became known, to the margins of probation practice, to be replaced by accredited programmes that, it was claimed, had been rigorously evaluated and were proven to be effective in reducing the offending behaviour of participants. Where the 'kudos' of implementing accredited programmes was not sufficiently motivating for local areas to ensure their wide implementation into probation practice, the subsequent introduction of 'cash-linked' targets based on the number of offenders who commenced and completed programmes certainly was.

There emerged a number of theoretical and cultural conflicts between the ambitions and pursuits of local probation areas when juxtaposed with the national approach. First, the Pathfinder models promote an individualistic explanation for offending behaviour and therefore place a greater emphasis on the pathology of the individual, paying scant regard to the social context within which the behaviour exists (Durrance and Williams 2003). This has resulted in the disengagement of the individual from their social, personal and cultural context, which undermines the significance of racism, discrimination and inequality for offending behaviour. ... Therefore, locally, the drive to utilise the groupwork programme as a mechanism to address inequality and discrimination was curtailed with the implementation of the Pathfinder process.

... The Pathfinder models make redundant the language of 'empowerment' for the less menacing 'preparatory' to describe the sessions undertaken prior to the offending behaviour module of the Pathfinder programmes. The aims of the 'preparatory' sessions are to aid the compliance of the participant through the programme, by acting as a motivator to engage programme participants (Stephens *et al.* 2004). Given the comparable completion rates for empowerment programmes, the Pathfinder employment of preparatory sessions to facilitate offender motivation and completion is somewhat misguided. Moreover, the partial inclusion of the experiential effects of racism, discrimination and wider societal inequality, within preparatory sessions, as a mechanism to facilitate programme compliance is inappropriate.

Second ... the increasing heterogeneity of Black people, as evidenced through the continuing diversification of British society, significantly reduces the capacity to include materials to meet the cultural, religious and ethnic needs of all eligible groupwork participants for whom empowerment would be beneficial. ... It is therefore important that the increasing diversification of the programme participants is not utilised as a justification for not pursuing the empowerment approach by rendering impractical the pursuit of offender empowerment.

Conclusion

The exploration of self-identity, the challenging of negative views of the self and the wider community, the re-framing of the offender perception from that of victim to agent, and facilitating the development and exploration of pro-social (and pro-community) choices are prerequisites to reduce the feelings developed as a result of the experiences of racism, discrimination and socio-economic inequality. Moreover, it is exposure to the empowerment process that can facilitate the desistance process.

Further, there is an imminent threat to the continuation of the Pathfinder enterprise in relation to Black and Asian offenders. The arrival of the National Offender Management Service (NOMS) has led to a restructuring of the Research, Development and Statistics Directorate (RDS), which had previously been committed to the evaluation of the projects. Regrettably, this has resulted in the devolution of research responsibility for the Pathfinder projects to local probation areas. The capacity of local research departments to fully engage with the issues discussed within this chapter is questionable, given the constraints on local resources and in the light of the revised methodologies employed that confine the evaluation to monitoring the throughput of participants in the Pathfinder models. Clearly the celebration and pursuit of 'equitable, fair and accessible practices both within the [probation] workforce and for those receiving its services' is being undone through an overemphasis and reliance upon micro-managerialist methodologies to push through the objectives of the NPD Diversity Strategy (Nellis and Gelsthorpe 2003).

… The NPD must now facilitate local areas to reconnect with their communities and develop effective interventions that match the community's needs. It is clear that this must be undertaken at a local level, as the composition of race and ethnicity varies by locality. This will require us to embrace and acknowledge the centrality of the social, personal and identity constructs of *all* offenders to illustrate our commitment to addressing offending behaviour in all its forms. A wider question that requires exploration is the extent to which issues discussed in this chapter relate also to the generic caseload – whether there is an urgent need to revisit and engage with the interplay of class and the dynamics of social exclusion as a context for all probation clients in relation to offending behaviour.

> From Patrick Williams, 'Designing and delivering programmes for minority ethnic offenders', in S. Lewis, P. Raynor, D. Smith and A. Wardak (eds.) Race and Probation (Cullompton: Willan), 2006, pp. 145–163.

References

Calverley, A., Cole, B., Kaur, G., Lewis, S., Raynor, P., Sadeghi, S., Smith, D., Vanstone, M. and Wardak, A. (2004) *Black and Asian Offenders on Probation.* Home Office Research Study 277. London: Home Office.

Dunn, M. (2000) *Recidivism: Report of the Black Offender Group Pilots.* Birmingham: West Midlands Probation.

Durrance, P., Hignett, C., Merone, L. and Asamoah, A. (2001) *The Greenwich and Lewisham Self-development and Educational Attainment Group: Evaluation Report.* London: London Probation Area.

Durrance, P. and Williams, P. (2003) 'Broadening the Agenda Around What Works for Black and Asian Offenders.' *Probation Journal,* 50(3): 211–24.

HMIP (Her Majesty's Inspectorate of Probation) (2000) *Towards Race Equality: A Thematic Inspection.* London: Home Office.

——(2004) *Towards Race Equality: Follow-up Inspection Report.* London: Home Office.

Home Office (2003) *Statistics on Race and the Criminal Justice System 2002.* London: Home Office.

ILPS (Inner London Probation Service) (1993) *The Black Groups Initiative 1992–93: Evaluation.* London: ILPS.

Mitchell-Clarke, V. (1998) *Groupwork with Black Offenders.* Unpublished Master's Dissertation. Leicester: Scarman Centre.

Nellis, M. and Gelsthorpe, L. (2003) 'Human Rights and the Probation Values Debate', in W. H. Chui and M. Nellis (eds) *Moving Probation Forward.* Harlow: Pearson.

Payne, M. (1991) *Modern Social Work Theory.* Basingstoke: Macmillan.

Stephens, K., Coombes, J. and Debidin, M. (2004) *Black and Asian Offenders Pathfinder: Implementation Report.* Home Office Development and Practice Report 24. London: Home Office.

Williams, P. (2001) *Evaluation of the Black Offender Groupwork Programme.* Manchester: Greater Manchester Probation Service.

——(2003) *Evaluation of the Think First Black and Asian Offenders Programme.* Manchester: Greater Manchester Probation Service.

64 Dealing with diversity (2007)

Loraine Gelsthorpe

Introduction

The issue of diversity is never far from media reports at present whether or not one is talking about race, gender, mental health or sexual orientation, for example, and a host of issues spring to the fore: is there evidence to suggest discrimination? How can we best interpret the evidence on the basis that no facts speak for themselves? Other questions revolve around the various attempts to avoid negative discrimination and to ensure that anti-discriminatory policy is translated into practice. Moreover, there are substantive issues as to whether or not any one group of offenders deserves to be dealt with differently on grounds of their differential needs and risks.

These questions are not easily answered because there might be different issues depending on whether or not one was talking about racial discrimination, gender, sexual orientation, mental health or, indeed, age. Moreover, the very notion of 'dealing with diversity' demands attention from other directions too, for it cannot be assumed that equality of penal outcome is, in fact, the most desirable goal, although we might agree that a broadly equitable approach is necessary to ensure that sentencing and the criminal justice system as a whole achieve legitimacy for the public, offenders, sentencers and other criminal justice professionals themselves. Thus one question is how diversity can be addressed without completely dislodging the principles of justice, fairness, and equity in approach. This chapter focuses on race and gender issues, although the broader precepts and principles find resonance when dealing with other forms of diversity too.

The concept of discrimination

First, it is important to consider ways in which diversity amongst offenders is already dealt with and here we turn to notions of negative discrimination. Discrimination is a notoriously difficult concept to define. In the criminal justice context the term is commonly taken to mean unfavourable treatment based on a person's sex, gender, social class, 'race', ethnicity, age, or disability, for instance. It is a concept that is frequently tied to the concept of prejudice against particular people on the grounds that they are, for example, 'inferior' or 'difficult'. Under the Race Relations Act 1976 (revised by the Race Relations (Amendment) Act 2000), *direct* racial discrimination arises when a person treats another less favourably on racial grounds than that person would treat someone else. 'Racial grounds' under the Act meant on grounds of colour, race, nationality (including citizenship) or ethnic or national origins. *Indirect* discrimination, on the other hand, consists of treatment which may be described as equal in a formal sense (say between black and white offenders) but discriminatory in its actual effect. Arguably, indirect discrimination is far more significant and pervasive than direct discrimination, and this is as likely to be the case in the field of criminal justice as it is in other areas of social policy.

Complaints relating to the treatment of BME (black and minority ethnic) offenders in the criminal justice system often lead to claims that there should be *less disparity* in the delivery of justice; complaints about the treatment of women in the system often lead to the opposite conclusion. Here it suggested that women and men should be treated *rather more* differently than they are. Thus 'dealing with diversity' is challenging and especially so in attempts to avoid dislodging notions of fairness, equality and justice in the process.

Concerns about discrimination

… A number of studies have pointed to notable differences in the trajectory of white offenders and black offenders (particularly African-Caribbean offenders) through the criminal justice system. It shouldn't be assumed that these differences are always evidence of clear discrimination however; indeed, taken together, the available research findings suggest that some differences may be explained by a combination of legal factors and social factors. Nonetheless, in many studies, residual, unexplained ethnic differences remain after these differences have been taken into account. …

There have also been concerns about race equality issues within court reports (formerly social inquiry reports, now pre-sentence reports; HM Inspectorate of Probation 2000). And there is concern about differential access to community penalties for BME adults and young offenders (Bowling and Phillips 2002; Feilzer and Hood 2004), as well as the suggestion that BME offenders' needs have been neglected. Indeed, there are now a number of forceful accounts that BME offenders have experienced considerable social exclusion (Social Exclusion Unit 2002) and that the particularities of the disadvantages that they have experienced are not captured either by risk assessment instruments or by the caring gaze of probation officers (Cole and Wardak 2006; Raynor and Lewis 2006).

Concerns about negative or neglectful treatment of BME offenders have been so great as to suggest that there is 'institutional bias' whereby organisations fail to provide a professional service to people on the basis of their 'colour, culture and ethnic origin'. Whilst the claim originally concerned the police in response to a catalogue of police failures following the murder of black teenager Stephen Lawrence (Macpherson 1999), it is a term which has been taken up by other criminal justice system agencies too in their attempts to deal with diversity (Bowling and Phillips 2002; Lewis *et al.* 2006).

Turning to *gender*, there is a popular view that women receive lenient treatment in criminal justice compared to men, but little to support this claim beyond superficial analysis of criminal statistics which show that more women than men receive cautions (or reprimands and warnings in the case of young offenders in the English and Welsh system) and conditional discharges and probation, and that fewer women than men receive custodial penalties. But what such claims ignore is the fact that these differences reflect the seriousness of crimes committed and the number of previous convictions and so on. As a result of varying views, debates about whether women receive lenient or harsh treatment have abounded (Gelsthorpe 2001). ...

More recently, there have been huge concerns about the increase in the number of women sentenced to custody; the number has almost tripled in the last decade and is way out of proportion to the level of increases in crime or seriousness of crimes committed by women (Fawcett Society 2004; Gelsthorpe and Morris 2002; Home Office 2003). Women generally commit less serious offences than men and are far less likely to commit violence or sexual offences or to persist in crime. Moreover, it is thought that women's routes into crime are often quite distinct from men's ... (see chapters in McIvor 2004 for an overview). ...

Needless to say, it is important to consider how ethnicity and gender (and indeed social class) might inter-relate, but few studies have got anywhere near the methodological sophistication and robustness required for this (see Gelsthorpe 2006 who writes about the other 'other' – the experiences of female minority ethnic offenders).

To summarise, the evidence is that BME offenders have been treated in a discriminatory way that undermines equality and fairness and the possibility of distinctive needs and disadvantages have not been properly explored. Women have been treated differently from men, but not always on the basis of *relevant* factors, instead reflecting gender-role stereotyping. Whilst some women benefit from gender-role stereotyping, some are disadvantaged by it. The criminal justice system appears to neglect women's needs, and subjects women to sentencing provision and prison regimes which to a large extent have been designed for men (and white men at that). What does it mean to 'deal with diversity' then? ...

Dealing with diversity: policy and practice

... [A]ccording to Denney (1992) probation policy ignored ethnic minority offenders until the late 1970s. It wasn't until the mid-1970s that the Home Office encouraged the appointment of specialist officers in each area to develop services for ethnic minorities. The thinking at the time was that specialists could mediate any 'cultural misunderstandings'. Following the urban disturbances in the 1980s (the Brixton riots) there was emerging acknowledgement of the need to recognise institutional forms of racism and to promote anti-racist probation practice – mainly through local initiatives and projects. ...

There was relatively little research on BME offenders' needs and on what might 'work' for them until the early 1990s, but since then there have been a number of significant developments in efforts to address perceptions of inequality in provision (Williams 2006) and to establish more clearly what BME offenders' needs and experiences might be. One such development involved a survey of Probation Service provision (groupwork programmes and so on) specifically targeting black and Asian offenders (Powis and Walmsley 2002), but whilst some staff showed a preference for running separate programmes for BME offenders, others advocated mixed groupwork provision and there was little empirical evidence (in terms of effectiveness) to substantiate either position. Unfortunately the research did not include a focus on offenders' views. But another study did involve interviews with nearly 500 black and Asian offenders under supervision by the Probation Service in order to produce some evidence on their 'criminogenic needs' (Calverley *et al.* 2004). The research found that black, Asian and mixed heritage offenders showed less evidence of crime-prone attitudes and beliefs, and lower levels of self-reported problems than white counterparts. Interestingly, only a third of the offenders wanted to be supervised by someone from the same ethnic group whilst most thought that it would make no difference. Moreover, there was very limited support from those attending programmes for groups of offenders containing only members from ethnic minority groups. Given this, it will be important to ensure that the Equality Act 2006 does not lead to ready assumptions that ethnic diversity *has* to mean difference in delivery. But it is another story when we turn to gender.

There has been no shortage of proposals to deal with female offenders in a way which would reduce the use of imprisonment and reflect more closely what we know about women's pathways into crime. ...

Welcome as such proposals are, there is also the need to question whether or not such moves are enough, and whether or not initiatives which promulgate new policies for women but not for men run the risk of creating as many discrepancies as they resolve. Whilst claims that women commit less serious crimes and pose fewer risks than men are grounded in incontrovertible evidence which legitimates calls for the differential treatment of men and women, there is some difficulty in applying this same logic of differentiation on the basis of women's *social* backgrounds. Few would dismiss indications of social hardship amongst men in prison. ...

Importantly, there has been a general push to ensure that provision is 'gender-sensitive' in Home Office sponsored initiatives such as the Government's Women's Offending Reduction Programme (WORP) which attempts to co-ordinate work across departments and agencies in working more effectively with women offenders in the community and reducing imprisonment. The Fawcett Society's Gender and Justice Policy network – working with both Home Office departments and voluntary organisations – similarly serves to bring women's distinctive needs to the foreground in policy and practice.

Given what is known about women's distinctive needs the implications for practice in work with offenders are unmistakable but not easy to address. The relatively low number of women given community orders or prison sentences points to generic offender intervention programmes (on grounds of logistics and cost). The Home Office continues to focus on similarities rather than on differences (e.g. in relation to Enhanced Thinking Skills: Cann 2006) but 'What Works' principles (McGuire 2002) suggest that targeting and responsivity are important. As Anne Worrall amongst others has pointed out, 'women who commit offences are often driven to do so not by "cognitive deficits" but by the complexity of the demands placed upon them' (2002: 144). ...

Conclusion

... [C]onsideration has been given to ways in which the criminal justice system *does* give consideration to ethnic and gender differences and the possibility that there are ways in which the system *should* perhaps make differentiated provision. Whilst the focus has been on race and gender issues, it is possible to extrapolate from this points which are relevant to sexual orientation, religion, disabilities and mental health factors. The conclusion is to suggest that the system needs both to avoid negative discrimination and to accommodate diversity in order to work out 'What Works' (or at least might work) and in order to promote legitimacy.

From Loraine Gelsthorpe, 'Dealing with diversity', in G. McIvor and P. Raynor (eds.) Developments in Social Work with Offenders, *Research Highlights 48 (London: Jessica Kingsley), 2007, pp. 290–304.*

References

Bowling, B. and Phillips, C. (2002) *Racism, Crime and Justice.* Harlow, Longman.

Calverley, A., Cole, B., Kaur, G., Lewis, S., Raynor, P., Sadeghi, S., Smith, D., Vanstone, M. and Wardak, A. (2004) *Black and Asian Offenders on Probation.* Home Office Research Study 277. London: Home Office.

Cann, J. (2006) *Cognitive Skills Programmes: Impact on Reducing Reconviction Among a Sample of Female Prisoners.* Home Office Findings 276. London: Home Office.

Cole, B. and Wardak, A. (2006) 'Black and Asian Men on Probation: Social Exclusion, Discrimination and Experiences of Criminal Justice.' In S. Lewis, P. Raynor, D. Smith and A. Wardak (eds) *Race and Probation.* Cullompton: Willan.

Denney, D. (1992) *Racism and Anti-racism in Probation.* London, Routledge.

Fawcett Society (2004) *Women and the Criminal Justice System: A Report on the Fawcett Society's Commission on Women and the Criminal Justice System.* London: Fawcett Society.

Feilzer, M. and Hood, R. (2004) *Difference or Discrimination? Minority Ethnic Young People in the Criminal Justice System.* London: Youth Justice Board.

Gelsthorpe, L. (2001) 'Critical Decisions and Processes in the Criminal Courts.' In E. McLaughlin and J. Muncie (eds) *Controlling Crime.* London: Sage/Open University.

——(2006) 'The Experiences of Female Minority Ethnic Offenders: the Other "Other"'. In S. Lewis, P. Raynor, D. Smith and A. Wardak (eds) *Race and Probation.* Cullompton: Willan.

Gelsthorpe, L. and Morris, A. (2002) 'Women's Imprisonment in England and Wales: A Penal Paradox.' *Criminal Justice* 2, 3, 277–301.

HM Inspectorate of Probation (2000) *Towards Race Equality: A Thematic Inspection.* London: HM Inspectorate of Probation.

Home Office (2003) *Statistics on Women and the Criminal Justice System.* London: Home Office Section 95 Report.

Lewis, S., Raynor, P., Smith, D. and Wardak, A. (eds) (2006) *Race and Probation.* Cullompton: Willan.

Macpherson, Sir William (1999) *The Stephen Lawrence Inquiry.* Cm. 4262–1. London: Stationery Office.

McGuire, J. (ed) (2002) *Offender Rehabilitation and Treatment.* Chichester: John Wiley and Sons.

McIvor, G. (ed) (2004) *Women Who Offend.* London: Jessica Kingsley Publishers.

Powis, B. and Walmsley, R. (2002) *Programmes for Black and Asian Offenders on Probation: Lessons for Developing Practice.* Home Office Research Study 250. London: Home Office.

Raynor, P. and Lewis, S. (2006) 'Black and Asian Men on Probation: Who are They and What are their Needs?' In S. Lewis, P. Raynor, D. Smith and A. Wardak (eds) *Race and Probation.* Cullompton: Willan.

Social Exclusion Unit (2002) *Reducing Re-offending by Ex-prisoners.* London: Office of the Deputy Prime Minister.

Williams, P. (2006) 'Designing and Delivering Programmes for Minority Ethnic Offenders.' In S. Lewis, P. Raynor, D. Smith and A. Wardak (eds) *Race and Probation.* Cullompton: Willan.

Worrall, A. (2002) 'Rendering them Punishable.' In P. Carlen (ed) *Women and Punishment: The Struggle for Justice.* Cullompton: Willan.

Part F

Effectiveness

Introduction

The question of whether or not probation and its cognate approaches to dealing with offenders are effective is an issue that for at least half of its history was – to all intents and purposes – ignored. There were several studies carried out during the first 50 years of probation's existence which attempted to grasp the nettle of whether or not probation 'worked', but these tended to be limited in scope. For the most part, probation was simply taken for granted as an effective way of dealing with offenders; effectiveness was assumed as a matter of faith – somewhat appositely given probation's beginnings in the Church of England Temperance Society. But with the ability of the Home Office to fund criminological research (introduced by the 1948 Criminal Justice Act), the creation of the Home Office Research Unit in 1957 with its early focus on exploring the treatment of offenders, and rising crime rates with consequences for prison numbers, the effectiveness of probation became a matter of some significance. It also became tangled up inexorably with debates about how effectiveness might be measured and with political argument.

The first major assessment of probation's effectiveness was carried out by the Cambridge Department of Criminal Science in collaboration with the Home Office (Reading 65). It is important to note that this study immediately makes the point that measuring effectiveness can be done in a number of ways, some of which are more exacting than others – and this is an issue that has continued to dog efforts to assess effectiveness. In general, probation was more successful with females than males, and with older offenders than with younger ones. Probation at this time was used mostly for first offenders, and we should not be surprised at a fairly high success rate amongst such a group: almost seven out of ten male first offenders and almost 90 per cent of females 'completed their supervision and were not reconvicted during the subsequent three years', which is a demanding level of achievement. For those with previous convictions, the success rate fell so that for juveniles with two or more previous convictions, only four out of ten (42 per cent) were successful – and both juveniles and adults with two or more previous convictions were unlikely to complete their period of supervision. The impact of previous sentences on success is an important factor – previous custody and previous failure on probation not being particularly promising. Adding a condition of residence was also not conducive to success, although it is emphasised that this was unlikely to be because the condition was a failure but because those who received such a condition were likely to be more high risk cases.

Leslie Wilkins was one of the outstanding criminologists of the second half of the twentieth century with an unerring tendency to cast new light on an issue by examining it from a slightly different perspective. His piece here (Reading 66) – an overview of studies of treatment – notes that there are few signs of correctional treatment being successful, but goes on to draw some pertinent conclusions: that better research is needed; that failure can be valuable if the research is rigorous enough for lessons to be learnt; that far more research is needed into what actually goes on in 'treatment' (what we would now refer to as process evaluation); that we need to begin to ask questions about the unit costs of treatments (questions that have still to be answered). Typical of Wilkins' work is his somewhat iconoclastic claim that the least that is done with offenders the more likely it is to be successful, so perhaps the best approach is to keep it simple – more is not always more effective and the interaction between the elements of a sentence may not be positive.

Robert Martinson's 'What Works? Questions and answers about prison reform' is probably the most notorious article ever published about probation – yet is it important to emphasise immediately that it is *not* just about probation. The article covers all forms of treatment including prison. In the excerpt reproduced here (Reading 67), it is clear that despite the belief that 'Nothing Works', Martinson points to several studies that did work. The problem is that such studies are rare, have not been replicated, and when examined closely have limitations. The research is all too often flawed, so that more rigorous methods need to be applied when evaluating effectiveness. To complicate matters further, the assumption has been that effectiveness is due to the type of treatment or programme an offender receives, but Martinson shows the significance of individual probation officers' practice – what he terms a 'policy effect' as compared to a treatment effect. Like Wilkinson he proposes that we do less with offenders, and bear in mind that community treatments are usually much less expensive than custodial. The impact of Martinson's article in the UK seems to have been confined to academics and criminal justice policy-makers; there is little evidence that probation officers had any knowledge of it all.

At the same time as Martinson's article was being published, community service (CS) was being introduced in England and Wales. Rehabilitation was not the aim of CS, diversion from custody was, although that was more of a hope than a carefully planned system. The experimental period of CS was examined in some detail by researchers from the Home Office Research Unit, the first report looking at the approaches taken by the different areas while the second focused on a reconviction study (which concluded that there was no evidence of any reduction in offending after a community service order), and an assessment of how far CS acted to divert offenders from custody. The difficulties of measuring diversion from custody are just as complicated as measuring reconviction (Reading 68) and the researchers used four different methods – all of which were estimates. Overall, they conclude that at best around 50 per cent of those given CS were diverted from a custodial sentence but this is difficult to see as unequivocal evidence of success. The problem is where the remaining 50 per cent came from; and they must have been heading for a sentence that was lower on the tariff than CS. In other words, they were 'up-tariffed' and were examples of what became known (following Stan Cohen) as net widening – a phenomenon that has driven a great deal of criminological research and theorising ever since. By the end of the 70s then, there was little solid evidence for the effectiveness of probation or for CS.

Five years after his original article, Robert Martinson published a follow-up piece which has been widely seen as a recantation of his original views. Our extract from this follow-up (Reading 69) suggests that recantation might not be the appropriate term. Different criteria were used to select studies for inclusion in the new study and a different measure of effectiveness was used: the reprocessing rate which was defined to include a further arrest, conviction or imprisonment. Martinson concludes that it is not the programme or treatment itself that is helpful or harmful, but 'the *conditions* under which the program is delivered' – which is not so far from some of the points made in the original article. It seems unlikely that many in the UK saw 'New Findings, New Views' but if they took note of it and thought that it perhaps absolved probation from the judgement of Nothing Works, they ought to have noticed that the evidence provided in Table 1 applied to juveniles and covered shock probation only.

The IMPACT experiment signalled the end of a ten-year period of research by the Home Office Research Unit which had focused heavily on probation. IMPACT (Intensive Matched Probation and After-Care Treatment) was one of the earliest intensive probation schemes in England and Wales, but in this case intensive meant more social work rather than the more control it means today. The lead researcher on the IMPACT studies was Steven Folkard who reflected (Reading 70) on the issues raised by it five years after the publication of the second and final IMPACT report which was widely seen as disappointing due to its lack of positive results (Folkard *et al.* 1976). In fact, as Folkard points out, there were some interesting findings to emerge but it seems that these were lost as the second report was published immediately after the publication of Stephen Brody's *The Effectiveness of Sentencing* (1976) which was very much the UK equivalent of Martinson.[1] Folkard's thoughtful assessment of IMPACT and its significance highlights the increasing complexity of trying to assess the effectiveness of correctional treatment: the different aims of sentencing had to be taken into account and diversion from custody was now an important objective. Folkard presciently notes that if we expect probation or community service to divert offenders from custody, then these will need to become more controlling or new and more controlling sentences will need to be introduced.

The next contribution (Reading 71) represents yet another attempt to exorcise the Nothing Works demon. George Mair argues that Nothing Works was never a claim that was made by Martinson; instead, it was a cultural construct that fitted with the times and encouraged academic debate. Martinson's reliance on recidivism is flawed, as are the lack of process evaluations of the studies he examined. Mair goes on to propose a new approach to the evaluation of sentences which would begin with a process evaluation which would supply the context for the explanation of outcomes, and then encompass primary and secondary outcome measures, although how these might be combined or prioritised was never worked out in practice. The evaluation of the Intensive Probation initiative (IP) that was introduced in nine probation areas in April 1991 was intended to operationalise the approach suggested by Mair, but in the event the introduction of the combination order in the 1991 Criminal Justice Act meant that the Home Office lost interest in IP and only a process evaluation of the initiative was completed.

From the early 1990s the What Works initiative began to take over community penalties, and by the end of the decade the Home Office had bought into what had begun as a grass-roots probation movement. Effectiveness, as illustrated by the contribution from Tim Chapman and Mike Hough (Reading 72), was reduced to a series of bullet points, of boxes that had to be ticked. In the process, the messy, frustrating and complicated task of trying to change offenders who are human beings seemed to get lost; effectiveness essentially became a series of procedures that, if achieved, led to success. The difficulties, as far as Chapman and Hough are concerned, are virtually non-existent although even they are forced to concede that given the number of individuals who might be involved in working with offenders – 'assessors, case managers, programme deliverers, partners, administrators, and managers' – it might prove complicated to deliver a coherent and consistent programme to offenders. Indirectly, this excerpt helps to illuminate what would be lost if working with offenders in the community was reduced to a mechanistic procedure which followed a list of curt instructions.

By the early years of the new century, the What Works bandwagon was rolling but this did not mean that everyone had been converted to its nostrums. Academics and practitioners debated the advantages and disadvantages of Nothing Works in books and articles and the first contribution by Peter Raynor (Reading 73) is a spirited attack on those who questioned the What Works movement. There is no denying that the seven criticisms discussed by Raynor existed, but the issues are how significant they were in practice and how far they posed a threat to the What Works hegomony; given the weight of government behind What Works, the response is surely 'not very much'. With the benefit of hindsight, some criticisms look like paper tigers and some are perfectly valid critiques. Raynor is fairly optimistic about the future, but as his second contribution shows (Reading 74), such optimism did not last long. By 2008, the Crime Reduction Programme (CRP) was a bad memory, and the Pathfinder programmes that had made up the CRP with regard to community penalties had failed to demonstrate the positive results that had been expected. As Raynor carefully shows, the Pathfinder evaluations were doomed from the start: Home Office guidance on evaluation methodology was overly prescriptive and relied on quasi-experimental approaches, time-scales were short, there were implementation problems, expectations were pitched too highly, and the response to results that failed to match these expectations was to blame the researchers. Part of this blaming strategy resulted in the Home Office imposing standards for evaluation research, with the preferred approach being randomised control trials (RCTs). Raynor points to some of the limitations of such an approach and – perhaps more significantly – notes one highly significant consequence of the Pathfinders perceived failure: the potential for a return to Nothing Works, which could spell serious trouble for the probation service.

The evidence for effectiveness was not overwhelming as Steve Stanley suggests (Reading 75). Stanley discusses the available evidence for What Works in 2009 and while he concludes that the picture is more promising than it had been in earlier reviews of progress, he notes that matters 'have still not moved much beyond the stage of "promising leads"'. He claims that there are still remarkably few major studies of the impact of community penalties; where positive results are found they are all too often subject to methodological reservations; outcomes other than (or in addition to) reconviction rates are needed; some aspects of the What Works paradigm required re-evaluation. So effectiveness has neither yet been demonstrated, nor has there been any definitive conclusions about how it might be measured.

And the arguments over effectiveness and how to measure it most accurately and appropriately continue. Mike Hough (Reading 76) pulls together the main current debates and tries to resolve them in the final contribution. He notes the limitations of RCTs but also their advantages. The problem with relying on RCTs alone to measure the effectiveness of something like probation is that working with offenders and trying to change them is a complex, messy, human activity which is never likely to be contained by a few rules; it is a craft not a science and its outcomes will always be contested, contingent, temporary, tentative. Hough lists the factors that might go towards shaping effectiveness but makes the vital point that interventions or programmes are 'unlikely to be the major determinant of institutional outcomes'. There are a number of other factors in the mix that will affect outcome. In the final analysis it is not just community penalties that will be in trouble if the question of effectiveness is not tackled appropriately, but – Hough argues – the discipline of criminology itself.

Note

1   Interestingly, the Foreword to IMPACT vol. 2 was written five months before the Foreword for Brody's report, which might suggest some delay in publishing the former.

References

Brody, S. (1976) *The Effectiveness of Sentencing.* Home Office Research Study No. 35. London: HMSO.

Folkard, M.S., Smith, D.E. and Smith, D.D. (1976) *IMPACT Intensive Matched Probation and After-Care Treatment, Vol. 2: the results of the experiment.* Home Office Research Study No.36. London: HMSO.

65 Assessing the effectiveness of probation (1958)

Cambridge Department of Criminal Science

In order to assess the effectiveness of imprisonment or any other treatment involving deprivation of liberty such as preventive detention, corrective training, borstal or approved-school training, it is usual to examine the conduct of persons so sentenced over a number of years following their release; as a general rule success or failure of the treatment is assessed according to the proportion of offenders not reconvicted during this follow-up period; misconduct while undergoing detention, even if it amounts to a breach of discipline, is not normally taken into account. As regards the absolute discharge or the fine, the degree of effectiveness is usually measured by the proportion of offenders not reconvicted during a certain period immediately following the making of the orders.

An assessment of the results of probation, however, generally calls for a somewhat different approach; here two stages have to be distinguished. During the first stage, that is, while the order is in force, the offender is under an obligation to report regularly to a probation officer; he may also have to comply with certain other requirements imposed by the court. The outcome at this stage can be a straightforward one if he satisfactorily completes the period of supervision; but, unlike the case above of offenders deprived of their liberty, the issue is complicated because of a need to take into account any breach of the order or commission of a further offence, which may bring him again before a court. During the second stage, which follows the completion or termination of the order, again he may either choose to abide by the law or he may revert to crime and be reconvicted. Consequently, an accurate evaluation of the effects of probation necessitates an examination of conduct during both these stages. It must take into account, first, the proportion of those offenders who have satisfactorily completed the prescribed period of supervision and, secondly, the proportion of those offenders who have not only favourably responded to probation while under supervision but who have had no indictable offences recorded against them throughout the follow-up period.

Test of success and the degree of success achieved

The first major conclusion to be drawn from the facts brought to light by the enquiry is the remarkably favourable response to treatment by probation during the first stage. As many as 79 per cent of the adults and 73 per cent of the juveniles successfully completed their probation. This means that not one of these offenders was brought before a court either for a breach of the requirements of the order or for the commission of a further offence during the period of supervision; an encouraging result, considering that the time of supervision ranged from one to three years. This assessment, however, does not go far enough because the decisive test of effectiveness must be the extent to which those who are subjected to probation refrain from committing further offences once the orders have been terminated; for many offenders may respond to probation while under supervision and yet lapse again into crime. When this more rigorous criterion is applied and the conduct over a period of three years following the termination of the orders is scrutinised, the rate of success naturally becomes lower, but is nevertheless still very encouraging. In the case of 70 per cent of the adults and 57 per cent of the juveniles, probation proved to be successful in the strictest sense of the term; all of these offenders kept a clear record from the time they were put on probation up to the end of the follow-up period; this means that none of them was found guilty of either a breach of the order or the commission of a further offence while under supervision, nor of an offence during the subsequent three years.

But it may be objected that this test is too exacting, inasmuch as offenders should not be regarded as having failed to respond to probation if they completed the period of supervision prescribed by the courts and were not reconvicted during the following three years, even though they might have been found guilty of a breach of the order or the commission of a further offence while under supervision. Four per cent of the adults and 5 per cent of the juveniles belong to this class; and if these cases are included among those which proved to be completely successful then the general rate of success becomes as high as 74 per cent for adults and 62 per cent for juveniles.

Test of failure and the extent to which probation failed

Probation may be regarded as having failed to fulfil its purpose either when a breach of the order or the commission of a further offence has led to the revocation of the order; or when a further offence has been committed during the period of three years following the completion of supervision. Eighteen per cent of the offenders had their orders revoked and a further 14 per cent reverted to crime after their orders had been terminated. These two percentages added together give the general rate of failure,

Table 1

	Adults	Juveniles
Successful completion of probation with no appearance in court while the order was in force and no reconviction during the follow-up period	70.0%	57.9%
Successful completion of probation in spite of appearance in court while the order was in force and no reconviction during follow-up	3.8%	4.5%
General rate of success	**73.8%**	**62.4%**
Failure while on probation due to breach of order	3.1%	4.0%
Failure while on probation due to reconviction of a further offence	12.6%	16.5%
Failure following the completion of probation due to a reconviction during the follow-up period	10.5%	17.1%
General rate of failure	**26.2%**	**37.6%**

which amounts to 32 per cent of the total number of offenders put on probation; the proportion of adults was lower than that of juveniles, 26 per cent as against 38 per cent. But, in fact, not all cases classified as failures should necessarily be regarded as such. In particular, 250 offenders, or three per cent of all those under supervision, had their orders revoked and were again put on probation, or even fined or discharged, and yet reached the end of the three years without any further convictions recorded against them. If these cases are excluded, the rate of failure becomes lower: 24 per cent for adults and 34 per cent for juveniles.

Response according to sex and age

Satisfactory as the rates of success are with respect to both sexes, the general rate for females seems to be considerably higher than that for males: 83 as against 64 per cent. This difference holds good for each age group, and throughout the survey the rates of success in the case of females are approximately 15 per cent higher. It also appears that not only are these rates substantial in every age group, but they also show an increase from the lower to the higher: from 57 to 74 per cent for males, and from 73 to 88 per cent for females. Thus, while the results are better for women than for men and for the older than for the younger offenders, yet probation emerges unquestionably as a generally effective measure of treatment whatever the sex and age an offender happens to be.

Table 2

Offenders age group		Males %	Females %
8 and under 11 –	success	57.1	81.0
	failure	42.9	19.0
11 and under 14 –	success	58.9	73.0
	failure	41.1	27.0
14 and under 17 –	success	64.0	79.9
	failure	36.0	20.1
17 and under 21 –	success	68.7	82.1
	failure	31.3	17.9
21 and under 30 –	success	67.4	82.5
	failure	32.6	17.5
30 and over –	success	74.1	87.6
	failure	25.9	12.4
All offenders –	success	64.3	82.7
	failure	35.7	17.3

A measure for dealing with first offenders

Probation is primarily applied to first offenders: 66 per cent of the adults and 75 per cent of juveniles who were put on probation had no previous convictions for indictable offences recorded against them. That probation should be very useful in helping first offenders to overcome any propensity to commit crime is a conclusion which might be anticipated. The extent to which it fulfils this function may be gathered from the fact that among first offenders 69 per cent of the males and as many as 86 per cent of the females completed their supervision and were not reconvicted during the subsequent three years. But what is particularly noteworthy is the value of probation in dealing with adolescent and adult first offenders. It proved effective for nearly 80 per cent of the men and 90 per cent of the women, aged 17 and over; and indeed its effectiveness appears to be somewhat greater when used for adults aged 21 and over, than for any of the younger offenders. The rates of success according to sex and age are as follows.

Table 3

Age groups of first offenders	Males %	Females %
8 and under 14	60.5	77.0
14 and under 17	69.2	80.8
17 and under 21	74.8	86.6
21 and over	78.5	90.4
All first offenders	68.6	86.3

Probation for offenders with previous convictions

A substantial proportion of offenders who were put on probation had been previously convicted. As many as 34 per cent of the adults and 25 per cent of the juveniles had at least one previous conviction for an indictable offence. Indeed among these recidivists half of the adults and a fifth of the juveniles had no less than two previous convictions, that is to say they were put on probation on the third or even fourth occasion on which they were found guilty of an indictable offence. It is only to be expected that, on the whole, recidivists will not react as favourably to probation as first offenders, and yet the general rate of success for those with previous convictions shows that almost 6 in 10 not only satisfactorily completed their supervision but also completed the follow-up period without the commission of a further offence. It is perhaps interesting to note that among the recidivists as well the rate of success was somewhat higher for adults than for juveniles: 59 per cent as against 52 per cent.

There is certainly much scope for the use of probation in dealing with offenders with one previous conviction on their records. Their rate of success, while lower than that of first offenders, is nevertheless sufficiently high to support the view that probation could usefully be applied on a more extensive scale to this class of offender. And more favourable results might even be expected if it were possible to improve still further the methods of selection and the system of supervision, particularly with regard to the juvenile offenders.

However, the use of probation has not been confined to those who have been convicted on no more than one or two occasions; it has also been tried with respect to a considerable number of recidivists with several convictions on their records, many of whom had already been subjected to this very method of treatment, or to training in a borstal institution or an approved school, or had even undergone a sentence of imprisonment. One thousand, or 10 per cent of the total belong to this class and more than 700 were adult offenders.

Table 4

	Rate of success – first offenders (%)	Rate of success – offenders with one previous conviction (%)
Adults – men	76.8	66.1
Adults – women	89.2	72.1
Juveniles – boys	64.1	55.0
Juveniles – girls	79.1	63.3

Previous treatment of recidivists placed on probation upon their third conviction

Table 5

Previous treatment	Total		Adults		Juveniles	
	No.	%	No.	%	No.	%
Imprisonment	311	31.2	310	42.4	1	0.4
Approved school/Borstal	150	15.0	107	14.6	43	16.2
Probation order	248	24.8	134	18.3	114	42.8
Fine/discharge	267	26.8	172	23.5	95	35.7
Other methods	22	2.2	9	1.2	13	4.9
Total	998	100.0	732	100.0	266	100.0

Twenty-five per cent of these recidivists had already been placed on probation; more than 30 per cent of them had been in prison, and a further 15 per cent had been in approved schools or borstal institutions. After these methods of treatment had failed they were then given another chance by being put on probation. In fact, 57 per cent of the adults and 17 per cent of the juveniles had on previous occasions been unsuccessfully subjected to institutional treatment of one kind or another.

Decreasing effectiveness when applied to recidivists

The general rate of success for recidivists with two or more previous convictions is hardly encouraging: almost half of the adults and as many as 6 in 10 of the juveniles reverted to crime by the end of the follow-up period. Furthermore, among this group of recidivists who failed, the proportion of those who never completed their probation was high; it amounted to nearly 70 per cent for juveniles as well as for adults. The following tabular statement, which gives the variations in the rates of success according to previous records, shows the decreasing effectiveness of probation when applied to recidivists.

That no less than half of the recidivists who were placed on probation upon their third conviction again reverted to crime is a fact that cannot be ignored.

A comparison of the rates of success among recidivists, when classified with respect to the methods of treatment applied for the offence immediately preceding the one for which they were put on probation, reveals that the variations are much less marked than might have been expected. The rates were, however, somewhat less satisfactory for those who had been previously subjected to institutional treatment than for those who had been previously put on probation, discharged or fined. Fifty as against 55 per cent in the case of adults and 35 as against 44 per cent in the case of juveniles.

Table 6

	First offenders	Offenders with 1 previous conviction	Offenders with 2+ previous convictions
Adults	81.2	67.3	51.5
Juveniles	65.7	55.3	42.1
All offenders	72.4	60.3	49.0

Table 7 Rates of success of recidivists who were placed on probation upon their third conviction (showing previous treatment)

Previous treatment	Adults			Juveniles		
		Not convicted subsequently			Not convicted subsequently	
	Total	No.	%	Total	No.	%
Imprisonment	310	151	48.7	1	–	–
Approved school/Borstal	107	55	51.4	43	15	34.9
Probation	134	73	54.5	114	49	43.0
Fine/Discharge	172	96	55.8	95	42	44.2
Other methods	9	2	22.2	13	6	46.2
Total	732	377	51.5	266	112	42.1

A second chance of probation

The results with respect to recidivists who were given a second chance of probation directly following the first period of supervision are naturally of great interest. This was a substantial group amounting to nearly 900 offenders, equal to 3 in 10 of all recidivists who had been subjected to probation. Here, as might be expected, the rate of success was lower than the general rate for all offenders put on probation: 62 per cent against 74 per cent in the case of adults and 50 per cent as against 62 per cent in the case of juveniles. Indeed, as may be seen from the tabular statement which follows, the rates of success of probation, when ordered for a second time, differ little from the general results obtained for all recidivists.

Table 8

	Offenders with 1 previous conviction	Offenders with 2+ previous convictions
Adults – general rate of success	67.3	51.5
Adults – rate of success following a second chance of probation	65.9	54.5
Juveniles – general rate of success	55.3	42.1
Juveniles – rate of success following a second chance of probation	52.3	43.0

Thus, it appears that probation may still play a useful part when applied to recidivists who have already been put on probation and failed, although the view can be held that, especially in such cases, probation should not be used merely as a substitute for constructive institutional treatment of longer duration.

It is important to note that the effectiveness of probation decreases in the case of those who have failed to respond in the first instance to supervision. 700 offenders, or nearly 8 per cent of the total, had been found guilty of a breach of the order or the commission of a further offence and yet were kept on probation by a continuation or extension of the period of supervision. They may also be regarded as having been given a second chance; and, on the whole, their conduct following initial failure was such that the resulting rates of success were lower than the general rates for all offenders put on probation.

Table 9

	First offenders	Recidivists
Adults – general rate of success	81.2	59.4
Adults – rate of success following an initial failure during probation	72.5	57.4
Juveniles – general rate of success	65.7	52.5
Juveniles – rate of success following an initial failure during probation	48.1	53.6

Among all adult first offenders who were put on probation 81 per cent did not revert to crime, but among those whose initial response to probation was unfavourable, a greater proportion continued to commit offences, and for them the rate of success dropped to 73 per cent. A like deterioration is noticeable among adult recidivists, but it is apparently slight; their rate of success was 57 per cent compared with the general rate of 59 per cent. Among the juveniles, the decrease in the effectiveness of probation was more marked in the case of first offenders and the rate of success fell from 66 per cent to as low as 48 per cent; the rate for recidivists is slightly higher than their general rate, but even so it does not exceed 54 per cent. The unexpected drop to 48 per cent among first offenders is rather disappointing, but it is probably due to a tendency for courts to continue on probation this class of offender.

Probation in conjunction with requirements of residence

The courts may sometimes impose probation orders which contain conditions of residence, and when they do so the offenders are required to stay in some kind of institution such as approved or voluntary hostels and homes, or sometimes in approved lodgings; they usually stay for a period varying from 6 to 12 months. These requirements of residence were ordered by the courts in 600 cases, or 7 per cent of the total. The imposition of such conditions may be taken to mean that the courts expected to increase the chances of success if supervision were combined with a measure of this nature. It is also not unreasonable to assume that requirements of residence are usually imposed in the more difficult cases. This is to some extent corroborated by the fact that they are more frequently attached to orders of a longer duration and are more often imposed on recidivists than on first offenders. In the table which follows, an attempt has been made to assess the results of the imposition of such probation orders containing requirements of residence; adults and juveniles are shown in four groups, according to their sex and previous records.

Table 10 Rates of success for adults and juveniles grouped according to whether or not requirements of residence were attached to their orders

	Rates of success			
	Males		*Females*	
	First offenders	*Recidivists*	*First offenders*	*Recidivists*
Adult offenders – orders without a residence requirement	77.6	59.5	91.7	71.0
Adult offenders – orders with a residence requirement	53.8	32.4	68.0	44.7
Juvenile offenders – orders without a residence requirement	64.5	53.5	81.1	55.2
Juvenile offenders – orders with a residence requirement	56.5	40.7	57.6	*

*Only 7 in all, of whom 2 failed

The trend is unmistakeable: offenders who had to comply with conditions of residence reverted to crime more often than those whose probation orders contained no such requirements. And this tendency was observed in all groups: males and females, adults and juveniles, first offenders and recidivists. Among adults the differences in the rates of success between those who were and those who were not required to comply with conditions of residence amounted to no less than 17 per cent and among the younger offenders to almost 12 per cent. Adult and juvenile male offenders with previous convictions show the lowest rates of success; in both groups as many as 6 in 10 were reconvicted during the period of supervision or during the follow-up period of three years. These figures may suggest that in many of the more difficult cases the reinforcement of probation by combining it with conditions of residence has not proved to be particularly effective. That conditions of residence may play a useful part in probation cannot be doubted, but it seems that, with respect to certain classes of offender, a more drastic mode of institutional treatment is needed.

From Cambridge Department of Criminal Science, The Results of Probation
(London: Macmillan), 1958, pp. 1–11.

66 Summary reviews of treatment and its effects (1969)

Leslie T. Wilkins

Although it has been possible for some time to see how evaluation could be developed in the penal-treatment field, little serious work has yet been attempted. Few administrations are prepared to put money into research concerning the treatment of offenders, and although there are a few notable exceptions, even these are of recent origin. The pattern for research and evaluation as it is now seen is closely related to the work of the 1950s. More recently there have been a few developments in methods for the analysis of problems in criminology and a number of surveys on the state of knowledge. Some excellent information retrieval information systems have also recently been established. Criminological research is becoming an aspect of national significance in the United States. What has been the nature of this growth, and how do those who have viewed the general scene assess the position?

Institution studies

One interesting fact to be noted from the searches of the literature is that while studies of criminals, recidivists, juvenile delinquents, and deviants abound, there is a poverty of material discussing and describing different types of treatments. Exactly what goes on in prison, what takes place in group counselling, what a probation officer does and similar questions have not been given much attention. In this sector we have had to rely mainly upon the work of former inmates whose views may not be representative, because the proportion of inmates who have written books and found publishers is extremely small and atypical of the majority. Few if any of the works describing treatment processes seem to consider that there is any remedial effect in the components of the prison or other systems. Of course the public demands other features in the penal system than the therapy of treatment, and these demands must be considered in the type of system provided. But exactly how much security does the public obtain at how much unit cost? What is a 'unit'? What is meant by 'cost'? These would seem to be important questions, but apparently they have seldom been asked, and few attempts to answer them can be traced.

One hundred studies examined

There has been much more concern with the outcome of prison treatment than with what goes on inside the institution. This stage may be passing as certain forms of experimental work begin to be developed. Several hundred studies of outcome were published in English in the twenty years from 1940 to 1960. The US Health Service recently sponsored a large-scale investigation of the literature of correctional outcome studies. Walter C Bailey and his associates (1966) examined 100 such reports, which they classified according to methods utilized and outcomes reported. Bailey recorded: 22 experimental studies; 26 systematic empirical; 52 non-systematic empirical. It is not without some regret that it is to be noted that the treatment he classified as 'harmful or no effect' increased from 4 per cent for the non-systematic group to 23 per cent for the group classified as experimental. Only 9 of the studies reported results that were claimed to be statistically significant; but as it is noted later, some of these were significant only in the statistical sense, because of the method of defining outcome. Bailey concluded that 'the effects of wishful thinking become progressively less controlled as the rigor of the research design decreases'.

It is not known whether the 100 studies that formed Bailey's sample were in any way representative of all recent correctional outcome studies, and what may be more important, how representative his sample was of correctional procedures. An element of conscious selection must be expected in the selection for assessment by means of a research project of a certain form of treatment. Are such selected procedures representative or are they more likely to represent treatments that are believed to be 'good' treatments? Is it likely that research workers would be asked to evaluate a treatment program that was believed to be no more than average? Bailey further noted that 'evidence of the effectiveness of correctional treatment is inconsistent, contradictory and of questionable reliability'. Unless we are to believe that uninvestigated correctional procedures are generally superior to those investigated among the 100 projects, his conclusion is most disturbing. Perhaps on the evidence supplied by Bailey we might conclude that most or all correctional treatments are increasing rather than decreasing the probability of recidivism.

On the evidence set forth by Bailey, the hypothesis that all or most correctional treatments are harmful cannot be rejected. This hypothesis is not to be lightly dismissed as nonsense, nor is it a simple matter to test. By reason of the philosophy of jurisprudence and the practice of law, *something* must be done about the offender, and it is not possible to permit spontaneous recovery as an alternative to action. The problem of selection of treatment may reduce to the selection of the form of disposal that has the least amount of content, since all content is likely to have undesirable effects. By doing as little as possible we may be doing as little harm as possible. The best (but illegal) treatment for offenders may be a placebo.

British survey

It may be claimed that this analysis is a little too hard on the studies examined and that this may be the result of a particular enthusiasm for rigorous research that this writer apparently shares with Bailey. But Bailey is not alone in coming to conclusions of the kind reported above, nor does all the evidence of this type come from the United States. The Baroness Wootton of Abinger (Professor Barbara Wootton), who was also a magistrate, was concerned with a similar study in the field of treatment research and published her analysis in 1959 under the title *Social Science and Social Pathology*.

Barbara Wootton's approach was, as she says, essentially practical: 'My original interest in the subject matter of this book sprang from practical experience ... it was the unanswerable questions which forced themselves upon my attention as a magistrate serving both adult and juvenile courts in London ... while on the other hand eight years as Head of a University Department training students for social work provoked much reflection'. Whether one agrees with Professor Wootton's conclusions or not, it must be agreed that her experience is almost unique in this field and qualifies her to speak with authority.

After a very thorough search of the literature, Professor Wootton selected 21 pieces of research in the areas of crime prevention and treatment. Her reasons for rejection of a much later larger body of material are quite sound, even though she excluded many works previously respected in the field. She had certain requirements for each study: that it deal with at least 200 subjects (not, surely, an unreasonable number if any generalizations are sought), that it contain data on not less than half or nearly half of that number (this is a very generous allowance indeed in view of the bias that loss of information for a much smaller percentage could entail), and that the hypotheses under study be sufficiently substantial and include accounts of both the findings and the methods used.

These requirements do not seem unduly severe when it is realized that far more exacting standards are required in almost any acceptable piece of marketing research. Yet, Wootton states:

> ... a few of the better known studies of delinquency had to be omitted on one or more of the following grounds: because they produced insufficient material, because their statistical findings could not be divorced from the text or were presented in a form which defied comparative use, or because the samples used were inadequate. [Thus] Shaw and McKay's famous ecological study and Lander's Baltimore investigation were excluded on the first ground, Stott's work on Delinquency and Human Behavior on the second and Bowlby's celebrated study of affectionless thieves on the third.

From the viewpoint of assessment of treatment outcomes, the majority of those accepted according to Wootton's criteria are no longer admissible today, and many others that have since appeared should also be excluded on the more rigorous expectations of research design. Thus, although she admitted Healy's work *The Individual Delinquent* (1915), the 1,000 cases dealt with were those 'about whom sufficient data were available', doubtless a highly biased sample.

Despite references to about 400 articles and books, Wootton concludes that 'we have little solid factual evidence'. Moreover, many other summary works were considered, and that of M. Metfessel and C. Lovell (1942), is quoted with approval where they say that 'the longest lasting [theories] are those which deal with vague categories ... [the] more concrete measurable factors which can be more easily put to the test are seen to lose their significance as soon as they are subjected to really vigorous [*sic* – rigorous?] scrutiny'.

It is difficult to find any reasonable grounds for disagreement with the conclusion that the major achievement of research in the field of social pathology and treatment has been negative and has resulted in the undermining of nearly all the current mythology regarding the effectiveness of treatment in any form. As Wootton points out, however, this is no excuse for not giving careful consideration to treatment policy.

It is not surprising that Bailey concludes his study of the 100 research reports on the outcome of penal treatment:

If one were to eliminate from the 'successful outcome reports' all studies characterized by questionable research methodology and procedures, the percentage of successful outcomes based upon reliable and valid evidence would be small indeed … Perhaps, it is time for correctional treatment personnel to re-evaluate some of their basic assumptions regarding the nature and etiology of delinquent and criminal behaviour.

In the years that have passed since Bailey's summary and Wootton's analysis and critical survey of work in this field is there any new development that has more promise?

Trend toward rigor and complexity

A distinct trend *can* be noted. At about the time that Bailey and Wootton were reporting the state of ignorance and the sorry situation regarding methodology, a few studies were beginning to appear that showed promise of developing into a reasonable means of evaluating treatment and social action. The trend began with the application of some modification of the prediction methods. Some of the results of this approach raised questions on which there was further enlightenment from some experimental design studies conducted by the US Navy Retraining Command. The relationship between information and decisions was beginning to be noted and utilized. The questions that began to be asked were better questions in that they were more closely related both to the methods available and to the practical aspects of the problems studied.

Adams (1967) summarized the outcomes of eleven projects carried out by the California Board of Corrections, five projects by the Los Angeles County Probation Department, three by the California Youth Authority, and three federal probation studies. He noted that in nearly all cases the initial studies revealed no differences between the experimental treatment and the conventional program. Only later studies began to reveal significant programs and significant pay-offs from the innovation. It is perhaps also reasonable to summarize this result by noting that after the initial studies which were 'unsuccessful', it was possible to devise more complex models on the basis of the information generated by the earlier research. Thus, it may well be that without the *lack of success* of the earlier studies, there would have been no basis for the later successful studies! There was a tendency in each project to begin testing relatively simple theories, and, perhaps not surprisingly, the simple explanation was shown to be inadequate.

It is perhaps a feature of research workers that they become experts in one area of applied research and enthusiastic about a particular form of analysis, system of experimentation, method of measurement, or type of problem. Give any problem to some psychologists and they will immediately factor analyze it! Suggest some other area to some criminologists and they will set out at once to predict it. Although prediction is a form of classification, those who have followed the prediction interest have failed to take much interest in other forms of classification. Those who are interested in forms of classification have not been particularly interested in prediction or risk categorization.

Only in the most recent work have we found the relationship between risk categorization and other forms of classification of types of offender. In other studies the risk factor was taken care of, to some extent, by randomization of the input to the different treatment systems that formed the demonstration program.

Clearly the more complex the model, the more complex the information necessary to enable control of the model. Early failure to prove what was desired seems to have provided incentives needed to collect more sophisticated information and to spend the necessary funds in the provision of information. A further means whereby information has been brought into line with the situation is by simplification of the problem through increased specification and limitation of its conditions. Initially a common fault had been in attempts to cover the big problems with little information, perhaps because they were considered as 'really very simple'. The demonstration of complexity with the proof that failure was mainly due to a belief in simple solutions provided information as to how to proceed. Thus, the unsuccessful studies were, perhaps, the more valuable and useful.

In England and Wales, the official research unit began in 1953 with a prediction and evaluation study which seemed to demonstrate the kind of thing that every humanitarian social worker wanted to have 'proved' – that treatment in open conditions was superior to treatment in closed conditions. This inference was possible from the study by Mannheim and Wilkins (1955). There was then a tendency, as expressed by one newspaper, for people to believe that 'research workers labour for years ... they study many figures ... only to conclude what every reasonable person knew already'. Perhaps California was more fortunate in that their early studies were 'unsuccessful', tending to throw doubt upon what 'everybody knew already'.

Attendance centres study (Cambridge)

A very interesting result was obtained by McClintock *et al.* (1961) in their study of attendance centres in England. They calculated two different prediction tables, one of which they termed the 'penal score' and the other the 'social score'. The two scores utilized different items of information, but both provided good discrimination between subsequent successes and failures. The attendance-centre sentence is a court order requiring the young offender to spend a given number of hours during weekends at a centre that is usually administered by the police department. In addition, some offenders are placed on probation for 1, 2, or 3 years – normally 2 years. McClintock *et al.* noted that the offenders who were required to attend the centres and who at the same time were on probation were more often failures than those who were only required to attend the centre.

Those who had the double requirement of probation and attendance were, as might be expected, worse risks on average than the others. However, using the 'penal score' they found that after allowance for the class of risk, those who also served probation were still more frequently failures than expected. With the 'social score' an exactly similar result was found. Their data are summarized in Table 1.

The consistent pattern of the results for both types of prediction score and the fact that they are derived from a sample size somewhat larger than has been usual in this field are both very important points. The authors calculated a combined 'social and penal prediction score' and again compared the outcomes with the expectation in terms of the calculated risks. The results were exactly similar, the range for probation cases being from 30 per cent failure to 61 per cent failure and for the non-probation cases from 18 per cent failure to 55 per cent failure. In further support of this evidence it was noted that 'the rates of success were fairly high in cases where the attendance-centre orders were imposed independently of probation; 75 per cent among first

Table 1 Comparison of offenders not on probation and on probation

	Penal score			Social score		
Score	Percentage of failure rates		Score		Percentage of failure rates	
	No Probation	Probation			No Probation	Probation
1–8	48	62	Under 21		52	61
9–10	41	57	22–25		31	45
11–12	35	47	26+		23	35
13–14	30	37				
15–16	23	35				
Total No.	632	545	Total No.		632	545

Source: adapted from F.H. Mclintock *et al. Attendance Centres* (London: Macmillan, 1961)

offenders and 50 per cent among recidivists'. Where the attendance-centre order was combined with a probation order the success rates were 69 per cent for first offenders and 48 per cent for recidivists. Thus, even the single piece of information regarding the prior record of the offender gives a result of a similar kind to that obtained by the more complex and powerful prediction scores. The authors of the Cambridge study do not develop any theories on the basis of these findings, but they do provide three suggestions (one as a footnote):

1. Probation is causing the failure rate to increase.
2. Various factors other than those included in the investigation have influenced the magistrate in placing the boy on probation.
3. A conflict between the aims of probation and attendance centre orders may account for this anomaly.

They regard 2 as the 'more plausible', and suggest that the 'attitude of the offender in court' may be one of the factors related both to selection for probation and to the chances of 'failure' under the attendance-centre order. Thus, they opt for a 'residual information' explanation; other factors were utilized subjectively that were also predictors of failure, and in cases where these applied, the courts tended to award probation as well as make an attendance-centre order.

Since the court was not required to make any subjective assessment of likely outcome, it is impossible to test this explanation. In all studies to date there has been a conspicuous failure of subjective prognosis to account for more than a very small proportion of the variance in subsequent behaviour. The authors' belief that the subjective utilization of information *additional to that used in the building of the scores* provides the 'most plausible' explanation would seem to ascribe almost divine insight to the magistrates concerned. Indeed, the authors (McClintock *et al.* 1961: 95) themselves reported that 'officers themselves tried to assess or predict the after-conduct of the offenders sent to them by the juvenile court'. Such 'predictions were successful in 66 per cent of the cases … no better than if every offender had been indiscriminately classified or predicted as successful'. If the subjective assessment of the officers whose task was the treatment of the offender were so notably unsuccessful in 'prediction' (although no worse than is usually reported), how can the magistrates be considered so much superior in theirs? It does not appear that the 'residual information' explanation is very plausible; rather, the results that show a combination of treatments to be poor treatment might be interpreted on face value. It may be convenient to believe that two obviously good things together must be better than one singly, but the study's evidence is to the contrary.

The first interpretation that 'probation is causing the increase in failure' has no support from the data, because the project did not include cases where probation alone was applied. For this explanation to be made even in the most tentative terms, it would seem necessary to have comparisons between cases given (1) probation alone, (2) attendance centre alone, (3) attendance centre plus probation. The simplest hypothesis that can be put forward as an interpretation of the results is that *the least that it is possible to do with offenders, the better the outcome!* Alternatively, because attendance centres are essentially simple in terms of operation and the requirements made of their attendees, and give little or no attention to therapeutic concepts, the *simpler the setting for treatment*, the better it is for these young offenders. Probation alone is more complex than attendance centre alone, and probation plus attendance centre is even more complex. This is in accord with the third explanation suggested by the authors; the role expected of the offender by the attendance centre authorities is very different from the role expected of him by his probation officer.

The methods used in this study are among the most sophisticated found in the literature to date. A particular note should be taken of the calculation of two styles of prediction tables, the use of these to partial out differences between the risk classes of offenders dealt with in two ways by the courts, and the fact that it was subjected to a validatory test against a different sample of 208 cases. The validation sample continued to show results similar to those quoted above in respect to the attendance-centre orders with and without probation, although the overall failure rate was higher, particularly for the poor risks, in the second sample. The second sample was analyzed to test whether the higher failure rate could have been due to the greater proportion who were also given probation, but this did not appear to be the complete explanation.

Perhaps the study of attendance centres was the first to indicate from a prediction viewpoint the necessity for examination not only of an interaction between the offender and the 'treatment', but the possibility of interaction between elements within a treatment that may militate *against* the rehabilitation of the offender.

From Leslie T. Wilkins, Evaluation of Penal Measures
(New York: Random House), 1969, pp. 74–84.

References

Adams, S. (1967) 'Some findings from correctional caseload research'. Anaheim: paper presented at the National Institute of Crime and Delinquency.

Bailey, W.C. (1966) 'Correctional treatment: an evaluation of 100 correctional outcome studies', *Journal of Criminal Law, Criminology and Police Science* 57: 153–160.

Healy, W. (1915) *The Individual Delinquent.* Boston: Little, Brown & Co.

Mannheim, H. and Wilkins, L.T. (1955) *Prediction Methods in Relation to Borstal Training.* London: HMSO.

McClintock, F.H., Walker, M.A. and Savill, N.C. (1961) *Attendance Centres.* London: Macmillan.

Metfessel, M. and Lovell, C. (1942) 'Recent literature on individual correlates of crime', *Psychological Bulletin*, March.

Wootton, B. (1959) *Social Science and Social Pathology.* London: Allen and Unwin.

67 What Works?

Questions and answers about prison reform (1974)

Robert Martinson

… What we set out to do in this study was fairly simple, though it turned into a massive task. First we undertook a six-month search of the literature for any available reports published in the English language on attempts at rehabilitation that had been made in our corrections systems and those of other countries from 1945 through 1967. We then picked from that literature all those studies whose findings were interpretable – that is, whose design and execution met the conventional standards of social science research. Our criteria were rigorous but hardly esoteric: A study had to be an evaluation of a treatment method, it had to employ an independent measure of the improvement secured by that method, and it had to use some control group, some untreated individuals with whom the treated ones could be compared. We excluded studies only for methodological reasons: They presented insufficient data, they were only preliminary, they presented only a summary of findings and did not allow a reader to evaluate these findings, their results were confounded by extraneous factors, they used unreliable measures, one could not understand their descriptions of the treatment in question, they drew spurious conclusions from their data, their samples were undescribed or too small or provided no true comparability between treated and untreated groups, or they had used inappropriate statistical tests and did not provide enough information for the reader to recompute the data. Using these standards, we drew from the total number of studies 231 acceptable ones, which we not only analysed ourselves but summarized in detail so that a reader of our analysis would be able to compare it with his independent conclusions.

These treatment studies use various measures of offender improvement: recidivism rates (that is, the rates at which offenders return to crime), adjustment to prison life, vocational success, educational achievement, personality and attitude change, and general adjustment to the outside community. We included all of these in our study; but in these pages I will deal only with the effects of rehabilitative treatment on recidivism, the phenomenon which reflects most directly how well our present treatment programs are performing the task of rehabilitation. The use of even this one measure brings with it enough methodological complications to make a clear reporting of the findings most difficult. The groups that are studied, for instance, are exceedingly disparate, so that it is hard to tell whether what 'works' for one kind of offender also works for others. In addition, there has been little attempt to replicate studies; therefore one cannot be certain how stable and reliable the various findings are. Just as important, when the various studies use the term 'recidivism rate', they may in fact be talking about somewhat different measures of offender behaviour – i.e. 'failure' measures such as arrest rates or parole violation rates, or 'success' measures such as favorable discharge from parole or probation. And not all of these measures correlate very highly with one another. ...

With these caveats, it is possible to give a rather bald summary of our findings: *With few and isolated exceptions, the rehabilitative efforts that have been reported so far have had no appreciable effect on recidivism.* ...

Probation or Parole versus Prison

... [B]y far the most extensive and important work that has been done on the effect of community-based treatments has been done in the area of probation and parole. This work sets out to answer the question of whether it makes any difference how you supervise and treat an offender once he has been released from prison or has come under state surveillance in lieu of prison. This is the work that has provided the main basis to date for the claim that we do indeed have the means at our disposal for rehabilitating the offender or at least decarcerating him safely.

One group of these studies has compared the use of probation with other dispositions for offenders; these provide some slight evidence that, at least under some circumstances, probation may make an offender's future chances better than if he had been sent to prison. Or, at least, probation may not worsen these chances. A British study, by Wilkins (1958), reported that when probation was granted more frequently, recidivism rates among probationers did not increase significantly. And another such study by the state of Michigan in 1963 reported that an expansion in the use of probation actually improved recidivism rates – though there are serious problems of comparability in the groups and systems that were studied. ...

[Some studies] indicate a pessimistic general conclusion concerning the limits of the effectiveness of treatment programs ... they found that the personal characteristics of offenders – first-offender status, or age, or type of offense – were more important that the form of treatment in determining future recidivism. An offender with a 'favorable' prognosis will do better than one without, it seems, no matter how you distribute 'good' or 'bad', 'enlightened' or 'regressive' treatments among them.

Quite a large group of studies deals not with probation as compared to other dispositions, but instead with the type of treatment that an offender receives once he is *on* probation or parole. These are the studies that have provided the most encouraging reports on rehabilitative treatment and that have also raised the most serious questions about the nature of the research that has been going on in the corrections field.

Five of these studies have dealt with youthful probationers from 13 to 18 who were assigned to probation officers with small caseloads or provided with other ways of receiving more intensive supervision (Adams 1966 – two reports; Feistman 1966; Kawaguchi and Siff 1967; Pilnick *et al.* 1967). These studies report that, by and large, intensive supervision does work – that the specially treated youngsters do better according to some measure of recidivism. Yet these studies left some important questions unanswered. For instance, was this improved performance a function merely of the number of contacts a youngster had with his probation officer? Did it also depend on the length of time in treatment? Or was it the quality of supervision that was making the difference, rather than the quantity?

Intensive supervision: the Warren studies

The widely reported Warren studies (1966a, 1966b, 1967) in California constitute an extremely ambitious attempt to answer these questions. In this project, a control group of youths, drawn from a pool of candidates ready for first admission to a California Youth Authority institution, was assigned to regular detention, usually for eight to nine months, and then released to regular supervision. The experimental group received considerably elaborate treatment. They were released directly to probation status and assigned to 12-man caseloads. To decide what special treatment was appropriate within these caseloads, the youths were divided according to their 'interpersonal maturity level classification', by use of a scale developed by Grant and Grant. And each level dictated its own special type of therapy. ...

'Success' in this experiment was defined as favorable discharge by the Youth Authority; 'failure' was unfavorable discharge, revocation, or recommitment by a court. Warren reported an encouraging finding: Among all but one of the 'subtypes', the experimentals had a significantly lower failure rate than the controls. The experiment did have certain problems: The experimentals might have been performing better because of the enthusiasm of the staff and the attention lavished on them; none of the controls had been *directly* released to their regular supervision programs instead of being detained first; and it was impossible to separate the effects of the experimentals' small caseloads from their specially designed treatment, since no experimental youths had been assigned to a small caseload with 'inappropriate' treatment, or with no treatment at all. Still, none of these problems were serious enough to vitiate the encouraging prospect that this finding presented for successful treatment of probationers.

This encouraging finding was, however, accompanied by a rather more disturbing clue. As has been mentioned before, the experimental subjects, when measured, had a lower *failure* rate than the controls. But the experimentals also had a lower *success* rate. That is, fewer of the experimental as compared with the controls had been judged to have successfully completed their program of supervision and to be suitable for favourable release. When my colleagues and I undertook a rather laborious reanalysis of the Warren data, it became clear why this discrepancy had appeared. It turned out that fewer experimentals were 'successful' because the experimentals were actually committing more offenses than their control. The reason that the experimentals' relatively large number of offenses was not reflected in their failure rates was simply that the experimentals' probation officers were using a more lenient revocation policy. In other words, the controls had a higher failure rate because the controls were being revoked for less serious offenses.

So it seems that what Warren was reporting in her 'failure' rates was not merely the treatment effect of her small caseloads and special programs. Instead, what Warren was finding was not so much a change in the behaviour of the experimental youths as a change in the behaviour of the experimental *probation officers*, who knew the 'special' status of their charges and who had evidently decided to revoke probation status at a lower than normal rate. The experimentals continued to commit offenses; what was different was that when they committed these offenses, they were permitted to remain on probation.

The experimenters claimed that this low revocation policy, and the greater number of offenses committed by the special treatment youth, were *not* an indication that these youth were behaving specially badly and that policy makers were simply letting them get away with it. Instead, it was claimed, the higher reported offense rate was primarily an artefact of the more intense surveillance that the experimental youth received. But the data show that this is not a sufficient explanation of the low failure rate among the experimental youth; the difference in 'tolerance' of offenses between experimental officials and control officials was much greater than the difference in the rates at which these two systems detected youths committing new offenses. Needless to say, this reinterpretation of the data presents a much bleaker picture of the possibilities of intensive supervision with special treatment.

'Treatment effects' vs 'Policy effects'

This same problem of experimenter bias may also be present in the predecessors of the Warren study, the ones which had also found positive results from intensive supervision on probation; indeed, this disturbing question can be raised about many of the previously discussed reports of positive 'treatment effects'.

This possibility of a 'policy effect' rather than a 'treatment effect' applies, for instance, to the previously discussed studies of the effects of intensive supervision on juvenile and youthful probationers. These were the studies, it will be recalled, which found lower recidivism rates for the intensively supervised.[1]

One opportunity to make a further check on the effects of this problem is provided, in a slightly different context, by Johnson (1962a) ... Johnson, like Warren, assigned experimental subjects to small caseloads and his experiment had the virtue of being performed with two separate populations and at two different times. But in contrast with the Warren case, the Johnson experiment did not engage in a large continuing attempt to choose the experimental counsellors specially, to train them specially, and to keep them informed about the progress and importance of the experiment. The first time the experiment was performed, the experimental youths had a slightly lower revocation rate than the controls at six months. But the second time, the experimentals did *not* do better than their controls; indeed they did slightly worse. And with the experimentals from the first group – those who *had* shown an improvement after six months – this effect wore off at 18 months. In the Johnson study, my colleagues and I found, 'intensive' supervision did *not* increase the experimental youths' risk of detection. Instead, what was happening in the Johnson experiment was that the first time it had been performed – just as in the Warren study – the experimentals were simply revoked less often per number of offenses committed, and they were revoked for offenses more serious than those which prompted revocation among the controls. The second time around, this 'policy' discrepancy disappeared; and when it did, the 'improved' performance of the experimentals disappeared as well. The enthusiasm guiding the project had simply worn off in the absence of reinforcement.

One must conclude that the 'benefits' of intensive supervision for youthful offenders may stem not so much from a 'treatment' effect as from a 'policy' effect – that such supervision, so far as we now know, results not in rehabilitation but in a decision to look the other way when an offense is committed. But there is one major modification to be added to this conclusion. Johnson performed a further measurement (1962b) in his parole experiment: He rated all the supervising agents according to the 'adequacy' of the supervision they gave. And he found that an 'adequate' agent, whether he was working in a small *or* a large caseload, produced a relative improvement in his charges. The converse was not true: An *in*adequate agent was more likely to produce youthful 'failures' when he was given a *small* caseload to supervise. One can't much help a 'good' agent, it seems, by reducing his caseload size; such reduction can only do further harm to those youths who fall into the hands of 'bad' agents.

So with youthful offenders, Johnson found, intensive supervision does not seem to provide the rehabilitative benefits claimed for it; the only such benefits may flow not from intensive supervision itself but from contact with one of the 'good people' who are frequently in such short supply.

Intensive supervision of adults

The results are similarly ambiguous when one applies this intensive supervision to adult offenders. There have been several studies of the effects of intensive supervision on adult parolees. Some of these are hard to interpret because of problems of comparability between experimental and control groups (general risk ratings, for instance, or distribution of narcotics offenders, or policy changes that took place between various phases of the experiments), but two of them (California Department of Corrections 1966; Stanton 1964) do not seem to give evidence of the benefits of intensive supervision. By far the most extensive work, though, on the effects of intensive supervision of adult parolees has been a series of studies of California's Special Intensive Parole Unit (SIPU), a 10-year-long experiment designed to test the treatment possibilities of various special parole programs. Three of the four 'phases' of this experiment produced 'negative' results. The first phase tested the effect of a reduced caseload size; no lasting effect was found. The second phase slightly increased the size of the small caseloads and provided for a longer time in treatment; again there was no evidence of a treatment effect. In the fourth phase, caseload sizes and time in treatment were again varied, and treatments were simultaneously varied in a sophisticated way according to personality characteristics of the parolees; once again, significant results did not appear.

The only phase of this experiment for which positive results were reported was Phase Three. Here, it was indeed found that a smaller caseload improved one's chances of parole success. There is, however, an important caveat that attaches to this finding: When my colleagues and I divided the whole population of subjects into two groups – those receiving supervision in the North of the state and those in the South – we found that the 'improvement' of the experimentals' success rates was taking place primarily in the North. The North differed from the South in one important aspect: Its agents practiced a policy of returning both 'experimental' and 'control' violators to prison at relatively high rates. And it was the North that produced the higher success rate among its experimentals. So this improvement in experimentals' performance was taking place only when accompanied by a 'realistic threat' of severe sanctions. It is interesting to compare this situation with that of the Warren studies. In the Warren studies, experimental subjects were being revoked at a relatively *low* rate. These experimentals 'failed' less, but they also committed more new offenses than their controls. By contrast in the Northern region of the SIPU experiment, there was a policy of *high* rate of return to prison for experimentals; and here, the special program *did* seem to produce a real improvement in the behaviour of offenders. What this suggests is that when intensive supervision *does* produce an improvement in offenders' behaviour, it does so not through the mechanism of 'treatment' or 'rehabilitation', but instead through a mechanism that our studies have almost totally ignored – the mechanism of *deterrence*. And a similar mechanism is suggested by Lohman *et al.*'s study (1967) of intensive supervision of probationers. In this study intensive supervision led to higher total violation rates. But one also notes that intensive supervision combined the highest rate of technical violations with the lowest rate for *new* offenses.

The effects of community treatment

In sum, even in the case of treatment programs administered outside penal institutions, we simply cannot say that this treatment in itself has an appreciable effect on offender behaviour. On the other hand, there is one encouraging set of findings that emerges from these studies. For from many of them there flows the strong suggestion that even if we can't 'treat' offenders so as to make them do better, a great many of the programs designed to rehabilitate them at least did not make them do *worse*. And if these programs did not show the advantages of actually rehabilitating, some of them did have the advantage of being less onerous to the offender himself without seeming to pose increased danger to the community. And some of these programs – especially those involving less restrictive custody, minimal supervision, and early release – simply cost fewer dollars to administer. The information on the dollar costs of these programs is just beginning to be developed but the implication is clear: *that if we can't do more for (and to) offenders, at least we can safely do less.*

There is, however, one important caveat even to this note of optimism: In order to calculate the true costs of these programs, one must in each case include not only their administrative cost but also the cost of maintaining in the community an offender population increased in size. This population might well not be committing new offenses at any greater rate; but the offender population might, under some of these plans, be larger in absolute *numbers.* So the total number of offenses committed might rise, and our chances of victimization might therefore rise too. We need to be able to make a judgement about the size and probable duration of this effect; as of now, we simply do not know.

Does Nothing Work?

Do all of these studies lead us irrevocably to the conclusion that nothing works, that we haven't the faintest clue about how to rehabilitate offenders and reduce recidivism? And if so, what shall we do?

We tried to exclude from our survey those studies which were so poorly done that they simply could not be interpreted. But despite our efforts, a pattern has run through much of this discussion – of studies which 'found' effects without making any truly rigorous attempt to exclude competing hypotheses, of extraneous factors permitted to intrude upon the measurements, of recidivism measures which are not all measuring the same thing, of 'follow-up' periods which vary enormously and rarely extend beyond the period of legal supervision, of experiments never replicated, of 'system effects' not taken into account, of categories drawn up without any theory to guide the enterprise. It is just possible that some of our treatment programs *are* working to some extent, but that our research is so bad that it is incapable of telling.

Having entered this very serious caveat, I am bound to say that these data, involving over two hundred studies and hundreds of thousands of individuals as they do, are the best available and give us very little reason to hope that we have in fact found a sure way of reducing recidivism through rehabilitation. This is not to say that we found no instances of success or partial success; it is only to say that these instances have been isolated, producing no clear pattern to indicate the efficacy of any particular method of treatment. And neither is this to say that factors *outside* the realm of rehabilitation may not be working to reduce recidivism – factors such as the tendency for recidivism to be lower in offenders over the age of 30; it is only to say that such factors seem to have little connection with any of the treatment methods now at our disposal.

From this probability, one may draw any of several conclusions. It may be simply that our programs aren't yet good enough – that the education we provide to inmates is still poor education, that the therapy we administer is not administered skilfully enough, that our intensive supervision and counselling do not yet provide enough personal support for the offenders who are subjected to them. If one wishes to believe this, then what our correctional system needs is simply a more full-hearted commitment to the strategy of treatment.

It may be, on the other hand, that there is a more radical flaw in our present strategies – that education at its best, or that psychotherapy at its best, cannot overcome, or even appreciably reduce, the powerful tendency for offenders to continue in criminal behavior. Our present treatment programs are based on a theory of crime as a 'disease' – that is to say, as something foreign and abnormal in the individual which can presumably be cured. This theory may well be flawed, in that it overlooks – indeed, denies – both the normality of crime in society and the personal normality of a very large proportion of offenders, criminals who are merely responding to the facts and conditions of our society.

This opposing theory of 'crime as a social phenomenon' directs our attention away from a 'rehabilitative' strategy, away from the notion that we may best insure public safety through a series of 'treatments' to be imposed forcibly on convicted offenders. These treatments have on occasion become, and have the potential for becoming, so draconian as to offend the moral order of a democratic society; and the theory of crime as a social phenomenon suggests that such treatments may be not only offensive but ineffective as well. This theory points, instead, to decarceration for low-risk offenders – and, presumably, to keeping high-risk offenders in prisons which are nothing more (and aim to be nothing more) than custodial institutions.

But this approach has its own problems. To begin with, there is the moral dimension of crime and punishment. Many low-risk offenders have committed serious crimes (murder, sometimes) and even if one is reasonably sure they will never commit another crime, it violates our sense of justice that they should experience no significant retribution for their actions. A middle-class banker who kills his adulterous wife in a moment of passion is a 'low-risk' criminal; a juvenile delinquent in the ghetto who commits armed robbery has, statistically a much higher probability of committing another crime. Are we going to put the first on probation and sentence the latter to a long term in prison?

Besides, one cannot ignore the fact that the punishment of offenders is the major means we have for *deterring* incipient offenders. We know almost nothing about the 'deterrent effect', largely because 'treatment' theories have so dominated our research, and 'deterrence' theories have been relegated to the status of a historical curiosity. Since we have almost no idea of the deterrent functions that our present system performs or that future strategies might be made to perform, it is possible that there is indeed something that works – that to some extent is working right now in front of our noses, and that might be made to work better – something that deters rather than cures, something that does not so much reform convicted offenders as prevent criminal behavior in the first place. But whether that is the case and, if it is, what strategies will be found to make our deterrence system work better than it does now, are questions we will not be able to answer with data until a new family of studies has been brought into existence. As we begin to learn the facts, we will be in a better position than we are now to judge to what degree the prison has become an anachronism and can be replaced by more effective means of social control.

From Robert Martinson, 'What Works? Questions and answers about prison reform',
The Public Interest, *35, 1974, pp. 22–54.*

Note

1 But one of these reports, by Kawaguchi and Siff (1967), also found that an intensively supervised juvenile, by the time he finally 'failed', had had more previous detentions while under supervision than a control juvenile had experienced.

References

Adams, S. (1966) *Development of a Program Research Service in Probation.* Research Report No.27 (Final report, NIMH Project MH00718). Los Angeles County Probation Department.

California Department of Corrections (1966) *Parole Work Unit Program: an evaluative report.* A memorandum to the California Joint Legislative Budget Committee.

Feistman, E.G. (1966) *Comparative Analysis of the Willow-Brook-Harbor Intensive Services Program, March 1, 1965 through February 28, 1966.* Research Report No.28. Los Angeles County Probation Department.

Johnson, B. (1962a) *Parole Performance of the First Year's Releases, Parole Research Project: evaluation of reduced caseloads.* Research Report No.27. California Youth Authority.

——(1962b) *An Analysis of Predictions of Parole Performance and of Judgements of Supervision in the Parole Research Project.* Research Report No.32. California Youth Authority.

Kawaguchi, R.W. and Siff, L.M. (1967) *An Analysis of Intensive Probation Services – Phase II.* Research Report No.29. Los Angeles County Probation Department.

Lohman, J.D. *et al.* (1967) *The Intensive Supervision Caseloads: a preliminary evaluation.* The San Francisco Project: a study of federal probation and parole. Research report No.11. University of California, School of Criminology.

Pilnick, S. *et al.* (1967) *Collegefields: from delinquency to freedom.* A Report on Collegefields Educational Center. Laboratory for Applied Behavioral Science, Newark State College.

Stanton, J.M. (1964) *Board Directed Extensive Supervision.* New York State Division of Parole.

Warren, M. (1966a) *The Community Treatment Project after Five Years.* California Youth Authority.

Warren, M. *et al.* (1966b) *Community Treatment Project, an evaluation of community treatment for delinquents: a fifth progress report.* CTP Research Report No.7. California Youth Authority.

Warren, M. *et al.* (1967) *Community Treatment Project, an evaluation of community treatment for delinquents: a sixth progress report.* CTP Research Report No.8. California Youth Authority.

Wilkins, L.T. (1958) 'A small comparative study of the results of probation', *British Journal of Criminology* 8(3): 201–209.

68 Displacement from custody (1977)

K. Pease, S. Billingham and I. Earnshaw

Introduction

In every case in which a new sentence is used it displaces an 'old' sentence. To a degree, penal policy is designed to provide the courts with a range of sentences reflecting the concerns of Parliament and, thereby, to influence in broad terms (although emphatically not in individual cases) the way in which offenders are dealt with. Parliament is therefore able to prescribe to some extent the range and limits of judicial freedom. A major concern of the last decade has been to bring about, wherever appropriate, a reduction in the use of custodial sentences. New sentences have been introduced for the explicit purpose of reducing the number of offenders sent to prison.

After the introduction of a new non-custodial sentence it is not easy to determine what other sentences it has replaced and in what proportion. Statistical analysis of sentences passed can offer one solution, as demonstrated by Oatham and Simon (1972). They showed that 'courts have used the suspended sentence both to replace immediate imprisonment, and as a sentence in its own right ... it has been estimated that of all persons awarded a suspended sentence, only somewhere between 40% and 50% would, but for the new provision, have been sentenced to imprisonment for the original offence'. Sentence substitution can also be estimated by quasi-experimental means – for example by matching offenders given a particular disposal, with others sentenced by the same court in preceding years, then following up the sentences passed on the earlier 'twin'; or alternatively by inducing courts to say what they would have done if new alternative sentences had not been available. Finally, sentence substitution can be estimated by circumstantial evidence. That is what has been attempted here. It is argued that in order to estimate the number of those given community service orders who would otherwise have been given a custodial sentence, it is necessary to consider the penal measures imposed on the following groups of offenders:

(a)   Those for whom an assessment existed of the sentence thought likely if a community service order were not made.

(b)   Those who were in breach of the requirements of a community service order.

(c)   Those in respect of whom the courts asked for an assessment of suitability for community service.

(d)   Those recommended by probation officers as suitable for community service, but who did not receive a community service order.

Relevant information from all six experimental areas was not available for each of these groups. Details of their respective data sources are given below in considering each group.

Judgements by probation officers of what sentences would otherwise have been passed on those sentenced to community service orders

In only one of the experimental areas was there an exercise which allowed assessment of displacement from custody on the basis of guesses about the sentence which would have been passed had community service not been available (Durham County Probation and After-Care Service, 1974). In that area, in cases where a community service order was made, the probation officer who wrote the social inquiry report was asked before sentence was passed 'if an order is not made, do you think a custodial sentence – excluding a suspended sentence – would be probable, possible or very unlikely?' Of the 39 cases on which information is available where an order was made, the officers said a custodial sentence was probable in 19 cases, possible in 13 and very unlikely in 7. Making the crude assumption that 'probable' effectively means certain custody and 'possible' means certain non-custody, and also assuming that no one for whom custody was very unlikely would be given a custodial sentence, then in 19 out of 39 cases (48%) community service displaced from a custodial sentence. The accuracy of this estimate clearly depends upon the accuracy of probation officers in predicting sentences. It is therefore important to note that in the group for which predictions were made and sentences other than community service were passed, six out of six cases predicted as probable custody were given custodial sentences. Three out of four 'possible' custody cases were given non-custodial sentences, as were three out of three cases where custody was judged 'very unlikely'.

Those who breached the requirements of a community service order

Section 16 of the Powers of Criminal Courts Act 1973 allows revocation of an order (or fine with order to continue) for breach of requirements of the order. For the purpose of the present analysis, breaches which have been dealt with by the continuance of the order were excluded. Given this exclusion, in cases where the breach occurred early in the order and sentence was passed for the original offence, the sentence imposed gave indirect evidence about the sentence which community service had replaced. If the community service itself had been an alternative to custody, then early breach of the order would have been expected to lead to a custodial sentence. It should be noted that revocations of a community service order under section 17 of the Act were not included. Since offenders who commit further offences are characteristically dealt with under section 17 and not under section 16, the seriousness of the further offence would have been an additional variable and a potential source of confusion in this analysis.

The evidence to hand is somewhat fragmentary but is summarised in Table 1. Data are included from Durham (32 cases relating to the period 1 March 1973 to 20 July 1976), Merseyside (24 cases relating to the period 1 February 1973 to 15 August 1976), Kent (53 cases relating to the period 1 April 1973 to 20 July 1976) and South Yorkshire (6 cases relating to the period 1 April 1975 to 30 June 1976). No data are included from Shropshire because at the time of writing, no section 16 breach proceedings had

Table 1 Sentences passed on those whose orders were revoked after section 16 breach proceedings under the Power of Criminal Courts Act 1973, by hours ordered and hours worked (excluding deferred sentences)

| | Hours ordered | | | | | | | | | | | |
| | < 100 | | | 100–199 | | | 200 + hours | | | Total | | |
Sentence passed	*Active custodial*	*Suspended sentence*	*Non-custodial*	*Active custodial*	*Suspended sentence*	*Non-custodial*	*Active custodial*	*Suspended sentence*	*Non-custodial*	*Active custodial*	*Suspended sentence*	*Non-custodial*
< 10%	1	–	2	15	5	10	10	3	2	26	8	14
10–19%	1	–	–	6	–	6	–	–	2	7	0	8
20–49%	–	–	–	7	1	13	3	2	2	10	3	15
50%+	–	–	1	3	5	7	3	1	–	6	6	8
Total	2	–	3	31	11	36	16	6	6	49	17	45

Percentage of hours worked which had been worked before breach resulted in revocation of a community service order in that area. It will be seen that in 54% (26) of the cases where less than 10% of hours ordered had been worked a custodial sentence was passed. This compared with 47% where between 10 and 19% of hours ordered had been worked, 36% where between 20 and 49% of hours ordered had been worked, and 30% of cases where half or more than half of the hours ordered had been worked. It will also be noted that the longer the order, the more likely is a custodial sentence to be passed after a section 16 breach. This is as would be expected. The data therefore suggest that for the 46% of people given non-custodial sentences (including suspended sentences) following breach of a community service order when less than 10% of the required hours had been worked, the sentence was not in the first instance an alternative to an active custodial sentence. However, since the proportion differs as between lengths of order, and since breaches occur disproportionately among those given longer orders, it would be appropriate to correct the percentage on the basis of the actual distribution of lengths of order previously made (see Pease *et al.* 1975, p. 28). Correcting on this basis,[1] the percentage of people assessed as having received a community service order instead of a custodial sentence is 50%.

There is, however, at least one argument that the assessment, by this method, that half the sample had been diverted from custody is an over-estimate. It would be reasonable to suppose that the courts may pass custodial sentences after a section 16 breach, not because they would originally have imposed a custodial sentence, but because the offender's failure to take advantage of the order is seen as evidence of the need for a custodial sentence.

Those in respect of whom the court asked for an assessment of suitability for community service

Table 2 summarises information available to the Home Office Research Unit on 1 June 1974 in respect of those with whom the court took the initiative in considering community service orders, but where a community service order was not ultimately made. There are too few cases to justify a breakdown of numbers by area.

Further evidence from the post-experimental period is available (as a result of the way records are kept) from only one of the experimental areas. During the period between early September 1974 and the middle of May 1976 there were 29 cases in which the courts requested that the offender's suitability for community service be considered. In 11 of these cases a community service order was recommended but not

Table 2 Disposal of cases (excluding those given community service orders) where courts specified that probation officers writing social inquiry reports should consider suitability for a community service order

	Probation Officer recommended Community Service	Probation Officer did not recommend CS
Immediate custody	8	6
Suspended sentence	6	4
Non-custodial sentence	16	33
Total	30	43

made. Of these 11, four received custodial sentences, two received suspended sentences and five received other non-custodial sentences. Of the 18 offenders for whom no community service order recommendations resulted from the court's initiative, four received suspended sentences and the remaining 14 received other non-custodial sentences. Taking all the available data together, and ignoring the distinction between those recommended and those not recommended for community service, of the 102 cases considered, 18 (18%) attracted a sentence of immediate custody, in 16 cases (16%) the sentence was suspended imprisonment and in 68 cases (67%) a non-custodial sentence was passed.

This group is important in that it consists of offenders for whom the courts regarded community service as an option, in view of current offence and criminal record. If the court had not taken this view, the request for an assessment of suitability for community service would have been a waste of the court's time and that of the probation service. The sentences passed on those who are assessed for community service suitability on the court's initiative, but who do not attract a community service order, are thus relevant to the place of community service in the range of sentencing alternatives. It is an assumption of this method that those for whom the court asks for a judgement of community service suitability and who do receive an order are similar in all relevant respects to those for whom such a request is made but no order results. If that assumption is invalid, the group has much less relevance, although there is no reason to suppose that even if differences do exist they would make for more lenient sentencing in those not given community service.

Those recommended for community service by probation officers but who did not receive such an order

This group must, at least in the opinion of probation officers, have been potentially within the range of offenders for which a community service order was at least an arguable proposition. To recommend such an order for offences which were excessively trivial or excessively serious would have been to invite the derision of the court. However, it is assumed that those recommended for but not given community service orders are similar to those recommended and given community service orders. In so far as the court deals differently with the two samples, the assumption may be invalid.

On 1 June 1974 information was available to the Home Office Research Unit on 305 cases in which recommendations of community service orders had been made by probation officers and followed by different sentences. Table 3 summarises that information.

The proportions of those recommended for community service who were given an active custodial sentence do not differ significantly between on the one hand the three areas whose policy was to regard community service as an alternative to a custodial sentence, and on the other hand the three areas with a different policy (see Pease *et al.* 1975, p. 54). This is to be expected given a range of opinion about the place of community service, relative to other outcomes, held by probation officers within each area (see Pease *et al.* 1975, Table 33, p. 54).

More recent information is available from three of the six experimental areas, namely Nottinghamshire, Kent and Durham. In all cases it is more convenient to add together the information available from all the areas. Thus in all three cases the data

Table 3 Disposal of cases where probation officers' recommendations of community service were not taken up

Area	Custodial sentence	Suspended sentence	Non-custodial sentence
Co. Durham	12	4	10
Inner London	10	10	8
Kent	24	16	15
Nottinghamshire	57	35	44
Shropshire	6	8	14
South-west Lancashire	4	7	21
All areas	113	80	112

presented below include all that were available to the Research Unit from the beginning of the experimental scheme to the last available date (middle of May 1976 in the case of Nottinghamshire, 15 July 1976 in the case of Kent and 1 August 1976 in Durham).

For Nottinghamshire there were 317 cases where recommendations of community service orders by probation officers were not taken up. Of these, 149 (47%) were given immediate custodial sentences, 74 (23%) were given suspended sentences and 94 (30%) non-custodial sentences. As for Kent there were 623 cases where community service recommendations were not taken up. Of these, 300 (48%) were given an immediate custodial sentence, 118 (19%) a suspended sentence and 205 (33%) a non-custodial sentence. Information was available on 47 relevant cases in County Durham. Of these 23 (49%) were given immediate custodial sentences, five (11%) suspended sentences and 19 (40%) non-custodial sentences. As an additional piece of information, it is interesting to note that in the one non-experimental area for which data were readily available, South Yorkshire, between 1 April 1975 and 31 March 1976, 119 offenders were recommended for community service but otherwise sentenced. Of these 69 (58%) were sentenced to immediate custody, 23 (19%) to a suspended sentence and 27 (23%) to other non-custodial sentences. Thus combining all available data from all six experimental areas, plus South Yorkshire, in 1,194 cases where a probation officer's recommendation was not taken up, 561 (47%) were given immediate custodial sentences, 245 (21%) were given suspended sentences and 388 (32%) were given non-custodial sentences.

Conclusion

In assessing the proportion of those given community service orders who were displaced from custody three of the four methods used produced estimates within the range 45% to 50%. The similarity is seductive. It would be encouraging to regard this as conclusive evidence that the true displacement figure lies in or very close to this range. However, there are a number of arguments which cast doubt on such a conclusion. In two of these three estimates, there may be factors which would tend to reduce the proportion of those diverted from custody. It is not likely that all those given custodial sentences after a section 16 breach of a community service order would originally have received a custodial sentence. Further, it is possible that probation officers tended to recommended community service orders in many cases where such a recommendation was a forlorn hope in the face of an offence for which imprisonment was almost certain. To the extent that these considerations are true, they tend to reduce the estimated proportion of those diverted from custody.

It is very interesting that the one estimate which yielded a different figure was the one derived from cases where the court initiated consideration for community service. In so far as these results can be relied on at all, given the small numbers on which they are based, the implication of this particular result may be that courts placed the community service order in a lower position on the tariff than did probation officers. That is to say, courts considered a community service order to be an alternative to a non-custodial sentence in a higher proportion of cases than did probation officers, at least in cases where courts initiated consideration for community service. Nevertheless one could argue that these were cases where upon reflection the courts regarded community service as excessively severe, and therefore passed another non-custodial sentence. One could also point to the discrepancy between the court's behaviour in initiating consideration of suitability for community service and the way in which the court deals with offenders in breach of orders.

From K. Pease, S. Billingham and I. Earnshaw, Community Service Assessed in *1976. Home Office Research Study 39 (London: HMSO), 1977, pp. 3–10.*

Note

1   This is done by calculating, for each sentence length band, the proportion of those estimated as having been diverted from custody in that band (using sentence on breach when less than 10% of hours worked had been performed, see text) and multiplying by the number of orders occurring in each band, summing across bands, and expressing as a proportion of all orders made.

References

Durham County Probation and After-Care Service (1974) *Community Service Orders.* A progress report of the first 12 months of Community service by offenders in County Durham.

Oatham, E. and Simon, F. (1972) 'Are suspended sentences working ?', *New Society* August 3rd.

Pease, K., Durkin, P., Earnshaw, I., Payne, D. and Thorpe, J. (1975) *Community Service Orders.* Home Office Research Studies 29. London: HMSO.

69 New findings, new views (1979)

Robert Martinson

Treatment programs: some help, some harm

Any conclusion in scientific inquiry is held provisionally, subject to further evidence. My original conclusion concerning the importance of treatment programs in criminal justice was derived from a survey accomplished for the State of New York covering the period 1945–1967. This survey led to a book, *The Effectiveness of Correctional Treatment (ECT)*, which summarized research from 231 studies. I coauthored ECT. The conclusion I derived from ECT is supplied in an article which has been widely quoted and reprinted. However, new evidence from our current study leads me to reject my original conclusion and suggest an alternative more adequate to the facts at hand. I have hesitated up to now, but the evidence in our survey is simply too overwhelming to ignore.

Different procedures were used in the two surveys. ECT is based primarily on the findings of evaluation research – a special kind of research which was applied to criminal justice on a wide scale for the first time in California during the period immediately following World War II. This research is experimental – that is, offenders are often randomly allocated to treatment and nontreatment groups so that comparison can be made of outcome. Our current study, however, compares the reprocessing rates of groups receiving treatment with roughly comparable groups who receive the 'standard processing' given to most offenders across the United States.

ECT excluded about 90 per cent of the research it had available because it was not evaluation research. Only evaluation studies were included on the ground that only this kind of study can truly unearth causality. Our current study, on the other hand, includes any study which contains a verifiable reprocessing rate for a group of at least ten sentenced offenders. By including annual follow-up studies we increase the number of rates for persons given standard processing. In comparison with ECT, our sample is much more representative of criminal justice nationally.

In brief, ECT focused on summarizing evaluation research which purported to uncover *causality*; in our current study we reject this perspective as premature and focus on uncovering *patterns* which can be of use to policymakers in choosing among available treatment programs. These patterns are sufficiently consistent to oblige me to modify my previous conclusion.

The authors of ECT laboriously summarized hundreds of evaluation studies, but astonishingly the book itself contains no general conclusion. It is a compendium of findings displayed in hundreds of subparagraphs, and, in my opinion, it defies summary as a whole. I undertook, on my own responsibility, to supply what the authors of this work could not or would not supply – a conclusion. I limited my summary to recidivism, and included with the summary brief discussion and analyses of the research on which the summary was based. My conclusion was: 'With few and isolated exceptions, the rehabilitative efforts that have been reported so far have had no appreciable effect on recidivism.'

This conclusion takes the usual form of rejecting an hypothesis, i.e., the hypothesis that treatment *added* to the networks of criminal justice does in fact have an *appreciable* effect. The very evidence presented in the article indicates that it would have been incorrect to say that treatment had *no* effect. Some studies showed an effect, others did not. But, all together, looking at this entire body of research, I drew this conclusion, and thought it important that the conclusion be made public and debated. It surely was debated.

On the basis of the evidence in our current study, I withdraw this conclusion. I have often said that treatment added to the networks of criminal justice is 'impotent,' and I withdraw this characterization as well. I protested at the slogan used by the media to sum up what I said – 'nothing works.' The press has no time for scientific quibbling and got to the heart of the matter better than I did.

But for all of that, the conclusion is not correct. More precisely, treatments will be found to be 'impotent' under certain conditions, beneficial under others, and detrimental under still others. The current study, by enabling us to uncover a major category of *harmful treatment*, is an advance on ECT. It enables us to indicate, at least roughly, the conditions under which a treatment program will fall into one of three categories: (1) beneficial (the program *reduces* reprocessing rates); (2) neutral (*no impact*, positive or negative, can be determined); and (3) detrimental (the program *increases* reprocessing rates).

The most interesting general conclusion is that no treatment program now used in criminal justice is inherently either substantially helpful or harmful. The critical fact seems to be the *conditions* under which the program is delivered. For example, our results indicate that a widely-used program, such as formal education, is detrimental when given to juvenile sentenced offenders in a group home, but is beneficial (decreases reprocessing rates) when given to juveniles in juvenile prisons. Such startling results are found again and again in our study, for treatment programs as diverse as individual psychotherapy, group counselling, intensive supervision, and what we have called 'individual/help' (aid, advice, counselling).

Table 1 illustrates some of these contradictory patterns. A 'mean effect size' reports the average tendency of a treatment to fall above or below the mean reprocessing rate for standard treatment across the United States. In this table we examine treatments under three conditions: group home (preprison community treatment residences), prison (standard training school confinement for juveniles), and shock probation (brief period of confinement followed by standard probation).

A negative effect size indicates that a treatment is below the mean of standard processing and has a beneficial effect. All but two of the treatments have *beneficial* effects when given in prison (and when compared to standard youth confinement *without* treatment). On the other hand, all but one of the treatments have *detrimental* effects when given in the group home conditions. One treatment, job training, is beneficial under both conditions.

Table 1 Mean effect sizes for three locations (juvenile sentenced offenders)

Treatment	Group Home	Prison	Shock probation
Job placement	+1.46	+0.07	
Benign custody	+0.12	+0.01	−0.96
Reduced supervision		−0.12	
Increased custody	+0.62	−0.13	
Job training	−0.32	−0.25	
Volunteer/help		−0.36	−1.49
Group counselling		−0.43	
Psychotherapy	+2.09	−0.45	−1.73
Milieu therapy		−0.51	
Group therapy	+0.51	−0.66	
Behavior modification	+0.09	−0.88	
Intensive supervision		−1.00	−1.42
Education	+0.46	−1.37	
Individual/help	+1.62	−1.79	

1. A positive (+) mean effect size indicates a treatment mean higher than the standard processing mean.
2. A negative (−) mean effect size indicates a treatment mean lower than the standard processing mean.
3. Mean effect sizes for the group home are computed using standard probation as a comparison group.
4. Mean effect sizes for prison and shock probation are computed using standard juvenile prison as a comparison group.

Treatments do seem to differ when given in prison, individual/help having the largest beneficial effect (−1.79). Yet when this treatment is given in a group home, it becomes substantially detrimental. Four comparisons are possible between treatments given in youth prison and under the condition of shock probation. In all four cases, shock probation is superior, and in one case (benign custody) the sign of the mean effect size changes from plus to minus.

The group home and shock probation can be called 'locations'. Recent reforms have introduced them into criminal justice as *alternatives* to standard processing. The treatment programs examined in ECT were primarily *additions* to standard processing. The patterns of treatment effects under these locations offer clear evidence that reforms in criminal justice can be either beneficial or detrimental. The patterns in Table 1 should be a warning to policymakers and local decisionmakers. One can no longer assume that innovations (or treatments) will differ primarily in the degree to which they are beneficial. Certain types of reform programs can have a strongly harmful effect on those to whom they are administered.

Table 1 also warns against confining juvenile offenders without some kind of treatment. The pattern of effects does not indicate that *any* treatment will work (for example, job placement and benign custody are questionable). But most treatments for incarcerated juveniles have negative effect sizes and one suspects that a *common process* may be at work. Future research should compare these various treatments and seek to discover what this common process might be.

Perhaps the most extreme case of radical tinkering with the system of criminal justice is the nationwide movement to abolish parole release, and with it, parole supervision of released offenders. As part of our study, we were able to make 80 controlled comparisons between parolees and roughly comparable offenders released maxout. In 74 of these 80 comparisons, parolees had lower reprocessing rates than those released without parole supervision. Our conclusion is cautious. We have stated that these results 'should give pause to those policymakers and legislators who have been operating on the unexamined assumption that parole supervision *makes no difference*' (Martinson and Wilks 1977: 27).

The evidence that parole supervision *works* (reduces reprocessing rates) is more convincing than the bare assumption that it does not. I suggest that it can work better if the courts and the sentencing reformers stop trying to reduce it to impotence. Indeed, parole supervision should be extended to misdemeanor and felony offenders who are currently released maxout as part of a definite sentence so that parole will be properly *limited* both in duration and in its function, which is to reduce crime through surveillance and quick action when danger threatens.

Conclusion

The current system of sentencing in the United States must be reformed. Not only are individual offenders treated disparately, but classes of offenders are treated disparately as well. Yet any reform must be approached with caution. The reprocessing rate is low and while some programs are beneficial under certain conditions, others can be distinctly harmful. In fact, some recent reforms show evidence of increasing the reprocessing rate, rather than decreasing it. Thus great care must be taken when introducing alternatives to our standard procedures – probation, imprisonment, and parole supervision. Those treatments that are helpful must be carefully discerned and increased; those that are harmful or impotent eliminated.

From Robert Martinson, 'New Findings, New Views: a note of caution regarding sentencing reform', Hofstra Law Review 7(2), 1979, pp. 243–258.

Reference

Martinson, R. and Wilks, J. (1977) 'Save parole supervision', *Federal Probation*, September.

70 Second thoughts on IMPACT (1981)

Steven Folkard

Introduction

Many of the traditional assumptions of social work have been questioned, because research has increasingly cast doubts on whether expressed objectives have been achieved in practice. Traditional assumptions have been questioned, too, in probation, where the situation is in some respects more complex: although probation officers are social workers, they are also officers of the court, and evaluation of their work requires consideration of criteria related to social justice on the one hand and to criminal justice on the other. In the criminal justice field evaluation has usually been based on the use of reconviction rates. As discussed below, there is now little evidence to suggest that penal treatment, including probation, is likely to be effective in these terms. The IMPACT experiment to which reference is made in this chapter has already been completed and reported. While it is briefly summarised here, it is used mainly as a point of departure to consider some of the broader issues and problems relating to the objectives of social work in a penological context.

The IMPACT experiment

IMPACT, which stands for Intensive Matched Probation and After-Care Treatment, was an experimental project carried out by the Home Office Research Unit, and described in two short volumes (Folkard *et al.* 1974, 1976) published in the Home Office Research Studies. It arose from three general interests. The first was an interest in situational treatment, which had been highlighted in previous research. It had been shown that many probationers had severe situational problems relating to work and family, etc.; the presence of these tended to be associated with high failure rates; a relatively small amount of probation officers' time was devoted to these problems; and efforts to ameliorate them apparently made little difference to failure rates. There was no evidence to show that more situational treatment would necessarily produce better results, but research had shown a need which perhaps could be answered in this way.

The second interest was in differential treatment. It seemed possible that the failure to demonstrate general treatment effects might be due to the heterogeneity of each treatment group, given variations in sentencing practice. In these circumstances one type of treatment might be effective for one type of offender but not for another, and those who failed to respond to one type of treatment might respond to a different approach. The positive and negative results would then cancel each other out in any general comparisons, and perhaps mask any differential treatment effects. If such interaction effects could be established, a closer matching of type of treatment to type of offender might produce improved success rates.

The third interest was in diversion, or the attempt to find alternative treatment in the community for offenders who might otherwise have been sentenced to prison. Prisons had become overcrowded and increasingly expensive, and there was a growing belief that many offenders sent there could be dealt with as effectively in the community if suitable alternative treatment could be provided. The development of more intensive and varied treatment was conceived as one way in which the probation service might contribute to this objective.

The IMPACT project, which started in 1971, was carried out in four probation and after-care areas – Dorset, Inner London, Sheffield and Staffordshire – to evaluate the provision of more intensive situational treatment for relatively 'high risk' offenders. Emphasis was given to situational treatment in the family and in the areas of work and leisure. In London and Sheffield the experimental treatment was provided through specialised units comprising one senior probation officer and five probation officers. In Dorset and Staffordshire an experimental officer provided special treatment in each of four probation offices within each county. For the duration of the experiment all experimental officers worked with reduced caseloads and were relieved of other office duties. The maximum experimental caseload was 20 cases, which in some offices, if much additional travelling was necessary, was reduced to 15. Experimental and control groups were set up in each area by random allocation procedures, the control cases being given normal supervision on normal caseloads. Evidence was produced to show that these groups were comparable, and that the experimental cases did in fact get more attention and more situational treatment. In IMPACT Volume II (Folkard *et al.* 1976) reference was made to seven criteria thought by Logan (1972) to be the minimum necessary as a test of effectiveness of any research concerned with evaluating penal treatments. Tested against these criteria the design of IMPACT seemed sufficiently viable to enable fairly reliable conclusions to be drawn from the findings.

In operational terms, the feasibility and acceptability of this kind of treatment in probation practice were demonstrated. The exercise required close collaboration between probation officers, administrators and researchers, and this was achieved with relatively few problems. However, the results showed no significant differences overall in one year reconviction rates between the experimental and the control cases, therefore producing no evidence in these terms to support a general application of more intensive situational treatment.

A typology of offenders was produced, based on the two dimensions of 'criminal tendencies' and 'personal problems'. The first of these was derived from probation officers' ratings and the second from scores on a problem check-list completed by probationers. A differential treatment effect for different types of offender was apparently demonstrated. Offenders with moderate or high criminal tendencies and average or few personal problems did significantly worse (in terms of one year reconviction rates) under intensive situational treatment than under normal probation supervision. There was a suggestion that an offender with low criminal tendencies and many personal problems had a more successful outcome under the experimental treatment, though this was based on a relatively small number of cases and was not statistically significant.

There is a need to consider these results, not in isolation, but in the wider context of other research on penal treatment and of general penal policy. There have been several literature surveys which have cast increasing doubts on the effectiveness of penal treatment. In an evaluation of 100 studies of correctional outcome Bailey in 1966 concluded that 'it seems quite clear that, on the basis of this sample of outcome reports, with all its limitations, evidence supporting the efficacy of correctional treatment is slight, inconsistent, and of questionable reliability'. Martinson, in his 1974 consideration of 231 studies, reported that 'with few and isolated exceptions, the rehabilitative efforts that have been reported so far had no appreciable effect on recidivism'. Similar conclusions are reached from a survey of published research carried out by the Home Office Research Unit (Brody 1976).

Palmer in 1975 criticised Martinson for not focusing on the subjects of 'differential value' and 'degree of effectiveness', for which it is claimed some evidence does exist. It is suggested that in preference to asking 'what works – for offenders as a whole?' research workers must increasingly ask 'which methods work best for *which* types of offender, and under *what* conditions or in what types of setting?'. The findings from IMPACT are consistent with Martinson's conclusion that no general effect from treatment can be demonstrated, but also not inconsistent with Palmer's view that some pointers can be provided to suggest differential effects for different types of offender.

The treatment model

As a consequence of the cumulative negative evidence about penal treatment, it is necessary to look critically at the concepts and criteria employed in attempts at evaluation. One of the most commonly used criteria has been that of reconviction rates (which was used in the IMPACT study), and there has been a good deal of agreement about its relevance to research on individuals who had already committed offences and been convicted. However, there are many difficulties when attempts are made to use reconviction rates as measures of success or failure following particular treatments. When considered by themselves in relation to particular individuals or groups, it is not possible to show how far subsequent behaviour has been influenced by treatment or would have occurred in any case. In many studies attempts have been made to control for factors extraneous to treatment by matching groups on variables thought to be relevant to reconviction, sometimes making use of prediction techniques for this purpose. However, this is severely limited by the failure to produce powerful predictors. When two or more groups being compared have been sentenced in different ways, although 'matched' on several variables, one cannot eliminate the possibility that any differences in outcome between them are due, not to treatment effects, but to initial differences in risk which have not been taken account of in the matching or prediction formula used. Where there is evidence of some systematic difference – for instance, one group has been sent to prison and another put on probation – this may seem the most likely explanation. Controlled experiments making use of random allocation (as in the IMPACT study) overcome this problem of systematic bias, but there are a limited number of situations in which this method can be used. A further difficulty in the use of reconviction rates is the well-known problem of low detection rates, so that there may be as many failures in the 'success group' as in the 'failure group'.

In the light of problems of this kind there have been suggestions that attempts should be made to identify criteria other than reconviction for the purpose of evaluating penal treatment. Of course there is nothing new about this, and in the past consideration has often been given to looking at changes in personality, social adjustment, work performance, etc. Part of the probation research in the Home Office in 1961 included a search for alternative criteria, as did also the IMPACT project. There are perhaps three general points to make about this. First, there is a fairly strong tendency for other personality and social problems to be correlated with reconviction rates, so that similar results are obtained in any case. Second, it seems difficult to avoid the conclusion that in attempting to evaluate penal treatment of offenders, reconviction is the most *relevant* criterion, and that at best other criteria are secondary ones. Third, there has been an increasing questioning not merely about what criteria to use in evaluating penal treatment, but about whether the treatment model itself is an appropriate one in the field of penology.

For more than a century rehabilitation through treatment has been one of the primary objectives in sentencing and penal practice, and had become so widely accepted that it seemed to require little justification. However, over the last few years, apart from the negative results from research, there have been moral objections as well. It may seem a paradox that the rehabilitative model should be criticised on moral grounds, for, as Hirsch (1976) says, it was a scheme born to optimism, faith and humanism. Yet it is on these grounds that some of the most serious objections have recently been raised. Hirsch says that despite its emphasis on understanding and concern it has been more cruel and punitive than a frankly punitive model would probably be. In referring to the empirical evidence he also makes the point that it cannot be rational or fair to sentence for treatment without a reasonable expectation that the treatment will work. In criticising individualisation of treatment he points to the wide discretion on which this is based, which leads to great disparity. This raises a fundamental moral objection that individuals may receive sentences they do not deserve.

Similar points are made in *Struggle for Justice* (American Friends Service Committee 1971), where the individualised treatment model is seen as systematically discriminatory in administration and inconsistent with some of our basic concepts of justice. Here also discretion is seen as the core of the problem. Norval Morris (1974) suggests that the rejection of the treatment model as part of crime control flows not from lack of power or competence to influence the criminal's behaviour, but from historical evidence about the misuse of power and from more fundamental views of the nature of man and his rights to freedom. Bean (1976) says the rehabilitative ideal is manifestly unjust because it is unfair, and shows a strong tendency to service purposes that are essentially incapacitative rather than therapeutic in character. The common objection would seem to be that sentences which purport to be rehabilitative in aim are often more severe and longer than they would have been if the aim had been one of retribution. This objection would still stand even if there were evidence to show that the treatment worked.

The justice model

Advocates of a justice model place renewed emphasis on retribution, which has its roots in individual vengeance but has become socialised under the criminal law. It is recognised that in current penal practice retribution is still a primary objective. Retribution is not the same as vengeance, for it prescribes limits to the punishment to be inflicted. Some writers (Hirsch 1976) prefer to discuss the concept in terms of desert: the offender should receive the punishment he deserves; no more and no less than he deserves for the crime he has committed. This is justified not in utilitarian terms of reducing crime, but in moral terms because it is thought to be right and fair. It is suggested that 'Justice-as-fairness represents the superordinate goal of all agencies of the criminal law' (Fogel 1975). This is seen as a fairer and more humane way of dealing with offenders than one motivated by rehabilitative goals. It is claimed that many offenders agree with this proposition, as most of them do not see treatment which is imposed as something which they want or which is in their interests. On the contrary, many of them feel that treatment is a disguised form of punishment, which turns out to be longer and more severe than punishment they would have received on the basis of deserts or retribution. Some evidence along these lines is provided by Alison Morris (1978) from research on juvenile offenders.

This is not to say that offenders should be denied treatment altogether, only that it should not be part of a sentence of punishment. Coercive treatment is seen as wrong because it may involve punishment which is not deserved. However, the view is taken that treatment should be available to all those who wish to avail themselves of it, in the same way as it is available to non-offenders. This should be provided not because it is expected to reduce criminal behaviour, but because the individual wants it and has a right to it. These rights are more part of general *social* justice than criminal justice. An offender's participation in a treatment programme should therefore be completely voluntary, and should not be expected to influence the course of his punishment or its outcome. Many therapists would take the view that treatment cannot be effective if it is enforced. From both points of view it would seem desirable to separate punishment and treatment.

One of the main features of a justice model centres around the use of discretion, which is seen as the core of the problem (American Friends Service Committee 1971). The treatment model required judgements about how long it would take an offender to respond to the treatment given. Individuals would vary in this respect (even if they had committed similar offences) and discretion has led to indeterminate sentences. While the treatment model requires maximum discretion, the justice model requires minimum discretion. In the case of the former an attempt is made to make the punishment fit the individual, in the latter to fit the crime. It is suggested that in the interests of justice similar crimes of similar severity should be punished in similar ways and that discretion should be eliminated (American Friends Service Committee 1971), reduced (Fogel 1975), or only allowed in the interests of clemency (Morris 1974). Allowance may be made for mitigating or aggravating circumstances (Fogel 1975), but these should be carefully defined and applied in all cases.

There may be something to be said for a model less concerned with utopian solutions than with devising short-term and middle-range solutions to shape a rational and acceptable set of correctional policies (Fogel 1975). But whatever the merits of the justice model, many people will retain reservations about it. The rehabilitation model has been strongly supported by many practitioners, administrators and criminologists associated with penal practice, and not all of these are likely to be rapidly converted by the evidence or arguments. Moreover, some critics of the present system would probably reject the justice model as well.

Justice and treatment

At first sight the justice model may not seem to have many implications for the probation and after-care service. Many of the concepts have been developed in response to the problems presented by prisons, and much of the discussion is about prisons, particularly in the United States. From one point of view it can be claimed that probation has always formed a central part of the liberal and humane tradition in penology, and as a form of social work there has always been stress on self-determination. From another point of view, it is firmly based on the rehabilitation model, which seems to be diametrically opposed to the justice model. It has been argued that these differences can be reconciled and the two models held together in some kind of balance (Parsloe 1976). It has also been argued that many of the criticisms which have been made of the rehabilitative ideal in other contexts can be made about probation as well (Bean 1976).

Probation, as a form of social work, is one of the most treatment-oriented penal disposals. Insofar as this is seen as serving the rehabilitative ideal to prevent further criminal behaviour, it would be incompatible with the justice model. Insofar as it is a form of *compulsory* treatment it would also be incompatible. It is true that the offender has to give his consent to being put on probation, but this does not mean that the offender *wants* to be put on probation, and subsequently he has no choice of probation officer or the treatment he receives. To conform to the justice model treatment would have to be available but not imposed, something like the present arrangements for voluntary after-care (Bean 1976). It is further suggested that 'only if there is a clearer distinction between the probation or parole officer's supervisory (police) role and his supportive (social welfare) role can he be free to relate usefully to such offenders as may gain from his assistance to them' (Morris 1974). There is no *necessary* conflict between punishment and treatment, but problems arise when attempts are made to combine them. Given a clear separation, offenders (like non-offenders) have a right to such 'treatment' as they may need.

Discretion is regarded as the core of the problem, producing disparities in practice, and therefore conflicting with notions of fairness. The probation officer has considerable discretion in deciding how frequently to see each case, the amount of time spent on each contact, the content of treatment in general and in detail, and whether to seek termination of the order for good progress. The discretion exercised in all these respects may be justified in terms of treatment, but not in terms of justice. Justice would require that the amount of time forfeited by an offender should be assessed in relation to what was deserved for committing a crime of a particular kind. For crimes of a similar kind and severity the forfeited time would be the same in terms of length of order, and number and length of reporting sessions. Any treatment needed would be given separately, independent of any requirements of the probation order, and only on a voluntary basis. Parsloe (1976) has suggested that there is a need to confine, structure and check discretion in the context of probation.

Responses of the probation and after-care service

The research findings on the effectiveness of treatment, together with the increasing emphasis given to justice, raise questions about the work of the probation and after-care service. Attempts are being made to reconcile probation practice with current evidence and emerging ideas. In reviewing the IMPACT experiment Thomas (1977) suggests that 'the credibility of the probation service rests increasingly on its ability to provide and co-ordinate a range of alternatives to custody only some of which may come within a traditional definition of social work'.

An article by Bryant *et al.* (1978) entitled 'Sentenced to social work?' recognises that the concept of differential treatment, once used to describe a range of social work skills, is now taking on a much broader meaning, encompassing provision based on concepts such as justice, reparation and punishment, where social work in the traditional sense may have a limited place. The authors suggest a redefined probation order, in which the court would determine the length of the order and the frequency of reporting to the probation and after-care service. The essential ingredients of the justice model would be met in this proposal. The probation order would be seen as a form of punishment, separate from social work treatment, and the latter would be available but voluntary. It remains to be seen how far these ideas would be regarded as feasible by the courts and the probation and after-care service.

Diversity of views and practice

While some people would no doubt welcome a return to retribution, others would strongly object to it. Penology is a mixture of beliefs and practices which do not conform to a simple rational system, and some practices will persist even when evidence suggests they are not effective. Treatment objectives linger on among practitioners, administrators, academics and researchers. However, there seems to be a shift in emphasis within the total pattern, with rather less weight given to treatment and rather more to justice. Whether this will be reflected in changes of practice is a matter for further research. There are often discrepancies between belief and practice, and it is possible for people to change the ways in which they talk about what they do without changing what they actually do. On the other hand, if a change of belief brings it closer to existing practice there may be advantages in achieving greater consistency. It has been argued that much penal practice has been supported by the treatment ideology, but that the underlying motives have often been those of retribution. A more explicit recognition of these motives, even if they are not accepted as the sole basis for penology, might also lead to some change in practice. Utopian solutions are not likely, and all 'models', whether they are those of treatment or justice, are theoretical concepts or abstractions from reality, and do not occur frequently, if at all, in a pure form. This does not mean that everything which is done is equally viable and acceptable, as it does seem desirable in a democratic society to achieve some degree of consistency in penal practice, broadly acceptable to society in general and also to offenders. The justice model suggests one direction in which progress along these lines might be achieved.

Support and control

Assessed needs of support and control are likely to influence sentencing decisions. Courts take account of many factors such as the nature and seriousness of the offence on the one hand, and an offender's personal and social problems on the other. If it is thought that the offence is not very serious, but that the offender has a lot of personal problems, it may be decided that he needs more help or support than control. On the other hand, the offence may be regarded as a more serious one, whether or not there are also personal problems, and it might be thought that some form of control is needed. In the context of 'the tariff' there may be a need to take account of the punishment thought to be deserved. Such decisions are of course matters of judgement, and the views on which they rest vary widely. Different positions can be and sometimes are taken: that all offenders should be punished; that they should all be helped; that most of them need a mixture of the two; that this is a false or undesirable distinction and that cases cannot or should not be categorised in this way. Whatever the truth of the matter (if this could ever be agreed), the reality would seem to be that assessments and decisions are made, choosing between existing options, and however difficult or complex an assessment might be the decision about disposal has got to be a specific and clear-cut one, even though at times it may also be felt as an arbitrary one.

There is evidence that the distinctions which have been suggested between treatment and justice, and between support and control, are fully recognised by offenders themselves. Parker (1979) notes that the results of research concerning the perceptions from the 'receiving end' suggest consistently that young offenders and their families expect the juvenile courts to operate on a justice model, and for sentences to be awarded according to tariff criteria rather than those of individualised treatment. The courts seem frequently to take a similar view, as the great majority of juveniles continue to be brought before the court under criminal rather than care proceedings.

Diversion

One of the aims of IMPACT was to explore whether the experimental type of treatment developed might be of value in relation to diversion, or the attempt to find alternative treatment in the community for offenders who might otherwise have been sentenced to prison. IMPACT could not, of course, provide direct evidence on this, because it was a post-sentence experiment of offenders all of whom had been placed on probation. However, many were high risk cases who had already served prison sentences, and who because of variations in sentencing practice might well have been sent to prison on this occasion. As already indicated, there was no evidence that high risk cases had lower reconviction rates when given more intensive treatment in the community, compared with normal probation. From the standpoint presented here, however, the main question is not whether treatment in the community is more likely to reduce recidivism, but whether probation officers are prepared to recommend non-institutional placements, whether courts are prepared to give non-institutional sentences, and whether the community is prepared to accept the consequences. It may not be enough to demonstrate that offenders have personal problems, and to suggest that their needs might be met as adequately or more adequately in the community. There is probably a need to show that facilities and conditions of treatment in the community meet the requirements of the courts for offenders who would otherwise be sent to prison. These requirements might well include elements of retribution or control, as it is unlikely that many offenders are sent to prison entirely for their own good or welfare. If they are sent there because it is thought that this is what they deserve, some alternatives in the community may be seen as too soft an option for these cases and not used for them. If the assumptions about retribution are valid, a viable alternative to prison will be judged, not by its expected therapeutic effects, but by whether it is seen as sufficiently controlling.

The Report of the Committee of Inquiry into the United Kingdom Prison Services (May Report 1979) has recently stressed the urgent need to reduce the prison population by such action as redirecting from prison categories of inmate who, it is argued, might be better dealt with elsewhere, and also by developing existing or fresh non-custodial alternatives. It has been suggested in this paper that some offenders probably need help rather than punishment, while others probably need punishment rather than help. For social inadequates or petty persistent offenders the primary need might be for the kind of help provided by the probation service or the practical supportive schemes set up by the National Association for the Care and Resettlement of Offenders.

It is sometimes said that such cases are sent to prison only because everything else has been tried, unsuccessfully, or because courts do not know what else to do with them. However, if it is felt that there is some need for punishment or control, any alternative scheme in the community not incorporating these features may not be used. This problem may become paramount when considering alternatives for those offenders who are thought to need punishment more than help. For these cases a form of support in the community will not seem a viable alternative to custodial punishment, but rather a soft option, and giving a reward instead of a punishment. An alternative might be more readily used if it clearly incorporated punitive or controlling features (even if to a lesser degree than prison), in view of the need to reduce the prison population for reasons of cost and overcrowding. Alternatives which would satisfy these requirements may need to take the form of senior attendance centres or more controlling types of supervision in the community.

Evaluation

As already mentioned in the Introduction, evaluation may be more complex in probation than in many other forms of social work, since probation officers are social workers as well as officers of the court, and evaluation of their work requires consideration of criteria related to social and criminal justice. These criteria are different, and sometimes conflicting, and in the attempt to reconcile them (as within the treatment model) inappropriate criteria have been used for evaluation, and usually the results have been negative and disappointing. The current debate about the justice model at least helps to clarify some of the issues and suggests the way in which some of the dilemmas might be reduced.

In terms of criminal justice it would seem that too much was expected from the methods used, or the wrong kinds of results were expected. On the other hand, and to put the matter in perspective, most sentences of the court are straightforward penalties, with fines comprising about half of the total. It is doubtful whether in most of these cases there is any therapeutic intent. Ultimate or long-term objectives in penology are problematic, in that there is disagreement about what they should be, doubts about whether they can be achieved, and great difficulties of evaluation. It may be more fruitful to set short-term or medium-term objectives, and one of the most pressing of these is the reduction of the custodial population.

A prior step to evaluating the effectiveness of alternatives to custody would be exploring how far a particular scheme had been fully implemented, whether there were any obstacles to implementation, and how these might be overcome. Klein (1980) reviewed over 200 published accounts of diversion programmes for juvenile offenders in the united States, and came to the conclusion that they had not been adequately tested, because they had seldom been implemented, the main impediment being inappropriate selection of offender groups.

The use of alternatives to custody could be evaluated in terms of changed court decisions in respect of offenders who would otherwise have been given a custodial sentence. Reconvictions would be taken into account, not to show any 'treatment effects', but to show whether alternatives to prison could be used without disastrous consequences. Also any follow-up study could compare sentences given on reconviction to see whether further non-custodial sentences were given, and therefore whether diversion could be regarded as more than temporary respite.

It is not easy to demonstrate specific changes in sentencing, but a number of pointers might be provided. Magistrates who use an alternative could be asked (if they are agreeable to this) what sentence they would otherwise have given. It is also possible to show statistical changes in local sentencing patterns compared with previous years, and for many purposes this probably provides the most valid and reliable measure. Also, if there are more referrals than places available on a particular scheme, it would be possible to show which alternative disposal was used. In a situation of financial constraints one important criterion is that of comparative cost. Generally custodial placements are more expensive than non-custodial ones, but some of the latter rely on intensive use of resources and can also be very expensive. Costing is a complex matter but it may be possible to demonstrate, taking account of objectives and requirements, that one alternative is as effective as another and at the same time a good deal cheaper.

The main point to emphasise about alternatives to custody is that they are not likely to be more effective in terms of reconviction rates, which are likely to be a bit higher (because of the longer period of risk and opportunity), although not a lot higher. But if alternatives to custody were cheaper, more humane, and generally no less effective, these alone would seem to be substantial benefits. However, to satisfy the requirements of justice, and to ensure that particular disposals or schemes are used for their intended purpose (for some types of case), they may need to be seen as alternative forms of punishment.

The requirements of social justice are, of course, different, and social work has a relevant and legitimate role. The purpose here is to help and not to punish, although there may be difficulties in deciding what type of help to provide and in showing whether there are any lasting benefits. Some critics have questioned whether special provision should be made to meet social work needs of offenders other than facilities available to anyone (offenders and non-offenders alike). This is obviously a matter for debate and judgement, but positive discrimination might be justified if certain conditions can be met. First, if it can be shown that offenders tend to be a specially disadvantaged group. Second, if it can be shown sentencing makes them more disadvantaged, by creating or increasing such problems as unemployment or homelessness. If special provision for offenders is justified, on these or other grounds, the issue then becomes whether it can be offered in such a way that it does not conflict with the requirements of justice. Evaluation of social work for offenders would then be by the same criteria as in other types of social work. This is not to imply that once a need for social work has been demonstrated its provision and evaluation are simple matters. On the contrary … The purpose here is to emphasise that however social work is justified, and whatever the criteria used, this should be seen as separate and different from the requirements of criminal justice.

Wider implications

Although the issues discussed here have been mainly concerned with social work in probation, they have implications for other types of social work and other types of treatment. There are parallels in the field of psychiatry, where questions of justice as well as of welfare can arise. Just as overcrowded mental hospitals contributed to the development of various forms of community care, so overcrowded prisons are leading to the search for more feasible and acceptable forms of community containment. Problems common to psychiatry and penology are presented by mentally disordered offenders for whom society does not yet seem to have reconciled the needs for containment and care. Similar considerations apply to offenders categorised as socially inadequate, and to juvenile offenders. In the 1969 Children and Young Persons Act the assumption was made that juvenile offenders should be treated and not punished. In spite of this, the majority of juveniles continue to be brought before the court under criminal proceedings rather than care proceedings. Also, what is intended as help or treatment by those who provide it may be seen as punishment or control by those who receive it. Thus the issues considered here in the context of probation may also be relevant to an evaluation of other types of social work. Some cases may become involved in both social support systems and social control systems. If and when this happens there may be particular difficulties in reaching agreement about objectives, treatment practice, and methods of evaluation.

From Steven Folkard, 'Second thoughts on IMPACT', in E.M. Goldberg and N. Connelly (eds.) Evaluative Research in Social Care *(London: Heinemann), 1981, pp. 81–97.*

References

American Friends Service Committee (1971) *Struggle for Justice.* New York: Hill and Wang.
Bailey, W.C. (1966) 'Correctional outcome: an evaluation of 100 reports', *Journal of Criminal Law, Criminology and Police Science* 57: 153–160.
Bean, P. (1976) *Rehabilitation and Deviance.* London: Routledge and Kegan Paul.
Brody, S.R. (1976) *The Effectiveness of Sentencing: a review of the literature.* Home Office Research Study No.35. London: HMSO.
Bryant, M., Coker, J., Estlea, B., Himmel, S. and Knapp, T. (1978) 'Sentenced to social work?', *Probation Journal* 25: 110–114.
Fogel, D. (1975) *We Are the Living Proof.* Cincinnati: Anderson.
Folkard, M.S., Fowles, A.J., McWilliams, B.C., McWilliams, W., Smith, D.D., Smith, D.E. and Walmsley, G.R. (1974) *IMPACT: Volume I.* Home Office Research Study 24. London: HMSO.
Folkard, M.S., Smith, D.E. and Smith, D.D. (1976) *IMPACT: Volume II.* Home Office Research Study No.36. London: HMSO.
Hirsch, A.V. (1976) *Doing Justice.* New York: Hill and Wang.
Klein, M. (1980) 'Deinstitutionalization and diversion of juvenile offenders: a litany of impediments', in N. Morris and M. Tonry (eds.) *Crime and Justice: An Annual Review of Research*, Vol. 1. Chicago: University of Chicago Press.
Logan, C. (1972) 'Evaluating research in crime and delinquency: a re-appraisal', *Journal of Criminal Law, Criminology and Police Science* 63: 378–387.

Martinson, R. (1974) 'What works? – questions and answers about prison reform', *The Public Interest* 35: 22–54.

May Report (1979) *Report of the Committee of Inquiry into the United Kingdom Prison Service.* Cmnd 7673. London: HMSO.

Morris, A. (1978) *Juvenile Justice.* London: Heinemann.

Morris, N. (1974) *The Future of Imprisonment.* Chicago: University of Chicago Press.

Palmer, T. (1975) 'Martinson revisited', *Journal of Research in Crime and Delinquency* 12: 133–152.

Parker, H. (1979) 'Client-defendant perceptions of juvenile and criminal justice', in H. Parker (ed.) *Social Work and the Courts.* London: Edward Arnold.

Parsloe, P. (1976) 'Social work and the justice model', *British Journal of Social Work* 6: 71–89.

Thomas, C.H. (1977) 'Review of *IMPACT*', *Howard Journal* 16: 117.

71 What Works – nothing or everything?

Measuring the effectiveness of sentences (1991)

George Mair

The doctrine that 'Nothing Works' has had a profound impact upon penal policy and practice during the past 15 years, and continues to do so today. Quite simply, 'Nothing Works' asserts that no penal disposal (and no disposal more than any other) has any significant effect upon recidivism and it has thus become a synonym for penal pessimism. For better or for worse, the name of Robert Martinson has been inextricably associated with the 'Nothing Works' doctrine since the publication in the USA of his paper 'What Works? Questions and answers about prison reform' (Martinson 1974). This paper, together with research in this country such as the review carried out by Brody (1976) and the IMPACT study (Folkard *et al.* 1976), has been confidently assumed by many to demonstrate that community-based sentences (as well as imprisonment) have no effect in terms of reducing re-offending. This assumption, of course, has serious implications for such sentences as probation and community service, and may be particularly important at the present time as the government aims to increase the use of community disposals for all but the most serious offenders.

'Nothing Works', however, is a doctrine with no real foundations. Indeed, its title alone should signal a warning. No-one would claim that everything works, yet it is equally absurd to claim that 'Nothing Works'. The 'Nothing' is quite meaningless, and the 'Works' is based upon recidivism – a crude and problematic criterion for assessing the effectiveness of sentences.

In this paper I propose to look at the origins of the thesis and how it came to be accepted so rapidly. I will then discuss some of the problems surrounding the measurement of the effectiveness of penal disposals, and suggest a way forward which attempts to capture the complexities of the situation. Although others have attempted to demolish 'Nothing Works' it retains a powerful influence; no apologies are needed for yet another attempt to counter its depressing and stifling implications.

'Nothing Works'?

It is notable that nowhere does Martinson state unequivocally that 'Nothing Works'; his own summary of the evidence was not set out without qualifications:

> With few and isolated exceptions, the rehabilitative efforts that have been reported so far have had no appreciable effect on recidivism.

It is questionable whether this can be reduced to the simple statement 'Nothing Works'. However, given the evidence he considers, Martinson's summary itself goes a little too far in its negativity. The article is littered with phrases such as 'hard to interpret', 'no clear evidence', 'difficulty of interpreting', 'ambiguous results', 'suggestive', 'equivocal', 'problem of interpretation', 'important caveat'. A reading which takes full account of such cautionary notes would come to a suitably cautious conclusion. Martinson's interpretation was somewhat skewed in one direction, but the article was available for public consumption. So where did the simplistic misinterpretation come from and how has it persisted?

A key factor in explaining the attention given to the thesis that 'Nothing Works' is the media treatment the article received in the USA. Partly because of its content, but partly because of the convoluted process which lay behind its publication (those who commissioned the report refused to publish it and a subpoena was needed for Martinson to get his hands on the document), there was a good deal of media interest. As Palmer (1978) shows, it was very much as a result of the interaction between Martinson and the media that 'Nothing Works' became a fixed and definite finding. There is a certain irony here in that it is precisely *because* of its public availability that the article was misinterpreted.

Achieving a certain degree of notoriety, however, is not an adequate reason to account for the rapid appropriation – or misappropriation – of Martinson's work. For this, one has to consider the period in which it was published. As Cullen and Gilbert (1982) demonstrate, Martinson – quite unintentionally – found a remarkably receptive audience from both sides of the political spectrum in the USA. On the right, the period from the second half of the sixties into the seventies was seen as a time of serious disorder and instability: Vietnam, black power and youth protest were seen to threaten the traditional order. And out of all this 'crime assumed new meaning and significance ... [it] became a codeword for all that was wrong with American society' (Cullen and Gilbert 1982). The right, therefore, welcomed Martinson's attack on the rehabilitative ideal which was seen as being soft on offenders and looked forward to new, tougher methods of punishing criminals. The perspective from the left was, of course, rather different. Here, the benevolence of the state was subject to sustained questioning, a process which inevitably touched upon criminal justice. Rehabilitation and treatment became suspect; they were criticised as theoretically faulty, discriminatory and unjust (American Friends Service Committee 1971), and the unfettered discretion entrusted to criminal justice professionals was attacked as leading to abuse of power and injustice.

The penological agenda was shifting its focus. The medical model of deviance (whereby crime was perceived as a 'disease' of the individual who therefore required treatment), which had been the major theoretical basis for much criminal justice policy and practice for most of the century, was increasingly under attack. Its replacement by the justice model, with its emphasis on just deserts and standardised punishments for similar crimes – with some scope for flexibility – was underway (see von Hirsch 1976). Decriminalisation, diversion and crime prevention were appearing more often on the criminal justice agenda. The idea that 'Nothing Works' could only encourage such developments, and it fell, therefore, upon exceptionally fertile ground.

Another important factor in the rapid acceptance of the idea that 'Nothing Works' was undoubtedly the seductive clarity of a neat and simple formula. A great deal of social science research comes up with conclusions which are equivocal – 'on the one hand, on the other hand', 'more research is needed' and so on. This is not a result of social scientists' congenital inability to be plain-spoken, but a reflection of the caution which must be shown in the face of complex realities which rarely have clear-cut solutions. And dealing with offenders effectively is not a simple process. 'Nothing Works' was clear and unvarnished, it was a simple lesson which could be easily learned, and because of its clarity it almost immediately spawned an academic industry.

Opponents of 'Nothing Works' quickly appeared, as indeed did defenders, and debate began. Although the opponents tried hard it has proved remarkably difficult to dislodge a claim which seemed to be set in concrete (see especially Gendreau and Ross 1979; 1987). Generally, opponents have tended to take the very studies which Martinson had used and carry out some re-analysis which, it was argued, showed that Martinson was wrong – some things worked; or collect new examples of initiatives which were claimed to demonstrate success. Ultimately, such formulations were never likely to threaten seriously 'Nothing Works'; they were unclear and messy in comparison to the hard-edged clarity of 'Nothing Works', and could only tinker with parts of the doctrine rather than attack its foundations. Many opponents pointed to the significance of differential treatment (also known as interaction effects), whereby some programmes worked for some offenders at some times, but this common-sense – but not clear-cut – formulation has been all too often marginalised. Opponents are fond of claiming that Martinson recanted his views (1979), although modification may be a more appropriate term; but even this claim has been the subject of some debate (see Doob and Brodeur 1989 and the response by Gendreau 1989).

Thus nothing has been settled and the debate has continued ever since; the point which it has reached at present is as good as any for exemplifying the process. The latest stage began with a paper re-analysing 50 studies of juvenile correctional treatment which concluded that 'correctional treatment has little effect on recidivism' and therefore supported the 'Nothing Works' thesis (Whitehead and Lab 1989). This was attacked by a further re-analysis of these studies with the addition of some 35 other studies concerned with adults, which concluded that appropriate correctional treatment does work (Andrews *et al.* 1990a). Lab and Whitehead have responded (1990) and Andrews and his colleagues have offered a rejoinder (1990b). And so it goes on, the raking over of old fires while new ones need to be started or are ignored.

Essentially, then, 'Nothing Works' is a reading of Martinson which is not borne out by the detail of the paper. The times were right for such a simple formulation, however, and the exigencies of academic careers have helped to keep it in the forefront of criminology up to the present day. But this can only go part of the way to countering 'Nothing Works'. A closer look is needed at the evidence used by Martinson.

Inadequate evidence

Martinson's argument is fundamentally flawed in two ways: first, by reliance upon recidivism as the sole measure of success of a sentence; and second, by a failure to address the issue of how sentences are implemented and operate in practice. Both of these weaknesses are as much due to the methods employed in the studies used by Martinson, as the way the studies were utilised by him.

Recidivism has traditionally been the criterion used to measure the success of a penal disposal. There is a real issue as to whether it is the right criterion, and whether it should apply to all sentences. Certainly, a major object of all probation-based disposals is to reduce re-offending; whether this is the case for prisons and fines is debatable. But even if one accepts that recidivism is an appropriate indicator of effectiveness, it is by no means simple and easily understood. It can mean several things in practice: the commission of a new offence which comes to the notice of a criminal justice agent, a further conviction in court, breach of the requirements of an order. It is important to emphasise that none of these possible meanings actually measures the amount of an individual's re-offending.

The usual measure of recidivism is the reconviction rate – the percentage of those given a certain sentence who are reconvicted of a further offence within a specified period (usually two years after sentence or release from custody) – but even here there are difficulties. What about those who offend but are not apprehended or convicted? What about those who are reconvicted but whose offences took place before the imposition of the order under investigation? Conversely, what about those who re-offend during the specified period but are not reconvicted until after that period has ended? Should we be using a rather crude, dichotomous measure whereby a reconviction equals failure and no reconviction equals success? And what about the impact of policing practice upon the likelihood of apprehension, prosecution and reconviction?

Equally significant is the failure of many researchers to examine in any detail the operation of the sentence under investigation. If, for example, a considerable number of the disposals investigated in the research reports included in Martinson's analysis had failed to be properly implemented as planned, had been starved of resources, had used badly trained and uncommitted staff, and had been studied in the first year or so of operation, would it be any surprise that the sentences had failed? Only by studying how a sentence or treatment programme has been put into practice, how well it is meeting its immediate objectives, how it functions in organisational terms can we begin to interpret the meaning of any outcome measures (such as the reconviction rate) which might be used. Such a *process* evaluation enables us to understand more clearly *why* a penal measure may be working successfully or – equally important – why it may be failing.

The kind of review carried out by Martinson and those who have followed him (both supporters and opponents) tends in any case to reduce a complex situation to a simple one. There is little space to discuss the subtleties of sentence implementation in a review which includes 50 or 100 separate studies. And how should those measures which show no change be interpreted? Some authors place them in the successful category while others consider them as failures. In the detail of some research reports there can be interesting and useful findings although the programme as a whole may be a failure, and such optimistic details are all too often missed or lost in re-analysis.

Starting again

The solution which begins to take shape for measuring the effectiveness of a sentence is to use several measures of success; and to interpret them the sentence or treatment must be set in context. How might this approach work in practice?

For a community penalty such as a probation order with a day centre requirement which aims to deal with offenders at high risk of custody and reduce re-offending, two levels of criteria of effectiveness might be devised. Primary measures would be reconvictions during the period of day centre attendance (for offences which took place *during* that period), as well as time to reconviction after sentence, the kind of offences for which offenders were reconvicted, and the pattern of reconvictions during the subsequent period of supervision; how far centres acted to divert offenders from custody; the financial costs of centres; sentencer satisfaction with the disposal; and the views of offenders. Secondary measures would include the specific objectives of centres such as help with accommodation, employment, social skills, addictions, use of leisure time, etc. Essential for the interpretation of such outcome measures would be a study of the operation and organisation of day centres; how do they fit into the structure of the local probation service, staffing levels, target groups, premises, regimes, staff commitment, etc. By studying the context in which centres operate as well as the outcomes associated with them, a fully informed evaluation of probation day centres could be made. It should be emphasised that the primary measures for day centres would not necessarily be the same as those for other sentences. For prison sentences, diversion from custody and reconvictions might be left out and incapacitation added as a primary measure; reparation might have to be included for community service and so on.

An approach of this kind to measuring effectiveness is not wholly free of problems of its own. In the first place, agreement will be necessary about the official aims and objectives of a penalty or treatment programme. There can be considerable advantages in having vague and ambiguous objectives, particularly when introducing a penal measure, but clarity of objectives is necessary to allow evaluation to be carried out. If re-offending is agreed to be the key criterion by which a sentence is to be judged then this should be made clear and the limitations and problems associated with this measure accepted.

Another issue which will have to be agreed (and may have to be reconsidered for different evaluations and at different times) is how the primary measures may be combined to give an overall index of effectiveness and whether or not they are of equal weight. For example, are the five primary measures which have been suggested for day centres equally important or are some more important than others? If diversion from custody and cost are taken to be the key factors, then success on these two criteria will outweigh failure in terms of reconviction rates, the views of sentencers, and those of offenders. Similarly, agreement will be necessary over the relationship between secondary and primary measures; for example, how would a day centre be judged which was found to be achieving successfully its aims of helping offenders with accommodation and employment, but was failing in terms of diversion from custody, had a high reconviction rate, was very expensive and not seen as helpful by sentencers?

It may be argued that this multi-dimensional approach will only confuse the basic question of whether or not a penalty is successful. But this is to miss the point. Sentences of the court have objectives other than the reduction of re-offending; by focusing upon several criteria the complex nature of the objectives of sentences is recognised. Indeed, one might envisage a situation where, using the approach suggested here, a penalty is seen to be reaching all of its objectives but one; and this problem area can then be investigated and efforts made to improve it. By using a multi-dimensional approach there is a much better chance of finding out just how far sentences are successful at attaining various objectives, and therefore targeting sentences more effectively. And it may also help to produce more realistic expectations of what a court sentence can achieve.

Conclusion

For an emperor who has been scantily clothed, 'Nothing Works' has had a long reign. Almost since the publication of Martinson's article there have been attacks upon this simplistic interpretation, although these have tended to be ignored probably because their message tends to be a more complicated one. The question posed in the title of this paper is intended to expose the absurdity of the 'Nothing Works' formula: 'Nothing' is meaningless, and 'Works' is only considered in terms of recidivism.

The time is right for a new generation of evaluations of penal initiatives which leaves behind the sterile debates and re-hashing of the same research findings associated with 'Nothing Works'. It is encouraging to note that some researchers are beginning to move in this direction. Colin Roberts, in his study of the Hereford and Worcester Young Offender Project (Roberts 1989), looks at time to reconviction and the new offences which are committed. It should be added that this refinement is not particularly new – Cornish and Clarke (1975) utilised such an approach in their study of the Kingswood Training School. And Peter Raynor considers a variety of measures of success in his study of the Afan Alternative Project (Raynor 1988). The RPU evaluation of intensive probation will use a variety of measures of effectiveness, and it is hoped that this will provide a useful test of the ideas discussed here (see Mair *et al.* 1994).

This paper presents a very preliminary outline of how measuring the effectiveness of court sentences might be refined. Details of this approach have yet to be worked out in a coherent way – practical, policy and methodological problems have yet to be confronted. Indeed, the problems of the approach may only become apparent as it is used and developed, and some difficulties may never be completely resolved. But it would seem to offer a more comprehensive and flexible approach to capturing a complex phenomenon. Most would agree that penalties do work much of the time; what we need to know is how, why, with whom, when – and the approach to evaluating effectiveness outlined here will help to answer such questions.

George Mair, 'What Works – nothing or everything? Measuring the effectiveness of sentences', Home Office Research Bulletin 30, 1991, pp. 3–8.

References

American Friends Service Committee (1971) *Struggle for Justice: a report on crime and punishment in America.* New York: Hill and Wang.

Andrews, D.A. *et al.* (1990a) 'Does correctional treatment work? A clinically relevant and psychologically informed meta-analysis', *Criminology* 28: 369–404.

——(1990b) 'A human science approach or more punishment and pessimism: a rejoinder to Lab and Whitehead', *Criminology* 28: 417–429.

Brody, S. (1976) *The Effectiveness of Sentencing: a review of the literature.* Home Office Research Study No.35. London: HMSO.

Cornish, D.B. and Clarke, R.V.G. (1975) *Residential Treatment and its Effects on Delinquency.* Home Office Research Study No.32. London: HMSO.

Cullen, F.T. and Gilbert, K.E. (1982) *Reaffirming Rehabilitation.* Cincinnati, Ohio: Anderson.

Doob, A.N. and Brodeur, J.-P. (1989) 'Rehabilitating the debate on rehabilitation', *Canadian Journal of Criminology* 31: 179–192.

Folkard, M.S., Smith, D.E. and Smith, D.D. (1976) *IMPACT: Vol.II The results of the experiment.* Home Office Research Study No.36. London: HMSO.

Gendreau, P. (1989) 'Programs that do not work: a brief comment on Brodeur and Doob', *Canadian Journal of Criminology* 31: 193–195.

Gendreau, P. and Ross, R.R. (1979) 'Effectiveness of correctional treatment: bibliotherapy for cynics', *Crime and Delinquency* 25: 463–489.

——(1987) 'Revivification of rehabilitation: evidence from the 1980s', *Justice Quarterly* 4: 349–408.

Lab, S.P. and Whitehead, J.T. (1990) 'From "Nothing Works" to "The appropriate works": the latest stop on the search for the secular grail', *Criminology* 28: 405–417.

Mair, G., Lloyd, C., Nee, C. and Sibbitt, R. (1994) *Intensive Probation in England and Wales: an evaluation*. Home Office Research Study 133. London: HMSO.

Martinson, R. (1974) 'What Works? Questions and answers about prison reform', *Public Interest* 35: 22–54.

——(1979) 'New Findings, New Views: a note of caution regarding sentencing reform', *Hofstra Law Review* 7: 243–258.

Palmer, T. (1978) *Correctional Intervention and Research: current issues and future prospects*. Lexington, MA: D.C. Heath and Co.

Raynor, P. (1988) *Probation as an Alternative to Custody: a case study*. Aldershot: Avebury.

Roberts, C.H. (1989) *Young Offender Project: first evaluation report*. Hereford and Worcester Probation Service.

von Hirsch, A. (1976) *Doing Justice: the choice of punishments*. New York: Hill and Wang.

Whitehead, J.T. and Lab, S.P. (1989) 'A meta-analysis of juvenile correctional treatment', *Journal of Research in Crime and Delinquency* 26: 276–295.

72 Summary of research evidence for principles of effectiveness (1998)

Tim Chapman and Mike Hough

1.27   There are different levels of evidence of effectiveness. There are programmes which have been tested (usually in North America) and found to reduce recidivism. From meta-analyses of these evaluations principles of effective programme design and delivery have been isolated but have yet to be tested fully in Britain or Ireland. These principles include:

- The risk principle; intensity of supervision should be appropriate to the level of risk
- The need principle; the content of intervention should be designed to effectively address criminogenic needs (those factors which have a direct link to offending)
- The responsivity principle; interventions should be delivered in ways which match the offenders' learning style and engage their active participation
- The principle of programme integrity; interventions should be rigorously managed and delivered as designed.

Risk and criminogenic needs are discussed in Chapter 2 on assessment and responsivity in Chapter 4 on programme delivery.

Effective methods

1.28   In addition meta-analysis identified other critical success factors:

- Effective programmes were multi-modal (employing a variety of methods to address a range of criminogenic needs)
- Effective programmes were skill oriented
- Effective programmes drew upon theories and methods of cognitive-behavioural psychology
- Effective programmes were generally but not solely community based
- Effective programmes were delivered by staff who were adept at pro-social modelling
- Monitoring and evaluation were built in from the outset.

Multi-modal work

1.29   It is often assumed that effective programmes are based upon group work. However, this is not specified in the research. Individual and family work can be as effective when used appropriately and delivered to high standards of integrity.

1.30   It is important to select the most effective method to achieve each objective set and address the specific issue or need. In doing so a clear and testable rationale should be recorded. In this way the effectiveness of each component of a programme can be measured.

1.31   Group work is appropriate for:
- Role play and rehearsal of appropriate behaviour
- Peer education
- Peer challenge and support
- Cognitive and interpersonal skills training
- Reflection on common difficulties.

1.32   Individual work is appropriate for:
- Offenders requiring high levels of intervention and surveillance to protect others from the risk of serious harm
- Reflection on some personal disclosure
- Self-monitoring and self-instructional training
- Tutoring or applying learning outcomes from group work to personal circumstances
- Managing personal obstacles to programme participation.

1.33   Family work is appropriate when criminogenic needs originate in the family or when the family is or could be a key protective factor.

1.34   Experiental learning can enhance outcomes if used appropriately. Care should be taken to ensure that activities are closely aligned to objectives of change and address criminogenic needs. If they are offered as a simple diversion unconnected to any change programme, they are no more effective than surveillance or punishment similarly detached from an effective programme.

1.35   Drama, art therapy, outdoor pursuits and sport projects, if purposefully and carefully designed and delivered, can address a range of criminogenic needs including:
- Anti-social attitudes, beliefs and values
- Anti-social associates
- Lack of pro-social role models
- Cognitive and interpersonal skills
- Dependence upon alcohol and drugs
- A sense of achievement and community integration
- Employment
- Social isolation
- Mental health.

These activities should be carefully marketed and evaluated to convince the public that they are effective in reducing offending.

Skills

1.36   The acquisition of skill empowers people with a sense of control, achievement and potential whether it is in relation to employment, relationships or recreation. Such skills might include:
- Cognitive skills such as consequential thinking, problem solving and critical reasoning

- Interpersonal skills such as self-control, conflict resolution, empathy and communication
- Literacy and numeracy skills
- Vocational skills e.g. computer skills
- Creative or physical skills.

Cognitive and behavioural psychology

1.37   This refers to a range of personality and social psychology theories including social learning theory. It addresses the complex relationships between thoughts, feelings and behaviour. An individual learns to manage these relationships from experience and from the example of significant others. This process of socialisation can result in deficits which reinforce anti-social behaviour. Such deficits can be corrected through training which reinforces positive behaviour rather than negative in a consistent way. The training is essentially:

- Cognitive, i.e. learning thinking skills
- Emotional, i.e. learning self-awareness, self-expression and self-control
- Behavioural, i.e. learning pro-social ways of acting to achieve goals.

Community-based projects

1.38   A programme based in the community facilitates the application of learning to real, current difficulties, the opportunity to practice what has been learnt and access to resources, activities and relationships which can support positive change. It is clear from research into institutional treatment that anti-social influences can subvert much of the positive effects of programmes. This is not to say that it is not worth delivering programmes in custodial institutions. Such programmes should be part of a sentence plan which connects with resources and programmes available on release.

Pro-social modelling

1.39   According to Trotter (1993) pro-social modelling 'involves the practice of offering praise and reward for clients' pro-social expressions and actions ... the probation officer becomes a positive role model acting to reinforce pro-social or non-criminal behaviour.' Research indicates that pro-social modelling results in higher levels of compliance with supervision programmes as well as lower reoffending rates. It is important that the probation officer explicitly identifies with the offender the pieces of behaviour to be learned and practised. The approach emphasises the importance of demonstrating respect for individuals, by being punctual, reliable, courteous, friendly, honest and open. These are characteristics which offenders value in their supervising officers and which may encourage them to undertake a threatening process of change.

Other critical success factors

1.40 *Duration and intensity.* Duration and intensity, increasingly referred to as 'dosage' should match risk of offending and be sufficient to fully cover all required outputs. Research (Lipsey 1995) indicates that the most effective treatments for high risk offenders last at least six months in which there is at least 100 hours of programmed intervention. Further research is needed to set firm standards for effective practice.

1.41 *Choice.* The research into principles of effectiveness strongly suggests that Services should develop a portfolio of accredited programmes of differing duration, intensity and content in order to address different levels of risk and criminogenic need.

1.42 At the most intensive level there should be cognitive and behavioural skills courses linked to programmes for the most persistent offenders i.e. sex offenders, domestic violence, other forms of violence, and habitual property or car offenders. These programmes may need to be further divided according to gender, race and age.

1.43 A middle range could contain shorter programmes addressing specific criminogenic needs. These could be delivered as modules tailored to the needs of individual offenders. They could address victim awareness, alcohol/drug use, relationships, oppressive behaviour or beliefs linked to offending etc.

1.44 The basic level of intervention should address issues obstructing community reintegration, e.g. accommodation, employment, education, family, health, leisure etc.

Effective practice generates knowledge

1.45 Knowledge about what works can only be tested and developed by clearly defining what one is striving to change, by specifying in concrete terms how one is setting about the change process and then rigorously measuring achievement against the original objectives. A learning organisation not only delivers superior practice now but holds out the prospect of even better quality and effectiveness in the future.

The principle of integrity

1.46 Effective practice is not ideological or purist. It is not one theory or method which seeks to dominate and extinguish all others. It is responsive to ever-changing needs and requirements. It requires of staff a commitment to the programme and yet also a readiness to improve and innovate. It develops through cross-pollination, partnership and, above all accountable performance. What prevents this approach disintegrating into anarchy is integrity.

Integrity is the organising concept of this Guide

1.47 Programme integrity has been defined as the delivery of a programme as intended in theory and design (Hollin 1995):

> Treatment integrity refers to what is actually delivered and is evaluated against a treatment plan that specifies what is intended.
>
> (Lipsey 1988)

Research findings indicate that the level of integrity is a significant variable in determining outcome. This is not surprising as it is very difficult to measure the effects of a programme whose content and delivery is arbitrary and subject to unanticipated change.

This deceptively simple concept has been identified as an essential element of effective practice. Yet the word, integrity, carries with it connotations of quality, morality and connectedness. These meanings help to integrate effective practice.

Integrity as quality

1.48   HM Inspectorate of probation has adopted the following definition of quality:

> The search for quality is a process of sustained and persistent improvement to ensure that the totality of features and characteristics of services provided continue to satisfy the needs and requirements of users.

If it is accepted that the protection of the public and the reduction of reoffending are the core purposes of community supervision, this concept of quality is very close in definition to the concept of programme integrity.

1.49   Other writers have already commented on the link between 'What Works' and total quality management (Thomas 1996 and Kemshall 1996). Hollin (1995) provides a useful discussion of programme integrity which links the demands of programme delivery, empirical research and management. Integrity enables the supervision practice to be observed, measured against theory and design and evaluated, improved and replicated.

1.50   Integrity is served by:
   - Clear procedures and practice manuals which are designed to meet specific targets and objectives (quality as science)
   - The knowledge, skills and commitment of staff (quality as human resource management)
   - Responsiveness to the public's concerns about risk, the courts' requirements and offenders' criminogenic needs and learning styles (quality as consumerism).

1.51   The programme must serve the public, the court and the participant. The practitioner must, first and foremost, serve the programme. This requires a redefinition of professional discretion and autonomy. The temptation is to confuse subjectivity with creativity, and personal satisfaction with professionalism. The reality is that the pursuit of a structured, effective programme increases both creativity and professional satisfaction.

Integrity as honesty

1.52   Before credibility and trust are established and an authentic working relationship can begin, the community, courts and offenders need to know what probation services stand for and for what they can rely on their staff. The values which underpin effective practice must be accepted and understood by different stakeholders whose interests do not necessarily always coincide.

Table 1

Effective practice depends upon the following values:

- An uncompromising stance against the harm caused by crime
- A strong belief in the capacity of people to change
- The importance of taking personal responsibility for behaviour
- The necessity of learning from experience
- The value of partnership
- Social inclusion
- Public accountability

(See also Underdown 1998: 131 for Features of Staff Culture which Support Effective Practice)

1.53   Research (Trotter 1993, Rex 1997) has confirmed the importance of practitioners modelling appropriate values and behaviour in enabling people to change. Staff who lack integration between their values and their actions lose credibility with the people with whom they are working.

1.54   Integrity enables practitioners to persist in the face of offenders' resistance. Nothing is more important in the process of change than the determination to follow the programme when it is tempting to give into resignation in the face of resistance. Moral integrity can be defined as doing the right thing in the absence of surveillance or coercion. This is, of course, the aim of all rehabilitative work. It is essential that practitioners model this integrity to offenders.

1.55   The relationship between offenders and staff in the supervision process is not one of equals. This imbalance of power can be perceived as oppressive and demotivating. Clear values honestly expressed and legitimately implemented and enforced can counter this perception and increase active participation in the process of change.

Integrity as the integration of the whole

1.56   The concept of integrity reinforces to managers and practitioners that every component of the supervision process, no matter how apparently trivial, should be directed by a commitment to the principles of effectiveness. The pursuit of this concept integrates the various tasks of assessors, case managers, programme deliverers, partners, administrators, and managers into a holistic and seamless process.

Such a process is much more difficult to deliver than the work of a single supervisor. Yet, there is no doubt if we get it right, effectiveness will increase. This Guide is offered as an aid to this process.

Table 2 A Framework for Effective Practice

PSR prepared using approved Assessment Tool

- Structured and systematic
- Identifies levels of risk and areas of need

Case Management System

- Allocation based on levels of risk and needs

Medium to high risk/need	*Low risk/need*
• Intensity of contact is based on level of risk/need • Both 1:1 and groups used • Core curriculum of programmes, i.e. cognitive skills, anger control • Involvement of specialist staff and partners	• Contact levels to National Standards. Resource efficient • Case manager co-ordinates the case worker in the day to day running of the order • The emphasis is on referrals to and accessing of community resources for the work identified • Low level of in-house 1:1 work, emphasis is on the necessary work based in groups

Supervision Plans

- Specific, achievable objectives
- Method clear, plan adhered to
- Emphasis on evidencing change
- Reviewed regularly
- Intensity and type of work clearly linked to the assessment
- Re-assessment using approved tool

Period of Supervision

- Any programme of work clearly based on research evidence
- 1:1 and group based
- Core elements/modules on offer; induction module – structured and replicable
- Accreditation of core elements
- The whole programme of supervision is integrated and systematically worked
- Cognitive behavioural in approach where appropriate

Community Reintegration

- Maintenance of behaviour change and protective factors
- Integrated approach from all agencies to gain acceptance within the community

In-Built Evaluation and Monitoring

- Practitioner evaluation of individual cases
- Team/division based plus area wide evaluation and monitoring using assessment tool and other information
- Learn from results and implement agreed changes

Checklist for programme integrity

- A manual or detailed guidelines for supervision procedures specifying:
  - Testable theoretical premises or hypotheses
  - Targets for change
  - Objectives of change
  - Specific tasks or sessions to be undertaken each with specific objectives or learning outcomes
  - Methods to be used

- Appropriate staff:
  - Competent in the knowledge and skills necessary
  - Committed to the programme's integrity
- Appropriate management:
  - Understand and committed to the programme's integrity and values
  - Able to support, prepare, coach and debrief staff
  - Monitors programme integrity through records and observation
- Appropriate information systems:
  - Checklists for criteria of programme integrity to be completed by staff and independent observers
  - Participant feedback forms.

From Tim Chapman and Mike Hough, Evidence Based Practice: a guide to effective practice *(London: Home Office), 1998, pp. 14–21.*

References

Hollin, C.R. (1995) 'The meaning and implications of "programme integrity"', in J. McGuire (ed.) *What Works: Reducing Reoffending.* Chichester: Wiley.

Kemshall, H. (1996) 'Quality in probation: getting it right first time', *Vista*, May: 2–14.

Lipsey, M.W. (1995) 'What do we learn from 400 research studies on the effectiveness of treatment with juvenile delinquents?', in J. McGuire (ed.) *What Works: Reducing Reoffending.* Chichester: Wiley.

Rex, S. (1997) 'Offenders and their supervisors views of probation: help within a restrictive framework'. Paper presented at the British Criminology Conference.

Thomas, M. (1996) 'What Works: quality management and professional protocols', *Vista*, May: 54–61.

Trotter, C. (1993) *The Supervision of Offenders: What Works.* Melbourne: Victoria Office of Corrections.

Underdown, A. (1998) *Strategies for Effective Offender Supervision: report of the HMIP What Works project.* London: HMIP.

73 Evidence-based probation and its critics (2003)

Peter Raynor

The background: 'What Works' and the rediscovery of rehabilitation

Recent history's most spectacular example of a wholesale conversion to evidence-based practice can be found in the National Probation Service of England and Wales. The story of probation's rediscovery of rehabilitation and of the 'What Works' movement towards evidence-based policy and practice in working with offenders has been told in more detail elsewhere (see, for example, McGuire, 1995; Raynor and Vanstone, 2002) and there is no need to repeat it in this article. Most readers will remember how, by the early 1990s, the consensus that 'nothing works' to rehabilitate offenders was being challenged from a number of directions. Practitioners in Britain had begun to develop some learning-theory-based methods of active and practical work with offenders which prefigured the later development of 'programmes' (for example, McGuire and Priestley, 1985) while more extensive research in other countries had begun to identify some characteristics of work which was proving to be effective (Andrews *et al.*, 1990; Lipsey, 1992; Ross and Fabiano, 1985). Some relatively successful and adequately evaluated local projects from the 1980s (Raynor, 1988; Roberts, 1989) were followed by a more systematic pilot of a developed Canadian programme, with modestly encouraging results (Raynor and Vanstone, 1996, 1997).

Meanwhile the political context was changing rapidly, and not in probation's favour: a largely constructive and liberal Criminal Justice Act in 1991, which promised the probation service a 'centre stage' role in reducing reliance on custodial sentencing, was quickly modified and its central principles swept away by a sudden lurch into populism orchestrated by an electorally insecure right-wing government. In these circumstances the probation service (regularly briefed against by ministers, attacked in the press, struggling to defend its training arrangements and threatened with effective abolition by merger into the larger prison service) needed a new message and a new rationale. Largely through the tireless efforts of the Chief Probation Inspector of the time, the late Sir Graham Smith, opportunities were created to redefine what the probation service could offer to the criminal justice system. The principles and methods of evidence-based practice and the new 'What Works' research seemed to offer a new foundation for the development of a valued and constructive role.

From the mid-1990s developments accelerated rapidly. Some key events were Gill McIvor's review of evidence on effective sentencing for the Scottish Office (McIvor, 1990); the first 'What Works' conference in 1991; the launch of the Effective Practice Initiative in 1995; and the publication in the same year of McGuire's edited collection of papers from the 'What Works' conferences (McGuire, 1995); the 'Underdown Report' on effective supervision in 1998 (Underdown, 1998); the launch of the 'What Works' pathfinder projects and the Joint Accreditation Panel in 1999; and the launch of the National Probation Service for England and Wales in 2001.

Faced with such rapid changes and such powerful demands that they should alter the way they worked, some practitioners have questioned many aspects of the 'What Works' movement. Many of the criticisms are helpful and point to real problems which need to be addressed (for example, Merrington and Stanley, 2000) but many also appear to rest, to some degree, on misunderstandings either of what the available research supports, or of how the new developments are being implemented. Some misunderstandings have acquired a broad currency, and the main purpose of this article is to explore the debate by considering seven of the more widely repeated concerns, and what evidence might be available to address them. I consider these in three groups: first, concerns which express or inform some practitioners' resistance to the new methods; second, some misunderstandings which seem to flow from a managerialist orientation and seem likely to cause difficulties in the implementation and 'roll-out' of new practices; and finally the nostalgic mythology which argues, impossibly, that it would be better not to change.

Scepticism and resistance

One of the more obvious manifestations of the move towards evidence-based probation has been the widespread introduction of cognitive-behavioural programmes for medium-risk and high-risk offenders ('risk' here means risk of reconviction). This has also led to the first of the critical reactions I want to explore: the belief that programmes are *inherently conservative, pathologizing individual offenders and ignoring social causes of crime*. This is a widespread concern, spelled out for example in NAPO's policy statement on accredited programmes (NAPO, 2002) and by other critics such as Gorman (2001) and Kendall (2002). NAPO refers to 'a simplistic model of offending that isolates individual behaviour from its social, economic and political context', and 'a medical model which labels people who commit offences' (NAPO, 2002: 2). Certainly, a model which concentrated exclusively on individual responsibility for offending and ignored social context would fit well with a neo-liberal anti-welfare political stance, but there are many ways in which neither contemporary political realities in Britain nor the criminological assumptions behind evidence-based probation fit such a model. For example, even a cursory examination of instruments developed to assess offenders' needs for rehabilitation, such as the Canadian LSI-R (Andrews and Bonta, 1995) or the Home Office's own OASys (2001), shows that many of the factors taken into account are social and environmental, including various consequences of disadvantage. Some authors (such as Hudson, 2002) have rightly pointed out that the use of such factors in risk assessments can further disadvantage the poor if the consequences of assessment include greater severity of punishment or longer confinement. However, where such instruments are appropriately used to support rehabilitation, assistance and the least custodial option, this danger is reduced.

As for pathologizing offenders, the need for rehabilitative services exists mainly among relatively persistent offenders who are frequently convicted, and it would be perverse to deny that a number of these have difficulties in the areas of self-management, problem solving and social skills, as well as social disadvantages. The former may derive partly from the latter, and may also contribute to them. Individuals in similar social circumstances may involve themselves in very different amounts of offending, and we need to be particularly interested in the characteristics which help to distinguish those who offend to a significant degree from those (the rest of us?) who offend less. A large volume of reputable research documents the interacting mixture of social and personal factors which is associated with significant offending (see, for example, Farrington, 2002; Andrews and Bonta 1998), and a recent Home Office evaluation of resettlement 'pathfinder' services for short-term prisoners suggested that the most effective projects were those which *combined* attention to prisoners' social resources and opportunities with attention to cognitive factors such as beliefs and motivation (Lewis *et al.*, 2002).

Those who argue for spending on social programmes instead of on programmes for individual offenders (Kendall, 2002) may be setting up a false dichotomy – of course social programmes are needed, but some of them will have their impact on crime in the next generation, when today's children are growing up. In the meantime we also need to be doing something for people who need help now to escape from a pattern of offending. This is often not simply a matter of opportunities, but of how and whether they use them. Cognitive-behavioural programmes, being based on social learning theory, assume not so much that offenders are inherently pathological as that they learn in ways which are fundamentally similar to the ways the rest of us learn. It is also an everyday experience that individual learning styles differ: people learn different things with different degrees of ease or difficulty. To notice this does not imply 'pathologizing', or a 'medical model'. The language of 'cognitive deficits' may not be the most elegant way ever devised to describe learning needs, but it is a bizarre misrepresentation to portray it as some kind of Lombrosian search for atavistic 'criminal characteristics'.

A related misunderstanding portrays the process of programme development and accreditation as *dominated by psychologists* and consequently only interested in cognitive-behavioural programmes (Mair, 2000). Of the 12 appointed members of the Joint Prisons and Probation Accreditation Panel in 1999–2002 (13 including the Chair), only seven were psychologists, and only one of the seven nominated members was a psychologist. The panel accredited or recognized not only cognitive-behavioural programmes but also twelve-step addiction programmes and therapeutic communities. Not all were group programmes, some were for one-to-one use. Eventually new criteria were developed for 'integrated systems' of provision that contained a variety of elements which needed to be combined with appropriate assessment, case management and matching; the first of these to be recognized, Enhanced Community Punishment, contains no conventional 'programme' (though it does use methods such as pro-social modelling) and one of its intended outcomes is an improvement in basic skills to enhance employability. Half of the probation service's target number of accredited programme completions are intended to come by this route. The assertion that only cognitive-behavioural programmes are supported is simply a mistake.

A third regularly advanced criticism is that *the 'What Works' agenda is indifferent to diversity*; in other words, the particular needs of women or of minority ethnic offenders are likely to be insufficiently recognized by risk assessment methods (Shaw and Hannah-Moffatt, 2000) or programme designs (Kendall, 2002) which are based on research that has primarily involved white male offenders. NAPO (2002) has also referred to 'potentially discriminatory' content and 'racist and sexist language and assumptions' (NAPO, 2002: 1; 4). It is certainly true that research tends to start where large numbers are available, so that majorities are often studied before minorities, and much the same can be true of programme provision where there are targets to be met. However, it is also clear that the amount of work being done by the probation service to try to address diversity issues in effective practice is far more than can be summarized here, and has already included a diversity review of programme content and extensive research on programmes for minority ethnic offenders (Powis and Walmsley, 2002). A current project is surveying Black and Asian experiences of probation, and 'pathfinder' projects incorporating different models of specialized provision are in progress and being evaluated. Development work is also under way concerning racially motivated offenders (Perry, 2002). We do not know how successful this work will be, but the conditions are in place for learning to occur.

More work is also needed in the area of programmes which reflect specific needs of women offenders: some early attempts were not successful in attracting support or accreditation because their good intentions were not matched by convincing programme content, and another design is at the pilot stage. The theoretical basis of such gender-specific provision is also the subject of strongly held positions and active debate, well summarized by Gelsthorpe (2001). Studies of effective practice with women offenders (e.g. Dowden and Andrews, 1999) and of risk factors associated with women's offending (Clark and Howden-Windell, 2000) suggest some overlap with what we know from research on men, together with some differences reflecting the different circumstances and motivations of some women's offending and the different opportunities open to women in society. It would seem odd to argue that what we learn from men can never have any relevance to women, or indeed vice versa. In a recent Home Office evaluation of risk-need assessment instruments in probation (Raynor *et al.*, 2000) the LSI-R (Level of Service Inventory Revised) predicted reconviction almost as accurately for women as for men, but this only means that some of the same risk factors are relevant for both, not that their needs are identical. It was also clear, from this and other studies, that for a given LSI-R score the associated risk of reconviction is lower for a woman than for a man, suggesting a real risk of over-predicting reconviction if the same instruments are applied to both groups without appropriate modification. Overall, the critics who concentrate on diversity issues have helped to ensure that these questions are not ignored or sidelined. The more evidence-based the debate becomes, the more likely it is to lead to real improvements.

The fourth and last criticism to be examined in this section is that *the implementation of 'What Works' in probation is running too far ahead of the evidence.* This has been carefully argued by Merrington and Stanley (2000), who point out that many of the programmes now being implemented on a large scale have not yet been subject to a full reconviction study. The Accreditation Panel in particular has been aware of conflicting drives: on the one hand to be sure about the effectiveness of programmes, and on the other hand to 'go to scale' as soon as possible where there is judged to be a reasonable amount of evidence. In a context driven by Treasury targets it is not very practical to wait for the necessary three years or so which would be needed for a full reconviction study between the end of every pilot and the decision to implement more widely.

In these circumstances the Panel has reviewed other evidence of the effectiveness of methods used in a programme, and has made quite frequent use of 'recognition' rather than full accreditation ('recognition' enables a programme to be used pending resubmission with fuller evidence within a specified time). In every case the evaluation is in place and the results are being collected, so evaluation and implementation are proceeding side by side, and even full accreditation is reversible, being subject to revision in the light of emerging evidence. An important test of the evidence-based approach over the next three years will be how the service reacts when some programmes do not produce the expected results. (For example, a number of conference presentations have indicated concern about whether the original version of the 'Think First' programme had the intended impact on reconviction rates, although the full evaluation is not yet published at the time of writing.) It is to be expected that not everything will work; more time would have been helpful, but was not available. Already the investment in ongoing evaluation has been unprecedented in its scope and thoroughness, and this in itself seems a promising sign for the future.

The perils of management

At this point it seems right to turn, in the interests of fairness and balance as well as thoroughness, to two misunderstandings which seem particularly likely to affect managers, of both the national and local varieties. They can be summed up as the beliefs that *only programmes matter* and *there is a technical fix for everything*.

The first of these, 'only programmes matter', is the same belief that has been criticized by the Chief Probation Inspector as 'programme fetishism' (Her Majesty's Inspectorate of Probation, 2002). It consists of an exclusive focus on the delivery of programmes at the expense of other essential elements of practice, such as case management and the maintenance of appropriate contact and communication with offenders under supervision. The origins of this lie partly in the influence of earlier programme delivery practice in the prison system: the emphasis there could be primarily on programmes as the prisoners were already in prison, being to some degree looked after, and not simultaneously struggling with all the practical problems they would meet in the community. Delivering programmes outside institutions invites very high non-completion rates unless offenders are helped to comply: the case manager's role becomes essential in helping to maintain motivation and commitment, and helping people to deal with problems and challenges which are otherwise likely to disrupt their attendance on programmes and prevent them from benefiting. None of this can be done without contact. It is easy to understand why the early focus of 'What Works' was on delivering programmes, since that involved the largest cultural shift in the service, but case management now needs to become a priority. In some areas, case management seems to mean little more than assessing an offender and assigning him or her to a programme, which is then meant to carry the whole supervision task. In other areas, case management continues throughout the order, and there is at least suggestive evidence that this can mean higher completion rates (Heath *et al.*, 2002). It is important to remember that when programmes were first introduced into British probation (see, for example, Raynor and Vanstone, 1997; Vanstone, 2000) they were intended as a supplement to 'normal' supervision or an enhancement of it, not as a substitute for it.

Concerning the second belief that 'there is a technical fix for everything', this shows itself mainly in an exaggerated optimism about information technology and other 'scientific' procedures which on occasion has proved counterproductive. It is natural and appropriate that a newly unified service will aspire to greater uniformity of practice through central control, and there is no shortage of examples from the past where a more consistent approach would have helped (see the discussion of 'myths of nostalgia' below). However, even Napoleon's insistence on common weights and measures throughout the Empire had to compromise with reality sometimes. Recent years have seen a number of examples of essential new procedures being hugely delayed by dependency on commissioned software which is never delivered on time or in full working order (a lesson which could surely have been learned from other Government departments in advance). Case recording and management software (CRAMS) and 'interim' accredited programmes software (IAPS) have both experienced major problems and delays, interrupting the introduction of important practices such as monitoring the effectiveness of programmes, and sometimes forcing a resort to unsatisfactory interim paper versions. However, the most important example may turn out to be the delay in introducing a systematic approach to risk and need assessment.

The crucial role of risk/need assessment in the matching of programmes and services to offenders has been widely recognized since the early 1990s and available in Britain (in the forms of LSI-R or ACE – see Raynor *et al.*, 2000; Roberts *et al.*, 1996) since the mid-1990s. By 1999 at least half of the probation areas were using LSI-R or ACE, but these developments were interrupted by the announcement that the Home Office would develop its own instrument for roll-out in 2000 (Robinson, 2001). The result of this process was OASys, which is undoubtedly an impressive instrument with substantial scientific support, but is much larger than its predecessors and cries out for software support, which has been severely delayed. The result is that roll-out of OASys to probation areas is only beginning at the time of writing, and the prisons will not adopt it for general use until 2004 at the earliest. Meanwhile the critical years for the introduction of evidence-based methods into probation areas have passed without the consistent use of any form of evidence-based risk/need assessment, although simple and feasible methods were available eight years ago. (Other jurisdictions which adopted good-enough methods in the 1990s have had a rather different experience: see, for example, Heath *et al.*, 2002.) No doubt many lessons about implementation are being learned in what is, to be fair, still a fairly new national management structure.

Nostalgic illusions

The seventh and final source of misunderstanding which needs to be mentioned here is at least partly a myth of nostalgia, the belief that everything was better in the old days when practitioner autonomy and 'established methods' (NAPO, 2002: 2) provided all the guarantees of effectiveness that were needed. I can certainly remember the attractions of the relative autonomy I experienced as a probation officer in the 1970s (though even then we complained about bureaucracy and interference, questioned whether senior probation officers were necessary and grumbled about heavy caseloads and having to keep records up to date). Autonomy may allow good practice to flourish, but unfortunately it does exactly the same for bad practice. However, the strongest arguments against the 'autonomous practitioner' model rest on evaluation of its results. Whilst there is evidence that well-designed programmes can reduce reconviction rates below expected levels, national studies of the reconviction rates of people supervised by probation officers compared to those released from prison consistently show little or no difference in outcome when differences in initial risk of reconviction are taken into account (for example, Kershaw *et al.*, 1999; Lloyd *et al.*, 1994; Prime, 2002). The overall performance of the service has not matched the achievements of some pioneering special projects. Similar problems have arisen when instead of systematically following practices *designed* to be effective, officers have been left largely to provide whatever services they pleased.

One of the clearest examples of this was the IMPACT study (Folkard *et al.*, 1976) which began the 'nothing works' era in British probation. This famous study allocated probationers at random to standard or 'intensive' caseloads to see if the results were better when probation officers had more time to work with offenders, but did not specify what the officers should do with the extra time. Instead they seem to have offered a mixture of more of what they would normally have done ('established methods') with a few innovations they would not normally have had time to try. The overall result was that the experimental (intensive caseload) group reconvicted slightly but not significantly more than the control (normal caseload) group. The only group which appeared to benefit from experimental status was a fairly small number of offenders who combined high self-assessed problems with low 'criminal tendencies', which suggests that a number of officers may have been using counselling-based methods which met some needs of this group, but not of other groups more typical of the offender population (Folkard, 1981; Raynor, 1978). Overall, getting more probation input was slightly less beneficial than getting less.

A more recent example of the results of local autonomy in the development and implementation of practice is Andrew Underdown's survey of 'effective practice' initiatives for the Probation Inspectorate (Underdown, 1998), which paved the way for the introduction of much more central direction and leadership in the promotion of 'What Works'. Briefly, the survey identified 267 projects and programmes which were claimed by local probation areas (then relatively autonomous rather than, as now, part of a national service) to be examples of the application of 'effective practice' principles. Out of these 267, even a relatively benign scrutiny could find only *four* which had been competently evaluated and showed some positive results. Other researchers around the same time found that many probation areas which claimed to be running effective programmes were unable to say how many offenders had completed them (Hedderman and Sugg, 1997).

Other issues which should give rise to concern about the effects of local autonomy include the 'down tariff' drift of probation orders (now community rehabilitation orders or CROs) to include more and more low-risk offenders. The proportion of probationers who are first offenders has been rising since 1991 (Raynor, 1998) in spite of the 'risk principle' and long-established research evidence that first offenders on probation reconvict about twice as much as first offenders who are fined (Walker *et al.*, 1981). This almost certainly reduces the overall effectiveness of probation/ CROs. Wide variations in performance are also known to exist, both between officers (at least in Australia, see Trotter, 2000) and between local probation areas now that these are being measured by audit and by national 'performance reports' (for example, Wallis, 2002). More examples could be given, but this should be enough to indicate that the empirical support for practitioner autonomy is not strong.

So returning to the past is unlikely to be the answer. Nevertheless, the difficulties of the present are very real and immediate: the rapid roll-out of new programmes and methods has coincided with major reorganization to set up a national service, with new management and funding arrangements, new area boards replacing probation committees, and a redrawing of boundaries which has created newly-amalgamated areas still struggling to bring different systems and structures together. Whether it was wise to try to tackle all these problems at the same time is a management question which lies outside the scope of this paper, though there are examples of services which have improved their effectiveness without such major restructuring (Heath *et al.*, 2002). One particularly unnecessary touch, insisted on by politicians, was the decision to confuse practitioners, sentencers and the public by changing the familiar names of probation and community service orders to community rehabilitation orders and community punishment orders, when some continuity in a period of major change might have been more helpful.

The current period of transition in probation services is full of paradoxes: at the same time as probation officers have been taking industrial action over workloads, the Home Office has recently published evidence that both probation and prisons are on course to meet the ambitious crime reduction targets agreed with the Treasury (Prime, 2002). Developing knowledge and enthusiasm about new methods coexist with serious resource problems in many areas. It is also important to recognize that not all the strains and difficulties are consequences of evidence-based practice. Often, as in the example of name changes, they are quite the reverse. In short, the way forward for probation services seems more likely to be found by broadening and extending the evidence-based approach than by abandoning it. If the National Probation Service wants to pursue the reforming mission shared by most of its staff by providing alternatives to more punitive and less constructive sentences, it is not enough to show that an ever-increasing prison population is not cost-effective. It is also necessary to *demonstrate* (not simply to claim) that community penalties can provide greater tangible public benefit through more reparation to the community, greater opportunities for offenders to change their behaviour, and in the long run a reduction in offending.

From Peter Raynor, 'Evidence-based probation and its critics', Probation Journal, *50(4), 2003, pp. 334–345.*

References

Andrews, D.A. & Bonta, J. (1995) *The Level of Service Inventory – Revised: Manual.* Toronto: Multi-Health Systems Inc.

——(1998) *The Psychology of Criminal Conduct.* Cincinnati: Anderson.

Andrews, D.A., Zinger, I., Hoge, R.D., Bonta, J., Gendreau, P. & Cullen, F.T. (1990) 'Does Correctional Treatment Work? A Clinically Relevant and Psychologically Informed Meta-Analysis', *Criminology* 28 (3), pp. 369–404.

Clark, D. & Howden-Windell, J. (2000) 'A Retrospective Study of Criminogenic Factors in the Female Prison Population'. Unpublished report to the Home Office.

Dowden, C. & Andrews, D. (1999) 'What Works for Female Offenders: A Meta-Analytic Review', *Crime and Delinquency* 45 (4), pp. 438–452.

Farrington, D. (2002) 'Developmental Criminology and Risk-focused Prevention', in Maguire, M., Morgan, R. and Reiner, R. (eds) *The Oxford Handbook of Criminology.* Oxford: Oxford University Press.

Folkard, M.S., Smith, D.E. & Smith, D.D. (1976) *IMPACT. Intensive MatchedProbation and After-Care Treatment. Volume II. The Results of the Experiment.* Home Office Research Study 36. London: HMSO.

Folkard, S. (1981) 'Second Thoughts on IMPACT', in E.M. Goldberg and N. Connelly (eds) *Evaluative Research in Social Care.* London: Heinemann.

Gelsthorpe, L. (2001) 'Accountability: Difference and Diversity in the Delivery of Community Penalties', in A. Bottoms, L. Gelsthorpe, and S. Rex (eds) *Community Penalties: Change and Challenges*. Cullompton: Willan.

Gorman, K. (2001) 'Cognitive Behaviourism and the Holy Grail', *Probation Journal* 48 (1), pp. 3–9.

Heath, B., Raynor, P. & Miles, H. (2002) 'What Works in Jersey: the First Ten Years', *VISTA* 7 (3), pp. 202–8.

Hedderman, C. & Sugg, D. (1997) *The Influence of Cognitive Approaches, with a Survey of Probation Programmes*, Part 2. Home Office Research Study 171. London: Home Office.

Her Majesty's Inspectorate of Probation (2002) *Annual Report 2001–2002*. London: Home Office.

Hudson, B. (2002) 'Gender Issues in Penal Policy and Penal Theory', in P. Carlen (ed.) *Women and Punishment*. Cullompton: Willan.

Kendall, K. (2002) 'Time to Think Again About Cognitive-behavioural Programmes', in P. Carlen (ed.) *Women and Punishment*. Cullompton: Willan.

Kershaw, C., Goodman, J. & White, S. (1999) *Reconvictions of Offenders Sentenced or Discharged from Prison in 1995, England and Wales*, Statistical Bulletin {19/99}. London: Home Office.

Lewis, S., Vennard, J., Maguire, M., Raynor, P., Vanstone, M., Raybould, S. & Rix, J. (2002) *The Resettlement of Short-term Prisoners: An Evaluation of Seven Pathfinders*. Report to the Research, Development and Statistics Directorate, Home Office. Unpublished at time of writing (July 2003).

Lipsey, M. (1992) 'Juvenile Delinquency Treatment: A Meta-analytic Enquiry into the Variability of Effects', in T. Cook, H. Cooper, D.S. Cordray, H. Hartmann, L.V. Hedges, R.L. Light, T.A. Louis and F. Mosteller (eds) *Meta-Analysis for Explanation: A Case-book*. New York: Russell Sage.

Lloyd, C., Mair, G. & Hough, M. (1994) *Explaining Reconviction Rates: A Critical Analysis*. London: HMSO.

Mair, G. (2000) 'Credible Accreditation?' *Probation Journal* 47 (4), pp. 268–271.

McGuire, J. (ed.) (1995) *What Works: Reducing Reoffending*. Chichester: Wiley.

McGuire, J. & Priestley, P. (1985) *Offending Behaviour: Skills and Stratagems for Going Straight*. London: Batsford.

McIvor, G. (1990) *Sanctions for Serious or Persistent Offenders*. Stirling: Social Work Research Centre.

Merrington, S. & Stanley, S. (2000) 'Doubts about the What Works Initiative', *Probation Journal* 47 (4), pp. 272–275.

National Association of Probation Officers (2002) *Accredited Programmes Policy*. London: NAPO.

OASys Development Team (2001) *The Offender Assessment System (OASys)*. London: Home Office.

Perry, D. (2002) 'Racially Motivated Offenders: The Way Forward', *Probation Journal* 49 (4), pp. 305–309.

Powis, B. & Walmsley, R. (2002) *Programmes for Black and Asian Offenders on Probation: Lessons for Developing Practice*. Home Office Research Study 250. London: Home Office.

Prime, J. (2002) *Progress Made Against Home Office Public Service Agreement Target 10*. Online Report {16/02}. London: Home Office.

Raynor, P. (1978) 'Compulsory Persuasion: A Problem for Correctional Social Work', *British Journal of Social Work* 8 (4), pp. 411–424.

——(1988) *Probation as an Alternative to Custody*. Aldershot: Avebury.

——(1998) 'Reading Probation Statistics: A Critical Comment', *VISTA* 3 (3), pp. 181–185.

Raynor, P. & Vanstone, M. (1996) 'Reasoning and Rehabilitation in Britain: The Results of the Straight Thinking On Probation (STOP) Programme', *International Journal of Offender Therapy and Comparative Criminology* 40 (4), pp. 272–284.

——(1997) *Straight Thinking On Probation (STOP): The Mid Glamorgan Experiment*. Probation Studies Unit Report 4. Oxford: Centre for Criminological Research.

——(2002) *Understanding Community Penalties.* Buckingham: Open University Press.

Raynor, P., Kynch, J., Roberts, C. & Merrington, M. (2000) *Risk and Need Assessment in Probation Services: An Evaluation.* Home Office Research Study 211. London: Home Office.

Roberts, C. (1989) *Hereford and Worcester Probation Service Young Offender Project: First Evaluation Report.* Oxford: Department of Social and Administrative Studies.

Roberts, C., Burnett, R., Kirby, A. & Hamill, H. (1996) *A System for Evaluating Probation Practice.* Probation Studies Unit Report 1. Oxford: Centre for Criminological Research.

Robinson, G. (2001) 'Power, Knowledge and What Works in Probation', *Howard Journal* 40, pp. 235–254.

Ross, R.R. & Fabiano, E.A. (1985) *Time to Think: A Cognitive Model of Delinquency Prevention and Offender Rehabilitation.* Johnson City, TN: Institute of Social Sciences and Arts.

Shaw, M. & Hannah-Moffatt, K. (2000) 'Gender, Diversity and Risk Assessment in Canadian Corrections', *Probation Journal* 47 (3), pp. 163–172.

Trotter, C. (2000) 'Social Work Education, Pro-social Modelling and Effective Probation Practice', *Probation Journal* 47 (3), pp. 256–261.

Underdown, A. (1998) *Strategies for Effective Offender Supervision: Report of the HMIP What Works Project.* London: Home Office.

Vanstone, M. (2000) 'Cognitive-behavioural Work With Offenders in the UK: A History of Influential Endeavour', *Howard Journal* 39 (2), pp. 171–183.

Walker, N., Farrington, D. & Tucker, G. (1981) 'Reconviction Rates of Adult Males After Different Sentences', *British Journal of Criminology* 21 (4), pp. 357–360.

Wallis, E. (2002) *National Probation Service Performance Report 6.* London: National Probation Directorate.

74 Community penalties and Home Office research

On the way back to 'nothing works'? (2008)

Peter Raynor

Introduction: the shifting focus of research in community penalties

The history of research on community penalties in Britain falls into several distinct stages, which correspond to shifts in official and sometimes professional perceptions of the role, purpose and nature of community penalties. For the purposes of this article, community penalties can be understood as originally (since 1907) probation orders, to which were added from the 1970s onwards a range of derivatives which now offer, under the 2003 Criminal Justice Act, 13 different ways of supervising an adult offender in the community. To these, which can in principle be combined in thousands of different 'packages', can be added new hybrid sentences such as 'custody plus', which combines a short period of imprisonment with a longer period of supervision in the community. (Many of the orders which can be made in respect of young offenders can also be regarded as community penalties, but are not central to the argument of this article because their recent evaluations have been commissioned by the Youth Justice Board rather than directly by the Home Office: see, for example, Wilcox (2003).)

The earliest studies of the outcomes of probation in Britain were carried out in the context of a treatment model influenced by the psychological theories of the time and particularly by developments in American social casework theory (for fuller accounts see Raynor, 1997; Raynor and Vanstone, 2002; Vanstone, 2004; Raynor and Robinson, 2005). Radzinowicz described probation as 'a form of social service preventing further crime by a readjustment of the culprit' (1958: xi–xii) and his study of outcomes, which lacked a comparison group, reached broadly positive conclusions. Wilkins' study carried out around the same time (Wilkins, 1958) used a comparison group and did not find clear differences in favour of probation. Both studies essentially saw probation as a form of penal 'treatment' intended to reduce re-offending and evaluated it in these terms. The Home Office Research Unit (an ancestor of RDS-NOMS) shared the contemporary enthusiasm for probation as treatment, and carried out a series of studies through the 1960s and early 1970s, which are still among the most detailed and interesting of their kind (for example, Davies, 1969 and 1974). However, with the exception of Sinclair's (1971) study of hostels and Shaw's (1974) random allocation study of pre-release help for prisoners, they contained few positive findings about effectiveness. Eventually a probation study with a random allocation design was tried: the IMPACT study (Intensive Matched Probation and After-Care Treatment) was set up in the hope that it would provide evidence of lower reconviction rates among probationers supervised in lower caseloads (Folkard *et al.*, 1974, 1976).

By the time the results of this experiment were published in 1976, the climate had changed: Martinson (1974) had published his rather selective and one-sided summary of the very wide-ranging and systematic New York research review, which found little evidence of successful methods for the rehabilitation of offenders (Lipton *et al.*, 1975). A similar review with similar results was carried out by Brody (1976) of the Home Office Research Unit. In this new context the results of the IMPACT study (probationers did slightly but not significantly worse on lower caseloads) began a long period during which the Home Office showed no interest in carrying out further research on how probation affected the future behaviour of probationers. As the Director of the Unit put it: 'Penal treatments, as we significantly describe them, do not have any reformative effect' (Croft, 1978: 4). It should also be noted that 'nothing works' was the right message for the changing political climate of the times, and achieved the status of orthodoxy particularly in those countries like Britain and the USA where political developments were taking an anti-welfare, lower-public-spending, pro-market turn.

Instead, the questions asked by official research on community penalties changed. From the mid-1970s onwards, research on community penalties was mainly concerned to find out whether they had an impact on the criminal justice system by diverting offenders from expensive custodial sentences, rather than to investigate their impact on the behaviour of offenders. (This reflected emerging government thinking: if nothing worked, cheaper was better.) The new focus was clear in research on Community Service, which measured diversion effects in four different ways but did not look at reconviction rates (Pease *et al.*, 1977). In 1984 the first attempt by the Home Office to define objectives and priorities for the probation service made it clear that its purpose was to allow as many offenders as possible to receive non-custodial sentences (Home Office, 1984). These changes also demonstrated the near-monopoly of the Home Office in the funding of probation research: studies that questioned the prevailing orthodoxy and continued to look for impacts on offenders tended to be small and local (for example, Raynor, 1988; Roberts, 1989). In other countries where funding streams were more diverse (most notably Canada, but also Australia, Germany, Spain, the USA) large studies of the impact of rehabilitation continued to be done, often in new ways, for example by meta-analysis (Andrews *et al.*, 1990; Lipsey, 1992). Practitioners, by the way, seem never to have stopped believing that they could influence offenders' behaviour (Vanstone, 2004).

From 'nothing works' to 'what works'?

'Nothing works' was a powerful, resilient and simplistic doctrine capable of attracting support from a range of positions: not simply monetarist welfare cutters, but also radical criminologists opposed to the pathologizing of offenders as objects of treatment (Taylor *et al.*, 1973) and liberal advocates of justice models which prioritized desert over attributed need (American Friends Service Committee, 1971; Hood, 1974). This consensus facilitated a certain amount of what Andrews and Bonta (1998) have described as 'knowledge destruction': for example, the very promising Midlands prison experiment (Shaw, 1974) was not followed up, after a partial replication with different resources in a different kind of prison came up, not surprisingly, with a different result (Fowles, 1978). However, 'nothing works' did not provide a strong enough basis for resistance to the next big change of policy, when Michael Howard in

1993 sensed more popular support for punishment and incapacitation than for diversion, and announced that 'prison works'.

The threat that this represented to rehabilitation in general and the probation service in particular has been fully described elsewhere (for example Mair, 2004; Raynor and Robinson, 2005). To cut a long story short, a number of people in and around the probation service were becoming aware of research done in other countries on effective rehabilitation. They began to disseminate it (McIvor, 1990; McGuire, 1995) and to apply it in local experiments (for example Knott, 1995; Raynor and Vanstone, 1996). Other key steps in this transition were the election of a New Labour government with a stated commitment to evidence-based policy; the preparation of a wide-ranging review of research to inform policies on crime (Goldblatt and Lewis, 1998); a study of probation projects by the Inspectorate which showed a need for more central direction and quality control in what are now called 'interventions' (Underdown, 1998); and the official launch of the 'what works' initiative. Home Office researchers had to become quickly familiar with a new research literature, much of it published abroad (Vennard *et al.*, 1997).

The quasi-experimental pathfinders

In 1999 the investment in 'what works' dramatically increased through funding provided by the Crime Reduction Programme (CRP). For community penalties this took the form of several pathfinder projects designed to test various strands of thinking about effective practice. All were externally evaluated, and together they constituted the largest programme of research into community penalties ever attempted in Britain, covering as they did offending behaviour programmes, basic skills, community punishment and the resettlement of short-term prisoners. The perceived political importance of the CRP for future Home Office funding meant a high degree of RDS involvement in trying to 'manage' the associated research projects, with more steering groups, interim reports, commenting and redrafting than most of the external researchers were used to, and the size of the programme meant that sometimes quite junior Home Office researchers found themselves required to 'manage' large and complex projects. RDS also produced guidance on methodology, in the hope that diverse projects might produce comparable data on impacts and cost-effectiveness.

In the light of more recent methodological pronouncements, it is interesting to note that the guidance produced for CRP evaluations, and particularly for interventions with offenders, was firmly based on quasi-experimental methodologies (Colledge *et al.*, 1999). For example, advice was provided about selecting suitable comparison groups and matching relevant characteristics such as age, sex and criminal record. Random allocation was mentioned but largely rejected as an impractical approach:

> In rare circumstances it may be possible to set up control groups by random allocation of offenders to the programme of interest and to a control group which does not receive the programme. However, usually such randomised control groups are not possible for practical reasons.
>
> (Colledge *et al.*, 1999: 16)

As an alternative, the authors of the guidance suggested using a standard reconviction predictor to generate expected reconviction rates for programme and comparison groups, correctly pointing out that because of local variations in reconviction rates this comparison can be misleading unless local comparison groups are used – in other words, the important finding is not whether predicted and actual rates differ, but whether they differ by different amounts, and in what direction, in programme and comparison groups. (The method of comparing predicted and actual reconvictions had been used by Lloyd *et al.* (1994) and was also a feature of an early local evaluation of an offending behaviour programme, the STOP study (Raynor and Vanstone 1996, 1997). The use of multiple local comparison groups to allow for local error in predictors had also been pioneered in the STOP study.) There was no suggestion that evaluation might include studying the impact of a project on the use of custodial sentences: this was Oldspeak, discouraged among Home Office officials and probation managers since 1993, and apparently forgotten by most researchers too.

The difficulties of the CRP and the associated evaluations have been well documented by now (Homel *et al.*, 2005; see also Raynor, 2004a for specific discussion of the probation pathfinders). Briefly, for the community penalty and resettlement pathfinders the three-year time-scale of the CRP was too short for full evaluations of properly implemented projects to be undertaken, and evaluations were over-dependent on early data from projects which all suffered from slow start-up and implementation problems (Hollin *et al.*, 2002, 2004; Lewis *et al.*, 2003; McMahon *et al.*, 2004; Rex *et al.*, 2004). Some of this could have been predicted from international research, which has pointed to the importance of implementation (Bernfeld *et al.*, 2001), and to the capacity of poor implementation to undermine potentially successful programmes. One meta-analysis which compared 'demonstration' (i.e. pilot) programmes with 'practical' programmes as rolled out for general implementation (Lipsey, 1999) found that the rolled-out programmes were about half as effective as the pilots, and pointed to a number of features of their implementation which helped to explain this. (Earlier British research also contained some warnings: for example, McIvor (1995) argued that unless practitioners were involved in research, their support for evaluation and evidence-based development could not be taken for granted.)

In the pathfinder studies, the impact of implementation problems on the evaluation process was very clear. For example, in the projects concerning basic skills and offending behaviour programmes, rates of attrition were so high that only minorities (sometimes tiny minorities) of the programme groups completed their programmes, leading to difficulties in distinguishing programme effects (changes attributable to the programme) from selection effects: offenders who survive to complete the programme are likely to be better prospects, and more likely to succeed independently of any beneficial effects of the programme. In some studies involving several different types of intervention, such as the resettlement pathfinders, it was possible to compare outcomes for different intervention groups, and characteristics or features of services associated with better outcomes could be tentatively identified in retrospect by logistic regression, but none of these provided a clear and unambiguous endorsement of the 'what works' initiatives.

In the prisons, a series of three studies of offending behaviour programmes (Friendship *et al.*, 2002; Cann *et al.*, 2003; Falshaw *et al.*, 2003) suggested first that they reduced reconvictions, then that they did not and then that they did so for those who completed the programmes. Clearly more time and more studies, both in prisons and in the community, would be needed to reach a clearer understanding of what benefits could be expected under what circumstances. However, policy makers and Home Office officials had been hoping for quick and positive answers, and were clearly disappointed. There has also been a good deal of soul-searching about the reasons for the mixed findings (for further discussion of these see Raynor, 2004b). Were the theories wrong, or the implementation, or the research?

Reacting to disappointing results

Continuing positive results from international research and new meta-analyses (such as Lipton *et al.*, 2002) make the hypothesis of 'theory failure' unlikely. Some aspects of implementation failure attributable to the short timescale have already been mentioned; others included a target-driven over-concentration on programme development which led both to neglect of supportive and motivational offender management of the kind probation officers had traditionally provided, and to the inclusion of people in programmes for which they were not even in theory suitable (Hollin *et al.*, 2004). A further design and implementation issue was the fact that although evaluation was central to the CRP enterprise, the community punishment and resettlement projects did not seem to have been designed to facilitate evaluation. Examples of this were that it was often hard to identify appropriate comparison groups, and that it was usually impossible to gather the same information in comparison groups that was available for programme or intervention groups.

In the resettlement pathfinders, internal comparisons between different types of service could be made, but not for women, because only one women's prison was included and there was nothing with which to compare it. It was also difficult to match intervention and comparison groups on anything other than basic static risk factors, as the risk/need assessment system OASys was not yet in general use and information about needs and dynamic risk factors was usually available, if at all, only for intervention groups. In short, those who designed the projects were primarily interested in getting them into operation and using the CRP money, and did not seem to have been thinking of ways to make evaluation easy and reliable. A further very clear example of *not* building in evaluation occurred when a new form of Enhanced Community Punishment, building on the pathfinder but very different in many details, was accredited by the Correctional Services Accreditation Panel on the understanding that it would be implemented gradually and fully evaluated. Instead it was 'rolled out' quickly in all areas (making impossible any comparisons between areas where it was available and those where it was not), and the evaluation was cancelled, after tenders had been prepared and submitted, because the money to finance it could not be found.

However, the explanation for disappointing findings which was most often put forward by RDS spokespeople was neither theory failure nor implementation failure, but research failure, that is, that the evaluation studies were badly carried out or of the wrong kind. This explanation conveniently overlooked the fact that many decisions about methodology were either pre-empted by project designs, or already determined in the Home Office's own advice to researchers (e.g. Colledge *et al.*, 1999) and in the design and budget decisions taken within RDS before invitations to tender were sent out. However, what is more important for the purposes of this article is that the perceived failure of much of the correctional 'what works' research to show positive outcomes, and the consequent questions raised about the status and value of research within the Home Office, constitute the background and partial explanation for the emergence of a new and more cautious methodological orthodoxy.

The new orthodoxy

During the second half of 2003 and the winter of 2003–4, RDS staff began to work on a new strategy to standardize approaches to evaluation which was eventually to inform the publication of a new guidance document described as 'Standards for Impact Studies in Correctional Settings' (Home Office, 2004). This also provided the underpinning rationale for a new review of 'what works' research in Home Office Research Study 291 (Harper and Chitty, 2004). The shift to a more managerial language is interesting: what had been *guidance* for evaluators (Colledge *et al.*, 1999) was replaced by *standards* for impact studies. More important, however, were the methodological shifts. The new 'Standards' were heavily influenced by the Maryland Scientific Methods Scale (Sherman *et al.*, 1998), which was originally devised to provide guidance on how much weight to attach to the findings of studies with different methodologies when carrying out a systematic review of crime reduction measures. All systematic reviews need threshold standards to determine which studies to count, and the Maryland scale and its close relations (such as the criteria used by the Campbell Collaboration) are based on the level of certainty afforded by different methodologies when testing the hypothesis that an observed difference in offending rates is actually a result of a particular intervention rather than of some confounding factor such as selection effects.

The highest levels of certainty are provided, it is argued, by random controlled trials (RCTs) which offer 'the only method of assignment [to experimental and control conditions] that controls for *unknown* and *unmeasured* confounders as well as those that are known and measured' (Farrington, 2002: 6, emphases in original). Next come the familiar quasi-experimental methods, which depend on matching intervention and comparison groups on as many known relevant criteria as possible but may still be affected by unknown or unexpected differences between them. Without going into exhaustive detail, the Maryland scale has five levels, with random control trials at the top, then quasi-experiments with well-matched comparison groups, then quasi-experiments with less well-matched comparisons, then two levels of designs lacking comparison groups. Results from the top three levels (not simply random controlled trials) were taken into account in the review for which the scale was designed. Such scales, then, were designed to assess the validity of *particular kinds* of research carried out for particular purposes, and not as an all-purpose guide to the quality of evaluative research.

This approach to measuring the quality of evaluation research has been heavily criticized by, among others, Pawson and Tilley (1997, 1998) who advocate a more descriptive and pluralistic research strategy. In essence they propose a 'realist' methodology, which focuses on contexts and mechanisms: 'what works for whom in what circumstances' (Pawson and Tilley, 1998: 85), and *how* it works, with a strong emphasis on detailed documentation of what is actually happening. They contrast this with what they regard as 'black box' approaches that try to measure outcomes without unpacking processes. Their approach has in turn been criticized as likely to be weak in the demonstration of causal relationships (Farrington, 1998), and in reality the arguments in favour of RCT designs are persuasive if certain conditions are satisfied:

for example, that the intervention is actually delivered as intended, that it is uniform in nature and quality and that there are not other factors introduced by its implementation which are likely to undermine its effects. Unfortunately it is often not possible to be sure of these conditions, particularly in the messy context of the probation CRP pathfinders, and investigating such projects requires a different kind of research. It appears that RDS staff, in a search for methodological certainties following the supposed failures of the 'what works' evaluations, have adopted the most rigorous-looking experimental methodology they could find and promoted it as a touchstone of good research, when many of the problems of the field in which they are operating need to be studied in other ways. For example, it is doubtful whether the pathfinder interventions are best understood and tested as discrete 'treatments': they were part of an overall experience of supervision in a particular penal context, and there is a need to investigate and understand the whole experience, what changes for whom, what range of activities and qualities of intervention actually occur under the umbrella of the 'pathfinder', and how the people involved (primarily practitioners and offenders) understand and make sense of what is being done. This requires a social research approach, and would make the results of any subsequent experimental evaluation far easier to interpret. The problem posed by the outcomes of the pathfinder evaluations could be summed up as having plenty of results and not being sure what they mean.

The literature and practice of criminal justice evaluation is not in fact lacking in suggestions that might have supplemented or enhanced the Home Office's approach. For example, in a rather polemical attack on the methodology of 'what works' research, Farrall (2003a) argues for detailed qualitative study of *how* probation impacts on offenders and their circumstances, and of what has been helpful and why. In a further article (Farrall, 2003b) and a subsequent book (Farrall and Calverley, 2006) it is suggested that our understanding of how rehabilitation 'works' needs to be informed by research on the process of desistance from crime, and that this could help to add depth to our understanding of outcome studies. (There have in fact been some attempts to do this within the pathfinder studies (see, for example, Maguire and Raynor, 2006), but these are probably regarded by Home Office sponsors as somewhat peripheral to the main purpose of the research.) In another example of a contextualized and socially informed approach to the understanding of outcomes, Lipton (2002, personal communication) has described using anthropologically trained social researchers to investigate the nature and social setting of an intervention before sending in evaluators armed with experimental methodologies. Even one recent Home Office report suggested:

> ... design of future evaluation needs to take into account the process of intervention research and development. While progress straight to an outcome evaluation might work for 'off the shelf' products ... it is less helpful for more innovative work. Rush to an outcome evaluation may be premature ... Where work is based on sound principles, clearly targeted, documented and monitored, and aimed at relevant service outcomes ... then separate reconviction outcome testing for individual interventions may not always be a priority.
>
> (Stephens *et al.*, 2004: 15)

In addition, one important task for evaluation research in corrections is to develop the evaluation tools and methodologies which will help managers and practitioners to measure the effects of what they are doing as they do it. A preoccupation with RCTs, which most managers will never have the opportunity or authority to set up, is unlikely to deliver what is needed here either. A more pluralistic, comprehensive and triangulated multi-method approach to evaluation seems more likely to improve our understanding than a premature narrowing of the agenda to concentrate on RCTs. A broad approach is also more able to accommodate other possible goals of correctional intervention such as change in sentencing patterns, which is still omitted from RDS guidance on assessing 'impact'.

Methodological closure and information management

One particularly worrying aspect of the emerging orthodoxy is that it has coincided with an approach to publication and dissemination which sometimes looks suspiciously like a loss of interest in results which do not fit. This is different from the familiar (though often prolonged) process of comment and modification before a report is published. Recently there have been several cases of reports that have gone through this process and through peer review, but have not been published because publication was no longer seen as a priority. This happened, for example, to the reconviction study of the Community Punishment pathfinder, to the whole of the Phase 2 resettlement study and to the reconviction study of resettlement Phase 1. (The resettlement studies were later published by Policy Press instead (Clancy *et al.*, 2006).) A new term, 'sunsetting', has been coined to describe this process of deciding to do nothing with a report. This is worrying, as well as frustrating for researchers who felt they had been virtually promised full publication when they took on the pathfinder evaluations. It is also strange that the final stage of these studies, seen as so important when they were set up, was seen on completion as suitable only for 'sunsetting', or at best dissemination within the Home Office and not outside. Taking this together with the obvious persistent anxiety about how to 'handle' reports, it is hard to avoid the conclusion that the publication of Home Office studies is no longer driven by a culture of openness about the results of publicly funded research, but instead by the culture of information management which has become characteristic of the New Labour governments in several fields.

A related problem has been an emerging selectivity about the results that *are* published. The publication of the reconviction results of the offending behaviour programme evaluations (Hollin *et al.*, 2004) followed an argument between the research team and its RDS 'managers' about which groups should be included in the published results. The researchers' view was that they should present results for the comparison group and for two intervention groups: an 'intention to treat' group comprising all those who were supposed to do the programmes, and a 'programme completers' group. The Home Office preference was to compare the first two groups only and to omit the programme completers, on the grounds that the impact of a sentence can only be measured by looking at its effect on everybody sentenced to it, rather than on those who successfully complete it. The researchers preferred a three-group analysis in order to include the effect of the programmes on those who actually experienced them (with the obvious warnings about possible selection effects). They eventually persuaded RDS to allow this, and methodologically it seems sound practice to publish results for both intervention groups ('all sentenced' and 'all completing') as was done in earlier studies (e.g. Raynor and Vanstone, 1996); however, the new

RDS preference for omitting data on programme completers was followed throughout a recent review of the 'what works' studies (Harper and Chitty, 2004). This seems a narrow and somewhat dogmatic approach in a report that presents itself as a follow-up to the wide-ranging and influential study that marked the beginning of the 'what works' approach (Goldblatt and Lewis, 1998). It also risks distorting the results of some of the summarized studies.

It is, of course, fair to ask what should be expected of a government research unit producing research for internal customers, and operating within the current expectations regarding the relationship between civil servants and politicians. We may regret recent changes, but we can hardly expect RDS researchers to be unaffected by them. However, history also shows that Home Office research on community penalties has always tended to operate within the policy assumptions of the time, and has often not produced the studies that have informed the next policy shift. These have come from other countries, or from local initiatives independent of Home Office funding. Home Office research tends to remain within the policy box: that is its job, and thinking outside the box usually has to come from elsewhere. The emergence of public sector managerialism inevitably moves RDS researchers closer to the policy world and further away from the academic world: the realistic response is not to expect them to behave differently, but to try to ensure a variety of sources of support for a variety of approaches to criminal justice research rather than a Home Office near-monopoly.

In some other countries where responsibility for probation (or equivalent) services is more devolved to state or local level, there appears often to be more diversity in the provision and funding of evaluative research. For example, in Scotland a new Centre for Crime and Justice Research links together a number of university departments with interests in evaluating developments in Scottish criminal justice policy, but seeks a variety of funding and has no directive approach to methodology. In countries such as Germany and the USA where individual states run all or most probation services, research studies are often set up with regional or local universities, and, in a much smaller but interesting example, the relative autonomy of probation in the British Channel Island of Jersey has allowed the development of new approaches to measuring the impact of all its probation provision (Raynor and Miles, 2007; see also www.gov.je/Probation/Publications). If similar decentralized approaches were prevalent in England and Wales there would be less need to worry about Home Office attempts to prescribe the rules of research. It may in fact be the *limited* power of researchers within the Home Office that motivates both the search for foolproof methodologies, and the over-management of external researchers and the information they produce.

One further danger is worth pointing out. The perceived (though arguably not actual) failure of the pathfinder evaluations risks a reaction in the direction of 'nothing works', or at the very least the adoption of market mechanisms for quality improvement through contestability rather than through the evidence-based development of effective methods, which was the model underpinning 'what works'. A narrow and over-cautious approach to evaluation research could feed this tendency by underplaying positive findings. Over 20 years ago Ken Pease pointed out that the anxiety of researchers to avoid 'type 1' errors (false claims of effectiveness) was probably masking a high rate of 'type 2' errors (false findings of ineffectiveness), and that this reinforced beliefs that 'nothing worked': 'to stack the odds against the recognition of real differences for what they are has the direct effect of making the demonstration of correctional efficacy unlikely, and to make the spurious demonstration of correctional inefficacy more likely' (Pease, 1985: 74). It seems at least possible that we are heading in this direction again.

From Peter Raynor, 'Community penalties and Home Office research: on the way back to "nothing works"?', Criminology and Criminal Justice, 8(1), 2008, pp. 73–87.

References

American Friends Service Committee (1971) *Struggle for Justice: A Report on Crime and Punishment in America.* New York: Hill & Wang.

Andrews, D.A. and J. Bonta (1998) *The Psychology of Criminal Conduct.* Cincinnati, OH: Anderson.

Andrews, D.A., I. Zinger, R.D. Hoge, J. Bonta, P. Gendreau and F.T. Cullen (1990) 'Does Correctional Treatment Work? A Clinically Relevant and Psychologically Informed Meta-Analysis', *Criminology* 28(3): 369–404.

Bernfeld, G., D. Farrington and A. Leschied (eds) (2001) *Offender Rehabilitation in Practice.* Chichester: Wiley.

Brody, S.R. (1976) *The Effectiveness of Sentencing.* Home Office Research Study 35. London: HMSO.

Cann, J., L. Falshaw, F. Nugent and C. Friendship (2003) *Understanding What Works: Accredited Cognitive Skills Programmes for Adult Men and Young Offenders.* Home Office Research Findings 226. London: Home Office.

Clancy, A., K. Hudson, M. Maguire, R. Peake, P. Raynor, M. Vanstone and J. Kynch (2006) *Getting Out and Staying Out: Results of the Prisoner Resettlement Pathfinders.* Bristol: Policy Press.

Colledge, M., P. Collier and S. Brand (1999) *Programmes for Offenders: Guidance for Evaluators.* CRP Guidance Note 2. London: Home Office.

Croft, J. (1978) *Research in Criminal Justice.* Home Office Research Study 44. London: HMSO.

Davies, M. (1969) *Probationers in their Social Environment.* Research Study 2. London: HMSO.

——(1974) *Social Work in the Environment.* Research Study 21. London: HMSO.

Falshaw, L., C. Friendship, R. Travers and F. Nugent (2003) *Searching for 'What Works': An Evaluation of Cognitive Skills Programmes.* Home Office Research Findings 206. London: Home Office.

Farrall, S. (2003a) 'J'accuse: Probation Evaluation-Research Epistemologies. Part One: The Critique', *Criminal Justice* 3(2): 161–79.

——(2003b) 'J'accuse: Probation Evaluation-Research Epistemologies. Part Two: This Time It's Personal and Social Factors', *Criminal Justice* 3(3): 249–68.

Farrall, S. and A. Calverley (2006) *Understanding Desistance from Crime.* Maidenhead: Open University Press.

Farrington, D. (1998) 'Evaluating "Communities That Care": Realistic Scientific Considerations', *Evaluation* 4(2): 204–10.

——(2002) 'Methodological Quality Standards for Evaluation Research', paper presented to the Third Annual Jerry Lee Crime Prevention Symposium, University of Maryland, April.

Folkard, M.S., A.J. Fowles, B.C. McWilliams, W. McWilliams, D.D. Smith and G.R. Walmsley (1974) *IMPACT. Intensive Matched Probation and Aftercare Treatment: Volume I. The Design of the Experiment and an Interim Evaluation.* Home Office Research Study 24. London: HMSO.

Folkard, M.S., D.E. Smith and D.D. Smith (1976) *IMPACT Volume II: The Results of the Experiment.* Home Office Research Study 36. London: HMSO.

Fowles, A.J. (1978) *Prison Welfare: An Account of an Experiment at Liverpool.* Home Office Research Study 45. London: HMSO.

Friendship, C., L. Blud, M. Erikson and R. Travers (2002) *An Evaluation of Cognitive Behavioural Treatment for Prisoners.* Home Office Research Findings 161. London: Home Office.

Goldblatt, P. and C. Lewis (1998) *Reducing Offending*. Home Office Research Study 187. London: Home Office.

Harper, G. and C. Chitty (2004) *The Impact of Corrections on Re-offending: A Review of 'What Works'*. Home Office Research Study 291. London: Home Office.

Hollin, C., J. McGuire, E. Palmer, C. Bilby, R. Hatcher and A. Holmes (2002) *Introducing Pathfinder Programmes into the Probation Service: An Interim Report*. Home Office Research Study 247. London: Home Office.

Hollin, C., E. Palmer, J. McGuire, J. Hounsome, R. Hatcher, C. Bilby and C. Clark (2004) *Pathfinder Programmes in the Probation Service: A Retrospective Analysis*. Home Office Online Report (66/04). London: Home Office.

Homel, P., S. Nutley, B. Webb and N. Tilley (2005) *Investing to Deliver: Reviewing the Implementation of the UK Crime Reduction Programme*. Home Office Research Study 281. London: Home Office.

Home Office (1984) *Probation Service in England and Wales: Statement of National Objectives and Priorities*. London: Home Office.

——(2004) *Home Office and YJB Standards for Impact Studies in Correctional Settings*. London: RDS.

Hood, R. (1974) *Tolerance and the Tariff*. London: NACRO.

Knott, C. (1995) 'The STOP Programme: Reasoning and Rehabilitation in a British Setting', in J. McGuire (ed.) *What Works: Reducing Reoffending*, pp. 115–26. Chichester: Wiley.

Lewis, S., J. Vennard, M. Maguire, P. Raynor, M. Vanstone, S. Raybould and A. Rix (2003) *The Resettlement of Short-Term Prisoners: An Evaluation of Seven Pathfinders*. RDS Occasional Paper 83. London: Home Office.

Lipsey, M. (1992) 'Juvenile Delinquency Treatment: A Meta-Analytic Enquiry into the Variability of Effects', in T. Cook, H. Cooper, D.S. Cordray, H. Hartmann, L.V. Hedges, R.L. Light, T.A. Louis and F. Mosteller (eds) *Meta-Analysis for Explanation: A Case-Book*, pp. 83–127. New York: Russell Sage.

——(1999) 'Can Rehabilitative Programs Reduce the Recidivism of Juvenile Offenders? An Inquiry into the Effectiveness of Practical Programs', *Virginia Journal of Social Policy and the Law* 6(3): 611–41.

Lipton, D., R. Martinson and J. Wilks (1975) *The Effectiveness of Correctional Treatment*. New York: Praeger.

Lipton, D., F. Pearson, C. Cleland and D. Yee (2002) 'The Effectiveness of Cognitive-Behavioural Treatment Methods on Offender Recidivism', in J. McGuire (ed.) *Offender Rehabilitation and Treatment*, pp. 79–112. Chichester: Wiley.

Lloyd, C., G. Mair and M. Hough (1994) *Explaining Reconviction Rates: A Critical Analysis*. Home Office Research Study 136. London: Home Office.

McGuire, J. (ed.) (1995) *What Works: Reducing Reoffending*. Chichester: Wiley.

McIvor, G. (1990) *Sanctions for Serious or Persistent Offenders*. Stirling: Social Work Research Centre.

——(1995) 'Practitioner Evaluation in Probation', in J. McGuire (ed.) *What Works: Reducing Reoffending*, pp. 209–19. Chichester: Wiley.

McMahon, G., A. Hall, G. Hayward, C. Hudson and C. Roberts (2004) *Basic Skills Programmes in the Probation Service: An Evaluation of the Basic Skills Pathfinder*. Home Office Research Findings 203. London: Home Office.

Maguire, M. and P. Raynor (2006) 'How the Resettlement of Prisoners Promotes Desistance from Crime: Or Does It?', *Criminology and Criminal Justice* 6(1): 19–38.

Mair, G. (ed.) (2004) *What Matters in Probation*. Cullompton: Willan.

Martinson, R. (1974) 'What Works? Questions and Answers about Prison Reform', *The Public Interest* 35, 22–54.

Pawson, R. and N. Tilley (1997) *Realistic Evaluation*. London: SAGE.

——(1998) 'Caring Communities, Paradigm Polemics, Design Debates', *Evaluation* 4(2): 73–90.

Pease, K. (1985) 'The Future of Research and Information in the Probation Service', in E. Sainsbury (ed.) *Research and Information in the Probation Service*, pp. 72–5. Sheffield: University of Sheffield.

Pease, K., S. Billingham and I. Earnshaw (1977) *Community Service Assessed in 1976*. Home Office Research Study No. 39. London: HMSO.

Radzinowicz, L. (ed.) (1958) *The Results of Probation*. A Report of the Cambridge Department of Criminal Science. London: Macmillan.

Raynor, P. (1988) *Probation as an Alternative to Custody*. Aldershot: Avebury.

——(1997) 'Evaluating Probation: A Moving Target', in G. Mair (ed.) *Evaluating the Effectiveness of Community Penalties*, pp. 19–33. Aldershot: Avebury.

——(2004a) 'The Probation Service "Pathfinders": Finding the Path and Losing the Way?', *Criminal Justice* 4(3): 309–25.

——(2004b) 'Rehabilitative and Integrative Approaches', in A. Bottoms, S. Rex and G. Robinson (eds) *Alternatives to Prison: Options for an Insecure Society*, pp. 195–223. Cullompton: Willan.

Raynor, P. and H. Miles (2007) 'Evidence-Based Probation in a Microstate: The British Channel Island of Jersey', *European Journal of Criminology* 4(3): 299–313.

Raynor, P. and G. Robinson (2005) *Rehabilitation, Crime and Justice*. Basingstoke: Palgrave Macmillan.

Raynor, P. and M. Vanstone (1996) 'Reasoning and Rehabilitation in Britain: The Results of the Straight Thinking on Probation (STOP) Programme', *International Journal of Offender Therapy and Comparative Criminology* 40(4): 272–84.

——(1997) *Straight Thinking on Probation (STOP): The Mid-Glamorgan Experiment*, Probation Studies Unit Report No. 4. Oxford: University of Oxford Centre for Criminological Research.

——(2002) *Understanding Community Penalties*. Buckingham: Open University Press.

Rex, S., L. Gelsthorpe, C. Roberts and P. Jordan (2004) *What's Promising in Community Service: Implementation of Seven Pathfinder Projects*. Home Office Research Findings 231. London: Home Office.

Roberts, C. (1989) *Hereford and Worcester Probation Service Young Offender Project: First Evaluation Report*. Oxford: Department of Social and Administrative Studies.

Shaw, M. (1974) *Social Work in Prisons*. Home Office Research Study 22. London: HMSO.

Sherman, L., D. Gottfredson, D. MacKenzie, J. Eck, P. Reuter and S. Bushway (1998) *Preventing Crime: What Works, What Doesn't, What's Promising*. Washington, DC: National Institute of Justice.

Sinclair, I. (1971) *Hostels for Probationers*. Home Office Research Study 6. London: HMSO.

Stephens, K., J. Coombs and M. Debidin (2004) *Black and Asian Offenders Pathfinder: Implementation Report*. Development and Practice Report 24. London: Home Office.

Taylor, I., P. Walton and J. Young (1973) *The New Criminology*. London: Routledge & Kegan Paul.

Underdown, A. (1998) *Strategies for Effective Supervision: Report of the HMIP What Works Project*. London: Home Office.

Vanstone, M. (2004) *Supervising Offenders in the Community: A History of Probation Theory and Practice*. Aldershot: Ashgate.

Vennard, J., D. Sugg and C. Hedderman (1997) *The Use of Cognitive-Behavioural Approaches with Offenders: Messages from the Research*. Home Office Research Study 171. London: Home Office.

Wilcox, A. (2003) 'Evidence-Based Youth Justice? Some Valuable Lessons from an Evaluation for the Youth Justice Board', *Youth Justice* 3(1): 19–33.

Wilkins, L.T. (1958) 'A Small Comparative Study of the Results of Probation', *British Journal of Delinquency* 8(3): 201–9.

75 What Works in 2009

Progress or stagnation? (2009)

Steve Stanley

Introduction

In 2000, What Works, and particularly the delivery of cognitive-behavioural programmes, was seen as a key element in the work of the emerging National Probation Service (NPS). A range of programmes and interventions was developed; some were evaluated and the evaluations published, some were based on evidence from previous evaluations while some, it appears, were neither. Since 2004 the renewed emphasis on offender management following the Carter Report (2003), the incorporation of the NPS into the National Offender Management Service, and the development of the National Offender Management Model, have all tended to shift the emphasis away from accredited programmes as such and perhaps also from What Works as a whole. Meanwhile the concepts and implementation of effective practice have been subject to a range of criticisms. In such a changing environment, has What Works survived?

In 2000, Simon Merrington and I published a brief review of the evidence then available to support the What Works Initiative (as it then was) (Merrington and Stanley, 2000). We followed this in 2004 with a review of the evidence, particularly from early programme evaluations that had been published in the interim (Merrington and Stanley, 2004). This article is a follow-up to these publications and attempts to bring the story up to date. In it, I review the history and progress of What Works, recapitulate on our previous articles and attempt to assess the present state of What Works. It is now nearly a decade since Effective Practice or What Works began to be incorporated into government policy for the treatment of offenders. Has this movement delivered what it appeared to promise?

A brief history of What Works in probation

The central premise of What Works was that programmes, and specifically cognitive behavioural programmes, would deliver worthwhile reductions of between 5 and 10 per cent in reoffending for those who went through them. The evidence for this proposition was based largely on American and Canadian research and meta-analyses of relatively small-scale studies. The key United Kingdom review of the literature was in McGuire (1995), who highlighted key principles for effective programmes. Over time, these have undergone some development; a recently published list (adapted from Hedderman, 2007 after Vennard *et al.*, 1997) is as follows:

- Risk   Match programme intensity to risk;
- Responsivity   Match programme delivery to offenders' learning styles;
- Integrity   Programmes should be delivered consistently;
- Needs   Address factors contributing directly to criminal behaviour;
- Modality   Multi-modal intervention to improve cognitive and other skills;
- Community focus   As effects are stronger when delivered in the community.

In 1998, the Probation Inspectorate produced two documents, *Strategies for Effective Offender Supervision* (Underdown, 1998) and *Evidence Based Practice – a guide to effective practice* (Chapman and Hough, 1998). In the context of what happened later it is worth noting that Chapman and Hough stressed the importance of delivering good programmes integrated to the supervision of offenders.

Initially the Inspectorate took the lead in promoting and introducing What Works, sponsoring the two papers above as well as, later, a guide to evaluation (Merrington and Hine, 2001). Despite this central and 'top down' sponsorship, the initial introduction of What Works relied heavily on local initiatives. Individual probation services were encouraged to submit promising programmes as pathfinders for subsequent accreditation.

It is indicative of the importance then attached to What Works that the 1999–2001 Crime Reduction Strategy included a commitment to spending £21m over three years on developing a 'national curriculum' (as it was called at the time) of programmes to reduce offending (Merrington and Stanley, 2000). The first wave of accredited Pathfinders – three general offending behaviour programmes based on cognitive behavioural principles – was rolled out to local services in 2000. The emerging National Probation Directorate incorporated this commitment into its first What Works Strategy (Home Office, 2000) and included cash-linked targets for programme completion in its performance management system (McGarva, 2007; Merrington and Stanley 2007).

We commented then (Merrington and Stanley, 2000) on the ambition of the programme set out in these documents. We also noted the risks in using reconviction as the sole criterion of success. One reason for this lay in the difficulties of measurement (not least because of apparent gaps in the two databases then used, the Police National Computer and the Probation Index, to track offenders' convictions). A second reason was the importance we attached to intermediate factors such as attitude change and employment, both in helping the reform of offenders and as indicative and more timely measures of a possible effect on reconviction.

A quick review of our articles

Our first article (Merrington and Stanley, 2000) expressed concerns, referred to above, about this developing process. In addition to our caution about relying on reconviction as the only measure of success in judging programmes, we believed that the evidence base for launching these programmes nationally was insufficient and that the scale of the roll out was a risk in itself, given the importance of local factors in ensuring successful implementation. We recognized the political imperatives that were perceived at the time and called for open sharing of evaluation findings. Reviewing the position some three to four years later (Merrington and Stanley, 2004), we found only limited evidence of progress, but nevertheless some grounds for encouragement and others for concern.

None of the pathfinder evaluations then published had found unequivocal evidence that accredited programmes were effective in reducing reconviction. There were promising leads to be sure. Offenders who completed programmes appeared to do better than predicted and better than the comparison group. In the case of Think First, it appeared that lower than expected completion rates could be attributed to a fault in its design. But by comparison with offenders sentenced to other community sentences, those sentenced to Think First did no better on the reconviction measure (Ong *et al.*, 2003).

There had been some promising results from programmes delivered in prisons but these had tended to decay over time; that is the same programme returned less satisfactory results (and no evidence of a reduction in reconviction) in a repeat study (Cann *et al.*, 2003). The authors attributed this to factors to do with selection of offenders on the one hand and with the motivation of the offenders on the other.

In this second review (Merrington and Stanley, 2004), we therefore drew some preliminary conclusions from the evidence then available:

1.   There was no consistent evidence of a reduction in reoffending.
2.   Some studies showed improvement in intermediate outcomes such as skills and employment, but did not show that these were related to a reduction in offending.
3.   There was evidence that some programmes had a short-term effect, which faded over time.
4.   There was no strong evidence of the value of different models of intervention.
5.   We judged that the What Works risk principle of focusing intensive interventions on those at greater risk of reoffending was validated.
6.   Most studies showed that offenders who completed programmes were less likely to be reconvicted than those who did not, but completion rates for the programmes studied were low. This raised the question of whether the effectiveness of programmes might improve if completion rates were to improve.
7.   There were some doubts about the validity of the comparison groups used in the studies (none used a random control trial design). It was possible that participants in some groups differed from non-participants on some key factor, such as motivation, not controlled for in the comparison.
8.   We suggested that the quality of case management, including offender-driven assessment and allocation to programmes, and then effective support to improve the chances of successful completion, was a key factor and that more attention needed to be paid to it.
9.   There was a continuing issue about the publication of evaluations and about the openness of the work of the Correctional Services Accreditation Panel (CSAP). (This has since been met, at least in part, by the publication of annual reports by CSAP before it was abolished (Correctional Services Accreditation Panel, 2008).)

Our conclusions were that it was still too early to say what did or did not work, what was a dead end and what was a promising lead. We thought however that the evidence then available suggested that the risk principle at least was valid and that a stronger offender focus and good case management should improve results.

On the methodological side, we felt that while the quality of evaluations had improved there was still too much concentration on the single outcome measure of reconviction at the expense of other measures. We also felt there was a need for more open and exploratory studies to examine why and how interventions help reduce reoffending to supplement the prospective and retrospective evaluations already commissioned.

Developments since 2004

Since then the probation service has gone through yet more changes with the unfolding and one might say unravelling of the original concept for a National Offender Management Service (NOMS) as set out in the Carter Report (2003). The 2003 Criminal Justice Act replaced community rehabilitation, punishment, etc. with a single community order which can include combinations of 12 different requirements, including one to attend an accredited programme. The research that has been published has still not shown a consistent positive effect for structured interventions; the programmes tested as part of the Crime Reduction Strategy did not produce unequivocal results (see below).

In a review of evaluation in the probation service (Merrington and Stanley, 2007), we argued that probation practice required evaluation using a range of methods, including those of performance measurement, inspection and review as well as formal research studies. The latter needed to address the same issue for a range of perspectives as was done in the STOP project (Raynor and Vanstone, 1997).

The fate of the Pathfinders

In the heady days of What Works and as part of its crime reduction strategy, the Home Office had commissioned a range of 'pathfinders' to test out different aspects of effective practice. These included general offending behaviour programmes in probation (already discussed) and programmes on employment, basic skills, community punishment and resettlement after release from custody. All were to be evaluated; the research designs for these evaluations were effectively specified by the National Probation Service and the Home Office Research Development and Statistics Directorate (RDS). As Raynor (2008) has noted, few of these evaluations were published by the Home Office and fewer still of these publications included reconviction follow-ups. Some of the Pathfinders can be categorized (if unfairly) as examples of implementation failure as they produced too few cases for analysis. In none of them were the results unequivocally supportive of programmes or strategies that were adopted in these areas. Raynor (2008) comments that the introduction of 'Enhanced Community Punishment' owed little to the findings of the Community Punishment pathfinder and its roll out was not accompanied by an evaluation.

We can summarize the results of the pathfinders as follows:

- *Think First* – a retrospective analysis showed no evidence for a positive overall programme effect but a 'completion effect' – that is offenders who completed the programme were less likely to be reconvicted. The researchers tentatively identified factors that supported programme completion and successful outcomes but also others, including aspects of the design of the programme, that inhibited it (Ong *et al.*, 2003).

- *Effective Thinking Skills (ETS)* – again there was no overall programme effect but a completion effect was identified. Due to difficulties with matching samples, there were some doubts over the validity of the comparison group (Hollin *et al.*, 2004; Merrington and Stanley, 2005).
- *Resettlement* – this was an assessment of the impact of seven different projects for the resettlement and rehabilitation of adult offenders sentenced to short (under 12 months) custodial sentences (Lewis *et al.*, 2007). Again, there was no consistent programme effect but a 'completion' effect. The researchers noted that offenders who completed a short cognitive motivational programme were less likely to be reconvicted, as were those who received (that is to say accepted) continuous supervision 'through the gate' – before and after release. The researchers concluded that what worked was 'skilled and systematic work ... in relation to thinking, attitudes and motivation as well as practical problems' (Lewis *et al.*, 2007: 49) delivered 'through the gate'. Programmes alone were not enough but neither was person-centred one to one contact.
- *Community Punishment* – the pathfinder results were set aside and Enhanced Community Punishment introduced in 2004, a rather different scheme from those tested in the pathfinder (see Raynor, 2008).
- *Basic Skills* – too few cases went through the programme for a full evaluation.
- *Employment* – again too few cases went through the programme – arguably because of the complexity of the design as well as through implementation issues.

Overall, therefore the pathfinders did not produce the kind of evidence that had been hoped for. Some were dogged or inhibited by design and implementation problems; others were overtaken by shifts in government policy. They did however give many useful lessons in design and implementation for those who wished to learn from them and gave some promising leads.

The pathfinder projects have been criticized, not least by the NOMS RDS (Harper and Chitty, 2005) for using weak experimental designs so that the results, positive, negative or inconclusive, could have arisen by chance or were susceptible to more than one explanation. The fact that they showed only completion effects if any positive effects at all has been written off as a 'selection effect' – perhaps these were offenders who would have desisted whatever intervention they received. Equally, however, it can be argued that completion effects were what should have been expected if the pathfinders had worked. The reason for having a long and complex programme, with rules about how to deal with participants dropping out and restarting, is that, in theory, only the full programme will be effective in bringing about cognitive and behavioural change. By contrast, those who do not receive the full programme are less likely to change. (Some will because even an incomplete programme will have an effect but others will not and may become 'worse' because they will reject the programme, while others will have been prevented from receiving the programme by factors extraneous to the programme.)

So if a programme has effects only on the group who complete it, this is at least a demonstration that this programme is effective for some offenders. Nevertheless, this demonstration does not rule out the possibility that a different intervention will also be effective. Conversely, if a programme has no demonstrable effect on completers this should perhaps be read as evidence that it is not effective (or at least ineffective for the group to whom it was delivered). And finally if a programme is equally effective for completers and non-completers this can perhaps be read as evidence that the programme itself is redundant or trivial and that any positive effect lies elsewhere in the process.

It follows from this that any 'programme effect' will be the effect of the programme on those who complete it, less negative or neutral effects on those who start but do not complete. Judging a programme solely on 'intention to treat' (i.e. its impact on all sentenced to it), as is current RDS orthodoxy, therefore risks misinterpreting the findings.

Reviews and meta-analyses

The National Audit Office (NAO) commissioned an independent review of the effectiveness of probation work as part of the evidence base for its review of the supervision of community orders in England and Wales (NAO, 2008). This review was carried out by RAND Europe. This review (Davis *et al.*, 2008) was in fact primarily a review of reviews. Its methodology was based on examining international review articles, systematic reviews and meta-analyses published over a considerable time span. It included prison studies despite some doubts about the transferability of their findings to community orders and, given the source material, it appears that there was a bias towards North American studies. So there was a multiple filtering process in the selection of evidence, with studies being excluded or included according to the multiple and varied criteria used in the different kinds of reviews. The report does reference some individual studies (e.g. Cann *et al.*, 2003) but excludes some others such as Hollin *et al.* (2004), which one would have thought worth including.

Nevertheless, the review came up with positive conclusions on the potential for cognitive behavioural programmes (general offending behaviour programmes) and drug treatment to reduce reoffending. It judged that there was only 'weak' evidence for the effectiveness of domestic abuse programmes, Employment and Basic Skills training, intensive supervision and unpaid work. These were thought unlikely to have a positive effect on reoffending.

For four types of intervention the RAND review judged there was as yet insufficient evidence – in effect that there might be a positive impact but the evidence was not strong enough, mainly because the quality of research was too low to show or validate strong positive effects. These were Anger Management programmes, unstructured probation, alcohol treatment and mental health treatment. These were seen as deserving of more and better research.

Whether this report takes us much beyond the original claims of the What Works Movement is less clear but it is at least a valuable corrective to any pessimism about effectiveness in the corridors and open plans of the Ministry of Justice.

Evidence on programme outcomes

Even if the RAND review was positive it is a sobering thought that, as we have seen, relatively little has been published that could stand as evaluations of programme impact in the community.

The main piece of new, if flawed, evidence is an analysis by NOMS RDS of the outcomes, in terms of predicted and actual reconviction rates, for accredited programmes delivered by the probation service in 2004 (Hollis, 2007). This report on the outcomes of accredited programmes was based on data collected through the IAPS[1] database. A total of 25,255 cases were included in the sample but a further 6000 had to be excluded because of poor data quality. There are therefore bound to be biases in the sample both at the offender level (more compliant offenders are probably more likely to provide better quality information to offender managers) and at the area level (areas that manage programmes better are more likely to provide better data). As both offender compliance and quality of programme delivery are positive factors the bias in the selection is towards successful programmes and outcomes. Unfortunately, no estimate of this bias is made in the report. There is a further methodological caveat that must be entered here. There is no comparison group and this must be counted as a major weakness in the report.

The report compares actual reconvictions with predicted reconvictions for a set of offenders 'engaged with' the full range of accredited programmes in 2004. Of the 25,255 cases analysed, 5243 (21%) were referred but failed to start, 12,000 (48%) started but failed to complete and 8012 (32%) completed their programme. It seems plausible that a number of cases sentenced to accredited programmes but failing to start were not recorded as referrals in IAPS. (This is a risk that arises from collecting data about programme attendance in a system separate from the main offender management database and so requiring the same data to be entered more than once.) It is therefore possible that the report understates the rate of drop out between sentence and starting the programme. This in turn means that the report may overstate the overall effect of being sentenced to an accredited programme. Of the 20,012 cases recorded as starting, 8012 (40%) completed their programme. The overall completion rate is therefore some way below the target of 70 per cent set in the original What Works strategy.

The results appear generally positive. The reconviction rate for all offenders recorded as referred to programmes was 54.9 per cent, compared with a predicted rate of 61.2 per cent, while the reconviction rate for those completing any programme was 37.6 per cent compared with a predicted rate of 50.7 per cent. So while those who completed programmes presented a lower risk of reconviction than the total sample referred, the gap between their predicted and actual reconviction rates (13.1 percentage points) was greater than the gap for all offenders who were referred (6.3 percentage points). In other words, those who completed programmes were considerably less likely to reoffend than expected and did relatively better than those who did not complete.

On the face of it, and even allowing for the biases noted above, this looks like a positive result and a demonstration of the impact of accredited programmes. Not all programmes were equally successful however. Domestic Violence programmes in general failed to show a significant reduction in reconviction for those referred. Conversely anger management, sex offender, Drink Impaired Drivers and general offending behaviour programmes showed a reduction in reconviction rates of more than 10 per cent in the cases analysed.

With all these reservations, the results are still worth noting. The report also presented data from the two-year reconviction follow-up of offenders commencing community orders in the first quarter of 2004; see also Cunliffe and Shepherd (2007). The full set of results is summarized in Table 1 below.

These figures suggest that referrals to accredited programmes have a slightly higher predicted rate of reconviction than a subset of all community orders (which includes programme referrals). The actual reconviction rate is also higher but the reduction in the rate of reconviction (here and elsewhere defined by the Home Office as the percentage change between actual and predicted rates) is also higher – 10 per cent for accredited programmes as against 7 per cent for all community sentences.

Table 1 Reconviction rates for accredited programmes and community sentences

	No. of cases in sample	Percentage reconvicted after 2 years	Predicted reconviction rate at 2 years (%)	Percentage difference between actual and predicted rates	Rate of change in reconviction from predicted to actual (%)[1]
All programme referrals[2]	25,255	54.9	61.2	−6.3	−10.3
All programme completers	8,012	37.6	50.7	−13.1	−25.8
Programme non-completers	12,000	63.9	66.7	−2.8	−4.3
Referrals who did not start	5,243	60.9	64.6	−3.7	−5.7
All community sentences[3]	30,968	50.5	54.1	−3.6	−6.7
Community Punishment[4]	11,548	37.9	43.5	−5.6	−12.9
DTTOs[5]	1,658	82.3	82.9	−0.6	−0.7[6]
Community Rehabilitation[7]	17,492	55.9	58.3	−2.4	−4.2

Sources: Hollis (2007) and Cunliffe and Shepherd (2007)

1. This is calculated by dividing the actual difference between actual and predicted reconviction rates by the predicted reconviction rate. A negative number indicates a reduction in reconviction rates. This is the outcome measure used in national measures of performance. (See also Merrington and Stanley 2004.)
2. Programme referrals are those entered on to the IAPS database as being 'involved' with accredited programmes in 2004.
3. Community sentences are all community sentences commencing in the first quarter of 2004 (see Hollis 2007).
4. Cited by Hollis 2007 (Appendix A).
5. Cited by Hollis 2007 (Appendix A).
6. Not statistically significant.
7. Figures for Community Rehabilitation taken from data in Cunliffe and Shepherd (2007). They include cases with a requirement for accredited programmes.

Hollis also presents data for reconviction rates for Community Punishment Orders (CPOs) (shown in Table 1 above). In the 2004 cohort (CPOs starting in the first quarter of 2004) the reduction in reconviction was also high (13%). However, those sentenced to CPOs are on average a different group from offenders attending accredited programmes. This is partly because the criteria of suitability are different and also because their predicted reconviction rate was lower (43.5%) compared with a predicted 61 per cent for the programme group.

Finally, given the figures for programmes, all community orders and Community Punishment, it is possible to infer that the actual reconviction rate for community rehabilitation orders which did not include accredited programmes was much closer to the predicted rate and that the reduction (if any) in reconviction was small.

This is not as unequivocal a result as may be thought. The reasons why community rehabilitation orders did not include accredited programme requirements would be both positive and negative; positive in that offenders were assessed as not requiring a programme (either in response to criminogenic needs or reflecting the seriousness of the offence) and negative in that offenders would have been judged unsuitable for programmes because of their behaviour, the complexity of their problems and/or the risks that they presented.

So there is a 'selection' effect. Offenders selected for accredited programmes should have had some characteristics that made them suitable for these programmes and lacked some characteristics that made them unsuitable. Within the group who were selected and referred, any success of accredited programmes is linked to a 'completion effect' – offenders who completed programmes were in general less likely to be reconvicted than those who did not or who were not selected. We can also hypothesize that a similar combination of effects applied in Community Punishment.

But even allowing for selection effects it is clear that accredited programmes are effective for some offenders and under some circumstances. The same can probably be said (on less evidence) for other interventions and sentences. Rather than attempting to 'prove' that one or another intervention (now from a large range of potential combinations of requirements in community sentences) 'works' RDS would arguably be better employed in studying how these different interventions achieve the effects they do.

So the question that needs to be asked is whether similar processes apply in other requirements in community orders. It has been argued (Stanley, 2007; Patel and Stanley, 2008) that the use of requirements in community orders can and should be made more responsive to the specific needs of offenders – with for example the potential for greater use of specified activity requirements in community orders for young adult offenders and for women. Research suggests that the use of requirements in community and suspended sentence orders has so far tended to follow established patterns (Mair *et al.*, 2007, 2008) in that the combinations most commonly used appear to replicate old-style community rehabilitation, community punishment, drug treatment and testing and community punishment and rehabilitation orders. It is not clear how far this reflects the 'conservatism' of probation staff in recommending orders and sentencers in making them, the lack of alternative provision or the fact that these are the types of sentences most appropriate to the needs of offenders and the seriousness of their offending. Given the range and complexity of offenders' needs, it seems likely that new combinations of requirements could be used which are more responsive to offenders' needs and circumstances and so more likely to reduce their reoffending.

Reconviction statistics

The most recent figures for the Government target for reducing reconviction (now PSA 23) appear to show that the one-year reconviction rate for adult offenders is below the predicted figure (Ministry of Justice, 2008). This is based on a follow-up analysis of offenders sentenced to community orders or released from custody in the first quarter of 2006. The report compares actual with predicted rates for community orders and for custody. Separate reports are prepared for adult and juvenile offenders and here I consider only the report on adult offenders. Predicted rates are calculated using a new predictor constructed from 2005 data. These rates are used as the comparator for custody and for the set of all community sentences. However, for individual order types, and particularly for new Community Orders, no predicted rates (either raw or corrected) are provided so more detailed measurement of the difference between actual and predicted reconviction rates of, for example, DTTOs is not possible.

The measurement innovations introduced in 2008 make these results incompatible with previous studies. Firstly and most critically, the measurement is taken at the one-year follow-up point as opposed to at two years as before. Secondly, a new predictor, calibrated to 2005 data has been developed, and thirdly the results of orders are measured not only in terms of whether offenders are reconvicted, but also in terms of the frequency and seriousness of reoffending. For these the following measures are used:

- Number of offences per 100 offenders in the sample;
- Number of offences per reconvicted offender;
- Number of severe offences per 100 offenders.

These measures of frequency of offending (or more properly frequency of conviction) lack at present any criteria by which we can judge whether they are better or worse than might be expected for the group of offenders in the sample, so their utility as a measure of performance is limited.

To deal with the impact of the shift to using one-year reconviction rates against a new predictor and with the introduction of other measures data has been presented retrospectively to 2000. The main headlines can be summarized as follows:

- One-year reconviction rates for offenders sentenced to court orders fell both absolutely and against predicted rates from a peak of 42.1 per cent for the 2003 cohort to 36.1 per cent for the 2006 cohort.
- For the cases sentenced in 2006, the actual reconviction rate was 4 per cent below the predicted rate.
- The numbers of offences 'committed' per person reconvicted also fell (from 414 per 100 in the 2003 cohort to 323 per 100 over two years in the 2006 cohort). This is to say that for example each person who was reconvicted in the year after sentence in 2006 was recorded as having committed just over three further offences during that year. How far this is a measure of police activity, and how far a measure of offender behaviour, is of course open to debate.
- The number of severe offences per re-offender does not appear to have fallen. (The number of severe offences per 100 offenders did fall slightly (from 0.7 to

0.6) but as the proportion of re-offenders in the cohort also fell, I estimate that the number per 100 re-offenders was around 1.7 – the same as for the 2003 cohort.)

Data on offenders released from custody shows a similar pattern where actual reconviction is lower than the predicted rate, although prisoners now have a higher prior probability of being reconvicted than do offenders given court orders.

The report also presents data for community orders and suspended sentence orders and within community orders for different combinations of requirements. However, these are hard to interpret at present as predicted reconviction rates are not given for any of these groups. We should therefore beware of using this report to say anything about the results of different community sentences or different combinations of requirements.

A concern is that the new measure of reconviction gives substantively different results from the old two-year measure. This can be illustrated by comparing the two-year results for the 2004 cohort as published in 2007 (Cunliffe and Shepherd, 2007; Hollis, 2007) with the retrospective analysis of one-year results for the same cohort. The two-year follow-up gives a reconviction rate for community orders 6.7 per cent below the predicted rate. The one-year follow-up gives a reconviction rate 1.8 per cent *above* the predicted rate. So on one measure community orders are effective; on the other, they are ineffective.

This incompatibility arises from several factors. It is possible that the introduction of a new predictor significantly changes the criterion against which reconviction is judged. As the rate of reconviction does not change equally over time, it is possible that both measures are factually correct even if they will be interpreted in different ways. It is also possible that offenders in the 2004 cohort were convicted more rapidly than expected and more often than expected in the first year of the follow-up. While it is obviously right to review and update predictive instruments there is thus no guarantee that the 2005 predictor is more accurate for cases commencing before 2005 than an earlier predictor was. Furthermore, it appears that choosing a different predictor and/or follow-up period gives substantively different results. This in turn throws doubt, unfortunately, on the value of the current one-year reconviction rate as a stand-alone measure of outcome.

Conversely, there is now no guarantee that the comparison between actual and predicted rates for the two year follow-up of the 2004 cohort (or any preceding cohort) is in fact sound. It is possible that the predictor used for 2004 was less reliable than the predictor developed on 2005 data.

As the observed reductions in one-year reconviction rates appear across the board they cannot in any case all be attributed to effective practice. Other factors need to be considered as well. First there is the question of whether this is the result of a shift in police (and court) behaviour since 2006. In this context, Hedderman (2008) observes that an apparent effect of the Offences Bought to Justice Target is that: 'While the "usual suspects" are developing longer records, it is not bringing additional offenders into the net'.

Thus, it is perfectly possible for more offences to be brought to justice and sentenced more quickly without more offenders being arrested. It follows that the overall conviction rate could rise without affecting the reconviction rate for offenders in the community. Hedderman also argues that observed reductions in reconviction may be a result of improved supervision, and so a demonstration of good work by offender managers, but not necessarily a consequence of particular sentencing decisions.

There is also the issue of enforcement. The reconviction data excludes breaches of orders or recalls to custody. More rigorous enforcement will result, directly or indirectly, in more offenders being taken out of circulation for a time without having committed a recognized offence. This means that the 'pool' of offenders available to be reconvicted is smaller than it appears and that the true reconviction rate is higher than it appears to be.

Finally, I must emphasize the question of whether these figures represent an accurate measure or are partly a statistical artefact of the way the reconviction predictor has been calculated. Retrofitting predicted scores against an index year of 2005 may tend to lower predicted rates before 2005 and of course we cannot tell whether the true rate for 2005 was lower than expected using an older predictor.[2]

Offender management

In 2004, we suggested that some evidence suggested that improved management of offenders would help them complete programmes and that, as the resettlement pathfinders seemed to show, was a critical factor in avoiding reconviction.

NOMS introduced the National Offender Management Model in 2005. This was planned to provide a consistent framework for managing offenders through their sentences. The key features of the model (National Probation Service, undated) are:

- that a single Offender Manager should be responsible for the offender for the whole of his or her sentence;
- that there should be a single sentence plan covering the whole length of a sentence – including both custodial and community elements;
- that resources should follow risk;
- that an offender's offender manager is based in the community, regardless of whether the offender is currently in custody or in the community.

The principle that resources follow risk means that different groups of offenders are associated with different modes of intervention (called tiers). These modes are, in increasing order of complexity: punishment, help, change and public protection. (Each tier includes the one(s) below it so that, for example, help includes punishment.) Offenders were to be assigned to tiers according to the level and types of criminogenic needs they were assessed as having, and also according to the level of risk of harm they presented.

Although this model appears to fit well with the needs of What Works (see Chapman and Hough, 1998), it was found to mesh less well in practice with the sentencing framework of the 2003 Criminal Justice Act. As a result, new guidance was issued to reconcile a tiering framework based on offender characteristics with the legal constraints of the Act. A consequence is that tier allocation is now dependent on the sentence the offender has received as well as on the levels of risk and criminogenic needs that they present (National Probation Service, 2008). This guidance is also evidently driven by concerns over the allocation of resources in probation work.

Despite the emphasis given in the guidance to the other principles of offender management there is the risk that by making the tier dependent in part on the sentence and thus applying only to a particular case, some key elements of continuity and responsivity will be lost for some offenders. And in fact this risk appears to be greatest when a 'tier 3' offender – the group most suitable for accredited programmes – receives a community order with only a single requirement. In many cases the guidance, especially when taken with the government's promotion of unpaid work, may limit the ability of the probation service to manage that case effectively.

Alternatives to What Works

Over time several critiques of What Works have been developed, offering alternative visions and standards of measurement. These critiques fall into roughly two groups, critical thinking about outcomes and critical thinking about processes.

Critical thinking about outcomes

While many commentators have called for a range of outcome measures to assess the impact of supervision and intervention in the community and in custody, in practice most of the literature on What Works has concentrated on the measure of re-offending, conventionally and where possible by a two year follow-up of reconviction (Merrington and Stanley, 2007). Reconviction is of course a measure of official not offender behaviour but it has generally been established that there is a strong relationship between official and self-reported offending (see Farrall, 2005). Measures of social well-being or adjustment have of course been used as an adjunct to reconviction or as an interim measure in many studies and the basis of What Works is that cognitive and/or behavioural change precedes a cessation of offending. (People stop offending because their thinking, behaviour or circumstances change although of course a decision to stop offending will in turn lead to other changes.)

Robinson and Shapland (2008) show how some of the procedures of restorative justice can fit the emerging models of desistance and so in theory support a reduction in reoffending. As restorative justice depends on the offender's consent, they argue, there is a predisposition to stop offending among those who take part – stronger than among those referred to accredited programmes – and this in turn has implications for how outcomes would be measured. They argue that it would be possible to reframe restorative justice to facilitate or consolidate a decision to desist from offending but warn that this is not the only or even the main goal for restorative justice.

However, personal change in the offender is not the only change that may result from Criminal Justice processes. In Restorative Justice, the key element is not a change in the offender but the dynamic of the exchange between offender and victim that may enhance the way society deals with offending without a necessary impact on the offender's future behaviour.

Other commentators (Bottoms, 2008; Clear, 2005) have argued, from different standpoints that the main impact of supervision should be in and on the community rather than on the individual offender. Clear's critique encompasses a general critique of 'casework' so will be reviewed below. Bottoms, however, argues for a re-orientation of casework towards greater community engagement and a reorientation of interventions (in his article primarily unpaid work but the same argument could be applied to others) towards benefiting the community. Bottoms' argument is persuasive but, as he admits, the chances of its being accepted at present by NOMS are low.

Critical thinking about processes – the place of case management

A significant amount of comment about processes of working with individual offenders has been driven by an assumed opposition between What Works on the one hand and individual work with offenders (Burnett and McNeill, 2005; Robinson and Raynor, 2006). Whatever obstacles to effective individual work with offenders may be perceived it must be noted that the seminal work by Chapman and Hough (1998) attempted to place cognitive behavioural programmes firmly within a context of desistance and individual casework. Of the five practice chapters in the *Evidence Based Practice Guide*, four deal with casework, one with programme delivery. The use of targets by the National Probation Service probably undermined this as an unintended consequence because it led to an emphasis on completing the group element in programmes, perhaps at the expense of the quality of engagement with individual offenders.

There are reasons for thinking that the balance is shifting from an over-reliance on programmes as the panacea. Davies (2006) and McCulloch (2005) have both argued that good casework is an essential component of effective practice. A belief in casework is, if shaken, still held by probation staff (Annison, Eadie and Knight, 2008). Perhaps this is a belief that will survive the over-prescription that is creeping into the National Offender Management Model.

A further critique of What Works has been through desistance research. The value of this (for example Farrall and Calverley, 2006) is that it has explored, in a way that NOMS RDS has been apparently unable to do, the processes by which offenders become ex-offenders and law-abiding citizens. The risk with desistance research is that, as it has relied heavily on accounts by participants who were willing to be interviewed some time after their index offence, it gives more weight to some routes out of offending than to others. While Farrall and Calverley recognize the cognitive processes and moral choices that underpin a decision to desist, there is a risk that the material they have collected has led to an underestimate of the part that cognitive behavioural programmes, properly designed and administered within an effective framework of case management, can play in desistance. If there are selection effects to be considered in interpreting programme outcomes, there are similar effects to be allowed for in generalizing from desisters' accounts.

There is also the point that some aspects of the What Works paradigm may have been given more emphasis than the evidence allowed. Wilkinson (2005) used data from the evaluation of a pre-accredited implementation of R&R to show an apparent dissonance between reconviction outcomes (which showed a completion effect) and the results of two psychometric tests where scores shifted in the 'wrong' direction so that those who did not reconvict were more pessimistic about their prospects than those who did. Wilkinson argued that this implied a flaw either in the theory behind R&R or in the use of psychometric tests as an interim measure. This study thus showed the risks of relying too heavily on intermediate outcomes as a substitute for reconviction. Numbers were very small but one possible alternative interpretation, which fits with the kinds of processes described by Farrall and Calverley, is that re-offenders were over-confident as a result of the programme while those who did not re-offend were more realistic about the obstacles they faced.

Annison (2006) has criticized the belief that offenders have 'active' learning styles and the effect of this on programme design and implementation. She argued that the evidence for active learning styles was weaker than claimed and risked over-generalizing and labelling of offenders. The implication was that if programmes were designed (as they appear to be) around 'active learning' they would be inappropriate for a proportion of participants. There would therefore be a tension between the principles of responsivity and programme integrity. This criticism seems to me to be well grounded. It strengthens the case for more research into the processes that underpin What Works. It does not in my view lead to a wholesale abandonment of structured learning. 'Unstructured' social interaction is equally problematic (see Stanley, 1991).

Finally there is the more comprehensive critique offered by Clear (2005). This is founded on the observation that there is no hard evidence that individualized casework is appropriate or effective. He therefore argues that the focus of probation work should be on communities and working to build relationships and alliances in the community rather than with individual offenders.

Knowledge and research

So does research into What Works and the impact of programmes still matter? As other commentators have noted, the Ministry of Justice Research team's obsession with Random Controlled Trial (RCT) experiments does not help. Personally, I find the arguments against these presented over thirty years ago by Clarke and Cornish (1972: 21) to be if not unanswerable then at least not answered.

> Because there has usually been little systematic attempt to study or monitor the 'black-box' of treatment it has been easy to conceive of treatment as a single unitary factor, and the label it is given is invoked to account for the results. It is only when the attempt is made to reach a better understanding of the treatment process ... that its complexity is revealed and the inappropriateness of the experimental design is fully appreciated.

We may have some better ideas then about What Works but we are still some way from the types of definitions of how, with whom and by how much that are needed before such research could show results.

If there are completion effects, we do not have the kind of rigorous 'realistic' evaluations that would tell us how they are achieved – is this simply separating the sheep from the goats or is the experience of going through a programme something that helps offenders turn away from crime?

So one might question how far RCTs are needed. Government of course likes simple answers, even though desistance studies and others show the complexities of offenders' journeys from crime and how contingent the impact of probation is on these. Nor on the other hand should probation retreat into the kind of atheoretical and *ad hoc* practice described by Fielding (1984). Investment in programme design and training staff to deliver is of course costly, but one lesson that should be learned from the studies that have been published is one we identified in 2000; the importance of local implementation. If this is so, then there is more scope for well-designed local research to see how programmes actually work in specific settings.

Ferriter and Hubbard (2005) and Hollin (2008) have queried whether RCTs are the only game in town. They argued that excessive reliance on RCTs in systematic reviews would miss promising findings shown in other research designs. Even if RCTs are accepted as the only valid research method (something I would not agree with) their results need careful interpretation. Not every failure to show a positive result is evidence that the intervention being tested does not work. The only interventions that should be rejected after a trial are those where there is a significant negative effect or where the positive effect fails to reach a threshold of substantive importance (Weisburd, Lum and Yang, 2003).

Even if the conceptual approach to research was correct, has it been well funded? Priestley and Vanstone (2006) observed that the Home Office (and by extension now the Ministry of Justice) has spent too little on research (less than one tenth of one per cent of their budget they estimate), and most of that is directed to studies of how the system operates rather than on how to improve effectiveness. No major private sector organization, they argued, would be able to survive on such an exiguous research investment. The current emphasis on reviews and 'rapid evidence' as well as 'process evaluation' while waiting for the ultimate RCT that will give the final answer is not a recipe for improving public protection, reducing crime or helping offenders to reform.

Conclusions

This article has tried to show that there is some evidence that cognitive behavioural programmes can produce positive results. We have still not moved much beyond the stage of 'promising leads' for interventions but, through research on desistance and related topics we can begin to understand better the processes by which offenders get out of crime.

It is fair to say then that the evidence about the impact of what works has advanced more slowly than Simon Merrington and I hoped when we published our last review. The state of play can be summarized as follows:

- Progress in the development of an evidence-based effective practice with offenders has been slower and more uncertain than the Home Office and the National Probation Directorate had hoped.
- The kind of developing reflective practice called for at the start (Chapman and Hough, 1998; Underdown, 1998; Merrington and Hine, 2001) and partly supported in the National Probation Service's original strategy has not been helped by organizational turmoil, the drive for standardization and a narrowing of the research focus.
- Government priorities for research have not led to a significant improvement in the quality of knowledge about What Works.
- Research on desistance and how offenders may learn or choose to reform does provide valuable insights.
- The introduction of the Offender Management Model has potential benefits for work with offenders but these may be at risk through too much central prescription and too few resources.
- It is increasingly evident that What Works, as operationalized through accredited programmes, is not the only or entire solution, although some have behaved as if it were.
- Conversely, What Works does appear to be part of the solution; the evidence for the positive results associated with the completion of programmes cannot be dismissed out of hand.

- And the motivation and commitment of probation staff, as recognized by the National Audit Office (2008) remain the bedrock of effective work with offenders.

The challenge is to develop the strengths that are there, build on new and diverse understanding of offenders, link these to the literature on intervention effects to improve our knowledge of what works when, for whom and under what circumstances.

From Steve Stanley, 'What Works in 2009: progress or stagnation?' Probation Journal, *56(2), 2009, pp. 153–174.*

Notes

1   IAPS stands for Interim Accredited Programmes Software. It is the database used to record offenders' progress through accredited programmes from referral to completion.
2   These comments on the predictors used in the national reconviction measure do not apply to OGRS3 – the predictor of offending introduced in 2008 (and replacing OGRS2, which had been launched in 2000). In essence OGRS3, based as it is on data about the subsequent sanctioning (including cautions) of offenders sentenced or released in 2002, is designed to measure the likelihood that an individual offender will commit further offences (if no further action is taken). It is based on a different sample of cases, uses a different criterion of reoffending and is intended to be part of an assessment process.

References

Annison, J. (2006) 'Style over Substance? A Review of the Evidence Base for the Use of Learning Styles in Probation', *Criminology and Criminal Justice* 6(2): 239–57.

Annison, J., T. Eadie and C. Knight (2008) 'Probation Officer Perspectives on Probation Work', *Probation Journal* 55(3): 259–71.

Bottoms, A. (2008) 'The Community Dimension of Community Penalties', *Howard Journal* 47(2): 146–69.

Burnett, R. and F. McNeill (2005) 'The Place of the Officer–Offender Relationship in Assisting Offenders to Desist from Crime', *Probation Journal* 52(3): 221–42.

Cann, J., L. Falshaw, F. Nugent and C. Friendship (2003) *Understanding What Works: Accredited Cognitive Skills Programmes for Adult Men and Young Offenders*, Home Office Research Findings 226. London: Home Office.

Carter Report (2003) *Managing Offenders, Reducing Crime – A New Approach*. London: Prime Minister's Strategy Unit.

Chapman, T. and M. Hough (1998) *Evidence Based Practice – a guide to effective practice*. London: HM Inspectorate of Probation.

Clarke, R.V.G. and D.B. Cornish (1972) *The Controlled Trial in Institutional Research – Paradigm or Pitfall for Penal Evaluators?* Home Office Research Studies No. 15. London: HMSO.

Clear, T. R. (2005) 'Places not Cases? Re-thinking the Probation Focus', *Howard Journal* 44(2): 172–84.

Correctional Services Accreditation Panel (2008) *The Correctional Services Accreditation Panel Report 2007/8*. London: Ministry of Justice.

Cunliffe, J. and A. Shepherd (2007) *Re-offending of Adults: Results from the 2004 Cohort*, Home Office Statistical Bulletin (06/07). London: Home Office.

Davies, K. (2006) 'Case Management and Think First Completion', *Probation Journal* 53(3): 213–29.

Davis, R., J. Rubin, L. Rabinovich, B. Kilmer and P. Heaton (2008) *A Synthesis of Literature on the Effectiveness of Community Orders*. Cambridge: Rand Europe.

Farrall, S. (2005) 'Officially Recorded Convictions for Probationers: The Relationship with Self-report and Supervisory Observations', *Legal and Criminal Psychology* 10: 121–31.

Farrall, S. and A. Calverley (2006) *Understanding Desistance from Crime: Theoretical Directions in Resettlement and Rehabilitation*. Maidenhead: Open University Press.

Ferriter, M. and N. Hubbard (2005) 'Does the Non-randomised Controlled Study have a Place in the Systematic Review? A Pilot Study', *Criminal Behaviour and Mental Health* 15(2): 111–20.

Fielding, N. (1984) *Probation Practice: Client Support under Social Control*. Aldershot: Gower.

Harper, G. and C. Chitty (2005) *The Impact of Corrections on Re-offending: A Review of What Works*, 3rd Edition, Home Office Research Study 291. London: Home Office.

Hedderman, C. (2007) 'Past, Present and Future Sentences: What Do We Know about their Effectiveness?' in L. Gelsthorpe and R. Morgan, *Handbook of Probation*, pp. 459–84. Cullompton: Willan Publishing.

——(2008) *Building on Sand: Why Expanding the Prison Estate is not the Way to 'Secure the Future'*, Centre for Crime and Justice Studies Briefing 7. London: Centre for Crime and Justice Studies.

Hollin, C. (2008) 'Evaluating Offending Behaviour Programmes: Does only Randomisation Glister?', *Criminology and Criminal Justice* 8(1): 89–106.

Hollin, C., E. Palmer, J. McGuire, J. Hounsome, R. Hatcher, C. Bilby and C. Clark (2004) *Pathfinder Programmes in the Probation Service: A Retrospective Analysis*, Home Office Online Report (66/04). London: Home Office.

Hollis, V. (2007) *Reconviction Analysis of Programme Data using Interim Accredited Programmes Software (IAPS)*. London: RDS NOMS/National Probation Service.

Home Office (2000) *Probation Circular (60/2000) What Works Strategy for the Probation Service*. London: Home Office.

Lewis, S., M. Maguire, P. Raynor, M. Vanstone and J. Vennard (2007) 'What Works in Resettlement? Findings from Seven Pathfinders for Short-term prisoners in England and Wales', *Criminology and Criminal Justice* 7(1): 33–53.

McCulloch, T. (2005) 'Probation, social context and desistance: retracing the relationship?', *Probation Journal* 52(1): 8–22.

McGarva, R. (2007) 'Performance Management', in R. Canton and D. Hancock (eds) *Dictionary of Probation and Offender Management*. Cullompton: Willan Publishing.

McGuire, J. (ed.) (1995) *What Works: Reducing Reoffending*. Chichester: Wiley.

Mair, G., N. Cross and S. Taylor (2007) *The Use and Impact of the Community Order and the Suspended Sentence Order*. London: Centre for Crime and Justice Studies.

——(2008) *The Community Order and the Suspended Sentence Order: The Views and Attitudes of Sentencers*. London: Centre for Crime and Justice Studies.

Merrington, S. and J. Hine (2001) *A Handbook for Evaluating Probation Work with Offenders*. London: Home Office.

Merrington, S. and S. Stanley (2000) 'Doubts About The What Works Initiative', *Probation Journal* 47(3): 272–75.

——(2004) '"What Works?": Revisiting the Evidence in England and Wales', *Probation Journal* 51(1): 7–20.

——(2005) 'Some Thoughts in Recent Research on Pathfinder Programmes in the Probation Service', *Probation Journal* 52(3): 289–92.

——(2007) 'Effectiveness: Who Counts What?', in L. Gelsthorpe and R. Morgan (eds) *Handbook of Probation*, pp. 428–58. Cullompton: Willan Publishing.

Ministry of Justice (2008) *Reoffending of Adults: Results from the 2006 Cohort, England and Wales*. London: Ministry of Justice.

National Audit Office (2008) *The Supervision Of Community Orders in England and Wales*. London: NAO.

National Probation Service (undated) *Offender Management: A Brief Guide for Probation Staff*. London: National Probation Service (available from the NPS website www.probation.justice. gov.uk).

—(2008) PC (08/2008) – *National Rules for Tiering Cases and Associated Guidance*. London: National Probation Service.

Ong, G., Z. Al-Attar, C. Roberts and L. Harsent (2003) *Think First: An Accredited Community-based Cognitive-behavioural Programme in England and Wales. Findings from the Prospective Evaluation on Three Probation Areas*, Report produced for the National Probation Directorate by Probation Studies Unit, Centre for Criminological Research, University of Oxford.

Patel, S. and S. Stanley (2008) *The Use of the Community Order and the Suspended Sentence Order for Women*. London: Centre for Crime and Justice Studies.

Priestley, P. and M. Vanstone (2006) 'Abolishing Probation – A Political Crime', *Probation Journal* 53(4): 408–16.

Raynor, P. (2008) 'Community Penalties and Home Office Research: On the Way Back to "Nothing Works"?', *Criminology and Criminal Justice* 8(1): 73–87.

Raynor, P. and M. Vanstone (1997) *Straight Thinking on Probation (STOP): The Mid-Glamorgan Experiment*, Probation Studies Unit Report No. 4. Oxford: University of Oxford Probation Studies Unit.

Robinson, G. and P. Raynor (2006) 'The Future of Rehabilitation: What Role for the Probation Service?', *Probation Journal* 53(4): 334–46.

Robinson, G. and J. Shapland (2008) 'Reducing Recidivism – A Task for Restorative Justice?', *British Journal of Criminology* 48: 337–58.

Stanley, S. (1991) 'Studying Talk in Probation Interviews', in M. Davies (ed.) *The Sociology of Social Work*. London and New York: Routledge.

—(2007) *The Use of the Community Order and the Suspended Sentence Order for Young Adult Offenders*. London: Centre for Crime and Justice Studies.

Underdown, A. (1998) *Strategies for Effective Offender Supervision: Report of the HMIP What Works Project*. London: Home Office.

Vennard, J., D. Sugg and C. Hedderman (1997) *Changing Offenders' Attitudes and Behaviour: 'What Works'*, Home Office Research Study No. 171. London: Home Office.

Weisburd, D., C.M. Lum and S.-M. Yang (2003) 'When Can We Conclude That Treatments or Programs "Don't Work"?', *Annals of the American Academy of Political and Social Science* 587. *Assessing Systematic Evidence in Crime and Justice: Methodological Concerns and Empirical Outcomes*, pp. 31–48.

Wilkinson, J. (2005) 'Evaluating Evidence for the Effectiveness of the Reasoning and Rehabilitation Programme', *Howard Journal* 44(1): 70–85.

76 Gold standard or fool's gold?

The pursuit of certainty in experimental criminology[1] (2010)

Mike Hough

This article was prompted by that of Larry Sherman (2009) which advocates a top-down system for developing experimental evidence about what works in reducing crime. The vision of a criminological equivalent of the National Institute for Health and Clinical Excellence (NICE) is seductively attractive to politicians and practitioners. It also contains an implicit criticism of mainstream criminology: how could we have failed so badly to have answered those questions that so obviously need answers? I want to suggest that the promise of experimental criminology in Sherman's article is an over-promise, and to explain why. I have restricted my discussion only to that part of the evidential jigsaw that covers the reduction of re-offending – attempts to reform, rehabilitate or deter people who are known offenders. I hope that what I have to say builds on responses to Larry Sherman's article by Tim Hope (2009) and Nick Tilley (2009), both of whose critiques I find very persuasive. And I should say that, like Tilley, I admire Sherman's research work as much as I am troubled by what I see as his oversell of the experimental method.

To anticipate the article's conclusions, there has been over-investment (both financially and intellectually) in a technocratic model of reducing reoffending that attaches too much importance in accredited programmes and packages, and under-investment in models that see the process of 'people changing' as a complex social skill.[2] The technocratic model seriously underestimates this complexity, and its advocates wrongly assume that experimental research can readily identify the causal processes at work in helping people to stop offending. They mistakenly suggest that *clinching* evidence[3] about 'what works' can be accumulated when in reality this is a field where evidence is perennially tentative and where knowledge is perennially labile. This is not to deny that there is a place for experimental methods in this field. They constitute one form of evidence about what works in reducing reoffending, and in some circumstances this can be very important evidence.

What Works? What research has told us

For as long as I have being doing criminology, there have been tensions between researchers at the 'applied' end of the spectrum and their more traditionally academic colleagues. Government research, and government-sponsored research, tends to be largely atheoretical, or rather, it implicitly accepts the conceptual frameworks within which political and governmental debate about crime and its control are conducted.[4] This body of work tends to be narrowly focused, and addresses specific policy questions. In general it is empirical, quantitative and increasingly incorporates a cost–benefit assessment. It is overwhelmingly short-termist – designed to answer the question as to whether whatever is being evaluated is having an immediate impact; and it tends to be uncritical, in the sense that it does not (or cannot) question general government policy. Rather, it assesses whether the evidence favours investment in one policy tactic as opposed to another. Traditionally this sort of research has either been carried out by Home Office (and now Ministry of Justice) researchers, by the NAO or the Audit Commission, or by academics on contract to government departments. Increasingly, though, 'niche consultancies' are also carrying out this sort of work.

In contrast, there is a growing body of academic research which is much more theoretically orientated, and substantially detached from policy dilemmas – even when crime policy is the focus of its attention, as indeed is often the case. Typically this work is concerned with conceptual rather than empirical analysis, and in so far as it engages with empirical work it is as likely to draw on qualitative as quantitative work. Probably the best known and the most cited British criminologist at the moment is David Garland (e.g. Garland, 2001, 2002).[5] His work is an extended commentary on government crime control policy that is nevertheless largely detached from the day-to-day questions with which politicians and their advisors have to grapple.

There is no necessary reason why this divergence should have occurred. Research can be both theoretically engaged and empirically grounded. Indeed it should be a source of concern if there were not a vigorous interplay between theoretical and empirical work. In practice, however, criminology feels as uncomfortably polarized as it has been at any time since the 1970s.

Over the last seven years or so this polarization has become more obvious, because the atheoretical empiricism of government criminology has become more obvious. Research managers at the Home Office and especially at the Ministry of Justice have nailed their colours to the mast of the Campbell Collaboration.[6] The basic idea behind this initiative, itself modelled on the Cochrane Collaboration in the healthcare field, is that one should be systematic in assembling and reviewing research evidence, admitting only those studies that achieve acceptable methodological standards.[7] The threshold for inclusion of studies should be set individually for each review, in the light of available evidence. For example, the Maryland Scale of Scientific Methods is often used as a filtering device.[8] In this, randomized controlled trials are rated as the gold-standard – the highest quality research. The ambition is that with sufficient investment in high quality research, a body of knowledge will be built up over time that would tell criminal justice managers what works in crime control in much the way that the National Institute for Health and Clinical Excellence (NICE) can give guidance to health managers about what treatments represent a good investment.

There are, of course, a wide variety of systematic reviews. Whilst those that are accredited by the Campbell Collaboration website have a bias toward evaluative research with experimental research designs, there is no reason why totally different approaches could not be adopted to the inclusion or exclusion of studies in reviews. It is hard to take issue with the principle of *system* in carrying out reviews of research evidence. It is important for reviewers to be clear and explicit about their rules for searching for evidence, and about their rules for admitting or rejecting evidence. It is systematic reviews that follow rules *inappropriate to the object of study* that are objectionable.[9] An important question to ask is whether the rules for sifting evidence that have gained currency in the Campbell Collaboration and in governmental criminology are the right ones.

What systematic reviews of evaluative research have told us

The most consistent finding to emerge from those examining programmes for reducing reoffending is that insufficient research has been conducted of high enough quality to say much with any confidence. The second most consistent finding – which is, of course, linked to the first – is that knowledge about what works is inconsistent and incomplete. The third finding that consistently emerges is that some programmes sometimes work. Those that have emerged as successful most frequently are cognitive behavioural programmes. This probably reflects the fact that they have been developed on a firm theoretical foundation – but also that in their nature, they are amenable to evaluation.

Advocates of the Campbell approach such as Sherman (2009: 16) argue that it is still early days, and that if we take the right decisions now about research strategy, in time the evidence base will develop. I would not want to belittle the importance of carrying out evaluations that demonstrate that a particular approach to reducing re-offending *can* work. This is a necessary building block in developing theories about how best to reduce reoffending. However an important series of studies carried out by the Home Office in the mid-1990s graphically demonstrated the limits in generalizability from evaluative research in this field. The first study (Friendship *et al.*, 2002), examining the first four years' experience of a cognitive skills programme working with offenders in prisons, showed considerable impact. However in a later replication of the evaluation (Cann *et al.*, 2003; Falshaw *et al.*, 2003), when the programme was rolled out to prisons on a larger scale, the effectiveness of the programme appeared to evaporate. The authors suggest, amongst other things, that changing levels of motivation amongst prisoners or staff could explain the difference.[10]

These studies graphically illustrate a potential problem for evaluative research: evaluations with robust methods of causal attribution, such as RCTs and quasi-experimental designs with properly matched control groups, tend to have high internal validity, but often have limited external validity. Let us accept, in this case, that the initial study had established incontrovertibly a link between the cause and the effect for the particular groups of offenders and workers under evaluation. However strong this internal validity, the study's external validity – the ability to generalize to other circumstances – may be quite limited. Even if the initial study reached the right conclusion, there are plenty of reasons for doubting whether the programme will work the same magic with other offenders and workers in other settings. In this respect, experimental research into criminal justice differs fundamentally from pharmaceutical trials, where generalizability, at least within broadly similar settings, is usually high.[11]

The implications for criminal justice research strategy are important. It is of great value for evaluative research to establish that something *can* work in reducing reoffending, but this is only the beginning of any serious evaluation. If a programme has been shown to be effective in one setting, the important next research step is to identify the mechanisms by which this impact was achieved.[12] The sort of evidence that one needs to search for in this enterprise may be distinctively different from that which one needs to establish whether a programme can work.

What is missing from systematic reviews in this field – as currently practised – is the development of 'middle level theories' to explain why some things work and others don't. The available systematic reviews are such disappointing documents to read, precisely because of their failure to grapple with the real evaluative issues. The main theory of evidence that underpins work of this sort is that the production of 'clinching evidence' based on RCTs and similar evaluative methods can result in an accumulation of generalizable hard knowledge about what works in reducing reoffending. There is a failure to recognize that work with offenders is a highly reflexive process in the sense that the meanings attributed to the process by those involved in it will affect the outcomes.[13] This means that the effectiveness of interventions will be highly context-specific. What works in one culture at one time may well be ineffective in other settings and at other times.[14]

What descriptive research has told us

More theoretically engaged descriptive criminology has contributed a great deal to academic understanding of the issues, but the impact on policy has been more limited than is desirable. I do not propose to offer a comprehensive review. Rather, I shall consider just two examples. One is concerned with the development of 'procedural justice' concepts in thinking about prison regimes; the other relates to desistance theories. The former has had a very marked impact on thinking within the Prison Service – but less within the Ministry of Justice and NOMS. The latter has achieved very little impact on policy thinking to date, but I expect this to change – not least because there are some important commonalities between this body of work and that concerned with procedural justice, relating to concepts of institutional legitimacy. I have labelled this research 'descriptive', to suggest that it is empirical but not experimental.

Procedural justice

Procedural justice theories are concerned with explanations for why people *comply* with the law, thus inverting the problem usually addressed by criminologists and criminal justice strategists. The key insights to emerge from writers such as Tom Tyler (e.g. Tyler and Huo, 2002; Tyler, 2003; Tyler, 2007) are that people comply with the law for normative as much as instrumental reasons, and that preparedness to obey the law is a function of perceived institutional legitimacy. The implication is that to promote compliance, criminal justice managers need to identify the drivers of institutional legitimacy, and to maximize the impact of these drivers. The survey evidence put forward by these researchers is good – but not incontrovertible – that preparedness to comply with the law is a function of the perceived fairness of procedures and the personal style of the officials carrying out these procedures as much as the perceived fairness of outcomes.

In the context of working with prisoners, there is an important body of British work in this tradition, by Richard Sparks and Tony Bottoms (Sparks, 1994; Sparks *et al.*, 1996), and in particular by Alison Liebling (2004). These researchers have been successful in describing institutional regimes and the important dimensions of difference that can be found across institutions. Regime quality (including levels of civility and the respect accorded by staff to prisoners) have a clear impact on prisoner perceptions of regimes, and there is some evidence that regime quality is linked to reconviction outcomes. The body of work has been important in supporting senior Prison Service managers' drive to push forward the 'decency agenda'. The evidence for this set of middle-level theories about institutional regimes could not be presented as incontrovertible 'clinching' evidence. It is circumstantial, but cumulative and persuasive. It is significant – and disheartening – that many systematic reviews would exclude this body of work from the 'admissable evidence' about approaches that work in reducing reoffending.

Desistance studies

Desistance studies focus, as their name implies, on the factors that lead offenders to stop offending. The empirical base on which their theorizing rests is typically but not exclusively qualitative in-depth interviews carried out with ex-offenders (e.g. Farrall, 2002, 2005; Laub and Sampson, 2001; LeBel *et al.*, 2008; McNeill, 2006; McNeill and Weaver, 2007; Maguire and Raynor, 2006). This body of work stresses the importance of understanding the centrality of offenders' *agency* (or capacity to exert control over their lives) in deciding to stop offending, and to appreciate that criminal justice agencies are only one of the many factors that impinge on offenders. Desistance theorists tend to stress that the process of change should be *offender-led*, with those helping offenders providing offenders with empathetic support to sustain their motivation to stop offending. Drawing on McNeill (2006), I would summarize the lessons from desistance theory for practice as follows:

- Work with offenders should aim to promote and support offenders' own efforts to stop offending.
- This work needs to respect and foster offenders' agency.
- It has to be grounded on legitimate and respectful relationships.
- It needs to focus on the provision of practical support as well as the development of motivation and capacity.
- It needs to adhere to certain 'practice virtues' that support the legitimacy of the enterprise in the eyes of the offender.

Procedural justice theory and desistance theory provide two examples of empirical criminological research playing an important role in developing and testing middle-level theories about criminal behaviour. It is a function of the complexity of the topic, however, that the theories rarely allow for conclusive verification – or even for conclusive (Popperian) disconfirmation. In this respect, knowing how to get offenders to stop offending is simply a special case of the general question about making other people do what we want. We know that this sort of knowledge is problematic. It is not easily acquired or easily stated or readily tested. I find it puzzling that this – fairly obvious – reality is not reflected in the research strategies of those responsible for reducing reoffending. I also find it worrying that a top-down experimental evaluation strategy as proposed by Sherman might be blind to the subtleties of both procedural justice and desistance theories.

A conceptual framework for thinking about reoffending

Let me first simply assert here that the effectiveness of any work to reduce reoffending is likely to be shaped by several interacting factors, including:

- the programmes (structured activities or interventions) to which offenders are exposed;
- the quality of the regime of the prison or the ethos of the probation office;
- the personal qualities and skills of the staff;
- the morale of staff, and the quality of leadership;
- the characteristics and mix of offenders under the supervision of the prison or probation office;
- funding and other resources available to the institution;
- the additional resources upon which prison and probation staff can draw from elsewhere to support resettlement; and
- the economic and social environment from which the offenders are drawn.

It is reasonable to expect that the interventions to which offenders are exposed will have *some* impact on their subsequent behaviour, but these are unlikely to be the major determinant of institutional outcomes. If one accepts the research cited above by Liebling (2004), and by Sparks *et al.* (1996), the quality of the regime will be a major factor in prison settings. Similar considerations are likely to apply in probation work, in that different probation areas and within them, probation offices, will have widely varying styles and work cultures. Perhaps more important, the (positive or negative) impact of friends and family is likely to be greater than the relatively brief encounters that offenders have with probation staff. Levels of resourcing within the prison and probation services will be relevant, as will be the external resources upon which they can draw, and the socioeconomic environments in which offenders live.

Models of working with offenders

There are at least three discernibly different approaches to work with offenders:

- the case-manager/interventions model;
- the therapeutic relationship model; and
- the caseworker/craft model.

The case-manager/interventions model is the one which is currently favoured by government. According to this, the most skilled of prison and probation staff assess offender needs and decide on a package of interventions tailored to this need. The interventions are then delivered by other staff under the overall direction of the case-manager. Within this model, it is the programmes or interventions which are assumed to be the things that really make the difference to outcomes processes so that they can be delivered by less highly trained and qualified staff (see Raynor and Maguire, 2006, for a discussion). The more weight that policy gives to this model, the greater the focus on a narrow sub-set of evaluation questions about 'treatment effectiveness' – equivalent to those answered by NICE-type systematic reviews.

This is not the only model of practice with any currency, of course. At the other end of the spectrum to the case-manager/interventions model is the therapeutic relationship model, where the relationship *is* the intervention. In this model, styles of engagement define the intervention. The prototype for this model is Freudian and Post-Freudian psychoanalysis, of course; its popularity has substantially waned in social work and cognate professions.

Between the two extremes is the casework model, where the 'craft' of the key worker is in managing a process of effective moral persuasion. In this model, caseworkers may well deploy interventions in support of their work, but they will not regard interventions as the primary means of effecting change. Clearly the casework model can be combined with the case-manager model up to a point. Caseworkers may often need to supplement their own skills by referral to specialist workers, but will continue to be the main player in the process.

There is very little narrowly defined *evaluative* evidence against which to test current policy preferences for the case-manager/interventions model – though plenty of useful evidence exists against which to evaluate the model. The National Offender Management Model (NOMM) has been subject to process evaluation (Matrix, 2006), but there has been no formal outcome evaluation. To my mind, the casework/craft model conforms more closely to our everyday experience in persuading others to do what we want. And it privileges a different set of evaluation questions about craft skills.

Craft skills

Too little attention has been paid to the *craft* of working with offenders. Within any preferred model for working with offenders, prison and probation staff have to choose tactics for engaging with offenders and for getting them (or helping them) to change. It is useful to think of these as constituting the *craft* of people-changing. These skills are obviously cognate to those required of managers in the workplace, of teachers and lecturers in the classroom and of police on the streets.

One can identify various levels of craft skill. For example there are *tricks of the trade*. These are common-sense tactics for working effectively with offenders, such as taking account of benefits pay-day in arranging meetings, or tailoring appointment times to early in their offenders' waking hours (1.00 p.m.–4.00 p.m.) rather than to the convenience of the worker (10 a.m.–1.00 p.m.). Then there are *skills in social interaction* that refer to those techniques for asserting control and authority – which can range from detailed attention to language, body-language and personal presentation to strategies which rely on analysis of the power dynamics in a relationship.

Third there are *casework styles or orientations*, by which I mean approaches such as Motivational Interviewing (see, for example, Miller and Rollnick, 1991; Prochaska and Diclemente, 1986), pro-social modelling (c.f. Trotter, 1999) or client-led approaches. Compliance Theory, or Procedural Justice Theory, provides a related but separate set of orientating principles (c.f. Bottoms, 2001; Tyler, 2003; Tyler and Huo, 2002); what is distinctive about these is the emphasis on securing normative as distinct from instrumental compliance.

Finally there are issues of *responsivity* and of *sequencing* to consider. The principle of responsivity is an important one (Andrews and Bonta, 2003). It is well established that different offenders have different learning styles – both at the individual and group level – and that work should be tailored to these differences. Sequencing decisions relate to the fact that offenders typically have multiple needs, and that effective practice is often a matter of arranging the right *sequence* of support (c.f. McSweeney and Hough, 2006). To our knowledge there is very little research that throws much light on sequencing, but we would expect to find a fair amount of professional wisdom on the topic.

The promise of experimental criminology?

What I have tried to do here is to demonstrate the complexity of questions relating to work with offenders. Sherman (2009: 16) sketches out the evidential utopia that the Campbell Collaboration will create as follows:

> Whether you are a crime victim, a police superintendent, a Magistrate or a probation officer, you will be able to go to www.campbellcollaboration.org to find out exactly the same kind of information [as is provided by the Cochrane Collaboration in relation to health treatments]. What is the most effective strategy to prevent auto theft? Do burglar alarms work? What can I do to protect my daughter from chronic domestic violence by her partner? What sentence is optimal for a chronic burglar? All these questions deserve to have answers from the Campbell Crime and Justice Group.

I doubt that we shall ever find answers to these questions which are good for all places and good for all time – or good even for the next ten years. Experimental criminology can provide valuable evidence of 'proof of concept' – for example that restorative justice meetings can reduce reoffending for some groups of offender in some settings (cf. Shapland *et al.*, 2008). However I doubt that it can offer with any certainty the answers to Sherman's questions, as the honest answer in all four cases are surely: 'It depends on the context'.

These questions are much more complex than those about the impact of pharmaceutical treatments. The right strategy for getting closer to answers is not to invest in a huge programme of randomized controlled trials, but to construct and test middle-level theories about how to change people's behaviour.[15] Choices about strategies and tactics need to be made on the basis of middle level theories about what is likely to work best.

What counts as a middle level theory? Well, this article is full of examples of partially-evidenced claims about approaches to changing people's behaviour: that achieving change is a human process, in that the quality of relationship will be a key determinant of outcome; that the personal qualities of the agent of change will thus also be critically important; that for change to occur the offender should confer legitimacy on the agent of change and on the process for achieving change; that legitimacy flows from fair and respectful treatment; and that structured programmes can sometimes be useful in helping the process of change.

The research strategy for testing such middle level theories needs to be as multi-faceted as the subject is complex. Evidence in support of them may *sometimes* be found in experimental research, sometimes in quantitative surveys, sometimes in qualitative work. If criminology is to remain healthy, it needs to do what it does best – which is to construct and test middle-level theories about the maintenance of social order. These middle-level theories can bring insight and perspective to policy. In my view this is the real contribution that criminology – whether theoretical or empirical – has actually made to policy.

Let me end with a political point. As we fall under increasing pressure to demonstrate impact and social utility, criminology needs as a discipline to develop a more inclusive and shared narrative about the value of criminology. This narrative needs to recognize the importance of questions about instrumental impact – 'what works?', in the narrow terms set by Treasury scrutineers. But we also need to recognize the narrowness of such questions, set against the breadth and diversity of the contribution that is actually made by criminology. If we over-promise clear answers to questions that are more complex than they appear, we shall pay heavily for this in the middle term.

> *Mike Hough 'Gold standard or fool's gold? The pursuit of certainty in experimental criminology'*, Criminology and Criminal Justice, *10(1), 2010, pp. 11–22.*

Notes

1 This article is based on a paper commissioned by the National Audit Office, and I am grateful to the NAO for funding this work.
2 Intellectual fashions ebb and flow. This article has some resonances with the backlash against 'positivist criminology' which occurred in the late 1960s and early 1970s – though I do not share the 'radical non-intervention' pessimism that critics of that era expressed.
3 I borrow the term from Nancy Cartwright, who makes a useful distinction between evidence that clinches conclusions and evidence that vouches for conclusions. She argues that in reality the most widely used methods for warranting causal claims – even in scientific work – involve vouching, not clinching (Cartwright, 2007).
4 See Morgan and Hough (2007) for a fuller discussion.
5 Despite being based in the US for many years.
6 See Hollin (2008) for a discussion. I and colleagues have argued elsewhere that this is best understood as an understandable response to the disappointing results of a very large-scale research programme established in the first years of the current administration for evaluating the Crime Reduction Programme. See Hough (2004), Maguire (2004).
7 See http://www.cochrane.org for details of the Cochrane Collaboration, and http://www.campbellcollaboration.org/ for details of the Campbell Collaboration.
8 The Maryland Scale assigns evaluative studies into one of five categories, according to the form of experimental control that is used to help to attribute causality. The highest score is reserved for studies that use randomized controlled trial methods. Systematic reviews usually exclude all studies that fall into the lowest two categories, and some include only the top, or the top two, categories. The scale provides a measure of internal validity, but does not take account of external validity.
9 The most common form of mismatch is to specify inappropriately restrictive rules. Our Home Office-funded evaluation of Drug Treatment and Testing Orders (Hough *et al.*, 2003; Turnbull *et al.*, 2000) is typically excluded from systematic reviews using the Maryland Scale, as lacking adequate comparison groups. So too is the Scottish equivalent (McIvor, 2004). In combination the two studies say a great deal about the order's effectiveness, however. But reviews which wastefully throw away such evidence necessarily exclude such comparative insights.
10 There are other possible explanations. There might have been problems of matching in the – quasi-experimental – design that biased the first study towards success, for example.
11 For example UK doctors would probably accept the clear US evidence about the effectiveness of statins in lowering cholesterol as a good guide to outcomes in this country.
12 The Home Office very sensibly mounted a qualitative study to get at the reasons for the differences between the two evaluations (Clarke *et al.*, 2004).
13 There is a discussion to be had about the extent to which the prescription of pharmaceutical drugs is a similarly reflexive process, but *on the whole* it is safe to assume that statins – or paracetamol or aspirin – will achieve their intended effect regardless of the meanings that participants construct of the process.
14 I suspect that cognitive behavioural (CB) programmes may have proved so successful specifically with offenders over the last 25 years because they typically – but not always – provide an apparently morally neutral framework within which offenders can think about their offending. They facilitate a covert moral dialogue, at a point in our cultural development when a more explicit moral dialogue would fail. Some CB programmes, such as ART (Aggression Replacement Therapy) specifically address moral values.
15 Ironically, Sherman's own work is full of very creative examples of such middle-level theories, as Tilley (2009) argues.

References

Andrews, D. A. and Bonta, J. (2003) *The Psychology of Criminal Conduct*, 3rd Edition. Cincinnati, OH: Anderson.

Bottoms, A. E. (2001) 'Compliance and Community Penalties', in A. E. Bottoms, L. Geslthorpe and S. Rex (eds) *Community Penalties: Change and Challenges*. Cullompton: Willan Publishing.

Cann, J., Falshaw, L., Nugent, F. and Friendship, C. (2003). *Understanding What Works: Accredited Cognitive Skills Programmes for Adult Men and Young Offenders*. Home Office Findings No. 226. London: Home Office. Available at: http://www.homeoffice.gov.uk/rds/pdfs2/r226.pdf.

Cartwright, N. (2007) *Hunting Causes and Using Them: Approaches in Philosophy and Economics*. Cambridge: Cambridge University Press.

Clarke, A., Simmonds, R. and Wydall, S. (2004) *Delivering Cognitive Skills Programmes in Prisons: A Qualitative Study*. Home Office Findings No. 242. London: Home Office. Available at: http://www.homeoffice.gov.uk/rds/pdfs04/r242.pdf.

Falshaw, L., Friendship, C., Travers, R. and Nugent, F. (2003) *Searching for 'What Works': An Evaluation of Cognitive Skills Programmes*. Home Office Findings No. 206. London: Home Office.

Farrall, S. (2002) *Rethinking What Works with Offenders*. Cullompton: Willan Publishing.

——(2005) 'On the Existential Aspects of Desistance from Crime', *Symbolic Interaction* 28(3): 367–86.

Friendship, C., Blud, L., Erikson, M. and Travers, R. (2002) *An Evaluation of Cognitive Behavioural Treatment for Prisoners*. Home Office Research Findings No. 161. London: Home Office.

Garland, D. (2001) *The Culture of Control: Crime and Social Order in Contemporary Society*. Oxford: Oxford University Press.

——(2002) 'Of Crimes and Criminals: The Development of Criminology in Britain', in M. Maguire, R. Morgan, and R. Reiner (eds), *The Oxford Handbook of Criminology*, 3rd Edition. Oxford: Oxford University Press.

Hollin, C. (2008) 'Evaluating Offending Behaviour Programmes: Does Only Randomization Glisten?', *Criminology and Criminal Justice* 8(1): 89–106.

Hope, T. (2009) 'The Illusion of Control: A Response to Professor Sherman', *Criminology and Criminal Justice* 9(2): 125–34.

Hough, M. (2004) 'Modernisation, Scientific Rationalism and the Crime Reduction Programme', *Criminal Justice* 4(3): 239–53.

Hough, M., Clancy, A., Turnbull, P.J. and McSweeney, T. (2003) *The Impact of Drug Treatment and Testing Orders on Offending: Two-year Reconviction Results*. Home Office Research Findings No. 184. London: Home Office.

Laub, J. H. and Sampson, R. J. (2001) 'Understanding Desistance from Crime', *Crime and Justice: An Annual Review of Research* 28: 1–70.

LeBel, T. P., Burnett, R., Mauna, S. and Bushway, S. (2008) 'The "Chicken and Egg" of Subjective and Social Factors in Desistance from Crime', *European Journal of Criminology* 5(2): 131–60.

Liebling, A. (2004) *Prisons and their Moral Performance*. Oxford: Oxford University Press.

McIvor, G. (2004) *Reconviction following Drug Treatment and Testing Orders*. Edinburgh: Scottish Executive Social Research.

McNeill, F. (2006) 'A Desistance Paradigm for Offender Management', *Criminology and Criminal Justice* 6(1): 39–62.

McNeill, F. and Weaver, B. (2007) *Giving up Crime: Directions for Policy*. Edinburgh: SCCRO. Available at: http://www.strath.ac.uk/media/media{_}64785{_}en.pdf.

McSweeney, T. and Hough, M. (2006) 'Supporting Offenders with Multiple Needs: Lessons For the "Mixed Economy" Model of Service Provision', *Criminal Justice* 6(1): 107–25.

Maguire, M. (2004) 'The Crime Reduction Programme in England and Wales: Reflections on the Vision and the Reality', *Criminal Justice* 4(3): 213–37.

Maguire, M. and Raynor, P. (2006) 'How the Resettlement of Prisoners Promotes Desistance: Or Does It?', *Criminology and Criminal Justice* 6(1): 17–36.

Matrix (2006) *Process Evaluation of the NOMS North West Pathfinder*. Report to the Home Office. London: Matrix Knowledge Group.

Miller, W. R. and Rollnick, S. (1991) *Motivational Interviewing*. New York: Guildford Press.

Morgan, R. and Hough, G. (2007) 'The Politics of Criminological Research', in R. King and E. Wincup (eds) *Doing Research on Crime and Justice*. Oxford: Oxford University Press.

Prochaska, J. O. and Diclemente, C. (1986) 'Towards a Comprehensive Model of Change', in W. R. Millar and N. Heather (eds) *Treating Addictive Behaviours, Processes of Change*. New York: Plenum Press.

Raynor, P. and Maguire, M. (2006) '"End-to-end" or End in Tears? Prospects for the Effectiveness of the National Offender Management Model', in M. Hough, R. Allen and U. Padel (eds) *Reshaping Probation and Prisons: The New Offender Management Framework*. Bristol: Policy Press.

Shapland, J., Atkinson, A., Atkinson, H., Dignan, J., Edwards, L., Hibbert, J., Howes, M., Johnstone, J., Robinson, G. and Sorsby, A. (2008) *Does Restorative Justice Affect Reconviction? The Fourth Report from the Evaluation of Three Schemes*. Research Series (10/08) (June). London: Ministry of Justice. Available at http://www.justice.gov.uk/restorativejustice-report{_}06–08.pdf.

Sherman, L. W. (2009) 'Evidence and Liberty: The Promise of Experimental Criminology', *Criminology and Criminal Justice* 9(1): 5–28.

Sparks, R. (1994) 'Can Prisons be Legitimate? Penal Politics, Privatisation and the Timeliness of an Old Idea', *British Journal of Criminology* 4(Special Issue): 14–28.

Sparks, R., Bottoms, A. E. and Hay, W. (1996) *Prisons and the Problem of Order*. Oxford: Clarendon Press.

Tilley, N. (2009) 'Sherman vs Sherman: Realism vs Rhetoric', *Criminology and Criminal Justice*, 9(2): 135–44.

Trotter, C. (1999) *Working with Involuntary Clients: A Guide to Practice*. London: SAGE.

Turnbull, P. J., McSweeney, T., Webster, R., Edmunds, M. and Hough, M. (2000) *Drug Treatment and Testing Orders: Evaluation Report*. Home Office Research Study No. 212. London: HMSO.

Tyler, T. R. (2003) 'Procedural Justice, Legitimacy, and the Effective Rule of Law', in M. Tonry (ed.), *Crime and Justice: A Review of Research*, 30: 431–505. Chicago: University of Chicago Press.

Tyler, T. (ed.) (2007) *Legitimacy and Criminal Justice*. New York: Russell Sage Foundation.

Tyler, T. R. and Huo, Y. J. (2002). *Trust in the Law: Encouraging Public Cooperation with the Police and Courts*. New York: Russell-Sage Foundation.

Index